THE HARTSHORNE FESTSCHRIFT

THE HARTSHORNE FESTSCHRIFT

PROCESS

AND

DIVINITY

Philosophical Essays presented to Charles Hartshorne
and edited by • William L. Reese & Eugene Freeman

OPEN COURT PUBLISHING COMPANY • ESTABLISHED 1887
LASALLE • ILLINOIS • NINETEEN SIXTY FOUR

Library of Congress Catalog

Card Number: 64-13547

PROCESS AND DIVINITY—THE HARTSHORNE FESTSCHRIFT

© 1964 by the Open Court Publishing Company

Printed in the United States of America

INTRODUCTION

THE ESSAYS which comprise this volume are by students, friends, and colleagues of Charles Hartshorne—not all, we might add, of those who fit into any one of these categories; but such a selection as the exigencies of space, time, and human nature have allowed. The essays have a wide ranging focus in the philosophy of organism, neoclassical metaphysics, and the metaphysics of religion. The volume makes a significant contribution, we feel, to the Whitehead literature of our time. The bibliography of writings on Whitehead in languages other than English and the Hartshorne bibliography deserve special notice. A heavy debt of gratitude is owed George L. Kline in the first instance, and Mrs. Charles Hartshorne in the second, for their presence here.

The *persona* of Peirce, Whitehead, and Hartshorne being what they are, the editors had rather expected to find these essays extending what some of us had begun to call the Peirce-Whitehead-Hartshorne axis in philosophy. A phrase comparable to this does occur in at least one of the essays. We had rather expected to find these essays dividing naturally into three sections, one on each of the persons we hold to exhibit a substantial unity. The reader will have no difficulty in discovering a section of this volume devoted to the analysis of Whitehead; and both within and beyond this section essays motivated by the writings of Professor Hartshorne. For whatever reason, however, although Peirce is mentioned not infrequently, only one of our essays moves substantially within the framework of his thought.

It is now quite clear that the underlying focus of these essays defies any ordinary table-of-contents classification; and the reason for this would seem to be that among the obligations this man has laid upon the philosophical community is one supporting independence of philosophical thought. Hence, the unity of this *Festschrift* volume is a unity of feeling; it is simply that each of the philosophers

v

represented in this volume, plus many others who would do him honor, has felt the significance of the person and writings of Charles Hartshorne. Among the facts of contemporary philosophy is the very pleasant fact that a sizable group of philosophers relate themselves to Professor Hartshorne through ties of respect and affection. Each is equal to the other; the respect and affection interfuse, forming a single complex property. This phenomenon is, we think, without rival in the contemporary American scene.

The essay by Albert William Levi reached the editors with an initial paragraph expressing so well the feelings of the students of Charles Hartshorne that we have gained the author's permission to allow that paragraph to speak for all of us:

I would not wish to begin this essay without a word about Charles Hartshorne. I studied with him at the University of Chicago between 1932 and 1934—metaphysics and aesthetics, and, I think, Kant. But it was then not possible to study any of those things without at the same time getting a generous dose of Peirce and Whitehead. Some of it "took." I am still never quite sure that aesthetics does not mean Peirce, and metaphysics Whitehead. Or is it the other way round? Much of what he taught was less a vaccination than a time-bomb. It took years for some of the insights to explode. But explode they finally did. I think there are few who studied with him who do not feel that his good influence upon us grows with the years. Who of us who worked with him does not feel gratitude and affection?

William L. Reese
Eugene Freeman
The Editors
January 15, 1964

TABLE OF CONTENTS

STUDIES IN METAPHYSICS AND LOGIC

STUDIES IN THE PHILOSOPHY OF RELIGION

THE CURRENT STATUS OF METAPHYSICS

EXISTENZ AND OBJECTIVITY

Necessities in the Intellectual Situation Today

IN PLATO'S dialogue which records the last day of the life of Socrates, near the midpoint of the account, Phaedo tells Echecrates that the argument about death and the soul's survival, itself nearly died. Two of the young men have given such telling counterarguments that a mood of intellectual discouragement falls upon the group in the prison. Only Socrates smiles. Attaching more importance to the mortality of the argument than to the approaching hour of his own execution, he says to Phaedo in the hearing of the others... "If this argument dies, and we cannot bring it to life again, you and I will both shave our locks" ...

Take this as a parable which touches one aspect of our present intellectual situation. The philosophical dialogue has often been strained between arguments for "science" and experimental objectivity and arguments for "the individual" and personal *Existenz*. The resulting tension has at times reached the stage of downright inconsistencies of attitude resembling those pointed out by Whitehead in his account of the Romantic mood of reaction against a machine view of nature. About the illogical attempt to conjoin *that* sort of science with "an unwavering belief in the world of men (and of the higher animals)," Whitehead judged that this "radical inconsistency at the basis of modern thought accounts for much that is half-hearted and wavering in our civilization."[1]

How is it with the dialogue today? Some are known to say that the argument has nearly died. They do not mean that one argument has overcome the other. The situation is more like that in the Athenian prison. Both arguments are there, but out of touch. They mean that the gap of blank non-comprehension which separates the attitude of scientific objectivity from the attitude of personal *Existenz* is so wide that it is senseless to speak of a single community of dis-

[1]A. N. Whitehead, *Science and the Modern World* (New York: The Macmillan Company, 1925), p. 110.

course including them. Not even the conditions which could make for responsible philosophic disagreement are met. Henry Johnstone's criteria for "controversy" of a philosophical sort fail. Recall his right comment: "A philosophy can be refuted only by someone sympathetic to it."[2] Is there enough sympathy between representatives of the two attitudes to bring the argument to life again?

At any rate, the community of our discourse *is* broken along this line. The break is partly concealed because among philosophers "scientific objectivity" mostly speaks English, and "personal Existenz" speaks Danish, or some other Continental tongue. To illustrate the point, glance again at Mr. Passmore's very useful book, *A Hundred Years of Philosophy*, written with disarming candor "from an English point of view." Eighteen of its chapters are devoted to our own well-known home environment, and the index shows the word "objectivity" as second or third most frequently cited. The nineteenth and final chapter adds with a nice *double entendre* "A Postscript on Existentialism." And there Mr. Passmore puts the case: "The fact we have to live with, then, is that if most British philosophers are convinced that Continental metaphysics is arbitrary, pretentious, and mind-destroying, Continental philosophers are no less confident that British empricism is philistine, pedestrian and soul-destroying." We've lost our souls, they've lost their minds, and there's no dialogue in us.

And this is where metaphysics comes in.

When the unity of the world of discourse is broken, there is a philosophical imperative to reconstitute the whole. The reconstitution of coherence in discourse is also the disclosure of the human situation in the cosmos. This aspect of the work of metaphysics, being linked with each intellectual situation as it arises from the past, records the itinerary of our minds' utterance.

The Achievement of Experimental Objectivity. .

Consider the two attitudes in turn, that of scientific objectivity, and that of personal *Existenz*, taking each as it discloses a conception of man's situation in the cosmos.

Scientific objectivity is an historical achievement arduously won. Regarded as an historical achievement, with its peculiar genealogy, it

[2]Henry W. Johnstone, *Philosophy and Argument* (Univ. Park: Penn. State University Press, 1959), p. 135.

may be thought to share the uncertain lot of such things. Whatever the staying power we care to attribute to this precious accomplishment, we do well to recognize that one condition of its endurance is that we understand it aright.

The logic of scientific objectivity, qua logic, is little help to understanding the history I refer to. We err if we ask such a thing of logic. What is involved, I think, is a venture in philosophical anthropology with open-minded attention to "the ontological weight" (to use Marcel's expression) which has attached to it in the modern West. A double interest is involved, at once metaphysical and historical.

The Scientific Revolution, as it is commonly called, centering in the 17th century (Whitehead's "century of genius"), made modern science centrally experimental science. It put the experiment in the midst of the search for objectivity. This revolution touched the very essence of our human being and not only our thoughts about scientific methodology. Francis Bacon, the prophet-spokesman for this change, conceived of his program in the *Instauratio Magna* as very considerably more than a new organon. Even in its fragments and supporting works it offers a new account of what it is to be human, an account of man facing futurewards, advancing both his learning and his own being on voyages of discovery.

Bacon was not conspicuously an experimenter himself, but managed to be sensitive to the subtle interplay of enlightenment and power that constitute an experiment in objectivity. The aphoristic thread of his account is: "Nature, to be commanded, must be obeyed." First of all, Bacon puts the stress on a disposition of mind to obey Nature, to be intellectually docile to the way things are. But the way things are is not superficially apparent. "The History of Nature wrought" discloses inner secrets not shown to mere looking. An obeying use of power is called for. Here Bacon sees the moral importance of giving proper dignity to the mechanical labor involved. An obeying use of power gives rise to "experiments of light" "that never fail" (for they answer disinterested questions) in contrast to utilitarian "experiments of fruit." Enlightenment *(theoria)* is the first aim. (Dewey's interpretation of Bacon seems to me to miss this point.) Experiment which does really enlighten has the after virtue that it also enhances human power. But the reasons for this, as Bacon judges the situation, are ontological. (Novum Organum, I, xxiii, cxxiv.) The objective world is a world of "signatures" "defined in matter by true and exquisite lines." Every-thing bears the mark of the divine ideas. An experimenting mind, swept clean of idols (preconceptions, including utilitarian wishes) can receive the messages there inscribed. And they are messages of the significant connectedness of the ongoing world within which men ex-perimentally place themselves. In Bacon's cosmological notion of the "interperceiving" of all things in Nature, we recognize the "ontological weight" which is connected with his doctrine of experimental man.

These Baconian recollections tell us evidently that the experimental objectivity which was achieved in the scientific revolution was a matter calling for intelligent and planned adventure, an unproud readiness to labor, and a self-forgetful welcoming of risk. The notion of ex-perimental man was a hopeful one by reason of the supporting cos-mology.

When we turn our attention to recent, prevalent, and positivistic accounts of scientific objectivity we find a thing much attenuated. Take, for example, our *International Encyclopedia of Unified Science,* as a programmatic expression of the newer objectivity. Clear-ly, the earlier theme of the Century of Genius has been muted. In the interval between Francis Bacon and Otto Neurath, the "ontological weight" of scientific objectivity has declined to the zero point. Bacon's words about discovering "the secret motions of things" may linger on, but not the ontology.

With this decline into positivity, there seems to have gone a con-comitant neglect of the anthropological presuppositions of experiment-al objectivity. It is significant that the great first positivist, Auguste Comte, who dispensed with metaphysics, also omitted from his scale of the basic positive sciences the science of human individuality, psychology. An exploration of the *International Encyclopedia of Uni-fied Science* is instructive as to this concomitance. There is a place in the scheme to be sure, for the objective study of human beings be-havioristically. The "physicalization" of the whole vocabulary of the science of psychology is envisaged. As a remarkable consequence the human beings who are concerned to achieve scientific objectivity are to be regarded as themselves objective material on which to exercise scientific objectivity. We find the program called, in this case, "the objective functional approach." The human, thinking, experimenting individual emerges as a complex of "negative feedbacks," "servomechanisms," cybernetic intricacies, in principle a thing wholly open to the inquisitions of scientific objectivity.[3]

I said at the outset that Scientific Objectivity, regarded as an historical achievement, is coupled with an anthropology and an "ontological weight." But it is in the nature of this objectivity that it calls for a self-effacing quality of mind. The Baconian "obedience" is an injunction to turn from all idols of self. In achieving experimental objectivity, the history of the achievement tended to be cloaked in official silence.

It is the unintended cloak of official silence about the fact that Objectivity is an historical achievement that has tended in addition to conceal from view the decline in the "ontological weight" of the ideal of Objectivity to which I have referred.

The Commitment of Socratic Existenz

Existenz philosophy arose as a corrective in a quite different situation. Kierkegaard gave it the character of a philosophical recoil from systematic philosophy. Kierkegaard was an anti-Hegelian Hegelian, rectifying "the System" on issues which seemed to him to call for sharpening the distinction between Objective Spirit and Individual inwardness. For him, *Existenz* meant a return to the roots of human history which lie in individual biography.

That against which Kierkegaard rebelled was itself part of a more majestic turning from the ahistorical perspective of Newtonian science to the life-centered and historical perspective of the post-Kantians.

In the century which has elapsed since Kierkegaard's generation, *Existenz* philosophy has so varied its forms of protest as nearly to lose a common character save that of protest itself. This is perhaps as it should be with expressions of protest. For our present purpose, let us

---

[3]A telling indicator of this decline into positivity is a proposed goal for scientific language which would perfect its objectivity by dropping all personal pronouns. It would be "a neutral language." Such a language of objectivity would thus have no linguists, or at all events no way of being linguistic about linguists. Reichenbach writes: "We are free (so he proposes: *"we* are free") to imagine a world in which there would be no ego." How? Quite objectively, surgeons could splice our nerves together so that sense-reception would lose its privacy; result,—no use for personal pronouns, hence no egos. [Hans Reichenbach, *Experience and Prediction* (Chicago: University of Chicago Press, 1938), p. 261.]

focus upon Socratic *Existenz* as found in the writings of Kierkegaard and Marcel.

Just as Socrates stood in the midst of the Greek discovery of man and of human authenticity, so did Kierkegaard in his generation. It was he who gave to the term *"Existenz"* its place as a category in a reborn anthropology. Someone recently remarked that Existentialism *"leans on* anthropology."[4] I prefer to say that *Existenz* philosophy *is* anthropological.

The haze that obscures the word *"Existenz"* can be largely dispelled by recalling its use in the ordinary idiom of the Scandinavian languages. A person's *Existenz* is his situation in life with all its ups and downs, joys, pathos and sudden turns. A person may say "My Existenz is grave" meaning poor health, unkind gossip, bad reviews, job-uncertainty. In any event, a person's *Existenz* is not just "something on paper." It is a certain stage in a life-journey, filled with circumstance and other people, and brought to the focus of that person's care and concern. In English we say, for the same meaning, "Situation."

The Socratic aspect of Kierkegaard's thought is his conviction that direct and objective communication is not competent to convey what it is to be a person in any degree. Such communication as *is* possible about human being is *in*direct of necessity, and hence of necessity a sort of communication by negation.

Kierkegaard's anthropology pivots on much the same conception of the moral person as we find in the Kantian ethics, the situation of a finite human individual faced with an unconditional moral command. But Kierkegaard, unlike Kant, thinks historically about the situation, or *Existenz*, of such a person. The historical journey, within which moral *Existenz* is a pivotal stage, is a journey which is to be read from within, in the manner of a diary. No objective sociology of knowledge is adequate to the metaphysics of this inner history; no objective behavioristic psychology either. An existential exploration of the history available for any finite person discloses a *pre*moral *Existenz*, that of the pragmatic hedonist, and a *post*moral *Existenz*, that of the person caught up in the dialectic of sin and grace.

The historical categories which Kierkegaard identifies remind one of the ancient theme of the primacy of will over intellect. One category, for example, is *Decision*. The well-known "Either-or" (illus-

[4]Henry Margenau, *Open Vistas* (New Haven: Yale Univ. Press, 1961), p. 53.

trated in biographical richness) is Kierkegaard's way of referring to acts of commitment not to be evaded through objective thinking. Another category is *Repetition*. In the inner history of a person, the profounder the *Existenz*, the more precarious. This is apparent enough in the moral situation, even regarded in a Kantian way, with all the moment-to-moment uncertainties about one's motives and inclinations. It is far more apparent in the post-moral, (religious) situation. "Repetition" here means "each moment's strenuous reacquisition of that which has once been acquired" in the way of being that sort of person. Kierkegaard adds "it is far more comfortable to be objective."[5] A third category is *"Venture"* (which might be called "risk"). Here is a human life's vector toward the future. The deeper, more inward, a person's *Existenz*, the more prospective. "If I risk everything in the medium of *Existenz*, this is by itself a lifelong task, and when I remain with my venture in *Existenz*, I shall repeatedly have to continue to venture."[6]

The theism which is Kierkegaard's chief concern is intentionally not stressed here. The aim here is to indicate that the categories which are his commonplaces belong to those of historical being, and especially are pertinent to the inwardness which constitutes the personal history of an individual.

The Socratic emphasis reappears today in Marcel's thought. His Socratic philosophy is marked by the stages of reflection through which a person passes in an inward history. It is not surprising that Marcel is persistently called a philosopher of *Existenz* in spite of himself. Like Kierkegaard he constantly keeps his focus upon the personal situation of an individual life. His own thinking takes the form of personal "research," or *search*, in the form of a diary (again like Kierkegaard.) The journal as a literary form is calculated to emphasize the breech with objectivity in the ordinary sense of that word. Marcel has a gift of language in identifying his categories, which carries over into English effectively. Like those of Kierkegaard they are categories of history in its biographical dimension.

One such term is *Exigence* (urgency). When we individually find ourselves becoming "organization men," we come to know a fear of

---

[5]Søren A. Kierkegaard, *Concluding Unscientific Postscript*, trans. D. L. Swenson (Princeton: Princeton Univ. Press, 1941), p. 35n.
[6]*Ibid.*, p. 381n.

becoming a mere number or interchangeable part in the administrative machine. Marcel associates the term *"exigence"* with this fear. Referring to "the state of universal continuous registration and enrollment, from birth to death," he says "such a bureaucracy cannot hope to inspire any other sentiment than a vague fear . . ."[7]

The Socratic character of this *"exigence"* becomes clear as Marcel's "search" discloses a deepened form of personal reflection which he terms *"recueillement"* ("re-collecting" oneself after the threat of being dismembered, in the literal sense of gathering oneself together again.) This "re-collection" is a reflection which follows upon the analyzing reflection and recovers the lost harmony of experience.[8]

One who is thus reflectively in-gathered learns to know the difference between the "problems" of selfhood and the "mystery" of selfhood. He realizes that the *"présence"* of self to self underlies the whole domain in which things and people are taken as technical problems. "Objects," including oneself as an object, pose problems for which solutions are forthcoming through reliance on the appropriate techniques. "When I am faced with a (scientific) problem, I work on the data in front of me; but everything proceeds, and quite rightly proceeds, as if I had no need to pay any attention to the 'I' who is at work; for the purpose in hand, 'I' am only a prerequisite."[9] "But a mystery is something in which I myself am involved," "a problem which calls its own conditions in question." The experience of personal *"présence"* arises. Only a re-collected self can make its presence felt to another. There is no teaching someone "the art of making his presence felt." Yet one may be quite deeply moved in the presence of a sleeping child.[10]

Thus, we have *exigence, recueillement,* and *présence* as categories of pilgrim *Existenz* and not of Objectivity.

One can hardly fail to notice in Kierkegaard and Marcel the conviction that individual life is an itinerary, and that a life, in its inner history, is a perilous and pressing thing. Insofar, these two are "process thinkers," with some kinship to Bergson for example. Intensity

---

[7]Gabriel Marcel, *The Mystery of Being* (London: The Harvill Press Ltd., 1950-51), I, 31.

[8]*Ibid.,* I, 83.

[9]Gabriel Marcel, *Être et Avoir* (Paris: Fernand Aubier, Ed. Montaigne, 1935), p. 169.

[10]Marcel, *The Mystery of Being,* I, 206, 216.

of freedom, memory, hope are inherent in the account. *But* so, too, is a certain sort of transcendence of the historical itself. This demarks an *Existenz* philosopher from other process philosophers. The interplay between what is historical and what is transhistorical, that which frustrates direct objective communication and calls upon a manner of Socratic irony, points to the subjective pathway to ontology, or in Marcel's words, "restores its ontological weight to human experience."[11]

Kierkegaard's reiterated themes of the Moment, and the Eternal in a moment in Time, correspond to Marcel's "Creative fidelity," acknowledging the permanency and mystery of Being as in some sense "intersubjective." Both thinkers are acknowledging an ontological necessity in the most concrete way. At times one is reminded of the ontological proof, but needs to remind himself that what is central here is rather an ontological insight in which thought and *"présence"* unite, in the "recognition" of "the transhistoric depth of history" (to quote Marcel.) [12] Kierkegaard's assertion that "God does not exist, He is eternal" carries the same import, for *"Existenz"* belongs only to the personal creature.[13]

Objectivity Regenerated by Existenz

At length I come to the two propositions which are the aim of this paper.

Having recalled that Experimental Objectivity, as an achievement of the Scientific Revolution, possessed at the outset an "ontological weight" that has been concealed by latter-day "positivity"; and that the commitment of *Existenz* arose in an ethical context as a corrective anthropology restoring another sort of lost "ontological weight" by a recoil into the historical categories of personal biography, I propose that: (i) the reaffirmation of Experimental Objectivity today can, and does, draw on Socratic *Existenz* for its regeneration, and reciprocally, (ii) that Socratic *Existenz* needs this sort of objectivity to support its own concept of human community. These two propositions disclose a sort of mutual involvement of Objectivity and *Existenz* betokening a wider categorial scheme, within which this reciprocal

---

[11]Marcel, *Being and Having,* trans. by Katherine Farrer of *Être et Avoir* (Westminster, London: Dacre Press, 1949), p. 103.

[12]Marcel, *The Mystery of Being,* I, 218.

[13]Kierkegaard, *op. cit.,* p. 296.

relationship has meaning. The interdependence is not an accident, but is proper to the intellectual situation which has given rise to these contrasting doctrines. In recent interpretation of science we have been seeing evidence that the original theme of Experimental Objectivity, with its risk-taking quality, is being reaffirmed. It persists with a gain in clarity over earlier formulations (like Bacon's) because of being re-thought in contrast to latter-day positivist objectivity.

For example, Michael Polanyi, in his Gifford Lectures,[14] speaking out of a scientist's experience, certainly restores the note of risk-taking commitment that goes into the achievement of scientific objectivity. What he calls "the fiduciary program" of such objectivity (in contrast to mere "objectivism") hinges on the affirmation: "I believe that in spite of the hazards involved, I am called upon to search for the truth and state my findings."[15] He points to the scientist's paradoxical impersonalness in the midst of personal "dedication." "In it," he writes, "a person asserts his rational independence by obeying the dictates of his own conscience." In conscious analogy to the dialectic of sin and grace, he writes of the scientific venture that: "The technique of our redemption (*qua* scientists) is to lose ourselves in the performance of an obligation which we accept, in spite of its appearing on reflection impossible of achievement." A remarkable way of speaking in behalf of objectivity!

In C. F. von Weizsäcker's account of Experimental Objectivity, the quality of solitary courage in each person who does experimental work is the major theme.[16] He puts more weight on the solitude than on the courage. The courage to face an uncertain outcome that enters into Experimental Objectivity is like in kind, however distinct in motive, that which launches practical, non-scientific ventures. But the solitude of the experimental man carries with it a peculiar burden. In his commitment to Experimental Objectivity, he, of his own will, undertakes to detach himself from the reassurance of his cultural surroundings, from the prevailing mores and aesthetic sensibilities. Furthermore he undertakes to suspend to the uttermost the influence of his own wishes and inclinations on his intellectual and manual acts.

---

[14]Michael Polanyi, *Personal Knowledge* (London: Routledge & K. Paul, 1958).
[15]*Ibid.,* p. 299.
[16]C. F. von Weizsäcker, *Zum Weltbild der Physik* (Leipzig: S. Hirzel, 1945), pp. 169-183.

He is to be as though his earthly circumstances were nothing and is to commit his mind and his labor to the artificial world of the experiment he has built. To complete this solitude a further detachment intervenes between the experimental man and his objects (whether they be uranium nuclei or a pure strain of laboratory mice).

He, of course, does not forego aesthetic delight in these objects, or a sense of intelligible harmony in their make-up. He *does* forego "the expectation of personal response." What is experimented upon cannot be "thou." In the experiment, the experimental man is ominously autonomous. The scientific revolution has brought with it this burden to be borne freely and without evasion.

A characteristic corollary of the risk-taking temper that accompanies experimental objectivity is the welcoming of provisional defeats through experiment, the experience of "falsification." This is an open and active seeking for possible disproofs of one's own hypothesis. Peirce expresses this attitude thus:

... the scientific man is above all things desirous of learning the truth and, in order to do so, ardently desires to have his present provisional beliefs (and all beliefs are merely provisional) swept away, and will work hard to accomplish that object. (In "The Logic Events," *Collected Papers*, 6.3).

Such openness to disproof bespeaks a strong personal center from which experimentation springs.

The common theme, in these examples, is the re-affirmation of risk, and with it the restoration of the "ontological weight" that was recognized in the adventurous conception of human being, at the time of the Scientific revolution.

The question I now invite is this: Are there elements of *Existenz* philosophy in its Socratic form which sustain the attitude of Experimental Objectivity? It seems to me that there are, and if this is so, the contribution should be recognized and enhanced.

Consider Kierkegaard's concept of Repetition. No doubt it refers, in his own thinking, to experiences and actions which are essentially religious, and religious in a very special context. But *is* there an analogy between the situation Kierkegaard has in mind and the situation of scientific experiment? It would seem so. No experiment, in the scientific exploration of nature, is immune from the hazard of being challenged. The thought and labor it involved stand always in need of redoing. This is all the more true, if we accept Oppenheimer's judgment that the advancing front of experiment in any natural science contains, funded within it, the history of antecedent experimentation up to that time. The achievement of experimental objectivity is precarious because it is historical. Kierkegaard's words about "each moment's strenuous reacquisition" apply to the achievement of experimental objectivity somewhat as they do to the "experiment" of religious inwardness which was his main concern.

What, for another example, of Marcel's concept of "re-collection" *(recueillement)*—the act of reflection raised to the second power? Is there any analogy to it to be found associated with the venture of experimental objectivity? I think so. The freely assumed solitude to which Weizsäcker refers, and the fiduciary commitment to which Polanyi refers, both testify to a powerful integrity of the individual self, an "ingatheredness" (to use Marcel's word), which should satisfy the exacting requirements of a "concrete philosophy" like Marcel's. If I misread these two scientists, and if one could plausibly take them as holding to the "cogito" of the Cartesian tradition and to the unindividuated subject of that "cogito," any suggestion of a parallel to Marcel's concept of "re-collection" would collapse at once. For Marcel means by the "recuperative" activity of personal reflection raised to the second power a return to one's *embodied* and unique inner self, in recoil from the abstract "knower as such" or "linguist as such" of the fashionable epistemologies. It is because Polanyi and Weizsäcker are at pains to relate experimental objectivity to self-possessed and risk-taking persons, that I think it worth suggesting a parallel to Marcel's more searching principle of *receuillement*.

Say that these and other Existential categories *are* pertinent to the scientific venture. What then? For one thing, the difference between "experiments of light" and "experiments of fruit" would be more cleanly kept, since the keeping of it would avowedly depend on personal integrity and motive. Then the great resources of Socratic *Existenz* could be brought deliberately to bear upon those inner conditions which save science from being engulfed in a vast technology and a vast technical way of carrying on life. Science rests on a teleological suspension of the practical which contains an echo of Kierkegaard's noted "teleological suspension of the ethical."

Readers of Kierkegaard and Marcel have good reason to enter

protests againt the foregoing proposal to regard Existential categories as contributing to the regeneration of Experimental Objectivity. One can gather evidence to show that Kierkegaard is incorrigibly anti-scientific. But, Kierkegaard's hostility is directed at intellectual pride, not at intellect. In the well-known chapters entitled "Something about Lessing" it is quite clear that the butt of his ridicule is a pretentiously completed intellectual system: ". . . now that the System is almost finished, or at least under construction, and will be finished by next Sunday: . . ."; ". . . a system which is not quite finished is an hypothesis . . ."[17] I read Kierkegard as having no animosity against hypothetical scientific thinking about nature, so long as it makes no total claim, and in particular does not pretend that human individuals are really computers and feed-back circuits.

Is Marcel not guilty of hostility to science? There are strong passages in which he is severely against the attitude of the objective spectator, and against the exploitative "having" for our own use of the externals of life, even including our bodies. But here too, as in the case of Kierkegaard, I think the warning is against letting these expressions of objectivity lead to a total claim. Scientific knowing may be a kind of "having," but, in its place, Marcel affirms rather than denies it. "Knowing as a mode of having," he writes, [is the] "possession of a secret. Keeping it, disposing of it . . ." "Knowledge as a mode of having is essentially communicable."[18] He does not deplore this as long as we see that the "présence" of person to person is not such knowledge, and underlies and makes possible such sharing of knowledge.

I have been suggesting that the purposes of objectivity are sustained by principles that seem far removed from the standpoint of objectivity. Insights into human *Existenz* are pertinent to our search for objectivity but are inaccessible to objectivity. There is a principle of "closure" here like Whitehead's "closure of nature" but operating in the opposite direction. Just as nature does not lose its autonomy in being pertinent to the mind's knowing of it, so personal *Existenz* does not lose its autonomy in being pertinent to the venture of objectivity. Personal inwardness is closed to objectivity, while being essential to it.

[17]Kierkegaard, *op. cit.*, p. 97–98.
[18]Marcel, *Being and Having*, Aug. 13, 1933, p. 145.

Existenz Requires Objectivity

The reciprocal proposition is: the philosophy of Socratic *Existenz* requires principles of Experimental Objectivity in order to make intelligible its own concept of human community and intersubjectivity.

All through the writings of thinkers like Kierkegaard and Marcel there runs the theme of *"concreteness."* A person's situation is a concrete historical situation. The proper mode of research into it seems to be thoroughly biographical and introspective. Swenson used to describe Kierkegaard's work as an exploration of the emotional cosmos within us. Marcel's journals are in much the same character and even more personal, since not complicated by pseudonyms. Such principles of order as emerge inductively from these explorations, whether the Kierkegaardian "spheres" of life, or the levels of "reflection" identified by Marcel, strike us as laws of inner personal history, not likely to give rise to any views of "world history" in a public sense, and not bound up with any doctrine of nature.

In the hands of Marcel, however, the emphasis upon a philosophy of the concrete leads to a lengthy phenomenology of "existing as an *embodied* person." Marcel's distinction between "having" and "being" centers around the issue of how a person stands to his own body. The corporeal fact becomes his concern. Negatively, Marcel sets aside "objective" accounts of one's body as a sort of instrumental apparatus, as well as "objective" behavioristic theories of human nature. His singular thesis, "I *am* my body" is a dramatic focus on the act of self-manifestation. It replaces "I have my body" (as a technique or instrument) by "I, *as* body, show forth a life." Being embodied is the same as being the "outcome or fixation of a history."[19]

Such a person-centered conception of 'being corporeal' has its puzzles. (In certain respects it is like Schopenhauer's concept of the identity of will and body.) For one thing, it raises the question: Why limit "my body," in this sense of "the fixation of a history," to just these bones and sinews? In principle, does not "my body" merge into the nearer natural environment to the extent that my environment is enlivened with outcomes and fixations of my history? (e.g., my home and garden, my favorite stretch of woods.) Here is a point at which the principle of concreteness, in the hands of an existential thinker,

19*Ibid.,* p. 84.

tentatively opens out the concept of "one's situation" to the *physical* cosmos. Nature enters as a party to the historical being of persons.

Kierkegaard is more elusive on this issue. He is no less insistent on the concretely historical character of each person's "situation" or *"Existenz."* He is too much the Kantian moralist to be easily drawn into Marcel's kind of exploration of 'being-corporeal'. But there is no difficulty in principle, it would seem, to understanding Kierkegaard's notion of a person's situation as indefinitely open to the natural environment. Consider his meditation, toward the end of *Purity of Heart is to Will One Thing,* on how to live as an 'individual' in one's *vocation.* There is no hint of world flight, either from the company of fellow men or from the physical conditions of human existence. Kierkegaard, in this work, is reflecting on each individual's *"eternal vocation"* (that is, the vocation of his religious inwardness), having in mind its bearing on each individual's *temporal* vocation. "This does not demand," he writes, "that you withdraw from an honorable vocation." "On the contrary, it is precisely that consciousness which will *sustain* and *clarify* and *illuminate* what you are to do in the relations of life." "The relations of life," the historically concrete principles of *Existenz,* include all the requirements of each ordinary vocation including all of its involvements in the natural environment. However, this acceptance of physical nature as party to existential history, is only tentative, and not explored.

I hold that the exploration is called for, in behalf of *Existenz* itself. The basis for this statement is the requirement, in *Existenz* philosophy, of a doctrine of intersubjectivity.

The more one follows Kierkegaard's exploration of various 'spheres' of *Existenz,* the more he realizes they are all achieved within pre-existing community. Even the extremest religious inwardness is indirect communication. The "incognito" is a relation with others.

Marcel's concept of *"présence"* is a way of saying that "We are" is prior to "I am." And the higher reflectiveness of *'recueillement'* (an individual's being ingathered) is the way to interpersonal *présence.* Intersubjectivity is the unintermittent support of each individual's situation or *Existenz,* even when it is overlooked.

The appeal to intersubjectivity in *Existenz* philosophy, however necessary, is unconvincing to the extent that the publicness of *nature* is not acknowledged as *that which makes intersubjectivity possible.* As long as research into 'being corporeal' remains tentative, Existential intersubjectivity remains so to speak, too angelic. It properly acquires its "ontological weight" by way of nature and cosmological principles.

Here, the doctrine of Experimental Objectivity can make a contribution, because being experimental toward nature is to be humanly within the public world. In this context, as Polanyi puts it, as experimenting persons we "pour ourselves into" the instruments of experiment, expanding our very selves within nature. Thus a community of experimenters literally interpenetrate each other in the unprivate "dwelling place" of nature.[20] The anthropological importance of Experimental Objectivity is that its world is the Public World. As public, it is the source of the "ontological weight" required for the Intersubjective World of *"Existenz."*

A Socratic Complementarity

Here is the course of the foregoing discussion in brief.

1. It is interesting that the contemporary intellectual situation furnishes so sharp a contrast as that between the doctrines of scientific objectivity and of existential subjectivity. But it is troubling that the positions seem often too far apart for philosophical controversy.

2. Rather than admit the death of dialogue here, we consider what each doctrine discloses about the nature of man. Clues given in reflection upon the "Scientific Revolution" lead to the current interpretations of Experimental Objectivity which discloses man as intellectual risk-taker in Nature, looking away from History. The Socratic type of Existential doctrine discloses man in forms of Individual Historical commitment, withdrawn from Nature.

3. In this anthropological light each doctrine can be seen as pertinent, and perhaps prerequisite, to the other, without reduction of either to the other. This is a relation of complementarity of man in nature and man in history. Each doctrine carries "ontological weight," but the reciprocal relationship of each to the other is such that it is difficult to bring both into a single focus.

4. If this, or something like this, is the situation as far as *Existenz* and objectivity are concerned, the dialogue lives in at least the responsible form of "philosophical controversy." Each position may

20Polanyi, *The Study of Man* (London: Routledge & K. Paul, 1959), p. 33.

claim controversial power (in Dr. Henry Johnstone's sense) as "a power that one can possess only by granting it to the other." If at least philosophical controversy is here possible, then a Socratic intensification of these opposites may win intellectual assent.

RICHARD HOCKING

EMORY UNIVERSITY

THE CRITIQUE OF ABSTRACTIONS AND
THE SCOPE OF REASON

THE STORY of modern philosophy is largely the story of the criticism of reason undertaken from many points of view and prompted by diverse motives. Thinkers as different in outlook as Kant, Hume, Kierkegaard, Freud and James have had a hand in criticizing the nature and status of reason in relation to our cognitive experience of the world and to the realization of our purposes and aims as active beings. Reason has been subject to internal criticism aimed at the disclosure of its structure and capacities and it has been judged in accordance with its success or failure in contributing to the self realization of the individual self. Although other ways than his have been discovered for carrying on the reflective critique of reason associated with the name of Kant, critical scrutiny of reason continues and the question of the scope of reason is in the center of discussion at the present time.

The philosophical thought of the last one hundred years has focused numerous problems about reason and its relation to our life and world. In the various forms of the Romantic movement, for example, the distinctions and arguments of reason were set over against the integrity of living experience and direct participation by the individual in the concrete situation. Wordsworth's identification of "murder" and the "dissecting" thought is typical of the Romanticist reaction to analysis; thought fragments and dismembers things, it kills and does not revivify. For others the issue was posed as that of the opposition between the partial character of thought and the wholeness and integrity of concrete situations. Or again, reason has been charged with dwelling in the sphere of the possible as opposed to the actual and of providing man with a means of avoiding decision and action in historical life. So understood, reason is able to weaken the will and spoil the "native hue of resolution." More recently with some of the philosophers of existence, reason has been described as a wholly "theoretical" power which by its very nature puts the individual at a distance from both himself and the world. The complaint is that reason can express only what is universal or, as Bradley put it, what is so true in general that it must be false in particular.

In addition the growth of modern science has had much to do with the evaluation placed upon reason in our current situation. The thought processes exemplified by mathematical physics have been regarded by many as the essence of reason so that it has come to be thought that reason is capable of dealing with nothing but high level abstractions. The identification, moreover, of reason with natural science leads to the belief that reason is confined to theoretical knowledge and that it must exclude from its domain the "practical" concerns of life—art, religion and ethics. If we are to recover a broader conception of reason in the modern world we shall have to reconsider it with particular attention to the meaning and status of abstractions. We must ask whether it is true that reason is confined to analysis alone and whether it is necessarily in conflict with immediate concrete life and experience. For much of the criticism leveled against reason has been based on the assumption that it is incapable of synthesis or constructive activity and that it is unable to provide us with safeguards against the confusion of its own abstractions with the larger concrete situation from which they have been drawn. This latter problem is most clearly evident in the modern educational situation where we are confronted with a multitude of bodies of abstract and specialized knowledge without very clear ideas of their relations to each other or their relative importance to the immediate situation we face.

Calling attention to the above plurality of problems centering in a common theme serves at the same time to point up the complexity of the topic. It is neither possible nor profitable to attempt to deal with all of the issues involved; we shall make more progress by singling out one basic problem. I propose to concentrate on abstractions, what they are, why they are necessary and what strategy is required for relating them to each other and to that concrete life and experience which is the ultimate referent of all serious philosophy. We may make a preliminary statement of our problem as follows: since the comprehension of ourselves and the surrounding environment requires analytic thought and this in turn means discrimination, selective focus and abstraction, what safeguards shall we devise in order to avoid confusing abstractions with the concrete reality from which they have been drawn and to which they ultimately refer? This question is not to be confused with the question of the verification of theories or the justification of statements containing abstract concepts. It goes much deeper. The issue turns on the status of abstractions in relation to each other and to concrete experience even when there is no question about the well-founded nature of these abstractions. The basic importance of the problem is signalized by the fact that Dewey and Whitehead, though their philosophies are based on different motives and have diverse orientations, each described philosophy as the enterprise whose proper business is the "criticism of abstractions" or the reflective inquiry which identifies abstractions and their kinds in order to show their relations to each other and to direct experience. For both thinkers philosophical vision is required to accomplish the result.

We scarcely need to be reminded that although the terms "abstraction" and "abstract" are often used as though their meaning were perfectly clear in contrast to the concrete, philosophers at least have not always understood these terms in a single sense. In order to clarify our problem, we must commence with some indication of the meaning of an abstraction. We shall not claim to give a definition: Kant was right on this point when he held that mathematics alone can begin with definitions and that philosophy, just because it has to cope with a concrete world, must postpone definitions until the very end of inquiry. We can, however, begin with a notion of abstraction sufficiently clear for our purposes.

Abstraction is both a rational process and a result fixed in a concept and expressed through language. Neither aspect can be neglected; one draws attention to the power of human reason and its intervention in an ongoing process, while the other focuses upon the outcome of the intervention, the final embodiment of knowledge. The abstraction in the sense of a result must not be disconnected from the process through which it arises because, as we shall see, no abstraction is intelligible entirely apart from the purpose of the thinker standing behind it. Abstraction in its generic character means discrimination and selection for emphasis involving both the inclusion or concentration upon an aspect or feature of a thing or collection of things, and the exclusion as not relevant of what is other than the selected feature. If, for example, our aim is to determine the number of items in a collection, we shall, in the first instance at least, concentrate on the counting and the identification of each item as one and only one, while paying no attention whatever to the colors and shapes of the things in question. The concentration upon each item as one and the neglect of the features of color and shape illustrate the inclusion and exclusion features of abstraction.

It is important to notice that there is no way of describing an abstraction which does not involve the notion of a purpose or a principle of selection; an abstraction expresses or includes what is relevant to a purpose in thought and excludes what is irrelevant to that purpose. Thus, for example, the determination of the value of a given national currency on the international exchange might largely exclude the esthetic value of many commodities, whereas an international art exhibit might succeed in its main objectives without any reference whatever to the economic value in exchange assigned to the works exhibited. In each case the features of things considered relevant and those irrelevant are determined by taking purpose into account.

In addition to the generic meaning of abstraction as inclusion and exclusion, there have been at least three ways in which this generic meaning has been interpreted. The differences are more than a matter of emphasis; they point ultimately to different ways of understanding the nature of things. First, an abstraction has been understood as the selection of a *part* of some whole—whether the whole of reality as with some idealists or some finite whole—such that the abstraction includes the part and excludes all of the other features that would go to make up the whole. In this sense, to be abstract is to be partial and thus incomplete. Secondly, an abstraction has been taken to mean a fixed or static element with clear and enduring boundaries carved out of a passing or flowing reality. In this sense to be abstract is to include a "frozen" excerpt or feature and to exclude the continuous process or flow of things which is in itself without convenient stopping places. Thirdly, an abstraction has been taken to mean a universal or generic feature which transcends the immediate situation or what is present for perception. In this sense to be abstract is to be an essence comprehensible in itself without regard to this or that occasion upon which it may be exemplified. All three senses involve the generic meaning of abstraction as selection but it is important to note that whereas the first and third senses stress the partial or incomplete character of abstractions, the second sense implies that abstractions are inherently *distortions* of a reality which can be apprehended only in an immediate way as an undifferentiated continuum. It follows that in accordance with the second sense abstractions are illegitimate and must finally be dispensed with whereas in the other two cases they are not only allowable but indispensable and the way is then open to show how they are related to each other and to the concrete reality from which they have been derived.

Underlying the special senses of abstraction we have noted is the generic description; abstraction means selection or inclusion and exclusion in accordance with some purpose in view. In every case the meaning of an abstraction is not independent of the purpose for which it was selected. Relevance or irrelevance of a given factor or aspect of a situation is always to be determined by reference to the purpose involved. Thus, for example, if we are interested in coming to understand the *temporal* character of our world and experience we must first identify that feature by abstracting. Now if our purpose is, as it undoubtedly would be in science, to understand temporality as a bare fact for a system of causal explanation, we would have to regard as irrelevant to that purpose our individual and personal sense of duration, the so-called psychological time, as well as the qualitative character of temporal position which in historical reality is described as the "right" time or the time that is "providential." The excluded elements are excluded on purpose at the same time that the relevant factors are selected on purpose. The difficult problem at this point is to guard against our tendency to think and act as if what we have disregarded as irrelevant for one purpose may safely be disregarded absolutely; this would be, from a philosophical viewpoint, the most disastrous justification of the proverb—"out of sight, out of mind."

The dual character of abstraction as both including and excluding needs further attention. Let us consider a piece of furniture, for example, and set as our purpose the determination of its fair market price. I take this to be attending to what can be called the economic aspect of the thing. To carry out our purpose we must select for attention and analysis certain aspects of that piece of furniture and also certain factors in the social and economic system in which it exists. What we select or abstract has its positive character in the fact that it is genuinely relevant to the accomplishment of our original purpose. And as such the abstracted elements have a legitimate status and function, since whatever else we may say about them they were selected for their relevance and because they enable us to achieve our stated aim. This I call the positive aspect of abstractions, that they include a portion of reality and that, when well founded, they enable us to understand, to describe and to manage things. Failure to take seriously enough this positive aspect has often led philosophers to think of abstractions only as "mere abstractions."

But there is the other side of the coin. To direct attention or select is to exclude as well as include and this fact is more problematic. In our illustration, the concentration upon the economic aspect of the piece of furniture means the exclusion from consideration of any aspect of the object which cannot be shown to be relevant to the determination of its fair market price. The object is being considered *only* in regard to its economic aspect and this aspect does not exhaust its being. This is what is meant by saying that an abstraction is partial and leaves something out of account.

Some decades of discussion about reductionism have taught us to be wary of our ineluctable tendency to identify anything with "nothing but" one of its aspects or features; we are less prone than we once were to identify the concrete and whole object or situation with an abstraction. And there is, I believe, considerable agreement as to the illegitimacy of such identification. We cannot correctly say, to use an old and well worn illustration, that the playing of a violin by a master is nothing but the production of sound waves from the friction between a horse's tail and a cat's gut. But in denying the identification, we must go on to consider what is implied by the denial. First, it is not false to describe certain features of a situation in terms of abstractions appropriate to, let us say, physics. For the fact is that the violin in the illustration has a physical constitution and when it is played, even when it expresses the most sublime music, certain purely physical conditions are being fulfilled. What is open to objection is the identification of an aspect with the whole, or a claim made in behalf of the abstraction to cover more ground than is stated and implied in the purpose for which it was made. We can, nevertheless, distinguish between well and ill founded abstractions made for a certain purpose and this fact precludes our saying that an abstraction is false merely because it is partial and does not express the whole. An abstraction is seen as partial, *not from within* the purpose which controls it since it was made precisely to fulfill that purpose, but only in relation to some wider purpose which takes more into account. But the fact that an abstraction does not fulfill some other purpose does not preclude its being well founded within its own intent and under the control of its own purpose. There are, however, more serious cases where an abstraction becomes materially altered when excluded elements are later brought into the picture. And here the genuine but thorny philosophical problem of internal relations presents itself, for when the omitted elements in a situation have the retroactive effect of altering a previous abstraction the concrete situation is not left standing where it was before. We are led at once to ask how the omitted elements, the exclusion of which make abstraction possible, are related to what we have already selected and clearly grasped. If philosophy is not to forfeit its claim to speak about and be relevant to concrete life and experience, it cannot avoid this problem.

The underlying issue is an essential one and is not posed merely as the outcome of this or that particular way of viewing the world. Precise and disciplined thinking in any domain requires clear concepts expressive of analytic distinctions and as soon as we attempt to carry out such thinking we are landed at once in abstractions. We are then faced with the problem not only of guarding against taking the partial for the whole, but of preserving the unity and integrity of experience at the same time. For analysis always breaks the unity of things directly experienced into a plurality of aspects and parts and we have continually to ask: How is the unity of experience and our own unity to be preserved? We are asking, in short, *whether reason has any synthetic function in construing the world or whether its activity is exhausted in analysis,* the dismemberment of what initially comes to us with integrity and wholeness.

It will be helpful to begin by calling attention to three responses which our basic problem has elicited from philosophers in the recent past. First, there is the refusal to acknowledge any problem here, either by claiming that it is "speculative" and beyond our reach, or by insisting that empirical inquiry is possible without our becoming involved in any such problem; thought, so this view runs, is thought and it is under no obligation to reproduce or duplicate reality. Here the identification of thought with analysis is accepted and there is no further problem; abstractions do not call for philosophical interpretation and they occasion no difficulty. In the second place we must recognize the position that does see a genuine problem here but poses it as an absolute antithesis between life, immediate experience or intuition on the one side and conceptual thinking on the other. This response not only acknowledges a problem, but does so enthusiastically and delights in finding every possible opposition and paradox between the abstractions of analytic thinking and the nature of things as disclosed in direct experience. Abstractions are then condemned as abstractions, reason in the form of analysis is limited to producing partial and distorted views of the world, and the proposed solution is that it is necessary to find a channel other than reason for grasping the nature of things. There is no attempt to reinterpret reason; it is left to its own self-destruction, a victim of its own abstractions. This approach acquiesces in the view that reason is no more than analysis; the only difference between this view and the first response is that while the first takes analysis as ultimate and legitimate, this view rejects analysis as distorting reality and seeks instead for some other form of insight. Acceptance of the claim that reason finds its whole being in analysis means avoidance of the hard problem of showing how abstractions may be related so as to reconstitute the wholes of direct experience. Intuition-type positions may have their heart in the right place as regards the criticism of abstractions but their failure consists in an over-readiness to surrender reason to the atomist while at the same time trying to make up the deficiency by appeal to an immediate apprehension which remains unconnected with analytic thought. Or if not completely unconnected, immediate apprehension remains so completely a matter of first person participation that general concepts expressive of general structures can be no more than distortions of the reality so disclosed.

The third response is by far the most complex; it is also the most rewarding. Like the second and unlike the first, it acknowledges a problem of major proportions in relation to abstractions and seeks to resolve it directly. It sets for itself the task of criticizing abstractions not in the sense of condemning them out of hand, but in the sense of exposing their partiality and then trying to find a strategy for relating them to each other so as to preserve the integrity of experience. This response, understood in its main aim, seeks to save reason from its own abstractions. It is the only approach that correctly grasps the problem and it alone can hope to deal effectively with the task of keeping concrete reality from being dissolved into abstractions and of saving reason from the just criticisms leveled against it when it relies uncritically upon its own abstract products.

I want to consider two solutions that have emerged in modern thought, each of which exhibits the general pattern of this third response. The first is the *way of dialectical recovery of the whole,* and the second may be called the *way of functioning or instrumentalism.* Each has its own truth, even if both have to be supplemented further.

1. *The Way of Dialectical Recovery of the Whole*

This solution finds its supreme illustration in Hegel and the key to understanding it is found in the thorough-going identification of the abstract with the partial and of the concrete with the whole. Isolated, atomic or self-enclosed existence is denied and the underlying strategy of this position is to show that abstraction can never be the same as complete separation. Discrimination does not mean the loss of all connection between the item or aspect discriminated and its environing context. Contrary to what has been said, this solution does not mean the denial of analysis, for Hegel always defended mediation and analysis, but it does mean that the results of analysis cannot stand as self-contained and independent results. From the other side, Hegel's approach means the ultimate justification of thought, but it is a very rich type of thought which includes showing how the abstractions produced by analysis are related to each other so as to re-establish the concrete whole which seems to be left behind by the understanding that distinguishes but does not unite. Hegel's way, in other words, means the removal of partiality through organic and systematic recovery of the whole as a system of intelligibly related aspects or parts. His doctrine that mediation or abstraction is "immediacy becoming" or the self-specification of the subject matter denies at the outset any difference in kind between an immediate and integral given experience on the one side and the conceptual distinctions demanded by reason on the other. His formula is: *First distinguish and then unite*; synthesis can be achieved because all intelligible aspects or parts are related to each other in the whole. We are invited by this strategy to complete the process of mediation and thus to reconstruct the concrete reality.

The truth in this approach is that the partiality of abstractions is revealed only when they are set against the wholes to which they refer or of which they are aspects. Partiality is never disclosed for what it is as long as we remain wholly within the specific or limited purpose that produces it. Physicists, for example, will never see the partiality of their abstract descriptions as long as they confine their vision to those features of things with which they can successfully deal. But the disclosure of partiality shows the inescapability of appealing to the concrete world and at the same time raises the question as to whether the criticism of abstractions can ever be carried through from a standpoint which regards all abstractions as on the same level. To this we must return.

If Hegel's strategy contains an element of truth it also involves a fatal error. To say that the concrete is the whole is to identify it with a non-differential concept; it is to identify it with what cannot be apprehended as such. For human reason, at any rate, the whole must always be grasped in some differential way, in one aspect or part; as soon as this is done, however, we no longer have the whole. Hegel saw this problem and it is precisely why the whole is left by him implicit until the process reaches its culmination in fully self-conscious spirit. But as later outworking of the position has shown, the recovery of the whole must then become a *program* for a process that is never completed. The concrete problem is this: How can we estimate the status and especially the importance of an abstraction when all we have to guide us is the concept of an ultimate totality? The answer is that we cannot do so; unless the whole is given some differential character such as being an organism, or a self, we have no way of saying how the various partial purposes behind all abstractions are related to each other. For every abstraction is, as such, equally abstract and the only way in which an abstraction can get to be "more or less" abstract is by reference not simply to the whole, but to the whole as characterized in some differential way. Hegel, of course, knew this and he sought to meet the difficulty by the differential conception of the whole as self or spirit. When it was necessary for him to place the emphasis on the wholeness or completeness of the concrete he put forward the Absolute as totality, but in order to keep the Absolute from falling into a bare or empty totality he brought forward the idea that the nature of the whole is spirit. It is in relation to this differential idea that he was able to judge that, for example, the category of quantity is less concrete than that of measure and all the categories of being are less concrete than those of essence. Put in this way, however, the criticism of abstractions is not merely an affair of discovering partiality and of relating it to the whole, but rather of determining the *relevance* of a given abstraction for expressing the whole taken as having some differential character. The difficulty here, and almost every critic of Hegel has made this point in one way or another, is that of establishing the importance of an abstraction in a finite and specific situation. To see the whole from the standpoint of God may be to relate everything to everything else so successfully that finite distinctions of importance simply disappear.

Dewey, above all other thinkers of the past 50 years, perceived the difficulty attaching to every attempt to criticize abstractions merely by confronting them with the concrete taken as the whole. He was uneasy in the absence of a differential concept or specific situation such as might provide special criteria for judging abstractions. Dewey went even further and began to doubt the legitimacy of a general *theory* of abstractions or what might be called a speculative resolution of the problem. In meeting the issue he brought forth his own alternative, the second way of approach to the criticism of abstractions, the way of functioning or instrumentalism.

2. *The Way of Functioning or Instrumentalism*

Without involving ourselves primarily in tracing historical influences, we can clearly see that Dewey was close to Hegel at several important points. Like Hegel, he rejected isolated or atomic existence and even defined philosophy as criticism aimed at the removal of "rigid non-communicating compartments"; isolation he regarded as unnatural and at the opposite extreme from that thoroughgoing interaction of all things which is of the essence of his metaphysic. Unlike Hegel, however, Dewey had no inclusive category save Nature and Nature was conceived by him in a thoroughly pluralistic way except for the unity it may receive from its being disclosed through a single method. He did not, moreover, conceive the process of criticizing abstractions as a purely logical one based on the interrelation of categorical structures alone. In criticizing the primacy and ubiquity of the knowledge relationship, Dewey had also to reject the exclusive emphasis placed by Hegel on knowing as the supreme expression of all reality. By contrast, Dewey's thought is thoroughly anthropological; in emphasizing the human situation or predicament he claimed that the generic traits of existence take on their proper importance when they become related to human concerns and figures in the success or failure of human plans and purposes. In place of Hegel's more exclusively logical interpretation of incongruity or conflict as contradiction in a dialectical scheme, Dewey focused on the active and progressive sense in which situations are incongruous or break down rather than on their static and structural aspect. He was led consequently to concrete, practical problems of a social and moral nature where the resolution of conflict so understood requires active and overt transformations of things. The bearing of these features peculiar to Dewey's approach upon our basic theme is not far to seek.

Abstractions or selective emphases, in Dewey's language, are inevitable wherever reflection occurs, but it seemed to him that their one-sidedness might be rendered harmless if only the fact and act of selection were taken into account along with the facts selected. Abstraction is regarded by him as one act of choice beside others and abstractions are set to work in a stream of activities so that the conditions and consequences of such selection will become manifest. In place of a general theory aimed at the logical relating of partial aspects to each other, we are to rely upon a public method of operation available to all who care to trace out the conditions and follow the consequences attendant upon a given act of abstraction. Everyone is invited to set the abstraction to work in the continuum of experience in order to see where it leads and what transformations it can effect. Thus, for example, in order to estimate the meaning and legitimacy of such selective biases—these are Dewey's favorite examples —as that the real is the simple, or that atomic sense data are experientially primitive, or that the knowledge relationship is omnipresent, we must trace out the results or consequences of assuming these selections to be true. In this way they are brought back into relation to concrete experience and we have an opportunity to decide whether experience is thereby rendered more intelligible or opaque or whether it becomes more or less subject to control. By taking abstractions neither as finalities nor as absolute starting points but rather as instruments or ways of handling things in order to achieve some purpose, practical or theoretical, Dewey was able to avoid some of the problems that have vexed other thinkers attempting to define, for example, the relations between the precise concepts of physics and the objects and situations disclosed in direct experience. This is more obvious in regard to the abstract concepts and theories of natural science than with respect to the selective emphases of philosophy and the distinctions of interest and purpose that so obviously confront us in the course of actual life. To interpret theory in science as instrumental is to focus upon its function in guiding inquiry and in enabling us to control nature, rather than upon its status as disclosing in descriptive terms the ultimate nature of things. Because of this functional approach, Dewey could never see the point of a theory such as Whitehead's method of extensive abstraction designed for the purpose of building a bridge between well founded abstractions and the presentational situation. Such criticism of abstractions seemed to him unnecessary because he viewed the problem of relating them to the concrete as a functional and dynamic affair having a specific focus in each case rather than as a theoretical affair to be resolved by formulating a conceptual relationship *überhaupt* between abstractions and concrete nature.

That the functional approach has made its own contribution to the task of criticizing abstractions cannot be denied, but it is not clear that a naturalism of Dewey's type has sufficient resources in itself for showing the relative *importance* of the various aspects of life to each other. The problem raised by the breaking up of integral experience into features which, when taken by themselves, are abstract, is not to be resolved merely by admitting that abstraction does occur and making the fact public property. Abstractions require criticism not only in the sense that we sometimes make errors and abstract badly, but in the broader and more urgent sense that we need to know the relative *importance* of the various partial aspects of life under which we live—the economic, political, religious, moral, etc. If it is true as we have said that every abstraction or selective emphasis is based upon and expresses some purpose in thought (cf. Whitehead: "Thought is one form of emphasis"), then the relating of various systems or sets of abstractions to each other in order to fix their relative importance will require critical comparison of basic purposes and cannot be done with a working pluralism harboring no values beyond the social. If Hegel was inclined to lose finite or differential distinctions of importance through an overweening emphasis upon the whole, the radical pluralism of Dewey's functionalism goes to the other extreme, thus avoiding the problem of a final context.

Nature and man's success or failure in controlling it provide us with as much of a final focus or standard as Dewey's pluralism can allow. But the lack of unity in his vision of human life begins to make itself felt; the only unity we find is that of method and this is in itself too abstract to provide the guidance that we need. Setting abstractions to work in order to exhibit their consequences does indeed make room for criticism in the sense that we are then able to see the fruits they produce. Moreover, exhibiting our principles of selection as a matter of public knowledge does enable each of us (at least in principle) to retrace for himself the functional meaning which the abstraction has. But an abstraction unmasked, so to speak, is not *ipso facto* made less of an abstraction, unless indeed it is held that self-consciousness all by itself effects a remedy and this is a thesis which I believe Dewey would scarcely want to advance. We still face the problem of having some unified view of things based on a concept of *ultimate* importance by which the *relative* importance of abstractions can be judged. For if we are to accomplish the criticism of abstractions by confronting them with concrete life, we shall not be able to avoid saying what we take the concrete to be.

I am unable here to develop a full solution to the problem of criticizing abstractions, especially since I believe it is more important to draw some implications from the foregoing discussion for current views of the status and scope of reason. I am able, however, to indicate the line I believe the solution should follow. We need to start with the contention that abstractions are inevitable; without them no understanding of anything is possible and this means that it is sheer folly to condemn them in any wholesale fashion. Secondly, abstractions are always made for a purpose and from this condition there is no escaping. We may, for example, consider one and the same individual man from an esthetic standpoint and express our apprehension in a portrait; we may consider him as a physical organism and express the results of investigation through an x-ray plate or an anatomical diagram; we may consider him as a moral being and describe him as untrustworthy or as not to be depended upon. In each case the context of consideration is dependent upon a purpose; concentration upon this feature or that of one and the same concrete individual is focused by an interest or an end in view. This interest or purpose controls the meaning and scope of the abstraction. Thirdly, we have the need in philosophy for a recovery of a sense of *importance,* for without a doctrine of the ultimately important there can be no treatment of the relative importance of abstractions to each other. No philosopher of recent years has seen this point more clearly than Whitehead.

But I wish to suggest that if we are to recover this sense we shall have to understand the ingredience of valuation and importance in concrete experience; it will be necessary to reverse a pattern of long standing. Ever since Kant, and perhaps earlier, the tendency has been to begin reflective inquiry with science, i.e., with our most precise and therefore most abstract type of thinking. We have set out from natural science as the archetype of safe, certain or near certain knowledge and have then entertained the hope that in some way an advance can be made to the good, or morality, or value which will enable us to estimate the importance or relevance of that knowledge and the ends to which the power it bestows should be directed. When we start with our most abstract and therefore our most precise thought we encounter great difficulty in moving to the concrete and to a sense of importance by a process of construction; the result is an indefinite postponement of all the urgent concerns and in fact they are often never allowed to enter at all. But surely this is to proceed in the wrong way. It is not true that we can reach concrete moral values by first beginning with the method or conclusions of science and attempting to extend it to the sphere of importance; on the contrary, scientific inquiry is itself incapable of being initiated and sustained without antecedent commitment to norms and values that are by no stretch of the imagination derivative from science. Without the commitment to the reality of a truth that no man has constructed and which is not the exclusive property of any nation or class, and a loyalty to the strict prosecution of a method for disclosing it, science is impossible. Science is a hard achievement just because it requires self-discipline, but this is a moral and, in many cases, a religious virtue; it is not a product of science but the life that sustains it.

We must start our philosophizing with the concrete human situation—man is the only being for whom the problem of abstractions and importance becomes explicit—we must start, that is, with man as the religious, moral, social, political being and then move from there to the abstractions of specialized knowledge which are directed to the realization of specific ends within these various aspects of the most concrete human situation. The real situation for man, in short, the concrete, is the moral, religious, political situation; all else is abstraction in relation to that and cannot be allowed to stand by itself. There is no way to the concrete concerns defining man's life and situation in the world if we first begin with the abstractions of theoretical knowledge any more than it is possible to reach the individual if we first begin with universals and then attempt some process of specification. To start with the abstractions of our most precise knowledge means that we shall be condemned to end with them as well and thus fail to reach the concrete. But if we start with the most important aspects of our experience and our life in the world we shall have a vantage point from which to view, criticize and evaluate the abstractions required by all reliable knowledge. If there are no abstractions apart from purposes, then purposes, valuation and importance are all present at the start; in the beginning was the purpose and Royce was right when he argued that there is no pure intellect but that all thought and knowledge stand essentially related to the will.

To return to the bearing of the earlier discussion upon the scope of reason, there is one central point to be made. To deny that there is any problem with regard to abstractions and to identify reason solely with analysis or, what amounts to the same thing, to hold that reality is basically atomistic in character, is most emphatically *not* to be a friend of reason at all, but to make a large contribution to its eventual dissolution. Contrary to what has been believed by most defenders of the sufficiency of analysis, it is the narrow view of reason that produces obscurantism, primitivism and explicit irrationalism. The more we abandon responsibility for the criticism of abstractions while at the same time acquiescing in the view which identifies the scope of reason with that of analysis, the more we invite those dealing with the most concrete human concerns to be done with rational criticism altogether. For those whose main concern centers in the problems of morality, religion, and politics see at once that if reason is exhausted in formal logic and the production of analytic distinctions without regard for either their relative importance or the integrity of experience, it becomes futile to think of rational criticism in these areas of thought. It is no pure accident that on the current scene the philosophy of existence appears side by side with highly formalized conceptions of reason and at a time when the dominant trend in philosophy identifies reason with analysis alone. Difficult and vague but highly important human questions do not remain in exile merely because they are banished by a formalistic reason. But under such circumstances discussion of them is bound to fall beyond the scope of rational criticism if we confine it to the horizon of analysis and assume no responsibility for those abstractions to which analytic thought inevitably leads. At present, therefore, nothing is more important than the recovery of reason in a sense broad enough to embrace both analysis and a doctrine of importance that will enable us to criticize abstractions in the light of our most concrete life and experience.

JOHN E. SMITH

YALE UNIVERSITY

THE DEATH AND REBIRTH OF METAPHYSICS

THE SUBTITLE of Charles Hartshorne's latest book sets the direction for my remarks. Titled *The Logic of Perfection*, the book is subtitled "Essays in Neo-Classical Metaphysics." Each ingredient in this characterization is pertinent. In declaring the book to be a metaphysical treatise the author dissociates himself from the positivistic suspicion that such inquiries are misguided in principle and cognitively can come to nothing. The qualification "classical," in turn, distinguishes the inquiry from dominant continental quests— Heidegger's, Jaspers', Sartre's, Marcel's—which, though engrossed with the problem of being, doubt that traditional tools (objective reason directed toward system construction) can effectively come to grips with it. There remains the prefix "neo," which announces that we cannot perpetuate the past. In method as well as in content, twentieth century metaphysics must break new ground.

Why? Necessarily? How? Fusing these questions, I wish to ask what has come over metaphysics in our time and what may be the discipline's future.

I

Deeply embedded in the history of Western civilization is a body of knowledge, conceived by the pre-Socratics, mid-wifed by Socrates, and born well-formed in the writings of Plato and Aristotle, whose name is metaphysics. The principles that have governed its growth have been abstractness, system, and scope. Scope signifies that it has taken all things—the total range of what is—as in some sense its province; system, that it has sought to make the categories of its 'scheme of things entire' hang together. Abstractness has been, simply, the inevitable price of generality: the more items you want your concepts to cover, the more the features that individualize them must be ignored. Two standard definitions summarize these traits as well as any: Metaphysics

is the endeavour to frame a coherent, logical, necessary system of general
ideas in terms of which every element of our experience can be interpreted.[1]

Metaphysics is concerned to reveal just that set of major classifications of
phenomena, and just those precise criteria of valid understanding, by which
the whole array of given experience may be set in order and each item (ideally)
assigned its intelligible and unambiguous place.[2]

Currently this discipline is virtually dead. British philosophy has
foregone metaphysics generally, continental philosophy the objectivity
which traditionally has been so much a part of metaphysics that the
definitions don't even trouble to mention it. America's contribution to
the demise has been her metaphysically-suspicious pragmatism. Before
mid-century, R. G. Collingwood could describe our times as "an age . . .
when the very possibility of metaphysics is hardly admitted without a
struggle."[3] More recently Iris Murdoch has written: "Modern philosophy is profoundly anti-metaphysical in spirit. Its anti-metaphysical
character may be summed up in the *caveat:* There may be no deep
structure. This is the lesson of Wittgenstein."[4]

The roots of this suspicion run back—to Kierkegaard, Nietzsche,
and Pascal on the Continent, and across the Channel to Hume. But
these were men before their time. It has remained for our generation
to see *as a generation* the import of their prophecies. A-cosmism at
large, lapping at the shores of thought's entire empire, streaming into
the inlets of every specialized discipline, breaking into spray which
salts the eyes of even the man on the boardwalk—a-cosmism in these
proportions is a twentieth century discovery.

In England the wave crested in logical positivism's 'elimination of
metaphysics' proclamation and has rolled on thereafter in the analytic
movement. Of the two, positivism *said* the ruder things about metaphysics, but only because it defined "metaphysics" and "meaning" in
ways that made them disjunctive. Actually it was less skeptical than
its successors have been, for it assumed that the world does have a
structure and that philosophy can perfect a language which, as used

---

[1]A. N. Whitehead, *Process and Reality* (New York: The Macmillan Company,
1941), p. 4.

[2]C. I. Lewis, *Mind and the World Order* (New York: Charles Scribner's Sons,
1929), p. 12.

[3]*An Essay on Metaphysics* (Oxford: Oxford University Press, 1940), p. 224.

[4]In D. F. Pears (ed.), *The Nature of Metaphysics* (London: Macmillan and Co.,
1956), p. 109.

to order the findings of science, can picture it without distortion. The 'ordinary language' movement doubts both points, assuming that it is profitable neither to ask after the structure of reality in general nor to dream of constructing a language governed by a single set of rules which is capable of doing justice to the full gamut of human experience and functionings.

Twentieth century American philosophy has been equally a-cosmic. Reviewing Dewey's *Experience and Nature* Santayana asked, ... "how comes it that ... cosmology is absent from his system, and that every natural fact becomes in his hands so strangely unseizable and perplexing?" His answer is: Because of "the dominance of the foreground ... Nature is here not a world but a story."[5] Or rather, many stories? Speaking to "The Way the World Is," Nelson Goodman concludes "the world is many ways ... There is no way which is the way the world is ... But there are many ways the world is, and every true description captures one of them."[6]

The existentialists on the Continent agree with this. Stressing to the extent they do that man is his relation to his situation, they are emphatic in insisting that as the life-situations men occupy differ markedly, traditional metaphysics' dream of a single world outlook relevant to everyone is misguided in principle. But they go on from here to make another point. Whereas British philosophy has tended to see metaphysics as rationally *deficient*—where not actually meaningless, then at least fatty or sloppy—continental philosophy sees it as *too* rational, too intellectual. For being cannot be laid before the mind as if it were an object. To the extent that it can be known at all, our knowledge of it must be of a special sort in which experience, with which thought must always be meshed to some degree, deepens to the point where the dichotomy between subject and object is transcended.

II

How are we to account for this near stampede from the endeavor which historically has been philosophy's central concern? The social

[5]Bernard Suits, "Naturalism: Half-Hearted or Broken-Backed?", p. 169, *The Journal of Philosophy*, 68, No. 7 (March 30, 1961).

[6]*The Review of Metaphysics*, 14, No. 1 (September, 1960), p. 55.

turmoil of our century may have played some part; also the extraordinary increase in our knowledge of history and cultural anthropology by making us aware of how variously the world can be, and under various skies has been, conceived. But these have been contributing causes at most. The central cause has been honesty.

Neither of the two directions in which metaphysicians have proceeded in their attempt to build their world views looks promising today. The deductive method used indubitable starting points—irreducible units of experience or self-evident principles of reason—as launching pads from which logic was projected to outline what was supposed to be being's necessary structure. The inductive method surveyed the full arc of man's experience and attempted to abstract therefrom characteristics (categories) which unite, divide, and structure.

How can we retain our faith in either approach today? Deductive metaphysics founders on the fact that there are no indubitable starting points; *cogitos,* matter/form dichotomies, sense data, all have been found to be open to intelligent questionings. This discovery unmasks deductive metaphysics' conclusions of their presumed certainty and throws them into camp with those of the economic analyst who takes a rough hunch and refines it to the seventh decimal place. Meanwhile the findings of inductive metaphysics command equally little conviction. The difficulty here arises not only from the deluge of information which, as a consequence of the systematization and subsidy of research has poured in upon us faster than we have been able to order it.[7] The problem is occasioned as much by the puzzling *character* of the new facts as by their number: particles that behave antiintuitively; ostensibly objective experiments that are affected by the experimenter's expectations;[8] thoughts that appear to transmit themselves without physical media,[9] and so on. In the absence of convincing

[7]Approximately two million scientific experiments are now being reported each year, and it has been estimated that the quantity of factual information in virtually every academic discipline is doubling about every ten years.

[8]The allusion is to Dr. Rosenthal's experiment at the University of North Dakota in which he assigned undifferentiated rats to his assistants telling some that they were being given genius rats and others that they were being given stupid ones with the result that the 'genius' rats learned to run mazes markedly faster than did the 'stupid' ones.

[9]Cf. C. D. Broad's attempt, which he admits comes to naught, to render an intelligible explanation for telepathy. *Religion, Philosophy and Psychical Research* (New York: Harcourt, Brace & Co., 1953), Chapter II.

syntheses to order the facts within departments of knowledge individually, how can we hope for a purview that will order them all? If Toynbee failed, what hope for a metaphysician?

These thoughts weigh heavily; so heavily that we might be tempted to abandon metaphysics forever, or at least for the time being, were it not for one fact. This fact is the nature of man. Man's knowing seems to reach out for something in the direction of metaphysics, and his life, which includes more than knowing, seems to as well.

III

Begin with life. Anthropologists have found that human life in the aggregate, which is to say human cultures, invariably include embracing outlooks on life and the world which provide their members with a sense of where they are and what is required of them. Psychologists find equal evidence of needs in this direction as they consider men individually rather than in groups. Erich Fromm says all men need "a frame of orientation." William Sheldon makes the point more emphatically. "Continued observations . . . in clinical psychological practice," he writes, "lead almost inevitably to the conclusion that deeper and more fundamental than sexuality, deeper than the craving for social power, deeper even than the desire for possessions, there is a still more generalized and more universal craving in the human make-up. It is the *craving for knowledge of the right direction—for orientation.*"

I find mid-century British and (to a large extent) American philosophers puzzling in their stance toward this need. They acknowledge that "man is a creature who makes pictures of himself and then comes to resemble the picture,"[10] while conveying the impression that philosophy's historic involvement in such picture painting, alongside that of theology and art, is no longer becoming. One of our most judicious philosophers recently extolled a deceased colleague as a man "not . . . driven by pathological anxieties about the cosmos or by a theological concern for the place of man in the scheme of things. Philosophy as he practiced it does not yield solace to bruised spirits; and it offers no apocalyptic vision of the universe, or a unified system of principles that provide categorical answers . . ." The implication is

---

[10]Iris Murdoch, in D. F. Pears, *op. cit.*, p. 122.

that attempts to locate man in his cosmic setting are compensations for intellectual or emotional weakness.

If any one of the following propositions is true, the current Anglo-American disconcern with overviews is justified:

1. The need for overviews is apparent only, not real.

2. The need for overviews may in some instances be genuine, but where it is thus genuine, it is pathological. Consequently attention should be directed to removing the need rather than catering to it. (John Wisdom?)

3. Overviews may be important, but reason can indicate nothing regarding them. They arise from faith, circumstance, chance, or naked decision. (Kierkegaard?)

4. Overviews may be important and reason competent *in principle* to work with them, but not yet. The premise here is that knowledge proceeds from part to whole; until we have clarified our understanding of aspects of experience that impinge on us directly and elementally, how can we hope to deal significantly with imponderables? (G. E. Moore?[11] Also Gilbert Ryle?[12])

But none of these propositions is true. The fourth is the most plausible, but the tide has turned against even it. Whether we listen to psychology, phenomenology, or the philosophy of science, the report is the same: there is no datum unpatterned, no figure without ground, no fact without theory. Psychology abandoned atomism with its discovery that there is no level of experience, perceptual or otherwise, that is free from what positivism called non-cognitive factors, and

[11]Professor Nagel has reminded us that Moore "never associated himself . . . with current revolts against the traditional conception of philosophy as an inquiry into the most general features of the entire scheme of things" ("The Debt We Owe to G. E. Moore," *The Journal of Philosophy*, 67, Dec. 22, 1960, 811). On the contrary, he maintained that one of the tasks of philosophy is to present "a general description of the *whole* of the universe" (G. E. Moore, *Some Main Problems of Philosophy* [London: Allen & Unwin, 1953], p. 1.) But he was convinced that such descriptions can command respect only when compiled or extrapolated from accurate knowledge of the world's parts. "That all truths about the universe possess to one another all the various relations which may be meant by 'unity', can only be legitimately asserted, when we have carefully distinguished those various relations and discovered what those truths are" (*Principia Ethica* [Cambridge: Cambridge University Press, 1954], p. 222).

[12]Our critics "scold us . . . for our sedulous refusal to talk about the cosmos . . . To this charge we had better plead guilty, though not, I suggest, with grave dejection. The time is not yet ripe for new global syntheses." In D. F. Pears (ed.), *op. cit.*, p. 156.

other epistemologically interested disciplines have followed suit with varying degrees of alacrity. Instead of a one-way process whereby through perceptual archaeology irrefrangible primitive elements— Hume's impressions, Russell and Moore's sense data—are first spotted and *then* built into wholes, knowledge (we now see) is polar. Part and whole are in dialogue from the start. And because this is so, philosophers cannot ignore metaphysics even if they abandon existential questions to psychologists and theologians forthwith. As long as they retain their interest in epistemology, questions of unrestricted scope (i.e. metaphysical questions) will inevitably intrude. For no man looks at the world with pristine eyes; he sees it edited, and editorial policy is always forged in the widest field of vision at command.

IV

If this is true, we should expect to find philosophers' recent attempts to take their epistemology 'neat' proving unsuccessful. And this, in fact, we do find. It is now generally agreed that the positivists were metaphysical with a vengeance.[13] As for their linguistic successors, if we take Gilbert Ryle as a sample can we not paraphrase Lenin's charge that "in Huxley agnosticism serves as a fig-leaf for materialism" and say that in Ryle ordinary language philosophy serves as a cover for behaviorism? Phenomenology's careful methodology has been no more successful in screening the biasses of its practitioners. Husserl proposed that we 'bracket' existence, that we empty our minds of belief in their heritage of assumptions, habits, and apparent cognitive certainties. But are we to believe that no assumptions intervened between his bracketing and his conclusion that consciousness constitutes the world? Heidegger and Sartre posit a direct, unreflective knowing through mood and affect. But do the moods of sombreness, hopelessness, and bitter, ascetic heroism through which they predominantly view the human predicament (why not, as Paul Pruyser has asked, simply the human situation?) do nothing to color (discolor?) the reality pictures that emerge from them? Are we to take it as accidental that the contemporary phenomenologist who does most justice to the joyous side of man's existence and his hope, namely Marcel, is the one who ap-

[13]Professor Hartshorne was among the first to point this out. See his "Metaphysics for Positivists," *Philosophy of Science*, 2, No. 3 (July, 1935), 287–303.

proaches his subject from an expressly Christian orientation? Apparently the attempt to elucidate being-in-general from being-human contains no inbuilt protection against the danger of generalizing from the way being-human strikes a particular phenomenologist. De Waelhens saw this twenty years ago when he wrote "so-called neutral descriptions are full of moral and philosophical presuppositions—phenomenology is often a 'point of view' rather than pure description."[14]

V

I suspect that as our century draws toward its close metaphysical interest will quicken to such an extent that rebirth will appear a not inapposite metaphor. I say this not only because I agree with Kant in his *Critique of Pure Reason* that men have a psychological need to ask the over-arching questions, but for logical reasons as well. It is one of the ironies of our time—completely understandable, but ironical nonetheless—that rising standards of scholarship and the explosion of knowledge have fragmented research in every field at precisely the moment that we see most clearly that knowing always involves a convergence between elements and the contexts that endow them with meaning. We are doing well with the elements. In the decades ahead philosophical endeavor will reflect a growing realization of the limited usefulness of advancing on this front while marking time on the other.[15]

What pointers might guide us as our interest in metaphysics revives?

1. No longer should we expect our systems to mirror the noumenal world (a) in its fullness or (b) even in limited features it may possess in itself. We have come to know too much about the relativity of knowledge to continue the traditional metaphysical ambition of bringing our thoughts into isomorphic congruence with reality as it exists apart from our perspectives. Insofar as we now think of reality-as-it-is-in-itself

---

[14]*La Philosophie de Martin Heidegger* (Louvain: Edit. de l'institut Supérieur de Philosophie, 1942).

[15]Already there are harbingers of recovery. Findlay's *Hegel*, Strawson's *Individuals*, and Hampshire's *Thought and Action* all go beyond piecemeal studies in the direction of syntheses, and it is said that toward the close of his life even Austin was coming around to more general questions in his Saturday morning discussions.

at all, we are inclined to imagine it as an un-ordered phenomenal wilderness—along the lines of Merleau-Ponty's "pre-objective world," perhaps, or the "buzzing, booming confusion" of the infantile mind as James envisioned it. Against this amorphous background we build our "coherent fairy-tales." From now on we shall regard any view of reality we construct as being the way it appears *from the human perspective.*

2. Or rather, "from *a* human perspective," we are likely to add in view of our greater awareness of the variety of ways in which the world can take shape in men's minds in different times and places. But it is important here to distinguish three levels at which world views can be attempted. (a) There may be some generic features which all world views must possess by virtue of the fact that they are framed by human beings. Cross-cultural studies, from perception and linguistics right over into comparative mythology, would appear to be the best means of discerning these features insofar as they exist. (b) Other elements in our outlooks will not be required by our basic humanity, but instead will derive their plausibility from a given cultural heritage: what it 'knows' about the world, its criteria of credibility, its prevailing assumptions and dominant expectations. (c) Finally, there are features of our outlooks which are, and should remain, idiosyncratic. A phrase, a metaphor, a *mantram,* each for reasons that are entirely personal might organize the world meaningfully for some individual without the slightest claim to do so for others.

Generic, cultural, and personal aspects of world views—traditional metaphysics has focussed on the first, existentialism on the other two. There is place for all three.

3. Wittgenstein's release of meaning from reference into use opens important possibilities for help from those who approach philosophy through linguistic analysis. I have yet to see an adequate statement of the valid *uses* of metaphysical discourse; even theological discourse seems to have received greater attention. A careful analysis of the functions and rules of metaphysical assertions should prove most valuable.

4. Along the lines just mentioned, analytic philosophy can help. It has another side, however, which is less auspicious. This is the side that gets tangled with the notion that philosophy is concerned exclusively with questions of form rather than content. The first (positivistic) version of this notion was grounded in the distinction

between analytic and synthetic: philosophy was to occupy itself exclusively with analytic issues while leaving synthetic ones to science. The second (Wittgensteinian) version draws the line between analyzing language games and using them for purposes other than such analysis; from there it goes on to suggest that the concerns of philosophy are exclusively with linguistic analysis. It is doubtful that either of these distinctions is air-tight; and even if they were, they would truncate philosophy if used to restrict its scope. Metaphysics' task is not over when the nature of metaphysical discourse is specified or even when the major modes of discourse are disentangled. The problems of metaphysics are not co-terminal with those of language unless language is equated with thought.

5. The error of supposing that we cannot profitably proceed to metaphysical questions until we get a number of smaller questions answered has already been remarked. It involves the fallacy of thinking that knowledge proceeds uni-directionally from part to whole. Kenneth Boulding's *The Image*[16] does a nice job of showing the extent to which throughout the various domains of knowledge our identification, valuation, and interpretation of data is controlled by our images of wholes. The attics of university buildings are crammed with research files which lie abandoned for eternity because changes in hypotheses render their data irrelevant. Meaning descends from whole to part as much as it ascends from part to whole.

6. The existentialist and phenomenological suspicions of objectivity and system need to be pondered carefully. They fear the right things—cynicism, relativism, nihilism—but have they correctly diagnosed their causes? "You cannot get everything into your system unless you have first gotten everything out of your system," they say, punning on the word "system" to make the point that to conceptualize a problem is to divorce oneself from it emotionally. But is this true—of Spinoza, of St. Thomas, of some Marxists and Vedantists I know today? Eric Heller says that the health of a culture (and by implication an individual) is determined by the number of values it takes so much for granted that it isn't even aware of them. This criterion makes every Hottentot healthier than Socrates. If existentialists and phenomenologists discover a method of building engagement into the very fabric of their theses, this will be a remarkable breakthrough: one

16Ann Arbor: The University of Michigan Press, 1956.

which neither poets nor religious writers have thus far managed. Short of this, we will do better to strive for good systems and the kind of objectivity that is not incompatible with commitment than to abjure these attributes of metaphysics while having no alternatives.

VI

As to the mode by which a new metaphysics might emerge, one thinks of two possibilities. If a dramatic new truth about the world were to come into view; if, in the succession of the copernican revolution, darwinian evolution, freudianism, or quantum mechanics, we were tomorrow to become completely convinced that extra-sensory perception, say, is a reality, or if we were to discover life on other planets so radically different that it threw the question of what life is into an entirely new perspective—if revolutionary discoveries of proportions such as these were to come into view I suspect that interest would swing rapidly from many of our present minute concerns toward working out the implications of the new discoveries for our view of life and reality in general. Short of this, the best prospect would seem to be to keep a careful eye on the basic concepts and theories of the various major fields of knowledge and try to formulate a general scheme of categories which will provide a perspective in which to view them all.

My single confidence is that the conviction to which Professor Hartshorne has devoted his intellectual life—that metaphysics is philosophy's central concern—will before long again be widespread in the philosophical community.

HUSTON SMITH

MASSACHUSETTS INSTITUTE OF TECHNOLOGY

STUDIES IN WHITEHEADIAN PHILOSOPHY

SCIENCE AND ITS HISTORY IN THE PHILOSOPHY OF WHITEHEAD

I

WHITEHEAD'S *Science and the Modern World* is certainly the most widely read and probably the most influential of his writings. This seems at first somewhat surprising, since much of the book deals with technical metaphysical issues of a peculiarly abstruse kind. On the other hand, the book is eminently quotable on a great variety of subjects, including mathematics, scientific method, English Romantic poetry, religion. And, indeed, *Science and the Modern World* is frequently quoted by those in search of authoritative support on any of these topics. Unfortunately, the misconstrued or misapplied quotations predominate; perhaps it is only the natural and appropriate tribute to a great and difficult thinker that he be cited more often for his aphorisms than for his passages of sustained argument and analysis. But it must be recognized that many of the chapters of *Science and the Modern World* do seem to be separable into two distinct and independent units: an opening historical discussion of some important topic relating to modern science followed by an elaboration of some leading ideas of the philosophy of organism (Whitehead's metaphysical system). The latter is, for the general reader, almost totally opaque; for the majority of contemporary philosophers, an unfortunate excursion into old-fashioned speculative metaphysics; and for the few serious students of Whitehead's philosophy, an incomplete and therefore only partly intelligible version of the system set forth in full detail in Whitehead's later book, *Process and Reality*. One suspects, therefore, that the usual way of reading *Science and the Modern World* is to ignore the metaphysical portion of each chapter, while treating the historical portion as a source of arresting epigrams on that always topical subject: "Modern Science—Its Implications and Presuppositions." Not that these epigrams should not be taken seriously: Whitehead was scarcely the thinker to indulge in rhetorical effects for their own sakes. Taken out of context, however, some of Whitehead's ideas and arguments will inevitably appear intellectually outrageous—justifiable, if at all, only by a kind of special poetic license granted to speculative philosophers. What can it mean, one might ask, to compare the role of mathematics in the history of thought to the role of Ophelia in *Hamlet* on the ground that both the "queen of the sciences" (to use Gauss's epithet) and the unfortunate young lady are indispensable, charming, and a little mad; or, to compare the performance of a crucial experiment in modern science to the performance of a Greek tragedy? But, I would urge, not only do these comparisons help to elucidate some of Whitehead's central themes; they also exhibit in action an essential feature of Whitehead's philosophical method, namely, the use of analogies drawing upon the most disparate areas of experience.

Science and the Modern World makes another claim upon our attention: it is the book which marks a transition from Whitehead's early work in mathematics and philosophy of science to his later work in metaphysics. And the transition is effected, I believe, precisely by means of the historical considerations with which most of the chapters open. Although I am not going to engage in textual explication of *Science and the Modern World,* we might take a close look at the opening chapter as a useful point of departure for subsequent discussion of Whitehead's conception of science, and at the same time as a way of throwing some light on the deep and much debated question of the origins of modern science.

Let me say at once that Whitehead offers us no simple thesis as an answer to the question. As many as ten different historical factors—economic, religious, philosophical, etc.—are mentioned in his discussion. Some of the factors will scarcely be news to students of the history of science, while others will seem far-fetched, even perverse, when judged by orthodox canons of historical interpretation. However, what specially characterizes Whitehead's analysis of the origins of modern science is not so much the inclusion or exclusion of some particular historical factor as *a general pattern of historical explanation.* Instead of the prevalent and often rather simple-minded listing of two non-overlapping sets of factors—the "positive", or those which tended to bring about a certain historical phenomenon, and the "negative", or those which tended to inhibit the occurrence of that phenomenon[1]—

1One or the other set may be empty. See, for example, the set of five (positive) factors which Gibbon proposes to explain the success of Christianity, *Decline and*

Whitehead gives us a single set of interacting factors, each of which may, in different respects, be *both* positive and negative in its effects. It must be emphasized, however, that Whitehead does not attempt to document adequately his historical analysis; neither shall I attempt such a documentation; and, indeed, I seriously doubt that any single contemporary scholar *could* adequately document (or refute) the analysis or even that the requisite historical data are currently available. Still, there are one or two things I am willing to assert rather positively: first, that no satisfactory explanation of why science emerged—and emerged only—in Western Europe in the sixteenth and seventeenth centuries can be much simpler than Whitehead's intricate scheme of interlocking hypotheses; and second, that each of these hypotheses considered separately would prove enormously stimulating and fruitful for future research in the history of science and in cultural history generally.

We may preface our account of Whitehead's analysis of the origins of modern science with a query as to the relevance of the topic in the broader scheme of *Science and the Modern World*. After all, Whitehead *begins* the book with a definition of the "new mentality" characteristic of modern science, namely, "a vehement and passionate interest in the relation of general principles to irreducible and stubborn facts"[2]; why not simply proceed to describe the impact of this new mentality on philosophy, poetry, religion, technology, and social affairs—in short, on the various institutions and modes of experience which make up the modern world? The answer, of course, is that it helps us to understand the nature of modern science and its influence if we first examine the slow growth of the new mentality in the centuries prior to its explosive manifestations during "the century of

Fall of the Roman Empire, Chap. XV, and the set of a dozen or so (negative) factors which S. Sambursky proposes to explain the decline of ancient Greek science, *The Physical World of the Greeks* (London, 1956), Chap. X.

[2]SMW, p. 3. Whitehead's works are referred to in this essay by the following abbreviations:

AI   *Adventures of Ideas* (New York, 1933).
ESP   *Essays in Science and Philosophy* (New York: Philosophical Library, 1948—there is another edition with different pagination).
FR   *The Function of Reason* (Princeton, 1929).
PR   *Process and Reality* (New York, 1929).
R   *The Principle of Relativity* (Cambridge, 1922).
SMW *Science and the Modern World* (New York, 1925).

genius" (Whitehead's name for the seventeenth century). Noteworthy, however, is the fact that Whitehead gives us this answer in the form of an exemplification of a general methodological principle to the effect that the history of thought—of which the history of science is a part—must always be traced both backward and forward for full understanding. Thus, to understand modern science we must understand both antecedents and consequences of the new mentality which is its necessary condition.

What are the ingredients of the new mentality? Whitehead distinguishes three:[3] (1) an instinctive belief in the existence of an order of nature; (2) a sense for what constitutes coherent, systematic thinking; (3) an active interest in natural occurrences for their own sakes. Each of these three factors has its own historical antecedents which may be briefly summarized as follows.

First, the ideas of fate and of the moral order in Greek tragedy, the Hebrew conception of a personal God, and the Stoic conception of nature combined to produce the rational God of medieval theology, from which was derived, unconsciously, the scientific belief in an order of nature. This belief provides the motivation for scientific research. (A negative instance supporting his argument, according to Whitehead, is the failure of the otherwise extraordinarily advanced Asiatic civilizations to develop either this conception of God or anything resembling modern science.) But, though inquiry into natural phenomena might be encouraged by belief in an omnipotent rational deity, the mixture of moral, theological, and philosophical ideas which gave rise to this belief tended to emphasize the role of final causes in scholastic cosmology, thereby delaying the development of the modern concept of physical law which is predicated on the elimination of final in favor of efficient causes.

Nevertheless, the predominantly dramatic, moral, and therefore antihistorical cosmology which the scholastics (rightly or wrongly) derived from Greek philosophy probably contributed to that "diffused sense of order"[4] which was so characteristic of medieval civilization. Intellectually, this sense of order manifested itself as a sense for coherent systematic thought, the most impressive historical antece-

---

[3] These ingredients must, of course, occur in just the right proportions; thus in SMW, p. 8, Whitehead refers to the "peculiar balance of mind required for science."
[4] SMW, p. 16.

dents of which were Greek mathematics and Roman law. Intense cultivation of this aspect of the new mentality resulted in an aptitude for analyzing clearly and pursuing cogently the various possible conclusions inherent in any given set of premises—"the priceless habit," as Whitehead calls it, "of looking for an exact point and of sticking to it when found."[5] Galileo, for example, was deeply indebted for his methodology to a long line of medieval thinkers at the University of Padua. On the other hand, an exclusive devotion to the lucid certainties of Greek mathematics conceived as the ideal of knowledge and an exclusive reliance on metaphysical analyses of the nature of things conceived as the preferred method for discovering truth tended to discourage patient and minute observation of natural phenomena and to degenerate eventually into a dogmatic and sterile rationalism. The latter provoked, by way of reaction, the anti-rationalistic spirit of many of the great founders of modern science, often expressed in their appeal to the evidences of the senses against the rationalistic excesses of their predecessors and opponents.

This anti-rationalism was, of course, in itself a purely negative attitude; nevertheless, I would suggest, it may have played a decisive role in the emergence of modern science by helping to confer intellectual respectability on that aspect of the new mentality which Whitehead describes as an active interest in natural occurrences for their own sakes. Such interest has certainly never been entirely lacking in human beings, but search for the antecedents of the new mentality discloses the special importance in this connection of three things: Roman technology, the practical activities of early Christian monks, and the naturalism of late medieval art. Once again, however, the "positive" influence of a certain historical factor is in part counteracted by a concomitant "negative" influence: in this case, the anti-rationalism of early modern science—which was probably a historical necessity—has long outlived its usefulness, but scientists and many thinkers in other fields continue to ignore the vital role of speculative reason in human culture generally, and in their own specialized disciplines in particular.

There are several striking things about Whitehead's discussion of the factors responsible for the rise of modern science. First of all, two of the three factors would seem to operate primarily at the level of feeling, namely, instinctive belief in an order of nature and active interest in natural occurrences for their own sakes. This should come as no surprise to anyone familiar with Whitehead's view that a civilization is always based much more on shared feelings than on shared conscious beliefs.[6] Thus, for Whitehead, the scientific revolution of the sixteenth and seventeenth centuries is not to be identified in terms of specific theoretical advances or the discovery of novel empirical data—such as the formulation of the principle of inertia, or the construction of a heliostatic system of the universe, or the recovery of ancient Greek mathematics, or the application of the microscope and telescope to the study of nature—but rather in terms of a general and only partly conscious shift in pervasive modes of thought, a change in the whole "climate of opinion." "The new mentality," says Whitehead, "is more important even than the new science and the new technology. It has altered the metaphysical presuppositions and the imaginative contents of our minds; so that now the old stimuli provoke a new response."[7]

The second point to note about Whitehead's list of factors is the somewhat surprising omission of mathematics. It *is* true, after all, that Huygens's powerful adaptations of Greek geometrical methods and Newton's invention of the infinitesimal calculus—to mention just two examples—were both designed, at least in part, as mathematical techniques for developing the new mechanics—a science which was in the vanguard of the scientific revolution. Whitehead, of course, is well aware of the significance of mathematics in modern science, and indeed very much in agreement with the commonly accepted view that makes of mathematics part of the essence of modern science. In fact, the second chapter of *Science and the Modern World* is devoted to a detailed analysis of the role of mathematics in the history of thought, and here Whitehead stresses the importance of mathematics as a factor in the scientific revolution.[8] I suggest that Whitehead may be making the following rather subtle point about the precise part played by

---

[6]See AI, p. 299.

[7]SMW, p. 3.

[8]This chapter was not one of the original Lowell Lectures on which SMW is based (see SMW, pp. x–xi). I take this as a piece of internal textual evidence supporting my interpretation above, namely, that Whitehead sees mathematics as an essential factor in the "Century of Genius" (Chap. III of SMW) but not as an essential factor in the origins of modern science.

mathematics in early modern science. Like many other historians of science, Whitehead identifies two of the first definite achievements of modern science as the heliostatic cosmology of Copernicus and the anatomy of Vesalius. (As often remarked, the representative character of these two great figures is enhanced by the fact that their respective monumental treatises, *On the Revolutions of the Heavenly Spheres* and *The Fabric of the Human Body*, were published in the same year, 1543.) But neither Copernicus nor Vesalius owed any of his innovations as such to mathematics (Copernicus, of course, made full use of the complex mathematical machinery of Ptolemaic astronomy, which he did not, contrary to an all too common opinion, notably simplify).[9]

Obviously, however, if scientific progress was to continue uninterruptedly and cumulatively after the initial triumphs of the scientific revolution, the conscious, intellectual factor in the new mentality had to become more explicit and more organized. To achieve this end, mathematics was the ideal intellectual discipline. One must agree with Whitehead's judgment that the birth of modern physics in the seventeenth century would have been impossible without the prior elaboration by mathematicians of ideas like those involved in the abstract theory of periodicity.[10] More generally, the abstract notion of a mathematical function served for the study of the order of nature in the form of mathematically expressed laws of nature. Examples would be Galileo's formulation of alternative laws of acceleration for falling bodies, and Newton's analysis of the mathematical consequences of hypothetical laws of force between two particles expressed as functions of the distance between the particles (that is, the inverse cube law, the inverse square law, and the law of direct proportionality). As Whitehead puts it, "Mathematics supplied the background of imaginative thought with which the men of science approached the observation of nature."[11] Nevertheless, in attempting to discover the most general features of the new mentality which made modern science possible, it is perhaps just as well to omit mathematics, thereby

---

[9]See, for example, O. Neugebauer, *The Exact Sciences in Antiquity* (2nd ed.: Providence, 1957), Appendix II, or D. J. Price, "Contra-Copernicus," *Critical Problems in the History of Science*, ed. M. Clagett (Madison, 1959).

[10]I would add that even Harvey's proof of the circulation of the blood depended essentially on arithmetical calculations.

[11]SMW, p. 46.

stressing the fact that although *some* systematic method is required in scientific inquiry, the particular kind of mathematics devised in the late seventeenth century (and almost universally employed in the physical sciences for the next two hundred years) is not sacrosanct and might well prove unsuitable for dealing with certain significant scientific problems.[12] It should be emphasized, however, that nowhere does Whitehead hold that any science (e.g., biology or psychology) is *intrinsically* incapable of mathematical formulation. It is rather a question of the proper role of mathematics in natural science. Hence Whitehead's remark, "There can be no true physical science which looks first to mathematics for the provision of a conceptual model. Such a procedure is to repeat the errors of the logicians of the middle-ages."[13] I shall return to this admonition later on, in connection with some of Whitehead's own work in theoretical physics.

Once science—or at least physics—has become fully mathematicized, is it still meaningful to speak of it as anti-rational? After all, isn't mathematics the rational discipline *par excellence*? Indeed, the scientific revolution itself has been plausibly described as a revolt *in favor* of reason and *against* the deliverances of the senses (including so-called "common sense"). Galileo, for example, refers to "the rape of the senses" which is involved in the acceptance of the heliostatic conception of the universe (because the sun, not the earth, *appears* to be moving through the heavens). Clearly we are here up against a terminological issue. In fact, Whitehead often distinguishes two different conceptions, or functions, of reason: one which he calls "practical", the other "speculative".[14] Reason in the practical sense refers to the devising of methodologies and schemes of abstraction designed to achieve various limited purposes (such as the discovery of the laws of physics). Reason in the speculative sense refers to the quest for a complete understanding of the world, and proceeds by comparison of the schemes of abstraction developed in different areas of experience in an attempt to elucidate the concrete facts from which

[12]Recent developments in both the physical and the non-physical sciences seem to have confirmed this view. That is, such mathematical disciplines as matrix algebra, set theory, tensor analysis, group theory, differential geometry, and topology have begun to supplement the classical theory of differential equations in such sciences as physics, economics, and psychology.

[13]R, p. 39.

[14]See FR for an elaboration of this distinction.

all the abstractions are derived. The ideal outcome of this attempt would be the construction of a system of speculative philosophy (such as the scholastic philosophy of the middle ages or Whitehead's own philosophy of organism) in which science as well as each of the other principal areas of experience finds its appropriate interpretation. In these terms, modern science was originally, and has remained, a revolt against the speculative use of reason but certainly not against reason in the practical sense. And in Whitehead's view, modern science has not only gained but also suffered from its long absorption in the perfecting of a highly specialized methodology—suffered from missed opportunities of theoretical revision, and from a weakening or distortion of its proper impact on the rest of human culture. For example, the dogma of mechanistic explanations impeded progress in physics during the nineteenth century; and the potentially salutary effects of science in de-mythologizing religion have been partly negated by a scientifically based positivism which relegates values to the realm of mere subjectivity and thereby fosters the indifference, if not the downright hostility, of many religious believers toward science.

The respective functions of the three factors which, according to Whitehead, jointly produced modern science may be summed up as follows: (1) instinctive belief in an order of nature served as the *motivation* for scientific inquiry; (2) a sense for coherent systematic thought developed into the *mathematical method* of analyzing natural phenomena; (3) active interest in natural occurrences for their own sakes stimulated detailed and precise *observation and experiment*.

II

Whitehead's treatment of the origins of modern science suggests some of the major themes in his philosophical analysis of science. If science is concerned with natural occurrences for their own sakes, the philosopher of science will have to be concerned with the general character of natural occurrences as such. If science is deeply committed to the mathematical formulation of natural laws, the limitations of such commitment at any given time must be subject to continuing scrutiny by the practicing scientist. If science depends on faith in an order of nature, it is up to the metaphysician to ask in what sense this faith can be justified. We shall proceed now to examine an important aspect of each of these three themes: first, Whitehead's analysis of natural occurrences; second, Whitehead's critique of Einstein's general relativity and his construction of an alternative theory; finally, Whitehead's attempt to provide an ontological foundation for the belief in an order of nature.

A natural occurrence for Whitehead is something observed through the senses or at least in principle so observable. The aggregate of such sense-perceptions is what we mean by Nature. Whitehead emphasizes that Nature is *not* to be identified with the whole of reality but is "an abstraction from something more concrete than itself which must also include imagination, thought, and emotion."[15] Each act of sense-perception involves as its terminus, or content, a specific totality of factors, some clearly defined, some vague, some fleeting, some persistent. Whitehead calls any such totality an *event*, while the factors distinguishable within any event are called *objects* or, synonymously, *adjectives*. This latter usage, which seems to eliminate the difference between "things" and their "qualities," is, of course, a part of Whitehead's deliberate repudiation of the traditional philosophical distinction between substances and attributes. I shall not pause here to explain Whitehead's analysis of this most complex and controversial topic beyond saying that for him an ordinary physical object (e.g., a chair or a star or the body of a living organism) is in every case to be identified with some common identity of character possessed by each member of a continuous sequence of events. It thus emerges that "objects" or "things" as ordinarily understood are abstractions; and, if the criterion of a substance is its concreteness, then the only true substances in Whitehead's philosophy of nature are events. To mistake objects—in particular scientific objects like atoms and molecules—for the concrete elements of nature is to commit the "fallacy of misplaced concreteness." This is the fallacy which vitiated the natural philosophy of the entire centuries-long period dominated intellectually by concepts derived from classical physics.[16] To recognize that the fundamental entities at any stage of the history of

[15]R, p. 63.

[16]See AI, p. 186: ". . . in the twentieth century this great notion [of material bodies], as shaped for use by Galileo and Newton, has completely collapsed so far as concerns its use as a fundamental notion for physical science. In the modern science, it is a limited notion confined to special purposes.

"This collapse of nineteenth century dogmatism is a warning that the special sciences require that the imaginations of men be stored with imaginative possibilities as yet un-utilized in the service of scientific explanation."

science are relatively abstract compared with events is, however, only the first half of Whitehead's proposed philosophical reformation; the other half lies in the recognition that events themselves are relatively abstract compared with actual experiences. Sense-perception rarely, if ever, occurs apart from feelings, emotions, and valuations; hence, any adequate philosophy must place such "subjective" states at the very heart of reality. We shall return to this point.

Suppose we now consider events as such, that is, apart from the various qualities which may characterize them. The only remaining differentiating characteristic of events is then simply how big they are. Thus, the full content of my sense-awareness of a particular landscape during a thirty-second interval is an event. A second event would be the full content of my sense-awareness of that landscape during the first half of the same thirty-second interval. A third event would be the full content of my sense-awareness of some circum-scribed portion of the same landscape during the original thirty-second interval. Using Whitehead's terminology, the first event is said to *extend over* (or *include*) each of the other two events. Events, then, are extended both in space and in time; events are four-dimensional entities. Also, events need not be "small" or "brief"; Whitehead cites the endurance of a block of marble as an example of an event. From the various possible relations of extension among events Whitehead claims to derive, in rigorous logico-mathematical fashion, all of the properties of space and time essential to the development of mathe-matical physics. I can illustrate the fundamental idea behind White-head's procedure (which he calls "the method of extensive abstrac-tion") by means of a simplified example using two-dimensional spatial regions instead of four-dimensional events.

Consider the concept of a point as it occurs in geometry. Clearly, points are inaccessible to sense-perception, since they are assumed to be literally unextended entities. Equally clearly, however, points are, if not indispensable, at least of very great utility in theoretical physics. Whitehead sees as a fundamental problem of philosophy of science the explanation of *how* points (and other similar entities) are related to events and objects and *why* such entities are important in natural science. Let's examine Whitehead's answer to the latter question first. Suppose we want to define the "distance" between two regions of a plane surface. Obviously, there is no unique value for this magnitude, since the distance will vary with one's choice of the termini of the straight line connecting the two regions. However, as one considers smaller and smaller regions the deviations in the various values representing the distance between the regions become less marked and eventually, perhaps, negligible. If, then, we could define some sort of a minimum (perhaps "infinitesimal"?) region in the plane, we might expect that the distance between any two such regions would be uniquely determined. In this way the introduction of points serves to simplify geometrical relationships.

But how shall we *define* points? The trouble with our formulation so far is that we have referred to "minimum" or "infinitesimal" regions which we have no reason to believe exist. Sense-perception always without exception reveals *finite* regions of space. Why not, then, make a virtue of necessity and define a point, not as a special sort of infinitely small spatial region but as a class of finite spatial regions? In particular, we might attempt to define a point P as that class of regions which would normally be said to "converge" to P. An immediate objection is that there are many classes of regions (even an infinite number) which "converge" to P. Consider, for example, a class of concentric circles with P as center; then, a class of squares inscribed in the circles; then, a class of hexagons circumscribed about the circles; and so on.[17] Which of these classes of convergent regions —the circles, the squares, etc.—shall we use to define the point P? Whitehead answers: all of them. In other words, Whitehead proposes to define the point P as the complete class of all the classes of regions which converge to P. Of course, in the formal definition of a point any reference to the point must be avoided; otherwise the definition would be circular. It should be noted that Whitehead denies that points are real in the sense in which events are real; hence, as far as we know, there is literally *nothing* to which the convergent classes of regions could converge. Instead, a point is to be identified completely with a class of regions (appropriately chosen) ; the success of the definition is measured by whether the defined entities turn out to possess all of the usual properties of points (and no unusual properties) .

It is perhaps worth stating here at least the central definition of

[17]For simplicity of description, only "regular" geometrical figures have been mentioned as examples of regions. In general, however, the regions may have any shapes whatsoever; nor must all of the regions in a given convergent set have the same shape.

Whitehead's method of extensive abstraction. Here, then, is the formal definition of an *abstractive class of events:*

First, of any two members of the class, one extends over the other; second, there is no event extended over by all the events in the class.

It follows at once from these defining conditions that an abstractive class of events must possess an infinite number of members—otherwise there would be a "smallest" event in the class, i.e., an event extended over by *all* the other events in the class. An infinite set of progressively smaller concentric circles will serve as a simple representation of an abstractive class of events. It is easy to see that two equivalent abstractive classes (say, the circles and a corresponding infinite set of inscribed squares) will be such that every member of the one class extends over some member of the other, and conversely. Thus, one can define sets of equivalent abstractive classes. The method of extensive abstraction deals with the "convergence properties" defined by such sets of equivalent abstractive classes of events.

I want to emphasize that the above sketch of Whitehead's analysis of points gives only a faint indication of the rather complicated and in some cases highly ingenious mathematical techniques that he develops in order to carry out his program of deriving all geometrical entities from relations of inclusion between events. Now, it cannot be denied that the effect of using Whitehead's mathematical techniques is to complicate geometry considerably. Whitehead's justification is that if points, for example, are really complex entities—as he thinks they must be on the relativistic view of space—then it is incumbent on the philosopher of science to exhibit this complexity and not to conceal it. Sometimes, however, Whitehead's philosophically motivated innovations lead to simplifications of existing theories. The most notable instance of this is his theory of relativity, proposed as a substitute for Einstein's general theory of relativity. I turn now to a discussion of this theory.

III

Einstein's special theory of relativity of 1905 replaced the absolute space and time of classical Newtonian mechanics with an infinity of possible space-time frameworks, each of them relative to a possible state of uniform ("inertial") motion of a material particle. (An alternative rather common but nevertheless somewhat misleading formulation is to say that each space-time framework is relative *to an observer* attached to such a moving material particle.) However, Einstein retained the Euclidean space of classical mechanics and the absolute character of accelerated (e.g., rotational) motions. (I am simplifying the actual situation: in fact, Einstein introduced a four-dimensional space-time which had the properties described by mathematicians as "pseudo-Euclidean".) Now, Newton's law of universal gravitation presupposes the existence of a unique value for the distance between any two particles regardless of their state of relative motion. To see this, consider a mathematical formulation of the law:

$$f = G\frac{m_1 m_2}{r^2},$$

where f is the force between the particles of masses m_1 and m_2 separated by *the* distance r, and G is the gravitational constant. Since, according to special relativity, the distance between two particles must be a function of their relative motion, Newton's law cannot be introduced without change into relativistic physics. In 1916 Einstein discovered a relativistic law of gravitation to replace Newton's, but in so doing he found himself compelled to throw off the limitations of his earlier special relativity theory. In particular, the new theory—called general relativity—involved non-Euclidean space (more precisely, space-time), and assumed the relativity of *all* motion.

In order to appreciate Whitehead's critique and rejection of Einstein's general relativity, one must have some understanding of non-Euclidean geometry. For simplicity, but at the risk of some misunderstanding, I confine this discussion to two dimensions. (Note that this implies a double simplification: ordinary space is three-dimensional and the space-time which figures in general relativity is four-dimensional.) Consider two two-dimensional surfaces: an ordinary Euclidean plane, and the surface of a sphere. In a rough, intuitive sense, these surfaces obviously have different types of "curvature". However, both are "uniformly" curved, again in this intuitive sense. What would a non-uniformly curved surface be like? Well, good examples would be the surface of an egg or of a potato. The generalized geometry capable of characterizing such a surface (on which the meaning of distance in a sense varies from point to point) is usually termed "Riemannian." Space-time according to Einstein's general relativity must be imagined (but not visually!) in terms of a four-dimensional

Riemannian geometry whose curvature varies as a function of the intensity of the gravitational field, that is, the deviation from "flatness" increases with the strength of the gravitational field and in the limit of zero gravitational field space-time is Euclidean (or better, pseudo-Euclidean) as in special relativity. It should be added that Einstein's method of deriving his new law of gravitation leans heavily on the formal mathematical properties of Riemannian geometry.

Whitehead's criticism of general relativity is that its conceptual model is derived from pure mathematics rather than from some pervasive and fundamental feature of the natural world. More specifically, the central mathematical assumption of general relativity—that the character of physical space-time varies from place to place in a way that can only be discovered by empirical investigation—is based on an analogy with abstract, or non-physical, Riemannian geometry in which the character of the manifold can vary arbitrarily from point to point. According to Whitehead, "our experience requires and exhibits a basis of uniformity,"[18] which in the case of Nature is the uniformity of spatio-temporal relations. Uniform space and time are *required* if the attribution of spatial and temporal properties to unobserved portions of the universe is to be meaningful; for example, we assume that the unobserved interior of a solid material sphere always has a definite geometrical center; and we assume that it makes good sense to talk about the distance between two stars even prior to the investigation of the regions which lie between them. Uniform space and time are *exhibited* in the extensive relations of events. This follows because the relation of inclusion between events (on the basis of which Whitehead constructs his geometry of space-time) is independent of any qualities which may happen to characterize these events, for example, color, or mass, or being starlike. As events are conceived in Whitehead's natural philosophy, there is no way in which the continuum of events which constitutes Nature *could* be anything but uniform in its extensive, i.e., spatio-temporal, relations. It is, according to Whitehead, precisely the error of many relativistic theories of space and time (such as Einstein's) that they derive spatial and temporal relations from relations among *objects*—which may be material things or sense-data or scientific entities like the gravitational field—rather than from relations among events. Hence Whitehead's

18R, p. v.

theory of relativity is constructed within the framework of special relativity, which implies that Whitehead's space-time is uniform and his three-dimensional space Euclidean. However, Whitehead points out that there is nothing in his philosophical outlook incompatible with the use of uniformly curved but non-Euclidean space, e.g., the three-dimensional counterpart of the surface of a sphere. (It is worth noting that later physicists have indeed succeeded in reformulating Whitehead's theory in terms of uniformly curved non-Euclidean spaces.) [19]

I shall now attempt a brief explanation of Whitehead's relativistic law of gravitation. That I make the attempt at all is a significant indication of the vast difference in level of mathematical difficulty between Whitehead's law and Einstein's; the latter is, I am convinced, really unintelligible without a substantial knowledge of higher mathematics—and this despite the best efforts of a host of skilled popularizers. Whitehead's law of gravitation can be formulated so as to bring out its close similarity to Newton's law of gravitation. In fact, one may interpret Whitehead's law as the simplest possible relativistic reformulation of Newton's law. Thus, suppose one rewrites Newton's law as follows:

$$F = G \frac{m_1 m_2}{R^2},$$

where F and R are now relativistic counterparts of the force f and the distance r respectively in the classical pre-relativistic law, m_1 and m_2 are now the so-called rest-masses of the two particles, and G has the same meaning as before. The problem now is to find an expression for R leading to the correct empirical consequences for all known gravitational phenomena. This expression for R must have the same numerical value in all permissible space-time frameworks,[20] from which it follows that the expression must have the form $R = R\,(r_1, r_2, t_1, t_2, v_{12}, c)$; that is, R will involve the spatial positions and times of m_1 and m_2, the relative velocity of m_1 and m_2, and the velocity of light c. Also, when m_1 and m_2 are at rest with respect to one another, the new law must reduce essentially to Newton's law.

[19]See Appendix IV of my *Whitehead's Philosophy of Science* (Chicago, 1960), for references.

[20]In mathematical terms, R must be Lorentz-invariant.

Beyond this, all I will say here is that Whitehead did succeed in find-ing a new law of gravitation and in working out many of the detailed mathematical consequences of this law.[21] Whitehead's gravitational theory is very different from Einstein's,[22] and yet surprisingly enough, the two theories give identical results for the gravitational field of a mass-point (usually termed the Schwarzschild solution) . This fact, first demonstrated by Eddington, accounts for the identical predictions of the two theories in each of the three so-called "crucial" tests of general relativity. The two theories are now known to make divergent pre-dictions in at least two cases: the motion of the moon (under the influence of sun and earth) and the motion of double stars. The divergences are so slight that present observations are incapable of deciding between the two theories.

I have so far neglected to point out that Whitehead's attitude toward Einstein's general relativity is not in fact purely negative. Whitehead is quite willing, he says, to adopt Einstein's law of gravi-tation if it turns out to be in better agreement with observations than his own law; furthermore, Whitehead claims that his natural philos-ophy is not incompatible with Einstein's law. How can this be? The non-uniform geometry of general relativity would seem to be irre-concilable with Whitehead's insistence on uniform space-time. Ob-viously, Einstein's law must be somehow reinterpreted, but Whitehead never explains just how. Perhaps, however, a recent reformulation of Einstein's law in *flat* space-time illustrates what Whitehead had in mind. S. Gupta has succeeded in constructing a law of gravitation equivalent mathematically to Einstein's law but involving only the pseudo-Euclidean space-time of special relativity (and of Whitehead's own theory of gravitation) .[23] (Incidentally, Gupta suggests that his

[21]For the actual formulation of Whitehead's law, see the Appendix.

[22]In particular, Whitehead's differential equations are linear in contrast to the non-linear differential equations of general relativity. This constitutes a marked simplification of Whitehead's theory compared with Einstein's from the purely mathematical point of view. Physically, Whitehead's theory can give a rigorous analysis of the two-body problem—something which, as far as I know, has not yet been accomplished in general relativistic terms.

[23]S. Gupta, "Einstein's and other theories of gravitation," *Reviews of Modern Physics,* **29,** 3 (July, 1957), 334. In this paper, Gupta first states three criteria for an acceptable theory of gravitation, leaving aside, as he puts it, "all philosophical con-siderations." The theory should (1) be Lorentz covariant, (2) reduce to Newton's theory of gravitation as a good approximation, (3) explain the three crucial tests (red shift of light emitted in a gravitational field, bending of light-rays as they pass near

formulation may actually be more convenient than Einstein's for dealing with certain physical problems, notably the quantization of the gravitational field.)

IV

We come now to Whitehead's attempt to discover an ontological foundation for the scientific faith in an order of nature. Whitehead's approach to this problem may be outlined as follows. During the course of its historical development modern science gradually became aware of its presupposition of an order of nature. In philosophy the questioning of this belief became known as "the problem of induction." It was demonstrated by Hume that the problem of induction is insoluble by the methods of science itself, since inductive solutions would be circular and deductive solutions can never outreach their premises. (Recently proposed solutions in terms of probability or statistics are merely complicated combinations of inductive and deductive arguments and hence must fail for the reasons given by Hume.) Kant attempted to substitute for the methods of science a special philosophical method, the so-called "transcendental method," in order to solve the problem of induction (and several similar related problems). The trouble with Kant's solution is that it is unduly subjective in the sense that Kant makes the existence and the characteristics of the world so largely a function of man's mental faculties. One significant source of the pervasive subjectivist bias of Kant's philosophy is its central concern with human knowledge and, in particular, the most sophisticated human knowledge, mathematics and natural science—after all, this kind of knowledge is a very special feature of the universe. Whitehead proposes to replace Kant's Critique of Pure Reason with a Critique of Pure Feeling, that is, to replace a subjective phenomenology of cognitions with an objective ontology of feelings, and in particular to replace the transcendental unity of apperception

the sun, and precession of the orbit of Mercury). Now, it is hardly remarkable that Whitehead should have stated exactly the same criteria in his book, *The Principle of Relativity*, pp. 84-5, but I am somewhat dismayed by the fact that Gupta seems unaware of the existence of Whitehead's theory, which he omits even to mention in his discussion of available theories satisfying the three criteria. A valuable comparative analysis of relativistic theories of gravitation, including Whitehead's, may be found in G. J. Whitrow and G. E. Morduch, "General Relativity and Lorentz-invariant Theories of Gravitations," *Nature*, 188 (1960), 790-94.

with the felt unity of aesthetic experience. Whitehead's philosophical method is that already alluded to above as the method of speculative reason. Specifically, Whitehead begins by appealing to "the immediate facts of our psychological experience" (a phrase from Chap. IV of SMW) from which are elicited a set of categories for his philosophy of organism. Then, the meaning of each category is generalized and deepened by discovering its role in a variety of diverse contexts illustrating different schemes and levels of abstraction. Thus, Chaps. IV through IX of *Science and the Modern World,* dealing successively with the phenomenology of sense-perception, English Romantic poetry, the theory of evolution, relativity, quantum theory, and modern philosophy—all from the point of view of the philosophy of organism—these chapters represent a definite order of increasingly abstract subject-matter, starting with the psychological actuality of our direct, pre-verbal intuitions, proceeding to the literary modes expressive of such intuitions, then on to the highly developed deductive sciences, and completing the circle, so to speak, with philosophy, whose task is "to exhibit the fusion of analysis with actuality."[24]

Whitehead's discussion of the problem of induction is best preceded by a short explanation of his central metaphysical category, the notion of organism itself. We note that the passage from analysis of science to metaphysical speculation involves the abandonment—or better, the transcending—of the categories of Whitehead's natural philosophy. In particular, natural occurrences (or events) give way to actual occasions of experience, the most concrete elements of reality in terms of which all explanations of any kind must ultimately be couched. It follows that an explanation of the order of nature must appeal to the main characteristics of actual occasions, and these are organisms in a double sense. First, actual occasions are synthesized into larger wholes in ways analogous to the synthesis of single cells into a many-celled living organism. The important point here is that there are always certain components of any organism which are also organisms whose character is influenced by the larger wholes of which they are parts; for example, Whitehead holds that electrons within a living body are probably influenced (very slightly!) by the mental states of that body and to this extent differ in their behavior from electrons outside a living body. The nature of this influence is explained by the second

24"Mathematics and the Good," ESP, p. 86.

respect in which it may be said that actual occasions are organisms. This has to do with the internal character of actual occasions, which, according to one of Whitehead's fundamental methodological principles, we must infer in the form of a generalization of what we know about our own internal experience. Suppose, in fact, we consider the higher animals in general rather than just human beings. It would be generally agreed that these organisms have an "inner" or "subjective" life in addition to their overt behavior; they feel, enjoy, will, and in some cases think, in addition to observing through their senses and moving their limbs and muscles. Some such inner life of feeling is what Whitehead attributes to *all* animals and in some degree to *all* actual occasions even at the so-called "inorganic" level. It is in this capacity of an actual occasion, no matter how primitive, to be—or better, to *become*—something in and for itself, "a unit of emergent value,"[25] that Whitehead locates the essential characteristic of reality; it is in this sense that becoming or process or creativity is the ultimate "stuff" of the universe; and it is in this sense that the term "organism" is analogically applicable to everything there is. That the fundamental entities of physics (e.g., electrons, protons, and photons) do not seem even remotely to resemble organisms even in the broad sense just specified is due to two facts: first, the materio-mechanistic terminology inherited from classical physics obscures the genuine organismic features of modern physical theory; and second, these features are in any case minimal because physics by its very method tends to abstract from what things are in themselves.[26]

Let us return for a moment to living organisms. To a modern biologist, two of their leading properties are, first, that living organisms interact in complex but definite and lawful ways with their environments, and second, that, as species, they evolve as a result of this interaction. To which Whitehead adds the perhaps less obvious truth that the environments of organisms also evolve[27], in part as a response to the behavior and evolution of the organisms themselves, so that adaptation is always of environment to organism as well as the other way around. It is in quasi-biological terms derived from the preceding account of organism-environment interaction that Whitehead attempts

[25]SMW, p. 157.
[26]See SMW, p. 220.
[27]See SMW, p. 163.

to explain the persistence of an order of nature and to justify inductive procedures. His argument goes something like this.[28] Inductive judgments assert that the future will resemble the past in certain definite ways. More precisely, such judgments take the form: a given species of organisms[29] known to behave in a particular way will continue to behave in this way at some future time. Every such judgment presupposes the future existence of a species closely analogous to, if not identical with, the given species. This is obvious because any complex pattern of behavior can only be ascribed to the organisms of a narrowly circumscribed species, so that if, for example, two species are not sufficiently similar, it may simply make no sense to ask whether their members share any common patterns of behavior (electrons move but do not eat, the sun rises and sets but does not move in quantized orbits). Now, in order for a species to be viable, an appropriately sustaining environment (itself composed of various interdependent species of organisms) is required; the latter will be characterized by a locally dominant set of natural laws. Thus, an inductive judgment can derive at least a modicum of support from the set of natural laws presupposed in the very formulation of the judgment. These laws, it should be noted, will be transmitted by inheritance from the present to the future time in question; to the extent to which the given species of organisms evolves, the surrounding environment and thereby the locally dominant set of natural laws will, of course, also evolve. Since *some* novelty, no matter how trivial, is a pervasive feature of all organismic development, no natural law can express more than a statistical regularity, and the universe must be continuously engaged in a gradual transition from one dominant set of statistical laws to another—in Whitehead's terms, from one "cosmic epoch" to another.

To illustrate: the prediction that the sun will rise tomorrow presupposes that both sun and earth will exist tomorrow, and hence that those general physical laws (e.g., Newton's laws of motion and gravitation) involved in any adequate definition of the sun and of the earth will continue to hold tomorrow—all of which makes it rather implausible to assume that the relative positions and motions of the sun

[28]The argument is hinted at in "Uniformity and Contingency," ESP, pp. 108–111, stated rather sketchily in Chap. IV of SMW, pp. 63–65, elaborated in PR, pp. 303–316, and very briefly restated in AI, p. 143.

[29]No essential restriction is involved in speaking only of organisms, since *all* entities are ultimately composed of organisms.

and earth will be radically altered tomorrow. Again, to predict that in a million years the behavior of electrons will still satisfy (in some suitable approximation) Schrödinger's wave equation presupposes first of all that there will be electrons in a million years; this in turn seems to presuppose a physical universe containing all or nearly all of the presently known elementary particles; and in such a universe, more or less analogous to our own at present, electrons would have to behave in accordance with some close analogue of Schrödinger's wave equation.

We have seen that the validity of inductive judgments rests on a presumed analogy between present and future cosmic epochs. But how shall one select from the potentially infinite set of natural laws characterizing, say, the present cosmic epoch, the locally dominant set to be used in defining the analogy; or, more simply, what is the ultimate inductive basis for natural laws? The question has an answer, according to Whitehead, only if the *relevant* aspects of the cosmic epoch are known to be specifiable by reference solely to spatio-temporal regions below a certain maximum and above a certain minimum size. Such regions provide the finite samples without which natural laws could never attain a finite probability. That such finite samples suffice for inductive purposes is known, according to Whitehead, by direct intuition of the local environment.

It would be a mistake, I think, to claim too much for the preceding argument. It is certainly no answer to that version—perhaps the commonest one—of the problem of induction which amounts to "The question, as to what will happen to an unspecified entity in an unspecified environment."[30] *That* question, according to Whitehead, can have no answer. Rather, his discussion of the problem of induction is designed to explain how the philosophy of organism expresses through its basic categories our instinctive belief in an order of nature.

One feature of the above discussion deserves special emphasis, namely, that there is no reason for expecting that natural laws will be strictly obeyed by the entities to which they apply; in other words, all natural laws are statistical in character. Is this conclusion compatible with the scientific faith in an order of nature—an order that, by all traditional accounts at least, is absolute and exact down to the last detail? To answer the question one must study the concept of natural law more carefully. This Whitehead does in two ways, first by a metaphysical analysis in terms of his philosophy of organism, and second by a historical analysis of the development of the concept of natural law. The metaphysical analysis leads to the result that in addition to the purely statistical basis of natural laws there is a non-statistical basis, namely, the fact that there is an intrinsic suitability about certain regularities in nature in the sense that they represent optimal conditions for the realization of value by the organisms involved in these regularities. But the optimal conditions cannot remain mere abstractions; they must be continuously and indeed eternally entertained and valued by some actual organism; furthermore, this valuation must somehow be capable of influencing all other organisms. Indeed, without such influence the universe would relapse into lawless chaos. What I have just been describing constitutes one of the primary functions of God in Whitehead's metaphysics. The relevant valuations of God are part of the initial data involved in the self-determining process of development of every organism; God's valuations, however, operate as "lures for feeling," not as the imposed fiat of an omnipotent being.

Historical study of the concept of natural law confirms Whitehead's theology on this point: " 'God' is that actuality in the world, in virtue of which there is physical 'law' ".[31] It is unnecessary for our purposes to undertake a detailed examination of Whitehead's history of the concept of natural law (in *Adventures of Ideas*). A few methodological points, however, are of considerable interest. First of all, the discussion in *Adventures of Ideas* is more detailed and more analytical than the earlier discussion of the origins of modern science in *Science and the Modern World* (which I have examined above). The later discussion is not so much a revision as a refinement of the earlier. Thus, for example, in *Science and the Modern World*, Hebraic and Greek conceptions of nature were mentioned as both contributing to the idea of an order of nature, but the two were not distinguished as notably different. Now, Whitehead sets forth an important philosophical distinction between the Hebraic and the Greek conceptions of the relationship of God to nature. To understand this distinction we must first mention a second significant methodological point.

It will be recalled that, according to Whitehead, the history of

[31]PR, p. 434.

thought must be read both backward and forward. In *Science and the Modern World* the history of modern science is read forward in terms of its origins; in *Adventures of Ideas* (Chaps. 7-8) the history of the concept of natural law is read backward in terms of the four main doctrines of natural law prominent in recent thought. These doctrines are: (1) law as immanent, (2) law as imposed, (3) law as mere description, (4) law as conventional interpretation. The last doctrine, associated especially with the name of Henri Poincaré, is of quite recent origin and hence may be safely ignored in a historical analysis going back to ancient Hebraic and Greek times; in any case, Whitehead argues that the interpretation of natural laws as mere conventions— even in the case of geometry, the stronghold of the conventionalists— is based on serious misconceptions and cannot be consistently maintained. The positivist doctrine of law as mere description, on the other hand, while expressing an important truth about the method of modern science, is incompatible with the actual practice of scientists in relying on the validity of natural laws beyond the immediate spheres in which they have been verified—in other words, the positivist doctrine is incapable of justifying induction.

The two remaining doctrines can be explained as follows: according to the immanence view, a natural law expresses an aspect of the mutual relatedness of some group of natural entities, and this mutual relatedness is part of the essence of what these entities are. This view "presupposes the essential interdependence of things."[32] To know what things are is equivalent to knowing the laws of their interaction. The imposition view asserts, on the contrary, that natural entities are what they are independently of any relations among them; a natural law is then a pattern of behavior imposed on these entities from without. An excellent illustration of an imposition interpretation of a natural law is afforded by Newton's attitude toward his law of gravitation. Newton held that mass (or inertia) but not gravity is an inherent property of all material bodies; gravitational attraction is due ultimately to God's imposition on inert matter of an active principle whose mathematical expression constitutes the law of universal gravitation. Furthermore, both the origin and stability of the solar system require active interference by a (non-physical) force external to the system itself, namely, God. By contrast, Einstein's law of

32AI, p. 142.

gravitation abolishes the distinction between mass and gravity—or at least that is Einstein's intent even if his proposed law is not completely successful in this regard. Also, Einstein hoped and expected that his theory of gravitation would serve to explain both the origin and the structure of the universe. Thus Einstein's work represents a deep commitment to the immanence doctrine of natural law, quite in keeping with his pantheistically inclined religious beliefs. As for Whitehead's view of his own law of gravitation, we shall see that it represents a fusion of the immanence and imposition interpretations of natural law.

In looking once more into the origins of modern science Whitehead finds a clear expression of the imposition doctrine in Semitic monotheism and a clear expression of the immanence doctrine in Plato's statement (in the *Sophist*) that the definition of being is simply power. In the *Timaeus,* on the other hand, Plato seems to be setting forth a fusion of the immanence and imposition doctrines of natural law (there is the creative demiurge and there is the presumed self-sufficiency of the universe as a whole). A still different account of natural law, emerging in Greek atomism, lent itself most readily to an interpretation fusing the imposition and mere description doctrines. Finally, we note the great popularity in the eighteenth century of deism, which implies a pure imposition doctrine of natural law. Newton himself was an adherent of this view of natural law, as we have seen. And this coincidence of a widespread belief in an imposition view of natural law with perhaps the greatest creative period in the history of modern science is no mere accident; only such a belief, according to Whitehead, can sustain scientists in their patient search for the regular patterns in nature which they instinctively *know* are there, waiting to be discovered. (Even such a confirmed devotee of immanence as Einstein retained a passionate faith in the exactness of natural law and in the strict determinism of natural occurrences, which of course was why he differed with most other physicists over the question of the ultimacy of the probability laws of quantum theory.) Thus, Whitehead's historical analysis, like his metaphysical analysis, suggests the importance for science of an immanence-imposition interpretation of natural law. As for the ontological status of Whitehead's law of gravitation, it seems to be intermediate between Einstein's general relativity (in which space-time and matter are, ideally at least, identified) and Newton's theory of gravitation (in which space, time, and matter are completely independent of each other apart from the influence of God). In Whitehead's theory, both space-time and matter are abstractions from the flux of events which constitutes Nature, the uniformity of Nature being expressed in the uniform, continuous structure of space-time and the contingent aspects of Nature in the non-uniform, atomic structure of matter.

Thus, according to Whitehead, there is an order of nature but it is not absolutely binding on finite occasions of experience, which are free within limits to determine their respective ways of responding to the fixed patterns of the past and in some instances to create novel patterns for the future. And so we have moved from the order of nature to a universe of interacting organisms and finally to concrete self-determining individual experiences—a progression characteristic of the philosophical enterprise but also essential to the fulfillment of the philosopher as a human being and indeed to the fulfillment of man as such. This conception of man in the cosmos is implicit in most of Whitehead's philosophical writings; one explicit expression of it occurs at the close of the first chapter of *Science and the Modern World*:

The faith in the order of nature which has made possible the growth of science is a particular example of a deeper faith. This faith cannot be justified by any inductive generalisation. It springs from direct inspection of the nature of things as disclosed in our own immediate present experience. There is no parting from your own shadow. To experience this faith is to know that in being ourselves we are more than ourselves: to know that our experience, dim and fragmentary as it is, yet sounds the utmost depths of reality: to know that detached details merely in order to be themselves demand that they should find themselves in a system of things: to know that this system includes the harmony of logical rationality, and the harmony of aesthetic achievement; to know that, while the harmony of logic lies upon the universe as an iron necessity, the aesthetic harmony stands before it as a living ideal moulding the general flux in its broken progress towards finer, subtler issues.[33]

Appendix

The formulation of Whitehead's law of gravitation given in the text above should not be taken too seriously except for heuristic purposes. Whitehead does not, in fact, formulate a law of gravitational *force* but rather a law for the gravitational *potential* at any point in space-

[33]SMW, pp. 27–28.

Fig. 1. A mass-point moving along the world-line L in space-time.

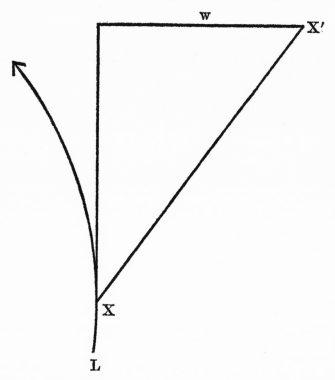

time due to a mass-point moving with any velocity less than that of light. Thus, suppose a particle of mass m is moving with a velocity v_m along the world-line L, and suppose we want to know the gravitational potential at X' (with spatial coordinates x'_1, x'_2, x'_3, and temporal coordinate x'_4) due to m. (See diagram.) We first follow a light-path from X' until it intersects L, say at the point X (with spatial coordinates x_1, x_2, x_3, and temporal coordinate x_4). At X we draw the tangent to L and then drop a perpendicular from X' to this tangent. This construction defines a Lorentz-invariant quantity w, which plays the role of "distance" from any point X' to the route of m. It can be shown that w has the form:

$$w = (1 - v_m{}^2/c^2)^{1/2} \{ c\,(x'_4 - x_4) - {}^1\!/c\,(x'_1 - x_1)\,\dot{x}_1$$
$$- {}^1\!/c\,(x'_2 - x_2)\,\dot{x}_2 - {}^1\!/c\,(x'_3 - x_3)\,\dot{x}_3 \}.$$

The gravitational potential ψ_m can now be written: $\psi_m = Gm/w$, which reduces to $\psi_m = Gm/r$ (i.e., Newton's law of gravitation) when m is at rest. This, then, is the form in which Whitehead makes use of his law of gravitation (in conjunction with the usual least action formulation of the law of motion).* It will be noted that Whitehead's law involves action-at-a-distance propagated with a finite velocity (the velocity of light, c). In other words, the gravitational potential at the place (x_1', x_2', x_3') at the time x_4' is determined by what happened at a different place (x_1, x_2, x_3) at an earlier time, x_4.

ROBERT PALTER

THE UNIVERSITY OF CHICAGO

*Whitehead's choice of an energy over a force formulation of his law of gravitation is dictated by the fact that there are no simple laws of force in special relativity mechanics corresponding to Newton's laws of force in classical mechanics.

SIMPLE LOCATION AND FRAGMENTATION
OF REALITY

THE term "fallacy of simple location" was coined by A. N. White-head in 1925 in his book *Science and the Modern World;* the two passages of the book that deal with this problem are worth being quoted in full and may serve as an introduction into our topic.

The Ionian philosophy asked, What is nature made of? The answer is couched in terms of stuff, or matter, or material—the particular name chosen is indifferent—which has the property of simple location in space and time, or, if you adopt the more modern ideas, in space-time. What I mean by matter, or material, is anything which has this property of *simple location*. By simple location I mean one major characteristic which refers equally to space and time, and other minor characteristics which are diverse as between space and time. The characteristic common both to space and time is that material can be said to be *here* in space and *here* in time, or *here* in space-time, in a per-fectly definite sense which does not require for its explanation any reference to other regions of space-time . . . In fact, as soon as you have settled, however you do settle, what you mean by a definite place in space-time, you can ade-quately state the relation of a particular material body to space-time by saying that it is just there, in that place; and so far as simple location is concerned, there is nothing more to be said on the subject.[1]

It is fairly obvious that the term "simple location" used in this passage is merely a new name for the old concept of *atomicity* of nature. Atomic theory of nature, whether in its classical speculative form associated with such famous names as Democritus, Lucretius and Pierre Gassendi, or in its modern scientific garb, claimed that nature is made of discontinuous solid entities moving through homo-geneous Euclidian space. At each particular moment each of these atomic entities occupies a definite portion of space with well-defined boundaries. The shape of these atomic volumes varied through cen-turies; at first, it was quite irregular because the Greek atomists needed hooks, indentations and various irregularities of surface in

[1]A. N. Whitehead, *Science and the Modern World* (New York: Macmillan, 1926), pp. 71-72.

order to explain the fact of cohesion; this tendency was also characteristic of the seventeenth century atomism whose main features were
consciously borrowed from its ancient ancestor. But in the modern
period, especially with the coming of the kinetic theory of gases, the
spherical shape was gradually more and more preferred. But no
matter what kind of shape was attributed to the ultimate particles
of matter, they always were regarded as *particles,* occupying a definite
place in space at each particular moment. A series of successive positions of one single particle constituted its trajectory in space; the
particle itself was regarded as immutable through time and the only
change which was admitted was change of its spatial relations in
respect to other particles or in respect to the Newtonian absolute
space.

It is clear that Whitehead's term "simple location" is in its meaning equivalent to what John Locke called *principium individuationis*
(principle of individuality).[2] For the only thing which differentiates
one atom from all others is its *spatial location* at a certain particular instant and nothing else. For atomists of all ages agreed that
atoms are made of the same qualitatively homogeneous stuff; the
idea of the *qualitative unity of matter* is one of the most characteristic features of not only atomism, but of the whole classical science
and philosophy which it inspired. The view that atoms are qualitatively different, that is, possessing inherently different qualities, was
always a sign of certain immaturity of the atomistic thought whether
we find it in Anaxagoras and Empedocles in antiquity or in Galileo's
contemporaries like Sennert and Berigard, or finally in John Dalton
at the beginning of the last century. The case of John Dalton is
especially instructive because, in spite of his authority as one of the
founders of modern chemistry, there were always scientists, not speaking of philosophers, who hoped that the qualitative differences
between chemical elements are only apparent and that they would
be eventually resolved into the differences of configuration of some
more basic elementary particles. The electron theory to a very considerable extent fulfilled these expectations. But if the basic units of
matter are made of the same stuff, then, as already stated, the only
differentiating features between such homogeneous particles are *differences in spatial location.* One and the same particle cannot be at

2John Locke, *An Essay Concerning Human Understanding,* Bk. II, Chap. XXVII.

the same time in two different places and two different particles cannot occupy one and the same position at the same time; if they do,
they cease to be different and their twoness itself disappears. Or,
more accurately, to speak of two different particles being simultaneously at one and the same location, means to apply two different
names to a single entity. It is clear that in the property of simple
location two basic features of classical science are united: the assertion of *impenetrability of matter* as well as *the denial of action at
a distance.* Classical physics and, in particular, philosophers inspired
by classical physics, were as reluctant to give up the first property of
matter as to accept any action at a distance. Space is lacking here to
show this in a sufficiently documented way: for our present purpose
it must suffice to state generally that every type of physical interaction was always interpreted in terms of solid and immutable entities being transmitted between bodies. From the old Democritus's
theory of εἴδωλα up to Newton's particles of light emitted by luminous sources, the pattern of explanation remained essentially the
same: every physical interaction was in the last analysis based on
contact or *impact.* But whether particles are touching each other as
in the entangled hook-like atoms of Greek atomists or whether they
are clashing together as in the modern kinetic models of light and
gravitation, their individuality remains preserved. They may be *adjacent* one to each other, but they never *merge* together; their impenetrability prevents their fusion while their confinement to certain
spatial regions prevents them from acting *where they are not.* Thus
the principle of simple location remains unviolated.

It is precisely this principle which Whitehead challenged:

I also express my conviction that if we desired to obtain a more fundamental
expression of the concrete character of natural fact, the element in this scheme
which we should criticize first is the concept of *simple location.* In view therefore of the importance which this idea will assume in these lectures, I will
repeat the meaning which I had attached to this phrase. To say that a bit of
matter has a *simple location* means that, in expressing its spatio-temporal relations, it is adequate to state that it is there where it is, in a definite finite
region of space, and throughout a definite finite duration of time, apart from
any essential reference of the relations of that bit of matter to other regions
of space and to other durations of time . . . This idea is the very foundation
of the seventeenth century scheme of nature. Apart from it, the scheme is
incapable of expression. I shall argue that among the primary elements of
nature as apprehended in our immediate experience, there is no element what-

ever which possesses this character of simple location. It does not follow, however, that the science of the seventeenth century was simply wrong. I hold
that by a process of constructive abstraction we can arrive at abstractions
which are the simply located bits of material, and at other abstractions which
are the minds included in the scientific scheme. Accordingly, the real error is
an example of what I have termed: The Fallacy of Misplaced Concreteness.[3]

If we read this passage attentively, we see clearly that Whitehead
is far from simply denying the reality of atoms. He was certainly
aware that the empirical evidence for the atomic structure of matter
is overwhelming and that it is impossible today to repeat the mistake
of Mach and Ostwald who denied the existence of atoms on spurious
epistemological grounds. But at the same time, he is equally aware
that the atomicity is only one aspect of nature. The dynamic connection of each individual entity with the rest of the universe is another equally essential aspect of reality which cannot be ignored. If
we ignore it, we commit, according to Whitehead, a fallacy of misplaced concreteness. In other words, we reify an abstraction; for, no
matter how justified and valid an abstraction may be, it remains an
abstraction which should never be confused with the richness and
fullness of the concrete fact. Or, as he says himself a few lines after
the quoted passage:

The disadvantage of exclusive attention to a group of abstractions, however
well founded, is that, by the nature of the case, you have abstracted from the
remainder of things. In so far as the excluded things are important in your
experience, your modes of thought are not fitted to deal with them.

The question of primary importance is then as follows: is it possible to construct a model in which nature is represented by an arithmetical sum of discontinuous and mutually external entities *or* is the
very concept of discrete atomic elements a result of artificial procedures by which we dissect the continuity of reality into discrete units,
disregarding all dynamical links which join them together? Or, more
simply: is simple location the intrinsic feature of reality or a result
of distorting abstraction and conceptualization? From the quoted
passages it is clear where Whitehead stands. But in order to understand better his position it is important to realize that no matter how
original his criticism of the concept of simple location was, it had
its antecedents in a wider movement, originating in the last decades

[3]A. N. Whitehead, *op. cit.,* pp. 84-85.

of the last century. This movement, which was present both in physical sciences and psychology, gained momentum around 1900 and Whitehead's philosophy was one of its later phases. The fact that the reaction against the atomistic conception occurred simultaneously, or nearly simultaneously, within such widely different fields as physics and psychology only increases its significance. It was a symptom that the traditional modes of thought had begun to change, and we know that the first indication of the incipient change is the appearance of doubt and criticism.

I

If we respect the historical chronological succession, then we have to consider the reaction against the fallacy of simple location first in *psychology*. This reaction is fairly well known under a more familiar name of *Gestalt-Psychology*. But before we analyze it, it will be useful to remember briefly how much the idea of the atomic entity dominated psychology in the last century. The atom in question was, of course, not a physical atom. The psychology of the last century was far less physicalistic than the American behaviorism and Russian reflexology is today; even physiological psychology recognized the existence of introspective data even though these data were interpreted as simple accompaniments of cerebral processes. But it is significant how these introspective data were treated; in this respect there is hardly any difference between naturalistically oriented psychology or its idealistic or dualistic opponents. The belief which the more idealistically oriented Herbart shared with the positivistic psychology of Wundt, Taine, both Mills, Bain and others was precisely the *atomistic* view of psychological processes. This psychological form of atomism, which is better known under the name of *associationism*, had its roots in the eighteenth century; John Locke and David Hume are its true ancestors. According to this view the basic elements of consciousness are *sensations* and the whole rich variety of psychological life results from various forms in which these basic elements are associated. Thus the difference between perception and thought is merely that of *degree of complexity* and *sensory vivacity;* thought is merely a more complex aggregate of less vivid sensations. Associationism and sensationalism were traditionally associated. The name of these basic elements of consciousness greatly varied; but no matter whether they were called *sensations, impressions, Vorstellungen,* or simply "mental states" or "elements", they always retained their quasi-atomistic character. Naturally, being of *psychological* nature, they were not regarded as entities existing in space; but in all other respects their resemblance to physical atoms was striking. Like physical atoms, they were well defined entities, mutually external and permanent in time; their disappearance from the field of consciousness was only apparent because they continued their existence under "the threshold of consciousness" until some accidental cause brought them back to "the surface of consciousness." To be sure, all these various spatial expressions were regarded as metaphors; but the choice of these metaphors only betrayed the close kinship of the physical and mental atoms. Even today our psychological language is imbued by the unconsciously adopted atomistic terminology; we speak about ideas *clashing* together, *sinking* under the level of consciousness, *re-emerging* from the *depth* of subconsciousness; we speak about the various degrees of complexity of our mental processes without realizing that we are borrowing this metaphor from physics and chemistry where the observed variety is a result of different degrees of electronic, or atomic or molecular configuration. A great part of the psychoanalytical language is *associationist,* that is, *atomistic* in its character. Thus although "the movement of ideas" or sensations was supposedly taking place *in time,* not in space, it was only natural to ask with Bergson to what extent the time of the associationistic psychology was not a verbally disguised space of Newtonian mechanics.[4] Both physical atoms and the atomic entities of the associationistic psychology were *substantial entities* moving through a homogeneous container; but while physical atoms were moving in space, psychological atoms were moving through time only. But in spite of verbal differences the imaginative background remained the same. Hume himself who so vigorously attacked the Cartesian concept of substantial soul, conceded explicitly that his "impressions" are substances too, although on a much smaller scale:

My conclusion . . . is that since all our perceptions are different from each other, and from every thing else in the universe, they are also distinct and separable, and may be considered as separately existent, and have no need of

4H. Bergson, *Time and Free Will,* trans. F. L. Pogson (New York: Harper, 1910), Chap. II, passim, esp. pp. 108-09.

any thing else to support their existence. They are therefore substances, as far as this definition explains a substance.[5]

This passage states clearly the principle of simple location applied to psychology; and because the definition of substance, which Hume applied, is Cartesian, we should designate Descartes rather than Hume as the thinker mainly responsible for introducing the principle of simple location into psychology. For the Cartesian "thinking substance", *substantia cogitans,* or simply *res cogitans* is only a species of substance in general which is defined as "an entity which does not need anything else for its own existence" *(res quae ita existit, ut nulla alia re indigeat ad existendum)*. In other words, the main characteristic of substance is its independence from the rest of the world; but this feature, as Hume himself conceded, belongs to his impressions as well. We can thus say without exaggeration that Hume merely cut the Cartesian substantial soul into small, but no less substantial, fragments; in spite of his criticism of substance, he did not basically depart from the substantialism.

There is not enough time to review even briefly all stages of the reaction against associationism in psychology. Let us recall only the most significant intellectual events. Although it is difficult to assign a definite date to the birth of certain movements, historians of psychology regard James Ward's article in the *Encyclopedia Britannica* in 1886 as the beginning of the new era.[6] This is not entirely accurate; James' brilliant analysis of the atomistic psychology appeared two years before in his article "On Some Omissions of Introspective Psychology" in the British review, *Mind.* Moreover, we do not have to forget that as early as 1874 Franz Brentano protested against the associationistic theory of judgement.[7] Judgement, or, as we say today, after adopting the nominalistic terminology, *proposition,* is, according to Brentano, a primary indivisible act irreducible to a mere aggregation of ideas. This does not diminish the significance of Ward's article which was characterized by one historian of psychology as "a blow from which the associationistic psychology never recovered."[8] Ward showed convincingly that what we call by a

[5]*Treatise on Human Nature,* Bk. I, pt. IV, sec. 5.

[6]"Psychology," *Encyclopedia Britannica,* 11th ed., 22 (1886), 547-604.

[7]R. Müller-Freienfels, *The Evolution of Modern Psychology,* trans. W. Beran Wolfe (New Haven: Yale University Press, 1935), pp. 83-84.

[8]J. C. Flügel, *Hundred Years of Psychology* (New York: Macmillan, 1933), p. 150.

rather misleading term "complexity of mind", comes about not through the combination of various elementary units, but rather as a result of a gradual differentiation of a primary unity. After Ward's article the attacks on associationistic psychology followed in rapid succession. In 1889 Bergson published his *Essai sur les données immédiates de la conscience,* in which the successive continuity of conciousness was stressed and the concept of arithmetical multiplicity rejected as thoroughly inadequate for psychology. If the mental states are "many," they are many in a sense different from that in which physical bodies or arithmetical units are many; they are without sharp boundaries; they pervade each other. One year later William James's *Principles of Psychology* appeared and, independently of Bergson, the continuity of "the stream of consciousness" was stressed again and psychological atomism under the name "mind-stuff theory" critically analyzed. In the same year Ehrenfels writes his article "Über Gestaltqualitäten,"[9] where the term 'Gestalt' appears for the first time. Three years later Wilhelm Dilthey writes his "Ideen über eine beschreibende und zergliedernde Psychologie" in which the unitary and comprehensive approach toward psychology is contrasted with the atomistic, associationist, analytical, or, as he says, 'dismembering' approach.[10] Gestalt-Psychology was thus founded; the subsequent work of Wertheimer, Koffka, Köhler is too well known to be dwelt upon.

Two features of this wide anti-atomistic trend in psychology are relevant to our topic. First, its empirical character. The associationistic psychology correctly claimed to be more empirical than the Cartesian theory of substantial soul; Hume observed that no such substantial entity is ever an object of introspective experience; what an introspective glance always discloses is a *particular* impression, *particular* feeling, *particular* idea, but never the bare "Ego" or pure "I". From this there is only a step to the conclusion that Ego is merely a verbal entity, that is, a collective name applied to the totality of concrete impressions, feelings and ideas. It is important to realize that the criticism of associationism was based not on some *a priori* speculative grounds, but on a more refined introspective experience. James significantly called himself a radical empiricist; he, like Bergson,

---

[9]*Zeitschrift für wissenschaftliche Philosophie,* 14 (1890), 249-292.
[10]Müller-Freienfels, *op. cit.,* pp. 98-101.

Ward, Dilthey and Gestalt psychologists, pointed out that psychological atoms, whether they are called *impressions, sensations, ideas, representations,* or simply *'mental states'* or *'elements',* are merely methodological fictions, artificial entities, carved out of the continuity of the stream of consciousness, and that by manipulating these entities we can obtain merely an inadequate and clumsy imitation of concrete reality. If we then concede that the associationistic sensualism of Hume and his followers is more empirical than rationalistic psychologies of Descartes or of Christian Wolf, it nevertheless remains true that Gestalt psychology and the related trends were even more attentive to experience, especially to some of its more elusive and non-sensory aspects. In particular it was Alfred Binet in France and the Würzburg school in Germany which by their investigations of imageless thought convincingly pointed out that the terms "experience" and "sensory experience" are far from being synonymous.

This empirical character of the anti-atomistic trend in psychology increases the significance of its *second* feature which is more closely related to our topic. The Gestalt approach in psychology directly challenges the principle of simple location, in particular, its application to time. According to this principle, each particular event is where it is, that is, in one particular moment, but it is *nowhere else*. In other words, its presence is confined to a narrow moment; but once this moment is gone, the corresponding particular event is gone irrevocably and forever. Once passed, it will sink into the abyss of the past, being completely and forever *excluded* from the present, completely *external* to the present. If this were true, then any influence of the past on the present would be completely impossible; consequently, neither causation, nor memory would be ever possible. This is at least what the principle of simple location requires when we apply it to time: the past event is the past event and the present event is the present event and both are mutually external; *the action at a distance in time* is impossible in the same sense in which the action at a distance is impossible in space in virtue of the same principle applied to space. Unfortunately, or, rather fortunately, this is not what experience discloses. Ehrenfels demonstrated it conclusively by analyzing our awareness of *melody*. At the first superficial glance melody appears to be an aggregate of successive individual tones; in this sense our awareness of melody would be built of gradual addition of successive auditory sensations each of which would be temporally external to all others. But if it were so, no awareness of melody would ever arise. Nothing would be present to consciousness except one single tone, living for one single moment; the fact is, however, that not only an immediately preceding moment, but *the whole antecedent musical phrase,* in spite of its pastness, is in an undefinable way present in the present tone which, without losing its musical individuality, acquires a peculiar coloration within its antecedent musical context. Remove this context and the consciousness of melody will disappear, or rather it will be replaced by another temporal *Gestalt,* i.e., by the sensation of the individual tone within the context of the antecedent silence. Deceived by our language and by the fallacy of simple location unconsciously applied, we speak of one and the same tone no matter whether it is embedded in a melody or preceded by a silence. But is it really "one and the same" tone? By no means: it is a *similar* tone, not an identical one. It is true that the differentiating features introduced by different temporal contexts are very elusive, so elusive that it was possible to ignore them for such a long time; this accounts for the plausibility of the associationist psychology. The fact, however, remains that by claiming a complete self-identity and self-sufficience of the individual sensations we can never successfully explain the continuity of our experience, the reality of temporal *Gestalten,* the fact of immediate memory, and that we are thus driven to all the absurdities to which the doctrine of external relations inevitably leads. The conclusions of Zeno of Elea are sufficiently known; the conclusions of Aenesidemus of Knossus are perhaps less known; and those of Herbart, although he lived in the last century, are nearly forgotten: they all agree that in the name of the principle of simple location, motion, change, becoming are impossible; if our experience shows the contrary, so much the worse for experience!

II

It is a peculiar coincidence that approximately at the same time when the notion of the independent simply located entity began to be questioned in psychology, some important changes began to take place in physics, the changes which eventually led to the question raised by Whitehead in his *Science and the Modern World.* Was it really a sheer coincidence? Or was it rather a symptom that the human mind began to become increasingly sensitive to certain inadequacies of traditional modes of thought? For in spite of all the differences between the methods of introspective psychology and methods of experimental and theoretical physics, it is the same human knower equally conditioned by the same influences in both cases. This truth has been shown, I believe convincingly, by Bergson when he pointed out that our logic is basically a *logic of solid macroscopic bodies* and that the very concept of *substance* or of *thinghood,* the Cartesian *res*—whether it is *res cogitans* or *res extensa*—has its roots in the concept of isolated simply located and impenetrable body.[11] It is true that when we speak of a certain thing, we do not necessarily think of a physical body, but also of some abstract entity; but this entity, though diaphanous and discolored, nevertheless retains some basic features which are characteristic of solid bodies. If we realize this basic principle of Bergson's epistemology, we shall also be less surprised by the otherwise unexplainable parallelism of certain trends in physics and psychology. As it was basically the same fallacy of simple location which colored the development of both physics and psychology in the last centuries, it is hardly surprising that the critical reaction against this fallacy has some analogous features.

First doubts about the adequacy of the corpuscular view of reality began to appear in physics in the last century. As early as in 1844 Faraday in his article "A Speculation Touching Electric Conduction and the Nature of Matter"[12] pointed out that the distinction usually made between solid material particles and forces which, so to speak, emanate from these particles, is artificial; for what will remain of matter if we take away its dynamic manifestations? Even the so-called impenetrability and inertia of material particles cannot be tested in any other way except by interaction with other bodies. And if we consider two other properties of matter, that is, its gravitational and electromagnetic actions which pervade the whole space, we can understand Faraday's conclusion that "matter is not merely mutually penetrable, but each atom extends, so to say, throughout the whole of the solar system, yet always retaining its center of force." The significance of Faraday's view did not escape Bergson who quotes it at least

[11]H. Bergson, *Creative Evolution,* trans. A. Mitchell, pp. XIX, 169-173; *Time and Free Will,* pp. 130f.

[12]M. Faraday, *Experimental Researches in Electricity,* 2, 293.

twice, in *Matter and Memory* and in *Creative Evolution;* similarly, Whitehead recalls Faraday's view about the ubiquity of atoms in *The Concept of Nature*[13] in a passage in which his future criticism of the fallacy of simple location is anticipated. Wolfgang Köhler, one of the outstanding representatives of Gestalt psychology, was also clearly aware of the affinity of his own attitude with the antiatomistic implications of the physical field-theories. He quotes the following passage of James Clerk Maxwell:

We are accustomed to consider the universe as made up of parts, and mathematicians usually begin by considering a single particle, and conceiving its relation to another particle, and so on. This has generally been supposed the most natural method. To conceive a particle, requires a process of abstraction, since all our perceptions are related to extended bodies, so that the idea of *all* that is present in our consciousness is perhaps as primitive an idea as that of any individual thing. Hence there may be a mathematical method in which we proceed from the whole to the parts instead of from the parts to the whole.[14]

But in the times of Faraday and Maxwell there still seemed to be a possibility to save the principle of simple location. Even if we admit that the particles are inseparable from the energetic field which surrounds them and that their very existence without their dynamic relations to the whole field is unthinkable, it was still conceivable that the field itself is *granular* in its structure, that is, made of some ultimate minute particles,—so-called aether-particles. In other words, it was hoped that the mechanical model of the aethereal field could be, in principle at least, constructed, and Maxwell himself tried repeatedly to provide such a model. The basic idea of atomism would thus have been preserved; it is true that the hypothetical aethereal atoms had to be pictured as having an extremely minute radius,—much smaller than the radius of the electron. The failures of all such attempts at mechanical interpretation of aether are sufficiently known and to survey them all would mean to write another history of the concept of the electromagnetic aether in the second half of the nineteenth century.

[13]*Matière et mémoire,* p. 233; *Creative Evolution,* p. 222; *The Concept of Nature,* p. 146.

[14]J. C. Maxwell, *A Treatise on Electricity and Magnetism,* 3rd ed., 2 (Oxford, 1891), 176-179; G. W. Hartmann, *Gestalt Psychology* (New York: Ronald Press, 1935), p. 39.

It may be objected that while corpuscular models of aether were unsuccessful, the corpuscular character of the elementary physical particles is established beyond any doubt; who today seriously doubts the reality of electrons, positrons, neutrons, mesons, etc.? On the other hand, does not the theory of quanta reintroduce the atomicity into the energetic field itself which acquires thus the granular character? In answering the second objection first we shall be less liable to be deceived by the superficial plausibility of the first objection. For it is clear that the quantization of energy does not mean in any sense a return to the corpuscular models of aether; the quantized electromagnetic field resembles the Huyghens or Maxwell models of aether as little as photons resemble the luminous particles postulated by Newton in his emission theory of light. Moreover, it is inaccurate to speak about "atomization" of energy; what is "atomized" is not energy, but its product with time, that is, a dimensionally different quantity which is called *action*. But it is precisely the atomic character of action which forces us to regard the adjective "corpuscular" as a mere metaphor and misleading metaphor at that. There is no place here for reviewing, even briefly, the history of quantum theory. Suffice it to say that the quantification, which was originally applied to the electromagnetic energy only, was later—but still before the advent of wave mechanics—applied to mechanical energy of translation and rotation as well. It was finally extended by Louis de Broglie even to "internal energy," which according to Einstein's equation $E = mc^2$ belongs to every mass, even to the mass at rest. It is sufficiently known how far-reaching and revolutionary were the changes brought about by the relativity and quantum theory and especially by wave mechanics in the very foundations of physics; but it is important to stress that especially the traditional concept of particles was transformed beyond recognition.[15] Here is the list of the most important changes to which the classical concept of corpuscle was subjected:

1. The solidity, impenetrability, constancy, indestructibility, uncreatibility—all these attributes which characterized the classical atom from the time of Democritus to that of Lorentz do not belong to the "particles" of contemporary microphysics. We know today that mass is not constant, but a function of its velocity; we know that even the

---

[15]Cf. my book *The Philosophical Impact of Contemporary Physics* (Princeton: Van Nostrand, 1961), in particular Chap. XIV.

nuclei, in which practically all mass of the atom is concentrated, are under certain conditions lacking impenetrability, being "transparent" to the slowly moving electrons (Ramsauer's effect); we know since Anderson's discovery of positive electrons in 1932 that the microphysical particles are *not* permanent as they can be either created or annihilated. Even if it is true that the corresponding "creation" is not *"creatio ex nihilo"* as a particle in question is a result of "materialization" of electromagnetic radiation into which it may be reconverted in the converse process of "dematerialization," it is quite clear that such entities do not possess the eternal solidity of the classical Lucretian atoms.

2. The boundaries of the microphysical "particles" in regard to their surrounding space are ill defined because their precise localization is impossible in virtue of the principle of indeterminacy (which is an unescapable consequence of the atomicity of action) and even their most fundamental properties such as mass and charge are inconceivable without their dynamic interaction with their environment into which their individuality is, so to speak, fused.

Faraday's view about the "ubiquity" of electric charge has been already referred to. It is not incidental that the conclusion about the relational character of not only charge, but even of mass was reached even before the contemporary revolution in physics. For, as James Clark Maxwell pointed out, the third law of Newton makes the concept of isolated force emanating from an isolated substantial entity —whether from a material particle or from an electric charge—physically meaningless. This is in a strange contrast to the general atomistic orientation of classical physics. We have to remember that Newton defined inertial mass as *vis insita,* that is, literally, as *force residing* within the location occupied by matter and constituting, so to speak, its substantial nucleus which is related *externally* to other particles. The belief in the simple location of sharply defined corpuscular entities could have hardly found more accurate formulation: the essence of material particle is its resistance to acceleration, reacting *hinc et nunc* against the *external* influences of other equally well defined corpuscular entities. This can hardly surprise us if we consider how much Newton and classical physics in general adhered to the atomistic tradition. But the situation becomes different when the third law of Newton—the concomitance and equality of action and reaction—is considered. According to this law every force is accompanied by an opposite force of equal magnitude. Maxwell clearly realized that both forces—action and reaction—are merely two partial and complementary aspects of one and the same dynamic phenomenon which he called *stress*:

If we take into account the whole phenomenon of the action between the two portions of matter, we call it Stress. This stress, according to the mode in which it acts, may be described as Attraction, Repulsion, Tension, Pressure, Shearing stress, Torsion, etc. But if . . . we confine our attention to one of the portions of matter, we see, as it were, only one side of the transaction—namely, that which affects the portion of matter under our consideration—and we call this aspect of the phenomenon, with reference to its effect, an External Force acting on that portion of matter, and with reference to its cause we call it the Action of the other portion of matter. The opposite aspect of the stress is called the Reaction on the other portion of matter . . . In commercial affairs the same transaction between two parties is called Buying when we consider one party, Selling when we consider the other, and Trade when we take both parties into consideration.[16]

In other words, to isolate one particle and force from the whole dynamical context is as artificial as to claim that buying may take place without selling. Even the alleged substantial core of matter, the *vis insita* of Newton, is a mere fictitious product of our substantializing habits of thought, a mere abstraction as long as we disregard the whole cosmic surrounding to which the individual inertial mass is related. This is what Ernst Mach saw in his famous criticism of Newton's rotating bucket experiment when he claimed that in the principle of inertia there is "an abbreviated reference to the entire universe" and that "the neglecting of the rest of the world is *impossible*."[17] The centrifugal forces in the rotating vessel arise, according to Mach, not in respect to the fictitious Newtonian void, but in respect to the great stellar masses of the universe. In other words, Mach, foreshadowing Einstein's principle of equivalence, suggested that the so-called inertial forces (of which centrifugal forces constitute one sub-class) instead of emanating from the interior of the particle are due to the gravitational effects of the stellar masses of the universe. Thus the "residing force" of Newton, allegedly confined within the narrow volume of the local particle, is in truth nothing but a mere

---

16J. C. Maxwell, *Matter and Motion* (New York: Dover, n.d.), pp. 26-27.

17E. Mach, *The Science of Mechanics*, trans. T. J. McCormack, 5th ed. (Chicago: Open Court Publishing Co., 1942), pp. 288-289. [6th ed. (LaSalle: Open Court Publishing Co., 1960), pp. 287-288.]

knot in the web of the universal dynamic interaction in which the remotest regions of the universe take part. J. B. Stallo, who anticipated Mach's criticism of absolute space by several years, rightly claimed that without the rest of the universe it would be meaningless not only to speak of the rotation of an isolated body, but even of a body itself:

A body cannot survive the system of relations in which alone it has its being; its *presence* or *position* in space is no more possible without such reference to other bodies than its *change of position* or *presence* is possible without such reference. As has been abundantly shown, all properties of a body which constitute the elements of its distinguishable presence in space are in their nature relations *and imply terms beyond body itself.* (The last italics added.)[18]

Thus it appears that what we used to call "particle", instead of being an isolated bit of material simply located in a certain region of space and time, is a product of the whole universe or, to use Leibniz's expression quoted by Bergson and Whitehead, "a mirror of the universe"; conversely, each "particle," instead of being confined within a certain region of space and time, pervades its whole cosmic context from which it cannot be separated except by an artificial process of abstraction:

In a certain sense, everything is everywhere at all times. For every location involves an aspect of itself in every other location. Thus every spatio-temporal standpoint mirrors the world.[19]

Thus the recent development in physics in its revision of the concept of simple location shows the same opposition toward an artificial fragmentation of reality as *Gestalt phychology* in its criticism of the associationistic "bundle theory." This is another instance of "the parallel development of method in physics and psychology" to which Professor Hartshorne called attention some time ago.[20]

III

But does not the last quoted passage suggest that the denial of simple location logically leads to the monistic idea of "the block uni-

---

18J. B. Stallo, *The Concepts and Theories of Modern Physics*, ed. P. W. Bridgman (Cambridge: Harvard University Press, 1960), p. 215.

19*Science and the Modern World*, p. 133.

20C. Hartshorne, "The Parallel Development of Method in Physics and Psychology," *Philosophy of Science*, 1, 420f.

verse," that is, to the idea of the cosmic whole which is wholly and indivisibly present in all its "parts"? Strictly speaking, such an universe does not have any autonomous parts because what we call its "parts" are merely partial aspects of one single whole. Individuality and autonomy of these aspects is purely spurious; it is merely a result of our analyzing attention which artificially carves them out of the indivisible unity of a single whole. In truth, the monistic assertion of one single whole and the denial of plurality and individuality is merely one statement in two different forms.

History of both Western and Eastern thought would provide us with practically an unlimited number of examples to illustrate what we just said. There are two assertions which are implicitly present in all monistic systems, although they are not always equally stressed: 1. Each alleged "part" of the universe is present in all other "parts"; 2. In each "part" of the universe all other "parts" are present. These two propositions are clearly not logically independent; you cannot assert one without another. The second proposition was explicitly stated by Spinoza. In his system not only the eternal substance necessarily implies each particular mode, but also even the most insignificant *modus* implies the whole eternal substance; or, in Spinoza's words which reveal the striking and ruthless logic of his system, the destruction of a single particle of matter would imply the destruction of the whole material universe.[21] The reason is obvious: according to Spinoza, unwittingly anticipating Mach, the totality of matter is indivisibly present in a single minutest particle. But then, as Professor Hartshorne stressed, the whole distinction between substance and its modes, between *natura naturans* and *natura naturata* disappears and the system of Spinoza becomes undistinguishable from the most extreme monism of the Eleatic type in which all plurality in space as well as in time is dissolved in the undifferentiated timeless unity of ἕν καὶ πᾶν, One and All.[22]

Is it not strange that practically the same statement is present in the genuinely pluralistic systems of Leibniz, Bergson and Whitehead? Does this perhaps mean that their pluralism is only apparent? This may be true of Leibniz in spite of the fact that he is regarded as a

[21]*Opera*, ed. J. van Vloten, 3, epistula IV.

[22]C. Hartshorne, "Contingency and the New Era in Metaphysics," *The Journal of Philosophy*, 29 (1932), 457-458.

textbook example of metaphysical pluralism and of the philosophy of discontinuity. If Leibniz says that "monads have no windows," he has also another statement which inspired both Bergson and Whitehead: every monad is a "mirror of the universe." Thus as Harald Höffding pointed out, the question of Leibniz is more complex than the conventional textbooks of history of philosophy assume and his difference from Spinoza is more apparent than real.[23] But what about Bergson and Whitehead? They both assert unambiguously the reality of succession, and to assert succession means always to assert plurality, at least *plurality in time*. It is true that pluralistic aspects in Bergson are somehow obscured by his constant emphasis on continuity; but we have to bear constantly in mind that this continuity is of *dynamic* type, altogether different from the static continuity of Spinoza. The monism of Spinoza as well as the "pluralism" of Leibniz is *timeless;* if we want to speak of the monism of Bergson or Whitehead, we have to join the adjective "dynamic" to the noun "monism." The monism of substance is altogether different from the monism of process; William James was right when he focussed attention on the pluralistic implications of Bergson's dynamism and when he pointed out that the denial of plurality and the denial of time are nearly always correlated.[24]

The concrete meaning of the pluralistic implications of the dynamic view of the world may be seen from the way in which the last quotation from Whitehead must be amended. It is true that "each particular event mirrors the world," but we must not forget that 1. the term "world" must not be taken in the sense of timeless, completed entity; 2. that the act of mirroring *takes time,* that it is itself a time-consuming process. These two qualifications require fuller explanation, which within the limits of this article must be necessarily brief.

1. Each particular event "mirrors the world," but this world is made of two heterogeneous parts: the first part is represented by the causal impact of the past events on the event in question; the second part consists of the virtual future events which may—but not

23H. Höffding, *A History of Modern Philosophy*, trans. B. E. Meyer, 1 (New York: Dover, 1955), 353.

24W. James, *A Pluralistic Universe,* Chap. VI; "The Dilemma of Determinism," *The Will to Believe and Other Essays in Popular Philosophy,* esp. pp. 150-152.

necessarily will—radiate from the same present event. In other words, each present event is pervaded by the causal impact of the past events and it implicitly contains the future events. But the manner in which the past is immanent in the present is altogether different from the way in which the future "pre-exists" in it. Future "pre-exists" only in a general, ambiguous and potential sense; the definiteness and *even the very individuality* of the future events as well as their causal efficacy is lacking as long as they remain future. On the other hand, the past events are by their own nature definite, complete and, in principle at least, causally effective. Future events do not act; the past does. In any genuine affirmation of the reality of process, futurity and potentiality are synonymous terms. This contrast between the definite, settled and causally effective character of the past and the ambiguous, indefinite and causally inefficacious character of the future is nothing but the consequence of the basic asymmetry of every temporal process. This contrast is obscured when the static and abstract term "world" is used; for the "world" which every spatio-temporal event reflects is, so to speak, made of two heterogeneous halves: of the completed past and of the virtual future. On the contrast between the irrevocability of the past and the plasticity of the future the irreversibility of time is based. This was clearly recognized by Aristotle when he limited the omnipotence of God by the following words: "Of this one thing God is deprived—namely to make undone the things that have been made." His disciple St. Thomas stated it even more incisively when he wrote: *Praeterita autem non fuisse contradictionem implicat.*[25] It was the same Aristotle who stressed the unreality and indefiniteness of the future to such an extent that he denied the applicability of the law of the excluded middle to the future situations. According to him the proposition: "There will be a seafight tomorrow" is neither true nor false *now;* it is merely possible *now;* but it *will be* either true or false *tomorrow.* According to the Laplacean determinism this proposition is either true or false even when we do not know it. As in René Clair's picture "It happened tomorrow" the future for a determinist has the same status as the past; it *already happened,* although we have an illusion that it

[25]St. Thomas Aquinas, *Summa Theologica,* Q. XXV, art. 4; Aristotle, *Ethica Nicomachea,* Bk. VI, ch. 2. Cf. also Hartshorne's article, "The Reality of The Past, The Unreality of The Future," *Hibbert Journal,* 27 (1939), 246-257.

did not. The whole difference between the static and dynamic view of reality is illustrated in these two different attitudes toward the future. In the dynamic view there is merely a *semantic* difference between the two following statements: "Each particular event mirrors the virtualities of the future" and "Each particular event does not mirror any specific future event at all."

2. Can we at least say that each spatio-temporal standpoint reflects the *whole present of the universe?* This was a natural belief until the discovery of the finite speed of all causal actions. Because there are no instantaneous interactions in the world, only that which is past can act on each particular event. When we contemplate the starry sky, the light of Polaris, which we perceive, is fifty years old, that of Sirius eight years, that of Neptune four hours, that of the moon one second. Using Leibniz's and Whitehead's expression, we say that only the cosmic past of the universe—never its present—is "mirrored" on the present sky of our planet. This is the meaning of our previous statement that "mirroring" is not an instantaneous process, but that it *takes time.* It would go beyond the scope of this essay to explain how this fact joined to the negative result of Michelson's experiment led to the denial of absolute simultaneity; for our purpose it suffices to say that the temporal relations are now redefined in causal terms: the relation "anterior to" is defined as "acting on" a certain event; the relation "posterior to" is defined as "being acted upon" by the same event; finally, the relation of simultaneity was superseded by that of causal independence. Thus the denial of simple location should be rephrased in the following way: each particular event reflects that part of the universe which acts on it as well as the potentialities of its own future effects; *but it remains causally unrelated to those events which neither act on it nor will be acted upon by it.* In no case can we say that it reflects the *whole* universe; the expression "the whole universe" is nothing but a remnant of the static, Eleatic and substantialistic terminology.

It is therefore clear that the denial of simple location implies the doctrine of "the bloc universe" only when this doctrine is assumed at the beginning. When Spinoza assumed that the destruction of a tiniest particle would imply the destruction of the *whole* universe; or when Chrysippus illustrated the same idea metaphorically by saying that "a drop of wine will eventually color the *whole* ocean," the concept of the universe as a completed whole was assumed without any discussion. Classical physics seemingly substantiated this assumption: the classical world was rigidly coherent along its temporal dimension because the iron link of necessity joined, and we may even say, *fused* its successive phases to such extent that even their succession, i.e. individuality in time, was in question. But the classical world cohered no less along its *transversal*, i.e., spatial dimension: the advance of time toward the future (as long as it was reluctantly admitted), had, so to speak, one single wave-front on which the single cosmic "Now," that is, all simultaneous events were carried together to the future. Whether moving or not, the classical world was one single huge bloc; the denial of simple location within such a universe necessarily entailed the spatial and temporal omnipresence of the smallest atom and, eventually, the *implicit identity* of each atom with the universe. ("The identity of Minimum and Maximum," as Cusanus and Bruno used to say.) The universe of modern physics is of a different type. There are definite indications that the cohesion of its successive phases is of a different kind from the rigid necessitarian bond of the Laplacean physics and Spinoza's metaphysics. The universe no longer seems to be a single unbending fact rigidly cohering along its temporal dimension. But the relativity theory loosened also its coherence along its transversal, i.e., spatial dimension when it replaced the relation of simultaneity by that of causal independence. It is possible that both types of loosening are interrelated. James saw this as early as 1884 when he linked the assertion of plurality with that of contingency. Fifty years later Whitehead, too, linked "contemporary independence" to the contingency character of the world.[26] In doing this Whitehead virtually modified his original claim that "each spatio-temporal standpoint mirrors the *whole* universe." In the dynamic universe—or rather "multiverse"—in which individual causal lines, partially separated by the gaps of causal independence, are being continually prolonged in the direction of the future, the concept of the absolutely coherent universe—coherent either in the temporal or spatial dimension—loses its meaning. In other words, *the principle of absence* limits to a certain extent the mutual immanence implied in the denial of simple location. In the language of James whose profound significance appears today even in a clearer light than fifty years ago:

26W. James, "Dilemma of Determinism," *op. cit.*, pp. 150-151, 181; A. N. Whitehead, *Adventures of Ideas* (New York: Macmillan, 1947), p. 255.

The monistic principle implies that nothing that is can in any way whatever be absent from anything else that is. The pluralistic principle, on the other hand, is quite compatible with some things being absent from operations in which other things are singly or collectively engaged.[27]

This recognition of the real absences in the world does not, of course, imply a return to the traditional atomism. The previously stated criticism of the artificial fragmentation of reality remains valid; but we have to be careful not to jump to the opposite extreme in believing that there are no articulations and no individualities in the universe. Reality is neither an undifferentiated and completed whole nor is it a bundle of externally related entities; it is a polyphonous process, never complete, never entirely one and never entirely many.

Mach's statement that in the principle of inertia there is "an abbreviated reference to the whole universe" should be now amended by replacing the word "the whole universe" by the words "that part of the universe which is causally affecting the material 'particle' here and now." When I perceive Sirius on the sky, my retina, my nervous system and my mind are affected by the event which is eight light-years away from me; using Leibniz's language, I can say that my consciousness "mirrors" an extensive spatio-temporal region affecting my particular present event. But the very same event *will remain forever independent* from the photon which will reach my eye tomorrow or after a week, a month, a year. The light from Sirius tomorrow will not reach my present moment, but its future causal successors. All future causal effects of Sirius will remain *forever absent* from this particular present moment. This is the meaning of *the principle of absence* which necessarily limits the denial of simple location; and from the illustration just given it is clear that this principle follows logically from the very fact that the universe is *always* incomplete, that no interaction can take place instantaneously and, *a fortiori*, that no causal action can move "backward in time." But to say that the universe is everlastingly incomplete and that every process exhibits temporal asymmetry is one and the same statement in two different forms.

MILIČ ČAPEK

BOSTON UNIVERSITY

[27]*Some Problems of Philosophy*, p. 144. The term "the principle of absence" was coined by Jean Wahl, *Les philosophes pluralistes d'Angleterre et d'Amérique* (Paris, 1920), p. 126.

BIOLOGY AND THE PHILOSOPHY OF SCIENCE

Introduction

IN PRESENTING this paper for the Festschrift in honor of my long time friend, Charles Hartshorne, I should state at once that I am writing as a biologist, specifically a geneticist, interested in the philosophical implications of his subject, but with only a superficial knowledge of philosophy in general. My justification for writing on this topic is the belief that the philosophy of science is necessarily a joint venture since it is obvious that advances in science provide data on the nature of existence which must be taken into account in philosophical consideration of this subject. This is most obvious in connection with the drastic revision of the basic concepts of physics since 1900, the impact of which on philosophy has recently been brilliantly developed by Čapek. There have also been great advances in biology. The resulting concepts do not strike at the very categories of thought and defy expression in language (other than mathematics) as do those of modern physics. Nevertheless they have a special importance from the facts that the only direct knowledge of mind that any one possesses is associated with a certain living organism, himself, and that in general, indications of the presence of mind are restricted to living organisms. The fact that while such indications are universally accepted in the case of other human beings but become progressively less convincing as we pass to animals closely similar to man, and from these to such forms as fishes, insects, clams, worms and protozoa, raises difficulties. Few see any indication of mind in plants.

The Subdivisions of Biology

There are many ways of subdividing the field of biology. The mode that is most instructive for our purpose is not by kind (zoology, botany and their subdivisions) but by problems that arise, in one way or another in connection with all of the kinds (Wright, 1953,59).

CLASSIFICATION OF FIELDS OF BIOLOGY (I)

Biological level		Climax phase	
		A. Description	B. Dynamics
VI. Ecologic system	b. World biota	Biogeography	
	a. Local biota	Theory of persistence	
V. Inter-breeding population	b. Species	Taxonomy	Theory of species stability
	a. Deme	Demography	
		Description	Statics 7a. *Population genetics*
IV. Multi-cellular organism	b. Individual	External character	Behavior 6. *Genetics of behavior*
	a. Organ Tissue	Anatomy Histology	Gross physiology
III. Cell	Cytoplasm and nucleus	Descriptive cytology	General physiology 4. *Physiological genetics*
II. Autonomous macro-molecule	Chromosome Gene DNA	3. *Theory of the gene*	
		Chemical composition	Chemistry of persistence
I. Non-autonomous molecule		Biochemistry	

CLASSIFICATION OF FIELDS OF BIOLOGY (II)

	History		E. Multiplication
	C. Description	D. Dynamics	
VIb. Paleontology		Biotic evolution	———
VIa.		Ecologic succession	———
Vb.	Phylogeny	Macroevolution Theory of transformation	Theory of species cleavage
Va.	Description	Microevolution Kinetics 7b. Population genetics	———
IVb.		Life history	Physiology of reproduction 1. Formal genetics
IVa. Descriptive embryology		Morpho-genesis Histogenesis 5. Developmental genetics	———
III.		2. Cytogenetics	Theory of cell division
II.	Description	Mutation Process	Duplication
I.		Biochemistry	

Table I presents a two dimensional classification: by level of organization and by similar problems that arise at some or all of the levels. These include (A) that of describing the persistent entities and (B) of accounting for their persistence; (C) of describing and (D) accounting for the orderly processes by which most biological entities develop from relative simplicity to complexity in their patterns, and (E) of describing and interpreting the processes by which the entities at some of the levels multiply. All of these involve the working out of the relations between levels. Genetics plays an especially important role in this respect and aspects of it are indicated in italics.

Biology began in the middle with interest in the external appearance of the larger forms, their behaviors, their life histories, and their modes of reproduction. From this it proceeded toward understanding of their structures in terms of organs (anatomy) and tissues (histology), of the functioning of these in the maintenance of life (gross physiology), and in the description and mechanism of the usually very complex process by which a fertilized egg becomes an adult (embryology). Reproduction sometimes occurs by budding but is usually from union of eggs produced by females and sperms by males.

In the course of study of fine scale structure, it became apparent about a century and a half ago, that the larger organisms, whether animals or plants, are composed of microscopic units that are essentially similar in all of them, and also similar to certain whole organisms of minute size (protozoa, protophyta). It came to be recognized that these cells, each a jellylike droplet, bounded by a membrane, containing numerous internal granules and membranes, and especially a large complex organ, the nucleus, are in a real sense, complete organisms. Each originates only by fission of a preexistent cell, and carries on its life processes, largely by and for itself. The validity of this view-point has been borne out by the long continued cultivation of cells in media as in protozoa. There is a flourishing branch of human genetics, devoted to the heredity of biochemical and other differences among human cells, multiplying in petri dishes. The cell has thus become an important object of study on its own account.

The concept that organisms are composed of suborganisms has become one of the most significant principles of biology. For many years, however, it seemed that the cell was the ultimate unit of living matter. It is now known that the characteristics of cells and, through them, of multicellular organisms depend largely on a vast number of entities known as genes that are autonomous in structure, but carried in linear strands (chromosomes) in the nuclei of cells.

Although believed to be essentially molecular in pattern of organization, genes have the most fundamental property of living organisms. Each duplicates its own specificity, irrespective of associated genes or of environmental conditions, along the succession of cells through which it is transmitted. They thus constitute the material basis of heredity. If by chance (perhaps once in a million generations for each gene) one does undergo change (a mutation), it duplicates thereafter as of the new sort. Each gene thus has an evolutionary history of its own.

There are cogent reasons for thinking that the structure of a gene is that of a giant molecule of the category known as deoxyribonucleic acid (DNA), a polymer in which each of the thousands of units (nucleotides) consists of a nitrogen base (purine or pyrimidine), a 5-carbon sugar (deoxyribose) and phosphoric acid. The x-ray diffraction pattern of DNA according to Watson and Crick (1953) indicates a double helix in which each strand has ten or eleven nucleotides per gyre with pentose phosphate backbone on the outside and connection with the other strand by means of a pyrimidine in one linked by hydrogen bonds with a particular purine in the other (cytosine with guanine, thymine with adenine). The basis for specificity is the order of succession of the four kinds of nucleotides in either strand, that in the other being necessarily exactly complementary. It is supposed that under certain cell conditions, there is uncoiling and separation of the strands followed (or accompanied) by recoiling separately, and synthesis by each of its exact complement from free nucleotides and thus duplication of the double helix. The multiplication of specific DNA, extracted from cells, has been carried out in cellfree solutions in the test tube by Kornberg and associates.

Under certain circumstances in the cell, DNA molecules also synthesize ribonucleic acid (RNA) in which uracil takes the place of thymine and ribose of deoxyribose. These determine the synthesis of correspondingly specific kinds of protein molecules (specific sequences involving about twenty kinds of amino acids) in a way that is in active process of analysis by biochemists. Proteins are the major constituent of living matter apart from water (which constitutes about two thirds). Certain proteins, the enzymes, behave as catalysts that guide the specific course of metabolism in each cell and thus ultimately determine all of the characteristics of organisms, except as these are modified by environmental effects. Because of the indirectness of the relation between gene and character, each gene tends to affect many characters and each character is affected by many genes.

It is to be noted that the molecule which is the physical basis of heredity (DNA) is composed wholly of a few common kinds of atoms (C,H,O,N,P,) as is also true of the proteins (C,H,O,N,S,). A few other kinds of atoms play important roles in the prosthetic groups of enzymes, in such processes as photosynthesis and oxygen transport, in regulating the body fluids and in the composition of relatively inert structures such as bone and shell. All of these atoms are continually being exchanged with the environment in the course of metabolism. There is no kind of elementary substance that is peculiar to living matter. The persistence of a living entity is thus that of pattern, not of a particular assemblage, of material units. According to the famous dictum of the great comparative anatomist and paleontologist Baron Cuvier, nearly a century and a half ago:

La vie est donc un tourbillon, plus ou moins rapide, plus ou moins compliqué, dont la direction est constante et qui entraine toujours des molécules de mêmes sortes, mais où les molécules individuelles entrent et d'où elles sortent continuellement, de manière que la *forme* du corps vivant lui est plus essentielle que sa *matière*.

It may be noted that in the structural hierarchy, gene, cell, large organism, the relation of gene to cell is utterly different from that of cell to large organism. In the latter case, one initial cell multiplies and by differentiation of its descendants gives rise to the large organism. On the other hand, two full sets of genes are assembled in the initial cell, one from the egg itself and one from the fertilizing sperm, and these two sets are in general, passed on to all of the cell descendants by duplication and segregation of duplicants at each cell division. There is one exception, the reduction to a single set in the formation of the germ cells by means of a unique sort of a cell division in which there is a pairing of maternal and paternal representatives of each kind of chromosome in place of a duplication. Exchanges occur between these paired chromosomes followed by random assortment and thus the production of a novel set of genes.

The hierarchic pattern of life is extended in the other direction by the existence of colonial organisms, resulting from the failure of complete separation of individuals after fission or budding. In some cases there is differentiation and division of labor among the zooids, and even, in certain bryozoa, development of a common nervous system by which the colony can react as an essentially single organism. It is probable that such complex segmental organisms as annelid worms and ultimately arthropods (such as lobsters, spiders and insects) trace to this process in their evolution.

Even when there is complete separation of individuals after reproduction, the group of relatives tend to form a population within which there is continued interbreeding. There are probably always many alternative forms of each basic gene (alleles), mostly with very slight differential effects, that arise by mutation and accumulate in the population. The recombination of these gives the potentiality for a vastly greater number of hereditary types in a population than there are protons and electrons in the visible universe. Thus it is reasonably certain that no two sexually produced individuals have exactly the same constitution. Nevertheless the group maintains its statistical characteristics generation after generation. It may be looked upon as a loosely knit organism with protoplasmic continuity of a netlike pattern in space-time. This important unit has been called the deme.

Such units of population are usually connected with many others by more or less frequent crossbreeding. The entire network, which may be continental in its range, or even worldwide as with man, is the very important unit; the species. There is still protoplasmic continuity but portions may be separated by thousands of generations.

As with individual organisms, this entity has a complicated history, its evolution. Some forms (e.g. certain brachiopods) have hardly changed for hundreds of millions of years. Many have gradually achieved considerable changes along a single line or perhaps a number of branching lines. In other cases, the process of change has been explosively rapid in terms of geologic time and has led, by branching, to types that differ enormously (as in the case of the orders of mammals in the paleocene). The essential condition at any time seems to have been ecologic opportunity. This is presented to the first forms that reach unoccupied territory, also to the few forms that survive a catastrophic change of conditions, but especially to a form that in the course of gradual perfection of adaptation to a very special way of life has acquired a character or cluster of characters that happens to give a general advantage and thus the possibility for branches that can specialize along many different lines. The evolution by certain marsh dwelling fishes of feet from fins as a means of crawling from one drying pool to another was one of the adaptations that opened up the dry land for exploitation. The great class of birds no doubt arose from the evolution of the wing from a reptile leg. The most successful forms (including man) have had a zigzag rather than a direct evolutionary history, because of a succession of such break-throughs.

As to the mechanism of evolution, the simplest view is that on which each mutation may be considered either as unequivocally favorable, or as unequivocally unfavorable in relation to the prevailing type. In the former case, the mutation gradually replaces the old type gene. Favorable mutations must, however, be exceedingly rare unless the adaptiveness of the old type has been reduced because of change in the environmental conditions, in which case this process may bring about rapid readaptation.

In general, relative selective values can properly be assigned only to genetic systems as wholes, since individual mutations that are favorable in some combinations are almost certain to be unfavorable in others. Evolution depends on the fitting together of a harmonious system of gene effects. There may be a vast number of different, more or less harmonious systems. Natural selection tends to hold the population to one, not in general the best one, that is possible from available genes. For an effective evolutionary process there must be a shifting balance between local random changes in gene frequencies and the local pressures of selection, and also a balance between local inbreeding and crossbreeding, that permits the continual selection among demes through differential population growth and migration. The most effective process either of perfecting an adaptation along a particular line, or of exploiting a major ecological opportunity is thus not, in the long run, the almost deterministic pressure of mass selection acting on recurrent mutations, but rather one of continuous trial and error, made possible by labile balance among all of the factors (Wright 1931, 48, 55, 59).

Branching of evolutionary lines comes about through relatively complete isolation of subpopulations by one means or another.

The evolutionary process results in categories higher than the species: genus, family, order, class and phylum and kingdom. In these there is no continuity, apart from rare hybridization, except in the remote past. They are not natural entities in the same sense as the deme and species but merely conveniences of classification.

In most animals, the deme is integrated not only by biparental reproduction but also by social relations. In some cases, this has led to a tightly knit organization almost comparable to that of a multi-cellular individual. The most extreme examples, apart from man, are found in the social insects such as ants (Wheeler, 1911), bees (von Frisch, 1950), and termites (Emerson, 1939).

In man, the capacity for symbolic speech, has made possible a still more far-reaching type of social organization (Gerard 1940), and a new sort of evolutionary process, that of ideas, enormously more rapid than biological evolution. The result is a multiplicity of social organisms, cutting across each other so that the same individual may belong to many different ones (state, church, profession, etc.). This is analogous to the intersection of organ and tissue as suborganisms at the level of the individual. There is also a hierarchic pattern: city, state, nation, now perhaps working painfully toward some sort of orderly integration of all mankind.

The representatives of the various species inhabiting each neighborhood form an ecologic system, Darwin's "web of life," which maintains its statistical properties year after year because of various limiting factors and self-regulatory interactions between predator and prey, and between parasite and host. After a catastrophic disturbance, there tends to be a developmental process in the form of an orderly ecologic succession, leading to whatever is the climax type of community under the prevailing conditions.

The ecologic systems of adjacent regions are connected. In the end, all life on the surface of the earth and in its waters may be considered one vast symplasm (Wheeler) of which the anatomy is described in biogeography and the evolution in paleontology.

A third dimension could be given to the scheme of classification by assigning a branch of pathology to each category for consideration of changes beyond the limits of adaptive capacity (Link, 1932).

Genetics began with the deduction from the results of breeding experiments of certain formal principles that accounted for the differences observed among organisms related by descent. Formal genetics (1) may be considered to be an aspect of the physiology of reproduction, at the level of the individual. Because of the central position of the mechanism of long-time persistence of type in biologic theory, genetics has ramified into nearly all levels of the biological hierarchy. This began when breeding experiments revealed the existence of a new ultracellular unit, the gene. It became a descriptive technique, that in some respects revealed more of the ultrastructure of the cell than the highest power of the microscope. The most remarkable thing, however, has been the detailed agreement in the conclusions from these very different techniques. The joint field is known as cytogenetics (2). Genetics has also joined forces with biochemistry in developing the chemical theory of the gene (3) and in a penetrating analysis of the metabolic processes of the cell, the subject of physiological genetics (4). Joint genetic and histologic studies have contributed much to the analysis of development (5). The genetics of behavior (6) brings us back to the level of the individual. All of the foregoing give a basis for the statistical genetics of populations (7) which in conjunction with studies of experimental and natural populations (Dobzhansky 1951) has brought about a more adequate understanding of organic evolution, along lines already touched on. Genetics more than anything else, binds the biology of all levels into a unity.

Biologic and Physical Entities

The hierarchy of biological entities may be looked upon as a continuation of the physicist's hierarchy: Planck's unit of action, photon and elementary particle, atom, molecule. The biological hierarchy from gene and other macromolecules to world biota is, however, to the side of the main physical hierarchy which procedes from molecule through systems with only point to point integration (crystals and geological formations, or bodies of water) to earth and solar system, or directly from atoms to stars on the way to galaxy and the universe as a whole, as the all embracing organism.

Intricacy of organization seems, however, to culminate in the multicellular individual in the middle of the biological hierarchy. The behavior of such individuals seems to transcend physico-chemical interpretation and the phenomena of consciousness in ourselves, as representative of such individuals, seems utterly inexplicable on this basis.

The Dualism of Mind and Matter

The physicist can accept a common sense dualism of mind and matter (or better of mental and physical action) without too much difficulty in his scientific work. This is also true of the social scientist and humanist in their fields. The biologist, bridging both worlds in an apparent unity, is continually in trouble. The philosophical biologist cannot escape from the problem of the relation of mind and matter.

It will be convenient here to list a number of possible relations.

At one extreme is solipsism. This, I suppose, is the viewpoint of a new born baby for whom all reality is encompassed in a single stream of consciousness: a kaleidoscopic medley of pressures, temperatures, colors, sounds, smells, etc. There is no way indeed, as Berkeley and Hume brought out, by which any of us can give a rigorous demonstration that anything else exists, but most of us became aware very early of constellations of sensations that persisted with such regularity, whether we wished it or not, as to give an overwhelming impression of external reality. Adults who relapse into a private world in which no distinction is made between fantasy and external reality must be shut up in institutions.

Anthropologists tell us that primitive man had a viewpoint toward nature, known as animism. In its most primitive form, all things were assumed to be of the same general sort as ourselves, merely more or less powerful. This was extreme anthropomorphism and application took the form of magic.

The capacity for spontaneous activity left the savage temporarily in sleep and was observed to leave others permanently in death. Animism tended to pass into a form in which mind and matter were considered to be separable. The dryads could come out of the trees, and the naiads out of the lakes. There was a beginning of the ultimately sharp distinction between two kinds of existence, each of which it was thought might occur alone as disembodied mind, or mindless matter but at least in man, in an association of body and soul.

The progress in the recognition of regularities in the world (natural science), has led to a continual decline in the role assigned mind and increase in that assigned matter, using the term to include all aspects of the physical world. Animism gave way to polytheism and this to increasingly impersonal monotheism and often, in science at least, to almost pure materialism.

There are several viewpoints which scientists have taken. There are still those who accept the intervention of disembodied spirits in the ordinary affairs of life. In relatively recent years this included such distinguished scientists as Sir Oliver Lodge and A. R. Wallace. The regularity with which apparently incontrovertible evidence has later been shown to rest on self deception or clever fraud has led most persons to profound skepticism with respect to disembodied spirits at this level, whatever may be their beliefs in religion.

The second viewpoint, vitalistic dualism which accepts mindless nonliving matter, and living matter, sometimes at least associated with mind, but does not accept disembodied mind (except perhaps for the Creator) has had wide acceptance among scientists. Descartes expressed clearly the underlying philosophy under which modern science has developed in his recognition of two sharply distinct modes of existence—matter, characterized primarily by extension in space, and mind as stated in his proposition "cogito ergo sum." Descartes restricted mind to man in the natural world. He held that animals were merely automata which along with plants and inanimate objects were subject to rigorous physical laws of cause and effect. He held, to be sure, that both extension and mind were created by God but in relation to science his viewpoint clearly belongs in this second category. It is a philosophy that has served admirably for more than three centuries in the development of physical science in harmony for the most part with humanism and theology.

Many biologists, especially those studying whole animals have postulated mind in animals other than man and have treated mind as an active factor in their science, not merely in the scientists. They have found no sharp break in mode of behavior between man and other animals and none between these and lower animals down to protozoa. Moreover they find no break in behavior between protozoa and the cells of which higher animals and plants are composed. Among leading modern biologists who have felt the necessity of postulating a vital principle not derivable from physics or chemistry are Driesch, Jennings (1953), Ralph Lillie (1945), and Sinnott (1955). Bergson (1911) has given appealing philosophical support for an "élan vital."

The prevailing trend among biologists, however, has been away from vitalism and toward increasing materialism and mechanism in interpreting physiology and behavior, and toward a decreasing role of the supernatural with respect to origins. Linnaeus accounted for the multiplicity of kinds of organisms by separate creation. Lamarck by advocating evolution, pushed creation back to the origin of life. His explanation of evolution was vitalistic as it involved an innate perfecting principle in life, diverted into branching lines by hereditary effects of the desires and actions of animals. Darwin gave a great impetus toward a wholly deterministic science (our third category) by accounting for evolution by random variation and selection. Jacques Loeb was the leader at the beginning of this century in insisting on the rigorous exclusion of any but physico-chemical explanations in biology.

The limit of this trend would seem to be complete materialism, the complete denial of mind as a category of existence. This however is contrary to the obvious facts of immediate experience. Our stream of consciousness is all that is experienced directly. Mind, even though denied any role in the course of events, must be retained as a category of existence, at least as an observer.

If the non-living world is completely devoid of mind, and if, as it seems necessary to believe, there was a time when no life could exist, how did mind appear? Lloyd Morgan (1933) (cf. Wright, 1935) treated the emergence of mind as a phenomenon of the same sort as the emergence of a new organ or physiological capacity, in evolution. A new organ, however, involves nothing more mysterious than differential growth, leading for example to an outpocketing from a flat surface, that turns out to be useful and may be elaborated by further differential growth. Similarly, loss, addition or rearrangement in the pattern of a macromolecule may enable it to bind certain other molecules in such a way as to catalyze a new metabolic process.

Emergence of either of these sorts, however surprising its consequences, offers no serious philosophical difficulty. Emergence of mind from no mind at all is sheer magic. Its postulation is as pathetically inadequate as the doctrine of Anaxagoras that mind depends on certain atoms that differ from others merely in being finer, smoother and more mobile.

The emergence of mind in the course of individual development presents a less extreme dilemma for dualism but nevertheless a serious

one and one that is an everyday occurrence instead of a single event
in the remote past. The fertilized egg, while a living cell, behaves
in a way that suggests a purely physico-chemical interpretation
rather than one involving mind. If the human mind is not to appear
by magic, it must be a development from the mind of the egg and
back of this, apparently, of the DNA molecules of the egg and sperm
nuclei that constitute its heredity.

Panpsychism

The only satisfactory solution of these dilemmas would seem to
be that mind is universal, present not only in all organisms and in
their cells but in molecules, atoms and elementary particles. This is
more plausible for the entities of modern physics than for the concept of matter that held essentially from Democritus to the end of
the last century. The ultimate atoms, constant in number, stripped
of all secondary qualities (color, smell, etc.) were conceived of as
particles each of which filled impenetrably a certain portion of otherwise empty space but which were capable of change of position in
space on due cause and of transferring motion to other atoms in such
a way that the total amount of motion remained in some sense unchanged. The dominant philosophy of science before 1900 is admirably expressed in the famous dictum of Laplace.

An intellect which at a given instant knew all the forces acting in nature and
the positions of all things of which this world consists—supposing the said
intellect were vast enough to subject these data to analysis—would embrace
in the same formula the motions of the greatest bodies in the universe and
those of the slightest atoms, nothing would be uncertain for it and the future
like the past would be present to its eyes.

The concept of events as occurring in a universal isotropic, three
dimensional space, which persists unchanged by these events, and is
thus independent of time has been replaced under Einstein's theory
of relativity by the concept of existence as consisting of multiple
causal chains of events, the spatial and temporal relations of which
may differ for different observers (except at intersections) in such
a way as to preclude any general meaning to simultaneity. Matter
and kinetic energy have become entities of the same general sort,
interchangeable in ways that now threaten the continued existence
of mankind. The wavelike properties of material units (protons,

electrons) as well as of radiant energy (photons) indicate that the ultimate physical reality consists of events in which oscillatory change (in themselves, as singularities in space-time) is of the essence. It has been shown that there is irreducible experimental indeterminism in the succession of events at the level of Planck's unit of action. While interpretation of Heisenberg's indeterminacy principle differs among physicists the simplest interpretation is that it implies emergence of genuine novelty at each instant, but novelty that is in statistical continuity with the past (above the level of Planck's unit). Under this view there can be no real vision of the future whether by the second sight of Highland seers or by extrasensory perception, but merely tentative extrapolation from past trends. Existence is a real adventure, not a mere unfolding before our eyes of a "future" that really exists now and always has existed.

We must go back to animism for a fresh start toward a fourth viewpoint. The earliest Greek philosophers, the hylozoic school, held that all that exists is alive, but in a less crudely anthropomorphic sense than primitive animism. This concept was further refined by Aristotle who seems to have been the only major philosopher who was also a major figure in biology. He was undoubtedly foremost in the ancient world as anatomist, embryologist and classifier of the animal kingdom. His concept of epigenesis (the step by step elaboration of the complexity of an adult organism from its simple beginnings) was based on observations of developing embryos. It was a great advance over the crude doctrine of preformation of Hippocrates (although the latter may be considered a remote precursor of the gene theory at a higher cycle in the advance of knowledge).

In his general concept of the development of phenomena as occurring through the association of a purposeful essence (form) with an inert substrate (matter) we recognize a biologist's philosophy in contrast, for example, with the more purely idealistic teachings of his master, Plato. With respect to man, his concept of the relation of mind to matter seems close to that of modern vitalistic dualism. His acceptance of contingency in the development of phenomena is in line with the indeterminacy of modern physics though it must be recognized that the detailed viewpoint of modern physics could hardly have been attained except on the foundation laid by a rigorous determinism more akin to the philosophy of Democritus than to that of Aristotle, whose physical concepts were in detail wholly erroneous.

Turning to relatively modern times we find the doctrine of universal association of mind and matter in the philosophy of Spinoza. This association was a necessary consequence of his identification of God and the universe and his specification of extension and thought as two of the attributes of God. Spinoza was more concerned with religion and ethics than with science, and his views did not seem to constitute as useful a philosophy of science as did those of Descartes.

The dualistic panpsychism involved in the universal association of mind and matter is not quite the same as what may be considered a fifth viewpoint, that of dual-aspect or monistic panpsychism, of which the first clear account that I have read was that by W. K. Clifford (1879) who however refers to an earlier statement by Wundt and doubtfully to a "suggestion thrown out by Kant that his *Ding an sich* might be of the nature of mind." As this viewpoint has long seemed to me to provide the most tenable philosophy of science it may be desirable to give my own approach to it. (Wright, 1921, 31, 35, 41, 48, 53.) As a student of science, I began with an acceptance of a determinism as rigorous as that of Laplace's dictum, although disturbed by the absence of any place in this scheme for the fact of consciousness. This mechanistic viewpoint was first somewhat shaken by reading (in 1912) Bergson's "Creative Evolution" which presented a viewpoint that seemed more satisfactory as a philosophy of Biology. I found, however, that I was unable to accept it as a philosophy of science as a whole. Similarly I looked with sympathy on Jennings's position in his famous controversy with Jacques Loeb on the interpretation of animal behavior: trial and error vs. tropism, but felt that the overtones of vitalism in his position were unsatisfactory. I began to see the possibility of a different approach on reading "The Origin and Nature of Life" by the biochemist Benjamin Moore (1912) who suggested that cells and higher organisms and societies might be looked upon as extensions of the series atom, molecule, colloid (p. 189), but the dilemma: absolutely deterministic laws of physics at one end of the scale, consciousness and apparent freedom at the other, remained. The key to a unified philosophy seemed to be provided by "The Grammar of Science" by Karl Pearson (1899), the leader of the statistical or biometric school of biology which I read a couple of years later. After emphasizing the subjective nature of all of our knowledge of the external world, he pointed out that the laws of nature could be looked upon, not as part of the eternal structure of the world, but as merely condensed statistical descriptions of how things are observed to behave. There need be no essential difference from statistical laws of voluntary human behavior such as the law of supply and demand.

If mind and matter are coexistensive, they may be looked upon as two aspects of the same reality. They do not, however stand on an equal footing. All that any of us can know directly is our own experience, mind, including our raw sensations, our perceptions, memories, emotions, thoughts and volitions. Matter (or physical action), is always a deduction from regularities that we find in our experience. In general, mind may be considered the inner aspect of the reality of the observer, matter the external aspect of a reality in the inner aspect of which the observer does not partake, except in so far as perception implies interaction.

FIELD OF MIND

Figure 1. Diagrammatic representation of interaction within and between two complex minds which lead each to interpret the other as matter.

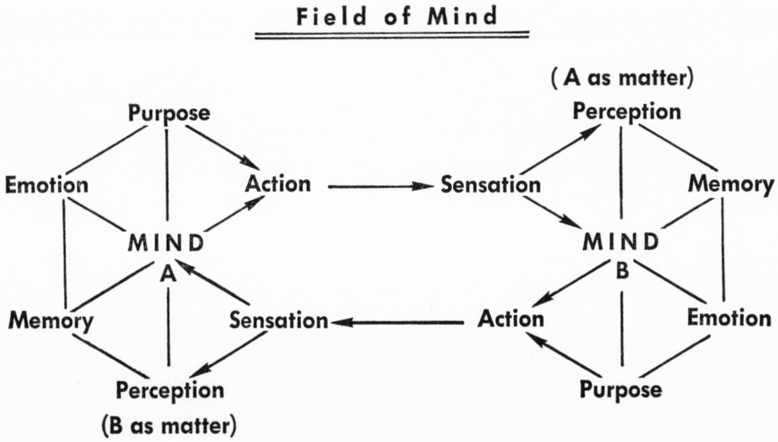

Field of Mind

This point of view is represented in figure 1. A and B represent two minds, largely private, but capable nevertheless of interacting either directly or through a chain. A perceives certain regularities in its stream of consciousness which it ascribes to an external reality, B, but as it does not enter into B's stream of consciousness, it tends to consider B as merely an unconscious source of disturbance, matter. B similarly deduces matter, A, from the regularities induced by the interaction in its stream of consciousness.

As each becomes aware of many external realities with varying interrelations, it locates them in a coordinate system of its own, consisting of two dimensions of direction in addition to one of remoteness and one of order of succession (time).

In certain cases complex minds recognize the behavior of external matter as paralleling their own inner reality so completely as to compel identification as their own bodies. In other cases, the behavior is so similar in kind, though not parallel, as to indicate matter inhabited by an alien mind, other men or higher organisms. In other cases there seems no indication of mind.

One of the clearest statements of this viewpoint that I later encountered was that of the psychologist Troland (1922) who traced it back to Fechner in the nineteenth century. I was also led to Clifford's statement to which I have referred.

It must be admitted that in discussions through the years I have found few biologists who seem at all attracted to this view. It was accordingly very gratifying to find far reaching agreement with Charles Hartshorne (1942, 1954) who had arrived at a similar view by a wholly different route. In Whitehead's "Science and the Modern World" (1925) to which I was now led, I found the most complete philosophical development of this point of view although I cannot say that I can penetrate into the full depth of his meaning.

As a working philosophy of science, dual-aspect panpsychism leads to two points of view. First is the psychical interpretation of the inner aspect of reality which the Australian zoologist Agar (1951) has attempted to apply. Second is the statistical description of the external aspect, in which Karl Pearson was long the leader. Statistical mechanics may be considered as the application in physical science (Margenau, 1952).

The psychical interpretation tends to be closely allied in modes of attack on problems to vitalism, and statistical description to determinism, but with a wholly different metaphysics in each case. The logical relation between psychical interpretation and statistical description is that of alternative points of view with respect to the same thing, while vitalism, determinism and either dualistic or dual-aspect panpsychism are mutually exclusive theories.

The two modes of interpretation under dual-aspect panpsychism cannot be combined in the same explanation. One cannot account for the behavior of an amoeba as due partly to physico-chemical factors and partly to what it wants to do without danger of duplication if the two modes are merely aspects of the same thing: as it appears to an outsider and as we imagine it appears to the amoeba itself.

The Hierarchy of Mind

Because of the hierarchic nature of biologic and physical entities it appears that my mind must be based somehow on the minds of my cells and these on those of their constituent molecules and so on down to elementary particles.

As atoms are continually entering and continually departing, the mind of the whole must depend on patterns of interaction in this whole rather than on the particular atoms. As noted, mind is really the inner aspect of actions rather than of things except as the latter are interpreted as bundles of actions.

It is obvious that the mind of an individual is not merely the sum of those of the cells. In one sense it is something much more, an integration or bundle of interactions, but in another, much less. I am not conscious of what all my cells are doing. My focus of consciousness shifts continually, now on a perception, now on a memory which has somehow been stored out of my mind, now on an emotional state, now on the construction of an abstract pattern of thought, now on the process of arriving at a decision or on the demands of action. I must suppose that the interactions within different, but overlapping cell groups of my brain somehow create a single, complex but continually shifting stream of consciousness, which, however, may be wholly interrupted in dreamless sleep, while those of the components continue.

When we pass from the individual to society as an organism, we at once perceive a serious difficulty. On the dual-aspect hypothesis, the interaction of individuals should constitute a mind, a stream of consciousness, at a higher level. We speak of the spirit of America, highly integrated at times, at others, sadly disintegrated by mutual suspicion. We think of this, however, only as a figure of speech, inconceivable as a reality comparable to our own stream of consciousness.

The very fact of interaction, at any level, implies however that minds are not entirely private. The entities cannot be the windowless monads of Leibniz. They exist as components of a more comprehensive mind in a pattern of relations to each other, which each represents to itself as a pattern in space and time.

There are many degrees of integration in nature, ranging from the mere point to point network of a crystal or of a sponge or higher plant, to the intimate integration of a higher vertebrate. A human society is intermediate in character, but enormously simpler and less intimate than that of the human nervous system. Much looser still is the pattern of a species or of an ecologic system.

The universe as a whole is the external aspect (to each of its components) of the all embracing world of mind that is a necessary postulate of this theory. It appears to us to be only very loosely integrated by its gravitational and electromagnetic fields through which interaction between remote parts requires periods of time of the order of hundreds of millions of years in contrast with a few hundredths of a second within a human being. It may, however, be as presumptuous of us to evaluate the universe as for a hydrogen ion in the blood stream of a man to evaluate the latter.

Freedom of the Will

Subjectively, mind seems to involve the continual exercise of choice, within, of course, a limited range of possibilities. How is this freedom to be reconciled with apparent determinism in the behavior of non-living things? Part of the answer is as already noted that the laws of nature are merely statistical and no more preclude choice on the part of the individual components than do statistical laws of human behavior.

There could not be statistical regularity, however, without at least some regularity in the behavior of individuals. Freedom of the will is sometimes considered to be equivalent to caprice, but mere chance is as little compatible with freedom of the will as determinism.

There are indeed two very different models which may be used for more or less predictable behavior. One is mechanical, such as the course of a billiard ball, struck by another, or the motion of a cogwheel, pushed by another. The billiard balls and the cogwheels are, however, aggregations rather than organisms and their highly regular behavior is that of statistical aggregates and need not apply to integrated entities such as single molecules. This is nevertheless the sort of model that is usually thought of in connection with determinism in science. At the opposite extreme, as a model, is the behavior of a man of firm purpose, who moves toward some goal, in spite of obstacles. His behavior under similar conditions may be predictable to a considerable extent and the more so, the stronger his will.

Conditions, however, are never exactly the same. As Pearson wrote: "The causes of any individual thing thus widen out into the unmanageable history of the universe. The causes of any finite portion of the universe lead us irresistibly to the history of the universe as a whole."

Every event must thus have a unique aspect. What happens may be one hundred percent the resultant of creative choices of the participants yet there may be sufficient similarities among conditions and among choices of behavior to give the appearance of almost complete determination in the statistics of large numbers.

As to the behavior of the individual entities, we have noted that physics itself, since Pearson wrote his *Grammar of Science,* has had to qualify the idea of complete predictability by Heisenberg's indeterminacy principle. Physical science thus has arrived at statistical mechanics as its ultimate form of statement, rather than deterministic equations. There seems to be nothing in physics that prevents the view that its particles are little creatures, acting essentially like the larger familiar organisms.

A human being appears to make choices that make enormous differences in the course of events. How can something that is composed entirely of molecules have a freedom that transcends the statistical regularity of an aggregation of molecules? The answer is, of course, that a tightly integrated organism operates through a hierarchy of switch or trigger mechanisms. In an action involving a very great exchange of energy, for example the flight of an aeroplane, all molecules may follow their customary modes of behavior, except in a small portion of the system (a lever and the pilot) which diverts the course of the whole in one way or another. Within this small portion there may in turn be no detectible swerving from customary behavior except in a switch mechanism of the second order of smallness (a neuro-muscular junction), and so on to transactions of the third order in neural and cerebral synapses. The portion of the total energy exchange involved in controlling the deviation from customary behavior may thus be of the nature of an infinitesimal raised to a high power. Yet the flight is all according to plan. A high degree of freedom of choice of the whole is *consistent* with highly regular behavior of the parts. On the other hand self-regulatory processes prevent control by minute indeterminacies.

The necessity for respecting the choices of the parts does set limits to the freedom of the whole. The dual-aspect panpsychist view requires that each event depend wholly on choice, as the inner aspect of action, but with the whole past history of the universe converging on it, it depends on the resolution of choices of innumerable entities, at all levels in the hierarchy of existence. One can dominate only by ways that involve concurrence of the others.

Philosophy and Methodology

Finally what difference in the methodology of science in general and of biology in particular is indicated by the dual-aspect panpsychist philosophy as compared with determinism?

It might seem that science should concern itself primarily with the inner aspect of reality. Unfortunately we cannot enter into any consciousness but our own. In the human case, we can indeed compare notes on our introspections and discover regularities. Psychoanalysis represents the most serious attempt at such a program. It would be absurd moreover in the social sciences not to avail ourselves of all the insight into human nature that we can obtain. The major emphasis must, however, be put on the objective, statistical account of what human beings actually do.

In the natural sciences, we cannot make any check on our interpretations of the inner life of animals, much less of single cells, molecules, atoms or elementary particles. Man is, indeed, an animal and by trying to separate out a residuum from those aspects of our minds that are associated with distinctively human traits—such as the use of symbolic speech and its consequences, we may perhaps derive some insight into the nature of the stream of consciousness of higher animals, taking due account of special capabilities as exaggerations of things that we perceive in ourselves.

This, however, must always remain a top dressing on the solid structure of science, and literary rather than scientific. Apart from this, science must restrict itself to the external aspect of things, largely to classification by kind, and to statistical laws relating to the so-called primary qualities of things: number and form, position in space, and motion, as those aspects of our perceptions on which it has been clearly recognized since the time of Locke, that men can best agree. We measure these in terms of such standard chunks of voluntary action and perception as are embodied in the operational definitions of centimeter, gram, second, etc. There is the philosophic difference from determinism that we now are to interpret natural laws merely as condensed statistical descriptions of the external aspect of behavior rather than accounts of reality in its totality.

A certain danger for science must be squarely faced. The acceptance of statistical description as ultimate may lead sometimes to premature abandonment of analysis in cases in which analysis would be pushed farther by one who believes firmly that there is a deterministic mechanism to be found.

Pearson, for example, undoubtedly felt more satisfied with a merely statistical account of the resemblances of individuals to their parents and more remote ancestors than did geneticists with a deterministic metaphysics. He violently opposed the Mendelian analysis of heredity after its rediscovery in 1900. The latter runs at once into mere probabilities in the Mendelian ratios but it carries analysis of the basis for these probabilities to deeper levels and gives more insight than a mere regression equation.

Pearson seems not to have recognized sufficiently the implications of the hierarchic structure of reality. The task of science is not complete until it has followed phenomena through all levels of the hierarchy, up and down as far as possible, and after obtaining the best statistical description at each, has tied them all together. In modern genetics, this has meant working down from the statistical rules at the level of the individual to those of chromosomes and genes and to the chemistry of these, and up again into the physiology of gene action at the levels of cell, tissue, organ and individual, and finally to the properties of populations. All statements are ultimately in terms of probabilities but all are related.

Acceptance of this point of view requires relatively little change in the actual practice of science, especially as determinism has never been more than an ideal admittedly unrealizable in full because of the invariable errors of observation and in many cases, practically irreductible probabilities like those in the fall of dice (or segregation and assortment of genes). The deterministic expressions do not lose their usefulness as approximations.

What we are given is a tenable philosophy of science and along with this a desirable humility in the recognition that science is a limited venture, concerned with the external and statistical aspect of events and incapable of dealing with the unique creative aspect of each individual event.

BIBLIOGRAPHY

Agar, W.E. *A Contribution to the Theory of the Living Organism.* 2nd edition. Melbourne: Melbourne Univ. Press, 1951.

Bergson, H. *Creative Evolution.* Translated by Arthur Mitchell. New York: Henry Holt & Co., 1911.

Čapek, Milič. *Philosophical Impact of Contemporary Physics.* New York: Von Nostrand & Co., 1961.

Clifford, W.K. *Lectures and Essays.* Edited by Leslie Stephen and Frederick Pollock. London: Macmillan & Co., Vol. II, 1879.

Cuvier, Baron Georges L. C. F. D. *Le Règne Animal Distribué d'après son Organisation.* Paris: Deterville, 1817, p. 13.

Dobzhansky, Th. *Genetics and the Origin of Species.* 3rd edition. New York: Columbia University Press, 1951.

Emerson, A.E. "Social Coordination and the Superorganism." *Amer. Midland Nat.* 21 (1939) 182-209.

Gerard, R.W. "Organism, Society and Science." *Sci. Monthly,* 50 (1940) 340-350.

Hartshorne, C. "Organic and Inorganic Wholes." *Phil. and Phenom. Research* 3 (1942) 127-136.

_____. "Mind, Matter and Freedom." *Sci. Monthly* 78 (1954) 314-320.

Jennings, H.S. *The Universe and Life.* New Haven: Yale Univ. Press, 1933.

Lillie, R.S. *General Biology and the Philosophy of Organism.* Chicago: Univ. of Chicago Press, 1945.

Link, G.K.K. "The Role of Genetics in Etiological Pathology." *Quart. Rev. Biol.* 8 (1932) 127-171.

Margenau, H. "Physical versus Historical Reality." *Phil. Sci.* 19 (1952) 193-213.

Moore, Benjamin. *The Origin and Nature of Life.* New York: Henry Holt & Co., 1912.

Morgan, C. Lloyd. *The Emergence of Novelty*. London: Williams and Norgate, 1933.

Pearson, Karl. *The Grammar of Science*. 2nd edition. London, 1899.

Sinnott, E.W. *The Biology of the Spirit*. New York: The Viking Press, 1955.

Troland, L.T. "Psychophysics as Related to the Mysteries of Physics and Metaphysics." *Jour. Washington Acad. Sci.* 12 (1922) 141-162.

von Frisch, K. *Bees*. Ithaca: Cornell Univ. Press, 1950.

Watson, J.D. and Crick, F.H.C. "The Structure of DNA." *Cold Spring Harbor Symposia on Quant. Biol.* 18 (1953) 123-132.

Wheeler, W.M. "The Ant Colony as an Organism." *J. Morph.* 22 (1911) 307-325.

Whitehead, A.N. *Science and The Modern World*. New York: Macmillan & Co., 1925.

Wright, S. "Origin and Development of the Nervous System." (A review of a book by C. M. Child.) *Jour. Hered.* 12 (1921) 72-75.

———— "Evolution in Mendelian Populations." *Genetics* 16 (1931) 97-159.

———— "The Emergence of Novelty." (A review of a book by Lloyd Morgan.) *J. Hered.* 26 (1935) 369-373.

———— "A Philosophy of Science." (A review of a book by W.M. Werkmeister.) *Amer. Biol. Teacher* 3 (1941) 276-278.

———— "Evolution, Organic." *Encycl. Brit.* 8 (1948) 915-929.

———— "Gene and Organism." (Presidential Address, American Society of Naturalists.) *Amer. Nat.* 87 (1953) 5-18.

———— "Modes of Selection." (Presidential Address, Society for the Study of Evolution.) *Amer. Nat.* 90 (1955) 5-24.

———— "Genetics, the Gene, and the Hierarchy of Biological Sciences." (Presidential address, X International Congress of Genetics, Montreal, August 20, 1958.) 1 p. 475-489. Also *Science* 30 (1959) 959-965.

———— "Physiological Genetics, Ecology of Populations and Natural Selection." *Perspectives in Biology and Medicine* 3 (1959) 107-151. Also in *Evolution after Darwin*, 1 429-475. Chicago: The University of Chicago Press, 1960.

SEWALL WRIGHT

DEPARTMENT OF GENETICS
UNIVERSITY OF WISCONSIN

WHITEHEAD AND THE THEORY OF FORM

WHITEHEAD'S theory of eternal objects or form is still perhaps the least appreciated part of his philosophy. He himself believed that he had made a significant contribution to the theory of form and that he had thereby advanced metaphysical thought in general. It seems to me that Whitehead was entirely correct in this belief. Moreover, the notion of form is as central in his metaphysics as it is in that of Aristotle. It is essential to most of his chief and novel doctrines, such as those of objectification, societies, the extensive continuum, propositions, etc. It is of interest that originally it was not primarily metaphysical considerations which brought Whitehead to the adoption of forms as integral to this philosophy, but considerations concerning the philosophy of science. In his later period, however, his theory of form was completely reshaped under the demands of metaphysical considerations.

I

Already quite early the entire unsatisfactoriness of a nominalistic conception of form was evident to Whitehead from scientific considerations which led him to his theory of 'objects'. The later metaphysical considerations left him in no doubt on this point. Nominalism in the end leaves the relevance of thought to things without any explanation. Whitehead saw clearly, with Plato, that to recognize an element of form exhibited in common by many actualities necessitates finally that we acknowledge form as a distinct metaphysical category. It is important to be clear what this involves.

To say that many actualities exemplify a form in common implies that in some fundamental sense the form must transcend the individual exemplifications. It is evident that the elucidation of 'transcendence' here is crucial.

It is not sufficient to maintain that this 'transcendence' consists merely in distinguishing form as an element in actuality, namely that element which constitutes the definiteness or character of the actuality, considered in abstraction from the actuality. For this does not account for the form being 'common'. Once we recognize this factor of form as common it becomes clear that we are concerned with an element in an actuality which is not existentially exhausted in that particular actuality.

This is clarified by a comparison with an element in an actuality which is existentially exhausted in a particular actuality. This is the 'act' of the actuality. The act of the actuality is absolutely individual to that actuality. That act is individual, and unique, in that it takes place and is over, completely and absolutely. *That* act can never be again. It came, and is gone for ever. There may be similar acts, but never again *that* act. The similar acts are other acts. An act can never, by its very nature, be repeated. Repetition involves other acts, and form. The act of an actuality is that which is existentially exhausted in that actuality.

By contrast with act, form is that element in an actuality which is not existentially exhausted in an individual actuality. In this respect, therefore, form is at the opposite pole to act. Form, it is true, is the form of *an* act, but form is not exhausted in that act. On the contrary, form in its nature transcends the individual act, the individual actuality. Form is what is common to different acts, whereby there is repetition; form is what is common to different actualities, whereby they are similar. Thus while act has the metaphysical nature of unique occurrence, form has the contrary metaphysical nature: it can 'be again'. In this respect act and form constitute opposite metaphysical poles: act is that factor in an actuality which is absolutely unique, while form is that which is general.

If we recognize that form is not existentially exhausted in individual actualities, that on the contrary, as that which can always 'be again', it transcends the individual actualities, we are thereby admitting form as having a distinct metaphysical status. That is to say, form must be admitted as a distinct metaphysical factor in the universe. It is not reducible to actuality. Whitehead insists on this admission, and in this respect he accepts the fundamental Platonic insight.

But to admit form as a distinct metaphysical factor is not necessarily to accept the doctrine of the Plato of the *Phaedo* and to regard forms as themselves separate actualities, as οὐσίαι. Here Whitehead agrees with Aristotle's criticism of Plato and with the Aristotelian doctrine that forms can *exist* only as the forms of οὐσίαι. This is an implication of his ontological principle. But Whitehead insists, contrary to Aristotle, that forms are not thereby to be understood as simply factors in actuality. Form *exists* as characterizing actuality, but form nevertheless transcends the actuality it characterizes. We shall discuss further implications of this later. For the moment I am concerned to stress the primary implication of this transcendence, namely that form must be a metaphysical ultimate, distinct from and not reducible to actuality or οὐσία. That is to say, form must be accorded a metaphysical status distinct from that of actuality—distinct from, but not separate from. For form cannot exist separate from actuality, since form is not itself an actuality, an οὐσία. Form is the 'what' and the 'how' of actuality. Form is that element in the total metaphysical situation whereby actuality is 'what' it is and 'how' it is. In other words, anything which can be conceived as contributing to the 'whatness' and the 'howness' of things, anything of the nature of 'pattern', 'structure', 'definiteness', or 'character' of things, belongs to the category of form.

A further basic implication of the transcendence of form is the eternity of form. This means that in its own nature *qua* form, form does not involve change, flux, or becoming. Things change; things, that is, exchange one character for another, but each character as such remains what it is, just that and nothing else. Red and green are respectively red and green, that and nothing else. Triangularity and squareness are triangularity and squareness, and there can be no alteration of their character as such. A thing can change from being circular to being oval, but circularity as such can never change. It is the things which are involved in flux, not forms. It is this feature of being intrinsically what it is which is fundamentally meant by 'eternity'.

The forms as that which constitute the 'what' and 'how' of things are necessarily eternal. That is, that the forms as such should be capable of change, of flux, is impossible. To be the form of changing things, form must itself be exempt from change, from flux. For it is in terms of form that we have to understand change; and therefore that the forms themselves should be capable of change is absurd, a contradiction. This is the argument of Plato against Heraclitus. Whitehead maintains, with Aristotle, that this argument is final and conclusive.

The same argument makes clear another aspect of the eternity of form, namely that forms as such can never become. That is, it is impossible that form as such should be capable of coming into being and ceasing to be. Actualities, οὐσίαι, monads, are that in the universe which come into being. Form, in its own nature *qua* form, involves no becoming; it transcends becoming; it is eternal. For if form is to be form, that is that in terms of which becoming is to be understood, it cannot itself become.

II

While it is important to insist on the necessary eternity of form, it is equally important to insist that form can *exist* only *as* actualized. That is to say, the transcendence of form is not to be understood as meaning the separation of form from actualization. This had been the mistake of the early Plato—an understandable mistake in the circumstances of the first epoch-making discovery of form. But, as Whitehead has it, by the ontological principle, form can exist only as actualized—in some or other actuality. Actualization is thus not merely accidental to the nature of form. To be at all, in any sense, it must be actualized, and being actualized means being the form of, the character of, some or other particular actuality.

But in its nature as form, it is neutral as to which actuality in particular it characterizes. That is to say, the *decision* as to actualization cannot lie in the nature of form *qua* form. For 'decision' implies agency, and, as Whitehead puts it, "agency belongs exclusively to actual occasions". [PR 42—Cambridge ed] Form is the form of a decision; it cannot itself *be* the decision. Form is form, and nothing else. Whitehead stresses this by insisting that the ontological principle must be borne clearly in mind. "The ontological principle declares that every decision is referable to one or more actual entities, because in separation from actual entities there is nothing, merely nonentity—'The rest is silence'." [PR 58] That is to say, form as such is not an actual entity, so decision cannot be referred to form *qua* form. Form cannot decide; only an actuality can decide. Only an actuality can decide which form is to be actualized in any particular case.

Now for an actuality to decide, form must be 'there' for the decision as to actualization; form must be 'given' for decision. This means that form *qua* form must have the status of a datum for actualization, a datum for decision as to actualization. To say that form *qua* form is a datum for decision is to say that form is in its own nature an 'object' for decision. Being an 'object' for actualization means that it does not in itself embody the factor of 'decision' as to actualization. This is why Whitehead uses the term 'eternal object' as an alternative to the more traditional 'form'. In its own nature form is 'eternal'—that is, it transcends all particular actualization; and it is an 'object'—that is, in its own nature *qua* form it has the status of a datum for actualization.

Further, to be an 'object' for actualization means to be 'potential' for actualization. Form is in its own nature 'potential', as opposed to 'actual': it is potential for actualization. As Whitehead has put it, "an eternal object is always a potentiality for actual entities; but in itself . . . it is neutral as to the fact of physical ingression in any particular actual entity in the temporal world". [PR 60] 'Potential' is the correlative of 'actual'. To be 'potential' is to be potential *for* actualization. This is one aspect of what Whitehead wishes to bring out in his doctrine of form as "always a potentiality for actual entities".

Actuality, he insists, requires potentiality. His fundamental metaphysical doctrine is that *actuality becomes*. Whitehead completely rejects the doctrine of actuality as 'static being'. Actuality *becomes*; it comes into being. Thus actuality necessarily requires potentiality as 'what it might become', that is, as what form it might actualize. Until an actuality is fully become, 'what' it *might* become is basically relevant: a potentiality to be actualized.

That 'potentiality' and 'actuality' are, in the metaphysical nature of things, correlative was clearly recognized by Aristotle in his doctrine of δύναμις and ἐνέργεια. But Whitehead makes a sharper distinction than Aristotle, and in this respect comes a bit closer to Plato. For Whitehead Aristotle has gone a little too far in his reaction against the doctrine of the *Phaedo*, and has not allowed sufficiently for form as necessarily having a distinct metaphysical status. That is to say, form cannot be consistently regarded as solely a factor in the analysis of actuality; rather, it must be explicitly regarded as having a nature transcending actuality.

This is where the big difference enters between Whitehead and Aristotle. One might put this by saying that Whitehead makes a deeper metaphysical distinction between 'potentiality' and 'actuality' than does Aristotle. For in ascribing to form the status of a fundamental metaphysical category, Whitehead wishes to go further—when maintaining that form is "always a potentiality for actual entities"—than merely to mean thereby that form *qua* form has the character of a potentiality for an actuality; further, that is to say, than only to hold that form must be realized in some or other actuality.

An intrinsic feature of his recognition of form as having a distinct metaphysical status is that form *is* potentiality. That is to say, Whitehead maintains that *form is that factor in the metaphysical nature of things whereby there is potentiality at all in contrast to actuality.* In other words, all potentiality in the universe, of whatever kind, is derivable from form. For example, when we speak of the potentiality of an actuality—that it has the potentiality to be this or that—the potentiality to which we refer is derivable from the element of form in the actuality, and not from the element of act.

What is ultimately—that is, metaphysically—required in order that the potentiality become actuality, is a 'decision', an *act* of decision. Whitehead has expressed this by saying: "Just as 'potentiality for process' is the meaning of the more general term 'entity' or 'thing'; so 'decision' is the additional meaning imported by the word 'actual' into the phrase 'actual entity'. 'Actuality' is the decision amid 'potentiality'." [PR 58-9] Act, the act of decision, is the ultimate metaphysical factor whereby there is actuality. Here we see again that 'act' and 'form' appear as ultimate metaphysical poles. They are the ultimate correlatives belonging to 'potentiality' and 'actuality'. And in saying that act and form are ultimate metaphysical poles I am intending to stress again Whitehead's doctrine that act is not ascribable to form. That is, form cannot act; 'actuality' does not become by virtue of the factor of form. Form *qua* form is devoid of the factor of act; form is the potentiality for act, and requires act in order that the potentiality be converted into actuality. Form itself cannot furnish the act necessary for that conversion.

I have dwelt on this point at some length because Whitehead here diverges most importantly from Aristotle, and the Aristotelian doctrine has in this respect become almost generally accepted, implicitly if not explicitly, for it has determined our customary terminology. Aristotle's position, it is true, is not unequivocal, but it cannot be denied that there is a strong tendency, at least, to ascribe act to form. Δύναμις, as the etymology of the word indicates, includes in its connotation a factor of 'potency', and Aristotle accepts this in his doctrine: δύναμις involves a 'potency' directed to the achievement of actuality. 'Ενέργεια, despite its derivation from ἔργον, work, tends for Aristotle to mean the achievement, the final outcome, the achieved, completed actuality. So that for him the factor of act is in the δύναμις rather than in the ἐνέργεια. But δύναμις is not only 'potency' but also 'potentiality', as opposed to 'actuality'—which is ἐνέργεια. Thus δύναμις is identified with form; and so act, as the 'potency' of δύναμις, is ascribed to form.

The Whiteheadian position, on the contrary, if I might put it so, would take more seriously the derivation of ἐνέργεια from ἔργον, work. That is to say, the act belongs to ἐνέργεια, and thus for Whitehead the factor of 'potency' is taken out of δύναμις, leaving 'potentiality'. Thus it becomes explicable that Whitehead uses the terms 'potentiality' and 'possibility' as largely synonymous. His doing so rests on a secure philosophical foundation.

III

In Whitehead's doctrine, therefore, while form is the form of actuality, the metaphysical status of form is not simply that of an element in the analysis of actuality. Form *qua* form transcends actuality, and it must have its own intrinsic nature as so transcendent. One important aspect of this nature we have seen to be expressed by the term 'eternity'. It is by virtue of this aspect that form is that factor in the universe whereby actuality has definiteness, character. Another important aspect of the nature of form is expressed by the term 'potentiality'. The intrinsic nature of form is that of potentiality for actuality. Form *qua* form is potential; but to exist at all it must be actualized. That is to say, as potentiality form necessarily requires actuality. And reciprocally, actuality necessarily requires form as potentiality. What I have been trying to bring out is that although actuality and form are thus reciprocal and correlative, they are distinct metaphysical ultimates, not reducible one to the other. Serious difficulties ensue if this be not accepted. On the other hand, much is explicable if we keep clear the metaphysical distinction amid ontological connection. This will be more readily seen when we have explored some further aspects of the nature of form *qua* form.

In this discussion I have mainly been using the term 'form' as a generic term covering all entities of a certain kind, namely those which in any respect constitute the 'what' and 'how' of actuality. This entails, it is evident, that although there is only one *kind* of entity which is form, there is not only one form. There are indefinitely many forms.

Now in regard to the manyness of forms Whitehead has some important differences with traditional doctrines. Since a particular form is in its intrinsic nature just that and no other, a frequent supposition, from the time of Plato onwards, has been that forms, *qua* forms, have a kind of unique distinctness as perfect archetypes. Connected with this supposition is the further one that there must be a specific definite number of forms. Whitehead rejects both these suppositions for reasons which become clear when two further aspects of the nature of form are elucidated.

The first is that although each form is in its essential nature just that which it is, there is no definite demarcation between forms *qua* forms, whereby one form is, as it were, separated off from another. Rather, in form *qua* form—as opposed to actualized form—there is a gradation, in which a definite demarcation *could be* made. That is, there are indefinite *possibilities* of demarcation, but in form *qua* form the demarcation *is not* made. In form *qua* form the demarcation is *possible*; it is only in form realized or actualized that a definite demarcation *is* made. The demarcation is the result of the act of actuality; in form *qua* form the demarcation is essentially only possible.

Another statement of this point is that form *qua* form constitutes a 'continuum'. That is, continuity is essential to the nature of form. This is readily seen if we consider an example, say, colour. Let us take 'red'. There is no single 'red'; rather there are an enormous variety of shades which are all red. Now these shades merge into one another; that is, there is a gradation in the shades, for instance, from dark to light, from one 'tone' to another. That is to say, there is an essential continuity in the colour; one shade is continuous with another, so that in the gradation one cannot say one shade quite specifically ends here and another begins there. But if we take a particular shade, for example by putting down a dab of paint, we see immediately that it is distinctly different from other shades. And further, if we were to put down another dab of paint, of an apparently contiguous shade, it is not difficult to see that it is possible to get a third dab in an intermediate shade. In these instances, however, we must be clear, we are concerned with actualized form, and not with form *qua* form.

In form *qua* form there is an essential continuity. The recognition of this leads to another point of great importance. This is that when we are concerned with continuity we are concerned with form. Continuity as such pertains to form, and not to actuality. In other words, the very meaning of 'continuity' is grounded in this aspect of the nature of form, namely that in itself form does not embody a definite demarcation; it is the essential nature of form that it is *possible* demarcation. Any actual demarcation is the outcome of the decision of actuality. This is what Leibniz saw clearly when he wrote: "But a continuous quantity is something ideal which pertains to possibles and to actualities only insofar as they are possible. A continuum, that is, involves indeterminate parts, while, on the other hand, there is nothing indefinite in actual things, in which every division is made that can be made. Actual things are compounded as is a number out of unities, ideal things as is a number out of fractions; the parts are actually in the real whole but not in the ideal whole. But we confuse the ideal with real substances when we seek for actual parts in the order of possibilities, and indeterminate parts in the aggregate of actual things, and so entangle ourselves in the labyrinth of the continuum and in contradictions that cannot be explained." [Letter to De Volder in *Leibniz: Philosophical Papers and Letters,* tr. L. E. Loemker, p. 879] Whitehead's terse statement of this point is: "Continuity pertains to what is potential; whereas actuality is incurably atomic." [PR 84] "What is potential" is form. Continuity is grounded in the nature of form as potential.

The other aspect of the nature of form relevant here is but a facet of the nature of form as potentiality essentially involving continuity. Each form is in its essential nature what it is, that and no other, and yet is also essentially continuous with other forms. In saying that it is the 'essential nature' of form I am meaning quite strictly that it is the nature which form has by virtue of which it is form. Now what I have distinguished here as the continuity essential to the nature of form is an aspect of an essential interrelatedness of forms.

An interrelatedness between forms is as essential to the nature of form as it is that the form be what it is. Whitehead has called these two respectively the "relational essence" and the "individual essence" of forms. [Cf. Chapter X of *Science and the Modern World.*] These two essentials are not disconnected; on the contrary, the one is required by the other, so that there could be neither without the other. One important aspect of this is that what a form is, its identity, does not belong to it simply in isolation; intrinsic to its identity is its difference from others. Hegel expressed this in his principle of "identity in difference".

But Whitehead goes further and maintains that this principle must be pushed to its full range. Not only, for example, is a particular shade of red what it is, that identical shade, in its difference from all other shades of red. But further, red as a colour has that particular identity as that colour in its difference from all other qualities. And colour as such has that particular identity in its difference from all other qualities. And qualities—for example such as the ones familiar to our senses—have that particular identity as those qualities in difference from, for instance, on the one hand, emotional qualities such as anger or pain, and on the other hand, all quantities and geometrical characters.

It is important also to appreciate that this 'difference' embodies a 'relation'. That is, it is not a mere difference: this and not that. 'Difference' is not merely negative. There is implied a positive relatedness. This can be seen by considering the previous example again. In the difference of sensory qualities from (say) geometrical characters, there is embodied an intrinsic feature of relatedness whereby a colour, for instance, is able to occupy a geometrical spread or volume. That is to say, that relation of occupation stands in the intrinsic nature of colour and of geometrical structure. It is not something which is extrinsic to them and can be superadded.

The basic principle I am seeking to bring out and stress here is that the possibilities of relatedness between forms are contained in the essential natures of the respective forms. In saying 'possibilities of relatedness' I do not mean that the forms are there, complete without relatedness, which can then be added to them. The forms as such, *qua* form, are possibilities, and the possibilities of relatedness belong to them intrinsically as possibilities. Thus the possibility of 'green' and 'square' being related as a 'green square', stands in the essential natures respectively of 'green' and 'square'. Likewise it stands in the respective natures of 'round' and 'square' that there is no possibility of their constituting a 'round square'. But, it should be noted, the exclusion of that possibility is also a relatedness.

A structure of relatedness is thus intrinsic and essential to form *qua* form. That structure of relatedness is there, complete. That is, not only is the relatedness intrinsic to the forms, but also there can be no addition of new possibilities of relatedness, and none can fall away. For forms, *qua* forms, are eternal, and the structure of relatedness is not something extrinsic to form; the structure of relatedness is intrinsic to the nature of form, and is thus equally eternal. A relatedness which has never previously been *actualized*, can in the course of time be actualized. But to be actualized, to be capable of being actualized at all, means that that relatedness must be an eternal possibility.

We thus have the nature of form as essentially continuous; and the nature of form as involving essential interrelations; and the nature of form essentially as possibility. Also, these aspects are essentially interconnected.

With this clear it is not difficult to see that there can be no specific determinate number of forms. We can say that there is an indefinite plurality of forms. But we can never say that there is such and such a number of forms. That is, we can never specify a determinate number as the totality of forms. To attempt to do so is to fail to keep distinct the fundamental metaphysical difference between possibility and actuality; as Leibniz said in the passage quoted above, "we confuse the ideal with real substances when we seek for actual parts in the order of possibilities . . . and so entangle ourselves in the labyrinth of the continuum and in contradictions that cannot be explained".

The confusion of potentiality with actuality lies at the root of the difficulty in dealing with form. For that difficulty consists precisely in being able to maintain the distinction between form *qua* form and the particular instances of actualized form. What is vitally important here is the insight of Plato that we are concerned with form *qua* form only in thought, not in experience. In Whitehead's terminology, form is the object of "conceptual prehension", not of "physical prehension". We can in thought abstract from actualization and so arrive at a consideration of form *qua* form. We are able to do so because of the ultimate metaphysical distinction of form and actuality. In being actualized form does not wholly cease to be form; as Whitehead remarks, "potentiality becomes reality; and yet retains its message of alternatives which the actual entity has avoided". [PR 207]

IVOR LECLERC

UNIVERSITY OF GLASGOW

BERGSON OR WHITEHEAD?

I would not wish to begin this essay without a word about Charles Hartshorne. I studied with him at the University of Chicago between 1932 and 1934—metaphysics and aesthetics, and, I think, Kant. But it was then not possible to study any of those things without at the same time getting a generous dose of Peirce and Whitehead. Some of it "took." I am still never quite sure that aesthetics does not mean Peirce, and metaphysics Whitehead. Or is it the other way round? Much of what he taught was less a vaccination than a time-bomb. It took years for some of the insights to explode. But explode they finally did. I think there are few who studied with him who do not feel that his good influence upon us grows with the years. Who of us who worked with him does not feel gratitude and affection?

I

IN A PREVIOUS paper, "Substance, Process, Being: A Whiteheadian-Bergsonian View" (*Journal of Philosophy*, Aug. 28, 1958) I attempted an exposition of the Whitehead-Bergson philosophy of process. I wished there to explore the strategy of the best worked out modern alternative to the Aristotelian or Cartesian conception of substance. And I appealed just to those subordinate metaphysical aspects under which the philosophy of process reveals itself most importantly: (1) a theory of time in which time enters into the essence of materiality, (2) a theory of relatedness in which the world enters into the constitution of each actuality, and (3) a theory of inheritance whereby continuance is explained as conformal inheritance of pattern. Essential temporality, total relatedness, and conformal inheritance were thus taken as the characteristic qualities of the philosophy of process. But these principles appear more in Whitehead than in Bergson, and subsequent reflection has caused me to recognize that I was too hasty in attributing to each an identical metaphysical commitment. The problem of time haunts them both, but for Bergson essential temporality qualifies the existence of only half of Whitehead's experient occasions, and in consequence the doctrine of total relatedness is applicable to Bergson's world only with

severe reservations. That they are both philosophers of process is
undeniable. That Whitehead found the Bergsonian speculations
sympathetic is clear. But when in the preface of *Process and Reality*
he claimed to be undertaking the task which should rescue Bergson's
thought from the charge of anti-intellectualism, his adjective was
not, perhaps, well chosen. He might better have said that his purpose
was to rescue Bergsonianism from the rightful charge of *dualism*.

The thesis of this paper is that the standpoint of these two philosophers of process is radically at variance, and that the clue to their
disagreement is to be found in their respective applications of two
distinct theories of time. Whitehead is unsympathetic to the distinction between a heterogenous *personal time* and a homogeneous *natural time* which is the cornerstone of the Bergsonian system. Whereas
Bergson's metaphysics is founded upon a bifurcation of nature which
distinguishes absolutely between the living and the non-living levels
of experience, Whitehead's relentless panpsychism denies all natural
bifurcation. And the ultimate consequence is that while Whitehead
can establish the unity of nature in a fashion congenial to the presuppositions of a thoroughgoing philosophy of science, Bergson emphasizes the disparity between mechanism and feeling in a fashion
profoundly sympathetic to the literary mind.

The issue here is partly the understanding versus the imagination,
the standpoint of the arts and humanities versus the standpoint of
science, but it is even more the purely metaphysical issue of pluralism versus dualism. My purpose is to examine the nature of the
quarrel, to inquire how the positions differ; if a choice is crucial,
what precisely is metaphysically at stake. And in the course of my
examination, I shall have reason to suggest that the differences between them represent a curious re-currence to certain modes of
seventeenth century thought.

II

Both Maritain and Whitehead have suggested (although not in
just these words) that Bergson is a kind of latter-day Faust who has
made his pact with the devil. The bargain? To avoid mechanism.
The price? To sacrifice the intellect. The charge is just, but it takes
no cognizance of the refinement of the Bergsonian empiricism. For

it is difficult to deny that the human intellect is at home among inanimate objects (especially "solids"), and that the natural congruence between a metaphysics of substance and accident and a logic of subject and predicate is evidence that the concepts of our logic are formed in the first instance as a logic of solids. If the moral of Euclid and the *Posterior Analytics* is the same, that only provides Greek verification that geometry is the point of intersection of logical thought and unorganized matter. Geometry is as frozen as architecture, and both are mute to the challenge of life and evolutionary movement. Not one logical category, not one of the forms of judgment which Kant isolated so carefully, applies exactly to life.

In Bergson the metaphysical impulse is pure. To pass beyond the "frames" of knowledge *(les cadres de la connaissance)* to a direct vision of the object is his ambition, provided that we understand the word "object" in a metaphorical sense. For the metaphysical ground-concept of "appearance and reality" must be translated first into the psychological terminology of an "inner" and an "outer" series of reality. Of other things our knowledge is external and superficial: of ourselves it is internal and profound. I change (in my sensations, feelings, volitions, and ideas) and there is no discontinuity in the actuality of the psychic life—it is only that my attention is *fixed* by separate acts. If you are an atomistic psychologist, you settle upon the separate acts (it is this settling which has made Hume famous), but if you are a contextualist, each state sums up the totality of the individual past, and the overlap of states only attests to the continuity of context which defines each actual occasion.

The insight of Democritus, on the other hand, expresses a permanent necessity of the scientific intellect. Material things are made of the unchanging (atoms) and the repeatable (elements). Whenever thought invokes a system of *elements* and *principles* there are operative those intellectual tools which Kant formulated as the laws of the understanding, and their structure reflects the influence of matter. Matter by definition is *isolated*, and for this very reason is patient of geometrical treatment, but the universe as a whole does not respond to chronometry—it *endures*. A truly universal interaction is reality itself and no algebra can exhaust it conceptually.

The real test is the case of the living body, for in this context we are dealing with what is *par excellence an individual*. Individuality, of course, admits of degrees, and an "ideal" individuality is not fully realized even in man. A tree lives, but it is a low grade society rather than an individual, since it does not realize itself within the ambience of a concrete time. The distinction between "concrete" and "abstract" time is here the crucial point. There is a current of being upon which each organism "rides through its life," and the tree, even without high grade individuality, is a "natural" rather than an "artificial" system. Matter is in some sense (as in the Aristotelian system) a universal substrate, but the continuity which Aristotle perceived in the scale of forms yields in Bergson to the central bifurcation—that between the "animated" matter of evolutionary development and the "inert" matter which defines a physical system. The principle of continuity (which Peirce took to be the essential presupposition of science) is broken and becomes here a split down the center of the universe which mind demands, and which it consecrates in the more or less trivial form of a distinction between a physical and a biological science. But the phrase "biological science" is less a description than a paradox. It represents the attempt to subsume the phenomena of life under the aegis of a universal mechanism; to bring the recalcitrantly *individual* within the domain of the law-imposed necessities.

But becoming has no number, no adjective, no *fixity* yielding to quantification or description. To count, measure, or dissect the living requires an act of dissociation—a denial of its intrinsic nature. For there is in the very nature of life a stubborn refusal of the concept, the formal pattern, the universal, and therefore of the intellect. "Cognition" and an "inert nature" read in terms of inorganic necessity are, like "causality" and "substance," but two sides of the same coin. Mechanism is thus refuted by an appeal to the experience of real time, and the intellect is seen to imply a Platonism which finds all ideas given in advance.

It is easy to understand why Whitehead felt that his philosophy of organism was to rescue Bergsonianism from its anti-intellectualist bias. Yet Bergson would have courteously but firmly denied the presuppositions of this "rescue." Whitehead's Platonism would have been the confirmation of his worst fears: the device of "the primordial nature of God" and a realm of "eternal objects" would have seemed to him a mere rationalization of that natural Platonism of the intellect which stands in irreconcilable opposition to the true means of comprehending life.

It is impossible, I think, to read Bergson without sensing in this civilized Parisian, this dandy of the Collège de France, the vestiges of that same imagination which inspired mythical thought before it was expurgated by the scientific mentality. "Life" breaks into individuals and species as a result of the explosive force (*l'élan vital*—the *vis a tergo*) with which it collides with the resistance offered by inert matter. The resistance of inert matter is the first obstacle to be overcome, and Bergson's account of this "overcoming" is the purest animism—the pathetic fallacy raised to a fine art. "Life," he says, "seems to have succeeded in this by dint of humility, by making itself very small and very insinuating, bending to physical and chemical forces, consenting even to go a part of the way with them, like the switch that adopts for a while the direction of the rail it is endeavoring to leave." The metaphor comes from an advanced technology, but the spirit behind it is surely that which Lévy-Bruhl long ago discovered in the mythical primitive mentality.

The encounter of "life" and "matter" is central to the Bergsonian philosophy. The role of life is to insert indetermination into matter, to make it inaccessible to the rational intellect. For intelligence always gives knowledge of a formal structure and so has as its chief object the unorganized solid. Therefore any table of categories will reflect at once the characteristics of matter and a catalogue of possibilities for intellectual thought. It is therefore useless to ask whether the intellect abstracts its categories from experience (as Scotus asserts), or Kantianwise imposes them upon it. The fact is that between the two there is a mutual adequation, and the characteristics of matter as thought by intellect will always be reducible to extension, externality, divisibility into parts, discreteness, atomicity. And if it be objected that this very extension and externality which characterizes matter requires space, and that space must be homogeneous, empty, infinite (and therefore infinitely divisible), the Bergsonian answer is that the continuity of the infinitely extended is never *perceived*; it is only *conceived* as a frame for action. What *is* perceived is always colored and resistent extension, and it is for this reason that our geometry and our logic have fashioned themselves upon solids.

It follows that for Bergson there will always be the most intimate relation between epistemology and metaphysics. The forms of reality demand their appropriate forms of knowing, and a dualism in the one area requires its corresponding dualism in the other. As matter is to life, so the intellect is to intuition. But this duality of our waking life is complicated by a monism of origins. When matter is perceived as an undivided whole, it must be a "flux" rather than a "thing," and this seems to promise a reconciliation between the inert and the living. If the intellect and matter have been formed by reciprocal adaptation, both have been derived from a wider form of existence. Development in time has meant a separation, a breaking asunder, a fragmentation. Mind separates into concepts. Matter separates into distinct bodies. But the metaphysical impulse struggles heroically against the mainstream of natural development—back toward the origins. At the root of most metaphysical speculations lies the ancient insight of Parmenides, flowering in Hegel and Spinoza, and supporting the strong idealist tradition: the double conviction that nature is a unity and that the function of mind is to embrace it in its totality.

There is an ocean of life in which we are immersed. Intelligence comes from it and philosophy tries to lead back to it. But opposition is Reality's fate. Matter and spirit remain at odds, and behind materiality and spirituality lie two processes opposite in their direction. Living beings (the bearers of real time) fall back exhausted in death as mere extension. Experience exhibits a constant regression of the "extra-spatial" *degrading* itself into spatiality, just as materiality is an interruption of the ever-renewed creation which reality, whole and undivided, accomplishes in advancing.

There is, I think, in Bergson a nostalgia for monism which is all the more poignant because his own ultimate outcome is so unrepentently dualistic. And one sees this exhibited in all its clarity in the interesting excursion into the history of philosophy with which *Creative Evolution* concludes. The topic is the metaphysical interpretation of modern science as provided by the philosophy of the seventeenth century. Bergson wants to show the unbridgeable gap between science and metaphysics, and his proof is to indicate the way in which real time (duration) as the very mobility of being escapes the hold of scientific knowledge. On the threshold of the modern world, he says, metaphysics hesitated between a time patterned upon the artificial extensionality of space and the unique temporality of the living being. The indecision is visible in Descartes. Bergson complains of

Descartes as a half-hearted mechanist who wishes to impose a universal deterministic necessity without compromising the free will of
man. But if this only shows how impossible it is to mingle consistently the traditions of Democritus and St. Augustine, Bergson
himself will not escape the censure he wishes to heap upon Descartes.
Bergson's uneasiness about the seventeenth century dualism which
severs bodies and souls, *res extensa* and *res cogitans* stems at least in
part from an unwillingness to admit his own obvious kinship with
Descartes. But when he objects even more strongly to the parallelism
discernible in Leibniz and Spinoza (as any consistent Cartesian dualist
should) it is because Spinoza's discovery of two attributes for a single
substance exhibits a monism which is a snare and a delusion, and
because Leibniz, in finding thought prior to, and more important
than, extension, seems to Bergson to be the victim of the intellectu-
alist fallacy.

Leibniz' unity is, however, only "the reciprocal complementarity
of monads" (as Whitehead's actual occasions are mutual data for
one another) and Bergson quite mistakenly makes a mechanist out of
Leibniz as, inversely (and just as mistakenly) Whitehead makes an
organicist out of Locke. But these curious readings of the history
of philosophy tell us more about their authors than their subjects.
When Bergson asserts that Leibniz differs from Spinoza only in that
he considers universal mechanism as our perspective upon reality
rather than (as in Spinoza) reality's perspective upon itself, he is
solidifying the distinction between body and mind in a mould as
unbreakable as that of Descartes. This shows itself unmistakably
in his further criticism of Kant.

Kant has one crucial advantage over Leibniz and Spinoza. His
concern is not the metaphysical maximum, but its minimum. He
applies Occam's razor to the reservoir of conceptual possibilities
in order to reduce to its most economical the epistemological structure required to make the physics of Newton and Galileo the model
of a universal science. But this again is only to reinstate a scientific
monism after the metaphysical debris has been cleared away. If
there is an Understanding, then (as the early positivists maintained)
there must be "a unity of science." Carnap's *Logischer Aufbau* only
spells out what is implicit in "The Transcendental Analytic." Or, to
put it in the simplest possible way, *there is only one experience* and
"science" explicates its structure. But the magician only removes

from the hat what he has previously carefully put in. Kant's initial data were mathematics and physics, *not* biology and certainly not psychology. This, according to Bergson, provided him with the categories of the intellect but prevented him from discovering *intuition*. Kant's treatment of "the Inner Sense" is mathematical and abstract; but if he had permitted himself a true empiricism here, he would certainly have stumbled upon the "lived time" which is *duration*. And this would have convinced him not of the unity, but the *duality* of science; it would have shown him how the mind must of necessity shift its gears as it moves from a physical to a vital and a psychical subject matter.

Bergson must always be opposed to any "unity of science" and always in favor of its duality. For his fight against a mechanistic view of mind and a materialistic view of reality places *the intuition of duration* at the absolute center of the philosophic enterprise. His criticism of the Kantian "Transcendental Aesthetic" is therefore radical, for it denies that time and space are categories on the same level of quality and generality. Real time is quite other than the spatialized time of our physics, and this duality of time indicates and symbolizes a duality of matter and life and their *contrary movements*—matter toward the perfect spatiality of necessity; life toward the perfect temporality of freedom.

It is clear, then, that Bergson has in no wise escaped the dilemma of Descartes. On the contrary, he is impaled upon the same historic horns. Descartes makes body and soul two separate substances, but leaves us with the riddle of their interaction. Bergson's matter and life are similarly metaphysically ultimate, and the problem of their interpenetration is one which neither the verbal magic of *Matter and Memory* nor of *Creative Evolution* can solve.

III

"These lectures," begins the Preface to *Process and Reality*, "are based upon a recurrence to that phase of philosophic thought which began with Descartes and ended with Hume." And a moment later: "The writer who most fully anticipated the main positions of the philosophy of organism is John Locke. . . ." But this is nonsense! In expressing his debt to the history of philosophy, Whitehead is obviously correct in his reference to the seventeenth century. But the philosopher to whom he should have made his chief acknowledgement is not Locke: it is Leibniz.

Whitehead's effort toward synthesis is apparent from the very beginning. A cosmology, he insists, must bring the aesthetic, moral, and religious interests of man into relation with the concepts of natural science, and in the end this must mean a heroic effort to somehow unify the operations of the Understanding and the Imagination. The enterprise undertaken in *Process and Reality* is nothing less than to bridge the gap between Kant's First and his Third Critique. In taking as his subject-matter the doctrines of space, time, causality, and perception, Whitehead is paying his respects to the foundations of natural science, while in seeking to "rescue" the thought of Dewey, James, and Bergson from anti-intellectualism, he wishes to do justice to doctrines of feeling, emotion, intuition, and immediate experience without compromising either the values or the purity of science. What price in turn must be paid for this unification?

Both Bergson and Whitehead repudiate mechanism and reject the doctrine of vacuous actuality, but in focusing upon the becoming, the being, and the relatedness of actual entities, Whitehead introduces an atomism into ultimate actuality which ill accords with the Bergsonian flux, and his assertion that the category of "relatedness" is dominant over that of "quality" shows him to be committed to that same relational logic which Bergson finds to be the chief resource of a mechanistic natural science. Whitehead says that his cosmology is a fusion of Plato's *Timaeus* and the Galileo-Descartes-Newton world view, but to attempt an elucidation of immediate experience while retaining at once the universality of the extensive continuum and the individual actual entities which atomize it, is to strain to the limits a discordant tension in the service of a metaphysical unity.

But the passion for unification and connectedness is just Whitehead's guiding principle, and he exploits it methodologically in his constant attack upon "incoherence." Incoherence for Whitehead is "the arbitrary disconnection of first principles," and he cites Descartes' two kinds of substance, *res cogitans* and *res extensa*, as an illustration of such incoherence. He might equally have directed his attack against Bergsonian dualism. He approves of Spinoza's single substance as an attempt to overcome the Cartesian incoherence,

and admits that the philosophy of organism is here closely allied to
Spinoza, although rejecting the subject-predicate logic, and sub-
stituting the notion of "process" for that of "substance." But this
substitution makes the appeal to Spinoza very strained indeed, and
in general Whitehead's use of the history of philosophy betrays an
engaging effort to appropriate for his metaphysics doctrines which
are in spirit enormously different from his own. (He asserts, for
example, that the recurrence to a plurality of actual entities is
"Cartesian," although he might much more appropriately have said
"Leibnizian," and his attempt to ground the ontological principle
in Locke is both quaint and unpersuasive.)

When Whitehead undertakes the analysis of actual entities into
prehensions which have vector character (and hence imply emotion,
purpose, and valuation) he admits the requirement of a one-substance
cosmology, but is curiously ambivalent as to its derivation. At one
moment he relates "prehensions" to Descartes' "mental cognitions"
and to Locke's "ideas," but since each maintained a two-substance
ontology, he is finally driven back to sounder grounds—to the moral to
be drawn from Leibniz' *Monadology*. But the criticism which he makes
of Leibniz that his monads are merely generalized from contemporary
(i.e., seventeenth century) notions of mentality holds *a fortiori* for
his own theory of prehensions. Whitehead's model of the ontological
unit is strongly influenced by the presuppositions of classical epistemology. That every prehension is analyzable into the three factors
of subject, datum, and subjective form, shows that the epistemology
is built into the metaphysics. And if there is some advance over the
Cartesian model, this consists less in the distinction between "physical"
and "conceptual" prehensions (which is, after all, Cartesian in spirit),
than in the attempt to deny the seventeenth century rationalism
by appropriating from Bradley and Schelling the special emphasis
upon "feeling." At this point Whitehead comes closer to Bergson,
for the Bergsonian "intuition" is saturated with just this feeling
character. Even a phrase like "conceptual prehension" smacks too
much for Whitehead of the austerities of a pure intellectualism,
and he prefers rather the term "appetition" which suggests not
merely application to the higher grades of mentality, but also the
lower forms of animal and vegetable life. Whitehead is sympathetic
to a generalization of Bergson's "intuition" which shall make it also
relevant to plant activity and animal instinct. And, ironically enough,

when he criticizes the meaning which Bergson gives to intuition, it it because it is too abstract—because it is insufficiently suggestive of ideas of emotion and of purpose!

The most important characterization of the Whiteheadean philosophy is that it is Leibnizian: in its attempt to generalize the concept of "perception" for all creatures whatsoever, in its analysis of universal becoming into a system of perspectives, in its insistence that the ultimate metaphysical truth is atomism. In noting that every occasion is dual—that it has a "physical" and a "mental" pole, Whitehead is using the Spinozistic device of "attributes" to do justice (as Spinoza also attempted to do) to the truth of Cartesianism without abandoning his preference for organic unification. But in emphasizing that the world consists of a plurality of atomic creatures, that atomism does not by any means exclude complexity and universal relativity, and that each atom is a system of all things, the appeal to Leibniz is no less obvious for being only intermittently explicit. That each actual entity "includes the universe by reason of its determinate attitude towards every element in the universe" is a pure Whiteheadean translation of the *Monadology*.

More than once Whitehead refers to Descartes' "disastrous classification of substance into two species," and he criticizes Locke also for his dualism, although admitting that Locke inherited it almost unconsciously from his predecessors. And he asserts (curiously) that if Locke had started with the one fundamental notion of an actual entity, then the complex of ideas which he found disclosed in human consciousness would have turned into the complex constitution of any actual entity disclosed in *its* own consciousness. But this is just to turn epistemology into metaphysics! The chief difficulty, however, does not lie here. It lies rather in Whitehead's treatment of the matrix of actual entities; of the extensive continuum as a general scheme of relationships. For just here, in contrast, the Cartesianism of Bergson takes another form, and shows itself in decided metaphysical opposition to the scheme of extensive relations which Whitehead has taken over from Leibniz.

The theory of relativity, with its corollary that from the standpoint of physical relations contemporary events occur in causal independence of one another, convinced Whitehead that any general system of extensiveness must be considered an abstraction from actuality. Thus his criticisms of Newton's concepts of space and time hinge upon his notion that Newton has confused potentiality and actuality. And it follows for Whitehead (as it would have for Leibniz) that continuity concerns what is potential, whereas actuality is incurably atomic. Extensiveness involves a general scheme of relationships beyond mere space and time, but this scheme is merely a matrix of possibilities. Actual entities "atomize" the extensive continuum. *It* is infinitely divisible, and it is precisely *they* who divide it.

Would such a theory of the relationship between extensity and actualities ever have arisen apart from the theoretical requirements of physical science? And is not the metaphysics of Whitehead therefore only a more recondite species of that same positivistic theory which insists that there is only one experience and that metaphysics cannot dispense with science as the ground and source of its intuitions? Bergson, I think, would have unhesitatingly said so, and the reason we have already seen. When reality is conceived as an undivided whole, it must be a flux rather than a thing, an infinite process and not a plurality of separable substances. When we strive to experience Being directly, we shall find it to be of the nature of duration. Every quality is a change, every permanence is but the repetition of numerous oscillations. Form itself is only a snapshot of transition. And if our perception solidifies into discontinuous images the fluid continuity of the real, this is only a requirement of practical existence and no insight into the nature of reality itself.

We are here, I think, close to the heart of that fundamental disagreement which divides the metaphysics of Whitehead from that of Bergson despite their common repudiation of mechanism, emphasis upon feeling, and commitment to a cosmology of process. And it springs from alternative readings of that principle which governs our experience of what is authentically given as real. For Whitehead it is a principle of *atomicity*. For Bergson it is a principle of *continuity*. And each, I think, would view the insight of the other as an instance of the fallacy of misplaced concreteness. Continuity for Whitehead characterizes the system of extensive relations only insofar as they represent an artificial construction—as they register the possible dimensionality of the *res verae* of nature. And conversely, atomicity for Bergson is the form which intellect imposes upon a reality utterly other—mobile, flowing, continuous; where states melt into one another so as to make the perspectives of past, present, and future one seamless web. Bergson sees in continuity the order of nature and in atomicity the form of intelligence. Whitehead sees in atomicity the mark of the ultimately actual and in continuity the matrix of actuality—the conditions of a community of contemporary actualities sharing a common world of mathematical relations. And the differences which these evaluations entail are ultimately expressible in a commitment to two divergent theories of time.

Bergson's entire metaphysical structure rests upon the distinction between time as mere quantity and time as qualitative differentiation—between that time mechanically registered upon the customary chronometers and the organismic experience of real duration. But despite this crucial distinction, Bergson does not abandon completely the classical theory of time. The *homogeneity* of time is denied, but its *seriality* and its *continuity* are not called into question. Whitehead comes to a different conclusion entirely. Since there is a "rhythm of process," the creative advance produces natural pulsation, and each pulsation forms "a natural unit of historic fact." Needless to say, the notion of "a natural unit of historic fact" implies a *quantum theory of actuality* where pattern is only actualized through an epoch—that is, through a specific extensive temporal unit. Therefore Whiteheadean "time" must be distinguished both from the continuity of mere extension and from the infinite divisibility inherently associated with the traditional properties of Aristotelian time. Time for Whitehead is not extensiveness—*it is sheer succession of epochal durations.* Any actual entity is the enjoyment of a certain quantum of physical time. But the process of its becoming is not explicable as temporal succession. Each phase in the process presupposes *the entire quantum,* and so does each aspect of each phase. This is the famous "epochal theory of time" and it presents serious problems in explanation and conceptualization.

The first of these stems from the requirement that any part of the succession implies the whole. That the realization of physical pattern requires a specific duration is obvious from modern quantum theory, but that "the epochal duration is not realized *via* its successive divisible parts, but is given *with* its parts" seems to deny the very concept of process for which the theory is meant to account. The second is even more serious and it would, I think, have been a specific target of Bergson's criticism. The philosophy of organism is, as Whitehead himself acknowledges, a "cell-theory" of actuality. And the atom or cell from which the actual world is built up is the "actual entity" or "actual occasion." But the surprising fact emerges that Whitehead identifies the atomized quantum of extension correlative to an actual entity with Newton's absolute space and absolute time—that is to say: *an actual entity never moves:* it is where and what it is. But it is quite obvious that in a physical cosmology meanings have to be found for "motion" and "moving bodies." This Whitehead does through the concept of the "nexus" or "event" which is a complex of actual occasions so that "change" becomes the difference between occasions comprised in some determinate event. But this, Bergson would have said, is only to reiterate once again that basic idea of ancient philosophy—the primacy of the motionless. To hold that the actual entity is the basic metaphysical unit, that it is motionless, and that motion means simply a complex of such basic units, is suspiciously akin to that illusion to whose criticism Bergson gave his best moments—the illusion that intellect may import a semblance of motion to its static foundations, and that the mobile may be explained by the immobile.

Whitehead's actual occasion is more primitive than the physical atom—for the latter is less an individual in the Leibnizian sense than a "society" with activities involving rhythms with their definite periods. And, as we have seen, the actual occasion can be identified with the Leibnizian monad precisely in that each actual occasion is a locus for the universe. But the immobility of the actual entity contrasts with the Leibnizian dynamism. And this is particularly interesting in terms of Whitehead's reading of the chart of metaphysical possibilities.

After his open repudiation of the Aristotelian notion of an enduring substance sustaining persistent qualities, Whitehead states that there remain two alternatives for philosophy: a monistic universe with the illusion of change and a pluralistic universe where change means the diversities among the actual entities which comprise it. The first alternative, which Whitehead repudiates, is clearly Spinozistic. The second, which he accepts, is Leibnizian. But it is Leibniz with a difference. For Whitehead's actual entity is constituted by the totality of its relationships and *it cannot move.* As he says: ". . . the creature cannot have any external adventures, but only the internal adventure of becoming. Its birth is its end." This is surely a theory of monads, but according to Whitehead it is not

Leibniz'. Leibniz' monads *change*; his own merely *become*. If the difference is real, it is enormous. In a generalized temporal theory (as in that of Aristotle's *Physics*) time is the measure of motion, the register of physical or organic change. Certainly growth, alteration, and local motion are alternative manifestations of such change. But a becoming which is instantaneous, or, at least, permits no register of the duration which it requires, makes of time itself but a static image.

The Whiteheadean preference for atomicity and the Bergsonian for continuity leads, as we have just seen, to alternative renderings of the temporal process. But this in turn only sets the stage for that other major conflict which sets these two views of the world at variance—in this case divergent readings of the status of mentality in nature. The position of Whitehead is, of course, the more extreme. For it is his belief that a certain development of mentality is characteristic of the actual occasions which compose the structured societies which we call material bodies. There is a strict correlation between "mentality" and "structure." And the consequence is that although any structured society may have more or less "life," *there is no absolute gap between living and non-living societies*. The reason for this conclusion is two-fold. In the first place, Whitehead accepts the Spinozistic solution to the Cartesian problem. This means that each actuality is essentially bipolar, physical and mental, and the particular grade of integration of the physical and mental side into a unity of experience defines the place of the organism in the *scala naturae* or great chain of being. And in the second place Whitehead reverses the strategy of mechanism so as to use the epistemic model of the higher organisms as his root metaphor for metaphysical entities. To the accepted doctrine of physical science that a living body is to be interpreted according to what is known of other parts of the physical universe, he adds the converse principle that other items of the universe are to be interpreted in accordance with what we know of the human body. With the customary Whiteheadean procedure of appropriating an epistemological analysis for a metaphysical description we are already familiar. When Whitehead candidly says: "In describing . . . an actual occasion, we have with Locke, tacitly taken human experience as an example upon which to found the generalized description required for metaphysics," the question arises: By what right? Whether Whitehead's interpretation of Locke is correct; whether in fact the latter made any metaphysical generalization beyond the restricted sphere of human understanding, is open to the most serious doubt. And in any case *the evidence* for such a cosmological extension of human characteristics is questionable and inconclusive. Bergson, with his sharp distinction between matter and life, obviously would have found it inadmissible.

The issue here, of course, is Whitehead's panpsychism—a panpsychism which is not crude and unbelievable, but subtly presented and refined. Whitehead's insistence upon the omnipresence of "feeling" in the universe is not meant to deny gradations in the scale of actual entities. He clearly distinguishes between actual occasions in so-called "empty space," primitive organisms like electrons, enduring living objects, and enduring objects with conscious knowledge. But the nature of his analysis turns every distinction of kind into a difference of degree. Every actual entity has the capacity for "knowledge," but there are gradations in the intensity of various items of knowledge. Not all actual occasions are conscious, but all have feelings, and in fact Whitehead at this point transforms Bergson's rather specialized qualities of "intuition" into a paradigm for the physical world. The primitive form of all physical experience is emotional: "blind emotion," "sympathy," "feeling the feeling *in* another and feeling conformally *with* another." What Bergson took as the highest product of the evolutionary process Whitehead finds inherent in the most elementary forms of material existence, and this is why, however mistakenly, he makes his appeal to Locke. For immediate experience is, in Whitehead's view, sufficient to reveal to us that just the feelingful, emotive, appetitive elements in human consciousness are those which most closely resemble the basic elements of *all* physical experience. The philosophy of organism attributes feeling throughout the actual world and in place of a hierarchy of thought categories, it finds a hierarchy of categories of feeling.

It is one of the ironies of modern philosophy that Bergson, whose account of ultimate reality requires a principle of continuity, should in his description of the world find the disjunction between spirit and matter absolute, whereas Whitehead, whose account of ultimate realities invokes Leibnizian atomism, finds in his description of nature just that continuity in the scale of feelings which Bergson denies.

IV

The new mathematical physics which began with Galileo and reached its culmination in Newton required both a new epistemology and a new metaphysics. To its elaboration the seventeenth century devoted itself. The first, and in many ways the most decisive, formulation came from Descartes. For our purposes what is important about it is not its reliance upon mathematical method, but its quite original complex of metaphysical notions. Some of the most important may be simply stated as follows: Self-evident, intuitive notions are expressed as our clear and distinct ideas. When we intuit an idea clearly we have a primary metaphysical factor, and thought and extension are two such basic metaphysical factors. Extension means figure, substance, endurance, but secondary qualities are too confused to be objects of knowledge. Matter is, thus, three-dimensional extension, and extension is not resolvable into ultimate atomic units but is homogeneous throughout. We must distinguish duration (the real quality of that which endures) and time (which is the way we think of that duration). The self is the mind's primary datum, and mind consists in perception, consciousness, and thought. Mind and body, finally, are independent and irreducible entities.

Cartesian dualism called out its appropriate response: the alternatives of Spinozistic monism and Leibnizian pluralism. The latter, in particular, is also an attempt to give metaphysical foundation to the new mathematical physics of the age, and it culminates in Leibniz' theory of monads. The basic "substantial" entity is the monad. But it is not extension: it is life and energy. An infinite number of indivisible monads constitute reality. They are the real atoms of nature, the elements of things, and they are not susceptible to external change, but only to creation and annihilation. Their activities are constituted by an internal principle of appetition, and their perceptions vary in clarity and massiveness. Nature is a continuum of monads and each monad mirrors the universe according to its own capacity and according to the adequacy of its perceptions. This means that the gradations of monads are infinite: there is an "inorganic" monad which is merely a center of force, and there are monads expressive of the full development of the soul. God is the primal unity from which all simple substances are derived, and in the smallest particle of matter there is a world of creatures, living beings, entelechies, perceptions.

The most recent scientific revolution which marks the period from Darwin to Planck has also required its metaphysical elaboration. And it is in consequence of this necessity that the systems of Bergson and Whitehead have been developed. But if my reading of the history of philosophy is correct, the modern crisis in thought has evoked consequences which almost exactly parallel the metaphysical alternatives of the seventeenth century. The fundamental thesis of this paper is that despite the obvious differences between them, there is an important continuity in French thought between Descartes and Bergson, and that in the dualism upon which his metaphysics is founded, Bergson is essentially Cartesian. And on the other hand, just as the *Principia Mathematica* falls in the great tradition of the *mathesis universalis* first envisaged by Leibniz, so the metaphysics adumbrated in *Process and Reality* is a perfect modern adaptation of the metaphysical alternative so brilliantly set forth in the *Monadology*. The contemporary metaphysical option "Bergson or Whitehead?" has, therefore, certain important analogies with the metaphysical option which confronted the declining years of the seventeenth century: "Descartes or Leibniz?"

I would not wish by this appeal to a doctrine of eternal recurrence in the history of philosophy to obscure those contrasts between Bergson and Whitehead which hinge upon purely contemporary issues. And surely, in those instances when metaphysical talent depends upon scientific knowledge, it is Whitehead who has the surer touch. Bergson's little known *Durée et Simultanéité,* an attempt to bend the theory of relativity to his own uses, is hardly an unqualified success, whereas the early interpretive efforts of Whitehead in this direction are still models of brilliant succinctness in the philosophy of physical science. But in general the contrast between Bergson and Whitehead is independent of appeals to the facts of physics or biology.

For both Bergson and Whitehead the universe is endlessly self-creative, but for the former this creativity means the continuous development of the life process; for the latter the atomic division of the extensive continuum by actual entities. As Leibniz in the *Monadology* found God to be the source of essences, and in the *Theodicy* the source of existences, so Whitehead has distinguished a primordial and consequent nature of God which almost exactly corresponds to this two-fold division. Whitehead's primordial nature of God (and the realm of eternal objects which is its expression) is his attempt to do justice to the notion of "possibility," but the rationalism and the Platonism expressed in this effort would have been completely uncongenial to the Bergsonian temperament. For Bergson there is always something incurably *artificial* about the intellect and its operations; therefore he will always find the universal *post rem* rather than *ante rem*. Thus where Whitehead according to his mathematical bent is a Platonic realist, Bergson, with the classificatory bias of the biologist, is a conceptualist. For Whitehead the explication of reality requires both actual entities and eternal objects: for Bergson it is enough that there is matter and life.

In Bergson and Whitehead alike there is particular emphasis upon sympathy and emotion, but in Bergson they are qualities struggling for achievement against the hindrances which matter imposes, whereas in Whitehead matter itself expresses in rudimentary form these self-same qualities. For Bergson (as for Descartes) there are selves and there are material objects. For Whitehead (as for Leibniz) material objects are themselves congeries of selves. What is metaphysically at stake? In one sense the appeal must surely be to "the facts." But in another the problem is simply one of the degree of generality which metaphysical theory requires. Bergson's dualism means that the two elements are recalcitrantly there, and their ultimate unification is impossible. Whitehead's metaphysics refuses to countenance this "incoherence." Whether Whitehead's "coherence" is bought at the price of a falsification of the facts, or at least by the assertion of a hypothesis which is quite unbelievable, remains an open question.

If one inquires how such divergencies arise in metaphysics, it is tempting to begin a genetic analysis—to trace back the theory to those sources of inspiration from which it springs. And here, even if one finds continuities between present-day positions and the philosophic tradition (as I have found continuities between Bergson and Whitehead and Descartes and Leibniz), even more to the point is the matter of those areas of experience upon which the metaphysical constructions depend. And here one cannot suppress the suspicion that the contrast between Bergson and Whitehead in some sense represents a bifurcation within the scientific revolution whose problems these alternative metaphysics attempt to solve. In referring to the contemporary scientific revolution, I have spoken of the period "from Darwin to Planck." But each of these key figures represents the dominance of a different natural science. The mould of Whitehead's mentality is that of mathematics and mathematical physics, whereas Bergson's first interest was biology, and he was always close to those psychological preoccupations which exercised his countrymen Amiel, Stendhal, and Proust. It is true that one might say of Whitehead's metaphysics that it ends as the transformation of physics into psychology, but psychology is the vantage point with which Bergson begins, and which he never abandons.

If it is indeed the case that the basic difference between Bergson and Whitehead lies in their respective application of two distinct theories of time, then it is perhaps not inappropriate to ask: Within what universe of discourse do theories of time arise? There are always at least two possibilities. And it is interesting, I think, to reflect that the genesis of the Western tradition represents a decided choice between them. In Aristotle the major treatment of time arises in the context of the *Physics* rather than the *De Anima*, and is thus related to the problem of physical movement in general rather than to the specific motions of the soul. Western thought has largely perpetuated this usage, and "the facts" upon which the philosophic analysis of time has traditionally depended have been those relating to the behavior of physical bodies. Bergson has, therefore, in fact instituted or at least made dominant a contrary model in which the facts (and therefore the conditions of certainty) have to do with a description of subjective states—the modes of awareness of the experiencing self. These two models of experience, physical and psychological, become criteria for the assignment of two sources of confirmation and thus the bases of two different philosophical theories. This is, perhaps, the ultimate explanation of the contrast between the theories of time of Bergson and Whitehead.

In *Process and Reality* Whitehead has stated very interestingly what he calls "the metaphysical rule of evidence"—"that we must bow to those presumptions, which in despite of criticism, we still employ for the regulation of our lives." But there is little in this criterion which permits us to choose between Leibniz and Descartes, dualism and pluralism, the continuity of duration and the atomism of actual entities. Such a pragmatic test will hardly work for metaphysical constructions, particularly when in general tone they are as closely allied as those of Bergson and Whitehead. One's ultimate choice will rather depend on factors which are intangible, highly individual, and probably in the long run chiefly aesthetic. To those to whom the Manichean dogma will always express a profound truth, Bergson speaks in clear and unmistakable terms. To those to whom dualism means "incoherence" and for whom division is not merely the sin of man but of the universe as well, the Whiteheadean unification will exemplify the deeper insight.

ALBERT WILLIAM LEVI

WASHINGTON UNIVERSITY

HOW DOES GOD ACT?: AN ESSAY IN
WHITEHEAD'S METAPHYSICS

THAT THE Christian God acts is one of the main themes of
contemporary theology. The Biblical conception of God as
Creator and Redeemer involves his purposive working in history. He
liberates a people and establishes a covenant with them. He with-
draws his favor from them when they are disloyal, he announces his
judgment and purpose through the prophets. He gives his son to live
and die for the world. He creates a new heaven and a new earth. It is
often remarked that such assertions about God mark the primary difference between Greek conceptions of time as cyclical, Asiatic conceptions
of the appearances of God in history as theophanies manifesting an
ultimate reality which lies behind the illusions of time and space, and
the Christian view of a history of redemption with a Beginning, Center, and End.

There are innumerable assertions in the Biblical record of specific
acts of God. The regularities of the times and the seasons as well as
miraculous suspensions of the expected occurrences in nature come
from God's sovereign will. He "sends his rain on the just and the
unjust," and he raises his Son from the dead. He clothes the lilies of
the field, and he ordains the powers which govern men, using them
as his instruments. As Holy Spirit God inspires and blesses, and he
holds before every moment as well as before the whole drama the
promise of ultimate judgment. In this intensely personal and realistic
way the Bible speaks of the acts of God. It has been the task of Christian thinkers to relate this Biblical outlook to rational interpretations
of the structure of nature and the occurrences of history. And this
has meant that the question of *how* the divine action is to be conceived, both in its "regular" and in its extraordinary manifestations,
has perennially exercised Christian thought and given it special
problems.

It may be granted that the acts of creation and of eschatological
judgment and deliverance are in a special category so far as rational
interpretation is concerned. They are generally held to be "events"

which cannot be interpreted as observable natural events. They deal with beginnings and endings and, as Immanual Kant claimed, we here move beyond the sphere of a possible basis of knowledge in experience. But most of the biblical assertions about God's action have to do with present experienced happenings in history, the destinies of men and nations, the powers, wonders, diseases, threats, and symbolic signif- icance of nature. Therefore the problem of giving a theological inter- pretation to the meaning of the divine action in relation to the powers and structures, causes and effects, which we can observe and which the sciences study is inescapable. Newton in the first edition of the *Principia* said nothing about God. He added the famous scholium to the second edition affirming God as *pantocrator*. But as to specific functions Newton could find nothing for God to do once the world was set in motion other than to keep the stars from collapsing in outer space, and occasionally to reorder the world when its motions led to too great a disorder. The problem of first and final causes, of the meaning of force, of the regularities of nature in relation to divine miraculous action, of creativity and evolution, of chance and purpose have thus become the standard problems of relating Christian theology to nature as scientifically understood. In this paper I shall express my con- viction that these are genuine problems for religious belief, and that Christian theology cannot assert that God acts without going on to a general interpretation of action in the world and of the meaning of God's activity within or upon the world.

It is a further presupposition of the approach in this paper that the problem of action has three dimensions, theological, scientific, and metaphysical, and that these are so related that the metaphysical analysis must take into account the scientific analysis, and the theolog- ical analysis must take into its range of vision both the scientific and the metaphysical analyses. It is less obvious that the metaphysical depends upon the theological and that the scientific depends also upon the metaphysical, although in the end I believe they are so related.

The problem of God's action involves the meaning of action, of cause and effect, of power and structure, of law and chance. Whether we start with scientific concepts or theological assertions we are led to a common ground where the meanings of these general concepts must be given some clarification. The problems are difficult. I shall confine my paper to an exposition which I hope has some measure of ac- curacy to Alfred North Whitehead's doctrine of action and causality, and then make some comments upon his doctrine and its implications for theology. Concerning its implications in relation to particular scientific concepts I am not able to speak above the level of a lay acquaintance with science, so many points are raised which will have to be pursued in discussion with scientific theorists.

I. *Whitehead as Metaphysician; his Concept of Speculative Philosophy.*

One of Whitehead's most interesting definitions of metaphysics occurs in *Process and Reality* in the opening chapter:

"Metaphysics is nothing but the description of the generalities which apply to all the details of practice."[1]

There are three points to note about this definition:

First, metaphysics is a description of what is experienced, or what is encountered in experience, such as structures, qualities, judgments, errors, minds, and bodies. Whitehead says the final tests of speculative concepts are in their applicability and adequacy to experience and their coherence with one another. That is, *practice* here means concrete observable, experienceable activity in the world.

Second, metaphysics seeks generality. Whitehead believes the chief task of philosophy is to elaborate categoreal schemes within which the world may be coherently spoken about. For Whitehead a category is a structure found in all experience. Hence the method of philosophy is to take some significant area of experience, for Whitehead this is primarily to take the human experience of knowing as a bodily-mental event, and then to elaborate a systematic scheme of concepts which will be adequate to make speech about this reality intelligible. Of course, if we begin with this human experience of bodily-mental knowing we must go on to examine everything within the range of human experience including all the specific data and theories disclosed in science and in the history of human institutions. The goal of the search is for a rational understanding, so far as reason can go, of the *being* of things, and of the ways things are related to one another. Thus Whitehead's fundamental doctrine that real things are actual entities, moments of experience which represent the outcomes of processes which aim at satisfaction, is his answer to the classical question about being. He seeks to give an account of all the conceptions which are

[1] Alfred North Whitehead, *Process and Reality* (New York: The Macmillan Co., 1936), p. 19. (Hereafter, *PR*)

necessary to understanding a world of actual entities related to one another and coming to be and passing away. It is this generality of intent in philosophy, its attempt to grasp the multiplicity of the world's phenomena, its dimensions of finitude and infinity, its goods and evils, its truth and illusion, its appearance and reality which distinguishes philosophy from science. And Whitehead explicitly says that philosophy is not a science.[2] But the concepts which philosophy seeks must be adequate to interpret the data and the meanings supplied by science. Of course we are here stating a goal of speculative philosophy which lies beyond any human attainment. Philosophy is an exercise in the construction and the criticism of metaphysical schemes.

Third, Whitehead's statement about metaphysics leads directly to the topic of this discussion, for the reference to the details of practice means that Whitehead accepts activity, function, and interaction as the context of all theory. In this statement he is very close to John Dewey's outlook. Philosophy itself is activity set in the context of a world of interactive processes. This pragmatic aspect of Whitehead's standpoint is important throughout his understanding of action.

II. Some Basic Concepts in Whitehead's Metaphysics

It is a fundamental doctrine of Whitehead's that if God is intelligible at all to us, he must exemplify the metaphysical categories and not be invoked just to "prevent their collapse."[3] Hence in seeking the categories we must arrive at generic concepts which in some way characterize all action including the divine activity. Therefore we must explore some of Whitehead's general concepts first and then see how they are used to interpret the action of God.

(a) Whitehead calls his standpoint the philosophy of organism. What he proposes is a social doctrine of being.[4] He envisions the world as an ongoing complex of real things which act upon one another within the patterns set by a primordial order which includes all the possibilities which may characterize the outcomes of particular activities in the world:

[2]"Mathematics and the Good" in Paul A. Schilpp (ed.), The Philosophy of Alfred North Whitehead (Evanston: Northwestern University Press, 1941), p. 681.
[3]PR, p. 521.
[4]Charles Hartshorne's illuminating characterization.

The notion of 'organism' is combined with that of 'process' in a two-fold manner. The community of actual things is an organism; but it is not a static organism. It is an incompletion in process of production. Thus the expansion of the universe in respect to actual things is the first meaning of 'process'; and the universe in any stage of its expansion is the first meaning of 'organism' ... each actual entity is itself only describable as an organic process. It repeats in microcosm what the universe is in macrocosm. It is a process proceeding from phase to phase, each phase being the real basis from which its successor proceeds toward the completion of the thing in question.[5]

In this quotation Whitehead rejects one approach to the interpretation of causation and interaction which has so often been stated in traditional philosophy. Given individual substances which have no relations to one another and which are not directly experienced by anything how do they act upon one another and how do they become known? The specific doctrine which Whitehead believes the seventeenth century finally worked out in following the implications of this question is that of "simple location." This means that each actual entity can be located in a specific time and place which has no necessary relation to any other time and place, or to any other entities which are in the past or present or future of the given thing. Whitehead believes this was the outcome of the application of the conceptual scheme of seventeenth century physics to the description of the material world, and he believes that Hume exposed the logical consequences of this view. Induction has no rational ground, for the present data have no inherent reference to any other state of affairs. It is impossible to account for living organisms, and valid inference from sense impressions to their origins or causes is impossible.

Whitehead declares that nothing in our experience gives any basis whatever for this doctrine of simple location.[6] He proposes to return to immediate experience and suggests the possibility of beginning with another set of concepts for describing the being of actual things. Further, Whitehead believes the logical and mathematical analysis of spatio-temporal structure requires the doctrine that every region involves a reference to, or "mirrors" every other region.

Through the appeal to immediate experience coupled with a logical analysis of spatio-temporal structure Whitehead gives a char-

5PR, p. 327.

6A. N. Whitehead, *Science and the Modern World* (New York: The Macmillan Co., 1931), p. 85. (Hereafter *SAMW*)

acterization of the metaphysical task which is quite close to Aristotle's.
He accepts as a point of departure a world of real things which function in relation to one another and to other realities in processes of
becoming. There are causes and effects, and these causes are complex.
Final causes are included among the interpretative principles of any
action. The problem of philosophy is to describe the interweaving of
the many strands of activity and structure in the one world. Where
Whitehead differs from Aristotle is in the conviction that the Aristotelian subject-object logic defeats itself by treating the qualifications
of substance as accidents which happen to characterize an underlying
reality which "possesses" and exhibits these qualities. Whitehead sees
no need for asserting an underlying reality beneath or behind the
process of the becoming of and passing away of "qualitied" things.
There is indeed one actual entity which does not pass away. God's
metaphysical status here differs in important respects from that of all
other things. His primordial nature, which is the structure of possibility, is eternal, and his concrete nature in interaction with the
world is everlasting.

(b) We can always begin with assumptions and it does not take
us far to say that we assume interactive processes in a world where
there are patterns of organic relatedness. The problem is to give an
account of this relatedness. It is here that Whitehead's distinctive
doctrines appear. They are illuminating, and they create their own
special problems.

Whitehead's term for the relation in which one thing is acted
upon by another thing is "prehension" and his distinctive doctrine is
that prehensions are "feelings." Actual entities are subjects. They are
centers of feeling which weld together the many strands of relatedness
to other things in one determinate outcome which is a specific satisfaction.

A feeling is the appropriation of some elements in the universe to be
components in the real internal constitution of its subject. The elements are
the initial data; they are what the feeling feels. But they are felt under an
abstraction. The process of the feeling involves negative prehensions which
effect elimination. Thus the initial data are felt under a 'perspective' which
is the objective datum of the feeling.[7]

Two kinds of things are "felt." One is the structure of possibility

7PR, p. 353.

which includes the logical orders and the qualities which can characterize particular things. These qualities Whitehead calls eternal objects. They are potentials for feeling until they are actually felt in some concrete process. The eternal objects are felt "conceptually." The other things that are felt are actual entities in the world and these are felt "physically." Thus Whitehead generalizes the body-mind duality in knowing. Further, he holds that every real subject-electron, cell, or human person grasps the structure of possibilities beyond itself and in the way in which it relates itself to the possibilities every actual entity makes a "decision," that is it has its world in its own way, contributing an element of its own novel self determination to the final outcome. There is always a way in which *that* subject unifies and possesses *that* set of prehensions. This involves final causation for it is possible for novel decisions to occur only as real things lay hold on a possibility of attainment which lies beyond the present activity.

It must be clear also that Whitehead regards the category of value as constitutive of every actual thing. Everything aims at being something, at realizing some unification of itself with other things and with its world. He writes "To be an actual entity is to have a self-interest. This self-interest is a feeling of self-valuation; it is an emotional tone."[8]

Whitehead has obviously derived his categories from human experience and has generalized them for all levels of nature. He appears to attribute feeling, valuation, subjectivity, decision, and even purpose to every actual thing, including the non-living orders. This may be criticized as naive imagination or speculative irrelevance. I suggest it is neither. Whitehead is quite explicit that he is not asserting consciousness below the human, or, perhaps in rudimentary form, the animal level. He is not a pan-psychist if that means the attributing of conscious decision and awareness to plants and atoms. He says explicitly the physical world consists of "blind" feeling.

This word 'feeling' is a mere technical term; but it has been chosen to suggest that functioning through which the concrescent actuality appropriates the datum so as to make it its own.[9]

It is in this sense that we can understand Whitehead's startling language about emotion when he says that the key notion with which

[8]*Religion in the Making* (New York: The Macmillan Co., 1927), p. 100.
[9]*PR*, p. 249.

cosmology should start is that "the energetic activity considered in physics is the emotional intensity entertained in life."[10]

What is fundamental here is the social analogy: the real things are the electronic and protonic occasions which form the societies, and their interactions are characterized by laws which "come into being by reason of the analogous characters of the members of the society."[11] ... "Thus our cosmic epoch is to be conceived primarily as a society of electromagnetic occasions, including electronic and protonic occasions ..." "The atom is only explicable as a society with activities involving rhythms with their definite period." And he also remarks that since the structural flow of energy has to do with the transmission of simple physical feelings, some sort of quantum theory in physics relevant to the existing type of cosmic order "is to be expected."[11]

One element of this description of actual entities deserves emphasis at this point. There is a novel element in the 'decision' of each individual occasion, which is its own contribution to the uniqueness of its perspective upon the universe. The weakest and most trivial occasion of an electron contributes a unique moment of being to the totality of the universe. Therefore the transcendence of God is not something absolutely peculiar to him. "Every actual entity, in virtue of its novelty, transcends its universe, God included."[12]

(c) We come now to the interpretation of cause.

It follows from the preceding analysis that every actual occasion is in one sense *causi sui*. We have to find the reason for things within the constitution of actual events, and their decisions. Every event prehends the universe in its own way, with some increment of novelty. Its outcome involves the way in which that actual occasion lays hold upon the structure of possibility which stands before it as the foundation of its subjective aim. Whitehead uses the term "final cause" to characterize this aspect of actuality. The feelings involved in any concrete process are to be understood as elements in the aim which is given concreteness by the "feeler" itself. Every process aims at its own satisfaction, that is, at being a certain kind of center of meaning, a

[10]*Modes of Thought* (New York: The Macmillan Co., 1938), p. 232. (Hereafter, *MT*)

[11]*PR*, pp. 121, 139, 141, 389.

[12]*PR*, p. 143.

unity of the universe at its place and from its perspective. "This final cause is an inherent element in the feeling, constituting the unity of that feeling."[12]

There is also efficient causality between one actual entity and another, for to prehend something is to have that something enter into the prehender as cause. The basic discussion here occurs in *Process and Reality*, pp. 361-365. I shall risk this brief summary:

"A simple physical feeling is an act of causation."[13] Actual entities are prehended, that is, felt, by other actual entities. What is experienced is not only the abstract form or quality which characterizes the other entity but in some measure we directly experience, Whitehead holds, the way the other entity entertains its own data. In experiencing the greenness of the forest we are experiencing the way in which trees and leaves entertain the eternal object, greenness. And the greenness of the forest enters as cause into the determination of the person who experiences it at this time and place. It is a constituent in the satisfaction which constitutes this phase of his being. Whitehead therefore terms the mode of perception in which the human body is organically conditioned by its prehension of another actual entity 'causal efficacy'. "Thus the cause is objectively in the constitution of the effect."[14] It should be emphasized that this organic experience of the greenness of the forest is a direct qualification of our organism and its structures by the actual occasions which they prehend. This organic experience is transmuted in the higher organisms into particular and discriminated sense data, which are then projected back upon their source. This later perception is the mode of "presentational immediacy." It is the way the world appears to us after the highly complex tranformation which organic experience undergoes in the body-mind organism. It is necessary to stress this because Whitehead is not declaring that what we consciously discriminate as the "greenness of the trees" is precisely what the trees entertain as greenness. Distortions, error, transformation, are all elements in the final outcome of our experiencing other things.

The primary mode of our experience of causal efficacy is our intuition of our own selves a fraction of a second before the present moment. The self at Time I has now become a datum for the self at

13*PR*, p. 361.
14*PR*, p. 363.

Time II, is prehended by the self at Time II, and enters as cause into the constitution of the self at Time II.

III. *God's Action Upon the World*

It will be necessary to give some general characterizations of Whitehead's doctrine of God's action before turning to its special aspects.

First, it is required in Whitehead's metaphysics that the notion of God as sole cause of all happenings is rejected. God exercises causality, and in a supreme way (also, I think it must be shown in some special ways) but he acts always in relation to beings who have their own measure of causal self determination in their interaction with other finite things and with God.

Second, the way in which God can act upon other things is categorically determined by the metaphysical order constituted by his primordial nature, and which he does not violate. It would be meaningless to speak of his violating his own essence. This means that God acts upon other things by objectifying his being for them so that he can be prehended by them. God acts by being felt by his creatures, and in this process he enters into the constitution of their successive moments of experience.

Third, the creatures enter into the constitution of God's experience as he prehends *them*. They become causes in his successive phases of experience. He receives from the world as well as gives to the world.

Fourth, causality is complex. This is of fundamental importance in any theological doctrine related to Whitehead's ontological outlook. Causality has complex aspects at the level of bare physical existence, for there are elements of final causation, through prehension of structure, and elements of self-causation, and of efficient causation. In the high grade organisms through their powers of abstraction, consciousness, with its transmutation of the modes in which experience is possible, introduces the complexity of emotion. Consider for example the feelings of mystery, of perplexity in the face of the variety of good and evils, the contemplation of ideals, the feelings of remorse. All these have causal aspects, and enter into the constitution of the occasions of personal experience. When we speak then of causality in God we are stretching our understanding of these structures of our experience far beyond any direct comprehension. But what Whitehead does insist is that if we are to speak intelligibly of God's action, and of God as cause, there must be some real analogy of structure between his being and that of the creatures.

Fifth, it must be shown that on Whitehead's terms there are identifiable ways in which the divine action differs from that of the creatures, differences rooted in the fact that God's metaphysical status is not identical with that of the creatures.

We now turn directly to Whitehead's doctrine of God. He distinguishes between the primordial and the consequent natures of God. I have always thought that his language here was improveable. It suggests two separate beings, or at least "natures" somehow joined together. But it is clear that the intent of Whitehead's view is quite different. The being of God is dipolar.[15] The primordial aspect of his being is his envisagement of the realm of possibility in its abstraction from all particular matters of fact. It is the order which characterizes the world so that it can be one determinate world, and at the same time be a process in which possibilities are realized and expulsion of incompatibles takes place. The primordial nature is actual, that is, there is a definite structure of possibility which characterizes every existing reality; but it is deficiently actual in itself for it has no concrete determination of matters of fact within it. It is the realm of possibility. It is also an order of value, for it includes the structure of relevance, the qualities, and the potential meanings which characterize the world, and it is an ordered realm in which gradations of value are structured.

How does God in his primordial nature act? The most obvious point is that he acts by presenting to the creatures the unity, the richness, and the limits of possibility as ordered by his vision. That is to say God acts in his primordial gift of structure to the world by "not acting." He acts by being. He is the order upon which everything existing must draw if it is to be at all. The primordial nature simply is what it is, and nothing can be anything in particular without prehending that order. Whitehead speaks of the primordial "appetition" which is the basis of all order.

The universe is thus understood as including a source of ideals. The effective aspect of this source is Deity as immanent in the present experience. The

15Again to use one of Charles Hartshorne's accurate phrases.

sense of historic importance is the intuition of the universe as everlasting process, unfading in its deistic unity of ideals.[16]

The view is then that God presents the individual occasions in the world with the possibility of participating in the society of being in certain definite ways, which involve elements of decision and novelty, but also strict conditions of limitation. Nothing is, for Whitehead, except by participation. Thus Whitehead, as in so many ways, repeats a Platonic theme, but on a realistic basis, rather than an idealistic one.

I will make two observations about this doctrine as it bears on the question of how God acts.

First, there is the question of the validity of stretching the category of feeling to cover non-conscious life. Does Whitehead throw any light on the question of how every physical event exhibits the structure expressed in the formula $E = mc^2$?

It is difficult in one sense to say that "feeling" which must be understood from the standpoint of our experience, belongs to non-conscious life. But the critical point is not whether "feeling" as we know it is attributed to electrons; but the point is that the description of an electron requires a doctrine of "physical memory" and of causal relationship in which there is a structural analogy to our remembrance of things past, and our knowledge of the inheritance of elements of our present actuality from that past. And it also requires some apprehension of a structure which is a form of possibility, applicable to an infinite number of occasions, but which characterizes this actual occasion in its immediacy. Further, Whitehead refuses to leave the problem of the evolution of organisms within the physical world simply with the name "emergence" to cover the mystery. Some kind of appetition toward further possibilities, some way in which even the physical world lays hold upon an order which lies beyond the present must belong to that world, else evolution is completely unintelligible. God, we may say, is that function of primordial order with its potentialities which makes evolution possible.

We note that the theme of the divine persuasion enters here. The primordial nature stands before the decision of each actual occasion; but in itself it does not determine the final outcome in its concreteness.

16*MT*, p. 132.

Thus the order of nature, by itself does not make anything happen. Physical law is not a cause, except as it becomes an order prehended by an actual entity. In the view of evolution here proposed then, one might observe physical structures which point toward the emergence of living organisms; but prediction at any given time that the new structure would emerge would be impossible, at least it would have only a probability status.

It can be emphasized that the primordial nature of God is the being of God on the side of absolute structure. No reason can be given for its existence. It is akin to Aristotle's Unmoved Mover. It moves the world by luring the multiplicity of efforts in the world toward as yet unrealized possibilities.

A second observation on the primordial nature of God concerns the problem of "miracle." I would interpret the position to be that every happening in the world has an element of novelty, of freedom. The notion of absolute laws governing existence is discarded in so far as it is taken to mean the exhaustability of meaning of any event through knowledge of law alone. Further, new kinds of beings do appear in history. There are new defining characteristics of new societies.

At the same time there is the primordial order with its ultimate logical structure ordering all potentialities and excluding what is really incompatible. All actions in the world and in God observe this order for without it the world would be no world.

This means that every act of God occurs within the ultimate structure of possibility which makes the world a unity. But any act might "violate", in the sense of transcend, some particular structure of a society of beings by introducing a new level of possibility. The one restriction is that it could not violate the essential unity of being. It could not in other words be a complete discontinuity, nor could it destroy the final possibility of rational understanding, though indeed that understanding might be far beyond the power of any creature.

Such a position does not directly bear upon the "religious" meaning of miracle as a sign pointing to the power and salvation of God. It is a metaphysical understanding which sets certain bounds to what miracle might be in relation to an intelligible world view. Nothing can happen which violates the community of being itself. But, as Schleiermacher saw, to take only extraordinary events as miraculous in a 'religious' sense is surely to limit greatly the religious understanding of the world. Every event which points to God, order as well as creativity, predictability as well as novelty may make manifest God's being. From this standpoint the experiences of order, and of possible rational understanding are also potential miracles pointing to God in his primordial nature and function.

IV. *The Principle of Concretion*

In his first essay on the nature of God in *Science and the Modern World,* Whitehead introduces the concept of God as the principle of concretion. He has discussed the structures of possibility which characterize every existing thing. Then he points to the fact, which is strictly in accord with Aristotle's view, that no amount of analysis of the structures of subjects can exhaust the full meaning of the subject. The "thisness" of this table can never be reached by multiplication of abstract structures of determination. Hence Whitehead argues that for a real world a metaphysical "principle of concretion" is required. There must be a metaphysical function by which a definite outcome is secured from the ambiguous and indeterminate possibilities which hover over every concrete matter of fact. And this function, he asserts, belongs to God.

In what sense, we may ask, is God's being as the principle of concretion a definite action upon the world? Can a principle act, in Whitehead's terms? And if it can, does it follow that God as this principle determines the outcome of every particular event? Whitehead has sometimes been interpreted in this way, and I must agree that some of his language is either unclear, or it leads to this conclusion. Certainly if the principle of concretion itself determines the outcome in every event, there is no freedom whatever except in God. But Whitehead's philosophy is so strongly assertive of radical freedom for the creatures that surely this cannot be his intent; however, his language may lend itself to this view.

In *Process and Reality* he identifies the principle of concretion with God's function as providing for every occasion that "initial aim" from which it takes its rise. That is, there must be an order of participation in an actual world with a definite presentation of this order before there can be a new occasion. Whitehead says, "Apart from the intervention of God, there could be nothing new in the world, and no order in the world."[17] And it is in relation to this doctrine that Whitehead makes his remark concerning the importance of the *secularization* of the concept of God's functions in the world.[18]

My conclusion is that we can keep the principle of concretion only in this sense of the offering by God of an *initial* aim to each creature, thus making its concretion in a new actual occasion possible.

V. *The Consequent Nature of God*

The consequent nature of God refers to God's concreteness as he is related to the world and as the world's events are objectified in him. God receives from the world the effects of the world's action but he receives them in his own way as subject, and in the decision of his freedom. There is a divine passivity as well as divine activity. The content of the divine experience changes with the happenings in the world. It is active, and passive, temporal as well as eternal, patient, judging and redeeming. The life of God is an infinite social order of concrete "havings" of the world in the divine way and in the pattern of the divine primordial nature which defines the order of value for all things.

We must pass over many questions which can be raised here in order to move to our central concern, how does God in his concrete, consequent nature act upon the world? Here he is not only structure, but conscious active and passive being.

On this important point Whitehead is not very explicit. There are a few tantalizing suggestions. He speaks of the "love of God flooding back into the world."[19] But does this mean that we are to add God as efficient cause to the other efficient causes in the world?

In some sense the answer must be yes, for God in his concreteness is in the total datum to which we respond and out of which our moments of experience are constituted. But how can this be construed?

The principle by which an answer can be sought is clearly established in Whitehead's philosophy. The consequent nature acts by being prehended, *felt* by the creatures. This means that not only the primordial structure but the concrete being of God in his relation to

[17]*PR*, p. 377.
[18]*PR*, p. 315.
[19]*PR*, p. 532 (cf. *RM*, p. 156).

the world is communicated to the creatures. God is, in a literal sense for Whitehead, "the love which moves the sun and the other stars," and "communicative immanence" is one mode of divine action (This last phrase is Robert L. Calhoun's in *God and the Common Life*).

We are asking how feeling is communicated and therefore we may legitimately turn to the "natural history of feeling" in human experience. In what ways does the community of feeling with another become an efficient cause of our own action?

If we look for suggestions on this point from depth psychology we are moving into an area which Whitehead does not explicitly deal with but for the interpretation of which I suggest he has made some fundamentally important contributions. In therapeutic psychology we have a great deal of knowledge about the significance of the exchange of feelings, and about its results, whether or not we have much insight into how it comes about. The mechanisms are only partially understood, but the results are observable. It may be that we have here some useful analogies for thinking of the divine action.

The central point is that the discovery of another person who will receive my feelings into his own feelings and neither reject them nor me, is a basic aspect of psychological therapy. The analysis of "acceptance" and of the resulting "clarification" confirms this. There is a transformative power in the knowledge, the *felt* knowledge, not bare conceptualization, that our feelings have entered into the "consequent" nature of another person. Of course we are talking about causal effectiveness, not about the possible evil as well as good in its exercise.

In interpreting this fact of experience we may distinguish three aspects:

(a) This process involves an objectification of the self, so that a position is established from which self-judgment can be made. This objectification seems to make it possible for the judgment to be known partly without the anxiety which normally attends it. The communication of feeling to the other in the accepting situation constitutes a new standpoint in which the self may reorder and reinterpret its experience.

(b) A second aspect involves this element of judgment in another way. To recognize the feelings of another which result from the communication of our own is to be brought up against a judgment which is independent of ourselves and is reflected back then into our being.

Accounts of the therapeutic situation do not always stress this, but it surely is one aspect of what happens. We are made aware of the significance of our acts by the way in which they are received in the feelings of others. We harden ourselves against this, or run from it but this only confirms the causal efficaciousness of the recognition that our feelings have a meaning in the feelings of others.

(c) Finally, there is a transmutation of feeling which qualifies both the aspects already mentioned. To have one's feelings taken in by another and reflected back is to experience a transformation of the meaning of the feeling. This is the central miracle of "feeling" that awareness of the other can result in strengthening or weakening, purgation or enhancement of my feeling. The way the other received my feeling is then a constitutive part of its outcome. When the feelings are received in "love" there is a transmutation which takes on the quality of the love which is given. This process has its conscious aspects; but it operates far below the conscious level. The child feels the mother's feelings long before the child is in any sense a discriminating person.

The use of the category of feeling to describe the relatedness of the world to God does not of course offer a full explanation; but it does sharpen the point that the experience we have of causality at the human level involves a transfer and transformation of energy in personal relationships. In Whitehead's view we do have some basis here for speaking about the way in which God acts. He says, "The power of God is the worship He inspires."[20] The feelings which enter into the constitution of our being are transformed through awareness of their reception in the consequent nature of God. We must speak of persuasion here also, for we can still reject, thwart, revise our reception of the new situation created by communion with God. But I think Dr. Hartshorne is right in stressing also the coercive aspects of our religious experience. To worship God in dependence on his holiness does transform the self, far beyond its conscious intent and understanding. When we oppose God we discover the boundaries of our action, which are starkly there, and the consequences which are visited upon us whether we will or no. There are large coercive aspects in the divine governance of the world. We might summarize by saying

[20]*SAMW*, p. 276.

that God is that metaphysical function in the world by virtue of which sanity becomes possible for the creatures.

VI. *Some Concluding Comments*

The greatest difficulty in relating a theological doctrine of God's action to scientific understanding lies in the problem of assigning specific, observable consequences in the world to divine causality. This always seems to imply an intervention of theological explanation in scientific inquiry. Science must surely restrict itself to the observations and categories of explanation which are appropriate to each special science. It seems meaningless or hopelessly confusing to a scientific physical theory to say that an electron behaves according to the pattern of the quantum theory because God induces it to do so. The statement can be made; but it seems to lie on a different level from that of scientific understanding. One thinks of G. K. Chesterton's remark that "the sun rises every morning because God says to it, 'get up'." This statement is religiously meaningful, but not intelligible scientifically.

But the problem remains because if we assign God's action upon the world to a level of metaphysical causality which lies in a different place from the particular actions and reactions in an observable world, we pay too great a price from the standpoint of religious faith. We are then saying that God's acts make no difference in the observable world. To say that God "judges the nations" or "raises his Son from the dead" would be saying that this all happens without altering in any way the understanding we have empirically of the course of events.

Whitehead seems to me to hold a position between these two extremes. There are specific metaphysical functions which God alone performs. These can be in some measure described. But they involve the assertion that God makes a specific and observable difference in the behavior of things. At the same time Whitehead describes God's actions in such a way that at least some of the traditional difficulties in relating this view to scientific understanding are overcome.

So far as the primordial nature is concerned, it acts only by being presented to the creatures as the integrity of the order of possibility by virtue of which there can be a world. No specific action is completely determined by the primordial order, it only sets limits to what any action may be. There is here no clash with scientific understanding.

The consequent nature acts by being concretely apprehended in feeling in such a way that God's specific response to the world becomes a constitutive function in the world. Here there is specific divine causality. It should be remarked that this assertion in no way denies the operation of all the other actual entities in the world as causes. God's causality is exercised in, through and with all other causes operating. There is no demand here to factor out what God is adding to the stream of events apart from those events. But there is the assignment of specific functions to God's causality. These include the presentation to the creatures of a supremely adequate center of feeling through which the meaning of every occasion is received into and transformed by the divine experience, and this is concretely known by the creatures in such a way as to qualify their experience. Verification here can hardly take the form of precise description of individual experiences. The problem is far too complex and the data are too obscure for that. Verification must take the form of observable results in cosmic history, in human history, and in personal experience. While we are looking for specific causes at the level of observable and controllable data, we also have the question of the interpretation of the meaning of the whole of experience. That interpretation has aspects of faith and commitment which go beyond any precise knowledge. But I have tried to show that the assertion that God acts is neither wholly outside the possibility of verification in the breadth and depth of experience, nor does it conflict with scientific description of any concrete event.

One final point. The standpoint here outlined is, I suggest, compatible with the biblical and Christian assertion about the acts of God. Indeed, such a metaphysical outlook owes its historical development in part to elements in the Christan perspective, as Whitehead and many others have acknowledged.[21] At the same time the development of scientific and metaphysical analysis in the Western tradition has led, and should continue to lead, to a profound caution concerning assertions about the divine action.

The caution has two aspects. One is that every "act of God" is presented to us in, through and with the complex of nature and life

21Ibid., chap. I.

in which we are. When we say God elected Israel, or that he sends his rain on the just and the unjust, we must not ignore the complex analysis of assignable causes and factors in Israel's history or in the cosmic record of rainfall. We have no way of extricating the acts of God from their involvement in the activities of the world.

The second caution is that to assign any particular historical event to God's specific action in the world is to risk ultimate judgment on our assertions. Faith leads us to take that risk. We say God sent his Holy Spirit at Pentecost. He spoke to Jeremiah, he heals diseases, he will send the Lord again. But all such assertions in so far as they conceivably refer to historical events require us to acknowledge the limits of our sight and our knowledge. In specific assertions about what God is doing now, or precisely how he has acted, and how he will act, we surely can be mistaken.

DANIEL DAY WILLIAMS

UNION THEOLOGICAL SEMINARY
NEW YORK CITY

THE CONCEPT OF GOD AS A DERIVATIVE NOTION

THE PRINCIPAL way to understand the concept of God in Whitehead's philosophy is to study its functions in his speculative system. We can ask what, according to the system, God does and does not do. In this way we can find out what attributes of God are permitted or required by the system. We can see what could be meant by saying, for example, that God is powerful or that God is good. Then we can compare these attributes with the attributes or properties which other conceptions of God, for example those of Aquinas and Spinoza, permit or require.

There is another way we might learn something about the concept of God in Whitehead's philosophy. That is by studying how the concept is introduced into his system. That is what I propose to do in this essay. These two methods are not mutually independent, but by concentrating on the latter, we may learn something we should not have learned by the former alone. I shall not be concerned with the way Whitehead's conception of God may have been formed in his own mind. I want to study the logical node at which the concept makes its first appearance in his system. So I shall be dealing with a logical question (in a broad sense of "logical") not a genetic question and hence with the logical structure of his system, not with its history.

First I shall explain how Whitehead introduces the concept of God into his system. Then (in II) I shall draw some conclusions about the concept from the way it is introduced. I shall ask what we can infer about it from the fact that it is introduced in this particular way. Finally (in III) I shall discuss some objections to certain parts of this argument.

I

In this part I want to show: (1) why the concept of God is not a part of Whitehead's categoreal scheme; (2) the function of "de-

rivative notions" in his system; and (3) some specific features of the
concept of God as a derivative notion.

1. One of Whitehead's convictions about philosophy was that
constructive thought, as well as criticism, was needed and that
the true method of philosophical construction is to frame a scheme of ideas,
the best that one can, and unflinchingly to explore the interpretation of
experience in terms of that scheme.[1]

This he proceeded to do, and the place for us to begin is with this
scheme, which he states in Part I of *Process and Reality*, Chapter II,
under the title, "The Categoreal Scheme." The scheme is composed
of four sets of categories, including "The Category of the Ultimate"
and three sets of "more special categories", namely categories of
existence, categories of explanation, and categoreal obligations. In
the rest of *Process and Reality* he develops these categories in a systematic way and uses them to interpret our experience of the world.

First we need to notice that the scheme does not itself include a
concept of God and to see why it does not. This can be done by
several steps which will also show something about the structure and
function of the scheme. (i) The term "God" does not occur in the
statement of the categoreal scheme (though it does occur in the
informal preface to the scheme). (ii) Further, a conception of God
is not introduced into the scheme by using some other referring expression. The scheme does not in any way single out some entity and
assign to it the distinctive functions which Whitehead later assigns
to God. This means that the conception of God is not immediately
deducible[1a] from the scheme taken by itself in its proper generality.
So there is no concept of God in the categoreal scheme.

(iii) To see why this is so we need to notice that, strictly speaking,
the scheme does not *mention* any entity whatever. This is in accord
with Whitehead's principle that the categories need to be stated with
the utmost generality, but it needs to be explained.

In the "category of the ultimate" the notions of "one", "many",
and "creativity" are conjoined. These are the logically primitive
notions which are "presupposed in" (PR 31) the categories of
existence, explanation, and obligation. For example Whitehead cannot

---

[1]Alfred North Whitehead, *Process and Reality* (New York: The Macmillan Co., 1936),
p. x. (Hereafter **PR**).

[1a]Later I shall argue that the scheme does not itself *require* the concept of God
either.

make a list of types of entities (i.e. of logical subjects of systematic statements) in his categories of existence without presupposing the primitive notions of "one" and "many." And he cannot supply categories of explanation which speak of "process" and "becoming" without drawing on the primitive notion of "creativity." The category of the ultimate is the matrix of the categoreal scheme.

Since these notions are presupposed in "the more special categories" it follows that they are not themselves examples of the more special categories. The terms "one", "many", and "creativity" are not being introduced as names of entities or even as names of types of entities.[2] For there are no proper names of entities anywhere in the categoreal scheme, and names of types of entities are given only in the categories of existence. Again, "creativity" is not being introduced, in the category of the ultimate, as a category of explanation.

Furthermore, for the purpose of systematic explanation these primitive notions are superseded by the special categories. For example the primitive notion "one" is superseded by the concept of the unity of an actual entity (categories of explanation ii, xxv-xxvii; categories of obligation i-ii, vii) as a principle of systematic explanation. Similarly the primitive notion "many" is superseded, for the purpose of systematic explanation, by the category of multiplicities which is listed in the categories of existence (vii) and carefully explained in category of explanation xvi. Again, the primitive notion "creativity" is superseded by the account of how actual entities come into existence by concrescence, in the categories of explanation and obligation.

By saying these primitive notions are superseded by systematic categories I do not mean there is no further use for them, but only that they are pre-systematic. Whitehead's aim in the construction of his system is not to eliminate pre-systematic notions but to elucidate them.

This conclusion is particularly important for understanding how Whitehead uses the term "creativity". For example, when in category of explanation xxv he is explaining the satisfaction of an actual entity and speaks of its objective character "for the transcendent creativity," the meaning of this phrase can be translated systematically into "for those other actual entities which prehend it." More generally, all that

---

[2]We have recourse to the category of the ultimate when we want to explain "the *meaning* of the synonymous terms 'thing,' 'being,' 'entity.' " (PR 31, my italics)

can be said about creativity can be put into systematic statements about the concrescences of actual entities.

Moving now from the category of the ultimate to the more special categories, we can see further how no particular entity is mentioned in the categoreal scheme. The list of categories of existence is a list of multiplicities. This list says, in effect, that there are (in a completely neutral sense of "are") actual entities, that there are prehensions, and so on for the rest of the eight types of entities which make up the categories of existence. Further, in the categories of explanation and obligation no particular entity of any of these types is mentioned. These categories do not single out any entity as having a function which other entities of its type do not have.

This is the general reason why the categoreal scheme does not include a concept of God. For this is a concept of an entity as having some functions no other entity has. It is a concept of a particular entity. So it is clear that the concept of God must be introduced into Whitehead's system in some other way than that in which the concepts which constitute the categoreal scheme are introduced.

2. Whitehead introduces the concept of God into his system not as a concept of the categoreal scheme but as a "derivative notion." What are "derivative notions", and what part do they play in Whitehead's system?

The subtitle of *Process and Reality* is "An Essay in Cosmology," but the categoreal scheme is not itself a cosmology. It is a scheme of concepts to be used in constructing a cosmology, to be used, that is to say, in giving a systematic interpretation of nature and human experience. Or we might put it another way: the construction of the categoreal scheme is only one stage, in particular an intermediate stage, in the construction of a cosmology. Changing the metaphor, it is the flight of the airplane in "the thin air of imaginative generalization."

The plane must have risen from the ground and it must come down to earth. The scheme is suggested by experience and will be used to interpret the world we experience, but it must be constructed before it can be used. It consists of definitions of concepts, definitions "of constructs in logical terms" (PR5), not propositions about the world.[3] Or, we might say, the scheme includes only systematic state-

[3]Except in category of explanation i: "That the actual world is a process, and

ments. It tells us only what Whitehead is going to mean by such terms as "actual entity", "eternal object", "nexus", and others. It does not show us *how* these are to be applied to the real world. It does not assert propositions whose logical subjects are human experiences, persons, electrons and galaxies and interpret these in terms of the concepts it defines.

To interpret the world in which we live we need something more than the concepts of the categoreal scheme; we need "Some Derivative Notions" also. This is the title of the chapter which follows "The Categoreal Scheme." One of the notions he explains there is the concept of God, but first let us see how some other derivative notions are introduced, namely extension and societies.

In the world we experience some things succeed other things in ordered ways. There are transitions from one state to another, so that we think of time as a perpetual perishing. We are not told this in the categoreal scheme; we know it from experience. Let me pause to explain the negative side of this point, namely that temporal succession is not a concept of the categoreal scheme.

In the scheme it is said that an actual entity is a process of becoming and this process (concrescence) is explained in detail. But, as Whitehead tells us over and over again later on, becoming is not the same sort of process as transition. In the world we experience, processes of the two sorts are intimately interrelated. But in the categoreal scheme we are not yet told that there are processes of transition in which one real thing succeeds another.[4]

At this point we find ourselves with the concept of actual entities as processes of becoming (this from the categoreal scheme) *and* with the fact that some things succeed others (this from experience). So we use the categoreal scheme to interpret this general fact of succession in the following way. We say that some actual entities have temporal beginnings and endings and that their becomings are finite durations. Such actual entities will be called "actual occasions" or "temporal actual entities." Then we can interpret temporal succession

that the process is the becoming of actual entities." This *announces* that the scheme is to be applied to the real world.

[4]Nor, of course, are we told that there are not processes of transition. See "Whitehead's Explanation of the Past," in George L. Kline (ed.), *Alfred North Whitehead: Essays on His Philosophy* (Englewood Cliffs, N.J.: Prentice-Hall, 1963).

in terms of the successions of actual occasions and thus develop the epochal theory of time.[5]

Similarly we learn from experience, not from the categoreal scheme, that the things we experience have a systematic spatial order as well as a temporal order. So we use the categoreal scheme to interpret this general fact of the spatio-temporal order of the world by saying that some actual entities have finite spatio-temporal regions, and we can develop the basic concepts of geometry by defining possible sets of relations among hypothetical regions.

In these ways extension is introduced into Whitehead's system as a derivative notion. (See also III below.) It is introduced after the categoreal scheme is (presumptively) complete. He is not now defining an actual entity. He is saying that, since we experience an extended world, at least some actual entities must have a certain feature in addition to those by which they were categoreally defined. They must have extensive regions interrelated to form an extensive continuum. Thus the categoreal scheme is being used to interpret a fact it does not state.

Another generic but contingent feature of the world is the fact that some things endure through time. Persons and stones, for example, persist through various successive states. (Compare Kant's schema of substance.) Again, this is not something we are told in the categoreal scheme. As far as the scheme itself is concerned there might, or might not, be enduring things, just as there might or might not be temporal transitions and spatial extension. We learn this in experience.

So Whitehead uses the categoreal scheme to interpret the contingent fact that there are enduring things. As he interpreted succession by saying that some actual entities have temporal beginnings and ends, and that some succeed others, so now he says that some nexūs of actual entities have "social order" and "personal order", which he defines with care. In this way the derivative notion of enduring objects is introduced into the system.

[5]The last clause of the paragraph which states category of explanation i is somewhat misleading. The last sentence reads: "Thus actual entities are creatures; they are also termed 'actual occasions.'" The last clause is misleading because it might suggest that "actual occasion" has the same range of application as "actual entity," which from Whitehead's clearly explained usage it does not have. See PR 102, 135, 378, for example. But my main argument is that, because of the sense the term is later given, it is premature to introduce it here.

So far we have seen how Whitehead introduces those derivative notions he will use in developing a philosophy of nature. This is the way he now approaches a problem with had occupied him since he first began to philosophize, namely the need to reinterpret the traditional concepts of space, time, and matter.

Constructing a philosophical system in this way presupposes that some of the generic features of the world, as well as its details, are contingent. In respect of these features, as well as in respect of the particular individuals it contains, the world is as we find it. The point is not that the categoreal scheme is incomplete; the point is that it leaves room for statements on a different logical level, i.e., for non-categoreal systematic statements. It not only leaves room for statements of this type; it also gives rules for forming them, in the categories of existence, explanation and obligation.

3. Now we are ready to see how the concept of God is introduced as a derivative notion. Here a difference appears. Instead of starting with a commonly accepted fact of direct experience, as he did in introducing the concepts of extension and of enduring objects, here Whitehead starts with a problem.

The problem is as follows. The scheme tells us that every actual entity has a subjective aim. Now, how can the subjective aim of a *temporal* actual entity originate? How is it possible for a novel aim at unity of feeling to occur? As Whitehead puts it: "In what sense can unrealized abstract form be relevant? What is its basis of relevance?" (PR 48) The fact that Whitehead begins here with a problem, instead of with a commonly accepted fact, means that the concept of God is explanatory in a different way than the way the concepts of extension and enduring objects are explanatory.

This problem does not arise within the categoreal scheme itself, strictly speaking. For the concept of temporal actual entities is not introduced in the scheme itself. But once we have said that some actual entities have beginnings in time, then it becomes a problem how *these* actual entities can satisfy the categoreal obligation of subjective unity. (cat. ob. i) .

Whitehead's solution of this problem, in the course of which his concept of God is introduced, is an argument for a "principle of concretion." It may be paraphrased as follows: By the ontological principle (cat. exp. xviii) actual entities are the only *reasons*. So if some novel (hence unrealized) possibility is relevant to every parti-

cular temporal situation, the basis of this relevance must be some
fact in the constitution of a primordial and everlasting actual entity.
This non-temporal actuality, Whitehead says,

is here termed 'God'; because the contemplation of our natures, as enjoying
real feelings derived from the timeless source of all order, acquires that
'subjective form' of refreshment and companionship at which religions aim.
(PR 47)

We might pause to notice the significance of this last point. The
initial term for introducing the concept is not "God" but "the primordial and everlasting actual entity" or some similar expression,
much as in the "five ways" of Thomas Aquinas the arguments first
reach "a first mover," "a first efficient cause", a necessary being, the
cause of perfections, and a directing intelligence. Then, somewhat
as Aquinas takes a further step and justifies the use of "God" as an
equivalent term for each of these ("This all men speak of as God"),
so Whitehead justifies "God" as a name for the non-temporal actual
entity. But instead of appealing to ordinary usage as Aquinas does
Whitehead's argument appeals to a theory of religion. The argument
might be paraphrased and expanded as follows: "God" is primarily
a religious term; an essential feature of religious experience is a sense
of "refreshment and companionship"; apprehension of the primordial
and everlasting actual entity generates these qualities; hence it is
justifiable to call it "God."

Why is it that in introducing the concept of God Whitehead does
not start with some fact of direct experience but instead with a problem?
For example, why does he not start with religious experience? The
reason is that he restricts himself to common and public facts as the
initial data for introducing derivative notions into his system. In our
experiences of successions, spatial extension, and endurance we have
facts of this sort. In religious experiences we do not.

He thinks religious experiences are themselves, as experiences,
genuine facts requiring interpretations such as he gives in the passage
above.[6] We use both categoreal concepts and derivative notions to
interpret religious experiences. But religious experiences do not give

---

[6]Also it is easy to argue that a religious vision is one of the sources of Whitehead's
system. It would be highly implausible to suggest that Whitehead himself arrived at
a conception of God only after he had conceived the categoreal scheme. See "On
Some Uses of Reason," in Ivor Leclerc, ed., *The Relevance of Whitehead* (London:
G. Allen and Unwin [New York: Macmillan], 1961). But we are concerned with the
logical structure of his system, not with its genesis.

us the kind of facts which justify the introduction of a derivative notion into the system.

So the concept of God is introduced at two removes from common public facts. It is not introduced as a direct interpretation of the experienced fact of successiveness, as the notion of temporal actual entities is. It is introduced at a later point, to explain these temporal actual entities. So it is an explanation of an interpretation. It gives an explanation of the concept of a temporal actual entity, which is itself used to interpret the fact of successiveness.

II

Now we can draw some conclusions about the concept of God in Whitehead's philosophy from the way it is introduced into his system.

1. It is a concept of a member of some multiplicity. Since the concept of God is the concept of an entity (and in this way unlike the concept of the extensive continuum) we know it is governed by some one of the eight categories of existence. "Every entity should be a specific instance of one category of existence . . . " (PR 31) It would be inconsistent with Whitehead's principles to introduce as a derivative notion either a new category of existence or some entity uncovered by any category of existence. Now the list of categories of existence is a list of multiplicities (PR 44) . Consequently the concept of God is a concept of a member of some multiplicity.

This does not mean that God must be construed merely as a member of a multiplicity but only that the predicate which defines the multiplicity must be true of him. For example the categories of explanation and obligation yield a complex predicate which defines the multiplicity of actual entities. So if God is construed as an actual entity this predicate must be at least as true of God as of any other actual entity. But this by no means excludes the possibility of saying other things of God also. Indeed, on Whitehead's principles it must be possible to say more than this of any mentionable entity. No entity is merely a member of a multiplicity.

Incidentally, it is somewhat misleading to say: "God is a member of a multiplicity," or "God is not beyond the categories." It is better to say: "The concept of God is a concept of a member of a multiplicity," or "The concept of God is not beyond the categories."

Saying that the concept of God is a concept of a member of a multiplicity does not have the same force as saying that God is a species of a genus. A genus in the traditional sense is a set of entities having some ordering relations among them. These ordering relations give a genus a unity which a multiplicity does not possess. This is why a multiplicity is not a "proper entity." (PR 44-45) Therefore it might be possible to construct a stronger doctrine of the transcendence of God than if God were said to be a species of a genus in the traditional sense.[7]

2. The concept of God is a concept of an actuality. Since it is introduced as an explanatory concept under the ontological principle, we know it must be the concept of an actuality, that is to say either an actual entity or a nexus of actual entities.[8] Hence all the categories of explanation which apply to actual entities (or alternatively to nexūs) must apply to the conception of God. Further, all the categoreal obligations (which define the conditions of the concrescence of an actual entity) must apply to God or, if God is a nexus, to the actual entities which constitute him.

The qualifying remark about the first conclusion above applies with added strength to actualities. Every actual entity is different from every other actual entity and every nexus is different from every other nexus. Whitehead has a strong doctrine of individuality with which to interpret Bishop Butler's saying: "Everything is what it is, and not another thing." So there is ample room for attributing to God properties which no other actuality possesses, for constructing a doctrine of the transcendence of God, and for developing analogies of various sorts between God and other actualities. The only limitation on this development is as follows: other predicates asserted of God must be compatible with the complex predicate which defines the multiplicity of actual entities (or, nexūs) .

[7]It is true that Whitehead speaks of there being only one "genus" of actual entities (PR 168), but he does not mean the traditional sense of genus here. He means all actual entities are members of the same multiplicity. For a parallel distinction between two senses of "class," one of which approximates the traditional concept of genus, the other being the concept of a multiplicity, see PR 348 and William A. Christian, *An Interpretation of Whitehead's Metaphysics* (New Haven: Yale University Press, 1959), pp. 248-250, 260n.

[8]I think the weight of both the textual evidence and systematic considerations is overwhelmingly on the side of identifying God as an actual entity, not as a nexus. This affects the way I develop the theme of this essay. But the concept of a *unique* nexus would be a derivative concept, and a parallel argument would then be in order.

3. The concept of God in Whitehead's philosophy permits and requires systematic references. This conclusion needs a good deal of explanation.

By a reference I mean an answer to a question of the form: "What do you mean by M?", when M has been used to stand for the logical subject of some proposition. And I shall suppose that making a reference involves offering some factual starting point, which connects with the experience of the asker of the question, and some interpretative category by which to move from this starting point to the goal of the reference. For example, "God is powerful" could not serve as a reference but "God is the cause of the world" might do so. Here it is hoped to move from "the world" by means of the category of causality to the goal of the reference and thus put the asker in mind of what is meant by "God." I shall show that the kind of references Whitehead's conception requires are much less simple.

But first let us notice that Whitehead does require references to God, and that his conception is different from those which eschew references. Sometimes when the term "God" is used, as in prayers and meditative utterances, it is not being used in a referring way. Further, sometimes even when theologians speak of God it appears that requests for references are not in order. Sometimes such requests are resisted or ignored if not indeed explicitly ruled out of order. In these cases we are led to conclude that the term is being used not in a referring way but in some other way, perhaps an expressive or evocative or prescriptive way. Sometimes it is said to be a "symbolic" term and this might mean, in part, that it is not to be used in a referring way.

In *Religion in the Making* Whitehead is clearly unfriendly to "assigning a merely personal significance" (65-66) to religious intuitions. "Justification" of its doctrines is even more necessary to rational religion that it is to science:

... science can leave its metaphysics implicit and retire behind our belief in the pragmatic value of its general descriptions. If religion does that, it admits that its dogmas are merely pleasing ideas for the purpose of stimulating its emotions. (85)

Progress in truth, he says, both in science and in religion is a progress in framing concepts "which strike more deeply into the root of reality." (131)

Now let us distinguish non-systematic references from systematic references. The following might function as non-systematic references: "the cause of the world," "the whole of which the soul is a part", and "the reality of which nature is the manifestation." If so, the interpretative categories (cause-effect, whole-part, reality-manifestation) are being taken over directly from general usage without systematic refinement. They are being used in a simple way. Their meaning does not depend on their place in some systematic categoreal scheme. They have the force of analogies, for they rely for their meaning on certain paradigmatic experiences (for example making a table, dividing a sphere into sections, expressing oneself by a gesture). But even if the paradigm is specified, no path of logical development from the paradigm to the reference is specified. It is taken for granted that we understand what causality, wholeness, and appearance mean.

In systematic references on the contrary the categories used to interpret the factual starting point get their meaning from their positions in an explicitly elaborated categoreal scheme. Thus "the final cause of all action," "the substance of which all things are modes", "the ground of the pre-established harmony of things", and "the ideal of reason" might presuppose the categoreal schemes of Aristotle, Spinoza, Leibniz, and Kant, and then they would need to be understood in the light of those schemes.

Hence systematic references do not rely on paradigmatic experiences for their meaning as non-systematic references do, at least not in a direct way. The schemes themselves may have been generated from paradigmatic experiences. But even so the direct and immediate contexts for the categories are not the paradigmatic experiences but the schemes.

A number of non-systematic referential expressions occur as allusions to God in Whitehead's writings, for example:
"the ground for concrete actuality" (SMW 249-250)
"the timeless source of all order" (PR 47)
"the totality of historic fact in respect to its essential unity" (MT 164)
"that power in history which implants into ... process ... a drive towards some ideal" (MT 164)
Many similar expressions can be found. Incidentally we might distinguish from these such passages as the following:

something which stands beyond, behind, and within, the passing flux of immediate things; something which is real, and yet waiting to be realised; something which is a remote possibility, and yet the greatest of present facts; . . . (SMW 267-268)

Such passages as this might better be regarded as conveying suggestions than as making references.

But it is clear that if these non-systematic expressions are found wanting in definiteness and clarity they can be explained by making use of the categoreal scheme. At least, they can be if Whitehead's cosmology is adequate. For one of his own norms for a speculative scheme is that it be capable of interpreting every item of experience. So any meaningful non-systematic expression must be interpretable in systematic terms. It follows that Whitehead is committed to giving systematic references to God as well as non-systematic ones.

Now we are ready to see what kind of systematic reference to God is implicit in Whitehead's introduction of the concept. A fully explicit reference of this kind could be developed by three steps, as for example the following:

Step 1. Consider your experience through a succession of moments.

Step 2. This stretch of experience is a nexus of actual occasions.

Step 3. The source of the subjective aims of these occasions is a primordial and everlasting actual entity for which the appropriate name is "God."

Step 1 gives the factual starting point of the reference and therefore must involve some *description,* using pre-systematic terms. Step 2 is an *interpretation* of this fact, using systematic terms, and is thus a post-systematic statement. Notice that this step must make use of the derivative notion of temporal actual entities (actual occasions) in order to pass to the next step, which moves on to the goal of the reference. This means that the factual starting point must be such that it calls in some way or other for the introduction of this notion. So the factual starting point must involve temporal process in some way or other. It must involve beginnings and endings. For if the fact (Step 1) did not involve temporal process in some way, there would be no call to introduce the concept of actual occasions (temporal actual entities) in the interpretation (Step 2).

Step 3 completes the reference by introducing the conception of God. It is not a purely systematic statement for it retains a connection with the factual starting point by way of "these occasions." So we may call it an indirect interpretation, falling between a direct interpretation like Step 2 and a purely systematic explanation like "Actual occasions derive their initial aims from God." It relates the conception of God not only to the explanatory system, of which Step 2 has already made use, but also to a particular fact.

This shows that the systematic references Whitehead's conception of God requires must include propositions, in his systematic sense of that term. Propositions are listed in the categories of existence (vi) and are explained as follows:

That a proposition is the unity of certain actual entities in their potentiality for forming a nexus, with its potential relatedness partially defined by certain eternal objects which have the unity of one complex eternal object. The actual entities involved are termed the 'logical subjects,' the complex eternal object is the 'predicate.' (cat. exp. xv)

They are explained further in Chapter IV of Part III of *Process and Reality*, which relates propositions to the theory of feelings. The point of particular interest is this: a prehension of a proposition (a propositional feeling) involves an "indicative feeling" (397) of the logical subjects of the proposition. This indicative feeling singles out these logical subjects, more or less completely, from all others. This is why a proposition is either true or false.

Now since a reference to God must not merely define the concept (as "God is the non-temporal actual entity") but must connect the concept with some factual starting point, propositions with indicated logical subjects are necessary. This brings with it the following consequence.

Any reference to God is made at some particular time and place, and the indicated logical subjects ("these occasions") of the propositions involved in the reference have definite positions in the extensive continuum. Now since God prehends all actual occasions as they occur, God as referred to from some one standpoint in nature will not be the same in all respects as when he is referred to from some other standpoint. Thus Whitehead's conception of God entails a certain relativity of references to God. This relativity is not due to any subjectivity of feelings; it is due to the fact that the content of the divine experience itself varies (objectively) with the passage of time. I believe this consequence has considerable importance for interpreting Whitehead's conception of God. Some confusions can be avoided by distinguishing systematic explanations of the term "God" (defining the concept) from referential uses.

4. The concept of God in Whitehead's philosophy is categoreally contingent, systematically necessary, and existentially contingent. This is another conclusion we can draw from the way the concept is introduced. By saying the concept of God is categoreally contingent I mean that the categoreal scheme permits but does not require the concept. I have explained how the concept is not introduced in the scheme and hence is not immediately deducible from it. In III below I shall argue that the concept is not indirectly deducible from (and in *this* way required by) the scheme. It is already reasonably clear how the concept is necessary to Whitehead's system as a whole. So my main business here is to show how the concept is existentially contingent. By this I mean that the proposition "God exists" is, if true, contingently true, not necessarily true.

In view of I above we can reconstruct Whitehead's argument as follows. Let us take as his conclusion:

P. There is a primordial and everlasting actual entity.

Then his argument for this conclusion must include premises like the following:

A. The real world is made up of actual entities.

B. Some real things have temporal beginnings.

C. Some actual entities have temporal beginnings.

The general shape of the argument is that C follows from the conjunction of A and B, and P follows from C as an explanation under the ontological principle.

Now if his argument is valid, we can tell whether the conclusion claims to be contingently true or to be necessarily true (and also give some definite meaning to these expressions) by examining these premises. For if some of the premises are contingently true then the conclusion is at best only contingently true, and only if all the premises are necessarily true can the conclusion be necessarily true. So let us consider the premises separately with this in mind.

A. The real world is made up of actual entities.

This is not a description, since it includes the systematic term "actual entities". To know the sense of this term we must read Whitehead's writings. And it is not a purely systematic explanation, since "the real world" is a pre-systematic term. It is an interpretation, with an extremely wide scope. It is a declaration of the general intention of Whitehead's scheme, namely that it is to be used to interpret the real world.

A is thus very like the first sentence of category of explanation i: "That the actual world is a process, and that the process is the becoming of actual entities." Especially since "actual" in this sentence (as in many other places) must be taken pre-systematically (to mean something like "real") and not systematically (as defined in cat.exp. xxi), in order to avoid tautology.

Now does *A* claim to be contingently true or necessarily true? And what would this mean? In *A* the truth-claim of Whitehead's system as a whole is epitomized. And Whitehead fails in two ways to claim necessary truth for his system. (In explaining these points I am also explaining what I mean by "necessary truth.") (i) He does not claim to have deduced his system from premises which are clear, certain and sufficient. (PR 11-12) He thinks no such premises are available for speculative philosophy. So he does not deduce his system; he constructs it. (ii) He does not claim that all possible alternatives to his system are absurd. He does argue against alternatives to *A*, for example:

A2. The real world is made up of bits of matter (impervious and inert atoms).

A3. The real world is made up of monads.

And (as against *A*2) he does challenge the significance of some of these (as in pronouncements on "vacuous actuality"). But some of his objections to others, as to *A*3, have a more empirical flavor. (We *do* experience real connections, he seems to say.) What is more to the point, nowhere does he claim to have exhausted the alternatives to *A*. Indeed, he explicitly leaves room for the possibility of progress in speculative philosophy. He is content to aim at showing that the philosophy of organism is superior to its main *known* alternatives. So if *A* is true it is contingently (not necessarily) true, in the sense just now explained.

B. Some real things have temporal beginnings.

This is a description, using only pre-systematic terms. Does it claim to be necessarily true? Let us look at one way it might be challenged:

Challenge: "Give me an example."

Response: "That sycamore tree. It wasn't in existence ten years ago."

Objection: "But you can't call things like that 'real.' It is only a manifestation of something real."

Notice that this kind of objection is not vulnerable to dialectical responses like:

Response 2: "Your utterance of a moment ago."

Does Whitehead admit this kind of objection? He does not seem to dismiss it as absurd. In arguing for a principle of concretion in *Science and the Modern World* he says:

The only alternative to this admission [i.e., of a principle of limitation], is to deny the reality of actual occasions. Their apparent irrational limitation must be taken as a proof of illusion and we must look for reality behind the scene. If we reject this alternative behind the scene, we must provide a ground for limitation . . . (249)

He carries on a running polemic against transcendental monism, saying for example that it is "in defiance of the most obvious deliverance of our intuitive 'prejudices.' " (PR 208) More specifically, relevant to temporal beginnings, he feels genuinely challenged by Zeno's arguments. He responds to objections against the reality of temporal beginnings in two ways: he constructs a system in which he hopes to express his own valuation of temporal things in a consistent way; and he appeals to "intuitive prejudices" and to the implications of practice on behalf of this valuation. These are serious arguments, against a respected opponent.

So it seems that *B* does not claim to be true necessarily in either of the senses mentioned above. Whitehead does not seem to claim it is a deduction from clear, certain, and sufficient premises; and he does not seem to claim that all its alternatives are absurd. Though there is no doubt he believes it is true.

C. Some actual entities have temporal beginnings.

It would not be in order to ask here a question like those we asked about *A* and *B*. For the point of *C* is to introduce the derivative concept of actual occasions. It is required as a separate premise because it is not deducible from the categoreal scheme (which has been brought in under *A*). The scheme itself does not require *C*. *C* is brought in to explain *A* in the light of *B*. If the real world is made up of actual entities, and if some real things have temporal beginnings, then some actual entities have temporal beginnings. That is to say, some actual entities are actual occasions.

From *C* it follows by a series of explanations under the ontological principle that there is a non-temporal actual entity, which is both primordial and everlasting. Hence *P* is systematically necessary.

To sum up:

i. Since the categoreal scheme permits but does not require *P*, *P* is categoreally contingent.

ii. Since *P* is systematically required by *C*, and since *C* is required by the conjunction of *A* and *B*, *P* is systematically necessary.

iii. Since the argument for *P* requires *A* and *B*, and since neither *A* nor *B* is necessarily true, *P* is existentially contingent.

Notice that this last conclusion does not amount to saying that God exists contingently. There are two important senses in which Whitehead's concept of God is the concept *of* a being which exists necessarily, as follows:

a. It is the concept of a being which has no temporal beginning or end, whose existence is effectively relevant everywhere and at all times, and whose character is constant. It is the concept of a being which never fails to exist.

b. It is the concept of a being which is an essential condition of the existence of every other actuality. More specifically, if any actual entity has a temporal beginning, God exists. (Contrast this with the argument—on which the major theologians have *not* relied: If the world had a temporal beginning, God exists.) Thus (since all actual entities but God have temporal beginnings) if any other actuality exists, God exists.

These provide a strong meaning for saying that God as conceived in Whitehead's philosophy is a necessary being. But saying the concept of God is the concept of a necessary being is not the same as saying the concept of God is a necessary concept. It is true that it is systematically necessary; without it Whitehead's speculative system would be inconsistent or incomplete or both. But it is categoreally contingent, since it is a derivative concept. And since its existential truth-claim depends not only on the consistency and coherence of Whitehead's system but also on its adequacy, the concept of God in Whitehead's philosophy is existentially contingent.

III

Now I must discuss some objections to certain parts of the foregoing argument. These objections argue that the concept of God is required by the categoreal scheme and is therefore categoreally necessary instead of, as I have argued, categoreally contingent. They would not affect the conclusion that the concept of God in Whitehead's philosophy is existentially contingent. I shall state the objections and then construct replies to them.

1. It seems that category of explanation v requires the concept of actual occasions (temporal actual entities) to explain the differentiation of "actual worlds." But if the scheme thus requires the concept of actual entities with temporal beginnings, it must also require the concept of God to account for the temporal origination of the subjective aims of these entities. Hence, though the concept of God is not introduced in the scheme it is required by the scheme.

2. It seems that categoreal obligation v (the category of conceptual reversion) requires the concept of God to account for the origination of conceptual novelty. Therefore the concept of God is categoreally necessary.

1. The real issue in the first objection is about its major premise. Does this category of explanation require the concept of temporal actual entities? The problematical part of the statement of the category is as follows:

> That no two actual entities originate from an identical universe; though the difference between the two universes only consists in some actual entities, included in one and not in the other . . . The nexus of actual entities in the universe correlate to a concrescence, is termed 'the actual world' correlate to that concrescence.[9]

Now if we read this with Whitehead's theory of actual occasions (as developed later) in mind we would interpret it as follows: Any two actual occasions, as M and N, have different standpoints in the ex-

---

[9]Notice that this systematic use of "the actual world" is different from the presystematic sense of the expression in category of explanation i.

tensive continuum. Hence, whether they are contemporary or successive they will have different (past) actual worlds. If they are contemporary, some of M's other contemporaries (those in other time-
systems) will be in N's past and thus in N's actual world but not in
M's actual world. Likewise some of N's contemporaries will be in
M's actual world but not in N's actual world. If N succeeds M, then
M is included in N's actual world but N is not in M's actual world.

There is no doubt this is the way Whitehead applies category of
explanation v in his theory of actual occasions. But our problem is
whether this category of explanation requires the theory of actual
occasions. For I have been arguing that the categoreal scheme does
not itself require a distinction between temporal actual entities and
a non-temporal actual entity, though it permits this distinction. The
reason it does not require the distinction is that it does not introduce
temporality. (The process of concrescence is not in physical time.)

Notice some of the assumptions we would be making in the above
interpretation. We would assume (i) that the actual world of an actual
entity consists of only those actual entities in its causal past. But we
are not told this in the categoreal scheme. Indeed the scheme does not
even include the concept of pastness.[10] Also we would assume (ii)
the theory of alternative time-systems. But I suppose no one would
argue that this is required by the categoreal scheme in itself, before
the scheme is applied to the real world. Most important and more
generally we would assume (iii) that actual entities are extended,
and that their extensive standpoints are coordinated in an extensive
continuum. But, as I shall show further shortly, the concept of the
extensive continuum is a derivative concept.

So, to understand this category of explanation in its own proper
generality, we need to think away these assumptions. And if we do
so, then no problem about explaining the differentiation of actual
worlds will arise. No categoreal explanation of category of explanation v is needed. Most generally, if we do not suppose that the uni-
verses of different actual entities are spatio-temporally coordinated, we
do not have to suppose that there are actual entities with temporal
endings or temporal beginnings, or both, in order to give this category
of explanation a meaning.

[10]As I have argued in "Whitehead's Explanation of the Past," *The Journal of
Philosophy*, September 14, 1961.

The categoreal scheme is not itself a cosmology but only a statement of some basic concepts Whitehead will use in constructing a cosmology, along with other (derivative) concepts he will introduce later on. The extensive continuum is not one of these basic concepts; instead, the extendedness of the world in space and time is a fact of experience to be interpreted by these basic concepts.

In support of this view I call attention to the following passages, most of them from Chapters II and III ("The Extensive Continuum" and "The Order of Nature") of Part II of *Process and Reality:*

The more likely opinion is that extensive continuity is a special condition arising from the society of creatures which constitute our immediate epoch. (53) [*A fortiori* it is not a categoreal concept.]

It is a "metaphysical[11] assumption"

that the real potentialities relative to all standpoints are coordinated as diverse determinations of one extensive continuum . . . This extensive continuum is 'real', because it expresses a fact derived from the actual world and concerning the contemporary actual world. (103)

The systematic scheme [of extension], in its completeness embracing the actual past and the potential future, is prehended in the positive experience of each actual entity. In this sense, it is Kant's 'form of intuition'; but it is derived from the actual world *qua datum,* and thus is not 'pure' in Kant's sense of that term. It is not productive of the ordered world, but derivative from it. (112)

The inclusion of *extensive quantity* among fundamental categoreal notions is a complete mistake. This notion is definable in terms of each systematic geometry finding its application in a geometrical society. (148-9)

2. Category of obligation v (conceptual reversion) is stated as follows:

There is secondary origination of conceptual feelings with data which are partially identical with, and partially diverse from, the eternal objects forming the data in the first phase of the mental pole. The diversity is a relevant diversity determined by the subjective aim.

The problem about this arises because Whitehead says later:

Thus, a more fundamental account must ascribe the reverted conceptual feeling in a temporal subject to its conceptual feeling derived, according to Category IV [conceptual valuation], from the hybrid physical feeling of the relevancies conceptually ordered in God's experience. In this way . . . a more

11"Metaphysical" here does not mean "categoreal." The last sentence makes this clear. Also, categoreal statements are not assumptions.

complete rational explanation is attained. The category of reversion is then abolished ... (PR 382)

This might be taken to mean that the categoreal scheme itself indirectly requires the concept of God. But, first, it is quite wrong to say the category is abolished, if this means it has no application in Whitehead's developed system. Indeed it is being applied in this very passage ("the reverted conceptual feeling"). It is needed both to explain the concrescence of an actual occasion and to explain the divine concrescence. Actual occasions *do* derive from their initial conceptual aims the relevant contrasts which make supplementary feelings possible. Furthermore, God derives from his primordial envisagement of eternal objects those conceptual feelings which continually supplement his physical prehensions of actual occasions.[12]

Second, more than this category is *not* needed within the categoreal scheme itself if taken in its bare generality. This category is a sufficient explanation within the limits of the scheme. As Whitehead himself suggests in the passage above, the problem arises only when we need to explain a reverted feeling *in a temporal subject*. For the statement of categoreal obligation v itself gives an ontological ground of reverted feelings, namely the subjective aim of the concrescence. And this is a sufficient explanation until the derivative concepts of actual occasions and of God are introduced. Now in the case of God, no *further* ontological explanation is needed, for his subjective aim is determined by his primordial envisagement of the whole multiplicity of eternal objects. The origination of the subjective aim of a temporal actual entity does require a *further* ontological explanation.

So, instead of saying that the category of conceptual reversion is abolished, Whitehead should have said that, in the case of temporal actual entities (with which alone he is concerned in this passage) conceptual reversion needs to be *connected* with an ontological explanation of finite subjective aims. But this problem arises only after the concept of temporal actual occasions has been introduced, whereas the scheme itself does not introduce this distinction.

In conclusion let me put the foregoing argument in a perspective. In saying the concept of God is a derivative concept we are

---

[12]See *An Interpretation of Whitehead's Metaphysics,* pp. 292-294, 353-354. At that time I did not see that conceptual reversion is needed for a categoreal explanation of these supplementary feelings.

saying something about the way it is introduced into Whitehead's system. It is not saying that in his cosmology the concept of God has a less important function than the concept of actual occasions, and it is not saying that in the world (according to Whitehead) God is less important than actual occasions. Neither of these would be true. Indeed Whitehead speaks of actual occasions as "derivative" from God (PR 46), having in mind the derivation of initial conceptual aims, and of God as the only "non-derivative actuality" (PR 48).[13] We are not speaking of the content of the concept but only of the logical order in which the concept is built into the system.

Nevertheless this is significant. It tells us that, if we want to understand the internal logical structure of the system, we had better not take the concept of an actual occasion and the concept of God as logically basic and construe the concept of an actual entity as a generalization from these. Instead we should begin with the concept of an actual entity as explained in the categoreal scheme, without reading into the scheme more than is there, and then see how the concept of an actual occasion and the concept of God are derived, as we have done.

These concepts specify in certain particular ways, in view of certain generic facts of experience which need to be interpreted, what is left quite general in the categoreal concept of an actual entity. Actual occasions, and God, are actual entities with certain specified features, features which are permitted but not required by the categoreal concept. If our experience were generically different from what it is—if for example we experienced no real temporal beginnings, or no real temporal endings—a different set of derivative concepts would be needed, and would be permitted by the categoreal scheme (though not any set whatever). There are other ways in which the concept of an actual entity might be systematically developed. *These* are the ways it needs to be developed, so Whitehead's thought runs, if we are to give an adequate interpretation of our experience in *this* world.

WILLIAM A. CHRISTIAN

YALE UNIVERSITY

---

[13]See *An Interpretation of Whitehead's Metaphysics*, pp. 311-312.

EXTENSION AND ABSTRACTION

WHITEHEAD'S philosophy of organism presents an alternative to a deterministic theory of causation. The attempt is made in this philosophy to provide an explanation of both novelty and determination. This explanation is based on three principal assumptions: a) there exist properties and relations of actual entities which are independent of position; b) the extensive relations which hold among actual entities govern the manner in which causal transmission occurs, but do not govern what is transmitted; and, c) physical feelings are the only agency of causal transmission. The following is a sketch of a theory which intends to elucidate these assumptions. The basic language used is set theory. In it we shall first sketch a theory of physical feelings, then one of extension. With the aid of these two theories we shall present a theory of definiteness. These theories shall be used to reformulate the above assumptions.

Our initial universe of discourse is set S and two subsets S_1 and S_2. Every feeling except satisfactions are members of S. S_1 is the set of all physical feelings and S_2 is the set of all conceptual feelings. We assume that S_1 and S_2 are disjoint and that the union of S_1 and S_2 is S.[1]

F is a many-one, asymmetric and irreflexive relation whose first place members are the members of S_1 and whose second place members are the members of S. If S_j is a subset of S_1, then '$F(S_j)$' is to mean 'the set of all second place members of F whose first place members are members of S_j'. Thus, we have that $F(S_1) = S$. "F" may be read "is a physical feeling of."

Every feeling must be felt physically.[2] Since we require F to be many-one, we do not countenance complex physical feelings. There is no x which is a member of S_1 for which there exist distinct y and z which are members of S such that Fxy and Fxz. This feature of F seems to be consistent with the category of objective diversity.[3]

[1]Alfred North Whitehead, *Process and Reality; An Essay in Cosmology* (New York: The Social Science Book Store, 1929), p. 365.

[2]*Ibid.*, p. 366.

[3]*Ibid.*, p. 39.

E is an equivalence relation whose field is S. "E" may be read "has the same subject as." The set A of all the equivalence subsets of S with respect to E is the set of all actual entities.[4]

If $X \in A$, then $X \cap S_1$ is the set of all the physical feelings of X and $F(X \cap S_1)$ is the set of all the objective data of X. The set of all $Y \in A$ for which $F(X \cap S_1) \cap Y \neq O$ is the set of initial data of X, or what is the same, the actual world of X.[5] If $X \in A$ and $Y \in A$, we may say that 'X feels Y' means 'there are x and y such that $x \in X$, $y \in Y$ and Fxy'.[6]

The following statements elucidate some of the basic properties of actual entities and feelings:

1. If Exy, then not Fxy and not Fyx.
2. If Exy, then there is no z such that both Fxz and Fyz.
3. If Exy, Ezw and Fxz, then not Fwy.
4. If $X \in A$, $Y \in A$ and $X \neq Y$ then world of $X \neq$ world of Y and world of X $\cap$ world of Y $\neq O$.
5. If X feels Y, then world $Y \subset$ world of X.

Statement 1 says that no actual entity feels its own feelings.[7] Statement 2 reproduces the category of objective identity.[8] According to 3, actual entities are asymmetrically ordered by their physical feelings.[9] Statements 4 and 5 reproduce some of the requirements of the fifth category of explanation.[10]

We may say that 'X directly feels Y' is to mean 'X feels Y and there is no Z such that X feels Z and Z feels Y'. Since feels is a transitive, irreflexive and asymmetric relation, then directly feels is an intransitive, irreflexive and asymmetric relation. Any two actual entities may be joined by a finite number of directly feels and directly feels[-1] steps. This is so, because the actual world of any two actual entities must overlap (4 above), hence there exists at least one other entity which they both feel.[11]

[4]Ibid., pp. 436–8.

[5]Ibid., pp. 33–34, 374, 435–6.

[6]Ibid., pp. 361–4.

[7]Whitehead distinguishes between integrations and feelings. See Categories of Explanation XXII, XXIII, XXVII. Ibid., pp. 38–9.

[8]Ibid., p. 39.

[9]Ibid., pp. 363–4.

[10]Ibid., p. 33.

[11]Ibid., pp. 127–167, 351–2.

According to the twentieth category of explanation, to function in an actual entity X is the same as contributing definiteness or position to X.[12] Position is to be explicated in terms of the relative status of X in a nexūs of other entities. The definiteness of X is to be explicated in terms of the illustration of selected eternal objects. The position which X occupies does not determine entirely the eternal objects which X illustrates. Conversely, the eternal objects which X illustrates do not determine uniquely the position of X.[13] The position of X relative to some other entities is defined by nexūs which lie in the actual world of X. The actual world of X is unique to X while eternal objects are not.

In order to explicate 'position' we shall make use of some of the predicates of the theory of extensive abstraction. 'Con' to be read 'is connected with' is the sole primitive predicate of this theory. The predicates 'Part' ('is a part'), 'Over' ('overlaps'), 'Diss' ('is a dissection of'), 'Excon' ('is externally connected with'), 'Abs' ('is an abstractive set'), 'Cov' ('covers'), 'Geo' ('is a geometric element'), 'Incid' ('is incident in'), 'Pnt' ('is a point'), 'Seg' ('is a segment'), 'Ln' ('is a line'), 'Ag' ('is an aggregate of'), 'Conn' ('is connected'), 'Ovoid' ('is an ovoid') are defined by means of 'Con'.

The definitions and some of the main features of these predicates are as follows:

6. Con is a non-transitive, reflexive relation such that for every x there is a y for which not Conxy.
7. $Con \subset Con^2$ and $SxS \subset Con^2$.
8. 'Partxy' means 'for every z if Conxz, then Conyz'; Part is transitive, antisymmetric and reflexive.
9. 'Over' means '$Part^2$'; Over is symmetric, reflexive, and non-transitive, $Part \subset Over \subset Con$.
10. 'Excon' means 'the complement of Over relative to Con'; Excon is symmetric, non-transitive and irreflexive.
11. 'Dissyz' means 'the members of y are non-overlapping parts of z such that for every w, Overwz, if and only if there is a u $u \epsilon y$ and Overwu'; Diss is many-one from subsets of the field of Con to the members of the field of Con.
12. 'Nontanpart' means 'the largest subset of Part which is disjoint from $Excon^2$'; Nontanpart is transitive, asymmetric, irreflexive

[12]*Ibid.*, p. 38.
[13]*Ibid.*, pp. 296, 440–1.

and every member of S is both a first and a second place member of Nontanpart.

13. 'Absy' means 'Nontanpart ∩ (yxy) is a series without initial members'; Abs is a set of subsets of the field of Con which cover it.

14. 'Coverxy' means 'for every z, z∈x, then there is a w, w∈y and Nontanpartwz'; Cover is transitive and reflexive, the field of Cover is Abs.

15. 'Geo' means 'the set of equivalence subsets of Abs with respect to Cover ∩ Cover⁻¹'.

16. 'Incidxy' means 'for every z and w if z∈x, w∈y, then Coverwz'; Incid is a transitive, antisymmetric and reflexive relation whose field is Geo.

17. 'Pntx' means 'for every y if Incidyx, then y = x'; Pnt ⊂ Geo.

18. 'Segx' means 'there exist y and z, Pnty, Pntz, Incidyx, Incidzx and for every u if u ≠ x and Incidux, then not both Incidzu and Incidyu'; Seg ∩ Pnt = O and Seg ⊂ Geo.

19. 'Lnx' means 'not Segx and for any y if x ≠ y and Incidyx, then Pnty or Segy'; Ln ∩ Seg = Ln ∩ Pnt = O and Ln ⊂ Geo.

20. 'Agxy' means 'for every z Overzx, if and only if there is a w, w∈y and Overwz'; Diss⁻¹ ⊂ Ag.

21. 'Connx' means 'there are no y, z and w such that not Conzw, y = {z, w} and Agxy'.

22. 'Ovoid' means 'the unique set z for which any y and x, y∈z, x∈z and Overyx, if and only if there is a u part of both x and y of which anything else which is part of both x and y is part of u and Connu (i.e. the largest common part of x and y is connected). Furthermore, if any x is not a member of z, then there exists some y, y∈z which overlaps x in such a way that the largest common part of x and y is not connected'. Ovoid ⊂ Conn.[14]

We assume that S ⊂ Conn and S is a subset of the field of Con such that every other member of the field of Con is the aggregate of some subset of S.[15] We also assume that for any X∈A, there exists a unique x such that Connx and AgxX. Such a unique aggregate of feelings is the satisfaction of X.[16] The satisfaction of an actual entity is divisible

[14]*Ibid.*, pp. 449–471.
[15]*Ibid.*, pp. 441–4.
[16]*Ibid.*, pp. 438, 448.

into feelings which are parts of the satisfaction; furthermore, there are no parts of the satisfaction which do not overlap some feelings.[17] Let S_3 be the set of all the satisfactions, then S_3 is the set of all the aggregates of members of A, and S_3 is a subset of Conn.

Some of the more obvious assumptions which must be made in order to accommodate Whitehead's theory of feelings are as follows:

23. If X feels Y, x is the satisfaction of X and y is the satisfaction of Y, then not Overxy.

24. x is the satisfaction of X, y is the satisfaction of Y and Exconxy, if and only if either X directly feels Y or Y directly feels X.[18]

A nexus is a subset A_j of A such that the aggregate of the satisfactions of the members of A_j is a connected entity. A_j is a nexus, if and only if there exists an $S_j \subset S_3$ such that every member of S_j is the aggregate of a member of A_j and conversely every member of A_j has an aggregate which is a member of S_j, where the aggregate of S_j is a connected entity.[19] Let the set S_4 be the set of all the connected aggregates of satisfactions, then the union of S, S_3 and S_4 is the set of all the entities which are connected: $S \cup S_3 \cup S_4 = $ Conn.

A feeling, a part of a feeling or any aggregate of feelings x has a unique set y of geometric elements associated to it. We may say that 'y is the geometric form of x' means 'y $\subset$ Geo and for any z, zϵy, if and only if x overlaps every member of every abstractive set which is a member of z and x also overlaps every member of every abstractive set which is a member of every geometric element incident in z'. The geometric form of any member of the field of Con is a subset of the geometric form of the aggregate of S. This is so because every member of the field of Con is an aggregate of some subset of S, hence every member of the field of Con is a part of the aggregate of S.

If x_1 and x_2 are distinct, then there is a part of x_1 which is not a part of x_2 or *vice versa*. Suppose Partux$_1$ and not Partux$_2$, then the geometric form of u is a subset of the geometric form of x_1 and not a subset of the geometric form of x_2. Therefore, the geometric forms of x_1 and x_2 are distinct. If y_1 and y_2 are distinct geometric forms of x_1 and x_2 respectively, then there is a geometric element which is a member of y_1, and not of y_2 or *vice versa*. Suppose g is a member of y_1 and not

17*Ibid.*, pp. 433–48.
18*Ibid.*, p. 468.
19*Ibid.*, pp. 351–2, 439.

of y_2, then x_1 overlaps every member of every abstractive set which is a member of g and also overlaps every member of every abstractive set which is a member of any h incident in g while x_2 does not. Hence there must be an entity u which overlaps x_1 and does not overlap x_2. Therefore x_1 is distinct from x_2. The geometric form of any x is unique to x.

The volume of a feeling, a part of a feeling or an aggregate of feelings x is a subset of the geometric form of x. We may say that 'z is the volume of x' means 'for any y, $y \epsilon z$, if and only if y is a point which is a member of the geometric form of some non-tangential part of x'.[20] The volume of x is composed of all the points which are "interior" to x. Since each x has a unique geometric form, each x also has a unique volume. The volume of any feeling is a subset of the volume of the aggregate of S.

According to Whitehead the volume of the aggregate of S, y_s, satisfies the following conditions: a) any two distinct points which are members of y_s are incident in a line that has among its members at least one abstractive set composed entirely of ovoids (i.e. every two points are incident in one straight line); b) there exists a set $S_c \subset Conn$ such that if $X \epsilon A$ and $X \cap S_c \neq O$, then $X \subset S_c$; c) there exists a $y_c \subset y_s$ such that the volume of every feeling which is a member of S_c is a subset of y_c and y_c is four dimensional; and, d) if $X \subset S_c$ and $X \epsilon A$, then every member of the world of X is a subset of S_c.[21] The set S_c is the set of all the feelings of our cosmic epoch, y_c is the four dimensional volume of the aggregate of S_c, and S_c stretches indefinitely into the past. The set y_s need not be four dimensional, but it must contain a four dimensional subset.

The condition that every two points of y_s be incident in one straight line imposes severe restrictions on the composition of the membership of S. S must be densely populated with ovoidal feelings.

The members of the field of Con impose an order upon the points which are the member of y_s. Since each member of the field of Con has a volume, let V be the set of all the volumes of the members of the field of Con. V is a set of subsets of y_s which has the following properties: a) $y_s \epsilon V$; b) if $V_j \subset V$, then the union of the members of V_j is a member of V; and c) if $V_j \subset V$ and V_j is finite, then the intersection of the

20 *Ibid.*, p. 458.
21 *Ibid.*, p. 464.

members of V_j is a member of V. In other words, the ordered pair (y_s, V) is a topological space.

Since we have assumed that S and all the aggregates of subsets of S are in the field of Con, then the aggregate of S must be a member of the field of Con. Therefore, y_s, the volume of the aggregate of S, must be a member of V. If V_j is a subset of V, then there exists a corresponding subset S_j of the field of Con such that the union of the members of V_j is the volume of the aggregate of S_j. Therefore, the union of the members of V_j is a member of V. If V_j is a finite subset of V, then there exists a finite subset S_j of the field of Con such that V_j is the set of volumes of the members of S_j. If there exists an $x \epsilon S$ such that x is a part of every $y \epsilon S_j$ and furthermore x is the largest common part of every y, then the intersection of the members of V_j is the volume of x. Such an x always exists if the members of S_j overlap each other and S_j is finite. If S_j were not finite, we could not guarantee the existence of such an x even if the members of S_j overlapped each other. For example, suppose S_j were an abstractive set, then there would not exist an x which is a part of every member of S_j, but the members of S_j would overlap each other. If the members of S_j do not overlap each other, then the intersection of the members of V_j is null. Of course we require that the null set of points, the volume of no member of the field of Con, be also a member of V.

The position of any feeling relative to others may be specified in terms of the relative position of the points which are members of their respective volumes. The position of an actual entity relative to other actual entities may be specified in terms of the relative positions of the points which are members of the volumes of their satisfactions.[22] The relative position of points may be specified by a metric. A metric is a distance function d which assigns to each pair of points of y_s a real number $\geq O$ and such that: a) $d(x,z) = O$, if and only if $x = z$; b) $d(x,z) = d(z,x)$; and c) $d(x,z) \leq d(x,y) + d(y,z)$.

The topological space (y_s, V) is metrizable if there exists a metric d such that the sets which are open in the sense of the metric are all and only the members of V. A condition sufficient to insure that (y_s, V) is metrizable is that (y_s, V) be a normal space with a denumerable base.

If x and z are two distinct points of y_s, then there must be an abstractive set $w \in x$ and an abstractive set $u \in z$ such that the members of the convergent tail of u and v do not overlap. Let us say x' and z' are members of w and u respectively and not Over$x'z'$. Then the volume of x' is a member of V and so is the volume of z'. Furthermore, x is a member of the volume of x' and z is a member of the volume of z'. Hence every two distinct points of y_s are members of disjoint members of V. Distinct points of y_s may be said to be "separated" by the members of V.

Let y_j and y_k be disjoint subsets of y_s such that $\overline{y}_j \in V$ and $\overline{y}_k \in V$. In other words, the complements of y_j and y_k are members of V. If $y \in V$ and $\overline{y}$ is the volume of x, then let z be the largest part of the aggregate of S which does not overlap x. Not Overxz and p is a point which is a member of the geometric form of z, if and only if p is not a member of the geometric form of any non-tangential part of x. Thus, any point is a member of the geometric form of z, if and only if it is a member of y and $\overline{y} \in V$. The set y_j is composed of all and only the points of the geometric form of z_j and the set y_k is composed of all and only the points of the geometric form of z_k. If Con$z_j z_k$, then the geometric forms of z_k and z_j must share at least one geometric element g. Every point which is incident in g must be a member of both y_k and y_j. This is contrary to the hypothesis that y_k and y_j are disjoint, hence not Con$z_j z_k$. This implies that there exists u_j and u_k such that Part$z_j u_j$, Part$z_k u_k$ and not Over$u_j u_k$ (see 12 above). Thus the set y_k is a subset of the volume of u_k, the set y_j is a subset of the volume of u_j and the volumes of u_j and u_k are disjoint members of V. Disjoint "closed" subsets of y_s may be said to be "separated" by the members of V.

If distinct points of y_s and disjoint closed subsets of y_s may be separated by the members of V, then (y_s, V) is normal. The space (y_s, V) has a denumerable base just in case there exists a $V_j \subset V$ such that V_j is denumerable and every member of V is the union of some members of V_j. If we suppose that the volumes of the physical feelings form such a base, then it follows that the set S_1 is denumerable. But of course the set of points y_s need not be denumerable. Perhaps it would be better to suppose that a subset S_j of the set S_1 of all physical feelings is denumerable and that the set of volumes of the members of S_j is a base V_j for the space (y_s, V). The set S_j may be called the set of primary feelings in that every other member of S is an aggregate of some subset of S_j.

Once a metric d is fixed for the space (y_s, V), then the interpretation that d receives depends upon the relations which hold among feelings.

If p_1 is a point which belongs to the volume of some feeling which is a member of an actual entity X and p_2 is a point which belongs to the volume of some feeling which is a member of an actual entity Y, then $d(p_1,p_2)$ is a spatiotemporal distance if X feels Y or Y feels X. The distance $d(p_1,p_2)$ is spatial if neither Y feels X nor X feels Y.[23] Further development of the theory of position depends on the choice of the metric for (y_s,V) and on the restrictions imposed upon the actual worlds of the actual entities by the existence of physical constants of transmission.

The notion of "actuality" explicated so far is non-relative. We may now introduce relative concepts of actuality and position. In terms of these concepts we will then explicate the notion of definiteness. The entities which are actual relative to some actual entity X are all of those which are members of the actual world of X. We may also say that the position of some actual entities is determinate relative to X if they are members of the actual world of X. More precisely, 'the members of A_j are positioned relative to X' means 'A_j is a subset of the actual world of X'. If x is a feeling or an aggregate of feelings, then we may say that 'the members of S_j are positioned relative to x' means: 'a) S_j is a subset of the field of Con; b) there exists a set $S_k \subset S$ such that every member of S_j is an aggregate of some subset of S_k and there is no member of S_k which is not a part of some member of S_j; c) there exists a set $S_i \subset S$ such that x is the aggregate of S_i; and, d) the set of all the actual entities whose intersection with S_k is non-null is positioned relative to every actual entity whose intersection with S_i is non-null'.

We shall assume that an eternal object is a subset of A or a subset of the field of Con that is not positioned relative to any actual entities nor positioned relative to any feelings and aggregates of feelings. If A_j is an eternal object such that $A_j \subset A$, then there exists a corresponding eternal object S_j which is a subset of the field of Con and S_j is the union of the members of A_j. Thus for our purposes we shall only need to consider eternal objects which are subsets of the field of Con. The definition of eternal object is as follows: 'S_j is an eternal object' means 'S_j is a subset of the field of Con and there is no x such that the members of S_j are positioned relative to x'.[24]

In our language eternal objects correspond to non-localized prop-

[23]*Ibid.*, p. 508.
[24]*Ibid.*, pp. 32, 38, 69–70, 283–7, 364–5, 443–7.

erties and relations. This is so because if 'F' is any sentential function and 'S' and 'S$_j$' are not free in F, then there is an axiom to the effect that given any set S, there exists a set S$_j$ whose members are the members of S which have the property F. F is independent of position if the set S$_j$ is an eternal object. F is localized or dependent on position if the set S$_j$ is not an eternal object.

The definiteness of an entity x may be thought of as the collection of all the properties of x which are independent of position. More precisely, we may say that 'D is the form of definiteness of x' means 'for any S$_j$, S$_j$ ∈ D, if and only if S$_j$ is an eternal object and x ∈ S$_j$'. If x is a feeling or an aggregate of feelings, then D is a set of subsets of the field of Con.[25] In those cases where X is an actual entity we shall consider instead the aggregate of feelings which are members of X. In other words we shall consider the satisfaction of X.

Let us suppose that Dx is the form of definiteness of x and that Connx. In other words: x is a feeling; or, x is a satisfaction; or, x is the aggregate of the satisfactions of actual entities which are the members of a nexus. We may divide Dx into five subsets as follows: a) if Partyx and Dy is the form of definiteness of y, then Dxy is the set of all the eternal objects which are members of both Dx and Dy; b) if Partxy and Dy is the form of definiteness of y, then Dyx is the set of all the eternal objects which are members of both Dx and Dy; c) Dxu is the set of all the eternal objects which are members of Dx and Dxy for every y; d) Dux is the set of all the eternal objects which are members of Dx and Dyx for every y; and e) Dxd is the set of all the eternal objects which are members of Dx and are neither members of Dyx nor members of Dxy.

We shall require that the sets Dxy, Dyx, Dxu, Dux, and Dxd be non-null; if and only if Connx. In other words, if x is a feeling, or x is a satisfaction, or x is the aggregate of the satisfaction of actual entities which are members of a nexus, then x, with respect to non-positional properties, has an individuality (i.e. Dxd ≠ O) and a unity (i.e. Dxy ≠ O, Dxu ≠ O) which arbitrary aggregates do not have.[26]

We are now in a position to consider physical feelings as transmission. If x is a physical feeling of y then the volumes v$_x$ and v$_y$ of x and y respectively are subvolumes of the volume of the aggregate of S. The

[25]*Loc. cit.*
[26]*Ibid.*, p. 348.

set V_x of subsets of v_x is the set of all the volumes of parts of x. That is to say that every member of V_x is the intersection of V_x with some members of V. Similarly the set V_y is the set of all the volumes of parts of y. It may be ascertained that the ordered pairs (v_x, V_x) and (x_y, V_y) are subspaces of (y_s, V). If x is a feeling of y, then there must exist a continuous transformation of (v_y, V_y) onto (v_x, V_x) such that the non-localized properties of y are transmitted onto x. More precisely, a physical feeling satisfies the following condition:

> 25. If Fxy, then there exists a homeomorphism H (i.e. H is bicontinuous and one-one) or (v_y, V_y) onto (x_x, V_x) such that for any z, v and D, Partzy, v is the volume of z and D is the form of definiteness of z, if and only if there is a w, Partwx, H(v) is the volume of w and D is the form of definiteness of w.

The feeling x and its objective datum y conform in the sense that the forms of definiteness of x and y are identical and the forms of definiteness of parts of x and parts of y which have corresponding volumes are likewise identical.[27] Corresponding points p_x and p_y of v_x and v_y respectively (i.e. $H(p_y) = p_x$) will belong to the volumes of parts of x and y which have identical forms of definiteness. Thus, to every point p_y of v_y and to the corresponding point $H(p_y)$ of v_x we may assign the set of all the forms of definiteness of parts of y such that p_y belongs to their volume.[28] This set of forms of definiteness is invariant under the transformation H.

Suppose the following: a) X and Y are actual entities and X feels Y; b) x is the satisfaction of X; c) y is the satisfaction of Y; d) Fx_1y_1 and $Partx_1x$, $Party_1y$; and e) Dx_1, Dy_1, Dx and Dy are the forms of definiteness of x_1, y_1, x, and y respectively. From assumption 25 we have that $Dx_1 = Dy_1$, hence $Dxx_1 \cap Dyy_1 = Dx \cap Dx_1 \cap Dy \cap Dy_1 = Dx \cap Dy \cap Dy_1$. It may be shown that a feeling is always a proper part of a satisfaction (see 4 above). The set S_3 of all satisfactions is disjoint from the set S of all feelings. S_3 is an eternal object which is a member of the form of definiteness of any satisfaction and not a member of the form of definiteness of any feeling. $S_3 \cup S$ is an eternal object which is a member of the form of definiteness of every satisfaction and feeling. Thus $\{S_3 \cup S\} \subset Dxx_1 \cap Dyy_1 = Dx \cap Dy \cap Dy_1 \cap Dy$. We may say

27 *Ibid.*, pp. 361–7, 441, 445–7.
28 *Ibid.*, pp. 472–3.

that X feels Y by abstracting a subset $D = Dxx_1 \cap Dyy_1$ from the form of definiteness of Y. D may be neither null nor equal to the form of definiteness of Y.

The assumption that feelings are the only agency of transmission may be worded as follows:

26. If neither X feels Y nor Y feels X, then the intersection of the forms of definiteness of X and Y is a subset of the form of definiteness of some actual entity Z such that both X feels Z and Y feels Z.[29]

In other words, the actual entities which do not feel each other share only those non-localized properties which they share with some third actual entity that they both feel.

LUCIO CHIARAVIGLIO

UNIVERSITY OF DELAWARE

[29]*Ibid.*, pp. 363–4, 375–77.

LANGUAGE AND WHITEHEAD'S CONCEPTION
OF SPECULATIVE PHILOSOPHY

THE CHESHIRE cat's advice to Alice is sound advice for the philosopher: the solution to any problem concerning method "depends a great deal on where you want to get to." In the beginning of *Process and Reality*, Whitehead is quite explicit when he tells us where the speculative philosopher wants to get to. His task is "to frame a coherent, logical, necessary system of general ideas in terms of which every element of our experience can be interpreted."[1] By 'interpreted' he means that "everything of which we are conscious, as enjoyed, perceived, willed, or thought, shall have the character of a particular instance of the general scheme."[2] Interpretation, however, is the task of both science and philosophy as Whitehead views them;[3] the difference between the two lies in the universality and necessity of the ideas of speculative philosophy. For this reason he adds to the two criteria of logicality and coherence the criterion of applicability—that is, some items of experience are thus interpretable—and the criterion of adequacy—that is, there are no items incapable of such interpretation. It is this latter criterion which seems to assure the universality and, consequently, the necessity of the philosophical scheme.

It is generally understood that such a scheme of general ideas, according to Whitehead, forms what has traditionally been called the categories of a metaphysical system. Some would, no doubt, question this particular definition of the metaphysical task. To argue, however, for the use of the terms 'metaphysics' and 'categories' in this particular connection, although it has obvious justification in the history of philosophy, is beyond the scope of this paper. Whatever name one wishes to assign to this particular task, it is certainly a legitimate philosophical endeavor. For the purposes of this essay, this definition

[1]Alfred North Whitehead, *Process and Reality* (New York: Humanities Press, 1951), p. 4.

[2]*Ibid.*

[3]Alfred North Whitehead, *Adventures of Ideas* (New York: Macmillan Co., 1933), p. 144.

of the task of speculative philosophy will be accepted as an explication of the traditional task of metaphysics.

When it comes to the problem, however, of method—*how* we can get to where we want to go—we are about as bewildered as Alice. Here Whitehead is not quite so explicit. He tells us that these general ideas are "inevitably presupposed in our reflective experience."[4] But rather than give us a precise method for obtaining this general scheme, Whitehead is generally more concerned with the application of his general ideas to the data of experience, what he calls the construction of a cosmology: "unflinchingly to explore the interpretation of experience in terms of that scheme."[5] Having accepted, however, the construction of such a scheme of general ideas as the goal of the metaphysical endeavor, it is the metaphysician's task to continue to seek the most effective method for getting there. The purpose of this essay is to suggest and explore a method which seems to promise some degree of precision and effectiveness.

Whitehead does not, however, leave us quite as much in the dark, concerning a possible origin of this scheme of general ideas, as it might at first appear. A key for the metaphysical task is found in the two conditions for the success of imaginative construction: "In the first place, this construction must have its origin in the generalization of particular factors discerned in particular topics of human interest; for example, in physics, or in physiology, or in psychology, or in aesthetics, or in ethical beliefs, or in sociology, or in language conceived as storehouses of human experience."[6] It is the latter, "language conceived as storehouses of human experience," which appears to be the most fruitful for metaphysical construction: "the general agreement of mankind as to experienced facts is best expressed in language."[7] It is language, after all, which we use to construct and systematize all of our theories, whether they be physical or ethical, physiological or aesthetical. Should not language itself, then, exemplify the most general ideas in terms of which we do in fact attempt to interpret "every element of our experience"?

The second condition given by Whitehead for the success of imag-

---

[4]Whitehead, *Process and Reality*, p. 27.

[5]*Ibid.*, p. x.

[6]*Ibid.*, p. 7.

[7]*Ibid.*, p. 16.

inative construction is the "unflinching pursuit of the two rationalistic ideals, coherence and logical perfection."[8] Unfortunately,
language, as we find it in common parlance, falls far short of this
ideal. It is too heterogeneous and, at times, hopelessly vague and
ambiguous. Its rules are far too incomplete for scientific purposes and,
in some cases, even contradictory. Much of philosophical analysis
today is concerned with the investigation and clarification of the
meanings of terms as they are used in ordinary discourse. Such philosophical investigations are, no doubt, quite valuable for ridding ordinary language of some of its ambiguities, but as Quine has pointed
out, "it passes over, as irrelevant, one important aspect of philosophical analysis—the creative aspect, which is involved in the progressive refinement of scientific language."[9] It is this "progressive
refinement" of language which has been one of the major factors in
the continuing advancement and success of the sciences and has been
the impetus for the contemporary construction of syntactical and
semantical metalanguages for formal theories. Thus philosophy, writes
Whitehead, "must redesign language in the same way that, in physical
science, pre-existing appliances are redesigned."[10] The language of
ordinary parlance will, of course, always be in the background as a
reservoir from which to draw, but since it is the refined, or formal,
languages which are the most effective tools which we have for the
construction of theories, it is to them and to their success that the
metaphysician must direct his major attention.[11] For Peirce, in a sense,
is right: "Metaphysical conceptions . . . are merely adapted from those
of formal Logic, and therefore can only be apprehended in the light
of a minutely accurate and thorough-going system of formal Logic."[12]
But the precise relationship between metaphysical conceptions and
those of formal logic needs to be made explicit. This is the major
burden of the present essay.

[8]*Ibid.*, p. 8.

[9]W. V. Quine, *From a Logical Point of View* (Cambridge: Harvard University
Press, 1953), p. 106.

[10]Whitehead., *op. cit.*, p. 16.

[11]The advantages of formalization have been ably discussed in R. M. Martin,
Truth and Denotation (Chicago: University of Chicago Press, 1958), pp. 8–15, and, I
trust, need not be argued here.

[12]Charles Hartshorne and Paul Weiss, *Collected Papers of Charles Sanders Peirce*,
1 (Cambridge: Harvard University Press, 1931), 344 (1.625).

Most of the work in contemporary syntactical and semantical theory has been done with a view toward constructing particular axiomatic systems, or languages, for the investigation and construction of particular scientific theories. Such work, however, is only preliminary to the distinctly metaphysical task as outlined in the beginning of this essay. The distinctly metaphysical problem is pointed to in a question which Charles Hartshorne has put to logical positivism: "What meanings are common to all languages? The definitions of these meanings will have universal, that is, metaphysical relevance."[13] It is perhaps asking too much—and in another sense far too little—of metaphysics to require it to discover those meanings common to all possible languages. But if metaphysics seeks to frame "a system of general ideas in terms of which every element of our experience can be interpreted," it must seek those ideas which are, in some sense, common to those theories, or languages, which have demonstrated some success in describing the world which is disclosed to us in experience. What is needed for this metaphysical task is a tool for analyzing entire families of languages—for example, those languages which are usually called first order languages—comparing and relating them to other families of languages.

A technique which immediately suggests itself, and with some hope of success, is the technique of mirroring theories, or languages, in algebras and exploring their relationships with the tools of modern abstract algebra. The possibility of mirroring theories in an algebra has been known since George Boole and the construction of the algebra which bears his name. The particular program of analysis used in this essay is based on the recent work of Paul Halmos on the algebra of logic,[14] a series of papers directed primarily to the mathematician, but which should be quite fruitful for the logician and philosopher as well.

Since Boolean algebras will form the basic tool of analysis, it is perhaps wise to have a definition of a Boolean algebra before us. The most general definition of 'an algebra' is 'a couple (S,O) consisting of a non-empty set S of elements and a set of operations O defined on S.'

---

[13]Charles Hartshorne, "Metaphysics for Positivists," *Philosophy of Science*, **2** (1935), 298.

[14]See particularly: Paul R. Halmos, "The Basic Concepts of Algebraic Logic," *American Mathematical Monthly*, **63** (1956), 365–387; and "Algebraic Logic, I. Monadic Boolean Algebras," *Compositio Mathematica*, **12** (1955), 217–249.

There are many different ways of characterizing a Boolean algebra, but perhaps the most convenient for the purposes of this essay will be the following:

D.1 'B* is a Boolean Algebra' for 'B* is a triple (B, $\wedge$, ') consisting of a non-empty set B of elements and a binary operation $\wedge$ and a unary operation ' defined on B such that it meets the conditions B1-B8.'

   B1. If α is in B, then α' is in B.
   B2. If α and β are in B, then $\alpha \wedge \beta$ is in B.
   B3. If α and β are in B, then $\alpha \wedge \beta = \beta \wedge \alpha$.
   B4. If α, β and γ are in B, then $(\alpha \wedge \beta) \wedge \gamma = \alpha \wedge (\beta \wedge \gamma)$.
   B5. If α, β and γ are in B and $\alpha \wedge \beta' = \gamma \wedge \gamma'$, then $\alpha \wedge \beta$
        $= \alpha$.
   B6. If α, β and γ are in B and $\alpha \wedge \beta = \alpha$, then $\alpha \wedge \beta' = \gamma$
        $\wedge \gamma'$.
   B7. If α and β are in B and $\alpha = \beta$, then $\alpha' = \beta'$.
   B8. If α, β and γ are in B and $\alpha = \beta$, then $\alpha \wedge \gamma = \beta \wedge \gamma$.

With such a set B and two operations meeting these conditions, the Boolean join $\vee$ can be defined in terms of meet and complement, '$\alpha \vee \beta$' for '$(\alpha' \wedge \beta')'$', the zero and unit elements by '1' for '$\alpha \wedge \alpha'$', and '0' for '$\alpha \wedge \alpha'$', and the ordering relation $\leq$ by '$\alpha \leq \beta$' for '$\alpha \wedge \beta = \alpha$.'[15]

Let us characterize a theory, or language, as a set S of declarative sentences. It seems reasonable to require that this set meet certain conditions. If s and t, for instance, are two arbitrary acceptable sentences of S, then Ns and Ast (where 'N' and 'A' are given the usual heuristic interpretation of 'not_____' and 'both_____and_____') should be acceptable sentences of the theory. Let us call these two conditions S1 and S2:

   S1. If s is in S, then Ns is in S.
   S2. If s and t are in S, then Ast is in S.

This characterization of a theory, however, is obviously too incomplete for any fruitful purpose. If s and t, for example, are two distinct sentences of a theory S, then Ast and Ats are also two distinct sentences

---

[15]These additional definitions, and the following analogous ones, will always be considered a part of the algebra under consideration.

of the theory. But we would like to be able to say that although Ast and Ats are two distinct sentences, they "mean the same thing." Thus another thing that is needed in order to characterize a theory is an equivalence relation. Let us consider any equivalence relation $\equiv^*$ which meets the conditions S3-S8:

S3. If s and t are in S, then Ast $\equiv^*$Ats.
S4. If s, t and u are in S, then AsAtu $\equiv^*$AAstu.
S5. If s, t and u are in S and AsNt $\equiv^*$AuNu, then Ast $\equiv^*$s.
S6. If s, t and u are in S and Ast $\equiv^*$s, then AsNt $\equiv^*$AuNu.
S7. If s and t are in S and s $\equiv^*$t, then Ns $\equiv^*$Nt.
S8. If s, t and u are in S and s $\equiv^*$t, then Asu $\equiv^*$Atu.

The need for all of these conditions should be obvious if the heuristic interpretation of the equivalence relation is to be "means the same as." There may be, however, many equivalence relations on a set S which satisfy these conditions. The equivalence relation, for instance, defined by s $\equiv^*$t for any arbitrary sentences of S meets these conditions. In order to avoid this triviality, and for other obvious reasons, what is needed is the intersection of all the equivalence relations on the set S meeting conditions S3-S8, or what amounts to the same thing, the smallest equivalence relation on S meeting these conditions. Let us denote this relation by '$\equiv$.' The pair (S, $\equiv$), considered in abstraction from any other properties which sentences might have, forms one of the most important structures in logic—the sentential calculus. We have, then the following definition:

D.2 'S* is a sentential calculus' for 'S* is a pair (S, $\equiv$) in which S is a set of declarative sentences meeting conditions S1 and S2 and $\equiv$ is the smallest equivalence relation on S meeting conditions S3-S8.'

A comparison of conditions B1-B8 and S1-S8 will disclose a striking similarity, but technically speaking the pair (S, $\equiv$) is not a Boolean algebra. Ast and Ats are two distinct elements of S which, according to the heuristic interpretation which guided the construction of the equivalence relation, "mean the same thing," whereas $\alpha \wedge \beta$ and $\beta \wedge \alpha$ are the same element in B*. What is needed is a trick for converting the two distinct elements, Ast and Ats, into one element. This can be done by forming the set of all equivalence sets of the pair (S, $\equiv$), which will be denoted by '(S/$\equiv$).' Whereas the elements of the pair

(S, $\equiv$) are sentences, let us call the elements of (S/$\equiv$) propositions. Since the equivalence relation $\equiv$ was interpreted for heuristic purposes as "means the same as," this definition of a proposition gives expression to the commonly accepted notion that a proposition is the "meaning of a declarative sentence." And if we define '[s] · [t]' as '[Ast]' and '$\sim$ [s]' as '[N]s', where '[s]' denotes the equivalence set of any arbitrary s of a pair (S, $\equiv$), then we are led to the following definition:

> D.3 'P* is a propositional calculus' for 'P* is a triple (P, ·, $\sim$) where P = (S/$\equiv$) and the pair (S, $\equiv$) is a sentential calculus, and '[s]·[t]' is defined as '[Ast]' and '$\sim$[s]' as '[Ns]' for any arbitrary s and t which are members of S.'

It is an easy matter to prove that the triple (P, ·, $\sim$) is a Boolean algebra, but a comparison of B1-B8 and S1-S8 should be sufficient. As usual, 'p v q' is defined as '$\sim$($\sim$p · $\sim$q),' where p and q are arbitrary elements of P—that is, equivalence sets of (S, $\equiv$). The Boolean elements 1 and 0 are defined as follows: '1' for '[NAtNt]' and '0' for '[AtNt]' or '$\sim$1.'

Although it is not particularly essential to the discussion which follows, it might be pointed out that the notions of proof, syntactical consistency and completeness, interpretation, and tautology can be mirrored in this algebraic structure. In order to mirror the notion of a proof, we must first discover the structure of a set of provable propositions.[16] One usually assumes that if both p and q are provable propositions, then p · q is a provable proposition; and if p is a provable proposition, then p v q is provable. This structure is available in algebra in the form of a sum ideal, or filter. A sum ideal is a subset SI of a Boolean algebra such that if α and β are members of SI, then $\alpha \wedge \beta$ is a member of SI; and if α is a member of SI, then $\alpha \vee \beta$ is a member of SI, where β is any arbitrary member of B*. This is precisely what is needed to characterize a proof. A set of provable propositions, then, forms a sum ideal of a propositional calculus. Two things, whose importance is obvious, should be noted: 1 is a member of every SI; and if p $\supset$ q (that is, $\sim$(p · $\sim$q)) and p are members of an SI, then

---

[16]This development and the one in the monadic case can be considered the dual of Halmos' development. Halmos uses the notion of an ideal, the dual of a sum ideal, in order to characterize the set of refutable propositions. Since logicians are usually concerned with provable propositions rather than refutable ones, this characterization seems preferable.

q is a member of that SI. With this notion of a Boolean sum ideal, we can formulate the following definition of a Boolean propositional logic:

D.4 'P** is a Boolean propositional logic' for 'P** is a pair (P*, SI) in which P* is a propositional calculus and SI is a sum ideal contained in P*.'

A Boolean propositional logic P** can be said to be syntactically consistent if the sum ideal SI of the pair ('P*, SI) meets the following condition: for any p in P* it is not the case that both p and ~p are members of SI; that is, SI is a proper sum ideal. P** can be said to be syntactically complete if the sum ideal SI of the pair (P*, SI) meets this condition: for every p in P*, either p or ~ p is a member of SI, or what amounts to the same thing, SI is a maximal sum ideal.

The two notions of consistency and completeness have been called 'syntactical' in order to emphasize the fact that neither of these definitions takes into account which sentences might be said to be true and which false. In fact, the discussion so far has abstracted from any consideration of the semantic notions of truth and falsity. Any set of sentences, however, in order to fully qualify as a theory, must have an interpretation—that is, we must know which of the sentences are true and which false. A truth functional interpretation can be defined as a Boolean homomorphism from a Boolean propositional logic P** into a two element Boolean algebra B_2, such that every proposition is mapped into the 0 or 1 element of B_2. A Boolean homomorphism is a mapping from one Boolean algebra into another which preserves the Boolean operations: $h(\alpha \wedge \beta) = h(\alpha) \wedge h(\beta); h(\alpha \vee \beta) = h(\alpha) \vee$ interpretation t, if $t(p) = 1$, and false, if $t(p) = 0$. Common sense would assume that any sentence of the form AtNt is obviously false and any sentence of the form NAtNt obviously true. A tautology can be defined, then, as any sentence of a sentential calculus S* which is a member of the equivalence set [NAtNt], or an element of proposition 1. Since one of the characteristics of a Boolean homomorphism is $h(1) = 1$—that is, the unit element is always mapped into the unit element—the tautologies of a theory, just as we would want it, turn out to be precisely that set of sentences of the theory which, in any interpretation, is mapped into 1, or that set which is true in any interpretation.

The primary motivation for D.2 and D.3 was to get us the definition of a proposition and the fact that a propositional calculus is a Boolean algebra; these will form the basis for an analysis of propositions and the lower functional calculus. "One practical aim of metaphysics," writes Whitehead, "is the accurate analysis of propositions."[17] Since a proposition is obviously "about something," it seems natural to interpret a 'propositional function' as a function on a given non-empty set X, the domain of the language, and whose value is in a propositional calculus P*. Let us consider, then, the set P*^{x} of all functions from a set X into a propositional calculus P*, the value algebra. This set P*^{x} is itself, in a natural way, a Boolean algebra. If Φ and Ψ, for example, are in P*^{x}, then $\Phi \cap \Psi$ and $- \Phi$ are defined by '$(\Phi \cap \Psi)(x)$' for '$\Phi(x) \cdot \Psi(x)$' and '$- \Phi(x)$' for '$\sim (\Phi(x))$' for each x in X. The zero element $\wedge$ and the unit element $\vee$ of P*^{x} are defined as those functions which are constantly equal to 0 and 1 respectively. Whereas the elements (s) of S* were sentences and the elements (p) of P* were propositions, the elements (Φ) of P*^{x} are propositional functions and the elements (x) of X are the entities of the domain of the language under consideration.

It now remains to be shown how quantification theory is mirrored in this algebraic structure. Let us denote the range of Φ by '$R(\Phi)$', defined as '$\{\Phi(x): x \in X\}$.' An existentially quantified propositional function Φ has as its value the suprenum of $R(\Phi)$ at every point x in X. Thus we can write '$\exists \Phi(x)$' for '$\cup R(\Phi)$'; and by dualization, '$_\wedge \Phi(x)$' for '$\cap R(\Phi)$.' Unless, however, the value algebra, P*, is complete in the lattice sense, the suprenum and the infinum of the range of a function need not be in P*. In order to avoid making the restriction that P* be complete, let us take a subalgebra F of P*^{x} such that for every Φ in F, the suprenum $\cup R(\Phi)$ and the infinum $\cap R(\Phi)$ are elements of P*. It turns out that $\exists$ can be characterized as a mapping of F into itself which meets these conditions:

E1. $\exists (\wedge) = \wedge$
E2. $\Phi \subseteq \exists \Phi$
E3. $\exists (\Phi \cup \Psi) = \exists \Phi \cup \exists \Psi$
E4. $\exists \exists \Phi = \exists \Phi$
E5. $\exists (- (\exists \Phi)) = - (\exists \Phi)$

And by dualization, the universal quantifier, defined in the usual way

17Whitehead, *Process and Reality*, p. 17.

by '$_\forall \Phi$' for '$- (\exists (- \Phi))$,' turns out to be a mapping of F into itself which meets the following conditions:

U1. $_\forall(\lor) = \lor$
U2. $\forall \Phi \subseteq \Phi$
U3. $\forall (\Phi \cap \Psi) = _\forall \Phi \cap _\forall \Psi$
U4. $_{\forall\forall} \Phi = _\forall \Phi$
U5. $_\forall (- (_\forall \Phi)) = - (_\forall \Phi)$

For the economically minded, it might be noted that both sets of conditions, E1-E5 and U1-U5, can be reduced to smaller sets, but these have, perhaps, greater intuitive value and will enable the reader to see some relation between these conditions and the usual rules for quantification. As a result of the preceding characterizations, we are able to formulate the following definition:

D.5 'F* is a monadic lower functional calculus' for 'F* is a pair (F, $\exists$) in which F is a subalgebra of a triple $(P^{*x}, \cap, -)$ in which P^{*x} is a set of functions from a given non-empty domain X into P* and P* is a propositional calculus; and $\cap$ and $-$ are operations defined by '$(\Phi \cap \Psi)(x)$' for '$\Phi (x) \cdot \Psi (x)$' and '$- \Phi (x)$' for '$\sim (\Phi (x))$'; and $\exists$ is a mapping of F into itself meeting conditions E1-E5'.

Since $_\forall$ can be defined in terms of $\exists$, there is no need to include it in the definition of a monadic lower functional calculus. The adjective 'monadic' is used in the previous definiendum since this characterization can accommodate only monadic functions; in effect, it can not accommodate relations. The polyadic lower functional calculus which can accommodate nadic relations is a rather complex extension of the monadic case and cannot be discussed in the limits of this essay.[18] It is hoped, however, that the point of the discussion will not be impaired by excluding it from consideration.

One of the most fruitful aspects of this characterization of the lower functional calculus is that it not only defines the existential and universal quantifiers in terms of a mapping of the set of functions into itself, but it makes possible the treatment of individuals in a similar

[18]For a brief summary of polyadic algebras, see Paul R. Halmos, "Polyadic Boolean Algebras," *Proceedings of the National Academy of Sciences*, 40 (1954), 296–301.

manner.[19] What is needed is a way of expressing algebraically the effect of replacing the argument-expression by an individual constant, the name of some fixed element of the domain. If Φ, for example, is a propositional function with domain X and x_0 is an element in X, then $\Phi(x_0)$ is a proposition whose function has only one value. What is needed is a mapping which associates with every such Φ, the function $I\Phi$ where $I\Phi(x) = \Phi(x_0)$ for each x in X. This mapping I turns out to be an endomorphism on the set of propositional functions, a mapping of the set F into itself which preserves the Boolean operations. Thus we have:

I1. $I(\Phi \cup \Psi) = I(\Phi) \cup I(\Psi)$
I2. $I(\Phi \cap \Psi) = I(\Phi) \cap I(\Psi)$
I3. $I(-\Phi) = -I(\Phi)$

It should be noticed that while $\exists$ preserves only the join $\cup$ and A preserves only the meet $\cap$, I preserves both operations. As such, it can be conceived as a homomorphism from the set F into a subalgebra of F, namely the range of I, $R(I)$. Since $\exists\Phi$ is always a constant function itself—that is, a function with one value, namely $\cup R(\Phi)$—then its value at x_0 is unchanged by an application of I to $\exists\Phi$. We have, then, as a further condition for I:

I4. $I\exists(\Phi) = \exists(\Phi)$.

Conversely, since $I\Phi$ is always a constant function, an application of the existential quantifier to it leaves its value unchanged:

I5. $\exists I(\Phi) = I(\Phi)$.

An individual I of a monadic lower functional calculus F*, then, is an endomorphism on the set F(conditions I1-I3) meeting the additional condition that it is the identity mapping on the range of $\exists$, $R(\exists)$ in F*(conditions I4-I5). A few other properties of individuals which are derivable from this definition will perhaps be useful: For all Φ in F*, a.) $II\Phi = I\Phi$; b.) $I\forall\Phi = \forall\Phi$ and $\forall I\Phi = I\Phi$; c.) $I\Phi \subseteq \exists\Phi$ and $\forall\Phi \subseteq I\Phi$; and d.) $R(\forall)$ is contained in $R(I)$ is contained in $R(\exists)$.

---

[19]It is difficult to know what to term this mapping. Halmos has used the term 'individual constant,' but this is somewhat misleading, for an individual constant is usually taken to be a name. As defined here, an 'individual' seems to correspond to what Carnap has called an 'individual concept.' Rudolf Carnap, *Meaning and Necessity* (Chicago: University of Chicago Press, 1947), p. 186.

A monadic functional logic can be defined in terms of a sum ideal in much the same way as a Boolean propositional logic. A sum ideal, it will be remembered, is a subset SI of a Boolean algebra B* such that if α and β are members of SI, then $\alpha \wedge \beta$ is a member of SI; and if α is a member of SI, then $\alpha \vee \beta$ is a member of SI, where β is any arbitrary element of B*. In order to formulate a monadic sum ideal, we must add the further restriction that if Φ is a member of MoSI, then $\vee \Phi$ is a member. In effect, then, a monadic sum ideal, MoSI, of a monadic lower functional calculus F* is a subset of F* such that if Φ and Ψ are members of MoSI (as before, interpreted as provable), then $\Phi \cap \Psi$ is a member (or, analogously, provable); if Φ is a member, then $\Phi \cup \Psi$ is a member, for any arbitrary Ψ which is a member of F*; and if Φ is a member, then $\vee\Phi$ is a member. With this explanation, we are able to formulate the following definition:

D.6 'F** is a monadic functional logic' for 'F** is a pair (F*,MoSI) in which F* is a monadic lower functional calculus and MoSI is a monadic sum ideal contained in F*.'

The notions of syntactical consistency and completeness are somewhat more complicated for a monadic functional logic than for a Boolean propositional logic. Here we must introduce the notion of a closed element of a monadic functional logic: an element Φ of a monadic functional logic is said to be closed if $\exists \Phi = \Phi$. The set of all closed elements of F* corresponds to the range of $\exists$ in F*, or R($\exists$). Remembering than R($\vee$) is contained in R(I) is contained in R($\exists$) and that the elements of R($\exists$) have only one value, it is easy to see that this set of closed propositional functions is, in fact, isomorphic to the set of propositions which are their values. Thus there is in a natural way a Boolean functional logic (B*,SI) associated with every monadic functional logic (F*,MoSI) where the algebra B* is a subalgebra of F* containing all the closed elements of F* and SI is the intersection of MoSI and B*. The monadic functional logic (F*,MoSI) can be said to be syntactically consistent if the associated Boolean functional logic (B*,SI) is syntactically consistent in the sense defined above—that is, SI is a proper sum ideal—and syntactically complete, if the associated Boolean functional logic (B*,SI) is syntactically complete, or SI is a maximal sum ideal.

The concept of an interpretation of a monadic functional logic is likewise somewhat more complicated. Rather than conceiving of a truth functional interpretation as a homomorphism into a two-element Boolean algebra as before, what is needed here is the notion of a simple monadic algebra. A simple monadic algebra is a triple (B*, ∃, {1}) in which B* is a Boolean algebra, ∃ is a mapping of B* into itself meeting conditions E1-E5 and such that if ∃Φ $\neq$ 0, then ∃Φ = 1, and {1} is the trivial monadic sum ideal in B*. An interpretation of a monadic functional logic F** is a monadic homomorphism t from the pair (F*,MoSI) into a simple monadic algebra such that $t(Φ) = 1$ whenever Φ is a member of MoSI. Here, of course, 1 is interpreted as true and 0 as false.

The main purpose of this essay is to suggest a relationship between language, or logic, and speculative philosophy as conceived by Whitehead. It was promised that the preceding, somewhat informal and perhaps too sketchy, analysis would suggest such a relationship. Can this claim be made good? In this analysis we have considered certain general ideas, or a general scheme, which all theories displaying the structure of a monadic functional logic have in common. But does this general scheme bear any resemblance, for example, to what Whitehead has called the metaphysical categories, or a cosmological scheme?

This question reveals an ambiguity in the phrase 'general ideas.' Take, for instance, the notion of an individual developed in the preceding discussion. If there is any truth in the thesis of this essay, it would seem that there should be some analogy between an actual entity, the fully concrete, or determinate, individual of Whitehead's categories, and what has been called an individual in this analysis. Unfortunately, this is not quite the case. In the preceding analysis an individual was defined as an endomorphism on any monadic lower functional calculus meeting conditions I1-I5. Such an individual is fully determinate relative to a particular universe of discourse only. It will be remembered that P^{*x} is defined as a set of functions from a particular non-empty domain X into a value algebra P* (D.5). An actual entity in Whitehead's sense, however, is a fully determinate individual relative to the universe itself: "Each monadic creature is a mode of the process of 'feeling' the world, of housing the world in one unit of complex feeling, in every way determinate."[20] This idea of the entire universe must somehow be incorporated in an explication of the concept of a cosmological scheme.

20Whitehead, *op. cit.*, p. 124.

In order to develop a more adequate explication of Whitehead's notion of a scheme of categories as a basis for a cosmology, "a view of the world,"[21] it seems we must specify the domain of the scheme—that is, the elements of X. The domain of a language is usually distinguished by specifying a common characteristic which delineates the entities under consideration, or fixes the range of the individual variables. Let us take, then, the set R, the set of all spatio-temporal regions as the domain and consider a monadic functional logic, C*, defined as follows:

D.7 'C*' for 'the pair ((C, ∃*), MoSI*) in which:
    i. the pair (C, ∃*) is a lower functional calculus;
    ii. C is a triple (P^{*R}, ∩, —) in which P^{*R} is the set of all functions from the set R into P*, where R is the set of all spatio-temporal regions and P* is a complete Boolean propositional calculus, and ∩ and — are operations on the set P^{*R} defined by '(Φ ∩ Ψ)(x)' for 'Φ(x) · Ψ(x)' and '— Φ(x)' for '~(Φ(x))';[22]
    iii. ∃* is a mapping of C into itself meeting conditions E1-E5; and
    iv. MoSI* is a maximal proper sum ideal contained in the pair (C, ∃*).'

It seems that C* could justly be called a cosmological scheme with a monadic functional logic as a base.

The ability to talk about the modalities, necessity, possibility, and actuality is usually considered one of the characteristics of a metaphysical, or cosmological, scheme. Let us, for a moment, enter into what at first might appear as a digression and reconsider the previous formulation of the propositional calculus defined in D.3. Add to this formulation an additional non-Boolean operation M (to be interpreted as, "it is possible that_____") defined as a mapping of P* into itself meeting conditions M1-M5:

    M1. M(O) = O
    M2. P ⊆ Mp
    M3. M(p v q) = Mp v Mq

---

[21]Alfred North Whitehead, *Science and the Modern World* (New York: Macmillan Co., 1947), p. ix.

[22]In this definition it is not necessary to specify a subset F, as in D.5, since P* is complete in the lattice sense.

M4. MMp $=$ Mp

M5. M($\sim$(Mp)) $=$ $\sim$(Mp)

In addition define 'Np' in the usual manner as '$\sim$(M($\sim$p)).' As a consequence, we can formulate the following definition:

D.8 'MP* is a modal propositional calculus' for 'MP* is a pair (P*,M) in which P* is a propositional calculus and M is a mapping of P* into itself meeting conditions M1-M5.'

This altered propositional calculus turns out to be an algebraic formulation of Lewis' propositional calculus S_5.[23] Unlike the propositional calculus D.3, MP* is not, strictly speaking, a Boolean algebra; it is a Boolean algebra with one additional operator, M. A comparison of D.8 with D.5 will be helpful, for the lower functional calculus F*, likewise, is a Boolean algebra with one additional operator, $\exists$. In fact, a comparison of conditions M1-M5 with E1-E5 and the definitions, '$_\forall\Phi$' for '$-$($\exists$($-\Phi$))' and 'Np' for '$\sim$(M($\sim$p))' will disclose an even more striking parallel. Algebraically the monadic lower functional calculus F* and the modal propositional calculus MP* have the same structure. $\exists$ acts, in fact, as a modal operator on the set F* of propositional functions.[24] The distinction between the modal operator M on a set of propositions P* and $\exists$ on a set of propositional functions F may be compared to Von Wright's distinction between alethic modalities *de dicto* and *de re* respectively.[25] One applies to propositions and the other to properties, or propositional functions.

In the cosmological scheme C*, if $\exists$* is thought of as a modal operator, then the sets defined by the intersection of R($_\forall$*), R(I) for any I, and R($\exists$*) with MoSI* are, respectively, the set of necessary properties, the set of actual properties, and the set of possible properties of the regions in R. In such a cosmological scheme C*, the natural counterpart to Whitehead's Category of Propositions is the set P where

[23]C. I. Lewis and C. H. Langford, *Symbolic Logic* (New York: Dover Publications, 1959), p. 501. For an algebratization of S_5 see Chandler Davis, "Modal Operators, Equivalence Relations, and Projective Algebras," *American Journal of Mathematics,* 76 (1954), 747–762.

[24]This correspondence has been noted by Carnap, *op. cit.*, p. 186, but developed in a somewhat similar manner by Chandler Davis, *op. cit.*, p. 753.

[25]Georg H. Von Wright, *An Essay in Modal Logic* (Amsterdam: North-Holland Publishing Company, 1951), pp. 8–28.

$$P = \{p{:}p \in P^*\} = P^*.$$

One would also naturally assume a correspondence between White-head's Category of Eternal Objects, "the pure potentials for the specific determination of fact,"[26] and the original set C, the set of proposi-tional functions, so that

$$EO = \{\Phi{:}\Phi \in C\} = C.$$

In addition, there is the set A, where

A = {$I{:}I$ is a mapping of the pair (C, $\exists\,*$) into itself meeting conditions I1-I5 and the intersection of R(I) and MoSI* is not empty}.

This set bears a resemblance to Whitehead's Category of Actual En-tities. An individual is a projection, or transformation, of the whole set of propositional functions onto a subset R(I) contained in (C, $\exists\,*$). This would correspond to Whitehead's notion that an actual entity is a perspective of the entire universe and "has a perfectly definite bond with each item of the universe."[27] The set of all ordered pairs $< \Phi, \Psi >$ which are members of some $I \in$ A, in turn, would seem to correspond to the Category of Prehensions. These are the bonds which an indi-vidual has with its universe: "Every actual entity is 'divisible' into an indefinite number of ways, and each such way of 'division' yields its definite quota of prehensions."[28] Consequently, we have the set

$$Pr = \{< \Phi, \Psi > : < \Phi, \Psi > \in I \text{ and } I \in A\}.$$

Remembering that C* contains a proper maximal sum ideal, MoSI*, the intersection of R(I) and MoSI* can be thought of as indi-cating the set of positive prehensions of I. And since MoSI* is maximal and proper, the intersection of R(I) and MoSI* is a maximal proper sum ideal contained in R(I). Thus each individual positively or nega-tively prehends every item in the universe. The set R(I) itself would be analogous to the subjective form: how that entity prehends its data, negative prehensions contributing to the subjective form. For the Category of Subjective Forms, then, we have the set SF, where

26Whitehead, *op. cit.*, p. 32.
27*Ibid.*, p. 66.
28*Ibid.*, p. 28.

$$SF = \{\Phi : \Phi \, \epsilon \, R(I) \text{ and } I \, \epsilon \, A\}.$$

In turn, the satisfaction, which adds "its character to the creativity whereby there is a becoming of entities superseding the one in question,"[29] would correspond to the maximal proper sum ideal in $R(I)$. The region "occupied" by that actual entity is that r_0 of R which the subjective form maps into P^*. Since the satisfaction, or to use Whitehead's other term 'superject,' is the entity considered as object, a nexus, a fact of togetherness of actual entities, might be defined in terms of a set of interrelated satisfactions, or more simply, as a sum ideal, not necessarily maximal, contained in $MoSI^*$. Thus corresponding to the Category of Nexūs, we have the set N defined as

$$N = \{SI: SI \text{ contained in } MoSI^*\}.$$

It is somewhat difficult to determine the role of Whitehead's other two categories, the Category of Multiplicities and the Category of Contrasts. There seems to be some analogy between the set

$$M = \{ \, < \Phi, \Psi, \Pi > \, : \, < \Phi, \Psi, \Pi > \, \epsilon \cup \, \},$$

and the Category of Multiplicities, which he tells us, are "pure disjunctions of diverse entities."[30] In turn, the set,

$$C = \{ \, < \Phi, \Psi, \Pi > \, : \, < \Phi, \Psi, \Pi > \, \epsilon \cup \, \},$$

seems to bear some resemblance to the Category of Contrasts, "modes of synthesis of entities in one prehension."[31]

These sets defined in C^* cannot, in any sense, be taken as a serious explication of Whitehead's own Categories of Existence. They are used here merely to illustrate the fact that the cosmological scheme C^* does bear a resemblance to Whitehead's own conception of a cosmological scheme. The primary concern of this essay has been to suggest a relationship between language, or logic, and such a scheme of categories, and to demonstrate a type of linguistic analysis which seems to offer a precise method for the task of speculative philosophy as conceived by Whitehead. The great advantage of this method, besides that of precision, is the possibility which it offers for mirroring alternative logical structures in algebra and examining their relationships and, con-

[29] *Ibid.*, p. 129.
[30] *Ibid.*, p. 33.
[31] *Loc. cit.*

sequently, for explicating and comparing alternative cosmological schemes. Perhaps the most that can be said for the particular cosmological scheme, C*, and its relation to Whitehead's own, as well as the method suggested here, is that it is in the spirit of the author of *Process and Reality* and *A Treatise on Universal Algebra*.

BOWMAN L. CLARKE

UNIVERSITY OF GEORGIA

WHITEHEAD IN THE NON-ENGLISH-SPEAKING WORLD

1. Introduction

ALTHOUGH Whitehead, like Russell, was known on the Continent as a mathematician, logician, and, to some extent, philosopher of mathematics as early as 1905, he was not recognized as a philosopher of science, epistemologist, or metaphysician until the 1930's—more than a decade after the publication of CN.[1] Even then commentators tended to class him as just another of the "British neo-realists"—along with Russell, Moore, Broad, and Alexander.[2] René Kramer, as well as Philippe Devaux and Jean Wahl—both of the latter having published substantial studies of Whitehead's philosophy around 1930—came to Whitehead from a close study of James and Alexander. The first articles on Whitehead's philosophy in French, German, and Italian appeared within a year or two of each other[3]—perhaps stimulated by the stir of the Gifford Lectureship, which had

---

[1]Titles of Whitehead's principal works will be abbreviated as follows:
  AE   *The Aims of Education and Other Essays* (New York: The Macmillan Co., 1929).
  AI   *Adventures of Ideas* (New York: The Macmillan Co., 1933).
  CN   *The Concept of Nature* (Cambridge: Cambridge University Press, 1920).
  ESP   *Essays in Science and Philosophy* (New York: Philosophical Library, 1948).
  FR   *The Function of Reason* (Princeton: Princeton University Press, 1929).
  MT   *Modes of Thought* (New York: The Macmillan Co., 1938).
  NL   *Nature and Life* (Chicago: University of Chicago Press, 1934).
  PNK   *An Inquiry Concerning the Principles of Natural Knowledge,* (Cambridge: Cambridge University Press, 1919).
  PR   *Process and Reality* (New York: The Macmillan Co., 1929).
  RM   *Religion in the Making* (New York: The Macmillan Co., 1926).
  SMW   *Science and the Modern World* (New York: The Macmillan Co., 1925).

[2]Cf. René Kramer, "L'Evolution du néo-réalisme en Angleterre," *Revue Néo-Scholastique de Philosophie,* 30 (1928), esp. 12, 16, 17.

[3]Philippe Devaux, "Une nouvelle phase du néo-réalisme anglo-saxone. A propos de *Science and the Modern World,*" *Archives de la Société Belge de Philosophie,* 1, No. 3 (1928-1929), 9–24. Edgar Wind, "Mathematik und Sinnesempfindung. Materialien zu einer Whitehead-Kritik." *Logos* 21 (Tübingen, 1932) 239-280. Cleto Carbonara: review of *Symbolism, Its Meaning and Effect* (1927), *Logos* 13 (Florence, 1930), 373–376.

issued (in 1929) in PR. Of these early studies the liveliest and most perceptive is undoubtedly Jean Wahl's.[4] Unfortunately, it has not been followed by French studies of comparable sophistication or penetration.

The first translation of Whitehead's philosophic works was into French, beginning with SMW in 1930. In contrast, the first German translations (of SMW and ESP) date from 1949. The intervening decades saw the first Spanish translation (of NL) in 1941, and the first Italian translation (of SMW) in 1945. Since the end of the War there have also been Italian translations of AE, CN, FR, and NL and Spanish translations of SMW, PR, AI, and MT; RM was published in French in 1939. (See Bibliography.) But no plans have been made for the translation of either AI, PR, or MT into French. In contrast, all of Whitehead's major philosophic works are to be included in a forthcoming German edition, edited by Charles Hartshorne, Ivor Leclerc, and Gottfried Martin.

Careful and competent book-length commentaries are now available in French and Italian.[5] Both bear comparison to Ivor Leclerc's *Whitehead's Metaphysics: An Introductory Exposition*, of 1958, although Cesselin's and Orsi's accounts of Whitehead's metaphysics are less thorough and systematic than Leclerc's, since both authors devote considerable space to a general survey of Whitehead's "philosophy of civilization" (drawn chiefly from AI and MT). There is as yet no similarly competent or comprehensive study in Spanish or German.[6]

It would, of course, be premature to assume that good translations and thorough commentaries will lead to an automatic enhancement of Whitehead's philosophic stature and influence in non-English-speaking countries. Conscientious students of Whitehead, whether they speak French, German, Spanish, Italian, Dutch, or Russian, will continue to turn to the original English texts—and to the excellent commentaries which already exist in English, e.g., those of Lowe and

---

[4]Jean Wahl, "La Philosophie spéculative de Whitehead," *Revue Philosophique*, 111 (1931), 341–378 and 112 (1931), 108–143. (Reprinted, with revisions, in *Vers le concret* [Paris: Vrin, 1932], pp. 127–221. Further references will be to this latter edition.)

[5]Félix Cesselin, *La Philosophie organique de Whitehead* (Paris: Presses Universitaires de France, 1950), 248 pp. Concetta Orsi, *La Filosofia dell'organismo di Whitehead* (Naples: Libreria Scientifica, [1956]), 159 pp.

[6]However, Leclerc's current study of philosophies of space and time, with special reference to Whitehead, will be published in German translation, probably in 1965.

Christian.[7] Still, translations and native-language commentaries are of great importance both to university students and to the "broader cultured public." Well-translated, competently-edited, and inexpensive editions of Whitehead's principal works in the major languages (including the Russian!) [8] would be desirable on many counts.

2. Whitehead and the Philosophic Tradition

It often appears that non-English-speaking philosophers, like some of their English-speaking colleagues, feel uncomfortable with Whitehead precisely because his thought defies ready classification.[9] Is he positivist or anti-positivist?—Existentialist or "essentialist"?—Kantian or anti-Kantian?—Hegelian or anti-Hegelian?—Subjectivist or objectivist?—Epistemological realist or idealist?—Ontological materialist or "spiritualist"? Is his ethics oriented toward individual autonomy or the collectivity of the "world-historical"? To most, if not all, such questions, it seems, the answer is no easy "either-or," but rather a hesitant "both-and" or an uneasy "neither-nor."

There is even a question as to whether Whitehead should be classed as an "English" or "American" philosopher. (All Continental commentators agree that he is "Anglo-Saxon.") Earlier writers tended to label him "English" without qualification; but a recent commentator calls him "one of the most original *American* philosophers."[10]

Classical terms like "axiology" and "finalism"—which French and Italian commentators like to apply to Whitehead's position—are cumbersome but not misleading. Recent European commentators seem to realize that the rough-and-ready label "neo-realist," persistently attached to Whitehead in the 1930's, has lost much of its meaning. It

[7]Victor Lowe, "The Development of Whitehead's Philosophy," in the Whitehead Volume of *The Library of Living Philosophers*, 1941, and *Understanding Whitehead* (Baltimore: Johns Hopkins U. Press, 1962), 398 pp. William A. Christian, *An Interpretation of Whitehead's Metaphysics* (New Haven: Yale U. Press, 1959), 419 pp.

[8]To date (1963) no Whitehead translation has been published in the Soviet Union, although a chapter of A. S. Bogomolov's book on theories of emergent evolution (1962) is devoted to Whitehead. SMW is being translated into Slovak by Jan Bodnar of Bratislava.

[9]The point was first made by Wahl in the introduction to *Vers le concret*, pp. 11f; it is repeated, rather polemically, by Marc-André Béra, *A. N. Whitehead: Un philosophe de l'expérience* (Paris, 1948), p. 3. Cf. also Cesselin, *op. cit.*, p. 162.

[10]Professor Antonio Aliotta in his preface to Orsi, *op. cit.*, p. iii. (Italics added.)

is now less ubiquitous in writings on Whitehead than it formerly was. But the term "organism" and its derivatives ("organic," "organismic," "organicistic," etc.) , are used more freely than ever—e.g., in the titles of the two solid academic commentaries already mentioned. This usage strikes me as vague, ambiguous, and seriously misleading; it has been curtailed in recent years by commentators writing in English, and with good reason. The expression "philosophy of organism," of course, was used by Whitehead to describe his own position, and it may be that he overused or even misused it. European commentators have surely managed to do both. A moratorium on its use for the next decade or so might prove helpful to all concerned.

Continental and South-American commentators, once past the stage of sheer exposition, have often been tempted to assimilate Whitehead's thought, as a whole or in part, to some established tradition. Jean Wahl's early claim that Whitehead was, on many points, a "phenomenologist"—close to Husserl and Heidegger—[11] has been repeated and elaborated upon by recent writers. Whitehead's relation to Leibniz, Kant, Hegel, and Bergson has been intermittently discussed. If commentators have sometimes overstated resemblances[12] or influences,[13] they have nevertheless offered a number of provocative and fruitful suggestions. (Some of these will be pursued below.)

Whitehead has noted his own closeness to Aristotle and to Hegel; Hartshorne, Leclerc, and others have explored the former relationship. But the latter remains in need of searching and critical examination, as does Whitehead's relation to Descartes, Spinoza, Leibniz, Kant,[14] and Schelling—and to lesser thinkers like Fechner, Lequier, and Lotze.[15]

[11]Wahl, *op. cit.,* pp. 215f.

[12]E.g., Enzo Paci's claim of similarities between Whitehead and Husserl. See his "Über einige Verwandtschaften zwischen der Philosophie Whiteheads und der Phänomenologie Husserls," *Revue Internationale de Philosophie,* No. 56–57 (1961), 237–250.

[13]E.g., Nicolà Abbagnano's stress on the "Romantic" influences in Whitehead. See the section on Whitehead in his *Storia della filosofia* 2 (Turin, 1950), esp. 614, 616. Whitehead's philosophy is also classed as "Romantic" by Carlo Mazzantini, "La Filosofia di A. N. Whitehead," *Quaderni di Roma* 2 (1948), 176; and by Ludovico Actis Perinetti, *Cosmologia e assiologia in Whitehead* (Turin, 1954), p. 56.

[14]One aspect of Whitehead's similarity to Kant has been suggestively explored by Hermann Wein. See his "In Defence of the Humanism of Science: Kant and Whitehead," trans. Eva Schaper, *The Relevance of Whitehead* Leclerc, ed. (London and New York, 1961), pp. 289–315.

[15]Concetta Orsi has pointed to the need for detailed studies of the relation of

3. Methodology and Philosophy of Science

In this and the following four sections, I shall explore briefly what seem to me the most interesting insights into, and criticisms of, Whitehead's philosophy put forward by commentators who have written in French, German, Spanish, Italian, Dutch, Slovak, and Russian.[16] These will be considered under the general headings: Methodology and Philosophy of Science; Epistemology; Metaphysics and Cosmology; Philosophical Theology; Philosophy of Civilization, Ethics, Aesthetics, and Educational Theory.

However, before proceeding to these topics, I should like to examine briefly an example of what is most regrettable (and, fortunately, not typical) in European Whitehead commentary, namely the brochure of Marc-André Béra, Agrégé de l'Université, and (as of 1948) Director of the French Institute of Scotland. Béra continues to figure in Whitehead bibliographies beside such serious commentators as Wahl and Cesselin; his slim volume appeared in the distiguished Hermann series of "Actualités Scientifiques et Industrielles," whose editors have included de Broglie and Mme. Curie. Yet Béra's book—though it is not without *aperçus*—is uniquely irresponsible and abusive.

In the process of charging Whitehead with inconsistency and incoherence, Béra manages to contradict himself on several points. Even his facts are wrong: He begins by asserting that nothing in Whitehead's teaching or writing before about 1920 foreshadowed an eventual commitment to philosophy (p. 4),[17] and that he was dramat-

Whitehead's thought to that of Bergson, Husserl, and Heidegger—as well as Alexander, Russell, Dewey, and Santayana. She feels that Whitehead shares with all of them a particular attitude toward Descartes and Kant, *op. cit.*, p. 145.

[16]There have also been commentaries in such exotic languages as Estonian, Welsh, Hebrew, Chinese, Japanese, and Korean. Whitehead's works have been translated into Dutch, Polish, Icelandic, Chinese, Japanese, Korean, and Arabic. (See Bibliography.)

[17]More recent commentators make the more reasonable claim that philosophic interests were present even in the earliest period (1898–1913) of Whitehead's work (the *Treatise on Universal Algebra* of 1898 being "rich in philosophic insights"), but deepened and broadened in the 1920's. Orsi, *op. cit.*, pp. 3, 4. Paci sees "significant metaphysical potentialities" in this early period, and calls *Principia Mathematica* a "philosophic experiment." Prospettive empiristiche e relazionistiche nel Whitehead prespeculativo," *Aut-Aut*, No. 16 (1953), 279. At the turn of the century Couturat had noted the Platonism of Whitehead's *Treatise on Universal Algebra*. Cf. *Revue de Métaphysique et de Morale*, 18 (1900), 325. Cesselin adds that the "hallmarks of

ically "converted" to philosophy at the end of the first World War.[18] Béra conjectures that Whitehead, seeking consolation for the "loss of his only son" (in fact, Whitehead had two sons), turned to religion, then to philosophy of religion, and finally to philosophy. To support his claim that Whitehead's philosophy is not genuinely speculative but "practical" and "moralizing," Béra alleges that in the midst of works of pure philosophy Whitehead took time to write "The Aims of Education" and "The Rhythm of Education" (p. 38). In fact, the former dates from 1916, the latter from 1922; Béra apparently assumes that they were written near the date of publication of AE (1929).

At one point Béra admits Whitehead's "originality" as a philosopher, but his last word is that Whitehead was not original at all, that his philosophic endeavors resulted in "simple variants of detail in existing theories, ideas which were in the air" (p. 54).

More serious, and more objectionable, is Béra's insistent claim that Whitehead is a typical English philosopher in the double sense of (1) an amateur, self-taught in philosophy, and (2) an "instinctive" empiricist," that is, an anti-rationalist—unsystematic,[19] analytic, casual, indifferent to "clear ideas and lucid systems," remote from "the close argumentation of French metaphysicians and the erudite and symmetrical constructions of German philosophers" (pp. 3, 13, 14, 16, 17). This amateurism, Béra suggests, is due to the paucity of chairs of philosophy in England and to the absence of philosophy courses in the secondary schools, both of which make philosophy a less important academic career in England than it is in France and Germany.

Whitehead's "instinctive empiricism"—which involves "respect for facts" and "fear of ideas" [sic]—is a feature of the businesslike British psyche (pp. 31f, 39). Englishmen distrust *esprit* and cleverness; they are muddling, moderate, and skeptical in religion and politics. Whitehead tries to expand his "moderate" rationalism to include what in France or Germany would be considered contrary positions (pp. 19f.).

philosophic genius" were apparent in Whitehead's earliest works; there was no sudden turn to philosophy, but only the development of "metaphysical thought which was present from the outset," Félix Cesselin, *La Philosophie, . . .* p. 8.

[18]Béra even asserts that *Russell* turned to philosophy after the first World War! (p. 6)

[19]Orsi goes perhaps too far in the opposite direction when she maintains that Whitehead's philosophic system is "absolutely unitary and organic," *op. cit.,* p. 40.

"What is a flagrant contradiction on this [French] side of the Channel," Béra exclaims, "becomes attenuated on the other until it is no more than one of the 'perplexities of facts' " [this last phrase appears in English in the original] (p. 25). For Whitehead pluralism means "complexity and richness"; for the lucid French mind it connotes "disorder and confusion" (p. 13).

Despite his own initial warning that Whitehead's thought defies ready classification in the traditional rubrics, Béra goes on to classify and misclassify it in several respects. He finds Whitehead a "vitalist in biology"[20] (ignoring the explicit rejection of vitalism at SMW 115) and a "faculty" psychologist. (Béra lists "wisdom, cognition, and feeling" as the faculties! [p. 12]) In AI, Béra writes, "[Whitehead] passionately discusses Marxist theories and accepts historical materialism in principle as an explanatory method" (p. 22).

Comment would be superfluous. But there is consolation in the fact that French students of Whitehead are not confined to Béra's fancies and crotchets; they can turn instead to the sophisticated interpretation of Wahl or the sober exposition of Cesselin.

European commentators have had relatively little to say about Whitehead's philosophic method. But two or three interesting suggestions have emerged. Gian Mario Crespi—one of the more thoughtful of Italian critics—distinguishes between metaphysics as *speculation* and as *description* (what Whitehead called "descriptive generalization"), and suggests that Whitehead's metaphysics is the result of a non-descriptive extrapolation (or "conjectural extension") to reality as a whole of categories drawn from human experience.[21] Crespi sees Whitehead as wavering between the theory and practice of a purely descriptive or analytic method and a speculative or inferential one. Two Whiteheadian doctrines which seem to him products of inference, though presented as "descriptions," are: (1) the claim that God "transcends every finite cosmic epoch" and (2) the ontological principle.[22]

A special kind of "inference"—namely, argument by analogy—is

---

[20]Abbagnano makes a similarly questionable classification, calling Whitehead's position a "neo-vitalism." Cf. his "Whitehead e il concetto della ragione," *Revue Internationale de Philosophie*, No. 56–57 (1961), p. 211.

[21]G. M. Crespi, "La Filosofia di Whitehead," *Rivista di filosofia neo-scolastica*, **40** (1948), 310, 325.

[22]*Ibid.*, pp. 321, 322.

singled out by Devaux as central to the philosophic method of both Alexander and Whitehead. He claims that this derives, perhaps indirectly, from Lotze.[23]

Another denial of Whitehead's characterization of philosophy as "descriptive generalization" comes from Paci, who, after defining philosophy, suggestively, though a bit vaguely, as "the invention and symbolization of new possibilities," goes on to offer a number of examples of Whitehead's symbolic inventiveness.[24]

Certain critics see Whitehead as tending, at least in his early works, toward positivism or even "scientism." Thus Actis Perinetti charges Whitehead with "an extension, (and in a certain sense, absolutization) of the validity of the concepts proper to science." The same writer goes on to assert that Whitehead confuses Newtonian physics with the "materialistic view of nature to which it has given rise, but which does not belong to it." He even accuses Whitehead of attempting to justify the insights of the Romantic poets by means of the Maxwell-Lorentz equations![25]

Related to Whitehead's conception of philosophic method is his theory of language, particularly philosophic language. European commentators have made much of Whitehead's similarities to Bergson on this point, although one critic notes that, since Bergson rejects the intellect altogether, because of its inevitable distortion ("spatialization") of real *durée*, he can consistently withdraw into mysticism.[26] Since Whitehead wishes to refashion rather than to reject philosophic discourse,[27] this path is closed to him.

Béra claims that for Whitehead "philosophic language is always obscure, because it is a symbolic and provisional language, the meaning of which cannot be made precise except in the course of philosophic investigation." He adds that, on Whitehead's Hegelian view, "philosophy, if it is true, is necessarily obscure, because reality itself is contradictory and incoherent."[28]

In contrast, Nédoncelle finds Whitehead's studies in the philoso-

---

[23]Philippe Devaux, *Lotze et son influence sur la philosophie anglo-saxonne* (Brussells, 1932), p. 46.

[24]Paci, "Prospettive . . . ," pp. 286-289.

[25]Actis Perinetti, *Cosmologia . . .* , p. 9.

[26]*Ibid.*, p. 33.

[27]Cf. Orsi, *op. cit.*, pp. 36, 37.

[28]Béra, *op. cit.*, pp. 15, 16.

phy of science written "with a magnificent clarity and simplicity, giving the lie to the reputation for obscurity which has been attached to him. He shares with Heraclitus the honor of being both cloudy and concise."[29]

Bubser, in a special study of "Language and Metaphysics in Whitehead's Philosophy," begins by characterizing Whitehead's philosophy of language as a compromised blending of three divergent positions: (1) the "rationalistic optimism" of the early mathematical logicians, (2) Bergson's anti-rationalism, and (3) American pragmatism. Bubser goes on to say that Whitehead supports his view of language with arguments which are foreign to all three.[30] In the end he finds Whitehead closer to Bradley than to any of these. Bubser rejects Whitehead's strictures on traditional language—as well as his characterization of the language of speculative philosophy as "metaphors mutely appealing for an imaginative leap"—with Wittgensteinian impatience.[31]

With respect to Whitehead's rejection of conventionalism in mathematics and physics, Italian scholars have offered two pertinent observations, one historical, one theoretical. Orsi points out that Poincaré had himself put forward (in *La Valeur de la science*, 1905) some of the criticisms of extreme conventionalism which Whitehead employs.[32] Paci notes that, although "the choice of conventionalism eliminates the problem of the reality of the object," it raises the "problem of the choice":—Why just this linguistic or mathematical convention rather than some other?[33] It was such difficulties, of course—coupled with the difficulty of accounting for the applicability of mathematical formalisms on purely conventionalist principles— which led Whitehead to develop the "method of extensive abstraction." Although this technical doctrine has been little discussed by non-English-speaking commentators, it has excited the admiration of

---

[29]Maurice Nédoncelle, *La Philosophie religieuse en Grand-Bretagne de 1850 à nos jours* (Paris, 1934), p. 109. We shall return to the question of Whitehead's "obscurity." (See below, pp. 259ff.)

[30]Eberhard Bubser, "Sprache und Metaphysik in Whiteheads Philosophie," *Archiv für Philosophie*, 10, No. 1–2 (1960), 87.

[31]*Ibid.*, pp. 102, 106.

[32]Orsi, *op. cit.*, p. 138.

[33]Enzo Paci, "Whitehead e Russell," *Rivista di filosofia*, 45 (1954), 16.

some of them—for example, Devaux, who calls it "a splendid theoretical success."[34]

Whitehead's views of space, time and extension (as set forth in PNK and CN) are competently expounded by a number of commentators, including Wahl, Cesselin, Paci, and Orsi; but I have found nothing particularly original or perceptive in their interpretations. On the other hand, a few provocative remarks have been made with respect to Whitehead's theory of relativity. Béra finds that Whitehead's alternative to Einstein's theory fails to attract adherents (which, by the way, was nearer the truth in 1948 than it is today) because of its "unnecessary and inexact complexity."[35] On the other hand, Orsi finds Whitehead's interpretation of relativity more convincing, because more philosophic, than Einstein's.[36] Actis Perinetti implicitly criticizes Whitehead for seeking an un-Kantian (and un-Machian) "event-*an-Sich*" behind the Einsteinian relativistic space-time metric.[37]

4. *Epistemology*: *Experience and Perception*

European commentators have seen clearly that Whitehead's position is anti-Kantian (in contrast to Bertrand Russell, who persists in seeing the later Whitehead as essentially influenced by Kant). Jean Wahl was one of the first to note that Whitehead's philosophy is "entirely opposed to Kantianism and to epistemological investigations . . ."[38] Nédoncelle judiciously qualifies this last remark by adding that Whitehead's "metaphysical realism is the result of epistemological reflection."[39] Actis Perinetti mildly rebukes Whitehead for adopting the "acritical" (i.e., non-Kantian) perspective of the "known" rather than the "knower," since this ascribes a tacit "ontol-

34Philippe Devaux, "L'Esprit du néo-réalisme anglais," *Revue Internationale de Philosophie*, No. 3 (1939), p. 534.

35Béra, *op. cit.*, p. 12.

36Orsi, *op. cit.*, p. 6.

37Actis Perinetti, *Cosmologia* . . . , p. 10.

38Wahl, *op. cit.*, pp. 127, 132, 213. Metz stresses Whitehead's opposition to Kant. Cf. *Die philosophischen Strömungen in Grossbrittanien* 2 (Leipzig, 1935), 159. English trans. *A Hundred Years of British Philosophy*, p. 613.

39Nédoncelle, *op. cit.*, p. 113.

ogism" (i.e., "objective ontological reference"?) to scientific statements.[40]

Cesselin has made it clear that Whitehead's opposition to Kant is integral to his repudiation of "bifurcation"—in this case the dualism of phenomena and noumena.[41] Like Pastore earlier,[42] Cesselin sees this as an aspect of Whitehead's "neo-realism." Crespi brings the point into clearer historical focus when he describes Whitehead's philosophy as "an attempt, going beyond modern criticism [i.e., Kantianism] to renew contact with the great metaphysical tradition, overcoming the provincialism of modern philosophy which springs from the predominantly epistemological character of its investigations."[43]

Various critics, beginning with Wahl, have accused Whitehead of returning, in his mature metaphysics, to a new form of the "bifurcation" of nature (into events and objects).[44] Orsi, among other recent commentators, emphatically denies this charge.[45] Cesselin borrows Northrop's distinction of (1) a "Newtonian" bifurcation between the object as sensed and the object as postulated, and (2) a "Lockean" bifurcation between the object (as postulated or as sensed) and the observer. Cesselin suggests, as had Northrop, that by rejecting the second and retaining the first—rather than rejecting both, as Whitehead did—one could meet the requirements of both science and common sense. Cesselin goes beyond Northrop only in asserting that it is possible to accept the Newtonian bifurcation and still maintain a realist position in epistemology.[46] It seems to me

---

[40]Actis Perinetti, *Cosmologia* . . . , p. 13. Metz had remarked as early as 1935 that Whitehead did not succeed in his announced program of considering nature as "closed to mind" (in PNK and CN), but in fact smuggled in mind through the category of "percipient event," *op. cit.,* **2,** 147.

[41]Cesselin, *La Philosophie* . . . , p. 201.

[42]Annibale Pastore, "Whitehead e Heidegger contro Kant circa la natura emotiva del tempo," *Rivista di Filosofia,* **38** (1947), 182.

[43]Crespi, *op. cit.,* p. 329.

[44]Wahl, *op. cit.,* p. 216. Cf. also Gianfranco Morra, "Religione e sociologia nel pensiero di Whitehead," *Filosofia e sociologia* (Bolgna, 1954), p. 236. Morra adds that the "final" Whitehead can be criticized, in the name of the "pre-speculative and relationist" Whitehead, for recurring to a form of the fallacy of misplaced concreteness, *loc. cit.* Cf. also Actis Perinetti, "Whitehead," *Enciclopedia Filosofica,* **4** (1957), col. 1753.

[45]Orsi, *op. cit.,* p. 143.

[46]F. Cesselin, "La Bifurcation de la nature," *Revue de Métaphysique et de Morale,* **55** (1950), 36, 49. Cf. F. S. C. Northrop, "Whitehead's Philosophy of Science," in

likely that both Whitehead and Northrop would have disputed this further claim.

Whitehead's distinction of three kinds of perception—in the modes of presentational immediacy, causal efficacy, and symbolic reference—has troubled European commentators no less than English and American critics. Carbonara, in his early discussion of *Symbolism*, complained that there were in Whitehead's theory too many kinds of perception or "activities of the mind."[47] Devaux remarks, more constructively, that perception in the modes of presentational immediacy and causal efficacy, respectively, are in effect "an epistemological reiteration (on the symbolic level) of the natural pair 'event-object'."[48] Cesselin is especially unhappy about presentational immediacy, going so far as to suggest that Whitehead should reject it as an "illusion" which is "artificial in the same sense as Bergson's spatialized time."[49]

Wahl notes that "perception is always at the extreme limit of creation," adding that in this doctrine "realism is on the point of turning into magical idealism."[50] Wahl also sees an echo of Hegel in Whitehead's general theory of perception. "All perception," he writes, "is perception of something as not being another thing, or as not having a certain character. It is negative perception. Conciousness is the sense of negation based on the contrast between the possible and the given. As Plato and Hegel saw, it presupposes the idea of the other."[51]

G. M. Crespi sees special ambiguity in Whitehead's notion of causal efficacy. It may mean (1) the immediate experience of causal connection, (2) the instinctive belief in causality, or (3) the (objective) fact of causal connectedness. Crespi concludes that Whitehead's appeal to the immediate experience of causal pressure establishes only that experience is "organic" (i.e., continuous) , not that there is

---

Library of Living Philosophers, ed. Paul A. Schilpp, 3 (1951), esp. 205–206. Cesselin does not explicitly refer to Northrop's article.

[47]Cleto Carbonara, *Logos*, 13 (Florence, 1930), 376.

[48]Philippe Devaux, "La Philosophie en Grande-Bretagne . . . ," in *Philosophy in the Mid-Century*, ed. Klibansky, 4, 195.

[49]Cesselin, *La Philosophie* . . . , pp. 213f, 71.

[50]Wahl, *op. cit.*, p. 177. The expression "magical idealism" is a (not wholly pejorative) reference to Novalis.

[51]*Ibid.*, p. 195n.

real causal efficacy in the third sense.[52] To establish that there is causal efficacy in either or both of the first two senses is not a conclusive answer to Hume—according to Crespi—since the first may be illusory and the second erroneous.

Cesselin, too, is critical on this point, asserting that causality must be explained, but neither in Hume's way nor in Whitehead's (on the basis of what he calls the "immediate intuition of an ontological mystery").[53] Cesselin's book, written some time before this article, though published in the same year, is less critical and closer to Wahl's interpretation of causal efficacy. Like Wahl, Cesselin finds Whitehead's account of the "lived" and "visceral" causal pressure of the past upon the present very close to Heidegger's description of *Dasein* and *In-der-Welt-Sein*. On this point, Cesselin declares, Whitehead is "an undeniable existentialist."[54]

I conclude with a comment on induction which provides a natural transition to the following section. Cesselin and Orsi adequately expound Whitehead's views on the grounding of induction (in SMW) and the four interpretations of laws of nature (in AI). But both mistranslate a crucial passage in Whitehead's discussion of the interpretation of law as "immanent." Whitehead writes: "Fourthly, a reason can now be produced why we should put some limited trust in induction" (AI 143). Cesselin translates: "We can have only a limited confidence in induction."[55] Orsi speaks of "a certain limitation of the value to be ascribed to the inductive method."[56] Both readings

---

[52]G. M. Crespi, *op. cit.*, pp. 309–310, 311. Earlier, Nédoncelle had written that Whitehead was at his most convincing in criticizing Hume's doctrine of causality, *op. cit.*, pp. 111f. In this connection, Wahl also notes that Whitehead's "empiricism" is un-Humean, while Hume's "empiricism" is "anti-empirical," *op. cit.*, p. 191. Paci adds that Whitehead's empiricism is "relational," replacing the Humean "impression" by a "complex fact in process," "Prospettive . . . ," p. 292.

[53]Cesselin, "La Bifurcation . . . ," p. 48.

[54]Cesselin, *La Philosophie* . . . , p. 72. Whitehead and Heidegger, according to Cesselin, share "le sens du concret, du corps, de l'organique, de l'importance du sentiment . . . , de l'immédiateté de la connaissance et de l'action causale," but Heidegger would reject Whitehead's Platonic doctrine of eternal objects, *ibid.*, p. 202.

[55]Cesselin, *La Philosophie* . . . , p. 138. (". . . nous ne pourrons avoir qu'une confiance limitée dans l'induction.")

[56]Orsi, *op. cit.*, p. 135. (". . . una certa limitazione del valore da attribuire al metodo induttivo.")

distort Whitehead's point, shifting the stress from "trust" to "limitation."

5. Metaphysics and Cosmology

European and South American commentators have discussed Whitehead's Platonism at some length. Angelo Crespi, repeating the London *Times'* characterization of Whitehead as "the last of the Cambridge Platonists," notes with specific reference to French and Italian philosophy, that "most significantly, after Bergson, Croce, and Gentile, it should have been recognized... that becoming is non-chaotic and compatible with induction and prediction only if it is rooted in the eternal, in an eternity which at the same time is immanent in and transcends it."[57] Others—such as Frondizi and Cesselin—have seen Whitehead's doctrine of "eternal objects" as more Aristotelian than Platonic. Whitehead's eternal objects are potential and abstract; Plato's forms are the "highest reality."[58] As Crespi puts it, Whitehead's objects, though "transcendent" (of actualities), are not "subsistent."[59] The point is pursued by Orsi: For Whitehead, she writes, "values do not exist apart from the world of becoming"; and this is an inversion of Platonism.[60] Cesselin adds that for Whitehead the eternal objects have no "reality" apart from actual entities.[61]

This claim would seem to rest on a misconception, based in turn on a misleading translation. Cesselin, following Wahl, translates "actual entity" as "entité réelle," in order to avoid the irrelevant con-

[57]Angelo Crespi, "Alfred North Whitehead: L'Ultimo dei platonisti inglesi," *Il Ponte*, 4 (1948), 1139, 1141.

[58]Risieri Frondizi, "Conceptos fundamentales de la metafísica de Whitehead," *Naturaleza y vida* (Buenos Aires, 1941), pp. 29f. Cesselin, *La Philosophie* . . . , p. 198. Cf. also I. M. Bocheński, *Europäische Philosophie der Gegenwart* (second ed.; Bern, 1951), p. 232.

[59]G. M. Crespi, *op. cit.*, p. 320.

[60]Orsi, *op. cit.*, p. 148.

[61]Cesselin, *La Philosophie* . . . , p. 209. Orsi seems to make the same mistake, for the same reason, when she writes: "Negare che gli oggetti eterni e la natura primordiale di Dio abbiano realtà fuori dell'inserzione nell'organismo concreto . . . significa negare l'esistenza stessa degli uni e dell'altra," *op. cit.*, p. 95, cf. p. 147. This passage appears to involve a surreptitious transition from actuality to reality, and from reality to existence. Orsi argues in effect that if eternal objects are not actual, they are not real; and if they are not real, they do not exist.

notations of the French "actuelle" (i.e., "present, contemporary").
Of course, unactualized eternal objects are not *actual;* but they are
perfectly *real* in Whitehead's sense. Objects are to events or actual
entities as abstract to concrete. This polarity is blurred by Wahl's
statement that "les uns ne sont pas plus abstraits que les autres."[62]
Wind seems to be guilty of a similar confusion when he characterizes
the "sense objects" and "perceptual objects" of PNK and CN as
"konkrete Gebilde" and "konkrete Objekte."[63] Metz repeats this confusion, speaking of sense objects and perceptual objects as "konkrete
Gegenstände."[64] This seems to me a misinterpretation of Whitehead,
but one to which Whitehead himself gave some support by overstres-
sing color qualities and understressing geometrical forms as examples
of eternal objects. Still, the epistemological distinction which apparently eluded both Wind and Metz (who follows Wind's discussion
closely on this point) is that between a particular *concrete* perception (experience, feeling) of redness or triangularity and the general,
abstract character of the redness or triangularity itself. This is simply
another case, for Whitehead, of the "ingression" of abstract forms
or eternal objects into concrete occasions of experience.

Wahl had noted that, historically, "Russell was discovering an
analogue of the Platonic ideas in the field of logic, and Husserl was
discovering them by an analysis of consciousness, while Whitehead
was bringing them to light by an analysis of our observation of nature."[65] Cesselin adds that Whitehead's doctrine of eternal objects
is central to his metaphysics and cannot be eliminated without muti-
lating the system as a whole.[66]

Other critics have pointed to some of the difficulties of detail
which Whitehead's doctrine involves. One of the earliest, as well as
the most penetrating and persistent, of these critics is Edgar Wind,
whose discussion focusses upon PNK and CN.[67] Wind holds that
Whitehead's "perceptual objects" are unstable, tending to dissolve
"down" into "sense objects," or "up" into "scientific objects." He

[62]Wahl, *op. cit.*, p. 178.

[63]Wind, *op. cit.*, pp. 253, 254.

[64] Metz, *op. cit.*, **2**, 154.

[65]Wahl, *op. cit.*, p. 182.

[66]Cesselin, *La Philosophie* . . . , p. 56.

[67]Wind, *op. cit.*, p. 247. Although Wind's paper was not published until 1932, it
was completed before PR had appeared (in 1929). *Ibid.*, p. 246n4.

makes the point, repeated by several later commentators, that what Whitehead regards as objects of sense perception are often products of "scientific imagination."[68] Further, Whitehead's dictum: "If the sense-object . . . be located in an area, it will be located in any portion of that area" (PNK 53.3), fails to distinguish between: (a) every portion of a red surface is red, and (b) a given red surface may be indefinitely contracted and still appear red. The second of these assertions, says Wind, is false. Yet Whitehead holds that color quality can be non-extensive and immutable, while remaining "visible."[69]

Many European commentators, as already indicated, consider Whitehead's theory of forms Aristotelian rather than Platonic. Cesselin remarks that Whitehead's characterization of "object" as "a sensible potentiality for actualization" comes "strikingly close to Aristotle."[70] Crespi sees Whitehead's Aristotelianism in the assumption that, "in order to make 'novelty' conceivable it is necessary that the world of becoming stand in a determinate relation to as-yet-unactualized possibilities."[71] Paci adds that Whitehead's "Platonism" must always be understood in its relation to the "temporality. . . or historicity of process."[72]

In a later work Paci claims to find a resemblance between Whitehead's eternal objects and Husserl's *Wesen*.[73] But Gottfried Martin seems closer to the truth when he cautions that, though Husserl and Whitehead both "went back to Plato," they stressed different dialogues and different doctrines—Husserl the *Phaedo* and *Republic*, Whitehead the *Sophist* and *Parmenides*. According to Martin, White-

[68]*Ibid.*, p. 276. Wind goes on to suggest (*ibid.*, p. 253) that what Whitehead calls "object" might better be called "Begriff," presumably in Kant's sense. (The *Hegelian* "Begriff" is characterized by a dynamism and self-activity entirely foreign to Whitehead's eternal objects.)

[69]*Ibid.*, p. 276. (In the original: color quality is "ausdehnungslos und unwandelbar . . . ohne dass seine Sichtbarkeit darunter litte.")

[70]Cesselin, *La Philosophie* . . . , p. 31.

[71]G. M. Crespi, *op. cit.*, p. 323.

[72]Paci, "Sul primo periodo della filosofia di Whitehead," *Rivista di filosofia*, 44 (1953), 409.

[73]Paci, "Über einige Verwandtschaften . . . ," pp. 242f. To reinforce the alleged similarity, Paci sometimes refers to eternal objects as "wesentliche Formen," *loc. cit.*

head's emphasis on the interrelatedness of eternal objects "excludes the Husserlian *Wesensschau*."[74]

Wahl criticizes Whitehead for assigning too large a role to possibility, for stressing purely "abstract" possibility, and for failing to recognize what Wahl calls the "concrete, Bergsonian" possibility "qui se fait en nous."[75] This would seem to be little more than an expression of preference for Bergson's non-Platonic (and, I would argue, incoherent) position. Actis Perinetti finds a general lack of clarity and a tinge of "syncretism" in Whitehead's doctrine of objects and events; but he fails to spell out his criticisms in specific detail.[76] In contrast, Wind discerns "no trace of eclecticism" in this doctrine.[77]

With respect to Whitehead's theory of actual entities, non-English-speaking critics have repeated most of the strictures of their English-speaking colleagues. Whitehead is charged with "anthropomorphism" and the "cosmologizing of feeling" or "cosmologizing of experient subjects."[78] His process-philosophy is attacked for "dissolving the [substantial] subject"[79] and "denying the intelligibility of being."[80] Actis Perinetti finds it natural that Whitehead, "in the last analysis . . . , should have come so close to those various forms of irra-

[74]Gottfried Martin, "Neuzeit und Gegenwart in der Entwicklung des mathematischen Denkens," *Kant-Studien*, No. 45 (1953–54), pp. 164, 161.

[75]Wahl, *op. cit.*, pp. 15, 16. Cesselin notes that Whitehead, like Aristotle, refers to *real* (not conceptual) possibility when he claims that "tout existant actuel est en même temps potentialité d'une nouvelle synthèse," *La Philosophie* . . . , p. 32.

[76]Actis Perinetti, *Cosmologia* . . . , p. 30.

[77]Wind, *op. cit.*, p. 279. Piero Bertolini also denies that Whitehead's philosophy is eclectic. "Aspetti e problemi dell'educazione in Whitehead," *Aut-Aut*, No. 28 (1955), p. 324.

[78]Actis Perinetti, *Cosmologia* . . . , pp. 20, 25. (The clumsy abstract term "cosmologizzazione" is twice expanded into the even clumsier "cosmologicizzazione.") For the charge of anthropomorphism see, e.g., Paul Ginestier, *La Pensée anglosaxonne depuis 1900* (Paris, 1956), p. 71.

[79]Actis Perinetti, *Cosmologia* . . . , p. 34. Wahl had put the point epigrammatically, declaring that Whitehead attempted to "construct a monadology without [substantial, enduring] monads, an atomism without atoms." He suggestively characterizes Whitehead's actual entities as "monades fluides," *op. cit.*, pp. 212n, 171. Bertolini points out that Whitehead insisted on the importance of personal identity partly to defend himself against "the charge, levelled at every form of historicism, that it destroys individual personality . . . ," *op. cit.*, p. 328.

[80]Wahl, *op. cit.*, p. 7. The point is put more tentatively by Cesselin, *La Philosophie* . . . , p. 209.

tionalism to which the path is opened by his theory of events which lack 'intelligibility'."[81]

Wind, who speaks of "events" rather than "actual entities," suggests two interpretations: either (1) events are theoretical constructs, which Whitehead would clearly deny, or (2) events are given in sense perception. If the latter is the case, then Whitehead is attempting to ground an ideal construct [e.g., point or line] by an appeal to facts, without noticing that the construct has already been included in the description of these facts. Put more simply, Whitehead's "concept of perception contains more than perception does."[82] This criticism has become familiar in recent years, but Wind seems to have been one of the first to state it in technical detail.

Actual entities differ from Leibnizian monads, as many European commentators have noted, in that they have "open windows," i.e., are causally interrelated. Jean Wahl saw this relatedness as a link with Hegelianism: "For Whitehead, as for Hegel," he wrote, "there is no strictly private term; whatever exists is linked to all the rest."[83] Wahl adds that, as a result of Whitehead's stress on the universal relatedness of actualities, "what at first strikes us as a realism,...comes to seem very close to the idealism of a Hegel," although Hegel ignores the "stubborn facts," resistant to reason, which Whitehead takes into account.[84] Crespi points out that in Hegel—but not in Whitehead—"organic relatedness" is associated with a denial of the principle of non-contradiction. How, then, asks Crespi, can Whitehead "explain the seemingly contradictory conception which makes *otherness* an *intrinsic* component of every entity?"[85]

Orsi notes that the problem of relating actualities, which Leibniz "solved" by positing pre-established harmony, recurs in another form in Whitehead: If a given actual entity prehends all other actual entities under its own subjective form, how can they enter it objective-

---

[81]Actis Perinetti, *Cosmologia* . . . , p. 14.

[82]Wind, *op. cit.*, pp. 264f.

[83]Wahl, *op. cit.*, pp. 198f.

[84]*Ibid.*, pp. 130, 134. Wahl adds: "Tout est social . . . Là est la vue profonde de la monadologie leibnizienne." But he notes that Whitehead differed from Leibniz in admitting internal, and many-term, relations among actual entities, *ibid.*, pp. 175, 176.

[85]G. M. Crespi, *op. cit.*, p. 313.

ly?[86] (One might formulate the question: how does Whitehead keep causal "objectification" from becoming a kind of "subjectification"?)

On the question of internal and external relations Jean Wahl set a pattern of careless interpretation which has been repeated by other commentators, assuming that Whitehead admits both internal and external relations indifferently, because any "scheme of relations is only an inadequate way of translating the real."[87] Bocheński goes even further, assimilating Whitehead's position to that of Bradley, for whom "no relations are purely external."[88] Wind was closer to Whitehead's doctrine: "Whitehead ascribes the internality of relations to events, their externality to objects."[89] Even this is not quite accurate; Whitehead holds that, of any two successive actual entities, the later one is internally related to (prehends) the earlier, while the earlier one is externally related to (provides data for) the later. Put more formally: If AE_2 is the successor of AE_1, the relation between them is external to (does not affect the "internal constitution" of) AE_1 but is internal to (does affect the constitution of) AE_2.

Crespi characterizes Whitehead's mature cosmology as "an attempt to reconcile the doctrine of internal relations with the opposed conception of the individuality or atomicity of the real."[90] And Paci, attempting to assimilate Whitehead to Husserl rather than to Hegel, declares: "The philosophy of universal correlation in both Husserl and Whitehead is grounded in a philosophy of time. . . ." The two positions, he concludes, are akin, "insofar as they are both philosophies of time and relation," Whitehead's process-philosophy being close to Husserl's "phenomenology of the temporal structure of the life-world."[91]

Non-English-speaking commentators have had relatively little to say about Whitehead's difficult "epochal" theory of temporality or becoming. Wind defines "epoch" in this sense as "an indivisible period which must become as a whole if the [eternal] object is to be

---

[86]Orsi, op. cit., p. 76.

[87]Wahl, op. cit., pp. 6n, 220n.

[88]Bocheński, op. cit., p. 237. G. M. Crespi also implies that Whitehead admits only internal relations and comments that this is unusual for a realist, op. cit., p. 305.

[89]Wind, op. cit., p. 279.

[90]G. M. Crespi, op. cit., p. 314.

[91]Paci, "Über einige Verwandtschaften . . . ," pp. 244, 250. (The German phrase is "Phänomenologie der zeitlichen Struktur der Lebenswelt.")

actualized at all."[92] Cesselin, while noting a "certain obscurity" in Whitehead's doctrine of durationless actual entities which yet give rise to duration, of non-temporal acts whose products are temporally extended, goes on to define an "epochal duration" as an "indivisible whole," corresponding on the physical level to a wave-length, and on the metaphysical level to the temporal realization of an eternal object.[93] In another passage, however, Cesselin speaks misleadingly of the time-span of an actual entity as "infinitely small."[94]

This brings us to Whitehead's interpretation of teleology and his theory of value. Abbagnano in his discussion of FR, admits that, in exalting reason to the status of a cosmic force, Whitehead is in good company—that of Anaxagoras, Heraclitus, the Stoics, and Hegel. But he criticizes Whitehead's "hypostatization of finalism" (even though an "open" finalism) as a concession to a doctrine (viz., teleology) which is unprovable as well as unfruitful in both science and philosophy.[95]

Actis Perinetti wrote in 1957 that the "revaluation of value" is, in a sense, the key to Whitehead's whole philosophy.[96] Earlier he had maintained that Whitehead had not formulated his value theory in terms of his process-cosmology, but had simply transposed an "acritical [i.e., non-Kantian] ontologism" from cosmology to axiology, thus attempting to overcome the dualism between "objective knowability and the concreteness of becoming."[97]

Other critics have taken a more positive view of Whitehead's value theory. Nédoncelle, in 1934, defined value in Whitehead's sense as "the union of a form to be actualized with a potency for becoming."[98] Wahl had made the significant historical point that for Whitehead there is a close connection between *actuality* and *value* —which places Whitehead among the Hegelians rather than the Kantians or Fichteans: "There is no existence which is vacuous or without

[92]Wind, *op. cit.*, p. 277. This definition would appear to be a reformulation of various remarks which Whitehead makes at SMW 183ff.

[93]Cesselin, *La Philosophie* . . . , pp. 41, 65.

[94]*Ibid.*, pp. 25f.

[95]Nicolà Abbagnano, "Whitehead e il concetto della ragione," *Revue Internationale de Philosophie,* No. 56–57 (1961), pp. 209ff.

[96]Actis Perinetti, "Whitehead," *Enciclopedia filosofica* (1957), col. 1754.

[97]Actis Perinetti, *Cosmologia* . . . , pp. 54, 56.

[98]Nédoncelle, *op. cit.*, p. 129.

value; it is Hegel's merit to have seen this."[99] Wahl speaks of White-head's "important new idea"—that all value is a product of limita-tion.[100] Cesselin writes that in Whitehead "a whole group of notions which at first sight seem a bit forbidding,...shape themselves into a lucid theory of values, a work of genius."[101]

Various commentators have pointed to affinities between White-head's categories and those of earlier philosophers. Wahl, taking a lead from Whitehead himself, early noted that Whitehead's Creativ-ity is Spinoza's Substance—but endowed with choice and purpose.[102] Orsi spells out the relationship. Creativity, she writes, is Spinoza's Substance "individualizing itself in a multiplicity of modes which are dominated by eternal objects variously synthesized in these modes."[103]

We have already noted Whitehead's points of contact with Hegel. Abbagnano makes the general (and controversial) point that for both Hegel and Whitehead "reason is reality itself, and,...the sub-stance of the reality to which [reason] assures order and progress to-ward perfection. But Whitehead lacks the sense of *necessity* expressed in the dialectical structure of reason, as a result of which what is real cannot fail to be rational."[104] The first half of this passage seems to go rather far in assimilating Whitehead's philosophy to the tradition of objective idealism.

Crespi approves Whitehead's rejection of the "rationalist pre-tense of deducing the entire system of philosophic truths a priori," but adds that, despite Whitehead's objections, "a minimum of a priori seems indispensable to the construction of a metaphysics."[105] This would seem less questionable than Abbagnano's assertion—re-peated by Actis Perinetti and Orsi—that Whitehead's philosophy as

[99]Wahl, *op. cit.*, pp. 196, 201.

[100]*Ibid.*, p. 199.

[101]Cesselin, *La Philosophie* . . . , p. 187.

[102]Wahl, *op. cit.*, p. 194. Wahl goes on to characterize Whitehead's philosophy as a "variety of Spinozism, on the condition that one free Spinozism of its obsession with the subject-predicate category and of its monistic prejudice," *ibid.*, p. 212.

[103]Orsi, *op. cit.*, pp. 90f. But Bocheński notes the originality of Whitehead's con-ception of creativity and of prehension, *op. cit.*, p. 233.

[104]Abbagnano, "Whitehead e il concetto . . . ," p. 208. This may be what various commentators have meant by Whitehead's "moderate rationalism"—presumably in contrast to the "immoderate rationalism" of Spinoza and Hegel. Cf. Actis Perinetti, *Cosmologia* . . . , p. 46.

[105]G. M. Crespi, *op. cit.*, p. 330.

a whole is "optimistic."[106] This claim is connected, of course, with Abbagnano's general charge of "Romanticism."

6. Philosophical Theology

Certain European commentators have repeated the familiar criticism that Whitehead's God is a "deus ex machina," a category introduced to save the system from collapse.[107] Others have been content to remark, and sometimes to deplore, Whitehead's "pantheism."[108] More serious students of Whitehead's philosophical theology have recognized, as Cesselin puts it, that Whitehead's conception of God meets systematic requirements of his metaphysics, serving to explain the fact of the continuing actualization of possibilities. The ground for actualization (or "principle of concretion") must be "an entity which is at once actual and non-temporal."[109] Devaux notes, more generally, that God serves to reestablish the equilibrium between the static and dynamic elements of Whitehead's cosmology.[110]

Béra characterizes Whitehead's God, misleadingly, in Aristotelian categories, as "material and formal, efficient and final cause" of the world.[111] Crespi, noting Whitehead's "substantial agreement" with the Aristotelian doctrine of the Unmoved Mover, goes on to say that in PR—"where the foundations of the theological doctrine exhibit the greatest affinity to the Aristotelian procedure"—Whitehead's conclusions are more anti-Aristotelian than in any other work.[112] Orsi specifies one of these conclusions: "Aristotle's pure actuality denies the value of becoming, whereas Whitehead's God reaffirms it."[113]

Whitehead's doctrine of "objective immortality" has often been

106Abbagnano, Storia della filosofia, 2, 614; Actis Perinetti, Cosmologia . . . , p. 14; Orsi, op. cit., pp. 118, 149f.

107E.g., Actis Perinetti, Cosmologia . . . , pp. 37f.; Bertolini, op. cit., p. 326.

108Cf. Béra, op. cit., pp. 29f. (Béra devotes a whole chapter, pp. 40-54, to Whitehead's "mysticism"); also José Pemartín, "Sobre el pensamiento de Whitehead," Revista de filosofía, 7 (1948), 604. (Pemartín's phrase is "panteísmo lamentable.")

109Cesselin, La Philosophie . . . , p. 82. Nédoncelle puts the same point in different words: "Dieu est nécessaire précisément parce que la métaphysique ne peut déterminer le résidu qui est la concrétion des choses," op. cit., p. 129. Cf. also G. M. Crespi, op. cit., p. 324.

110Philippe Devaux, "L'Esprit du néo-réalisme anglais," p. 539.

111Béra, op. cit., p. 45.

112G. M. Crespi, op. cit., p. 324.

113Orsi, op. cit., p. 97.

misunderstood, e.g., by Nédoncelle—an otherwise sensitive critic—who calls it an "immortality of objects" excluding subjective immortality.[114] Crespi seems much closer to Whitehead's intention when he describes God as the ground for the eternity of moral values, guaranteeing that, though "our actions perish in their immediacy, they live everlastingly in Him."[115] Crespi goes on to refute the charge, first made by Ely and repeated by many European commentators,[116] that Whitehead's God is "not religiously available." On the contrary, says Crespi, Whitehead's God is the God "to which religion aspires; the eternal beyond that which passes away and the eternalizing of that which becomes in time."[117]

With respect to Whitehead's philosophy of religion, there is a great variety of interpretations and evaluations. Actis Perinetti sees Whitehead as underestimating the role of dogmas and institutions in religious life.[118] Béra regards Whitehead as a "religious eclectic" and finds his discussion—"on the same level"—of "Jehovah, Allah, Brahma, and the philosophic deities" typically English.[119] Paci puts the point in sharper historical perspective when he notes the "profound Pythagorean religiousness" of Whitehead's thought: "From the start Plato and Pythagoreanism conjoin logical and aesthetic as well as mathematical and religious coherence. The same may be said, *mutatis mutandis*, of Whitehead's organicism."[120]

Nédoncelle writes appreciatively of Whitehead's "renewal of religion," comparing it with that of Spinoza: "The gravity of Whitehead's tone, the depth of his ideas, lend an unquestioned nobility to

---

114Nédoncelle, *op. cit.*, p. 137.

115G. M. Crespi, *op. cit.*, p. 325. Wahl, in loose and metaphorical language, stresses the "ambiguity" of Whitehead's conception of objective immortality: "Elle apparait parfois comme une sorte de dessèchement, d'éternité inerte, d'autres fois comme une éternité vivante," *op. cit.*, p. 198n.

116E.g., Angelo Crespi, *op. cit.*, p. 1142; Orsi, *op. cit.*, p. 98.

117G. M. Crespi, *op. cit.*, p. 325. Cesselin goes even further, finding in Whitehead's philosophical theology "la notion même de Providence et de Paternité divine. Dieu se penche sur toutes choses," *La Philosophie* . . . , p. 85. Cf. also Nédoncelle, *op. cit.*, p. 138.

118Actis Perinetti, *Cosmologia* . . . , p. 49.

119Béra, *op. cit.*, p. 47. (Béra refers to the passage at SMW 257.)

120Enzo Paci, "Definizione e funzione della filosofia speculativa in Whitehead," *Giornale Critico della Filosofia Italiana*, 32 (1953), 329.

his free profession of faith. Whether or not one accepts his rational
mysticism, one cannot deny its quality and its attractiveness."[121]

7. Philosophy of Civilization, Ethics, Aesthetics and Educational Theory

Certain of the major philosophers—one thinks of Plato, Descartes,
Leibniz—have been gifted with an acute and disciplined mathematical
imagination. Others—Hegel, Dilthey, Cassirer—have had a rich and
subtle sense of the complexities of cultural history. As as rule the two
talents have not been combined—though Pascal and Spinoza may
provide partial exceptions to this rule. Whitehead does combine
them to an extraordinary degree, and European commentators have
noted this fact in various ways.

Devaux observes that Whitehead was rare among English neo-
realists in his historical sense and his appeal to the history of philosophic thought,[122] having "effected an equilibrium between scientific
and historical culture in an exceptionally brilliant manner."[123]
Cesselin speaks of the "marvelous historical perspectives which [AI]
offers."[124] Pemartín notes the "paradoxical" quality of Whitehead's
admission that he had never read Hegel, since, despite Whitehead's
originality, his thought as a whole reminds one most of Hegel's.[125]

Orsi remarks that Whitehead overcomes the dualism between
(non-human) nature and spirit or culture,[126] and in that sense is
quite un-Hegelian. Cesselin finds Whitehead moving in his early
works "from the [physical] world to man," but in his later works
"from man to the physical world."[127] Actis Perinetti makes the same
point more critically, detecting in Whitehead's later works an "at-
tenuation" of his "primitive cosmologism," along with an increasing

---

[121]Nédoncelle, *op. cit.*, p. 142.

[122]On the other hand, Actis Perinetti finds Whitehead a superficial historian of
philosophy whose interpretation of Descartes, for example, is "almost a caricature,"
Cosmologia . . . , pp. 42, 43.

[123]Devaux, "L'Esprit du néo réalisme anglais," pp. 518, 519.

[124]Cesselin, *La Philosophie* . . . , p. 100.

[125]Pemartín, *op. cit.*, p. 600.

[126]Orsi, *op. cit.*, p. 70. Frondizi had made a similar point in terms of German
Lebensphilosophie, which, he says, tended to ignore nature in its preoccupation
with human life and culture. Whitehead takes *both* into account, *op. cit.*, p. 15.

[127]Cesselin, *La Philosophie* . . . , p. 70.

interest in human values.[128] In an earlier study Actis Perinetti had dismissed Whitehead's attempt to bring together "poetry and science, reason and myth" as impracticable.[129]

Cesselin is particularly interested in Whitehead's ethical views. He considers Whitehead's "aspects of freedom" (ch. iv of AI) "one of his richest and densest studies."[130] Cesselin insists that, although Whitehead wrote no special treatise on ethics, "ethical preoccupations were never absent from his thought."[131] And he makes the valid point that "a philosophy of organism" need not undervalue the individual, that in fact Whitehead places "an accent upon the person, upon the principle of individuality, which often reminds one of Kant."[132]

Whitehead's educational theory has been the subject of only one study in a language other than English, that by Piero Bertolini. Though largely expository, this article is of first quality. We may hope that Bertolini will return to the subject at greater length. He sees Whitehead as closer to Dewey in educational theory than in theoretical philosophy. Both emphasize the open and mobile character of the educational experience. But Dewey stresses growth for its own sake, whereas Whitehead emphasizes "progress toward the realization of universal values, above all a harmony which always remains vital and active."[133] Bertolini finds in Whitehead's three phases of the educational process ("romance, precision, and generalization") an echo of Vico and Hegel, formulated in an original way. He adds that many of Whitehead's criticisms of traditional educational methods—as focussing exclusively upon the second phase—are applicable to the present Italian scene.[134]

8. Problems of Terminology and Translation

Criticism of Whitehead's "obscure and difficult" style and his excessive use of neologisms is frequently voiced by non-English-speak-

---

[128]Actis Perinetti, "Whitehead," Enciclopedia Filosofica, col. 1756.

[129]Actis Perinetti, Cosmologia . . . , pp. 14f.

[130]Cesselin, La Philosophie . . . , p. 121.

[131]Ibid., p. 175.

[132]Ibid., p. 182. (Although he cites no text, Cesselin may have in mind such passages as this [ESP 164]: "Importance belongs to the one life of the one individual.")

[133]Bertolini, op. cit., pp. 323, 331.

[134]Ibid., pp. 334, 336.

ing commentators. One of the first, and most balanced, of such criticisms is to be found in Nédoncelle (1934), who notes that Whitehead's style is "not without charm and even a subtle precision," adding that its alleged obscurity is due not so much to the terms Whitehead uses as to the way in which he uses them: "Each lapidary formula is set in a disconcerting context."[135]

Metz was one of the first to claim that Whitehead's difficult technical style was more "German" than "English," and that certain key terms underwent changes of meaning from one work to another. In a sentence omitted from the English translation of his book, Metz remarks that it is hard to say whether the difficulty of understanding Whitehead is due to the obscurity of his language or to an insufficient "power of inner illumination" in his thought.[136]

Angelo Crespi describes Whitehead as "a highly original'" and "extremely concise thinker" who is "inevitably obscure."[137] Orsi declares that once the difficulties of Whitehead's style and terminology have been overcome, "the uncommon depth of his thought will shine through the ambiguities of expression." She adds that, although Whitehead sometimes overdoes neologism, it is necessary to his philosophic purpose.[138]

Routine references to the difficulty of Whitehead's style are also to be found in Abbagnano,[139] Devaux,[140] Paci,[141] and van der Horst.[142] G. M. Crespi contends that Whitehead's obscurity is not

---

[135]Nédoncelle, op. cit., p. 141.

[136]Metz, op. cit., 2, 140f. (The omitted sentence, which should appear on p. 594 of the English edition, reads as follows: "Es ist deshalb auch nicht leicht zu sagen, ob die Schwerverständlichkeit von Whiteheads Lehre lediglich durch die Dunkelheit seiner Sprache und nicht durch die mangelnde innere Leuchtkraft seines Denkens bedingt ist.") Metz also describes Whitehead's philosophy, somewhat hyperbolically, as a "gigantic cryptogram," which will take generations to decipher, ibid., p. 141.

[137]Angelo Crespi, op. cit., p. 1139. Earlier Frondizi had noted that Whitehead used familiar terms in unfamiliar ways, as well as new terms "which he rarely defined." Frondizi adds that Whitehead had clarified "most terminological difficulties" for him during a Harvard seminar in 1934–1935, op. cit., p. 9.

[138]Orsi, op. cit., pp. 2, 34.

[139]Abbagnano, Storia della filosofia, 2, 613.

[140]Devaux, "Le Bergsonisme de Whitehead," p. 227.

[141]Paci, "Definizione e funzione . . . ," p. 305.

[142]J. W. van der Horst, "De methode van de metafysica volgens Alfred N. Whitehead," Algemeen Nederlands Tijdschrift voor Wijsbegeerte en Psychologie, 52 (1959), 103.

just a matter of inadequate expression or neologism, but is due to the rapid development of his thought from work to work, and to "a fluidity and indefiniteness of concepts which is not casual, since [Whitehead] maintains that the clarity of definitions is always a false clarity, threatening to conceal the complexity of things."[143] Cesselin notes Whitehead's gift for turning a phrase,[144] and Müller remarks that the "exceptional, indeed inexhaustible fulness" of Whitehead's thought, like that of Plato, is not susceptible to simplification or popularization. "Whitehead's style is characterized by a sweet maturity and clear profundity—it always suggests more than it expresses.[145]

Considering the special difficulties of translating Whitehead's philosophic language, the general level of accuracy seems to me commendable. Of course, one finds minor inaccuracies and misleading renderings. Crespi remarks that he has noted about fifty such cases in the Italian translation of CN.[146] For example, where Whitehead writes: "The aggregate of event-particles forms a four-dimensional manifold," the Italian version has: "La totalità dell'evento punti-forme formerà varietà a quattro dimensioni." (Crespi suggests: "La totalità degli eventi particelle [formerà] un molteplice a quattro dimensioni.")

Whitehead's definition of value as "the intrinsic reality of an event" (SMW 116) is mistranslated by Cesselin as "la réalité intrinseque d'un *moment*."[147] The Italian translation of SMW misrenders Whitehead's phrase, "haunts time like a spirit" as "si burla del tempo come un fantasma,"[148] apparently through a confusion of 'haunt' with 'taunt'! Actis Perinetti, whose translations are generally reliable, transposes two adjectives in rendering Whitehead's statement that art "reveals as in a flash intimate, absolute Truth regarding the Nature of Things" (AI 350). (". . . risveglia in un intimo, assoluto splendore la verità riguardante la natura delle cose.")[149] Paci omits

---

[143]G. M. Crespi, *op. cit.*, p. 295.

[144]Cesselin, *La Philosophie* . . . , p. 122.

[145]Gustav E. Müller, *Amerikanische Philosophie* (second ed.; Stuttgart, 1950), p. 183.

[146]G. M. Crespi, *Rivista Critica di Storia della Filosofia*, 6 (1951), p. 240.

[147]Cesselin, *La Philosophie* . . . , p. 40. Italics added.

[148]*La Scienza e il mondo moderno*, trans. Antonio Banfi (Milan, 1945), p. 109. Actis Perinetti quotes this mistranslation without comment, *Cosmologia* . . . , p. 38.

[149]Actis Perinetti, *Cosmologia* . . . , p. 55.

a number of essential qualifiers, renders "seventeenth" as "eighteenth" ("diciottesimo") century and "particular instance" as "practical example" ("esempio practico").[150]

European commentators frequently misdate Whitehead's works. Wahl's pioneering study gave the date of SMW as 1927; this error has been repeated by many French and Italian writers. Metz placed the *Introduction to Mathematics* in 1908. Devaux, in his 1961 article, gives the date of CN as 1919.

Whitehead's special terms would seem no more difficult to translate than those of Spinoza, Kant, and Hegel, which have been somehow managed—not always well, to be sure—in English. "Feeling" is particularly difficult: most of the Romance-language terms miss the point, suggesting a state rather than a process, e.g., "sensibilidad" (Frondizi), "sensibilità" (Abbagnano), "sentimento" (Crespi, Paci) "sentiment" (Wahl, Béra, Cesselin). Less misleading are the infinitive forms—e.g., "sentire" (Paci)—and the compounds—e.g., "atto emozionale" (Actis Perinetti), "processo di sentimento" (Pastore), "sentiment-préhension" (Wahl, Cesselin). Sometimes the English term "feeling" is given without translation (Paci, Actis Perinetti, Wahl, Cesselin), a sensible practice already adopted in English with such difficult non-English terms as "natura naturans," "Ding an Sich," "Aufhebung," and "élan vital."

There would seem to be virtue in a degree of terminological standardization. I have counted at least seven Italian renderings of "fallacy of misplaced concreteness": "sofisma della falsa concretezza" (G. M. Crespi); "concretezza mal posta" (Orsi); "errore di concretizzazione" (Bertolini, Actis Perinetti); "concretizzazione mal posta" (Actis Perinetti); "concretizzazione male impostata" (Actis Perinetti); "illusione della concretezza mal posta" (Paci); "fallacia della concretezza mal posta" (Paci, Morra). This last would seem not only closest to the English original, but least misleading.

In Spanish there is "falacia de concretez fuera de lugar" (Frondizi); in French "sophisme [or "illusion"] de la concrétisation mal placée" (Cesselin), "aberration dite de la concrétisation mal placée" (Ginestier), and "erreur du concret mal choisi" (Devaux). In German: "Irrtum der falsch angesetzten Konkretheit" (Metz), "Täuschung durch das verstellte Konkrete" (Bochénski), and "falsch

<hr>

[150]Paci, "Definizione e funzione . . . ," pp. 313, 320, 321, 327.

angewandte Konkretisierung" (Paci). In Russian: "oshibka ne-umestnoi konkretizatsii" (Bogomolov).

The "fallacy of simple location" has not been quite so luxuriantly rendered. In French there is "location unique" and "emplacement unique" (both Wahl), "localisation simple" (Cesselin), "doctrine dite de la localisation simple" (Ginestier), and "simple localisation matérielle" (Devaux). In Italian I have found only "localizzazione semplice" (Crespi, Actis Perinetti, Orsi); in German: "Begriff der einfachen Setzung" (Metz) and "einfache Örtlichkeit" (Bocheński).

There is a special problem in rendering Whitehead's "actual entity" in the Romance languages—since 'actuelle,' 'attuale,' 'actual,' etc., all connote "present" or "contemporary."[151] We have already seen the difficulties generated by the Wahl-Cesselin substitution of 'réelle' for 'actuelle.' But no one seems to have tried 'active' (e.g., "entité active," "entità attiva," "entidad activa"), although Müller speaks of actual entities as "aktiven, sich bezeugenden Ereignissen."[152] Strangely enough, though the German 'wirkliche' would seem a close equivalent of Whitehead's 'actual,' writers using German have preferred 'aktuelle'—either "aktuelle Entität" (Metz, Bubser) or "aktuelle Wesenheit" (Paci). It is to be hoped that the forthcoming German edition of Whitehead's philosophical works, of which Charles Hartshorne is one of the editors, will employ an adequate and stand-ardized rendering of Whitehead's key terms.

9. *Conclusion*

The complexity of Whitehead's relation to Hegel is suggested by Jean Wahl in the remark that Whitehead, along with William James and Gabriel Marcel, attempted to restore the rights of immediacy (thus continuing Kierkegaard's endeavor). Whitehead's "empiricism" is characterized by "the affirmation of the non-deducibility of being, by the affirmation of the given, . . . of something immediate."[153] This last point Wahl sees as a link with contemporary phenomenology: Whitehead and the phenomenologists alike stress receptivity and im-mediacy, the "flux of the lived," *In-der-Welt-Sein;* Whitehead's "pre-

---

[151]A point made by Frondizi, *op. cit.,* p. 21n1, who nevertheless continues to translate "actual entity" as "entidad actual."

[152]Müller, *op. cit.,* p. 184.

[153]Wahl, *op. cit.,* pp. 3, 6.

hension"—as we have seen—is comparable to Husserl's "intentionality." "A kind of dialectic," Wahl remarks, "has carried phenomenology from a theory of eternal objects like Whitehead's to a theory of existence as duration" which echoes Whitehead's doctrine of causal efficacy.[154] Wahl also notes that both Heidegger and Whitehead have incorporated certain pragmatist themes: "The world is a world of obstacles and instruments, the mind reacts to it with anticipations, pre-perceptions, and hypotheses."[155] But Orsi maintains that Whitehead's similarity to the existentialists is external and superficial, since he assumes, and they deny, harmony and progress in history and nature.[156]

Appreciation of Whitehead's intellectual achievement goes back very far in France[157] (Wahl), Belgium (Devaux), and Germany (Metz). Metz declared in 1935 that few contemporary philosophers equalled Whitehead and none surpassed him. He saw Whitehead's philosophy as one of the summits of British thought, and declared that no British thinker had placed a higher value on speculative reason, or grasped its essence more profoundly. But though he found Whitehead strong in insight, and persistent and powerful in thought, he considered him weak as a system-builder. Metz even applies Whitehead's characterization of Plato—"greatest of metaphysicians but poorest of systematic thinkers"—to Whitehead himself.[158]

Whitehead's death was the occasion for the appearance of a number of appreciations in European journals. Angelo Crespi called him "the last of the great systematic English thinkers of the past generation"[159] and G. M. Crespi: "one of the most renowned of the thinkers of our time."[160] José Pemartín characterized Whitehead as "one of the most original, complex, and vigorous minds of . . . 'modern Anglo-

---

154*Ibid.*, p. 18.

155*Loc. cit.* Wahl fails to mention the opposed valuations which Heidegger and Whitehead place upon natural science, technology, and "contemporary American civilization." For Heidegger all three are an absolute wasteland; for Whitehead all three are expressions of cultural and intellectual vitality and adventure. Cf. Heidegger, *Introduction to Metaphysics*, ch. 1, esp. last few pages.

156Orsi, *op. cit.*, p. 150.

157Henri Dufumier, reviewing *Principia Mathematica*, Vol. I, noted that "les thèses essentielles du livre . . . s'imposent par leur courageuse précision et leur solide originalité." *Revue de Métaphysique et de Morale*, 20 (1912), 539.

158Metz, *op. cit.*, **2**, 130, 160f.

159A. Crespi, *op. cit.*, p. 1139.

160G. M. Crespi, *op. cit.*, p. 293.

Saxon philosophy,' " adding that whereas the epigoni of the Cartesian epoch—Anglo-Saxon neo-realists and European existentialists—seemed to exhaust themselves intellectually almost as soon as they were born, Whitehead's thought contains elements, "confused and unconnected" though they may be, for "a future synthesis."[161]

Gustav E. Müller, a European-born Professor at the University of Oklahoma, in his survey of American philosophy written for a German audience, spoke of Whitehead as "one of the most significant thinkers of all time," and referred to his "subtle and supple thought, proof against every dogmatism," adding that "measured by his absolute reasonableness, most contemporary philosophy seems coarse, awkward, and onesided."[162]

Similarly high evaluations are repeated by Cesselin,[163] Bocheński,[164] Xirau,[165] Ginestier,[166] and Orsi.[167] In contrast, Actis Perinetti finds Whitehead's thought bizarre, disorganized, incoherent, and lacking in philosophic rigor—though an original expression of "important needs."[168] Gottfried Martin places the matter in a large historical framework when he writes that "Whitehead's return to metaphysics and to 'the dialectical Plato' is one of the most important events in contemporary philosophy."[169]

When we turn from such individual evaluations to the general influence of Whitehead's thought in the non-English-speaking philosophic community, the question becomes much more complicated. Various sympathetic commentators have tended to overstate both Whitehead's influence in the English-speaking philosophic commu-

---

[161]Pemartín, op. cit., pp. 593, 603.

[162]Müller, op. cit., p. 183.

[163]Cesselin, La Philosophie . . . , pp. 1, 216; also Revue Philosophique, 77 (1952), 88: "La philosophie de Whitehead, malgré ses obscurités, semble décidément prendre une place de plus en plus importante dans la philosophie contemporaine."

[164]Bocheński, op. cit., p. 232.

[165]Ramón Xirau, "A. N. Whitehead: Tres categorías fundamentales," Filosofía y Letras, 23 (1952), 313.

[166]Ginestier, op. cit., pp. 70, 71.

[167]Orsi, op. cit., p. 143.

[168]Actis Perinetti, Cosmologia . . . , pp. 17f.

[169]Martin, "Neuzeit . . . ," p. 160.

nity[170] and the probable increase of his influence in their own countries.[171]

It seems clear that Whitehead's philosophy has had, and will continue to have, an unequal influence in various parts of the non-English-speaking world. At present, Whitehead enjoys unequal acceptance even *within* the English-speaking philosophic community, being much more highly regarded in the United States than in the United Kingdom. I shall consider briefly, in turn, the situation in French, German, Italian, and Spanish-speaking areas.

Despite the growing body of French translations and commentaries, Whitehead remains less well-known and less influential in the French-speaking philosophic community than, say, Bergson among English-speaking philosophers. The French, as Professor Randall has said, tend to be "provincial in their universalism." I see little likelihood that Whitehead's thought will make much impact upon French philosophy in the near future. This, of course, is no reason for French scholars not to press ahead with the task of translation, interpretation, and criticism of Whitehead's philosophic works.

In the German-speaking philosophic community Whitehead would appear to be nearly as well known—though probably not so influential —as, say, Husserl among English-speaking philosophers. The forthcoming German edition of Whitehead's philosophic works (edited by Hartshorne, Leclerc, and Martin) should considerably increase the interest in, and influence of, Whitehead's thought among German-speaking philosophers.

Whitehead may be better known in Italy than is Croce in English-speaking countries, and perhaps equally influential. The large number of Italian translations of Whitehead's philosophic works (more than in any other language), and the small but increasing number of competent and thoughtful commentaries, suggests that a renaissance of Whitehead

---

[170]E.g., Devaux, *Lotze* . . . , p. 39; Paci, "Definizione e funzione . . . ," p. 305; Cesselin, *La Philosophie* . . . , p. 70. Devaux makes the curious claim that Whitehead's influence in the United States was partly the result of American hospitality to a doctrine "qui érgierait avec succès la forme coopérative des sociétés coloniales en principe organique général et même (si possible) cosmique . . . ," *Lotze* . . . , p. 35.

[171]E.g., Paci, "Presentazione di Whitehead," *Aut-Aut*, No. 12 (1952), p. 517.

scholarship may already be in progress.[172] It is unfortunate that the influential "positive existentialist" Nicolà Abbagnano should have approached Whitehead's philosophy from a perspective that is both doctrinally peripheral and personally unsympathetic. It would seem that, with a little good will, he might have found common ground with Whitehead on many questions of metaphysics, ethics, and social philosophy.

Whitehead may be almost as well-known in the Spanish-speaking philosophic community (including, of course, both South and Central America) as, say, Unamuno among English-speaking philosophers— though probably less influential. In view of the informed interest of philosophers like Frondizi and Xirau, and of the fact that both AI and PR have appeared in Spanish, but as yet in no other foreign language, it seems likely that Whitehead's influence among Spanish-speaking philosophers, particularly in Latin America, may grow steadily in the years ahead.

The celebration of the centennial of Whitehead's birth has been impressively international. Ivor Leclerc included two German contributions (by Martin and Wein) in his centennial volume, *The Relevance of Whitehead*. The *Revue Internationale de Philosophie* published articles in French, German, Italian, and English in its special Whitehead issue. At the Whitehead session of the Extraordinary Interamerican Philosophy Congress in San José, Costa Rica, in July 1961 four papers were read in English (including two by Charles Hartshorne) and two in Spanish.[173] In Paris Jean Wahl presented a course of Sorbonne lectures on Whitehead's philosophy during 1960-1961, and André-Louis Leroy gave a special lecture on Whitehead's philosophy of science under the auspices of the Centre de Synthèse.[174] The recently-published anthology, *Alfred North Whitehead: His Reflections on Man and Nature* (New York: Harper & Brothers, 1961), edited by

[172]Actis Perinetti, a rather unfriendly critic, reports an increasing interest in Whitehead's philosophy (as of 1954) among Italian philosophers, *Cosmologia* . . . , p. v.

[173]The Spanish papers are: (1) Miguel Ángel Campos Sandí (Costa Rica) "El Método en el esquema de A. N. Whitehead"; (2) Quinter M. Lyon (University of Mississippi) "El Espíritu y la filosofía del organismo." All six papers will be published in the Proceedings *(Actas)* of the Congress.

[174]Published as "Science et philosophie chez Alfred North Whitehead" *Revue de Synthèse*, 3e Série, No. 22-24 (1961), 43-66.

Dr. Ruth Nanda Anshen for the "World Perspectives" series, will eventually be translated into French, German, Spanish, Italian, Dutch, Swedish, Danish, Norwegian, Serbo-Croatian, Chinese, Japanese, and Telugu.

All things considered, the prospects for a future increase of serious and informed interest in Whitehead's philosophy in the non-English-speaking world would seem brighter today than at any time in the recent past.

GEORGE L. KLINE

BRYN MAWR COLLEGE

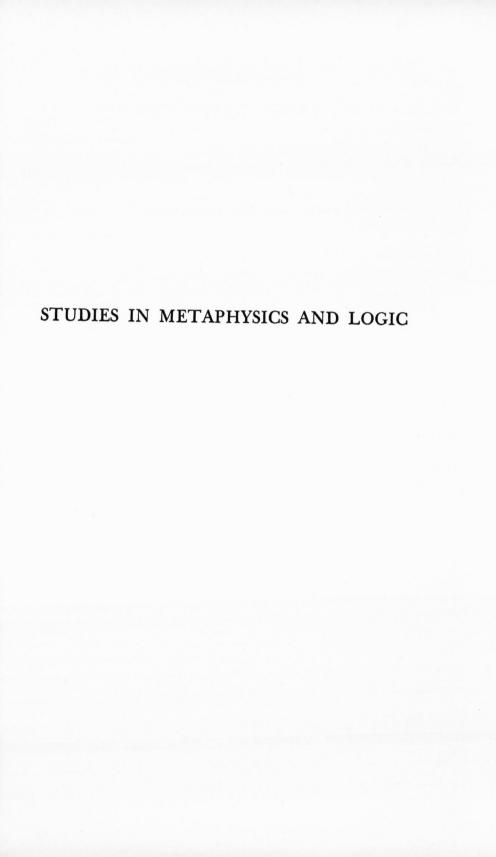

STUDIES IN METAPHYSICS AND LOGIC

ONTOLOGY, CATEGORY-WORDS, AND
MODAL LOGIC

I

In a recent essay Gottfried Martin has called attention to the traditional distinction between metaphysics as theory of principles, *scientia universalis*, and as theory of being, *ontologia generalis*.[1] Martin points out that historically metaphysicians have tended to be interested primarily in one or the other of these, rarely in both equally. He concludes by expressing preference for metaphysics as theory of being and gives several objections to metaphysics as *scientia universalis*. He thinks that "only regional systems of principles are possible, that is to say, that there are only systems of principles which are relevant to particular realms of being. If this assumption is correct," he continues, "it would be advisable to regard the systems of principles as belonging to the fundamental questions of the respective sciences. If we are dealing with very general systems of principles, and with general questions about systems of principles, then these had best find their place in the theory of science or in logic—logic here understood . . . in the modern extended sense." Hence it is "appropriate to loosen the old bonds between *scientia universalis* and *ontologia generalis* . . ." and to assign "theory of principles to logic in its wide sense, and to concentrate metaphysics essentially upon the task of theory of being."

By the *ontology* of a language-system *L* let us mean, following Quine in essentials, the domain of objects taken as values for its variables. By the *logical principles* of *L* let us mean the set of logical or analytic truths of *L*.[2] It might be thought that construing 'ontology' and 'logical principles' in this way does violence to traditional meanings, but this is doubtful. The modern semantical notion of an

[1]"Metaphysics as *Scientia Universalis* and as *Ontologia Generalis*," in *"The Relevance of Whitehead*," ed. I. Leclerc (London: Allen and Unwin, and New York: Macmillan, 1961), pp. 219-231.

[2]See especially the author's *The Notion of Analytic Truth* (Philadelphia: University of Pennsylvania Press, and London: Oxford University Press, 1959).

ontology renders explicit what has often been rather obscure. Likewise the modern notion of analytic truth may be regarded as a kind of paradigm to the precise characterization of which much of traditional logic has been devoted. Both of these comments require to be sure a detailed historical justification, which if we mistake not would not be too difficult to supply.

If the foregoing identifications are justified, it seems very doubtful that we should loosen the bonds between *ontologia generalis* and *scientia universalis,* as Martin recommends. In fact it is doubtful whether this is possible or even meaningful. The two—at least in their modern form—seem so indissolubly intertwined as to justify the maxim: No ontology, no logic.

Let us suppose that L is formulated as a first-order system, involving just the usual logic of truth-functions, quantifiers, and identity.[3] Such a formulation is designed with especial regard to ontology. In each such L, the only ontology involved is that of the particular discipline being formalized. In other words, no variables are introduced other than those having as their values the objects with which L deals. This is in contrast to other formulations of logic which involve variables over *propositions* (in some abstract logical sense) and perhaps other kinds of entities not pertaining to the subject-matter of L.[4] (Some comments against propositions will be given in §V below.) The formulation of L is such then as to involve the ontology of L, and none other, in a most fundamental way.

We see then that there is no specifically *logical* subject-matter. There is subject-matter only *of some L.* Hence there is no specifically logical ontology. Rather there are specific non-logical ontologies suitably described in appropriate L's.

Because of the generality of first-order logic, there is an important sense in which analytic truths are more than merely "regional." By 'regional truths of L' we could well designate the truths of L which are not analytic. Regional principles then are presumably not common to all disciplines and apply to only "particular realms of being."

[3]The formulations presupposed are those of the author's *Truth and Denotation, A Study in Semantical Theory* (Chicago: University of Chicago Press, Toronto: University of Toronto Press, and London: Routledge and Kegan Paul, 1958), Chapter II.

[4]See especially A. Church, *Introduction to Mathematical Logic,* 1 (Princeton: Princeton University Press, 1956). Unfortunately many of Church's formulations appear to be among the philosophically least acceptable expositions of modern logic.

It is the system of regional principles which "belongs to the fundamental questions of the respective sciences."

The converse maxim—No logic, no ontology—is also to be remarked. Any ontology and therewith system of regional principles gives rise to a logic, more specifically to a first-order *L*. Of course the required *L* may not actually have been formulated, but in principle such formulation can always be given.

It would seem then that there is no sharp, clear, or fundamental separation of *ontologia generalis* and *scientia universalis*, of ontology and logic, when each is understood in its proper relation to the other. The one without the other is impossible, and the other without the one, although possible, lacks the necessary refinement and precision of statement.

It is only the logical skeleton of metaphysical language, not its flesh and blood, that will concern us here. But it is just this skeleton that is so frequently found lacking in the metaphysical literature and which it is the function of the philosophic logician to provide. Logicians have for the most part disclaimed metaphysical interest and metaphysicians have not mastered the intricacies of the new logic. The result has been an unfortunate severance as complete as possible. Logic, divorced from its proper role as the *scientia scientiarum,* cannot thrive merely as an arid branch of pure mathematics, nor can the metaphysician hope to make progress disregarding the help which the modern logician has to offer. This present essay, written to honor Professor Hartshorne, is intended as a bridge-builder between these two great areas of philosophy. Each is here to stay. Not peaceful co-existence but intimate collaboration should be aimed at, for which the time seems now ripe. Professor Hartshorne has recognised the need for such collaboration more perhaps than any other contemporary philosopher.

II

Let us turn, by way of an example, to an area of metaphysics to which fruitful application of logic has yet to be made—namely, the theory of *categories.*

Some years ago Ryle noted that "doctrines of categories and theories of types [or sorts] are explorations in the same field. And the field is still largely unexplored . . . The matter is of some importance, for not only is it the case that category-propositions (namely assertions

that terms belong to certain categories or types) are always philosophers' propositions, but, I believe, the converse is also true. So we
are in the dark about the nature of philosophical problems and
methods if we are in the dark about types or categories."[5]

Carnap's more recent discussion of what is involved in the introduction of a new kind of entity and of the acceptance of a linguistic
framework is concerned with essentially the same problem.[6] Carnap
does not explicitly employ the word 'category', but he seems to use
certain general terms such as 'physical object', 'number', or 'proposition' as category-words in a more or less traditional sense.

Still more recently, Quine has stated that the "quest of a simplest,
clearest overall pattern of canonical [logical] notation is not to be
distinguished from a quest of ultimate categories, a limning of the
most general traits of reality."[7] "The same motives that impel scientists to seek ever simpler and clearer theories adequate to the subject
matter of their special sciences [a rather dubious description, is it not,
of what scientists do?]," Quine notes, "are motives for simplification
and clarification of the broader framework shared by all the sciences.
Here the objective is called philosophical, because of the breadth of
the framework concerned; but the motivation is the same."

Carnap describes with some care the method whereby new entities
are introduced into a language-system. An (interpreted) language-
system L is presupposed as already at hand and as formulated by
means of exact syntactical and semantical rules. The vocabulary of
L is specified and its variables are presumed to range over some well-
defined domain D of objects. The new entities constitute some new
domain D'. The two essential steps for the introduction of the entities of new domain D' are, Carnap notes, the specification of a "general term, a predicate of higher level . . . , permitting us to say of any
particular entity that it belongs to this kind (e.g. 'Red is a *property*',

5G. Ryle, "Categories," *Logic and Language* (Second Series), ed. A. Flew (Oxford:
Basil Blackwell, 1953), pp. 65-81. The material of this section and the next follows
in essentials the author's "Category-Words and Linguistic Frameworks," to appear
in the *Kant-Studien*.

6R. Carnap, "Empiricism, Semantics, and Ontology," *Meaning and Necessity* (2nd
ed.; Chicago: University of Chicago Press, 1956), pp. 205-221.

7W. V. Quine, *Word and Object* (New York and London: The Technology Press
of The Massachusetts Institute of Technology and John Wiley and Sons, 1960), p. 161.

'Five is a *number*') ." The second is the introduction of variables ranging over the entities of the new domain D'.

Strictly speaking, not both of these steps are needed. Either one alone may be made to suffice. Thus if the general predicate is introduced as a new predicate truly applying to all objects of the domain D', the range of the variables may now be regarded as D together with D' (i.e., as the logical sum of D and D'). No new variables are needed; the old variables are merely given a more extensive range.

On the other hand, if new variables are introduced ranging over just the objects of D', then no new general predicate for the objects of D' is needed. Such a predicate is in fact definable as merely a suitable expression for the universal class of D'. For this at least one other predicate applicable to the objects of D' is assumed available. In practise, such other predicates are usually needed anyhow. Without them, the modes of expression available for talking about the objects of D' would be rather limited. If 'P' is such a predicate applicable to the new objects and 'α' a new variable, then the new general predicate may in effect be defined as 'the class (or virtual class) of all objects α such that α has P or α does not have P'. In fact we could define 'D"' itself in this way if desired. (Throughout we are using 'D', 'D", etc., as meta-linguistic symbols but they may be defined as here within the object-languages also if desired.)

As an example, suppose D is the domain of physical objects in space and time. Let *L* be a linguistic framework whose variables range over the objects of D and whose primitive predicates are applicable to objects of D. *L* is presumed for the moment to contain no property or predicate variables. Suppose it is desired now to introduce into *L* (monadic) properties as a new kind of entity. The totality of such properties applicable to objects of D constitutes then the new domain D'.

Two methods are available. (i) A new kind of variable may be introduced to range over the objects of D'. Note that some names of specific properties, i.e., some one-place predicates, may already be available in *L*. The introduction of the new entities consists merely in the introduction of variables over these entities. If variables over dyadic relations applicable to objects of D are desired, the procedure is similar. Here we have a new domain D". And so on. Note that D' is in effect merely the universal class of properties, D" the universal class of dyadic relations, etc.

(ii) The second method consists in introducing a new general term and then extending the range of the variables of L, rather than of introducing a new kind of variable. Let 'x', 'y', etc., be the variables of L and let 'Prp' be the new predicate, to be read 'is a property'. 'Prp x' then reads 'x is a property'. The variables are now to range not only over the objects of D but over members of Prp as well. This second method is less familiar than the first. It is akin to methods used in axiomatic set theory. To see this let us use 'ϵ' as the converse of the relation of *applying to*. '$x \epsilon y$' then reads 'the property y applies to x' or 'x has the property y'. It then always holds in L that if $x \epsilon y$ then Prp y. No type distinction is explicitly required, although it may implicitly be used in framing axioms. Technically this second method is quite as suitable as the first and shows that no new style of variables need be introduced.

It should be noted that 'property' is being used here and throughout in the sense of 'property-in-extension' or 'class'. The main difference between properties and classes is in the condition of identity. If two properties are identical then every object which possesses one of them possesses the other, whereas two classes are identical *if and only if* every member of one is a member of the other. The latter condition gives both a necessary and sufficient condition for identity, the former a necessary one only. A sufficient condition for identity of properties is usually not given. To assure a clear necessary and sufficient condition, we construe properties as properties-in-extension and hence identify them with the corresponding classes.

We may, if we like, introduce, in addition to new variables and/or a new general predicate, some "names" for particular entities of D'. But Carnap notes that "this is not a sure sign of the acceptance of the new kind of entities," because "some such names may already occur before the introduction of the new framework." For example, 'Blue' may be introduced as a new predicate of L applicable to the objects of D. The introduction of 'Blue' in this way clearly does not involve the acceptance of a new kind of entity. Hence it is only to the new variables and/or to the introduction of a new general predicate that we must look as a sign that new entities are introduced.

As another example, let L be as above with D the domain of physical objects. Let D' be the new domain, say of positive integers. We may introduce a general predicate 'PI' ('is a positive integer') and extend the range of the variables, or we may introduce a new, second style of variables whose range is just the positive integers. The frameworks which result differ from each other only in minor technical ways.

III

Carnap seems to have in mind primarily systems based upon type theory. The examples he considers are for the most part examples of introducing entities of logical type higher than that of those at hand. In each such case, the new entities belong to an altogether new category of objects. If we think only of a simplified type theory for the moment in which relations are handled as classes of ordered couples, the introduction of a new category of entities at any stage consists merely of introducing all classes of entities of the highest type already available.[8] The customary method here is merely to introduce variables of the next higher type regarded as ranging over classes of the next higher type. No new category-word need be introduced as a primitive, for it is now definable as any expression for the universal class of next higher type.

Let 'V^n' be the expression for the universal class of type n. According to the type theory of the preceding paragraph, our categories are V^1, V^2, and so on, as far as one wishes.

For many scientific purposes it seems that these are the only categories needed. At any event, they may be made to suffice by suitable technical adjustments of detail and upon a suitable choice or suitable choices of V^1. For some purposes V^1 might be the class of physical objects, for others, the positive integers, for still others, qualities or values or human beings now alive or etc. Or V^1 could be taken as the logical sum of two or more of these domains. Thus it may be convenient to partition V^1 into as many sorts of individuals as are desired. But given V^1 in its totality, V^2, V^3, etc., are then wholly determined.

We need not put forward here specific suggestions as to how V^1 in its totality may be partitioned. This may be done of course in many ways, some of these ways yielding a more reasonable set of categories or sub-categories than others. Likewise each of V^2, V^3, etc., may be partitioned in ways which might be regarded as providing categories, although precisely how this is to be done is not obvious.

---

[8]See A. Tarski, "The Concept of Truth in Formalized Languages," *Logic, Semantics, Metamathematics* (Oxford: Clarendon Press, 1956), pp. 152-278, esp. pp. 242-244.

A theory of categories based upon a set theory rather than upon a theory of types might read somewhat as follows. The fundamental domain of objects including sets is subdivided into some mutually exclusively, jointly exhaustive domains $D_1, \ldots, D_n$. But this may be done in many arbitrary ways, and precisely how one would make such a subdivision so that each D_i could in some reasonable sense be called a category is not clear. Type theory seems to carry a clear doctrine of categories along with it, whereas set theory does not. Some *ad hoc* superimposition seems needed here, involving considerations extraneous to set theory itself.

To the preceding categories, whether based on type or set theory, may be added further ones for *syntax* and *semantics*, i.e., suitable categories of *linguistic* objects, such as *expressions, theorems, truths,* and so on. Here strictly the new category is merely that of expression, the others being suitable subsets of this. In particular, note that no new category for semantics is needed, merely a new primitive relation. Note also that no new categories for *classes* of expressions or relations between or among expressions or between or among expressions and the preceding objects are introduced. Such categories are simply not needed.[9]

For further purposes further categories may be required. For *pragmatics*, e.g., we should wish to add categories of *human persons* and *actions*, and perhaps of *social groups*. Human persons and actions are not to be handled merely as new kinds of individuals but *sui generis*.[10] Social groups are presumably classes (with a certain structure) of human persons.

Also it is very convenient to allow *time-stretches* or intervals to constitute a separate category. This is not indispensable perhaps but facilitates many forms of expression involving time.[11]

The preceding doctrine, as based upon type theory, possesses such "naturalness" or "unnaturalness" as might be thought to attach to that theory. The logical tradition has rightly differentiated among

[9]See *Truth and Denotation* and *The Notion of Analytic Truth.*

[10]Cf. the author's *Toward a Systematic Pragmatics (Studies in Logic and the Foundations of Mathematics,* Amsterdam: North-Holland Publishing Co., 1959); also his "Performance, Purpose, and Permission," *Philosophy of Science,* 30 (1963), 122-137.

[11]See *Toward a Systematic Pragmatics,* pp. 36-37. Also J. H. Woodger, *The Axiomatic Method in Biology* (Cambridge: Cambridge University Press, 1937), p. 56 ff.

individuals, classes, and relations in a way that is philosophically useful. If to these non-linguistic categories we add human persons and actions, times, and perhaps social groups, and then to these add suitable syntactical categories, we gain a linguistic framework of wide expressive power and utility. Such a framework might well suffice for the purposes of the unity of science and in fact provides the logical skeleton for a kind of restricted metaphysics. At any event, it seems to provide a suitable preliminary basis which may then be extended as needed.

Some provision must be made for epistemological objects, e.g., sensations, sense-data perhaps, etc. These may be handled as a special kind of individual, and hence no new category is needed for them.

IV

The foregoing approach to the theory of categories is akin in essentials to that of philosophers in the Peirce-Whitehead-Hartshorne tradition. The logic, syntax, semantics—and indeed pragmatics—involved are a development of work anticipated by Peirce. The doctrine of types implicit in one of the approaches sketched is essentially that of *Principia Mathematica* and seems closely related to Whitehead's doctrine of abstractive hierarchies.[12] Finally, the treatment of time and the logical skeleton suggested, as well as the doctrine of analytic truth, are not too remote from Hartshorne's treatment of and interest in correlative notions. And beyond such details is an underlying unity of purpose.

One of the most important features of the Peirce-Whitehead-Hartshorne achievement, it is sometimes said, is to have combined a form of Platonism with modern science. This Platonic or realist approach is of course explicit in the foregoing. Two alternative forms of Platonism have been sketched in logical dress. The adjudication between them is an open problem.

[12]See the author's "On Whitehead's Concept of Abstractive Hierarchies," *Philosophy and Phenomenological Research* 20 (1960), 374-382. In the theory of abstractive hierarchies Whitehead may have been employing not a simple theory of types, as suggested in this paper, but rather one modelled on the system in his "Indication, Classes, Numbers, Validation," *Mind* 43 (1934), 281-297, and 543.

Whether we take a type-theoretical or a set-theoretical basis, we must make sure that our categories are not too narrow. A tendency among recent logical analysts is to admit only very narrow categories, supposing or hoping that others can be "reduced" to these. But unless the explicit details of reduction are provided, it is by no means clear that this can always be done satisfactorily. With too narrow categories there is the constant danger of impoverishment if not sheer omission. Our categories must make ample room for human persons, for works of art, for striving after ideals both personal and social, and for the devotion to something afar from the field of our sorrow.

It emerges from the preceding discussion that the ancient problem as to what the ultimate categories are, "the most general traits of reality," is very much with us. Modern logic including semantics has shown how this problem is connected with language and has helped us to understand certain relations between language and non-linguistic objects. It has sharpened our insight and made us more critical as to details of formulation. But it cannot be said to have changed this ancient problem in any more fundamental way. On the other hand, we cannot hope to make much progress in limning the ultimate categories without using the framework which modern logic including semantics has provided.

V

The foregoing presupposes only the so-called *classical* logic. Let us conclude with a few comments concerning the unsuitability of *modal* logic as a philosophical tool.

Of course philosophers differ enormously as to just what they wish to include under 'logic'. Some wish to include the whole of mathematics, as developed, say, within the theory of types or an axiomatic set theory. Others wish to restrict logic to, say, a *second*-order functional calculus, within which (with appropriate non-logical axioms) mathematical analysis may be developed. Still others regard even such systems as involving too much, and condone using only a classical first-order logic. Intuitionists regard even this narrow kind of a logic as containing dubious laws and in its place have put forward the so-called intuitionistic logic. Others have attempted to develop many-valued logics, with one or more "values" intermediary between truth and falsehood.

To employ an underlying *modal* logic for the purposes of philosophical analysis is suspect, however, in the eyes of many. Mathematicians have been interested in modal logic because of the mathematical structure or structures involved. But philosophers who use a modal logic are not interested primarily in its mathematical structure. They must also provide a satisfactory *interpretation* of the calculus or calculi as needed for specific purposes. Of course we must clarify here just what is meant by 'satisfactory'. Roughly speaking, an interpretation is satisfactory if and only if it is provided by a metalanguage which is sufficiently "clear", "clean", and "simple". By this is meant roughly that it contain as values for variables no "dubious" entities or pseudo-entities and that its non-logical axioms and underlying logic be suitably economical and restricted. Further the interpretation must be explicitly formulated in the manner of modern semantics.[13] It is a controversial point as to whether any modal logic can be given a satisfactory interpretation in this sense.

Another basic objection to modal logic concerns *ontic* or *ontological commitment.*[14] Formulations of such a logic seem always to involve a kind of variable ranging over a kind of entity called *propositions.* But what these entities are remains rather obscure. It is perhaps not the task of modal logic itself to analyze propositions, being concerned as it is only with certain special operators upon them. But for a satisfactory interpretation of such a logic a clear notion of proposition is essential, which unfortunately seems not forthcoming. Modal logicians, it would seem, have not given a satisfactory account of what propositions are, *precisely.* They remain merely obscure and mysterious entities satisfying such and such conditions. And since modal logics utilize primitively variables (over such entities) which cannot be explained away as mere shorthand or as notational conveniences, the systems carry ontic commitment to such entities in a fundamental way.

[13]See, e.g., A. Tarski, "The Concept of Truth in Formalized Languages," and the author's *Truth and Denotation.* Points similar to those of these two paragraphs are contained in the author's review of Prior's *Time and Modality, Mind* **68**, No. 270 (1959), 271-272. Most of the material of this section, in fact, is borrowed, with the kind permission of the editors, from the author's "Does Modal Logic Rest Upon a Mistake?" *Philosophical Studies* **14** (1963), 8-11.

[14]The phrase is due to Quine (or Williams), but the notion involved presumably harks back to the ancients who first used variables.

The question arises also as to whether propositions and modal notions are ever really needed. Clearly they are not needed *in* mathematics, in the sense that they are in any way needed for the definition of specifically mathematical notions. Nor are they needed in discourse *about* mathematics, i.e., in metamathematics or *Beweistheorie*. Nor do they seem needed in natural science or in the logical or methodological analysis thereof. If a specific purpose can be exhibited in which they do seem needed, this purpose can often be better served by regarding propositions as suitable constructs and by identifying the modal operators with their semantical correlates.

Consider, for example, the notion of logical or analytic truth, already alluded to, as defined within a suitably formulated semantical metalanguage.[15] This notion provides a more or less exact semantical correlate of the modal operator *necessity*. And similarly for other modal notions. Most of the purposes for which the modal operators are used may be more easily and efficiently served by these semantical correlates. Hence most of the purposes of a modal logic itself are better served by an exact semantical metalanguage, which in turn utilizes or presupposes no propositions or modal notions.

It can be explicitly shown in fact, that no form of modal logic is needed for general semiotic, i.e., syntax, semantics, and pragmatics, or at least for these subjects as far as they have been developed to date.[16] And there is no reason whatsoever to suppose that their further development will reveal such need. Quite the contrary, it seems almost certain that it will not. Further, as we have noted in §III, a very broad categoreal framework is forthcoming without propositions or modalities.

It is sometimes claimed, as we have already observed, that modal logics themselves exhibit interesting mathematical structures. This is a claim difficult for anyone but a mathematician to assess. And indeed the very notion of being mathematically interesting seems obscure and subject to a good deal of variation. However this may be, a similar claim, it would seem, could be put forward for almost any well-developed logical theory of a sufficient complexity. If we mistake

---

[15]See, e.g., A. Tarski, "On the Notion of Logical Consequence," *Logic, Semantics, Metamathematics*, and the author's *The Notion of Analytic Truth*.

[16]Cf. *Toward a Systematic Pragmatics*, and also the author's *Intension and Decision, A Philosophical Study* (New York: Prentice-Hall, 1963).

not, modal logicians have not convinced the learned community that the mathematical interest of their subject is commensurate with that of classical logic or of set theory or recursive function theory or the like. Modal logic seems to have thrown little if any light upon any area of mathematics, pure or applied.

Often it is claimed that propositions are needed for the analysis of belief-sentences. But we have urged elsewhere that sentences of this and analogous kinds seem best handled in terms of a systematic pragmatics. Propositions, if needed at all, are handled as constructs of a special kind and relations such as belief, acceptance, etc., are characterized in terms of suitable pragmatical primitives without the use of propositions as values for variables.[17]

The classical, two-valued, logic of truth-functions and quantifiers (with perhaps identity, and classes and relations construed in accord with type theory or an axiomatic set theory) seems to provide the only basic logic needed for mathematics and natural science, and for syntax, semantics, and pragmatics. For discourse both *in* and *about* these subjects no modal logic with attendant propositions is needed. Perhaps some clear philosophical purpose can be exhibited for which a modal logic is needed or for which the use of a modal logic would have clear advantages over other methods. This would seem very doubtful and, if we mistake not, no such purpose has yet been exhibited by modal logicians.

To summarize: (1) It is doubtful whether a sufficiently clear, clean and simple interpretation of modal calculi for philosophical purposes can be given. (2) The analysis of logical or analytic truth seems best handled in terms of modern denotational semantics. (3) The use of propositional variables ontically commits us to an obscure kind of entity which, together with the modal notions, (4) are not needed for discourse in or about mathematics or natural science or (5) in or about syntax, semantics, pragmatics, or category theory. (6) Modal logics exhibit structures of only dubious mathematical interest. (7) Propositions and modal notions are not needed for the analysis of sentences expressing belief, acceptance, etc. (8) Classical logic seems

---

[17]See *Toward a Systematic Pragmatics, passim,* and the author's "Toward an Extensional Logic of Belief," *The Journal of Philosophy* 69 (1962), 169-172.

to provide the most suitable form of basic logic for the purposes of science and philosophical analysis.

These arguments—or rather outlines of such, for each should be given a fuller development—are not put forward in a spirit of intolerance. We must not "block the road to inquiry" nor "decree dogmatic prohibitions of certain linguistic forms." We must be prepared to accept modal logic if a compelling need for such can be shown or if the foregoing arguments can be shown to be unsound. But in the light of the detailed technical work presupposed, it seems doubtful that such a compelling need ever will arise.[18]

R. M. MARTIN

NEW YORK UNIVERSITY

[18]Note incidentally that a strong proponent of modal logic, Professor Ruth Barcan Marcus, says something not so very different after all in her "Extensionality," *Mind* 69, No. 273 (1960), 55-62, so far at least as concerns mathematics.

INTER-SUBJECTIVE TIME

TIME is now a central theme in philosophy. For after many centuries of bedazzlement by the eternal, by the "a prioris" conditioning everything, by insight into "necessary structures" suggesting even an ethics of insight which urged us to emerge from the cave of this world and see the eternal sun himself, or to pursue that blessedness which consisted in comprehending oneself and whatever existed *sub specie aeternatatis*, it seems the spell has been broken; it is almost now as if the eternal, the a priori, and the necessary are no longer even understood or, which is the same, are affirmed by *faith*, or perhaps worse, regarded as permanent features of Indo-European languages, the nature of consciousness, or even the mode of being of the Pyramids. But, be this as it may, unquestionably the eternal has for a moment lost its power, and if anything is distinctive of modern philosophy, it is a preoccupation with the temporal, with all that had been taken for granted, or loathed, or missed altogether by the predominant tendency of *philosophia perennis*. I should date the conspicuous turning point with Hegel; but in any event, time, becoming, existence, life, and history have been the preoccupations of a sequence of distinguished recent thinkers: Nietzsche, Dilthey, Bergson, Croce, Whitehead, Heidegger, and Professor Charles Hartshorne, to whom this essay is dedicated.

But perhaps something should be said to support the contention that time is a characteristically modern theme; for on the face of it, nothing could seem more extravagant. At the beginning of Western philosophy, was not time defined: the moving image of eternity, or, the number of motion? Newton conceived time and space as uniform and absolute receptacles, the sensorium of God, within which movement occured; Kant conceived them as pure forms of *our* sensibility, making individual intuition possible. In Schopenhauer they become the principles of individuation. For Husserl, time was one of the most general formal structures of consciousness. But what is striking in these views is that the purer, more formal, more a priori, time is conceived, the more it seems to resemble eternity itself; we finally end grasping time in its pure essence and as a whole only to see *another* time appear, that which is pertinent to *real* movement, *real* becoming, a time which itself "moves"—the time of the finite becoming world. But what is the *form* of this *new* time? And, no sooner is its "what" defined, but it too takes its place in the heaven of pure form only to generate *its* opposite, a newer time, temporalization, or whatever, which no doubt, when it is defined, will generate still another time, a more authentic time, etc. Time has always been conceived somehow, and yet has it?

This paradox is, I am convinced, irremediable on its own plane. What we shall attempt in this essay therefore is not to supply a new formal definition of time, but rather to consider the context in which the paradox of definition arises. My general contentions are that time is comprehensible only in an ontological context which can both distinguish and relate eternal timeless essence and contingent existence, that time names nothing but the mode of being of contingent existents, that there are as many "kinds" of time as there are types of existence, that the more appropriately *our* existence is comprehended, the more singular and less amenable to typification it is, and that the comprehension of time in these subjective senses is not through any abstractive or conceptualizing reason, but through modes of experience which are themselves as contingent, existential, singular, and diverse as the subjective existence of which they are aware.

First of all, time and its contrary, eternity, are not fundamental categories. To suppose that there is a single ultimate medium or receptacle called "time", within which we and the all world happen to find ourselves as though borne along some stream, carrying us against or with our will toward a final moment when we either vanish altogether or emerge out of that stream into another realm called "eternity", is to turn everything significant about the whole existent scene into an abstract absurdity. And the point of the absurdity has nothing to do with *where* that single formal medium of time is placed, whether in pure consciousness as with Husserl, or in sensibility as with Kant, or in the "sensorium of God" as with Newton, or simply in some ultimately irreducible fact of nature, a rocking of the receptacle as with Plato. For in all cases, we end with the notion that we "happen" to be "in" time; time is just there, like some monstrous fatality into which we and our lives have fallen by accident; and then the ethical problem seems to be what "attitude" we are to take toward this fatality: welcome it or regret it and seek blessedness by lifting the intellectual eye toward pure Being, toward eternal Substance. Life is seen as a "fever", the philosopher the physician not of but against life whose wisdom is the prescription to get out of it as soon as possible—by an *ascesis* of the will as in Schopenhauer, by the cultivation of insight into eternal Being as with Plato, or the intellectual love of eternal substance as with Spinoza.

But time and eternity are themselves non-entities. Both serve to *characterize* what genuinely is but they are not entities themselves. They say something about what is, but are not beings; hence, at the start, we should avoid all ideas of media, frameworks, a priori "conditions", "forms" or any variant of them, streams, weaving looms, consuming fires, fatalities, etc. Time is nothing but a synonym for the mode of being of existents, and that mode of being is not itself another being. Now, we can mean many things, or think a variety of kinds of thing: events, material substances, persons, political states, the "whole of nature", the "cosmos", God, laws of mathematics and physical nature, etc. Each of these can receive a more or less adequate definition, adequate enough at least for purposes of identification or further inquiry. And each sort of thing which we can mean has, *strictly correlative to its meant definition,* its own characteristic *way of being.* Its mode of being is that way in which it *must* be if it is to be at all. This general point can be seen by taking some extreme examples: it is not *possible* for numbers to be events. By this I do not mean that we can not count events, but that their number is clearly not an event but a collection, and the collection is exactly an act which collects together the events into a group, its number; that number is not itself a temporal event. Numerical ratios and formulas are thus atemporal in themselves although, obviously, temporal events may illustrate them temporally. And so it is absurd to date numerical formulas, although these formulas may describe events which can be dated. Similarly, it is equally impossible for events to be atemporal or eternal. To be an event *is* to occur, and that is the *only* way in which an event *can* be; but nothing *occurs* except temporally. It is similarly not possible for a symphony to be in an instant: its *form* may be apprehended non-temporally, and Mozart claimed to have seen whole works in an instant; but what is then apprehended is a *form* of that whose own being is in performance. On the contrary, many paintings are made to be apprehended finally in one apprehension; we may first have to explore them, but they are made for a non-sequential final apprehension.

Not everything then has such a nature that it *must* display itself or must be in time; and whether things *must* be in time if they are to be at all, or *can not* be in time is a strict correlate of *what* they are. Time therefore is no medium in which certain things find themselves existing by chance. It is not an accident that life "falls" into time— as though it could be lived otherwise! If we wish an answer then to the question why some things are "in" time, or how they must display themselves in time, or why others are "in" eternity, we should examine *what* they are; what they are strictly determines the mode of being open to them.

But this is itself preliminary. The next step is to re-examine the "in" when we say we are "in" time. For obviously, we aren't really "in" any such thing anymore than we are "in" existence. We exist, which is not the same as "being in existence" as though there were some prior thing called either time or existence into which we were thrown. We exist, and other things exist, and we all exist together. Hence there is neither a time nor existence into which we are thrown as into a pre-existent medium, but rather we exist together, and time names the distinctive mode in which we exist, a mode which is strictly correlative to what we are. *What, then, are* we, and what modes of being are open to us? For "we exist" is a statement which needs its own proper comprehension. For the truth is that if this were all that were to be said, we would have characterized *our* existences in the *worst* possible way. To say of a man that he "exists" is to say the *least* about his being, and is commonly understood to mean that he is barely alive, perhaps under an oxygen tent. The mode of being thereby expressed is the lowest biological plane on which he can be said to be living at all. And hopefully there are other modes of being than this; *each mode must correspondingly modulate "time."* The "time" of being under the oxygen tent bears the same relation to the "time" of decisive personal events, as the gasping, wheezing existence under the tent bears to the full flowering of life. Thus, to exist under the oxygen tent is not to have the "time of one's life."

From this point of view, nothing could be more sterile than the abstractive conception of a single, flowing medium within which everything seems to be carried. Such an abstraction *can be made*, and its making is easy and spontaneous: we simply restrict our attention to whatever all existents have *in common,* namely, "changing existence." The sterility of such an abstraction results from the very process by which it was generated; we have by thought reversed that whole *ontological* development through which bare spatio-temporal events, bare physical things have developed to become living organisms, and finally organisms which are not merely living, but living consciously, and freely, with memory, hope, histories and destinies, in short, living human persons and historical communities. That single uniform abstractive time is *useful* for certain specific purposes, mostly of a practical order; but it is utterly *useless* for characterizing the time which most specifically describes our lived experience. It provides a reference point common to both history and the stars, so that history can be dated in cosmic time; but historical time suffers by the reduction, and such a lowest common denominator has so little to do with the lived time of human history, that it should be regarded as more irrelevant than relevant, an accidental convenience rather than an appropriate characterization, more false than true.

Corresponding to the conceptualization of time as a single uniform medium in which all things are, is such a time's *ontology:* the ontology which looks for *being qua being:* that which all existents have *in common,* the universal categorization of everything just insofar as it is. It matters little for our present purposes whether such an ontology finds its categories clustering around substance or event, thing or process. In either case, *being qua being* aims at the universal. Next, it should be noted that *the universal is inherently objective.* That which is common to many possible instances, the universal, can only be exemplified by the objective. The objective to us subjects, is that which *for us* stands *independent of us.* But, we subjects are not independent of ourselves, and the idea "self" expresses this coincidence of each with himself in such a fashion that we can not be objects to ourselves *insofar as we are subjects.* If we alter our position with regard to ourselves in order to objectify ourselves, then, in that new position, we are no longer selves, but others-to-ourselves—objects. And so the subjective is precisely that which is subjectively identical with itself and therefore not an independent object to itself. Hence, the subject is *inherently* an *I my-*

self, and not an *other.* As I myself, I am only and uniquely myself; I am myself and not another. Now while each I *also* shares this I-structure with every other I, it is not *by virtue of* this universal I-structure that any I *is* an I. The universal structure therefore is but an accidental truth, true *of* every I myself, but true accidentally and irrelevantly. But objects for me must insofar as they are taken to be *objects,* be taken not as I-myself but as *independent out there,* which are out there *for* my experience or imagination or thought. I am not them, I am not in them, I do not project my own subjectivity into them, I do not vicariously share their own subjective point of view; they are essentially then, as objects, other-to-my subjectivity. As objects for me, or not-I's, I encounter them only as they can appear or show themselves to me. For me they can be nothing but their appearance to me, since I am not them and have no privileged access to their individuality and subjectivity. Their external objectivity means then that they are accessible only through their appearance, or put briefly, for me they *are* their possible appearance. Each object for me is only its function for me, and any other object functioning in the same way, is just as good. Hence, the very objectivity of the object decides how it can be for me, the subject, namely, by way of its functioning for me, its shareable phenomenal properties. To be object then is to be essentially substitutable; for I have bracketed the one thing which would single out this object as just this, namely, its subjectivity. Objects then are essentially indifferent to the singularity of one another, and are actually related only through substitutable functions. They inherently "universalize" one another, into a replaceability of function. An automobile works with this tank of gas, *or any other* tankful of the same properties.

Hence, subjects are inherently singular and only accidentally universalizable, and objects for me are inherently universalizable and only accidentally singular. Ontologies therefore which seek the categories of *being qua being* can only accidentally touch the singular subjectivity, and inherently characterize only the objective. They are then *because* of their universality inherently *objective* ontologies, and can touch upon the singular I-am-I only by way of objectifying and universalizing it too, that is, radically *distorting* it. Now the chief examples of objects for us are material things and events, spatially conceived. The time of such ontologies therefore invariably turns out to be the time of some general objective cosmic motion, the stars, the velocity of light, or the frequency of a band of light in the sodium spectrum. It is this cosmic time which is envisaged as a uniform medium, a motion moving equably in some unending cyclical rhythm. I can locate myself, as a subject, in this time, only through that radical misinterpretation of myself by which I objectify myself, range myself with other objects as one among them, and thereby become a member of the physical universe by the surrender of my subjectivity.

Cosmic time is arrived at through observation of objective continuous motions and calculation or extrapolation based upon one of these taken as standard. But, subjective time is apprehended neither through "observation" nor "calculation" but rather through our conscious involvement in experience or life itself, a participative consciousness. Hence, the character and texture of that life will determine its appropriate "time." But "life" is no more unambiguous than "time" or "existence." For, first of all, we mean here life as it is lived by him living it, and not as it might be objectively observed by another and least of all that which is common to all lives. And life so taken is not the name of some simple, literal, definable "process" or "experience" but is inexhaustible in depth and incomparable from case to case in quality. For again, even if comparisons are possible, it is not *through* any such comparison or generalization that the inherent singularity is touched, existence as it is to him who exists.

If life so conceived were a continuous circular motion or a uniform rhythmic repetitiveness, then a cosmic clock would measure it appropriately. And while life may at certain extreme phases almost seem to resemble such a uniform rhythm, such phases are experienced as unutterable boredom rather than as life properly so-called. Our own views should not be confused with those of Bergson, who analogizes this lived duration to a snowball rolling downhill, accumulating the past, moving toward a goal yet to be created. The experience of some life conceivably could resemble some such thing but life need not; and even at best, the analogy itself analogizes the time in life to a peculiar sort of objective process. Nor are we in search of Husserl's inner time-consciousness, with its uniform, essential structure. For such a structure is accessible only to the reflective, phenomenologically reductive consciousness in search of the essence of pure time consciousness, and finds such a structure to be a universal form of all inner consciousness. We are in search of the time which *inherently* characterizes life or existence in its singularity; and by inherently, we do not mean *universally*, but rather most *appropriately*; and the life to which time is to be appropriate is that of him who lives it, a singular, *his* life; and that singularity is its "essential" feature. By singularity, I do *not* mean that the singular life under discussion is atomically isolated from other lives, as though in a social or existential vacuum. Nor do we mean that the singularity is itself an objective property arrived at by comparison of this life with all other past, present, and future lives, a comparison impossible in principle, and in any case, utterly irrelevant to the sense of uniqueness and singularity here employed. We do mean that the existence in question is *mine* and *mine alone*, it is the life of that I which is and knows immediately that it is I *without* objective comparison. I know that I am I and not another not through any inference or induction, but immediately; if I could not know it immediately, I could not be the *self* I *am*. Now the *time* of life of such an I is as discrete as the I and its life of which it is the time. It is radically *my* time; and in the common phrase, to say "my time" is to say "my life" and that which is contemporary with it. It *begins* with my life and *ends* with it even though the stars move on. It is modulated by whatever meanings there are in my life, and is not characterized by the radical senselessness of cosmic time. It is oriented and centered upon my present, actual existence, and is "lost" in the endlessness of cosmic time. Its experience is my experience of my existence, and is properly characterized by whatever regret, nostalgia, joy, projects, hope or hopelessness there is in the very texture of my life. And while it is the time of an *individual's life* as he lives it, that life itself is not definable nor isolable *in itself* but is inherently intersubjective or *social*. Precisely how it is inherently social, we shall try to show next.

And our argument briefly is that the *now* which is essential for *any* sense of time, cosmic or subjective, can not be located by reason in any universal or cosmic time; and with *that* failure, all distinction between past, present and future fails; the *now* must be located in *singular experience*. This experience is the presence of *another subjectivity to me*. In the primordial presence of another subjectivity to me, the now is born as the now of that present. Time is therefore essentially a social event, an aspect of the encounter of two singular subjectivities in the mode "presence" (and not observation or inference). It is our time; I locate my time in our time, the time of singular human intersubjectivity, "communal" historical time. Our conclusion then is that lived historical time is prior to cosmic time in definition and in experience, and that that uniform, flowing medium in which we find ourselves, is rather based upon the observed motions of *things*, abstracted from a *prior* time, the time of the *life of human encounter and action* as it is lived and not observed.

Let me expand these remarks. They focus upon the difficulty of defining "now" rationally within an objective cosmic scheme. Without some "now," there is, of course, neither past nor future, since the past is the past of *now;* and the future is the future of the same now. Without *the* now, the actual present, we have only the general, universal serial structure in which any moment is indifferently in its own present, relative to which other moments are past or future. But every past moment is *for itself* present, and not past; and so with every future moment. Hence, *any* moment can be equally regarded as past to another, future to another, or present to itself. And so then, *which one* of all these cosmic nows, ranged in their endless sequence, is *right now?* Which is *really present?* For calculation then, time in its formal emptiness is a series of moments each of which is exactly like every other. Any one of these is indifferently past, present or future. But *even to say this* is ultimately impossible for reason; for to posit *any* moment means that that individual moment must be "selected out" provisionally so that the others may then be treated as past or future to *it*. But precisely how can reason ever select out even provisionally *any* single moment when, so far as it is concerned, they must *all* be formally identical? Hence reason in its incapacity to posit any single moment as a now, is equally incapacitated to regard any "other" moment as past or future to it, and the entire sequence of moments originally thought of as a series, collapses into one moment, the abstract now which is what all moments have in common, and which can not differentiate itself into an infinite series of serially related moments. This abstract now into which cosmic serial time collapses for reason is, of course, not *the* now we are looking for, but formally equivalent to eternity. This situation escapes us usually, since we are unaware in our thought that the very thinking of time as even a cosmic serial order presupposes that the thought in question be *directed* to some singular moment which is to serve as the basis for the rest; but it is the singular existing self which so directs its own reason, and not that reason of itself. And so then to "arbitrarily" select one moment as a now, requires that reason, equipped only with its definitions, be arbitrarily arrested at that now; what then is the *arbitrium* which arbitrates the matter, which enables reason to arrest itself provisionally on just this one singular moment, if not the existing, singular subjectivity? In a word reason together with its objective, cosmic, serial time order, is incapable of sustaining itself, and is therefore derived from another order of consciousness aware of another order of existence. In other words, upon analysis, cosmic time declares of itself that it is posterior, abstracted, and secondary to some other primordial experience.

The grasp of *some* moment *as singular* demands an *act* of consciousness, a *singular*, issuing from a singular existence. It may be a gesture, a word used in its indexical function, or an act of living attention or experience. The important thing is that the now can only be meant or experienced or grasped in any way by an act which itself is *in act*, and whose sense is inherently bound to its actual occurrence. It is not the *universal* meaning of the gesture which can locate the now, but the living gesture itself, interpreted as having its sense inherently determined by its *own singular occurrence*. Once the actual now has been located, then by transference we can imaginatively designate other instants as possible nows, again by *living* acts of attention or indices pointing to imagined other moments.

Time then is meaningful only *for* a temporal existent, and not for pure, formal reason. The formalization of time is never completeable since it always presupposes one non-formalizable existential act, a singular act of existence to locate some now, in order to confer sense on the supposed abstract differentiation between past, present, and future.

A second point should be considered. The determination of the now, as reference point for past and future nows, by something that exists now, is itself a preliminary characterization. There is no possible gesture, index or act of attention which can settle upon anything like a formal now. The now is always the presence not merely of a form, which would be empty, but the presence *of something*. Time is *filled* time; present existence is the present existence *of something*. And, so then, what *can* be *present to us?* In the first place, *we* are not present to objects, that is, to non-subjectivities; clearly, it is they which are present to us, this presence being the same as our awareness or experience of them. What can be present to *us*? And *who* are we to whom they can be present? When this problem is unravelled, I believe we shall have touched the origin of our own primordial grasp of our own time. The problem, it will be noted, has been shifted from some cosmic scheme of pure or formal time in which we are supposed to find ourselves but in which rather we lose ourselves, *to ourselves*, the living subjects, experiencing "things" as present to us. Out of this living experienced presence, we primordially grasp "now" as the most abstract name for our own existing. It is then *our own subjectivity*, in its existence that serves as the origin for the actual present now. "Now" names *our* living actuality and what is contemporary to us. But our own isolated, self-enwrapped subjectivity, the subjectivity of the *sum* in *cogito ergo sum* is itself *non-existential*. My *existence* is precisely my encounter with others, with the non-I. But the particular *kind* of non-I is decisive here. If my existence is my encounter with others, then the *kind* of others I encounter, live with, for, or against, determines the *kind* of life I lead; there are *levels* of myself called into play, and *levels* of otherness encountered. In short, encounter is not an unambiguous term; it suffers as many modulations of meaning as the term "life" or "existence" itself; and therewith, it modulates as many senses of the term, "time."

And so, on the very minimal level, we wind our way back to our mere encounter with physical things. We are now not interested in the supposed cosmic time they keep among themselves; we have located our own living subjectivity in encounter as the origin of the now; but, the dimension of the subjectivity operative is coordinate with the dimension of the world encountered. One level of encounter is simple sense-experience. I look, and the "now" is the now filled with what can be seen and only seen. It is the now of visible things, and of me as simple looker. My subjectivity is that of a perceiver. The future is the future of perceptive experience; the past that of past lookings. A reflective oyster provided with memory could do as well. Have we at last found a basic time in which all things which exist are? Am I now having the time of my life? I think not. But there are difficulties and obscurities.

Where are we to discover our primordial experience of the present? What sort of "object" *can be* present to us, present in the fullest and least derived sense, that is, primordially? Is everything on all fours with regard to its ability to be present to us, and therefore define a present? Are the barest objects of sensation as fully present as other *persons?* Can moving points of light serve equally with persons to define *the present?* If we could rid our reflections of bias, what would we say could be most *fully* present if not other *persons?* Must not that which is to be present to us fully, not merely be a something or other out there, inert and passive, but rather a *responsive* something or other which of itself *offers itself to us?* If in imagination we try to enter the world of the mere experience of nature, devoid of responsive persons or responsive things, do we not find our sense of being fully present attenuated? And, is it not attenuated to the exact degree that we do not experience such things of nature as offering themselves to us, but simply being there? In short, that vast otherness which we encounter in experience seems to become *timeless* to the degree that it is impersonal and unresponsive to us. We acquire the faces of animals, almost asleep, or that of naturalists so habituated to the world of stars, trees, animals, that they escape human time, the insistence of the present, and live now in the timelessness of nature, time itself regressing to the cycles of the seasons. But, as I have argued, this is not time, but timelessness. Preposterous as it may sound, it seems that *we* experience the actual present primordially in our experience of other subjectivities, subjectivities moreover which are present to us, i.e., *which present themselves to us,* in a free gift. The present then is in fact a present or gift of one subjectivity to another; it arises primordially in a mutual encounter, the presence of two presences as a present or gift. Is it purely by a happy accident that these terms are so intimately related?

In any event, such is our present analysis of lived time. It begins with some uniquely marked event which is a mutual subjective encounter; mutual presence is *the* event whose occurrence is the present. It is the irruption into mere uniformity of a determinative event; it is *the* event *par excellence,* whose time is only accidentally related to that cosmic time of things which is derived from such unique encounters. Such an abrupt event is an *origin;* it originates a now, in relation to which other times can be fixed as in *its* past or in *its* future. It is the time of existence, and as finite, singular and discrete as existence itself. It is inherently and not accidentally an encounter in existence; it can not be abstractly conceived. Such an event, originating human time, is filled time, filled with the other subjectivity. Its dimensions are the dimensions of existence related to that event, namely, categories such as regret, nostalgia, the memory of what has been, encounter, and hope or despair for the future of encounter; all are rooted in the decisive presence: the unique now of existential intersubjective encounter. These formulas, it now should be added, are themselves indices of singular events. Their final sense therefore is given not through themselves, as abstractions, but in the concrete historical singular life in which we are. Cratylus finally can not *say* what he *means*; he can only wag his finger.

WILLIAM EARLE

NORTHWESTERN UNIVERSITY

EXPERIENCE

DEWEY remarked that the experienced is not merely something private or psychological, the creation of man. He thought, though, that it embraced "all subject matters", "the history of this earth", "death" and "transcendental systems." But these, like the microscopic, are surely beyond the reach of experience. Dewey evidently made "experience" include many items which exist outside the borders of any man's experience. In apparent compensation for his generosity, he tended to exclude from experience realities in which he was not interested. He did not seem to find a place in experience for our feelings of strangeness, for our encounters with the prescriptiveness of ethical, logical and aesthetic ideals, or for our awareness and responses to the brute compulsions of existence. Like many another, Dewey thought that experience extended to but never went beyond the borders of his philosophic system. I think he erred in both directions.

Experience exhibits many stresses and strains; it has thick and thin areas, regions of high and regions of low intensity. There are areas in it where all seems muddled or undifferentiated, though it itself is not chaotic nor amorphous. It is complex, modulated, variegated, with evident foregrounds and backgrounds, heights and depths. It includes all that we immediately confront, whether we prepare for that confrontation or not. But it does not include the beings outside the reach of our confrontations, and thus the beings which ground or sustain what we have focussed on. If we are to get to these beings it must be in some other way than by experience. Experience does not encompass the realities to which we refer by means of our concepts, our intentions or our signs, though we do of course not only experience the use of these but what they terminate in, their referents, though not the external beings in which those referents are resident.

Our experiences have two ends—ourselves, the experiencers, and the content experienced. We can be so deeply immersed in an ex-

perience that we are oblivious of ourselves; nevertheless the experience is possible only because we are not entirely swallowed up in
what we are encountering. On the other hand, no matter how singularly private and intimate our experienced content may be, it stands
over against us who experience it.

Experience connects us with other realities. It terminates at them,
but it does not reach into them. No matter how much of them it
embraces, it stops short of them in their full concreteness, as independent entities having careers and rationales apart from our experiencing. Thinking is an experience which connects thinker and
object thought about. It stops short of that object thought about as
it exists in and of itself, and in contexts apart from the thinking.
Sometimes the objects about which we think are ideal entities—numbers, triangles, equations, virtues, peace, truth. These are not experienced. What we experience is the thinking of them and the content
they allow to be caught and qualified by that thinking. They yield
up content to the thinking and thereby qualify that thinking; conversely, the thinking abstracts from them and thereby obtains a
terminus, something which is the object of the thinking. Mathematicians engage in a distinctive kind of thinking, directed at a distinctive type of object. If they cut themselves off from their encounter
with such objects, there would be nothing to distinguish their thinking from any other kind. The mathematician does not experience a
number or a shape, but a way of thinking about numbers and shapes,
terminating in abstractions from numbers and shapes. The numbers
and shapes have a rationale of their own, apart from and over
against his thinking, and over against and apart from what that
thinking terminates in. Numbers and shapes are not creations of ours,
to do with as we like. Our thought, if it is to be reliable, must
keep in accord with the relations which the mathematical entities
have to one another, a matter which we can discover by thinking in
one of two ways. We can attend to the way the confronted content
dictates to the thought, compelling it to move in one direction
rather than another, thereby revealing that content to have a power
lying outside the control of the thinking. Or we can attend to what
was presupposed so as to enable such and such a content to become
the object of thought. The presupposed is here made the object of
a second thought and is then seen to have a nature which, as standing
apart from thought, makes possible a kind of abstraction at which the

first thought terminated. The first of these ways of thinking in consonance with what is outside the thought might be termed "phenomenological thinking"; the second "speculative thinking". Critical, constructive thought seeks to relate and eventually to adjust the one to the other.

Remembering, too, is an experience. It also stops short with experienced content, a content inseparable from our acts, on the one side, and external, independent realities on the other. The remembering, like other experiences, fails to encompass the sustaining, independent realities. It does not get to the remembered as something resident in the past; it encompasses only a facet of what has passed away, and then only so far as it has made it into the present terminus of a present act of remembering. The remembered is something now, experienced now, grasped as that which is related to something past, outside the reach of the memory.

The termini of our feelings or imaginings are also experienced. Objective counterparts of these are not experienced of course, for there are no such counterparts. Since most of what we do experience does have a counterpart, a ground outside the experience which it presupposes and in which it is oriented, and since we do tend to look to the termini of our experiences to tell us something about the nature of the counterpart, we do not usually use "experience" to refer to the termini of our feigning or imagining. An "experience" requires that there be something actually interplayed with, felt, suffered, met. It involves an experiencer, an experiencing, and something experienced; it presupposes someone who can experience, and something which can be experienced, neither of which is then experienced. A man's being is not exhausted in his career as experiencer; his experiencing is but one of the ways in which he is related to entities distinct from himself; the content he experiences rides on the surface of beings which are as ultimate, irreducible, independent as his own being. But though he and the other beings are outside the field of experience, they are not sundered from experience, cut off from it, alien to it in meaning and being. Experienced content is the real transposed, put into another context, given new affiliations, new neighbors, subject to new conditions.

Experience is inseparable from an experiencer; it is rooted in realities standing away from that experiencer. Such facts have led some to dismiss experience, and others to praise it. It has been said to be (a) illusory, a mere appearance; (b) to be something derivative or adventitious, which should be dispelled or replaced by something more real and basic; and (c) to be final and all-inclusive, precluding the presence of anything outside its confines, and thus to warrant the denial that there are any selves or external substantial realities. An examination of these views should make it possible for us to see whether or not there can be ways of going beyond experience, to the beings which ground it.

(a) A rather common view in the East is that what is sensed or known in daily life is an illusion. Since the illusion is recognized to have some kind of being distinct from the supposed reality beyond it, it must have some reality of its own, and cannot so far be an illusion. Also, it must be related to that reality, otherwise it would provide no warrant, no premiss, no evidence leading us to move from it to the real. Since commonsense, perception, politics and even religious institutions (not to speak of the instruction on how or why one should free oneself from illusions) are known in part through the aid of the senses and in the course of daily life, the theory that what we daily experience is illusory would, strictly speaking, preclude knowledge not only of what is, but of almost everything else we know. It would also stand in the way of our knowing that the theory was true or could be used. The rejection of daily experience would moreover be performed in the realm of supposed illusions and could therefore not be effective in getting us to the real.

The experienced is an appearance, and an appearance should be distinguished from what is real in and of itself. But this does not mean that the appearance is unreal, or that it is disconnected from the real as it is in itself. It does not warrant our putting all we encounter aside, or require us to deny that we can get to know the real from what we are experiencing. Appearances, experienced objects, are realities derived from more basic, external realities. Appearances are those external realities as caught inside the context of an experiencing. The external realities are not only knowable as the locus of the constraints to which we are subject when we experience and as the referents of speculative thought; they are confronted in the role of an experienced background and an experienced foreground.

Ultimate reality provides material for both an experienced background and foreground. The foreground—the experienced primarily as attended to by us but still under the control of something beyond us—is related to the real in itself via the background—the experienced as primarily oriented away from us but still caught in the context of an experiencing. Those who attempt to cut themselves off from the experienced foreground and the background can hope only, through paradox and negation, to lose themselves in something ineffable, inexpressible. There is no warrant for supposing this is ultimate reality or that it defines the experienced to be illusory. In the very nature of the case one who has lost himself in the ineffable has lost the opportunity to know that it is real or what relation it has to the experienced.

A good deal of what we daily take to be the case, to be sure, is confused, dubious, erroneous. That does not mean that experience is a poor mode of getting to know what is the case. On the contrary, it shows that what we daily take to be true is a distillate, a derivative from experience. Wherever there is error and so far as there is error, we have evidence of man imposing himself on what is real. Experience would not tell us the nature of an external reality were it solely man's creation. But an experience wholly created by man would be indistinguishable from a fiction. Mythology and mathematics, fantasy and physics are not on a footing.

But might it not be the case that experience is partly created and partly given, and that we have no sure way of distinguishing these parts? Ought we not then turn away from experience to pursue some more reliable guide to reality? It is, I think, desirable to try to reach the real through avenues other than experience. Inference, dialectic and speculation enable us to know the real in ways experience does not. But this does not show that experience is illusory or that we should try to abandon experience altogether when we find that the different parts of it bear no clear marks testifying to their degree of trustworthiness. Different parts of experience can be sifted out through the aid of what one has discerned of the real in other ways.

(b) It is better to view the experienced as a consequence or product of something more real than it is, than as an illusion which we ought to dismiss or oppose. The experienced has a centre of gravity outside experience. It offers us evidences, lures, guides and clues to the nature of that which it presupposes and on whose being its own being partly depends. It is not adventitious, unilluminating, to be replaced by what grounds it. Not only can it never be made to vanish entirely but it tells us much that an unmediated immersion in the real could not. Indeed, what would an unmediated immersion in the real be but an experience of it? Such an experience can be preferred to ordinary experience, but not because we will have nothing to do with any experiencing. And if we, in non-experiential ways, can or ought to get to a reality outside our experiences, we will not thereby disqualify those experiences.

We learn from experience, we learn by attending to parts of experience, we learn by reflecting on experience, and we learn by thinking about what lies outside experience. What we learn in one of these ways does not necessarily conflict with nor compromise what we learn in the other ways. They yield different data and involve the use of different criteria and "languages". I have an experience when I stub my toe. I then come up against a brute resistance and feel a pain. I learn from experience that there are resistant areas all about me. I learn too to attend to places in the immediate vicinity, to watch my step. I learn too by thinking about what could resist me in such a way as to be accompanied by a pain in my toe, and come thereby to think about stones. And I can speculate about the powers resident in stones and come thereby to understand what it is that exists over against me. Encountered resistance, awareness of resistant areas, an understanding of the nature of stones, and a knowledge of realities existing outside me, all deserve to be brought together in a single integrated account. No one of these exhausts the universe. No one of them disqualifies the others. None makes reference to the others unnecessary. Each in fact helps us either to discover features in the others, otherwise not discerned, or provides content to be united with the others to make possible a critically achieved knowledge of their sum.

(c) Phenomenologists, empiricists and pragmatists sometimes speak as though everything that is is experienced. Were they to persist in holding to this strange opinion they would be forced to deny that there are any hidden powers, any mysteries, any domain of ignorance, any dimensions of being lying outside observation or the promise of it. But then they would also have to grant that there can be no action, no motion, no making in their world, since these are possible only because there are potentialities in things, capacities to exhibit new features at subsequent moments. They could speak of regions where there is flux and regions where there is none, of areas of quiet

and of noise, but never of what makes these be, or what might replace them with something else. This fact is frequently overlooked
because the advocates of this position so concentrate on what they
confront that they tend to overlook the suppositions they make
regarding the nature of the knower. Their entire procedure rests
on the assumption that the knower is a substance with multiple
powers. Sometimes they even speak explicitly of his habits or of his
capacities to associate ideas, to infer, interact and plan. But then
evidently there is at least one being, the knower, who is more than he
is experienced to be. Whether or not one who takes this position
goes on to affirm that there are other substances which also have
capacities not yet exhaustively expressed in what is experienced, one
has given up the position that whatever is is experienced or even
experienceable. He who seeks to remain with experience has no right
to speak of a knower, the know*able,* or the experience*able,* since
these all require one to look outside any actual experiencing, to
attend to what is not in fact experienced. And they would still leave
undetermined the relation of the experienced to whatever was outside the being and the control of the knower.

Peirce, James and Dewey, in opposition to the traditional empiricists, affirmed that the experienced was no subjective, inert,
merely sensed content. They recognized and clearly said that it was
extended, dynamic, variegated. I think though that they did not
make it sufficiently clear that one could not only discern in it areas
where distinct careers were being carried out, but that it had a kind
of insistent rationale, that it imposed itself on us with brute compulsiveness, and that it forced us to submit to it and to whatever
else it made possible.[1] These pragmatists were so anxious to do justice
to the richness of experience that they tended to neglect the fact
that the experience testifies to realities outside it, making it possible.[2]

[1]Each of these experienced features lures one to act and thereby penetrate beyond
it; to hold oneself apart and thereby acknowledge the presence of other external
realities; to think about what is presupposed; and to make oneself part of a world
larger than oneself or one's experiences. Practical men stress the first, lonely men the
second, inquirers the third, and emotional men the fourth. Each move is, however,
tinged with the others. We go beyond experience in all these ways together; we always are to some degree practical, alone, curious and emotional.

[2]Peirce escapes from some of this criticism. Again and again he said that experience contained three distinguishable dimensions which he characteristically called
First, Second and Third,—an immediate, qualitative-like factor, brute compulsions,

Both Kant and Hegel did more justice to the real, and therefore to the experienced than their pragmatic followers did. Both knew that what was experienced did not exhaust reality. In Kant there was a tendency to suppose that the experienced in itself was ungraspable and could be dealt with only as a component inside a systematic, rationalistic, scientific, deterministic scheme. When he said that all viable discourse should begin and end with the experienceable he in effect meant that we should deal with the experienceable only so far as it had been caught and partly transformed by various alien forms and categories. This is one reason why he never could discover **how to relate the experienced to the reality** beyond, which he himself rightly said was presupposed by it. Hegel had a more muscular, more complete, a richer experienced world than Kant had. There was not in fact any type of entity or occurrence which it did not contain. Experience for him encompassed struggles, values, purposes, freedom, art, religion, philosophy. He saw though that the experience of any man at any time was incomplete, but then went on to suppose that it was incomplete only because other experiences were lacking, and that these others pulled on what was enjoyed here and now, forcing one to move on and on, until the whole range of the experienceable was covered. But what is not experienced is not identical in kind with what is experienced. Not only is it not being encountered now, but it has a power, a unity, an independence which the encountered does not have. Once it comes within the orbit of experience it fits in with the previously experienced; but before and apart from our experience, what is not experienced has a different nature, role and meaning. With Hegel one ought to affirm that the real is reachable from what we experience, but with Kant we ought to say that what is so reachable is not more experience or even the experienceable, but a reality as ultimate as the being who has not yet, but who can catch that reality in an experience.

and a law-abiding nature. But he did not note that his Second and Third testified to the reality of something outside and presupposed by experience, so that in the end, despite all his disclaimers, his realm of experience was, like the traditional, a First, though with facets of compulsiveness and rationality. Yet we cannot be compelled or prescribed to except by that which is at least as real as ourselves. He neglected also to remark on the presence of beings with distinctive careers, or to note the claim which experience makes on behalf of a reality beyond it. In short, he should have acknowledged five categories or dimensions, not three,—a First or qualitative, a Second or brutal, a Third or rational, a Fourth or individual, and a Fifth or representational.

Experience has fissures in it. It is pulled towards and away from the experiencer, thereby acquiring those fissures. We have no warrant for saying that as pointing away from the experiencer it faces continuations of itself any more than we have warrant for saying that it then faces what is entirely alien to it in nature and being. The experienced is distinct in nature and being from the experiencer, but it is not without relevance to him or he to it. Similarly, the experienced is distinct in being and nature from the real beyond it and the experiencer, but it is not without relevance to that reality, nor is that reality irrelevant to it.[3]

The experienced stands between two ultimates, the knower in himself and a reality beyond him. It is a function of the two of them, one of a number of ways in which they can be together. It has a nature, a rationale, a status of its own, distinct from that possessed by the beings[4] which made it possible. To get to those beings we must not dissolve the experienced, but must hold on to it and learn how to move through it to them. Our lives, however, are spent mainly with living in or living with experience. We live in experience when we relax, when we lose ourselves in a natural or supernatural mysticism;[5] we live through experience when we impose traditions, con-

---

[3]Pansychists, such as Hartshorne, see this. But they go on to suppose that the reality is a "psyche", and that the best or proper way in which the two of them can come together is by feelings. But why must the reality be a psyche, and why is thinking or acting a less legitimate way than feeling to get to that reality?

[4]Hegel and Peirce see that the experienced is not created by the experiencer, that it has a status apart from him; what they fail to see is that as apart from him it is, even as that which is to be experienced, distinct in being, place, career and nature from what it is as caught within an experience. We really have no alternative but to stay with experience and give up all attempts to show how it is possible, or to follow the lead of its fissures and move to what it presupposes. Indeed, only because we already know that there is a reality beyond what we experience are we prompted to look beyond the experiences we now have. We discover new areas of experience, new types of experience in the course of our effort to get beyond what we experience. Initially we have limited experiences and are driven to go beyond them by our awareness of a reality outside them. But in the course of an attempt to reach that reality we come to have experiences we otherwise would not have. (Towards the end of his *Critique of Pure Reason* Kant became aware of this fact and pointed out how Reason led the Understanding on to get more and more experiences.)

[5]These two mysticisms are often confused. The former is ours before we become mature and in defiance of all sophistication, thinking or learning; the latter is achieved when we have matured and know how to penetrate the veil of knowledge, discourse, practice and local interests, and let ourselves sink into a being distinct from our conscious selves.

ventions, memories, beliefs and the like on experience to constitute
the commonsense world of every day.[6]

So long as we are alive we have experiences. If we are unconscious,
their nature and import will not be known, though they will occasionally be made manifest in behavior and may eventually be recovered by us when we are conscious once again.[7] Nor do we ever free
ourselves from experience; even when we spin out idle fancies we have
many bodily and even emotional and cognitively tinged experiences.
The outside world and an inner one echo through the most idle
follies. We have experience of those worlds even when we turn away
from them. And we can get to those worlds as not experienced. We
need not stay with experience; indeed we can never wholly stay
with it. We not only imagine, day-dream, introduce arbitrary divisions
and useful distinctions in the data experienced, forge hypotheses and
build systems of knowledge, but are concerned with and live in fact
with realities outside the confines of experience.

[6]Kant thought of himself as accounting for a scientifically respectable world. He
identified it with a Newtonian one. In one stroke he committed two errors: he supposed that the world known to science is the most substantial of known worlds, and
that this was Newtonian in character. A Kantian philosophy would be impregnable
if it concerned itself with accounting for the commonsense world of every day, for
this is the product of a juncture of a given manifold and categories. But the categories are conventions, useful classifications. C. I. Lewis has perhaps seen this point
better than any other Kantian. However, with other Kantians he fails to note that
he has no way of talking about the experienced data that his categories help convert
into the stuff of daily life. To know what that experienced content is like, outside
the categories which structure it for daily use, one would either have to employ
other categories, engage in other modes of apprehending the content, or understand
what could be available for categorization by us. Scientists are interested in the first
approach, artists in the second, and speculative philosophers in the third. The Kantians make no provision for any one of these three alternative ways of dealing with
the content that we daily categorize, and therefore cannot know what this content
presupposes.

[7]It is characteristic of a number of anglo-saxon thinkers today to translate the
problem of experience into a problem of language. Most of those who take this position wobble between an Hegelian and a Kantian outlook, holding both that there is
nothing outside the language which they can acknowledge, and that language is
not the real, but only an indispensable structuralization of it. They are somewhat
matched on the continent by phenomenologists who seek to isolate in experience
various essences, isolated regions freed from their involvement in a larger world.
These not only lose something of the experienced content by their dissection of what
is given, but also all contact with the larger real world which they in the end seek
to know. Both the anglo-saxon and the continental schools fail to make provision for
experiences unconsciously undergone.

Discontent, sympathy, wonder, hope and reverence, and the like, are not purely subjective states. Nor are they agencies merely for providing us with new experiences, or which will enable us to leap the barrier of experience into some other region. They are relations which move in and through a present experience to what lies outside that experience. They pull us through the chinks of present experience to an external, independent and satisfying world beyond. It is desirable therefore to follow their lead. Where will they lead us? I think it will be to a substantial man, an insistent Ideal, a forceful realm of Existence, and a concerned God.

We are now having experiences; so long as we live we will continue to experience. When we move out of the area where we are now attending, we will experience what we then confront. But our experiences at our arrival will be quite different in tone, motivation, origin and outcome from what we presently experience, for that at which we arrive will make a difference to the nature of our experiencing and the contents we experience. We will be warranted then in speaking of our experiences of our deepest selves and of other men, of absolute standards, of energy, space, time, causation, and of grace, salvation, forgiveness. Nothing available to man escapes the mesh of experience, where experience has a multiplicity of tonalities and supports; much escapes experience, where experience has to do only with what is sensed, perceived, localized, or utilized.

PAUL WEISS

YALE UNIVERSITY

NON-BEING AND NEGATIVE REFERENCE

IN PLATO'S *Sophist* the Stranger, who patterns his style of thought after that of Parmenides, says:

"Do you see, then, that not-being in itself can neither be spoken, uttered, or thought, but that it is unthinkable, unutterable, unspeakable, indescribable?"[1]

Parmenides found the assertion, "Non-being is" a scandal to human thought. I do see the Stranger's point; and I find Parmenides' exasperation entirely natural: Being is, and non-being is not; it is incredible to believe "that things which are not are"—and that is the end of matter. But part of the exasperation—his, mine, and that of many others—may be traced to a lingering uncertainty that this *is* the end of the matter. The "not" in the expression, "Non-being is not" possesses, upon trial, a curiously expanding tendency which seems to make it refer beyond those limits, or limitations, of "being" within which we might hope to confine all of our references.

The situation appears to be this: In denying non-being, one is forced to recognize it; and in recognizing non-being one transforms it into the name of something. Consequently, the admission, "Non-being is," introduces inconsistency into the domain of the rational and the real. Hegel would authorize this admission, and allow the negative a role in generating truth and reality. In this respect, Hegel has gained a number of contemporary adherents. But the consequences following from this admission are so extreme that we must consider with care how it may be possible to deny non-being without implicitly recognizing its existence.

The puzzle of non-being turns upon two very ordinary facts: (1) discourse contains, and must contain, ways of expressing denial as well as affirmation; (2) more often than not the expressions of discourse refer extra-linguistically. Out of negation and extra-linguistic reference, then, the problem is somehow generated. And *ab initio* it

---

[1] *Sophist,* par. 238, trans. B. Jowett, *The Dialogues of Plato* (Oxford: Oxford University Press, 1920).

would seem that any sensible man would simply resolve to keep the distinction very clear between those terms which serve us by referring to realities beyond the conditions of discourse; and syntactical devices, such as negation operators, which serve us not by referring extra-linguistically but by qualifying the terms of discourse within discourse itself. The resolve to let terms refer extra-linguistically, and to confine the reference of operators to discourse, is so eminently sane that it is necessary to consider how the idea of negation ever became a substantive notion, requiring or seeming to require, nothingness as a kind of being.

Many of the terms we use are class terms; and most, at least, of the defining properties of these classes refer to positive aspects of things. The negations of such class terms define complementary classes, including everything not included in the original term, so that to be "non-tree" is as positive a way of being as to be a tree; it is to be positively almost everything, and almost anything you please. Fix the terms of discourse, then, in gradation beginning with proper names, and continuing with class terms of increasing generality. As one runs the grade, the references of these terms will be to larger and larger classes of things—the terms increasingly taking up the domains of their complements. The terms increase in range of reference; their complements decrease in this respect. As long as the term and its complement divide the universe between them, both continue to make positive reference to the world. At the limit, following the same abstractive procedure, one encounters the paradox of "non-being." The total abstraction of "being" is reached; and when one then affixes the negation operator, to define its complement, class and complement appear to stand for "everything there is" and "nothing at all." If "non-being" refers to "nothing at all" does not this assert, or come perilously close to asserting, that "nothing" is the name of something?

So it would seem; but "being" differs from terms of lesser generality in some respects; "being" is not definable, for example. Perhaps "being" also differs from other terms in having only a verbal complement. "Non-being" need be recognized as a complement, in fact, only if the relations of discourse require this reference. The requirement would be satisfied if in the affirmations and denials of ordinary discourse this reference should be found to be implicit. But if in every essential reference the term "non-being" can be replaced without loss of content, it can be assumed that "being" has no genuine complement.

It was our early resolve to permit terms to refer extra-linguistically, while confining the operation of negation within the boundaries of discourse. Plato's analysis in the *Sophist* fulfills this resolve by interpreting negation, whenever it appears to refer extra-linguistically, as a sign of "otherness." This interpretation is natural to our logic and language, and is operative in the term-complement relationship mentioned above. "Otherness" carries one an impressive distance; is it an adequate replacement for "non-being" wherever the latter may occur?

My denial that "All men are Caucasians" can surely be understood as standing for the positive ascriptions which make up the class of non-Caucasians. My affirmation that "No Delawareans are Pennsylvanians" yields without effort to "All Delawareans are non-Pennsylvanians," and a possible positive character—perhaps in this case, a somewhat tenuous character—is surely available, allowing a possible positive term to replace "non-Pennsylvanians." Furthermore, the double negation involved in the denial of an E statement makes no reference beyond discourse. The denial refers to the E statement; and the E statement is potentially a positive statement. Thus far, then, no non-being has appeared.

My denial that a girl is pretty will be understood, ordinarily, as a way of affirming that a different quality—unhappily—applies in its stead. My denial that an object is in one place may be taken as an affirmation that it is in another; it may also be understood as a way of saying that it does not exist. Is a reference to non-being present, when existence is denied? Possibly so, and yet it is worth pointing out that some denials of existence can be interpreted positively; for example, my denial that there are unicorns can be interpreted as a positive statement about the presence of unicorns in the literary imagination of the human race.

The thesis that all meaningful terms must be referable to something positive suggests that affirmations and denials of logically possible entities—such as round squares—be referred not to a null class; but that terms of this sort are to be understood as non-referable in themselves, since they are not meaningful units, but in their parts. Whatever is referable in the phrase "round square" must be referred to the classes of "round things" and "square things" and "attempts at mental construction." While the logic of impossibility is not clear to me, to refer contradictions to a null class may be merely a way of saying that what is meaningful in the term must be referred elsewhere.[2]

The instances are random, but three points are to be noted: (1) When a property is being denied of a substance—that is to say, when the denial is in the predicate—Platonic "othering" performs satisfactorily without any suspicion of a reference to non-being. (2) When the existence of a "substance" is denied—i.e., when the denial is in the subject—Platonic "othering" goes lame. It would not ordinarily be held that to deny the existence of an ash tray requires belief that something else exist in its place, as my denial that a girl is pretty requires that she be characterizable by an alternative quality. (3) If all denials of existence could follow the "unicorn" pattern where "othering" allows us to put literary unicorns in the place of real unicorns, no more than a slight wisp of a suggestion of non-being, if even that, would remain. But most denials of existence, from ash trays to Socrates, will not fit the "unicorn" pattern, exemplifying instead the second point.

Additional support for the first two points may be extracted from a consideration of Aristotle's *Categories:* My denial that an object is of a certain magnitude is ordinarily understood as affirming that it is of a different magnitude; or that it is an object to which considerations of magnitude do not apply, in which case it is supposed that some other considerations will apply; or that the object does not exist—the case in which no considerations apply and "othering" seems inapplicable.

My denial that an object is red is ordinarily understood as an affirmation that another color is appropriate, or as a denial that color is applicable at all (in which case, etc., as above).[3]

My denial that an object is in one place may be taken as an as-

2The null class includes indifferently what cannot possibly be, what might be but is not, what will be but is not yet, and perhaps what has been but is not now. Some of these sub-groups refer quite clearly to kinds of being. To group them as kinds of non-being is to fail in subtlety.

3For the sake of tedium reduction it will be assumed from this point on, that these necessarily repetitive qualifications will be introduced by the reader, as they become appropriate.

sertion that it is in another place, or that it is not a place-occupying object, or that it does not exist.

My denial that an object exists at one time may be taken as an assertion that it exists, has existed, or may exist in another time; or that it is not the kind of object that exists in time (could it, perhaps, subsist, for example?); or that it is nothing actual or possible.

My denial that an object bears one relation may be taken as an assertion that it bears another or—since I cannot conceive of a thing without relation to something other than itself—that it is nothing actual or possible.

The remaining categories, including even the basic category of "substance," introduce no new principles. If our denial that Socrates exists is not ordinarily understood as affirming that Plato, Aristotle, or anyone else, exists in his place, the denial of substance becomes one of the ways of understanding the denial of magnitude, quality, place, time, etc. Clearly, one manner of getting rid of a property is to get rid of the object whose property it is.

In sum, my denials give rise to three eventualities: (1) My denial of a given characteristic (say, red) implicitly affirms a characteristic of the same kind (say, green); (2) my denial of the whole of a kind (say, quantity) implicitly affirms a characteristic of a different kind (say, ideation); (3) my denial that Socrates exists seems not to refer to anything else whatever; hence, the legitimate suspicion that in the denial of the existence of a subject, there is a reference to non-being.

Once again, Platonic "othering" satisfies cases of denial in the predicate (eventualities one and two) while failing to apply adequately to denial in the subject. Is the denial of the subject explicable in terms of "otherness," or is it not? The issue can be stated by means of Aristotle's comments in the *Categories*. Concerning contraries Aristotle says:

'Socrates is ill' is the contrary of 'Socrates is well'; but not even of such composite expressions is it true to say that one of the pair must always be true and the other false. For if Socrates exists, one will be true and the other false, but if he does not exist, both will be false; for neither 'Socrates is ill' nor 'Socrates is well' is true, if Socrates does not exist at all.[4]

[4]Aristotle, *Categoriae*, 13b12-20, trans. E. M. Edghill (Oxford University Press, 1928).

And with respect to contradictories:

But in the case of affirmation and negation, whether the subject exists or not, one is always false and the other true. For manifestly, if Socrates exists, one of the two propositions 'Socrates is ill', 'Socrates is not ill', is true, and the other false. This is likewise the case if he does not exist; for if he does not exist, to say that he is ill is false, to say that he is not ill is true.[5]

Taking these two forms of contrariety together, we have three propositions to consider if we assume, and three if we deny, that Socrates exists.

Suppose Socrates' existence: "Socrates (exists and) is well," "Socrates (exists and) is ill." These assertions fail to raise the issue. "Socrates (exists and) is not ill." This is denial in the predicate, which can be understood as an instance of Platonic "othering."

Suppose Socrates' non-existence; again, we have three statements. "Socrates (does not exist and) is ill," "Socrates (does not exist and) is well," "Socrates (does not exist and) is not ill." Aristotle holds that the first two statements are false, and that the third is true. Contemporary logicians, agreeing that existential statements are false when their subjects fail to exist, would agree with Aristotle's judgments about the first two statements, while disagreeing on the third. From Aristotle's point of view the first two statements are saying of what is not that it is, and hence are false. The third statement is saying of what is not that it is not—i.e., in the given case I am denying a predicate to the non-existent—and hence the statement is true. With respect to all three statements Aristotle's claim would be, "If a thing does not exist, it has no properties." But does the denial itself name the non-existent? If it does, this fact is very far from our intentions. We want to hold that the denial of properties to the non-existent is merely a way of saying that "existing" and "possessing properties" are bound in chains of mutual entailment; so that once again the negation—which is a double negation—can be replaced by a positive statement. We would like to be able to hold that to deny properties to the non-existent is to say no more than that properties pertain to something else, i.e., to the existent.

But the phrase "something else," which allowed us to transfer the weight of our intention into a form of "othering" appears to carry the suggestion that "existence" is one kind of thing, and "non-exist-ence" another; what we might do in this situation is hold that one does refer fleetingly to non-being, while in passage toward a cancella-tion of double-nothing into something. One way of referring to being is as "the not non-being" whose negativity requires a momen-tary reference to non-being as we are in the process of transforming the double negate into a positive idea. But this contention seems largely verbal; and it would be well to avoid even the suggested momentary reference, if this is possible.

Twice in the preceding pages our interpretation of negation as "othering" led us to the use of mental constructions. Applicable to unicorns, and round-squares, may not this device apply as well to a non-existent Socrates? Consider first one of the simple statements presuming Socrates' non-existence: "Socrates (does not exist and) is ill." The statement can be considered in two stages. In the first stage the statement that "Socrates is ill" arises in the mind. Let us assume that it refers, at the very least, to some matter-of-mental-fact, a mental construct of some sort; perhaps the object of a dream, or the product of one's imagination. The assumption will fail if it is in fact not the case that epistemology requires both sentences and mental constructs as their immediate referents. Some contemporary modes of analysis consider such duplication unnecessary. Should they be correct the present account would be archaic "in so far forth." But I am not able to imagine how we can do without mental referring; until this is made clear to me I must suppose that the statement, "Socrates is ill," refers to a mental construct wherein a postulated Socrates is "illy" qualified. Since existence in the mind is obviously one manner of existing, we have thus far avoided non-being. In the second stage we shall refer the entire mental construct (this rather than merely the sentence which expresses it) to the world, to the realm of non-mental existence. The stage will be one of seeking, while failing to find, an appropriate counterpart. In this situation I shall have something in mind which I never succeed in fitting to the world. It is *not* here, *not* there, *not* anywhere, i.e., only in my mind. Put in such a context I no longer see how the case is different from the discovery that what I expected to find on the table is in an-other "place"—in this case, not a place in the world, but in the mind. And if these cases are not essentially different, then it follows that the failure of a subject to exist can be handled in the very same manner as the failure of a predicate to exist. Both can be understood as instances of Platonic "othering."

To be sure, when I fail to find in the world a counterpart to my mental construct of an existing Socrates, I entertain a feeling of disappointed expectation. But this is exactly so for every case of denial in the predicate, and that fact has thus far occasioned not the slightest suspicion of a reference to non-being. If I expect ice cream and receive tapioca pudding this, too, is "othering" mixed with disappointed expectation; and in the case of non-existent Socrates, I receive not a world with Socrates in it, to be sure, but a world of being, nonetheless. From this standpoint the attitude of Sartre over his disappointed expectations seems maudlin. The world is not *nihilated* or *neantised* by this experience. The world is full of its kind of being; while Sartre's—or Pierre's—mind is full of another kind of being; only, they are not counterparts. Hence, the reference to non-being reduces simply to the sense of shock, or surprise, upon experiencing incongruity where congruence had been forecast, disparity in the place of an expected parity. The failure of a subject to exist can therefore be treated on the same terms as this same failure in the case of a predicate. Both are instances of Platonic "othering"; in the case of predicate denials the "othering" takes place between a term and its complement; in the case of denial in the subject the "othering" takes place between the world and a mental construct. In neither case does a reference to non-being occur.

The only circumstance under which the failure of a subject to exist could involve a reference to non-being would be the case where a subject exhibits its failure to exist either in the world, or in the mind. But even to offer the suggestion is to speak nonsense, since such a case could not possibly be the object of a reference, could not exhibit itself, and hence could not be a case in point. Once more, non-being and nonsense tend to be coincident.

It is now obvious that the same analysis can handle the third sentence, "Socrates (does not exist and) is not ill." This virulently negative judgment yields placidly enough to our present position. "Socrates is not ill" refers to my, or your, or Aristotle's, mental construct; the negation in the predicate yields to the positive ascription "well" (or possibly "well, or in indifferent health"). "Socrates (does not exist and) is well" now fits the former analysis, and can be reduced, in its terms, to a case of Platonic "othering." But the consequence of our adopting this two-stage negation of predicate and subject, thereby reducing denials of existence to Platonic "othering," is that we are forced to side with contemporary usage, against Aristotle, in holding that the third denial sentence, "Socrates (does not exist and) is not ill" is false, as are the other two. Everyone agrees that "Socrates (does not exist and) is well" is a false statement. Since "Socrates (does not exist and) is not ill" can be translated into "Socrates (does not exist and) is well" the two sentences must have the same truth value; that is, both statements must be false.

Here we face a problem. It is obviously true that what does not exist has no properties. And it is tempting to believe that in denying a property to the non-existent, we are providing an instance of that truth. But two distinct cases are in fact at issue here. The first sentence involves denial of the subject. It would be illustrated by "Socrates does not exist," and explicated by my mental construct of a world containing Socrates from 469 to 399 B.C., which now no longer counterparts, but contrasts with, the contemporary world. The second sentence, denying a property to the non-existent, requires in this same context, a statement such as "Socrates is not ill." But this is a case of denial in the predicate; and would be explicated, as has been suggested, by qualifying my mental construct of Socrates with the property of "health." Through treating these very different expressions as though they were identical in meaning, Aristotle was able to conclude that "Socrates (does not exist and) is not ill" is to be construed as a true statement.

Having found a way of adjusting denial in the subject to Platonic "othering," I am ready to conclude that every sentence of the form, "Non-being is not," is simply an awkward manner of saying that "Being is;" and that the former can be translated into the latter without residue. But prior to drawing this happy conclusion let us consider three additional examples.

First, "Nothing exists." The assertion seems to refer openly to non-being; but in fact, since the assertion of the statement contradicts its content, there are no possible conditions under which the statement can be truly affirmed. It can be denied, but the denial of "Nothing exists" is the claim that something exists; so this statement is implicitly affirmative, and becomes explicitly so in keeping with the canons of double negation.

"Who was Immanuel Kant's wife?" "Nobody was the wife of Immanuel Kant." Is "Nobody," then, the non-existent wife of Immanuel Kant? Instead of this, the denial refers to the question; more exactly, it refers to a mental construct in the mind of the questioner. It is saying to the questioner: Some misinterpretation of your mental content has led you to pose a question which cannot be answered in a straightforward manner, as you intend; my denial informs you that your question fits the class of all other mistaken questions. Again, there is no reference to non-being; but in its place a complex assertion of the following sort: "There is an X such that X is a mental construct affirmed by Y; and X includes the notion that Immanuel Kant had a wife, while in the real world confronting this mental construct it is the case that Kant was a bachelor."

"What kind of ink was used by Homer to write the Odyssey?"[6] To mention a particular kind of ink, say Sheaffer's Skrip, would be to reply falsely. On the other hand to say "No ink was used by Homer to write the Odyssey," would be to suggest falsely that Homer did write the Odyssey; so we must judge this denial to be elliptical. And, indeed, if pressed, the reply might have been, "No ink was used by Homer to write the Odyssey, because he did not write the Odyssey." When the double negation is removed the answer to this question would present an appearance something like this: "There is an X such that X is a mental construct in the mind of Y; and X includes the notion that Homer used ink to write the Odyssey, while in the real world confronting this mental construct it is the case that Z wrote the Odyssey; and if there was a Homer, either he did not use ink, or he used ink for other purposes."

In sum the possibilities of Platonic "othering" are sufficiently rich to provide an adequate positive interpretation for any negative reference. It would seem, then, that we have arrived at our conclusion; and that "non-being" need not be taken seriously as the complement of "being." And this would be the case without qualification were the possibilities of reference to non-being confined to the class of negative statements. In fact there are positive assertions which raise the question of non-being in a temporal form. We must attend to these in a sort of postscript. But the success of our analysis thus far con-

---

[6]This example, and the one preceding, are mentioned by Henry Hiz, *Journal of Philosophy*, **59**, No. 10 (May 10, 1962).

firms us in agreeing with the Stranger that non-being is "unthinkable, unutterable, unspeakable, indescribable." And in agreeing with Parmenides that non-being is a scandal to human thought—a scandal, we might now add, which can be avoided.

If we are to agree with Parmenides it is appropriate to ask what status he gave to the assertions, "Being is" and "Non-being is." I suggest it is clear even from the fragments that "Being is" was accorded the status of a necessary truth, and "Non-being is" the status of a contradiction. Under what conditions have these assertions the appropriate values? If as our statements become more general and non-restrictive, they become more necessary, then "Being is" has the requisite generality to be unfalsifiable, necessarily true, and implied by any proposition. "Non-being is not" will have the same meaning, while the denial of this necessarily true judgment, "Non-being is" will have the status of a contradiction.[7] Ranging from the necessarily true to the impossible, that is, to the absurd and meaningless, between these two extremes lie the partially restrictive statements of ordinary discourse characterized by contingent factuality.

On this basis "being" has only a verbal complement and the philosophy of Hegel must be judged to be absurd. In the deduction of his categories, that simultaneous derivation of truth and reality, Hegel almost at once turns the idea of "being" into its complement, infusing the irrational quality of an existential non-being into every subsequent aspect of his thought.

We have discovered how well the philosophy of Aristotle lends itself to Platonic "othering." Are we to conclude that from this perspective it is possible to avoid turning non-being ino the name of something? A comment in the Metaphysics suggests a negative answer. After the listing of various senses of "being," including generation, destruction, and their negations, the following conclusion is drawn: "It is for this reason that we say even of non-being that it *is* non-being."[8] But an isolated passage retains an aura of opacity;

[7] I am employing here the doctrine of necessary truths as completely non-restrictive developed by Charles Hartshorne in "Metaphysical Statements as Non-restrictive and Existential," *The Review of Metaphysics*, 12, No. 1, Issue No. 45 (September, 1958), 3-47; and "Some Empty Though Important Truths," *The Logic of Perfection and Other Essays in Neoclassical Metaphysics* (LaSalle, Ill.: Open Court Publishing Company, 1962), pp. 280-298.

[8] Aristotle, *op. cit.*, *Metaphysica*, Book Gamma, 1003b 10. The point is strengthened by context: ". . . some things are said to be because they are substances, others be-

and hence an explication is required. It will be provided in the form of the postscript, already promised. Consider these assertions:

"Socrates (exists and) is ill, but will be well."

"Socrates (exists and) is well, but may become ill."

"Socrates (exists and) was well, but is now ill."

Here are positive statements, which make reference to non-being unless such reference is avoided by means of metaphysical decision. Certainly mental constructions, so helpful until now, find scant employment here. It is obvious, of course, that the properties of "health" and "illness," when actually characterizing Socrates, have as their primary reference not mental constructs, but aspects of the non-mental world. It is almost as obvious that references to these properties, even when not actually characterizing Socrates, which will, or which may, characterize him, cannot be regarded merely as mental constructs. They are not mental possibilities only, but real possibilities which will, or may, turn into real actualities. At this point reference to non-being can be avoided by granting to the possible its appropriate kind of reality. And while Aristotle strings his forms of contrariety out, as it were, on a line leading from thought to things, behind the forms of contradictories, correlatives, direct contraries, intermediary contraries, constitutive properties, and privatives-and-positives stands his doctrine of real potentiality.[9]

It would seem to be almost as obvious that our references to the past cannot be understood intelligibly as references to our own mental constructs; and that references to the past are not references to the possibilities of things, as some pragmatists would have it. Once again, there is a way of avoiding reference to non-being; one must grant the past its own mode of reality. But Aristotle does not authorize this step, and Whitehead characterizes Aristotle's doctrine of the past as a "perpetual perishing." Here, at least, there is reference to non-being in Aristotle. I think there are additional references. The type of opposition, called by Aristotle "privation," and

cause they are affections of substance, others because they are a process towards substance, or destructions or privations or qualities of substance, or productive or generative of substance, or of things which are relative to substance, or negations of one of these things or of substance itself. It is for this reason that we say even of non-being that it *is* non-being. The crucial statement is put still more vividly in Richard Hope's translation: "Thus, we declare even non-being to 'be' what-is-not."

[9]*Categoriae*, op. cit., 11b 19-13b 35.

the type involving constitutive properties, appear very strongly to require reference to non-being.[10]

If reference to non-being is the sign of contradiction in a philosophy, each such reference should be removed. Platonic "othering," including "mental constructions," the rejection of some expressions as contradictory and therefore meaningless, use of the modes of possibility and necessity, as well as actuality, and including the assignment of the referents of some expressions to the reality of the possible, or of the past: recognition of this variety of modes of being is an adequate substitute for any reference to non-being. It should not be overlooked that this solution leads one in the direction of the neoclassical metaphysic adumbrated in the writings of C. S. Peirce, and developed in the philosophies of A. N. Whitehead and Charles Hartshorne.

WILLIAM L. REESE

UNIVERSITY OF DELAWARE

[10]*Ibid.,* 12b 16-37.

THE INTER-RELATEDNESS OF 'TRUE',
'GOOD', AND 'BEAUTIFUL'

1. *The Problem*

Can that which is morally good be esthetically ugly? Can that
which is esthetically beautiful be morally evil? When we speak of
'morally evil' and 'esthetically ugly' are we speaking of one and the
same quality? Are 'morally good' and 'esthetically beautiful' two different qualities, or are they the same quality? And how are moral and
esthetic values related to truth values? Can that which is false be at
the same time good and beautiful, or must it have a negative moral
value and a negative esthetic value if it has a negative truth value?
These are some of the kinds of questions which press forward if one
examines the inter-relatedness of 'true', 'good', and 'beautiful'.

The present essay is a preliminary inquiry as to whether the qualities 'true', 'good', and 'beautiful' are one quality or many. For our
present purpose, we will limit our evaluations of 'true', 'good', and
'beautiful' to evaluations of truth value, moral value, and esthetic
value, listing broad grades or subqualities of each, namely, positive,
negative, or neutral. Within these broad limits, the present essay is
concerned with the question as to the relative inter-dependence or independence of the truth value, the moral value, and the esthetic value
which may be present, or which may be judged to be present, in a
specific empirical context. Specifically, if the truth value, or the moral
value, or the esthetic value which may be present is judged to be positive in grade, can either of the other two values which may also be
present be judged to be either neutral or negative in grade, or must all
three of these values, if judged to be present at all, be judged to be
present in the same grade as the first? If 'The True', 'The Good', and
'The Beautiful' *are One,* then in a given empirical context in which
grades of all three values are present as adjectival qualities, obviously
they must be present in the same grade—i.e., if one value is judged to
be present as a quality in the positive grade, the others which are
present must also be present in the positive grade, etc. However, if

'The True', 'The Good', and 'The Beautiful' are *not* One, then when all three are present as adjectival qualities in the same empirical context, their grades may vary independently of each other—i.e., whether a value is positive or neutral or negative has nothing to do with the grade of the other two values which may be present. Since there are three values (truth value, moral value, and esthetic value) which may be compresent (or absent) in a given empirical context, and since there are three grades of these values (positive, negative, and neutral) the number of possible combinations of various grades of these three values (including the absence or irrelevance of the value) which may be compresent in a specific empirical context is 4^3, or 64. The following table lists the 64 possible arrangements in which each of the three values (truth value, moral value, or esthetic value) is either present in one of its three grades (positive, neutral, or negative) or is not present at all.

(1)	Tp · Mp · Ep	(23)	Tm · Mn · En	(45)	Tp	*	Em
(2)	Tn · Mp · Ep	(24)	* Mn · En	(46)	Tn	*	Em
(3)	Tm · Mp · Ep	(25)	Tp · Mm · En	(47)	Tm	*	Em
(4)	* Mp · Ep	(26)	Tn · Mm · En	(48)	*	*	Em
(5)	Tp · Mn · Ep	(27)	Tm · Mm · En	(49)	Tp · Mp	*
(6)	Tn · Mn · Ep	(28)	* Mm · En	(50)	Tn · Mp	*
(7)	Tm · Mn · Ep	(29)	Tp * En	(51)	Tm · Mp	*
(8)	* Mn · Ep	(30)	Tn * En	(52)	* Mp	*
(9)	Tp · Mm · Ep	(31)	Tm * En	(53)	Tp · Mn	*
(10)	Tn · Mm · Ep	(32)	* * En	(54)	Tn · Mn	*
(11)	Tm · Mm · Ep	(33)	Tp · Mp · Em	(55)	Tm · Mn	*
(12)	* Mm · Ep	(34)	Tn · Mp · Em	(56)	* Mn	*
(13)	Tp * Ep	(35)	Tm · Mp · Em	(57)	Tp · Mm	*
(14)	Tn * Ep	(36)	* · Mp · Em	(58)	Tn · Mm	*
(15)	Tm * Ep	(37)	Tp · Mn · Em	(59)	Tm · Mm	*
(16)	* * Ep	(38)	Tn · Mn · Em	(60)	* Mm	*
(17)	Tp · Mp · En	(39)	Tm · Mn · Em	(61)	Tp	*	*
(18)	Tn · Mp · En	(40)	* · Mn · Em	(62)	Tn	*	*
(19)	Tm · Mp · En	(41)	Tp · Mm · Em	(63)	Tm	*	*
(20)	* Mp · En	(42)	Tn · Mm · Em	(64)	*	*	*
(21)	Tp · Mn · En	(43)	Tm · Mm · Em				
(22)	Tn · Mn · En	(44)	* · Mm · Em				

Table 1. 64 possible arrangements of grades of truth value, moral value, and esthetic value which may be compresent in a single empirical context. Legend: 'T', truth value; 'M', moral value; 'E', esthetic value; 'p', plus; 'n', neutral, 'm', minus; '*', absence or irrelevance of corresponding value; '·', logical conjunction.

I have designed various diagrams to represent as many of these classes in a single figure as can be done while retaining a reasonable degree of simplicity. Fig. 2 shows one of these diagrams which locates 44 of the 64 possible classes. The ones which cannot be shown are: 22, 23, 24, 26, 27, 28, 30, 31, 38, 39, 40, 42, 43, 44, 46, 47, 54, 55, 58 & 59.

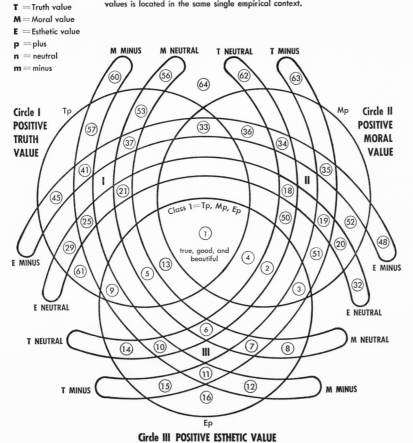

Figure 2. Diagram showing 44 of the 64 possible arrangements of the three grades of true, good, and beautiful when no more than one grade of each of the three values is located in the same single empirical context.

T = Truth value
M = Moral value
E = Esthetic value
p = plus
n = neutral
m = minus

2. Truth Values

Events or occurrences may be actual or potential. Actual events are empirical entities which have occurred or are occurring, that is, they are events of the present or the past, and thus they constitute the empirically real. Potential events, or events in the future, constitute the potentially real—they have not occurred, and whether or not they will occur can never be known with complete certainty in advance of their actual occurrence. Thus the prediction of the occurrence of a future event can never have more than a neutral truth value before the event has occurred. However, if the predicition conflicts with the prevailing established opinions concerning what events in the future are possible, then the prediction will have a tentative negative truth value until such time as it can demonstrate, by the occurrence of the predicted events, that the prediction was not false.

A report is a statement by an observer of what the observer takes to be the case. Reports of actual events may be true or false, depending on the reporter's perception and knowledge, and his accuracy in reporting it. The truth of a report is determined by what is the case rather than what is the report. If various reporters disagree in reporting an event, the truth value of their reports may be judged to be neutral (neither true nor false). Thus the truth value of reports may be positive, neutral, or negative. When the observer's report of what he takes to be the case agrees with what is the case, the truth value of the report is positive, when it disagrees with what is the case, its truth value is negative, and when it both agrees and disagrees with what is the case to a point where the agreements and disagreements cancel each other, its truth value is neutral (neither true nor false). Also, as mentioned above, a neutral truth value is the maximum grade which can be attributed to the prediction of a future event.

It should be noted that for truth values, as is also the case for esthetic values and moral values, the three grades of value which we have designated as positive, neutral, or negative are not separated from each other by clearly demarcated boundaries, but rather constitute three relatively arbitrary divisions (with intrinsically vague boundaries) which separate a continuum into three areas. In one area there is more plus value than negative, in the second there is about as much plus value as there is minus value, and in the third there is more minus value than plus. In each case, the ascription of a grade of value results from a decision or judgment made by an evaluator, whose judgments are the most fallible when he deals with boundary cases, and are the most accurate when he deals with cases which are the furthest from the boundaries (e.g., the middle of the neutral zone, or the far end of the plus zone or the far end of the minus zone).

There are two distinct questions concerning the truth value of reports which need to be clearly distinguished from each other. When a report contains a summary of the opinions of others, the first question involving truth value is a simple question of fact—namely, did the reporter quote correctly in ascribing opinions to others? This first question may be called the question of the *prima facie* truth value of the report, i.e., the accuracy of the reporting. The second question is concerned not with the reporter's own acuracy in quoting the opinions he is reporting, but is concerned with what we may call the *internal* truth of the report, i.e., the truth value of the opinions themselves.

3. Moral Values

While the term 'good' in a general sense may designate that which is useful for some end broader than a moral one, for the purposes of this paper the term 'good' and its correlates will be restricted to the context of morals, and will be referred to as grades of moral value, namely, morally positive, morally neutral, or morally negative. These three grades of moral value can be used to designate both actions and potential actions. Included under potential actions are not only future actions *per se,* but present motivations for action, present habits, and present dispositions which determine future actions, i.e., present character, or present institutions. Present character and present institutions comprise both summaries of past actions and predictions of future ones.

For evaluating a past action, all three grades of moral value ratings are appropriate. Whether the report of such an action is true or false is a question entirely of whether the action has occurred or not. If it has occurred, then regardless of what its moral value may be, the report that it has occurred is true.

However, the truth value of reports of past actions will vary depending on whether the report states what was the case as having been the case (thus being *true*) or whether it states what was not the case as having been the case (thus being *false*). We may have knowledge of past actions, or we may not, and that knowledge may be true, or it may be false.

Our predictions of future actions are present assertions which comprise integrated summaries of reports of past actions and which may be neutral or negative in truth value, depending on the average accuracy of the separate reports which are integrated in making the predictions, insofar as the predictions constitute reports of past occurrences.

4. Esthetic Values

In the present inquiry, grades of esthetic value will be limited to the three broad grades used to designate grades of truth value and grades of moral value, namely, positive, neutral, and negative.

An entity may be said to have positive or negative esthetic value ('beauty' or 'ugliness') if the contemplation alone of that entity is capable of producing a certain unique kind of delight or aversion in a sensitive observer, that is, one capable of making such a response. This response, which may be called the esthetic response, consists in a characteristic form of continuous delight or aversion in the sheer contemplation of the entity which produces this response—and any entity which produces an esthetic response is designated (or evaluated) as 'beautiful' or 'ugly' in terms of the quality and degree of the response it elicits. An esthetically neutral response is one of neither delight nor aversion, but merely indifference, in a situation in which it would be appropriate to anticipate a positive or negative esthetic response, e.g., in the contemplation of a work of art. The esthetically neutral response should not be confused with the response of esthetic indifference which will occur while contemplating an entity which is outside of the universe of discourse of esthetic evaluation. There are entities, such as simple factual statements like "This sample of iron oxide weighs 14.2 grams" such that the bare contemplation of the statement produces neither a positive nor a negative esthetic response. Clearly the response of indifference produced in such cases is a sign not of a neutral esthetic value of the entity being contemplated but rather a consquence of the fact that the entity being contemplated is outside of the universe of discourse of esthetic evaluations altogether.

While it is customary to designate the object which produces the esthetic response as beautiful if it produces delight, or ugly if it produces aversion, beauty is not so much a property of esthetic objects as it is, to use Dewey and Bentley's well-known term, a *transaction* between an observor and an entity to which he responds. Beauty is neither 'objective' nor 'subjective', but the product of a transaction involving a subject and an object which is contemplated by that subject, and to which the subject responds with delight or indifference or aversion.

We will follow the customary usage of designating the *object* producing these responses as beautiful, esthetically neutral, or ugly (in our more general terms, as having positive, neutral, or negative esthetic value) while recognizing the crucial role of the observer in the production of the response which defines and determines the grade of esthetic value of the object.

Thus, from the foregoing, it is evident that esthetic evaluations can be applied appropriately only to objects or entities which can be contemplated by an esthetically sensitive observer, and that the labelling of an object with a grade of esthetic value (positive, neutral, or negative) may be understood both as a summary of the esthetic responses actually made in the past to that object by observers who evaluated it and as a prediction of the esthetic responses which it is anticipated would be made by other observers should they contemplate it in the future. As a report of past evaluations, the truth value of the scale ratings ranges from positive through negative as determined by the responses and evaluations which actually were made in the past. The actual responses, which may run the whole gamut of the scale in reporting the responses to the same object as made by different observers, themselves exhibit, as pointed out above in the section on truth values, two distinct orders of truth value, *prima facie* truth value and *internal* truth value.

Prima facie truth value is determined by the accuracy of the reporting as to what judgments actually were made—as reported, for example, in a statistical poll of esthetic preferences. *Internal* truth value is determined not by the accuracy of the reports of what evaluations were made in each individual case, but by the appropriateness of the evaluations themselves—which is determined by the expertness of the evaluators rather than the accuracy of the reporters.

In considering the internal truth value of esthetic reports, we need to take into account two entirely different sources of variation which determine the appropriateness or correctness of esthetic evaluations. (a) There is a wide range of variation in sensitivity to esthetic stimulation, and a wide variation in the experiences and skill needed to make an appropriate esthetic judgment. Let us designate these ranges of variations in accuracy of making esthetic judgments as variations of esthetic *expertness*. (b) There is also a wide variation in the degree to which observers of relatively equal sensitivity and expertness will agree in their judgments. The resulting disagreements produce what we will term *idiosyncratic variations* among experts.

Thus the internal truth values of esthetic judgments may range from positive through neutral to negative depending on (a) the expertness of the observers and (b) the *idiosyncratic* variations among experts. The first variations are checked by comparing individual evaluations made by admittedly non-expert evaluators with those made by acknowledged experts, and the second is checked by determining the relative degree of agreement among those who by common consent are acknowledged to be expert evaluators.

Classic esthetic objects are those which have been available for contemplation and evaluation long enough so that a sufficient number of acknowledged experts have agreed that they are beautiful; accordingly, they become models of beauty for the training and indoctrination of the less expert.

It is, of course, well-known that on occasion, when esthetic objects are still young, they may be responded to with many negative or indifferent responses even by the "experts" but as they grow older they are "understood" or "appreciated" more, either favorably, or unfavorably —at first by the experts, and eventually even by the inexpert, who become conditioned to respond to them either favorably or unfavorably as the experts do, as these esthetic objects, and the "standard" or "classical" responses of the experts to them, become embedded in their culture.

The truth value of the designations of esthetic value (positive, neutral, or negative) when considered as predictions of future responses of other observers, can not have a positive truth value, since only an actual occurrence can have a positive truth value. As pointed out above, the truth value of any prediction is usually neutral, since until it is tested, the prediction is neither true nor false, although if the prediction conflicts with established knowledge and experience it is tentatively regarded as having a negative truth value until it is actually tested.

In the area of esthetic evaluations, due to the extraordinary range of idiosyncratic variations among experts, it would be rare to find esthetic evaluations which, when considered as predictions of future responses, would conflict sharply enough with established knowledge and experience to warrant being given a negative truth value, even if only the past reports of the experts are considered relevant, and even if we ignore the almost insuperable difficulties of determining who the experts are or what constitutes expertness other than the criterion used by some observers—namely, "the experts are the observers whose judgments agree with my own." Like moral judgments, esthetic judgments are culture-bound—and for the present, we will limit ourselves to the context of our own culture.

Summarizing the inquiry to this point, truth values are concerned with actual or potential occurrences of events (in the widest sense) and the accuracy with which they are reported or predicted. Moral values are concerned with a very limited kind of actual or potential entities or occurrences, namely, human actions, characters, and institutions, and their gradations in quality. Esthetic values are concerned with the transactions between objects and observers in which the bare contemplation of the object produces the unique kind of sustained delight or aversion which we call the esthetic response.

Thus truth values are concerned with objective occurrences and the reports made about these occurrences by human observers, who may be mistaken, but whose mistakes can within limits be detected by empirical methods. Moral values are concerned with the behavior of human subjects in their relations to each other as affecting what these subjects believe to be good for man. Esthetic values are concerned with the transaction between a subject and an object which he contemplates. In a word, then, on this view, truth is objective; falsity, and also moral values, are subjective; and esthetics is transactional.

One other preliminary consideration concerning esthetic evaluations is relevant to the present inquiry, namely, that there is an irreducible subjectivity or idiosyncracy at the core of esthetic judgments. Consequently, there are disagreements among experts which cannot be resolved by a majority vote, so that some of their judgments can better be graded as neutral in truth value rather than as true or false.

5. The Relatedness of Moral and Esthetic Values

To investigate the relatedness between moral and esthetic values we need only to examine an action of a person which it would be appropriate to evaluate on moral grounds. Then, for an observer in our own culture, whose moral and esthetic sensibilities were reasonably well developed, his responses on the esthetic scale would be parallel to his responses on the moral scale. For if this observer evaluates the action which he is observing as having positive moral value (i.e., as being 'good' in the moral sense) then his contemplation of that action will produce in him a corresponding degree of delight; while if he evaluates the action as having negative moral value (as being 'evil') then his contemplation of the action will produce in him a corresponding degree of aversion. These responses of delight and aversion are so linked that he cannot make a *moral* judgment without having it produce a corresponding esthetic response (but *not* vice versa, as will be pointed below). Expressed formally,

(1) $Mp \supset Mp \cdot Ep$
(2) $Mn \supset Mn \cdot En$
(3) $Mm \supset Mm \cdot Em$

From this it follows that for such an observer, all other possible conjunctions on the morality and esthetics scales are impossible, and that of the 64 theoretically possible arrangements of combinations of grades of truth, moral, and esthetic values tabulated in Table 1, only those can have empirical content in which, if E or M is present, they are both present, and in the same grade. These conditions are met only by the following arrangements, which are thus still empirically possible, namely, classes 4, 24, and 44. In addition to these dyadic classes which meet the above requirements, there are closely related triadic classes which contain parallel values for E and M, and as we shall see below when we consider truth values, these classes also meet our requirements. These are classes 1, 2, 3; 12; 21, 22; and 41, 42, 43. However, no other class which contains either E or M can on this view have empirical content.

When the object under scrutiny by the observer consists of a human action or character or institution which may be judged morally, then the moral and esthetic responses of the observer are so inter-related that *either* will elicit the *other*.

The esthetic response is intuitive, direct, and immediate—and the moral evaluation is rational, indirect, and mediated. Thus the observer can start with his intuitive esthetic responses as primary. He can make himself self-consciously aware of the esthetic delight or aversion which is produced by the contemplation of an action or character or institution which he is observing, and his esthetic response will trigger the corresponding moral evaluation which is linked to that response for him as his responses are structured by his culture. His esthetic sensitivity, on this view, becomes his moral conscience when it is his own action or character which he is observing and to which his immediate intuitive response is an esthetic one. Then by deliberately attending to the esthetic qualities of his response he will immediately discover its moral value as well.

6. The Independence of Esthetic and Moral Values

In diametric contrast to the relatedness which links an associated esthetic response to a primarily moral evaluation, there is no linked moral evaluation which is associated with a primarily esthetic response, that is, a response to an object of contemplation other than a human action or character or institution. As a matter of fact, the esthetic responses to what are primarily esthetic objects, such as, for example, works of art, are not only *not* linked to moral evaluations, but on the contrary, are so sharply demarcated from them that the very question of the moral worth of these esthetic objects is irrelevant, and it is a category mistake even to ask the question.

On this view, we would eliminate as empirically impossible any classes which exhibit the category mistake which would be made if we were to attempt to conjoin a reading on a scale of moral value with any reading on a scale of esthetic value. This excludes the following dyadic classes:

(4) Ep · Mp		(28) En · Mm
(8) Ep · Mn		(36) Em · Mp
(12) Ep · Mm		(40) Em · Mn
(20) En · Mp		(44) Em · Mm
(24) En · Mn		

Also excluded, on the same principle, are all of the triadic classes in Table 1, since in each of them a moral evaluation is linked (illicitly) to an esthetic evaluation. Thus the only classes which are not eliminated as empirically impossible on the basis of the above principle are the monadic or dyadic classes which do not contain moral evaluations, namely, monadic esthetic evaluations ((16) Ep; (32) En; (48) Em); monadic truth evaluations ((61)Tp; (62) Tn; (63) Tm); dyadic combinations of esthetic and truth values

(13) Tp · Ep   (31) Tm · En
(14) Tn · Ep   (45) Tp · Em
(15) Tm · Ep   (46) Tn · Em
(29) Tp · En   (47) Tm · Em
(30) Tn · En

and of course (64)***, which contains *none* of the three grades of value.

From the foregoing it follows that on at least a theoretical level we can now understand as category mistakes questions such as the following: (1) Does the fact that an artist is a scoundrel with a reprehensible lack of moral scruples diminish in any way the beauty of his works of art? For example, are the non-political poems of Ezra Pound any the less beautiful because of his Fascist-Nazi politics? (2) Recently some remarkable forgeries of the work of Vermeer were done by a previously unknown Dutch painter, Han Van Meegeren. His paintings were not copies of extant Vermeers, but new masterpieces indistinguishable from the work of Vermeer in theme and style and mannerisms and techniques. Was the beauty of the forged Vermeers diminished when the discovery was made that they were the work of a forger?

Obviously, the *objective* qualities of a work of art are not affected by the artist's morality or politics. In the loose sense in which we identify the objective qualities of a work of art as the locus of its beauty—as if for the sake of argument the beauty were independent of the expectations and perceptions and evaluations of the beholder—in this sense the beauty of the art object is totally unaffected by responses of the observer to the moral qualities of the artist. But on the transactional theory of beauty, the esthetic responses of delight or aversion produced by the contemplation of an object are constitutive of its beauty or its ugliness. It might very well be that an observer, listening to the voice of Ezra Pound reading some of his non-political poems, and either not knowing who the poet was or not knowing his politics, might find the poems very beautiful. However, if the listener knew that he was hearing the voice of an apologist for fascism, he might not be able to listen to the voice alone, dissociated from the man, but would respond to the voice as bringing him into the presence of a person to whom he responds morally with such aversion as to cancel out some degree of the esthetic delight he might otherwise have felt. True, it is not *really* the voice nor the poems which are ugly, but the Nazi-fascist politics; yet this truth is so refined and abstract that it has no empirical reference. As a practical matter, even though not "really" ugly, the voice of a fascist-sympathizer, like his politics, becomes ugly to the observer who abhors his politics.

Similarly, in the case of the forged paintings, it is the fraud and deception which are immoral and ugly, and the painting is "really" or "objectively" no less beautiful after the forgery is discovered than before the deception was found out. But as a practical matter, even though it is not "really" ugly, the picture loses some of its beauty when it is discovered to be a forgery. The responses of the observer who looks at the painting knowing that it is a forgery are complex. Part of his responses are responses not to the painting as an art object, but to the immoral human action of the deliberate fraud involved in the use of another man's signature or style (or both). The esthetic revulsion in response to the immorality has no effect on the objective qualities of the painting, and these qualities remain totally unaffected. Thus, loosely speaking, the real or objective beauty of the art object is undiminished. But as in the case cited of the voice of Ezra Pound, the painting or the poem is contemplated not only as a work of art, but as the product of an immoral action, or actor—and the contemplation of the immorality of the action or the actor produces a secondary esthetic response of revulsion. Thus even though the esthetic revulsion is a response to the immorality of the painter or the poet rather than to the ugliness of his works, for practical purposes it cancels out some of the delight which is elicited as the transactional response to his artistic creations. The net result is a possible diminishing of the total transactional beauty which some observers may find in the works of art created by an artist whose personal morality is sufficiently reprehensible as to be morally and esthetically offensive to the observer.

7. The Relatedness of Truth Values to Moral and Esthetic Values

What is the relation of the truth scale to the other two scales? If we consider the truth to be, in Wittgenstein's terms, "whatever is the case," then reports are true if they state what is the case—and false if they state what is not the case as being the case. For the sake of practical convenience—as a practical absolute—we may take as being the case what is agreed to by a majority of the recognized experts in a given field as being the case. On this view, a reported evaluation is true if it agrees with a majority of the experts and false if it disagrees with them—while if the experts disagree with sufficient diversity then no report can be considered to have either positive or negative truth value but instead is classed as having a neutral truth value.

Let us try to combine the truth scale with the other two scales if or where we can.

(a) Conjoint moral and esthetic evaluation of an act with moral significance.

If we know the opinions of the relevant experts, we can add to our previous analysis, Tp, Tn, and Tm ratings, on the basis of our knowledge as to whether the recognized experts in our culture would agree that the ratings made by the observer are correct—that is, of the same subquality or grade as would be made by the experts. Proceeding in this way, we could say that observer R says that action A is good and beautiful and (1) the experts would agree that what he says is true; or (2) the experts would disagree with each other to the extent that what the observer says would be rated as having a neutral truth value; or (3) the experts would disagree with the observer and the observer's evaluation would be rated as false.

Thus to the dyadic classes previously stipulated as being possible we can now add to each the three possible truth values of our truth scale. This gives as the possible classes which are not necessarily empty, classes 1, 2, 3, 22, 23, 41, 42, 43.

(1)   Tp · Mp · Ep   (23)   Tm · Mn · En
(2)   Tn · Mp · Ep   (41)   Tp · Mm · Em
(3)   Tm · Mp · Ep   (42)   Tn · Mm · Em
(21)   Tp · Mn · En   (43)   Tm · Mm · Em
(22)   Tn · Mn · En

(b) Esthetic evaluation of (extra-moral) art objects

We can also add truth value ratings to our previous conclusions concerning the classes which are empirically possible in making esthetic evaluations of extra-moral art objects. In addition to the monadic classes of esthetic value, namely, classes 16, 32, and 48, which we saw above were empirically possible, we can add to these classes the possible variations in truth value with which it is empirically possible they may be conjoined. These are classes 13, 14, 15, 29, 30, 31, 45, 46, and 47.

(16) Ep	(13) Tp · Ep	(31) Tm · En
(32) En	(14) Tn · Ep	(45) Tp · Em
(48) Em	(15) Tm · Ep	(46) Tn · Em
	(29) Tp · En	(47) Tm · Em
	(30) Tn · En	

(c) Monadic truth values

It is also possible to have monadic classes of truth value, namely, classes 61, 62, and 63. These are monadic classes, not related to beauty or goodness, where the report which has a truth value is a report about an entity which intrinsically has no moral significance and pro duces a minimum of esthetic response—examples are reports of pointer readings on scientific instruments.

(d) Inter-relatedness of truth, moral, and esthetic values

While monadic truth values are in their own right primarily non-moral and non-esthetic, slight secondary relations to esthetic or moral values can on occasion be discovered to be attached to them. The situation is very much the same as Peirce found to be the case when he discovered that his three categories, Firstness, Secondness, and Third-ness were not only conceivable as pure firstness, pure secondness, and pure thirdness, but that one could conceive of a secondness of firstness and a thirdness of firstness—of a firstness of secondness and a thirdness of secondness— and of a firstness of thirdness and a second-ness of thirdness—without thereby giving up the uniqueness of the three categories themselves. In much the same way, moral values and truth values and esthetic values each have their own unique identity (seen in the pure form in the monadic classes in Table 1) but there is a real sense in which we can find (in certain situations) esthetic values in truth values, e.g., when the "pointer readings" constitute a critical confirmation of a hypothesis and are consequently viewed by the observer not as bare true facts, but as critical evidence which has confirmed a hypothesis and is thus viewed with some of the same esthetic delight with which the observer views the hypothesis after it has been confirmed. That we can find esthetic values in moral values was developed in some detail in the section above on moral values. That we can find moral values in truth values is obvious from the fact that a lie has both a negative truth value and a negative moral value—thus the deliberate falsification of a report produces consequences which require moral as well as factual evaluation. And of course, as we have seen, we can find all three grades of truth value in reports of either moral values, or reports of esthetic values.

EUGENE FREEMAN

SAN JOSE STATE COLLEGE

POWER AND FORM

I

THE principal topics of metaphysics are power and form. The principal tasks of metaphysics are to clarify and develop the meaning of these terms; to trace their probable relations with each other; and to speculate on their place in the scheme or abyss of reality.

Major tendencies in philosophy can be identified by the positions they take in regard to these problems. They can be located at the reciprocal poles of knowledge and reality. At the one, rationalism emphasizes forms as abstract, general, and timeless. Empiricism favors them as concrete, particular, and temporal. Intuitionism of an experiential strain takes the concrete form and regards it as plastic and organic. And mysticism melts the boundaries of forms into an infinite formless. At the other pole, logical realism at its extreme point identifies abstract forms with reality, leaving no place for power. Materialism introduces power, since it admits motion and force; but it regards power as external to its preferred reality, which, as determinate bodies projected against determinate spaces, appears to be concrete forms related in contingent forms. Ontological idealism incorporates power in its notion of spirit, and gives power varying degrees of importance in relation to form. Rationalistic and empiricistic idealisms regard power as a means to the contemplation of form, in which power is made tranquil and perhaps is transcended. Voluntaristic idealism makes form a means to power, which is clearly paramount in this philosophy as long as will is firmly held to. And mystical idealism grasps the power of spirit in an ecstasy that annihilates forms. But beyond this is a neutral monism, in which spirit has no privilege. In this one substance and ground, power alone remains, bare and dark.

These philosophies seldom occur separate and pure. They are more persuasive and logical, more powerful and better formed, when they appear as conclusions rather than as premises, even though a conclusion may influence its premises. This paper therefore will approach the problems of power and form directly, beginning with the meaning of form and power and ending with the problem of their reality. It will conclude that power is the substance of the real and its ultimate value, but that form generally and spirit specifically are its indispensable allies. It will thus end on a strain of voluntaristic idealism, modified here and there in the direction of other and compatible tendencies.

II

The concept of form begins with that of a character, nature, or "meaning." The character may be of any sort, subject only to the stipulation that it be capable of bearing the further aspects of form that will follow in this analysis. As bearing these aspects, the character has form and may be called a form. The character may be a quality, such as red or joy; a relation, such as two or to the right of; or a mixture of quality and relation, such as table, father, or justice. It may be simple, like the hue of a single color, or complex, like the same color in regard to its hue, gray, and white or black. It constitutes the parts that are organized into a whole, any novelty that may result from organization, and the whole made from the organized parts. It may appear in a universal, such as whiteness; or in a particular, such as the white of a certain piece of paper; or in an individual, such as the piece of paper taken as a composite of particulars.

The second aspect of form is determinateness. A character is determinate insofar as it is definite; it is definite when defined; and it is defined when it has a limit or boundary. A boundary separates one character from another, so that when the character of man or of white is predicated of an individual, it is understood that it is that character and not some other that is meant. Every form is determinate, whether it is a genus, a species, a particular, or an individual. Only an infinite and undifferentiated whole, or mystical whole, is entirely indeterminate. But one form may be said to be more determinate than another, if it is more bounded and distinct than the other. A species is more determinate than a genus, for the differentia adds a limit to the limit established by the genus. Though color excludes sound and is thus far determinate, it is compatible with any hue and is therein indeterminate; but red excludes other hues as well as sound, and is more determinate by this greater definition and

distinction. Presumably particulars and individuals are more determinate than their respective species; and individuals are more
determinate than particulars.

The relation of exclusion is negative. But a limit is not simply
negative: it is a condition of the origin of character, which takes
place by a process of determination. This process, whether logical
or temporal, begins with something less determinate and ends with
something more determinate. The end is more defined and exclusive, but it is so by virtue of an increment of character: thus the
common dictum that determination is negation.

Completing the definition of form is the aspect that is most
commonly stressed: unity or structure. But though unity is the
potential and goal of form, it is not indispensable to form. If a form
is absolutely simple in character, it has no unity of character, having
no plurality to unify. But such a form has no discord, which is the
opposite of unity. And wherever there is plurality in form, there is
unity. The unity of form is the aspect that most readily commands
attention. Many characters have more character and value than one
character, and they have still more of these when they are united
as organisms rather than as aggregates. Discord threatens the determinateness of single characters, and unity is necessary to the determinateness of a plurality. Unity underlies control by the practical
intelligence, and it reduces the many to the few or the one for the
satisfaction of reason. It is the principle of economy and rest in a
world often crowded and worn. But unity has its perils. Practical
control favors means, types, and calculation rather than ends, individuals, and sympathy. Rational reduction simplifies at the expense
of variety and vitality. Rest ends in tedium. For these defects, the
remedy may be found within the scope of unity in a manner especially
conspicuous in the arts. The genius of art passes over harmony,
or unity based on qualitative similarity, to balance, or unity based
on qualitative contrast. In balance, the many are preserved in their
mutual exclusions but are used to contribute to each other at the
subtly sharp edges of their mutual contacts. Thus unity and determinateness go hand in hand. Borrowing from Nicolai Hartmann without the clear authority of his own use, it may be suggested that in
form determinateness is the stronger value and unity the higher value.

Whether as a major factor in unity or as an independent notion, universality usually is emphasized in accounts of form, and

characters then are admitted to the class of forms only when they are universals. But it appears that the universal is derivative first to unity and second to determinateness; that its service to these, though important, is ambiguous; and that it has no monopoly on form.

A universal is any character that is viewed as abstract in position, being separate in thought if not in reality from any given moment and the totality of moments in time; abstract in character, being separate from other characters that are regarded as dispensable for the given point of understanding or action; and general, or indefinitely capable of participation in positions in time and with other characters by virtue of the dual abstractness. A universal is determinate, having a boundary that separates it from all other universals, participant as well as not. But its abstract character makes it relatively indeterminate, and a high degree of abstractness in a universal, as in a superior genus, raises that trait to a corresponding power. What saves the universal from mere deficiency in regard to this trait of form is the psychological determinateness, as distinct from the logical and metaphysical, found in the clarity with which the outline of a stripped and filtered character can be discerned: there is a minimum of complication, distraction, and confusion from the superposition of other outlines, which tax the human mind. The universal is more fortunate in regard to unity. The presence of a given universal among many moments and with many sporadic characters constitutes to that extent homogeneity, which binds together the diverse moments and characters. But homogeneity and repetition are comparatively low forms of unity and fall under the criticism of harmony stated above. The universal as an instrument for unity is much more impressive when related in determinate ways to other universals, as in laws or general theorems and especially in deductive structures of these. But here the universal falls short of the proposed ideal unity. For connections of universals appear to be either analytic, going no further than exposition of the relation of a universal to its parts, or contingent, being borrowed from particulars. Thus the universal falls again into repetition, or it engages in compromise. It seems evident that the logical pursuit of form has its hazards in harmony and its disappointments about the synthetic a priori. In contrast, particulars and individuals, like tones, colors, and words in the arts, are determinate with a high degree of concreteness; enter into the tight unity of the work of art without sacrifice of their variety and vitality; and in that unity achieve a distinctive kind of necessity which is inevitable, undemonstrable, and plastic. The universal is not absent here, for characters, limits, and unities cannot be identified and controlled without some inflection of past awareness through memory and some systematization of it through conception. But the universal is dissolved in the particular and does not exhaust it, and an intuition of reciprocal standing defines limits and creates unities. Here is complex and satisfying form at a good distance from the universal.

The form of form as character determinate and unified can be summarized by the statement that form is the intelligible. Whether discovered or created, form is congruent with intelligence, or the cognitive power articulated and articulate; it is the sole appropriate object of this power. If knowing extends beyond the bounds of form, as perhaps in mysticism, its faculty and operation are of a quite different sort, which can be hinted at as a holistic interpenetration of parts that do not exist. From this cause mystical experience is inarticulate or ineffable, in contrast to the eminent expressiveness of intelligence. And it is evident that form as the intelligible has the same duality that intelligence has. Intellect sponsors logical or rational form, and imagination as the imaginal and figurative power sponsors aesthetic form. The one prefers identity, the universal, and rigorous necessity; the other prefers diversity, the particular, and a plastic necessity. These distinctions are not absolute, and they are in a manner reconciled in the general affinity of intelligence with character, determinateness, and unity. Thus form has a large domain. But it does not exhaust the topics of interest in metaphysics. Other than lucid, tranquil form is power, which never rests and has no face to show.

III

The first element in power is change, which is a relation of a complex and elusive kind. The terms in the relation are positions in space, or characters of any kind, or mixtures of the two. The positions or characters differ from one another in their respective modes, and change may be described initially as a species of diversity. This factor is thickened and tightened by its further determination as incompatibility. Residence at one position of itself excludes residence at another; and though white may share a position with oval and health, it excludes red as oval excludes circle and health excludes disease. Change proper is the additional factor in the relation whereby the incompatibility is surmounted without destruction of its inherent nature. The most that can be said of this final item is that it greatly increases the diversity of the world while promoting a characteristic unity: a unity which excludes chaos at one end, since it does not permit the joint being of incompatibles; excludes rational entailment at the other end, since it proposes no change of inherent nature and inherent antagonism of the terms; but maintains a discipline over its members, since change is not from health to red or oval, but only to disease. The item itself resists intelligence, whether intellectual or imaginative. The synonyms and partials of change: passage, becoming, motion, growth: take us no nearer to the center of change, which is indeterminate to the point of being characterless. The terms of change can be identified as determinate positions and characters, but their relation is radically indeterminate. As Bergson emphasized, intermediates of determinate nature can be placed between the original terms, but this takes us no closer to the supple flow. Intuition of some sort probably does so; but it does not lighten the mystery; it rather repeats it, being itself an instance of the changing and indeterminate. And the mystery is widened without limit when change is pursued from its derivative status among finites to its logically primordial status in the cosmos as a whole. Here the determinate terms of change melt away, being absorbed backward into an amorphous and anonymous sea of pure change, in which all is bare change and nothing in particular changes according to any particular pattern. In this condition, characters do not appear on the scene, and the scene has no mutually external positions to define space. Intelligence does not negotiate this condition. If mysticism has a cognitive function, it is to grasp this domain by a kindred disposition in the cognitive faculty.

Behind the manifest of change, whether derived or primordial, is the source of change, which is power. There is no change without power and no power without change. The first statement is speculative, since it claims a ground for change when there may be no ground, and identifies the ground with something that is not generally experienced and is subject to counterfeiting. It is indeed possible that change should have no ground, which is a kind of reason; but it is reasonable, though not certain, to propose for it such a reason, which is the first of reasons. Bare identification of the source of change with power is not speculative, but analytic: the notion of power as source of change is as close to a definition of power as the term admits. But power is not experienced among or within those changes that are open to public observation: the motions of bodies from one sensed position to another. The terms of mechanics are positions in space; changes of positions with velocities and accelerations; bodies, which appear to be mainly occupants of positions and patients of changes; and times, which are ratios of changes. Force occurs as a construction for which there is no experience and no intrinsic content. This is fatal to power in mechanics but not fatal, though admittedly injurious, to it in metaphysics, which is not limited by the terms of mechanics. But power is experienced among the changes open to private introspection. The experience of a source of change occurs in volition and emotion, and the experience reveals an intrinsic content of effort, strain, thrust, and consummation which is distinct from mere change and from the bare abstraction of source of change. But the experience may be illusory. In volition, the consciousness of power presumably is contained in the kinaesthetic sensation associated with muscular action. But the sensation does not occur until the action takes place; and like all sensation it reports on its object rather than causing it. If power is to occur, it must be in a prefatory image of kinaesthetic sensation experienced as the ground of the muscular action or the sensation or both. Apart from the psychophysical problem, it may be observed that an image has little authority; that it can occur, if at all, with or without the subsequent sensation; that its similarity in character to the sensation repeats the problem of power and postpones the solution; and that both image and sensation, as venturing to report beyond themselves, may be sensuous dreams foisted upon a nonsensuous action devoid of power. The case for emotion is better. The experience of pleasure and pain, of joy and sorrow, contains the forward impulse of emotion in time and the organic press of one nuance of the emotion into another. Here the feeling of power may well be the power of feeling, without counterfeit. But even in this highly immediate zone the apparent cannot guarantee that it is also real. Metaphysics can afford to take such a risk, having no alternative if it is to survive. Considerably more difficult is the pursuit of the footing thus gained into the more obscure recesses of the psychical, and beyond them into the physical. Without sharing Nietzsche's view of the epiphenomenal nature of the conscious process, it is clear that power cannot be limited to that area without jeopardy to its general and basic status as the source of all change. The sequel will recur to the problem.

Criticism of power is based partly on the supposition that power transcends the realm of change; is of itself detached in regard to change; and brings about change by a gratuitous and arbitrary act. Power then participates in an artificial bifurcation and in a mysterious bridging of the beings thus separated. Strict theism construes power in this fashion, and Christian theism in the form of the doctrine of the Trinity seeks to undo the error in the theory of the indwelling functions of the Son and of the Holy Spirit. The theory of material substance as made up of defined, rigid particles characterized by inertia and accelerating under external force has a similar dualism: less radical, since the power thus impinging is ascribed to other particles in the system, but more whimsical, since the power thus confined is never identified in its location. But power is immanent in change and of one fabric with it. It is committed to change and afire with it. And it brings about change by the inherent necessity of its own nature as power. If it appears not to be immersed in change, as in the theory of energy as potential, static, and quiet, it is because it has left its pure state and taken on organizing forms. These parcel it out for secondary and specialized modes of operation, in relation to which it is somewhat transcendent, detached, and contingent, and which conceal like a stratagem the abiding fusion of its basic nature and operation. No theory of the potential as the source of the actual can be metaphysically basic; for it assumes in the potential condition what is to be actualized. Thus it explains by repetition, which is a postponement of explanation; and it compounds this defect by seeking to generate by the same method. The distinction of potential and actual in regard to power belongs to the economy and mechanism of power, not to its essential nature.

The third and final item in the essential history of power is freedom. Power is fulfilled in freedom, and it is restricted, sometimes stunted, but never destroyed in compulsion. Power is free primarily, and change secondarily, to the extent that power is the sole source of the changes in which it participates. It is compelled to the extent that other power determines these changes and thus its operation.

Activity is the fused condition of change, power, and freedom: a condition of change as stemming from its own free power, or of power as freely operating in its proper changes. Passivity is a similar condition of change, power, and compulsion. Bare change is neither active nor passive. Power is one or the other, but only as consummated in change. And freedom and compulsion are abstract moments in action and passion, and become concrete as attributes of power and change.

Freedom is one of the most elusive targets of philosophy, as it is also of practice. In no useful sense, whether in philosophy or in the conduct of life, is it caprice. An item of caprice is completely separated from everything, so that a change is separated from other changes and from powers, and a power is separated from its changes and its own history. Caprice thus contradicts power and action. Freedom must then imply some sort of continuity among its terms; and this continuity is the minimum content of the causal relation, whether that relation be thought of as one of mere repetition of effect on cause, or of intrinsic rational necessity, or of productive efficacy or power. Though fraught with celebrated difficulties, the causal relation is not insuperably difficult when thought of as leading from one item to another. In the human sphere, freedom can readily be conceived as the causation of conduct by choice and of choice by self. But if the causal relation passes from self to the world, the concept of freedom is balked: the self that was free prospectively, in regard to its choice and conduct, is not free fundamentally, in regard to its own nature and being. Freedom therefore must consist in the condition of the self as an uncaused cause: one that has effects in accordance with its nature, but owes its nature and being to nothing other than itself. Power alone is free, for it requires nothing but itself to be and to act, and its being and acting are synonymous and require no foreign intermediary or trigger. Power needs no foreign being to secure its own being; for if the second has no power it is inferior, and if it has power it can provide nothing new in principle and it may compel in practice. As power is fulfilled in freedom, freedom requires power for its basis and meaning.

Freedom has degrees. Every substantial being has power, whether it be an electron or atom, a planet or galaxy, a human self or human society. But all identifiable beings are finites, each of which is limited by other finites. The power of each suffers the power of others, or is blocked and inhibited by it, or depends upon it for some action that exceeds its own magnitude. Thus compulsion subtracts from freedom. But it never reduces it to nothing; for power automatically is resistance at the point of collision with other power, and a power that dominates does so in terms of the nature of the power that suffers. A stone that is thrown moves in accordance with its own nature as well as that of the thrower. Freedom can be destroyed only when the power in question is destroyed. But power simple can not be destroyed. Only a mode of organization of power is destroyed, and with it the freedom appropriate to the mode. Thus every finite being has some degree of activity and some of passivity, though the proportion may in principle vary greatly.

Complete freedom can occur only in a being which has no limits and so is infinite. It is conceivable that finites can achieve a derivative infinitude, and a derivative completeness of freedom, by a method which presupposes form: this will be discussed later. But an original infinitude and freedom can be found in the power which is the source of the "anonymous sea of pure change" mentioned earlier. As changes with determinate terms presuppose logically if not temporally change that has no determinations, so powers identified with finite beings presuppose power that has no limits: and the original change proceeds from the original power. This power is the sole source of the change in which it participates, since there is no foreign power. It is the plenum of pure activity, to which the mystic wishes to return with an ardor which is an image of its goal.

IV

The relations between power and form are of three kinds, which form a logical sequence from mutual exclusion through polar reciprocity to cooperation.

It is evident from the analysis of power and form that the two are essentially exclusive of each other. Power, like the change it begets, is other than the characters related by change. When regarded in its basic form of original freedom, it is indeterminate not only in regard to character, but also to the distinctions of space that underlie the ordinary notion of the individual thing. It has no unity, having no parts to bind together into one: it is one without unity.

And characters do not themselves change. When regarded as non-temporal universals, they neither enter into nor leave the realm of change. When regarded as particulars or individuals in time, they do so enter and leave. But when a character, such as white, enters existence, it does not come from a realm of non-existence, and it does not change from another existent character into itself. Characters may move from one position in space to another; but the change is of the position of the character rather than in the character; a character is itself or it is nothing. Furthermore, characters have no power of themselves. As external to change they contradict the nature of power, which is fraught and congested with change. And determinateness and unity are indifferent to change if not opposed to it. As principles of intelligibility they are lucid to the point of diaphanous thinness: they have no dark recesses, no surds, no nests of power. Married to character, they perfect its intelligibility. The dualism of the intelligible and the dynamical is basic.

This distinction rises to polar reciprocity in the thesis that power and form are related to each other as creator and creature. Power is the source of change, and change is the introduction of novelty in character or position. When the introduction is of character and is of sufficient intensity to go beyond bare combination, it may be called creation: relative creation, or emergence, if the novel character has antecedent characters in combination to which it cannot be reduced; and absolute creation if there are no antecedent characters. The creator is power, and the character with its determinateness and unity is the creature. Power does not create power, and forms do not create. Power has a function, and form a need, and the two meet as reciprocals. But power exercises this function only under certain conditions. As a completely free being, unchecked by contrary power, power merely begets pure change in formless iteration and interpenetration. It is like light, which illuminates nothing until it is stopped. When power is stopped at the margin of other power, the result is a form, which is the joint creation of the powers involved. The powers are partly active and partly passive, and creation has that dual and somewhat ironic parentage. It requires activity but not pure activity. But forms are neither active nor passive.

The combination of action and passion in creation is accompanied by two further requirements for creation. Since power is checked only by other power, some sort of otherness and distinction is needed for creation. The plurality need not be that of discrete items in space, which are as clearly and completely separated from each other as the spaces they occupy. It may merely indicate that the original "interpenetration of parts that do not exist" has been slightly relaxed, leading to nascent schism in the plenum. This relaxation appears to be the first beginning of creation, which does not fall under creation in the full sense but is indispensable for it. How such otherness occurs is no more explicable than the operation of the final requirement for creation. This is that the creator must not contain the creature prior to the act of creation. Such containment is repetition, in which there is nothing new, no source of novelty, and no need for such a source or power. Intelligence in general, and logical intelligence in particular, succeed only when they establish repetition of one degree or another: the analysis of a whole into its parts, identification of a universal in a particular, explanation by derivation from the familiar, causal relation as constant conjunction, the potential as source of the actual by virtue of having the actual in germ, and emergence as novelty conditioned by abiding antecedents. None of these methods is appropriate to creation. It follows that the absolute creator, the primordial power which is the source of all character, determinateness, and unity, must be entirely void of these. Such status for power has already been claimed. Without reducing the darkness, which is not cold, of the greatest of mysteries, it seems that creation can be circumscribed as the function of power active and passive, plural, and radically indeterminate, from which form emerges as the creature.

The notion of form as the creature of power appears readily to hold of forms that may variously be designated as concrete, temporal, natural, actual. It is quite plausible in regard to particulars and individuals, such as a red and a star; to laws of nature as formulated in the special, empirical, and contingent sciences; and to categorial schemes thought of as immanent in, partly constitutive of, and valid only for the domain of nature. It is less plausible when applied to universals, and to universal relations of universals (as in logic and mathematics), when these are claimed to have some kind of being other than that of the temporal. The application to this problematic zone will be waived for the moment.

The reciprocal relation of creator and creature becomes one of interdependence and cooperation in the use that the first makes

Power + Form

color – hue   form   plurality in form = unity
              character

determination through definition
determination by exclusion, relationship + position

power – change   like   light
has no unity   + is checked only by power
freedom is not caprice –
is some kind of continuity with novelty

form is means + end for power

of the second. Form is not driftwood thrown on the beach in the struggle of powers. It is both a means and an end for power. Itself founded on division, it becomes the source of a comprehensive unity in which passivity yields by degrees to a new freedom: new because it belongs to individuals rather than the primordial whole. This relation of power and form can be traced through matter and mind, two major informations of power.

The elementary particle of traditional materialism, which alone unambiguously claims the name of matter, has several characteristics. It has position in space; shape, or limit in space; and size, or amount of space between the limits. It has motion, velocity, and acceleration, actual or probable, which imply time as well as space. It is homogeneous; rigid, or internally changeless; and indestructible. It is inert, changing in quantity and direction of motion only through the operation of incident forces. It exerts such forces on other particles. And it has or is a mass, which is occupant, possessor, patient, or agent of the foregoing traits.

Of these characteristics, those identified with space are eminently empirical, clear, and measurable. The same is true of those associated with time, since the mobility of motion is filtered out in favor of discrete points and instants and intervals between them of similar constitution. But inertia, force generally, and mass are not in themselves empirical; are measured only indirectly through reference to the empirical factors; and are highly obscure, since they are not experienced and elicit in measurement no proper content of which the measure can significantly be predicated.

The cause of the obscurity lies in the confusion in the concept of matter of form, which exhausts what is specifically material, and of power, which is antecedent to matter. The formal nature of matter is striking. The particle of traditional materialism is completely determinate in position, shape, size, motion, velocity, and acceleration. It is unified in its homogeneity and rigidity; in its inertia, which is repetition of condition with regard to motion; and in its admirable subservience to principles of quantity and of law. The determinateness and unity are of low complexity, since quality does not appear and character is restricted to relations which are reduced to those of space and time. But this elementary condition is appropriate to form in its beginning, and it has in its uniformity a simplicity and dependability that are important to power in its

first adventures in the difficult process of creating. And the obscure
factors in matter are derivatives of power. Force is power active in
relation to contrary power; it is power bare and abstract, acting only
as the reflex to mere otherness, apart from the nature and work of
the other; it is power systematized in law as a result of that abstraction and as a means to its most economical operation. Inertia is
power passive; it is similarly abstract and systematized, except that
it acts as the reflex to its bare identity and is systematized as a means
to the most economical maintenance of that identity. And mass is
power contained in the homogeneous forms of its first creation; in
that containment it is organized as a disposition which is neither
active nor passive, but potential for either; and its creatures serve as
a mask to others and perhaps to itself. These obscure factors ascribed
to matter are not matter, which has distinctive identity only in the
forms noted earlier; they are power at a relatively simple and homogeneous level of creation.

The further reaches of creation involve mind. The notions available to the concept of mind are those of power, consciousness, value,
and symbolic function. It is often thought that active power is the
hallmark of mind. But mind has no monopoly of power, and it is
possible for it to have power in the condition of passivity. Power is
not itself mind; consciousness, valuation, and symbolic function are
forms that power creates, which are contingent for power but essential for mind. Consciousness celebrates quality as matter does
relation. It differs from matter in certain respects. Matter is a
minimum accommodation to change; it is a mask for power; when
it is determined as this or that kind of matter, the determinations
are incidental to it and without genuine novelty. Consciousness is
in endless flux; it is charged with apparent power; it is determined
inherently in the infinitely varied and novel forms of desire, emotion,
and sensation. Here power is so intimately related to its creatures
that the bifurcation ceases: in emotion, quality and change, the intelligible and the dynamical, are fused in a single life. From power and
consciousness valuation arises. Valuation is the relation in consciousness of power to freedom. In valuation, power discerns freedom,
affirms it in the quality of pleasure, and moves implicitly in its behalf in desire. But consciousness and valuation are greatly extended
through semiosis, which underlies conception of universals and laws
and the operation of reason.

These forms of mind are effects of power at a high level of creation, and they serve power in complex ways. They are at first means and later ends. Consciousness enables power to redefine its relations to its environment; sensation precipitates on objects the attitude of power to them; reason simplifies and coordinates the environment. But power subsequently rises to the contemplation of these forms, admiring them sincerely for their own sake. It may seem that here power subordinates itself to form. But the forms it admires are the furnishings of its contemplation, and its contemplation is the serene exercise of power rather than its transcendence or abnegation. As means or as end, mind advances the freedom of the power that possesses it.

But intrinsic enjoyment and pragmatic function do not solve the problem of freedom in the multiplicity of powers that underlies all form. The contemplation of qualities and relations in pure art and science does not divide powers, minds, and men, but neither does it unite them: it is impersonal and uncommitted. Reason by itself assists a rational power to master other power and thus to increase its own freedom. But a power subdued declines in freedom and adds less than its own power to that of the master. Thus freedom and power are generally impaired. The remedy for this melancholy condition lies in the capacity of mind to identify itself with the distinctive consciousness and valuation of other minds and to desire them as it does its own. Through love, powers are united without deduction of power and with complete mutual freedom. But this union must be implemented by reason, which defines the means to the ends proposed by love. Thus power uses reason and love, products of form, to recover the freedom lost as the condition of form. But the freedom recovered is not identical with the freedom lost: the earlier is prior to individuation and the later is perfected in it. The one precedes creation; the other is creation consummate. Power creative begins as force in matter and ends as love in mind, and as it moves it becomes more truly power through its growth in freedom.

V

The nature and mutual relations of power and form shed light on the problem of their reality.

As the source of change and the motor of all that moves, power commends itself immediately as eminently real. The confrontation of power stirs conviction in the mind; power may not be ignored; it impresses the mind as that which must be taken into account for every act and for the achievement and even the definition of every value: without freedom in some degree no value is achieved, and if achieved it would be hollow. As the creator of form, power is more basic in reality than form; and if there are degrees of reality, power is more real than form.

Reluctance to accept these conclusions stems in theory of knowledge from admiration of reason, which is thought to be alien to power; in metaphysics from derogation of change because of its impermanence; and in ethics from criticism of force and compulsion, with which power is identified. But reason is not alien to power, being its creature, its instrument, and even the object of its admiring contemplation. Furthermore, reason of itself is a mere theorem or norm; it is incorporated in the world only in such instances as reasoning and law, which presuppose power. Specific instances of change, and the characters participating in them, have time before and after them; but change in essence is universal and everlasting; it has permanence without the death that seems inevitable in timeless beings. And power is force only at an early stage, and flowers far beyond force in rational and benevolent mind.

Form in itself has no credentials in regard to reality. It is properly thought of as an essence: that is, as something whose nature is grasped by the mind without any judgment of real or unreal. Character, determinateness, and unity can be exhausted as objects of awareness without any ontological judgment. Red determinate and unified can function in imagination, sense perception, and conception without intrinsic change. A judgment of reality will be determined proximately by the context of forms in which it is integrated, and ultimately by the service it renders to power. A form which satisfies power through a context of forms is more than mere form, and it is real. But as the creature of power, and as having its ontological credentials from power, it is less basic in reality than power and perhaps less real.

Exception to this view comes from those philosophies which believe that the universal has character and reality apart from the realm of time, nature, and concrete forms. For these philosophies, the universal is not the creature of power, but has a self-dependent integrity in timeless being. The universal then is regarded in any of three ways: as necessary; as the content of the timeless mind of God; and as possible. It is difficult to assign any meaning to the necessary status of universals, other than to regard them as related necessarily to each other in the fashion of a synthetic proposition. If universals are related to each other as universals, then they have a character and being other than that of particulars and individuals in time. But it is the despair of rationalistic philosophy not to be able to trace such necessary connections. If the universal is the content of the divine mind and has being thereby supposedly independent of time, it does not escape dependence on power, since mind human or divine is a form of power; nor does it escape relation to change, since power in any locus or garb is still committed intrinsically to change. Thus only the theory remains of the universal as the timeless possibility of character in time. The possibility no doubt is not existential, dependent on contingent laws of nature, but logical, consisting in absence of self-contradiction. A nisus toward actualization is not ascribed to the universal, and actualization depends on power. This view is plausible. But possibility is itself a form, and it seems to beg the question to use form to confer reality on itself. Furthermore, possibility appears to entail contrast with actuality, and the contrast may have being only for an actuality: that is, mind and power. And if the universal be conceded to have being after the mode of the possible, this surely is being pale and thin in comparison with that of power.

If this argument regarding universals is accepted, reality belongs first to power and second to form. But this order does not make form dispensable. Power is the abyss of reality and form its scheme: power constitutes the depth of reality and form its height.

ARTHUR BERNDTSON

UNIVERSITY OF MISSOURI

LOGICS

I

IN HIS ARTICLE on "Logic" in the Baldwin *Dictionary*, Peirce says that there are nearly 100 definitions of the word. Robert Blakey, in his *Historical Sketch of Logic*, published in 1851, makes the following statement: "The use of the word 'logic' is almost the only thing which logicians have in common; if we venture to step beyond this and ask for a definition of what is implied in it we are instantly stunned with a thousand discordant voices from all parts of the world." Blakey made this comment three years before Boole published his *Laws of Thought*, approximately 35 years before Bradley and Bosanquet wrote their logics, 50 years before Husserl developed his phenomenalism, about 70 years before Watson and Pavlov suggested a behavioristic interpretation of the learning process, and 87 years before Dewey published his *Theory of Inquiry*. When Blakey wrote, the ideas of the semanticists, not to mention the semanticists themselves, had not even been conceived. We may safely say, therefore, that there are now at least 106 discordant voices in logic.

To announce that this creates a scandal in philosophy is to be neither profound nor provocative. We are used to scandals in philosophy; in fact philosophy lives on scandals. But there are scandals and scandals, or, as I would prefer to put it, private scandals and public scandals. Every new philosophy is, in a sense, a private scandal, since it shocks, at least temporarily, the complacency of the older philosophers. But it soon becomes accepted, usually without too much change in the prevailing views, when we understand its origin and the framework within which it works. This I would call a private scandal. It is perhaps best illustrated by the claim of the logical positivists in their early innocence that all metaphysics is nonsense. This is no longer shocking since the older philosophers (among whom I count myself, chronologically if not ideologically) have conceded an inch or two here and there, and the logical positivists have conceded a mile or two there and here, and all are again living together at peace. But a public scandal is something quite different. In a public scandal many people seem to be conniving to produce something which will be shocking not only to those outside the clan but even to those inside, when they realize what is being done. It appears that logicians are deliberately trying to make the word 'logic' as confusing as possible. Not only are they inventing many-valued logics but they are making the word 'logic' itself into a many-valued term; "l" must always have a quantifier. The existential quantifier is more or less redundant since there are so many known logics that we gain nothing by saying that there is at least one, yet we cannot use the universal quantifier since there seems to be nothing in common among these many logics and therefore nothing that we can say about all of them. It would seem rather trivial to say with Blakey that the only thing that all logics have in common is the property of having been mentioned by logicians.

I am not here concerned with why logicians tend to make this favored word extend over a larger and larger area as time goes on. Perhaps they are only being pushed along by the force which impels all philosophical terms to increase in abstractness and generality with continued use; perhaps they are trying only to share in the prestige which logic has acquired in recent years. The problem of this paper is not to give a causal explanation of the ambiguities in the term 'logic', but to suggest a manner of eliminating them.

II

My reader, I take it, does not need documentation for the statement that the term 'logic' is many-valued. The citations which I gave in the first paragraph could be multiplied almost indefinitely. The problem is really one of discovering some sort of order in this confusion. What can the logician do to cope with the misunderstandings to which this ambiguity gives rise? Since definition is, in the final analysis, arbitrary one could, of course, settle the problem by this method. Then he would either honor his logical friends by defining the word so broadly as to include everything that they call 'logic' or scorn his logical friends by defining the word so narrowly as to include none of what they are doing. This would permit him to have precision or friends, but not both.

A much saner procedure would seem to be to start with a certain core subject-matter, which, presumably, everyone would agree to call 'logic', and then progressively add layers, step-by-step, losing logicians with each addition, but arriving, finally, at a position which would allow us to say: All logicians agree that logic is concerned with something, say A; of these, many admit that it is also concerned with B; a smaller number are willing to add C; others D; and so on. This might permit us to arrive at some conception of what the "essence" of logical subject-matter is, and then, using a loose Aristotelianism, go on to include the "properties" which might or might not be included in the study of logic, and end with the "accidents" which few would be willing to consider an important part of logical subject-matter. We could then divide logicians into the conservatives, who believe that logic is concerned with A and only with A; the middle-of-the-roaders, who are willing to admit that logic might also include B, or possibly B and C, or even B and C and D; and the logical liberals, who permit the logician to talk about almost anything that has some relation to A. Perhaps we might even quantify this series and thus be able to say *how* conservative or *how* liberal a logician is.

As an experiment, let us see how such an attempt might work out. At the very start I am, of course, on the spot. What would be accepted by all logicians as legitimate subject-matter for study? Let me suggest *deduction* and then, before you have a chance to tell me how many logicians would not accept this and for what reasons, permit me to inform you of what concessions I am willing to make in interpreting the word 'deduction'. Deduction is both a process and a result; let us include both. Deduction may be neither a process nor a result but a structure of marks on paper; let us include this. Deduction may be discovered introspectively or behaviorally; if we include both of these we shall have to say not only that anybody is deducing if he thinks he is deducing, but that a white rat is deducing when he pulls one lever rather than another, and that a man is deducing when he writes a p at the top of a page, then spends a certain amount of time frowning, chewing his pencil, scratching his head, and moving his larynx in a scarcely perceptible manner, and finally utters an "Aha!" and puts a q at the bottom of the page. From this it will be but a short step to including an electronic computer, certainly while it is operating and perhaps also as a structure which even when idle has the "disposition" to derive conclusions from premises. These have all been called 'deduction' and if we are to gain even a modest consensus of opinion among logicians we shall have to include them all.

This is the core; now for the first layer. You may insist that I have already added far too many layers, but I think it can be shown that our troubles have only begun. How about *induction*? If I read contemporary literature aright there is some tendency to exclude all considerations of induction from logic. It is not easy to do this since the term has taken on so many meanings in recent years that one hardly knows *what* he is excluding; indeed one is tempted to say that we should drop 'induction' from logic since we no longer have any idea what the term connotes and we should therefore exclude it simply because it is a meaningless sign. But the rejections are usually more firmly grounded. They claim to be justified by the fact that since induction presupposes the principle of the uniformity of nature, which can itself be established only inductively, induction is without deductive validation and therefore cannot fall in the field of logic. There may still be a problem of induction but it is either a pragmatic decision-problem involving such notions as predictive reliability or operational rule (I am thinking, of course, of such people as Feigl, Reichenbach and Braithwaite), or a psychological problem of why we utter generalizations in the presence of particular instances, as in the case of Billy, who is hit by Bobby and promptly says, "You're always doing that."

But there are many logicians who would include induction under a probability logic, so let us accept this meaning of the term. We have lost some logicians, but not too many. But if induction, why not also *abduction*? We can include this either in the sense of Peirce, who thought that the scientific method could not be understood without the trinity: induction, deduction and abduction; or in the sense of the traditional logic which apparently believes that a syllogism having a probable minor premiss and a probable conclusion is not strictly deductive. And if abduction, why not *eduction*—a term used by E. Constance Jones and others for what is commonly called 'immediate inference', and by W. E. Johnson for inference from particular to particular, which is what Mill believed induction to reduce itself to ultimately? And if eduction, why not *reduction*? Here again one might simply give up in despair because of the ambiguity of the term—reduction of ordinary language to

precise symbolism; reduction of second, third and fourth figure syl-
logisms to first figure; reduction (complete or incomplete) of statements containing non-observational terms to those containing only
observational terms; and reduction of the language of the humanistic sciences to that of the physical sciences. And if reduction, why
not *construction*? Carnap, in his *Logische Aufbau der Welt,* tried to
show that the world is a logical construction out of sense data; Goodman, in his *Structure of Appearance,* attempted to do the same
thing; and certainly Russell, in showing that classes as constructs
can be in all cases substituted for classes as inferred entities, commits
himself thereby to the notion that construction is some kind of
logical process.

Apparently this process of adding layers can go on indefinitely,
subject only to the limitations of the logicians in inventing "uction"
words. I hesitate to add just one more. Feigl, in his introductory
essay to *Readings in the Philosophy of Science,* insists that if there
is reduction there must also be *seduction*. Both are fallacious attempts
to explain the inter-relationships between the natural sciences and
the humanities. The former either ignores or explains away the most
essential human values by reducing the humanities to "nothing
but" the natural sciences; the latter insists that the humanities
contain a mysterious "something more", defined largely in wish-
ful and sentimental terms, and therefore beyond the scope of
scientific study. Feigl's insistence that we should approach the
problem in terms of a philosophy of "what's what", based on
"experience", is not too illuminating since both parties to the controversy would argue that this is precisely what they are doing. His
choice of the word 'seduction' clearly indicates the direction in which
he would swing if the two approaches are not dichotomous.

On the other hand, if we interpret 'seduction' as *any* fallacious
reasoning, then the question as to whether it should be included in
logic is simply one of whether logic should study the ways of reasoning badly as well as the ways of reasoning correctly. This seems
to me to be merely a matter of taste, or, perhaps, of pedagogy. Educational psychologists tell us that we should not teach our children
what they should not do, since this may only provide them with
suggestions for doing things which had previously never even occurred to them. My impression is that we do not run this risk in
teaching elementary logic. I am sure that my students can think of

more ways of reasoning badly than I could draw up in the most comprehensive scheme imaginable. When I talk to them about fallacies, therefore, I do not often feel regret because I may be suggesting to them new ways of committing logical sins. The reason the teaching of fallacies is important is that in logic (as in real life) sinning is so much more fun than living righteously. And in both areas the line between vice and virtue is often so fine that we can usually without the flicker of an eyelash transform a case of hoodwinking our listener by a logical trick into a skillful analytic argument.

III

Our attempt to get at logical subject-matter by starting from the core and working outward seems to have been only moderately successful. Let us try another approach—starting with the skin and removing successive layers. The skin of an apple is not really part of the apple, and when we have pared the fruit we certainly can still call what we have left an 'apple'.

Here again, I am on the spot. For where shall we start? We want cases where the word 'logic' is used in a very loose sense—perhaps in a very general sense, or a metaphorical sense, or a deliberately humorous sense which might be suggestive of a more acceptable meaning. Since we cannot, without trying, be sure that the outcome of this approach will be any more successful than when we started with the core, let us simply plunge ahead.

We may start with a meaning proposed by Russell in his *Sceptical Essays*. I think Russell has his tongue in his cheek when he mentions this, but I think we should make clear that his proposed meaning of the term 'logic' is hardly justifiable. Russell suggests that there is a certain political issue involved in logic. We want our citizenry to vote intelligently, and this requires them to reason. But the plain fact is that most people who reason draw false conclusions from true premises. We try to teach them logic in the hope that they will recognize that many of the conclusions which they draw do not *really* follow from the premises but only *seem* to. But apparently we are not successful in this teaching enterprise. Hence, says Russell, we should teach logic not as the art of *drawing* inferences but as the art of *abstaining* from inferences, since no matter how well people are taught they continue to draw invalid inferences. I must admit that after many years of teaching logic I am inclined to share Russell's feeling of futility in any attempts to make students into rational animals. But I do not think this quite entitles us to define logic as the art of refraining from all inferences—bad inferences, yes, but hardly *all* inferences. We could not live long without some inferences.

I proceed, next, to Tweedledee's definition of 'logic': "Contrariwise, if it was so it might be, and if it were so it would be; but as it isn't it ain't; that's logic." Now this may not be a good example of something on the fringe of logical subject-matter because every logician knows that there is a great deal of the core of the apple in this apparent description of the skin. For example, in this brief statement Tweedledee illustrates the distinction between implication and inference, that between actuality and possibility, and that between factual and contrary-to-factual conditional statements. Indeed, *mirabile dictu,* in the statement, "As it isn't it ain't", he shows how it is possible to draw a conclusion which is both necessary and novel, by using a tautology as the principle of inference. If you were to claim that this really conveys no new knowledge about the "it", I should argue that the statement presumably conveyed a lot of information *to Tweedledum,* and now conveys a lot of information to us *about Tweedledee*—and this is really what counts. I use the illustration simply because it is so well suited to express the opinion which most *non*-logicians have about logic, namely, that it is a mere jumble of "if's", "hences", "becauses", "not's" and "or's". When Mark Twain's wife tried to cure him of his profanity by adopting the same mode of speech, he pointed out that her argument was quite ineffective since she obviously had the words but not the tune.

But if we are to exclude the unsystematic use of logical words from logical subject-matter, shall we not also exclude their systematic abuse, namely, sophistry? Was the small boy right who defined 'logic' as proving what you know ain't so? Can logic prove false propositions; can it show paradoxes where there are none; and can it demonstrate absurdities? Unfortunately the word 'sophistry' is ambiguous. It may mean a kind of manipulation of the souls of rich young men, as in Plato. It may mean the use of fallacious arguments, arguments which appear to be valid but are really invalid. But 'sophistry' may also mean the valid proof of propositions known to be false. It is a kind of "as-if" procedure. Suppose a certain proposition were true (which we know it isn't), how would we prove it? Presumably if we know the proposition to be false the only way to make it appear to be true would be to argue validly from premisses which are also known to be false but appear to be true. Now I suppose one might argue for the right of logic to be concerned with the possible as well as with the actual. And the possible consists of what is and what is not. But since the possible is a rather large realm and designed to occupy our time for many years to come, perhaps we would be justified, as a mere economy measure, in dropping that portion of it which doesn't happen to coincide with actuality. At least a dominant concern with false propositions is certainly not in the first order of business.

What is the next layer? Dialectics? Here, again, the word itself leads up many avenues. In a certain sense dialectics is sophistry and sophistry is dialectics. For Mortimer Adler dialectics is simply arguing. For Hegel it was a process of things as well as of thoughts. For Plato it was a way of acquiring knowledge. Here I shall consider only one of its many meanings—hair-splitting. Samuel Butler said of Hudibras:

> He was in logic a great critic,
> Highly skilled in analytic;
> He could distinguish and divide
> A hair 'twixt south and southwest side.

Obviously one cannot dismiss from logic all hair-splitting. Hair-splitting gave us the distinction between material and strict implication, the theory of types, and the theory of metalanguages—all of which have proved to be very useful notions. The kind of hair-splitting with which logic seems to me to have no concern is that which provides an escape mechanism for getting oneself out of an embarrassing situation in debate. It is expressed by the Scholastic maxim, "When you don't know the answer to a question make a distinction in terms". This frequently results in a "distinction without a difference" and the argument is neither advanced nor retarded but simply stalled. Hair-splitting often plays essentially the same role in debate that pipe-smoking does. When the philosophical pipe-smoker finds himself in a tight spot he invariably discovers that his pipe is out, and must be slowly and deliberately emptied of ashes, rid of encrustations, refilled, tamped, and relit. By this time, if he is anything of a philosopher, he has some kind of answer ready. I do not think that logic should make a study of the social advantages of pipe-smoking.

IV

What, then, is left for the subject-matter of logic? We started with a core of deduction which we presumed to be acceptable to all logicians, and then added induction, abduction, eduction, reduction, construction and, finally, at least in the sense of deceptively valid reasoning, seduction. These are all, directly or indirectly, cognitive processes and structures, subtly interrelated, and jointly involved in the achieving and testing of knowledge. We then leapt to a broader conception of logic, including much, on the fringe, which had dubious status and was presumably rejected by most logicians. Paring away successively that logic which abandons hope in any logic, then omitting Tweedledee's logic, sophistry and dialectics, we rid ourselves of what most logicians would be inclined to call 'alogical' material, and arrived at something which logicians generally would accept. Note that these all concern themselves with what might be called either misconceptions or abuses of the cognitive processes and structures.

Let us call what remains 'cognition' or 'cognitive behavior'. It might equally well be called 'learning', 'investigation' or 'inquiry'. It has its outcome in knowledge, belief, a certain kind of conviction, and what we are pleased to call 'rational behavior'. In order to be as generous as possible let us include cognition both as process and as structure. Let us also admit that it may be discovered both introspectively and behavioristically, and that when it is known behavioristically it may be manifested in both linguistic and non-linguistic behavior. I am leaving all of these doors open since I do not want arbitrarily to close off any possible source from which we may get logical data. We may then say that as logicians we are concerned with our own cognition, discovered introspectively, and with the cognitive behavior of others, discovered observationally. This behavior of others is exhibited linguistically, as in creatures like ourselves, and non-linguistically, as in those creatures like ourselves and lower than ourselves in the evolutionary scale who manifest a certain complexity in their behavior responses.

I realize that although this attempted definition of the term 'logic' does tell us where to go to get the subject-matter of logic, it does not make any clearer what the terms 'cognition' and 'cognitive behavior' actually mean. And I further realize that these terms are themselves much less clear than we wish they were. I realize, finally, that no precise definition of 'logic', even when it is limited in its range of subject-matter to cognitive processes and cognitive behavior, can be achieved until we know which mental processes and which modes of behavior are cognitive and which are non-cognitive.

But while this is an important source of confusion in the meaning of the term 'logic' it is not my primary concern in this paper. I am disturbed, rather, by the use of the term 'logic' on the part of many philosophers to designate types of subject-matter which seem to have no relation whatsoever, or at least only a very remote relation, to cognition. I mention, for purposes of illustration only and without further elaboration, three types of instance. First is that of the linguistic analysts, who go to great lengths to clarify statements and then, having clarified them, drop them from consideration without bothering to determine whether they are true or false. This seems to me to overlook the fact that there is really no virtue in clarification as such; we clarify only because we want to know and we cannot know if we are confused. The second example is that of the symbolic logicians, who like to compare mathematics and other formal deductive systems to the playing of games, such as checkers. In both cases we start with something which is arbitrary—the postulates, on the one hand, and the rules of inference, on the other, the former corresponding to the positions of the men on the board and the latter to the rules for moving the men—and arrive at a conclusion which is necessary only within the arbitrary framework. Now I know that this type of symbolic structure *does* have an important relation to the cognitive processes, but I think it is misleading for logicians to disregard this relation and speak as though mathematics and logic had nothing whatsoever to do with the world. The third example is that of the very large group of logicians who dismiss from logic the question of how deduction can ever give us novelty, arguing that this is a purely psychological question and not worthy of the concern of the logician. I suspect that many of those who dismiss this problem do so because they find it too difficult to solve, and I have not found that the psychologists have been eager to take it on.

But it *is* an important cognitive problem, and a logic which disregards it is not worthy of being called by the name.

I feel, therefore, that nothing should be called 'logical' unless it has a statable relation to cognition or cognitive behavior. And I believe also that the approach to a definition of logic in terms of cognition and cognitive behavior provides a matrix by which various *kinds* of logic can be distinguished in terms of the nature of this statable relationship.

V

As a guide to a more precise definition of 'logic' I propose that we consider logic to be, in the most general sense, a science. The advantage of this approach, at least to me, is that there appear to be certain *kinds* of sciences which are quite sharply distinguished from one another, and we may use these as trial patterns for the purpose of examining whether logic also exhibits the same differentiating forms. I propose to examine five such patterns of the sciences. For the present I limit myself to pure sciences, excluding applied sciences.

The first classification of pure sciences divides them into descriptive, explanatory and formalized sciences. A typical example of a descriptive science is sociology, of an explanatory science is physics, and of a formalized science is mathematics. Perhaps we could find a more illuminating example (since no science exhibits itself in any one of these forms to the complete exclusion of the others) if we were to take a given science, say, physics, and consider it as descriptive when it states the law of falling bodies, as explanatory when it accounts for this behavior of falling bodies by the Newtonian theory of gravitation, and as formalized in its effort to develop a set of abstract postulates constituting a unified field theory which, when interpreted, would enable us to derive Newtonian theory, relativity and quantum mechanics in essentially the same way that Russell and Whitehead derived mathematics from logic in *Principia Mathematica*.

On the basis of this pattern descriptive logic will be closely identified with that part of descriptive psychology called 'psychology of reasoning' and 'psychology of learning', and will be oriented either introspectively or behavioristically according to the preference of the psychologist. Dewey's *How We Think* would fall essentially in this area, as would also Jerome Bruner's *Study of Thinking* and most of the books by Hadamard, Montmasson, Rignano, Wallas, Wertheimer and many others dealing with insight, invention and discovery. Studies in descriptive semantics could also be included, especially those which have to do with the informative role of signs rather than their evocative, ceremonial or directive roles. Much of the work of Piaget on judgment and understanding in children belongs here. Many books on symbolic logic, which do little more than show how words of ordinary speech may be translated into more precise logical equivalents, would probably fall naturally in this area. And, in this very general sense, all studies of the learning behavior of rats, insofar as they are purely descriptive rather than interpretive or formalized studies, would be types of descriptive logic.

Explanatory logic will, by definition, be identified with what has been commonly called 'theory of knowledge', since it is concerned with the attempt to devise a theoretical structure or to construct a conceptual scheme which will explain and account for our cognitive processes and behavior. Most of the great treatises in logic, by Bradley, Bosanquet, Hegel, Dewey, W. E. Johnson, J. S. Mill, the Thomists, and many others would be placed here, as would many of the writings of the phenomenologists. Indeed, a large part of the so-called 'traditional' logic, when its hypothetical structure has been laid bare, would also qualify for an explanatory logic. This has been done with an introspective orientation by H. W. B. Joseph, J. N. Keynes and R. M. Eaton, and with a formalistic emphasis by Bocheński and Lukasiewicz. We might also allow here the behavioristic studies in learning-theory carried on by Thorndike, Thurstone, Skinner, Hull and others. These have not been traditionally called 'logics' at all, but I see no strong reason why they cannot be. The behavior of a rat in getting himself out of a maze is not different in *kind* from that of a philosopher resolving an antinomy, and it would be the job of an explanatory logic to show precisely wherein the difference lies. Finally, certain studies in symbolic logic, considered as special types of semiotic, could well be placed in this area.

Formalized logic will, in general, be identified with symbolic logic. It will be a strictly formalized study of a formalized system of cognitive signs, such as found in *Principia Mathematica*. Whether more abstract, many-valued logics, divorced from any interpretation, should also be included here will depend on the logician. The point I wish to emphasize is that if they are considered to be logics they cannot be separated from all interpretation nor can they be completely unrelated to the normative aspects of cognitive behavior. The undefined terms must be capable of operational definition, the postulates capable of empirical interpretation, and the entire structure capable of evaluation as an effective tool in cognition. It is interesting to conjecture whether the idealistic logics of Hegel, Bradley and Bosanquet, or the pragmatic logic of Dewey, could ever be formalized. In attempting to do this the star to which one could hitch his wagon would be, of course, *The Mathematical Theory of Rote Learning*, by Hull and his associates. This is a formalized theory of a small part of cognition, but opinions seem to differ as to its adequacy as a representative of the actual learning process.

I turn now to a second pattern exhibited by the sciences. This is indicated by an ambiguity in the term 'descriptive science'. Sciences may be called by this name not only when, as above, they are contrasted with explanatory and formalized sciences, but also when they are contrasted with normative sciences. A normative science is one which, being a *science*, is concerned with truth-values in the way in which all sciences are, but which, being *normative*, studies values as well as non-values. In this sense physics is ordinarily considered to be descriptive but not normative, since it does not study values. But if we look at physics from the point of view of its historical origin in the needs of primitive man for better tools, weapons, shelter and transportation, and from the point of view of its technological role today we can see that values—instrumental values—to a great extent determine its content and direction. It is fair to say, therefore, that there is a normative physics in the sense that man finds certain natural objects to be useful for performing certain tasks, and objects which are not useful to be capable of being made into such by proper physical manipulation.

In very much the same way I think we can show a difference between descriptive logic and normative logic. At the descriptive level the relation between the methods of knowing and knowledge itself is disclosed to be a temporal one, or, possibly, a causal one. There is a suggestion of this in Dewey's "five stages of the complete act of thought", in Graham Wallas's famous "preparation, incubation, illumination and verification", and in all behavioristic descriptions of learning where the skill acquired by the animal is generally a function of the time spent in the conditioning process. These are

all descriptions of cognitive processes terminating in knowledge or
in conditioned response. A normative approach toward these processes would arise when we attempt to show that in all cases they are
activities directed toward ends. The normative element is certainly
more conspicuously present in the case of cognitive activities than
in the case of purely physical activities directed toward the manipulation of nature; thus while physics may have a normative aspect the
pure physicist can more or less completely disregard this in his
attempt to understand nature. But the logician cannot. Many of the
great historical attempts to explain cognition and cognitive behavior
seem to me to have been inadequate just because they tended to
overlook normative considerations. This is clearly indicated even
among those who called their studies 'logics', e.g., those who psychol-
ogized, like Bain and Mill, and those who formalized excessively,
like Carnap and Russell. Many of the behavioristic explanations of
learning seem to me inadequate because their perpetrators forgot
that in the experiments on which their conclusions were based the
rats were given food pellets. While it may be admitted that we cannot know whether the rats like food, or even what would be meant
by saying that they do, the presence of the food does have a distinctive role to play and cannot be disregarded in any adequate interpretation of the learning process. I find similar defects in the writings
of many of the linguistic analysts, who seem either to disregard
the normative aspects of our use of language, or to project into
it ends which seem to me to be there only in very rare and unusual
cases.

A third pattern exhibited by the sciences distinguishes between
pure science and applied science. But here again we have an ambiguity in the meaning of the term 'applied science'. 'Applied mathematics' usually means an interpretation of pure or abstract mathematics, as Euclidean geometry is one interpretation of Hilbert's
abstract geometry. In the same way an applied logic might be a
propositional interpretation of an abstract set of symbols. I shall
not use the term 'applied logic' in this sense. I shall employ it
after the pattern of applied physics, or applied chemistry, as a study
of the ways in which the knowledge of the laws and principles of a
pure science may be employed to produce a desired end. For example, pure physics, be it descriptive, explanatory or formalized,
tells us in various ways that heat causes expansion. Normative physics

tells us that when we want expansion we can introduce heat. Applied physics tells us how to introduce heat, how to modify it in order to modify expansion, and even how to prevent it in case we want to prevent expansion. In much the same way, and using a very crude analogy, pure logic, be it descriptive, explanatory or formalized, tells us in various ways that observation and inference produce knowledge. Normative logic tells us that when we want knowledge we can introduce observation and inference. Applied logic tells us how to produce and improve knowledge by using observation and inference as means.

Finally, this use of the patterns of science as a basis for determining kinds of logic may help us to see that just as there is a skill in using physical manipulations to produce better tools and weapons, so there is logical skill which involves modification of cognitive processes in order to make them effective in producing more and better knowledge. The difficult problem here is distinguishing between a normative science, an applied science and a skill. Physics becomes normative to the extent to which it recognizes that certain cause and effect relationships can also be interpreted as means-end relationships when the effects have value-properties. It becomes an applied science when the principles for the control of the means in the production of the valued end are discovered. And it becomes a skill when these principles are put into operation, as in the case of the engineer. We have seen that there is a normative logic and an applied logic. But is there an analogous logic which puts cognitive processes to work in the same way in which the engineer puts physical forces to work?

Take the case of the scientist who says that he arrived at a certain hypothesis by "using logic", or a student who says that he "uses logic" to solve a brain teaser. Logic is here *identified* with cognition. What the scientist and the student mean is that they reached their results by *thinking*. Now the plain fact of the matter is that thinking in this sense may be consciously recognized or not, may be skilled or unskilled, may be rapid or slow, and may or may not be dependent on a study of logic. Some people who "think out" conclusions do so very badly. Many of the great mathematical geniuses who are able to solve complicated mathematical problems with amazing speed protest that they do not know how they perform their miracles and are irritated when psychologists pester them to describe the method by which they do. Many students "think badly" at the beginning of a course in logic, yet do not seem to improve after being exposed to a study of the principles of argument. Indeed, there are even cases of individuals who have certain skills which function effectively only when they are *not* consciously directed and *not* subjected to analysis. For these people the development of the critical faculties might be a disaster.

The only way to avoid confusion here, I believe, is to distinguish between (1) a more or less *unconscious* use of cognitive skills to produce cognitive ends, (2) a *conscious and deliberate* use of improved cognitive skills to produce improved cognitive ends, all being based on knowledge of the laws of logic, and (3) a skilled *study* of the laws of logic.

To use 'logic' in the first sense seems to me to produce confusion, since it tends to encourage the extension of the word into areas where it has no legitimate application. Even if we do use cognitive processes in driving a car, building a house or playing bridge, I think it is misleading to speak of the "logic" of doing these things. Logic should not be identified with cognition (except in a sense to be designated in a moment), however successful it may be. Logic is not the *use* of cognition but the *study* of cognition. It should no more be identified with cognition than political science should be identified with political institutions and political skills, sociology with social institutions and social behavior, biology with life, or physics with matter and motion.

In the second sense I think the word 'logic' has a legitimate application. Here logic is being used to improve knowledge. In this sense we can use logic to win an argument, and we can use logic to increase the range, accuracy and reliability of scientific knowledge. Many applied logics designed to develop skill in reasoning are superficial, as indicated by the many "how-to" books on the market which we are assured will give us the required "know-how" —how to win an argument, how to be persuasive, how to think straight, how to solve brain teasers, how to study—all of which are reminiscent of the famous (or infamous) *How to Win Friends and Influence People*. But applied logic need not be superficial; it is shallow only for those who are unwilling to make a careful study of the laws and principles on which it is based. It presumes more than a knowledge of descriptive truths, just as engineering knowledge presumes more than a knowledge of physics and chemistry. Applied logic involves knowing how to produce something which doesn't exist in sufficient quantity (knowledge) and how to eliminate some things which exist in superabundance (error, ignorance and confusion). It presupposes, therefore, that the knowledge which exists can be improved by increasing its range, accuracy and reliability. And it assumes that the methods for attaining knowledge can be improved if we pay more attention to their instrumental status. In its emphasis on goals and skills applied logic requires consideration of man as a social and psychological being who can be operated upon by a kind of social engineering and made into something other than he happens at the moment to be. Applied logic *is not* this social engineering but it supposes that such engineering exists and can be improved by study. In our roles as scholars we endeavor to uncover the principles of this engineering, and in our roles as teachers we try to put them to work.

It is here, I believe, that the study of seduction should occur, for if we are to learn how to produce conviction by legitimate methods we ought to become informed of the many ways by which we customarily obtain deceptively valid knowledge by illegitimate methods. Hence I do not think that we are using the word 'logic' unjustifiably when we say that the army is the logic of kings, or when we speak of the logic of tears, or of the logic of the highwayman who places a gun at our head and demands our pocketbook, or of the logic of the traffic policeman who threatens with a ticket for speeding, or even of the logic of television commercials, which apparently attracts buyers who, by *being* attracted, prove thereby that they are intellectually too immature to be even looking at television. That men use logics of these kinds is, strangely enough, strong support for the belief that they *are* rational creatures. For who but a rational creature could conceive of so many methods by which to avoid being rational?

But we must not overlook the third meaning of 'logical skill', namely, the skill which the logician himself uses in his study of cognition. Because there is this skill we can utter the true metalinguistic statement that logic is logical. The corresponding statement that physics is physical could hardly be true, except in a Pickwickian sense. Logic *is* skilled cognition in, perhaps, the same way that physics is. But it is peculiar in the sense that it both *uses* skilled cognition and *studies* skilled cognition. And logic gets its name from *what* it studies, not from *how* it studies this.

Finally, we must provide a place for certain logical studies which are normative in character and thus seem to provide the basis for applied logics. However, they are concerned not with the study of logical means to produce desired cognitive ends, but with whether the cognitive ends of logic are really as important as they are often claimed to be. If the term 'logic' is to be pre-empted for the study of the most effective logical means for achieving the cognitive goal, we need some such term as the 'philosophy of logic' to designate those studies which attempt to evaluate cognitive goals among the many non-cognitive goals. Are there, for example, areas in which reasons of the heart may prevail? Are there spheres in which practicality or urgency for action may justify abandoning all cognitive criteria? Are there realms of privacy which the piercing eye of the scholar has no right to scan and the prying finger no right to touch? Are there experiences which justifiably evade analysis, not because they are private but because to analyze them is to destroy them? (I am thinking of the jokes which we do not "get" on first telling and at which we painfully try to laugh when their point is explained to us later). And do we *really*, as we sometimes claim, want to know the future, when we realize that while it might enable us to break the bank at Monte Carlo it would prevent us from enjoying a quiet game of bridge with our friends or experiencing the excitement of a philosophical debate? In this general area, in fact, lie all of the problems of the ethics of scholarship—whether there are any rules for playing the cognitive game, or whether the high value of the goal warrants arrogance, propagandizing, intolerance and iconoclasm. These are all important problems, which have been long thought about and should continue to be thought about. I submit that the man most competent to solve them is one who is *at least* a logician. That he must be *more than* a logician is obvious from the fact that perspective is required in their solution, and that the logician, in order to solve them, must emulate Matthew Arnold's friend (to whom he dedicated his Second Sonnet) "who saw life steadily and who saw it whole."

A. CORNELIUS BENJAMIN

UNIVERSITY OF MISSOURI

THE EMPIRICAL METAPHYSICS OF EPICURUS

I T HAS LONG been the standard opinion of Epicurean philosophy that its interest was purely practical or ethical and that Epicurus the founder either rejected or did not comprehend metaphysical speculation. That this view is largely a misconception can be seen from an examination of the chief and most authentic source, Epicurus' *Letter to Herodotus*, as reported by Diogenes Laertius. Epicureanism remained surprisingly orthodox in its faithfulness to the basic teachings of the master, although, of course, later Epicureans often were forced to devise new arguments and to make new answers to criticisms raised by Stoics and other opponents. One reason for the close adherence to Epicurus' position and method was undoubtedly the fact that these had been presented in a most clear and systematic manner by the master. Diogenes says that the Epicureans had no use for dialectic,[1] and there is frequently in Epicurus' writings the rejection of the type of metaphysical speculation that employed abstract theory and assumed general principles without empirical evidence and factual confirmation:

In the first place, Herodotus, you must understand what it is that words denote, in order that by reference to this we may be in a position to test opinions, inquiries, or problems, so that our proofs may not run on untested *ad infinitum,* nor the terms we use be empty of meaning.[2]

Epicurus had no use for hypothesis as such; the atomic theory was for him a certainty confirmed by the facts, which he would contrast, for example, with positions based on hypotheses or on a plurality of causes, as in the explanation of celestial phenomena.[3] He is concerned with citing carefully for each metaphysical principle or conclusion, as he gives it, the empirical evidence on which it is based. The *Letter to Herodotus* may be taken as an attempt at the development of a

---

[1]Diogenes Laertius, *Lives of Eminent Philosophers*, X, 31. Except where otherwise noted, the translation of Diogenes is that of R. D. Hicks in the Loeb Classical Library.

[2]Diog. Laert., X, 37.

[3]Diog. Laert., X, 86–87.

systematic empirical metaphysics in which Epicurus is presenting the
chief metaphysical ideas and principles which were to be mastered by
the pupil as the basis for subsequent ethical and social philosophy.
He is conscientious in documenting his statements by recourse to the
facts of experience, which he thinks confirm his principles and make
assumptions and hypotheses unnecessary:

Next we must by all means stick to our sensations, that is, simply to the present impressions whether of the mind or of any criterion whatever, and similarly to our actual feelings, in order that we may have the means of determining that which needs confirmation and that which is obscure.[4]

One is constantly reminded of the systematic procedure of another
materialist, Hobbes, who starts also with an empirical epistemology
and methodology, and deduces from a metaphysics of body and motion
his psychology, ethics, and political philosophy in due order.

Epicurus' Canon or Method is strictly empirical. Theory and reasoning are intended to explain or account for what really exists; and
without an appeal to experience we would have no means to infer
about objects and events outside our experience:

We must take into account as the end all that really exists and all clear evidence of sense to which we refer our opinions; for otherwise everything will
be full of uncertainty and confusion.

If you fight against all your sensations, you will have no standard to which to
refer, and thus no means of judging even those judgements which you pro-
nounce false.[5]

What is sure and real is the immediate data of sensation and feeling,
so these must needs be the criteria of truth and the bases from which
inferences are made by reasoning:

Nor is there anything which can refute sensations or convict them of error: one
sensation cannot convict another and kindred sensation, for they are equally
valid; nor can one sensation refute another which is not kindred but heterogeneous, for the objects which the two senses judge are not the same; nor
again can reason refute them, for reason is wholly dependent on sensation;
nor can one sense refute another, since we pay equal heed to all. And the
reality of separate perceptions guarantees the truth of our senses. But seeing
and hearing are just as real as feeling pain. Hence it is from plain facts that
we must start when we draw inferences about the unknown. For all our no-

4Diog. Laert., X, 38.

5Sovran Maxims, 22 and 23 (Diog. Laert., X, 146).

tions are derived from perceptions, either by actual contact or by analogy, or resemblance, or composition, with some slight aid from reasoning.[6]

Epicurus appeals to direct experience employing the method of verification (ἐπιμαρτύρησις) in the case of objects experienced, sometimes the method of analogy from experience in the case of objects falling outside our experience, and often the method of noncontradiction (οὐκ ἀντιμαρτύρησις), which consists in showing that experience does not conflict with a view or that the facts indicate that something cannot not be so. The method of showing the lack of evidence to the contrary or that facts conflict with the contradictory view is an empirical test as well as the direct method of confrontation with the facts of sense. It is not the test of rational noncontradiction. It is a way of extending our knowledge beyond immediate experience, and what is experienceable (but not immediately experienced due to time or circumstance), to objects which cannot be experienced by us. For example, that bodies exist, our senses immediately attest. However, that there is void or empty space is not directly observed. Here Epicurus must say that the empirical fact of motion proves the existence of void or space, since motion requires void or space in which bodies are moved. The absence or nonexistence of the void is contradicted by apparent facts—the existence of motion. Again, the metaphysical principle assumed by the pre-Socratic philosophers, that nothing comes into being out of what is nonexistent, is also a metaphysical principle for Epicurus but is not presupposed by him as a self-evident theoretical principle. Experience indicates clearly that there is something, viz., a world of existents, and that there is an order of nature. So Epicurus argues that if something came from nothing, then everything would come from everything, and things would not arise, as they are observed to, from their proper germs or seeds. Again, if what disappears is destroyed into the nonexistent, all things would have perished, that into which they were dissolved being nonexistent.[7]

The empirical basis of Epicurus' metaphysics may be further clarified by a more detailed examination of some of his metaphysical ideas and concepts.

[6]Diog. Laert., X, 32.
[7]Diog. Laert., X, 39.

1. *Substance*

Substance is, first of all, the self-existent, permanent subject of change. Something must remain solid and indissoluble amid the obvious dissolution of composite bodies. To prevent changes from the nonexistent to the nonexistent, which would conflict with our experience, the first-beginnings must be elements of a solid (i.e. without void), indivisible (without parts), unchanging nature out of which everything is composed and into which ultimately dissolution takes place:

These elements are indivisible and unchangeable, and necessarily so, if things are not all to be destroyed and pass into non-existence, but are to be strong enough to endure when the composite bodies are broken up, because they possess a solid nature and are incapable of being anywhere or anyhow dissolved.[8]

To account for the persistence of a world, then, the basic elements cannot be composite and cannot contain any void or empty space which would weaken them and make them subject to change and dissolution—hence the corporeal atoms. A limit to the divisibility of bodies or a minimum of physical existence is also required for the permanence of reality. Epicurus uses here an argument of analogy from experience, where a *minimum sensibile* is always found, to maintain also a minimum of existence.

Epicurus is careful to account for what is experienced. Different qualities of experienced objects can be explained by varying the sizes and shapes of the atoms which compose them. Yet, again, he cannot let the atoms admit of any and every size. Clearly, atoms are never seen by us. Since there appears to be a limit to variations within experience (i.e. types, species [9]), these can be accounted for by having the atoms vary indefinitely, but not infinitely, in size and shape.[10] The number of atoms in each size and shape, however, must be infinite. Besides admitting that atoms are not seen, Epicurus goes on to say that it is inconceivable that they be seen. For to be seen, an object must be composite in order to give off the corporeal films or idols which strike the eye and produce vision. Thus, to be visible an object

[8]Diog. Laert., X, 41.
[9]Lucretius, *De Rerum Natura*, I, 585 f.
[10]Diog. Laert., X, 42–43.

must meet the conditions of visibility, which we learn, again, from experience.

The sum-total of things is, however, infinite—the atoms in number, and the void or space in extent. An infinite void and a finite number of atoms would produce no world, such as we have, for then the atoms would be scattered throughout infinite space and remain nowhere in combination. Again, an infinite number of bodies in a finite space would have no place to be. From the infinity of atoms and the void follows the possibility of other worlds, both similar and dissimilar to ours, for clearly the infinite number of atoms has not been expended on this world.

The atoms, however, do not exhaust the meaning of substance. What exists in itself can either (1) act or be acted upon—i.e. a body, whether simple (atoms) or composite, or (2) not act or be acted upon —i.e. empty space.[11] The sum-total of existence consists of bodies and space. These are the only substances or self-existent things or whole natures:

Beyond these nothing can be conceived either immediately or by analogy from immediate impressions as whole natures, and not as so-called accidents or properties of these.[12]

Apart from the intangible void or empty space there can be no self-existent incorporeal nature or substance. The soul for Epicurus is material as it acts and is acted upon. The unreal produces no effects. What moves and is moved must be body:

Hence those who call the soul incorporeal speak foolishly. For if it were so, it could neither act nor be acted upon. But, as it is, both these properties, you see, plainly belong to soul.[13]

2. Quality

What is not body, simple or complex, or the intangible void, must be a property or modification of a body. The atoms possess none of the qualities of apparent objects except shape, weight, and size, and as many properties as are necessarily connected with shape.[14] The reason for this is that other qualities are observed to change or vary,

[11]Cf. Lucretius, I, 440–44.
[12]Diog. Laert., X, 40 (my translation).
[13]Diog. Laert., X, 67.
[14]Diog. Laert., X, 54.

while the atoms cannot change. The qualities of observed objects are due to changes of position or additions and subtractions of atoms—alterations in external relations of atoms producing the changes in qualities observed. The qualities of composite objects may be explained in terms of the different shapes and sizes of the constituent atoms and the amount of void contained in their combination and their motions. The atoms transposed cannot have the nature of a changing thing but must retain their own individual mass and shape. The primacy of shape is shown by an analogy with experience:

For in the case of changes of configuration within our experience the figure is supposed to be inherent when other qualities are stripped off, but the qualities are not supposed, like the shape which is left behind, to inhere in the subject of change, but to vanish altogether from the body. Thus, then, what is left behind is sufficient to account for the differences in composite bodies, since something at least must necessarily be left remaining and be immune from annihilation.[15]

Epicurus offers an empirical basis for his reduction of the qualitative differences of objects to quantitative differences of position, arrangement, motion, increase and decrease of atoms. Shape or figure and weight and size are permanent qualities of all objects experienced and unexperienced. The other qualities are due to combinations of atoms of various kinds and their varying movements.

Epicurus rejects Democritus' theory of atoms of any and every size as contradicted by experience or facts. Differences of size of atoms must be admitted to account for the facts of feeling and sensation (objects containing atoms of different shape and size produce different odors, tastes, etc.). But, Epicurus insists, more than this is not needed to help explain the differences in qualities of things and is indeed contradicted by the facts:

Again, you should not suppose that the atoms have any and every size, lest you be contradicted by facts; but differences of size must be admitted; for this addition renders the facts of feeling and sensation easier of explanation. But to attribute any and every magnitude to the atoms does not help to explain the differences of quality in things; moreover, in that case atoms large enough to be seen ought to have reached us, which is never observed to occur; nor can we conceive how its occurrence should be possible, i.e. that an atom should become visible.[16]

15Diog. Laert., X, 55.
16Diog. Laert., X, 55–56.

The qualities of composite objects are not to be regarded as separate existences (substances), or as nonexistent, or as incorporeal entities, or as parts of body. They are rather dynamically interpreted as what happens to bodies or as modifications of bodies. Both secondary and primary qualities are objective, as due to the various combinations, arrangements, and motions of atoms. All bodies as such have shape, size, and weight. All visible objects have color. Epicurus makes a distinction between qualities which are inseparable from bodies and those which are impermanent concomitants of bodies. But all its qualities give a body its permanent nature:

Moreover, shapes and colours, magnitudes and weights, and in short all those qualities which are predicated of body, in so far as they are perpetual properties either of all bodies or of visible bodies, are knowable by sensation of these very properties: these, I say, must not be supposed to exist independently by themselves (for that is inconceivable), nor yet to be non-existent, nor to be some other and incorporeal entities cleaving to body, nor again to be parts of body. We must consider the whole body in a general way to derive its permanent nature from all of them, though it is not, as it were, formed by grouping them together in the same way as when from the particles themselves a larger aggregate is made up, whether these particles be primary or any magnitudes whatsoever less than the particular whole. All these qualities, I repeat, merely give the body its own permanent nature. They all have their own characteristic modes of being perceived and distinguished, but always along with the whole body in which they inhere and never in separation from it; and it is in virtue of this complete conception of the body as a whole that it is so designated.[17]

Epicurus' view is in contrast with the position of Democritus that secondary qualities (colors, tastes, odors, temperatures) are conventional and subjective. He is also rejecting the Platonic view which gives separate, independent existence to qualities. Qualities do not exist apart from the bodies to which they belong; yet they are not parts of bodies as Aristotle regarded them. The combination of qualities gives the nature or character of bodies; but bodies are not combinations or collections of qualities as they are combinations of atoms. There is an unique unity and identity to the whole combination as such, which gives it its individuality. The last sentence of the quotation seems to imply that the combination of qualities, secondary as well as primary, constitutes the nominal essence of bodies by which

[17]Diog. Laert., X, 68–69.

the objects are identified and named and assume a concrete nature. One is tempted to call the real essence the atomic structure and motions which produce these qualities. However, for Epicurus, the experienced world of objects with all their qualities, changing and unchanging, is a real and objective world and is as our senses perceive it. He does not make the usual distinction between appearance and reality. The world as it appears to the senses is not an illusory or unreal world distinct from ultimate reality of atoms and void.[18] It is part of the sum of things and as the product of constituent 'reals', intimately connected with them, it can be used to acquire knowledge of the parts or elements of reality which do not enter directly into our experience either because of their remoteness in time or space or because of the minuteness of their nature. Atoms differ from bodies in our experience in their minuteness and their solidity; but as bodies they must possess the essential qualities of all bodies.[19] The gods, too, are configurations of atoms, which give off films or idols which are sometimes experienced by us, at least in part. Analogies may be made from bodies in our experience to the nature of atoms and gods, and to future and past objects.

Qualities often attach to bodies without being permanent concomitants.[20] Yet these temporary accompaniments are not to be classed among invisible or incorporeal entities, or to be considered as subjective and completely dependent upon the perceiver. These qualities Epicurus calls 'symptomata', a term suggestive of the medical influence on Epicurean empiricism. The temptation is to make the distinction of these as accidents in contrast with the permanent

[18]Compare the words that Plutarch (rather sarcastically) puts into the mouth of an imaginary Epicurean spokesman in *Adversus Colotem*, 1116 D: "But Epicurus more wisely than Plato uses the term 'being' of all alike, the intangible void, the resistant body, the elements, the compounds, holding that a common and single 'being' is shared by the eternal and that which is generated, by the indestructible and the destructible, by those natures which are affected by nothing, which are enduring, changeless, unable to cease existing, and those whose existence is in being affected and in changing, which do not for a moment remain the same."

[19]Cf. Philodemus, *De Signis*, xxxvii: "Since all things are the products of elements or of things derived from elements, or are related to elements in some other way, there is a peculiar connection between appearances and the unperceived . . . As a consequence of the fact that bodies in our experience rebound, we judge that atoms are heavy and solid, for we cannot conceive that bodies in our experience are of this kind and that similar ones (unperceived) do not have this quality."

[20]Diog. Laert., X, 70–72.

properties of objects; but Epicurus often prefers this term for qualities in general, perhaps to indicate their dynamic character and their empirical nature as 'signs'. Qualities are not static, even when they belong to bodies as such, but are movements, changes, and events that happen to bodies. Experience shows that some of the qualities of objects do not have the nature of the whole body to which they belong nor that of the inseparable properties without which the body cannot be conceived. These qualities, rather, are the result of certain peculiar modes of apprehension and are not perpetual concomitants. Thus they may be called properties of objects only as often as they are actually seen to belong to them. They need not be considered therefore as nonexistent or illusory, but are actually what sensation shows them to be. Bodies as such do not have color, but all visible objects have color. The color of an object does not have the nature of the whole body to which it belongs, yet it is an objective property which is produced by certain combinations of atoms and their movements affecting our sight, but not e.g. our touch (i.e. a peculiar mode of apprehension).

All independent real things capable of acting and being acted upon are bodies—composite bodies and the elements of which they are composed. Everything else that is experienced (and as experienced, is real) is a modification of a body, a property or occurrence. Epicurus avoids reification or hypostatization. A constantly changing universe of conjunctions of perpetually moving atoms of different shapes, sizes, and movements will produce varying properties or qualities to our senses and to the different sense organs by their contact. Yet as long as certain combinations of atoms remain entangled (as in the case of solid bodies) or stay enclosed in a protective sheath of other atoms (as in the case of liquids and soul atoms), certain properties of the whole complex are bound to remain as inseparable concomitants (shape, figure, size, weight, solidity). Others, depending upon the sense organ affected (as colors are seen but not felt), are not experienced as conjoined with the body at all times; and so cannot convey the nature of the body as such (as a solid, resistant corporeal entity), and cannot therefore be trustworthy bases for inference to objects outside our experience:

Therefore, we must not speak of wine as unconditionally productive of heat, but rather say that a certain quantity of wine will produce heat in a certain body which is in a certain disposition, or that a different quantity will produce cold in a different body. For in the compound body of wine there are certain particles out of which cold might be produced if, as need arises, united with different particles they could form a structure which would cause cold . . . Wine often enters the body without exerting any power either of heating or of cooling, but when the structure is disturbed and an atomic re-arrangement takes place, the atoms which create heat at one time come together and by their number give heat and inflammation to the body, at another they retire and cool it.[21]

Lucretius uses the term 'coniuncta' for the inseparable properties of things and the term 'eventa' for the impermanent concomitants. He reflects the dynamic aspect of Epicurean metaphysics by including as temporary qualities happenings or events such as slavery and war and historical events which, as accidents of body and place, the things to which they happen, are given no existence apart from the bodies and persons to which they belonged or in connection with which they occurred.[22]

3. Time

Time is not an object in itself but a quality *sui generis*. It differs

---

[21]Epicurus (Bailey edition), Fragment B V *(Symposium)*. Cf. also Philodemus, *De Signis*, xviii: "Similarly, bodies in our experience have color, but not as bodies; for tangible objects in so far as they resist the touch are bodies, but in so far as they are tangible they give no indication of color. Indeed, bodies in the dark have no color, yet still are bodies. Therefore from these qualities we do not infer concerning all bodies; but from other similarities, such as lightness and heaviness, we shall not be prevented from making inferences, provided that we use the method of analogy properly." Sextus Empiricus, *Adversus Mathematicos*, X, 220–3 (Bury's translation): "And such things as substances (like body and void) are self-existent; and such as are viewed as attached to the self-existents are what they call 'properties.' And of these properties some are inseparable from the objects whereto they belong, while others are naturally separated from them. Inseparable, for instance, from the things whereto they belong are the resistance of body and the non-resistance of void; for body can never be conceived as without resistance, or void without non-resistance; but each has a property that is eternal, the one resistance, the other non-resistance. But not inseparable from the things whereto they belong are such properties as motion and rest. For such bodies as are composite are neither in restless motion continually nor continually motionless, but have at one time the property of motion, at another that of rest, although the atom, when it is by itself, is in perpetual motion."

[22]Lucretius, I, 451–458: "That is a property [*coniunctum*] which in no case can be sundered or separated without the fatal disunion of the thing, as is weight to rocks, heat to fire, moisture to water, touch to all bodies, intangibility to the void. On the other hand, slavery, poverty, riches, liberty, war, concord, and other things by whose coming and going the nature of things abides untouched, these we are used, as is right, to call accidents [*eventa*]." Cf. also 478 f. (Bailey's translation of Lucretius is used throughout.)

from other qualities in that we cannot have a general concept of it derived from repeated experiences. Epicurus says that we must take account of the plain fact itself in virtue of which we speak of time as long or short (i.e. duration). We attach the attribute of time to days and nights, and their parts, and to feelings of pleasure and pain and mental states, and to states of motion and rest, conceiving a peculiar accident of them to be this very characteristic which we call 'time.'23 Time is thus not a thing or substance nor a first-order predicate; but an 'accident of accidents' that accompanies other qualities or events (day and night), our feelings and mental states, and involves the awareness of a succession of before and after in our experience of these. Time is not a concept or general notion but rather an immediate intuition or feeling which accompanies our immediate sensations and feelings, and their movement or succession.24

4. *Space*

Space for Epicurus is the void, which he also calls 'place' and the 'intangible nature.' It is regarded as a whole nature or separate existence (substance), not as a property or accident of things. He establishes the existence of void or empty space, which is not an

23Diog. Laert., X, 72. Cf. Lucretius, I, 459–463: "Even so time exists not by itself, but from actual things comes a feeling, what was brought to a close in time past, then what is present now, and further what is going to be hereafter. And it must be avowed that no man feels time by itself apart from the motion or quiet rest of things."

24Sextus Empiricus, *Adv. Math.*, X, 219: "Epicurus, as Demetrius the Laconian interprets him, declares that time is 'a symptom of symptoms, accompanying days and nights and hours and affections and non-affections and motions and rests.' For all these are symptoms attached to things, and as accompanying all these time may naturally be called 'a symptom of symptoms.'" 224–226: "Thus these things are 'symptoms' which time accompanies—I mean day and night and hour and affections and non-affections and motions and rests. For day and night are symptoms of the surrounding air, of which day is a property due to the illumination from the sun, while night results from the privation of the illumination from the sun. And hour again, being a part either of day or of night, is a symptom of the air, like day and night. And time extends parallel to every day and every night and hour; and for this reason a day or a night is called long or short, as we pass over the time which is a property thereof. The affections, too, and non-affections are either pains or pleasures, and on this account are not substances but symptoms of those who are affected either pleasurably or painfully, and not timeless symptoms. And besides these, motion and also rest are, as we have already established, symptoms of bodies and not without time; for certainly we measure by time the quickness and slowness of motion, and the greater or less amount of rest."

object of experience, on the basis of the empirical fact of motion. Motion requires space in which the movement occurs, and the presence of bodies requires a place in which to be. Void also makes up part of the constitution of composite bodies and accounts for their differences in weight and texture, and their destructibility. Sextus says that according to Epicurus one part of the intangible nature is named 'void', another 'place', and another 'room'. The same nature is termed 'void' or empty space when destitute of any body, 'place' when occupied by a body, and 'room' when bodies pass through it.[25] Lucretius, as his master, argues that no third nature or substance is possible besides body and space.[26] Epicurus again uses experience as the evidence for his metaphysical position. That bodies exist our senses immediately attest. That void or space exists is apparent from the fact of motion which is observed. The absence or non-existence of space would conflict with apparent facts. Therefore that there must be space is confirmed by the method of non-contradiction (οὐκ ἀντιμαρτύρησις) ; what experience attests cannot not be so, what conflicts with experienced fact is false or non-existent.

5. Motion

Motion is eternal for Epicurus, both in the ceaseless motion of the atoms and the constant changes taking place in the conjunctions and disjunctions of compounds throughout the universe and in their relative positions and arrangements. The atoms move downward because of their weight at equal speed through empty space, but are moved upward or laterally due to collisions with other atoms. Epicurus himself in his extant works does not mention the famous swerve of the atoms, but it seems clear that he did hold the view as it appears

[25]Sextus Emp., *Adv. Math.*, X, 2. Cf. also Lucretius, I, 426–28.

[26]Lucretius, I, 433–44: "For whatever shall exist, must needs be something in itself; and if it suffer touch, however small and light, it will swell the sum of body by an increase great or maybe small, provided it exist at all, and be added to its total. But if it is not to be touched, inasmuch as it cannot on any side check anything from wandering through it and passing on its way, in truth it will be that which we call empty void. Or again, whatsoever exists by itself, will either act on something or suffer itself while other things act upon it, or it will be such that things may exist and go on in it. But nothing can act or suffer without body, nor afford room again, unless it be void and empty space." 449–50: "For all things that have a name, you will find either properties [*coniuncta*] linked to these two things or you will see them to be their accidents [*eventa*]."

in other Epicurean sources.[27] The swerve is needed to explain the formation of the world in the first place by the union of atoms as well as to give the metaphysical basis for human freedom of choice and action.

Since all bodies are capable of acting and being acted upon, all bodies must possess motion and be able to come in contact with other bodies. Sextus attributes to Epicurus the view that the motion of change—that by which the body, while remaining identical in substance, receives different qualities at different times putting off one quality and putting on another—is a particular form of transitional motion—that by which the moving body passes from place to place.[28] The composite body which changes in quality changes as a result of the local and transitional motion of the atoms which compose it. The atoms are arranged in a new order and take up different positions, or additions and subtractions of atoms occur.

Again, the motions of external objects affecting by contact immediately or mediately the atomic constituents of our bodies produce the different effects of sensation and thought. All processes are explained as motions of atoms or complexes of atoms. The universe is characterized by process and change. What appears static is only a relative equilibrium, as far as our senses are concerned, produced by a continuity of movement in one direction or in continued unions of atoms amid changes. Again the analogy with Hobbes' materialism of motion is apparent.

6. Causation

Epicurus denies that formal and final causes are operative in the universe and has, as it were, assimilated the material and efficient causes. However, he rejects the necessitarianism of the physicists or natural philosophers:

Destiny, which some introduce as sovereign over all things, he laughs to scorn, affirming rather that some things happen of necessity, others by chance, others through our own agency. For he sees that necessity destroys responsibility and that chance or fortune is inconstant; whereas our own actions are free, and it is to them that praise and blame naturally attach. It were better, indeed, to accept the legends of the gods than to bow beneath that yoke of destiny which

27Philodemus, De Signis, xxxvi; Lucretius, II, 216 f.; Cicero, De Natura Deorum, I, 25.

28Adv. Math., X, 42–44.

the natural philosophers have imposed. The one holds out some faint hope that we may escape if we honour the gods, while the necessity of the naturalists is deaf to all entreaties.[29]

The defense of free will, or another causation than the mechanistic, is made on the basis of empirical evidence—the observed facts of human behavior where there is at times effective resistance to external compulsion, and of natural and celestial phenomena where the simple repetition of events and qualities from antecedent causes and conditions does not seem to occur. The presence of the swerve and the unpredictable behavior of atoms are attested by the presence of a world and the creation of worlds.[30] It is interesting to note how Epicurus sets himself in opposition to the naturalists who assert a strict determinism. He has not, however, deviated from his materialism as all processes of the human mind and will are of course also atomic movements. As in Whitehead, different combinations and different motions of atoms produce new activities and qualities in different contexts. One would not expect the atoms in the human body to act in the same way as the atoms in inanimate compounds. The procedure by which the will transmits motion to heart and nerves and limbs is again reminiscent of Hobbes. For the details we must look to the account as given by Lucretius.[31] Epicurus himself says that the cause of voluntary actions is not in the atoms but in certain products of the atoms. We have the first beginnings of initiating power in

[29]Diog. Laert., X, 133–34.

[30]Lucretius, II, 251–56: "Once again, if every motion is always linked on, and the new arises from the old motion in order determined, nor by swerving do the first-beginnings make a certain start of movement to break through the decrees of fate, so that cause may not follow cause from infinite time; whence comes this free will for living things all over the earth?" 284–93: "Wherefore in the seeds too you must needs allow likewise that there is another cause of motion besides blows and weights, whence comes this power born in us, since we see that nothing can come to pass from nothing . . . But that the very mind feels not some necessity within in doing all things, and is not constrained like a conquered thing to bear and suffer, this is brought about by the tiny swerve of the first-beginnings in no determined direction of place and at no determined time."

[31]Lucretius, II, 261–273: "For without doubt it is his own will which gives to each one a start for this movement, and from the will the motions pass flooding through the limbs . . . so that you see a start of movement is brought to pass from the heart, and comes forth first of all from the will of the mind, and then afterwards is spread through all the body and limbs. Nor is it the same as when we move forward impelled by a blow from the strong might and strong constraint of another."

ourselves, which leads to our choices and preferences and subsequent action.[32] Epicurus seems to advocate an open future:

We must remember that the future is neither wholly ours nor wholly not ours, so that neither must we count upon it as quite certain to come nor despair of it as quite certain not to come.[33]

To celestial phenomena, which are observed at a distance and so cannot be checked by close-hand observation, Epicurus ascribes a plurality of causes. He criticizes the 'vain astrology' which attributes causation to a divine agency or makes these phenomena themselves divine and those who tumble into myth in the attempt to pick and choose among the plurality of possible causes and reject others equally consistent with the facts. The atomic explanation is the only one of nature as a whole and is a certainty confirmed by the facts, not an hypothesis. But since in the case of celestial phenomena we know only the effects and not their causes (other than the principles which apply to all bodies), we must be content with alternative hypotheses. We cannot have the same certainty in assigning specific causes to specific cases. We must base our explanations on the facts which we have, not on empty assumptions and arbitrary laws. Epicurus is here again empirical and not dogmatic, recognizing the limits of human understanding and enquiry:

But one must not be so much in love with the explanation by a single way as wrongly to reject all the others from ignorance of what can, and what cannot, be within human knowledge, and consequent longing to discover the indiscoverable.[34]
We do not seek to wrest by force what is impossible, nor to understand all matters equally well, nor make our treatment always as clear as when we discuss human life or explain the principles of physics in general—for instance, that the whole of being consists of bodies and intangible nature, or that the ultimate elements of things are indivisible, or any other proposition which admits only one explanation of the phenomena to be possible.[35]

Epicurus would certainly maintain that the ultimate explanation of everything lies in the movements and combinations of atomic patterns; but this material causation was not causation in the strict sense

[32]See Epicuro, *Opere*, edited with Italian translation and notes by G. Arrighetti (Turin, 1960), Frag. [31 21], p. 333, and Frag. [31 31], p. 350.
[33]Diog. Laert., X, 127.
[34]Diog. Laert., X, 94.
[35]Diog. Laert., X, 86.

for him. Efficient causation is always the motion of atomic configurations in themselves and in contact with other configurations. The quantitative features of atoms produce the different qualities which composite objects reveal, and the effects of these composite bodies on our own bodies (by contact) produce again other movements and reactions. However, it would seem that the causation of particular events, while ultimately the result of atomic conjunctions which made our world in the first place, is not to be answered in terms of the 'why' of events but in terms of uniformities and sequences observed within experience and in the case of unobserved objects by analogy with observed events:

Hence, where we find phenomena invariably recurring, the invariableness of the recurrence must be ascribed to the original interception and conglomeration of atoms whereby the world was formed.[36]

Some phenomena within our experience afford evidence by which we may interpret what goes on in the heavens. We see how the former really take place, but not how the celestial phenomena take place, for their occurrence may possibly be due to a variety of causes. However, we must observe each fact as presented, and further separate from it all the facts presented along with it, the occurrence of which from various causes is not contradicted by facts within our experience.[37]

The determination of specific causes of specific events is thus a purely empirical matter—noting similarities, differences, and isolating the relevant from the irrelevant accompaniments:

But above all give yourself up to the study of first principles and of infinity and of kindred subjects, and further of the standards and of the feelings and of the end for which we choose between them. For to study these subjects together will easily enable you to understand the causes of the particular phenomena.[38]

Epicurus rejects the divine nature as an efficient cause along with any teleological explanation:

The divine nature must not on any account be adduced to explain this, but must be kept free from the task and in perfect bliss.[39]

To assign a single cause for these effects when the facts suggest several causes is madness and a strange inconsistency; yet it is done by adherents of rash

[36]Diog. Laert., X, 77.
[37]Diog. Laert., X, 87.
[38]Diog. Laert., X, 116.
[39]Diog. Laert., X, 97.

astronomy, who assign meaningless causes for the stars whenever they persist in saddling the divinity with burdensome tasks.[40]

Superstition and the fallacy of *post hoc, ergo propter hoc* are attacked:

The fact that the weather is sometimes foretold from the behaviour of certain animals is a mere coincidence in time. For the animals offer no necessary reason why a storm should be produced; and no divine being sits observing when these animals go out and afterwards fulfilling the signs which they have given. For such folly as this would not possess the most ordinary being if ever so little enlightened, much less one who enjoys perfect felicity.[41]
And further, let the regularity of their orbits be explained in the same way as certain ordinary incidents within our own experience.[42]

Epicurus sees no need for formal or final causes. What acts or is acted upon is always a body. The very nature of the incorporeal is to be inactive and incapable of being affected. Only knowledge of the very objectivity of phenomena can produce peace of mind:

Nay more: we are bound to believe that in the sky revolutions, solstices, eclipses, risings and settings, and the like, take place without the ministration or command, either now or in the future, of any being who at the same time enjoys perfect bliss along with immortality . . . Nor again, must we hold that things which are no more than globular masses of fire, being at the same time endowed with bliss, assume these motions at will.[43]

7. Soul and Mind

Soul and mind are corporeal, composed of fine atoms, smoother and rounder than other atoms, and so capable of greater speed and penetration, but which require the protective sheath of the body for their united activity. The soul particles which are scattered throughout the frame of the body most nearly resemble those of wind and heat. A third kind of particles, which exceed the others in fineness

[40]Diog. Laert., X, 113.
[41]Diog. Laert., X, 115–16.
[42]Diog. Laert., X, 97.
[43]Diog. Laert., X, 76–77. Cf. Lucretius, II, 174–81: "But when they suppose that the gods have appointed all things for the sake of men, they are seen in all things to fall exceeding far away from true reason. For however little I know what the first-beginnings of things are, yet this I would dare to affirm from the very workings of heaven, and to prove from many other things as well, that the nature of the world is by no means made by divine grace for us: so great are the flaws with which it stands beset."

and can therefore keep in closer touch with the rest of the frame, accounts for the mental faculties and the feelings. Sentience, sensation, and the various mental operations are the result of the motion of these soul particles. Differences in size, weight, shape, and mobility of the atoms thus produce different qualities and activities. While exhibiting some of the qualities of wind and fire, the soul atoms must be finer, lighter, more mobile, and round in shape. Epicurus seems to be thinking here of the warmth and breath attached to the living body. His theory of mind and soul he rests again on immediate experience:

Next, keeping in view our perceptions and feelings (for so we shall have the surest grounds for belief) we must recognize generally that the soul is a corporeal thing . . .
Hence those who call soul incorporeal speak foolishly. For if it were so, it could neither act nor be acted upon. But, as it is, both these properties, you see, plainly belong to soul.[44]

Part of the soul is irrational, that scattered over the frame; part is rational and located in the chest. This is attested by the experience of sentience throughout the body while our fears and joys are associated with the breast. The soul has the greatest share in causing sensation but it would not have sensation if it were not confined in the protective frame of the body. The body, too, has a share in sensation not only providing the protective sheath as an indispensable condition for the existence of soul atoms in union, but sentience is apparently imparted to the body atoms because of the close connection of the two. Sentience remains even with the loss of parts of the body and of some of the soul atoms; but the body loses sentience when the soul atoms have dispersed or when the whole frame is broken up. There can be no immortality of the soul because the soul is not an incorporeal substance nor can the soul atoms remain together and perform any operations of sensation and thought apart from the body. The soul is of the type of atomic compounds requiring a container of other atoms to maintain their union, identity, and to perform their peculiar activities. For more details of the Epicurean position we must look to Lucretius.[45]

44Diog. Laert., X, 63 and 67.
45Lucretius, III, 94–97: "First I say that the mind, which we often call the understanding, in which is placed the reasoning and guiding power of life, is a part of a man no whit the less than hand and foot and eyes are created parts of the whole

Lucretius goes on to say what kind of body the mind is—that it consists of very tiny particles of very fine texture, round in shape, and able to be moved by a little impulse very rapidly. The evidence for this is found in the nature of images, feelings, and thoughts and the rapidity with which they occur. Lucretius ascribes a triple nature of breath, air, and heat to the soul, since these qualities desert the dying, and a fourth nature of even finer particles which causes sensation.

Epicurus explains sensation in terms of motions produced by motions of particles coming from external objects: "We must also consider that it is by the entrance of something coming from external objects that we see their shapes and think of them."[46] Sensation is by touch or contact—immediate in the case of touch but mediate or by means of idols or images in the case of sight, hearing, and odor. Idols are corporeal films or outlines given off by external bodies preserving the same shape as the solid bodies from which they come, but of a thinness that makes them invisible in themselves to us. These idols are continually streaming off from objects, some of them affecting our senses and our mind. They retain for a long time the position and arrangement which the atoms had when they formed part of solid bodies, although occasionally they are thrown into confusion by collisions in the intervening air. The continued existence and identity of objects are guaranteed by the continual succession of idols received from them by our senses and mind. These idols enter into our eyes or minds, to whichever their size is suitable, and have the same color and shape as the objects themselves. Their very rapid motion explains

living being." 136–46: "Now I say that mind and soul are held in union one with the other, and form of themselves a single nature, but that the head, as it were, and lord in the whole body is the reason, which we call mind or understanding, and it is firmly seated in the middle region of the breast. For here it is that fear and terror throb, around these parts are soothing joys; here then is the understanding and the mind. The rest of the soul, spread abroad throughout the body, obeys and is moved at the will and inclination of the understanding. The mind alone by itself has understanding for itself, it rejoices for itself, when no single thing stirs either soul or body." 161–69: "This same reasoning shows that the nature of mind and soul is bodily. For when it is seen to push on the limbs, to pluck the body from sleep, to change the countenance, and to guide and turn the whole man—none of which things we see can come to pass without touch, nor touch in its turn without body— must we not allow that mind and soul are formed of bodily nature? Moreover, you see that our mind suffers along with the body, and shares our feelings together in the body."

[46]Diog. Laert., X, 49.

why they present the appearance of a single continuous object and
retain the mutual interconnection which they had in the object. Impressions of the senses are true in the sense that they are caused by
real external objects and are faithful resemblances of external objects.
Epicurus must insist on the reliability of sense perception since it is
the criterion and test for truth. The idols guarantee both the existence
and the nature of external objects. When the mind intrudes with
countermovements of its own and makes additions or subtractions
from the images received, or otherwise interprets them, error and
falsehood arise:

Falsehood and error always depend upon the intrusion of opinion when a fact
awaits confirmation or the absence of contradiction, which fact is afterwards
frequently not confirmed or even contradicted, following a certain movement
in ourselves connected with, but distinct from, the mental picture presented—
which is the cause of error. For the presentations which, e.g., are received in
a picture or arise in dreams, or from any other form of apprehension by the
mind or by the other criteria of truth, would never have resembled what we
call the real and true things, had it not been for certain actual things of the
kind with which we come in contact. Error would not have occurred, if we
had not experienced some other movement in ourselves, conjoined with, but
distinct from, the perception of what is presented. And from this movement,
if it be not confirmed or be contradicted, falsehood results; while, if it be
confirmed or not contradicted, truth results. And to this view we must closely
adhere, if we are not to repudiate the criteria founded on the clear evidence
of sense, nor again to throw all these things into confusion by maintaining
falsehood as if it were truth.[47]

Epicurus is often accused of being 'naive' in asserting that all perceptions are true. As existent, they cannot be false or illusory and must be
caused by real external objects. Even the perceptions of madmen and
of people in dreams are real for they produce effects (movements in
the mind at least) which the unreal never does. Taken as such they
are simply what they are and are the beginning of all knowledge and
the ultimate criteria of the truth of our opinions.[48]

     This does not mean that all our perceptions are equally valid for
knowledge or truth. Some idols are formed in the air by chance collisions of atoms and carry no guarantee of a real solid object which
they resemble. Images are often distorted by collisions, becoming worn

     [47]Diog. Laert., X, 50–52. The Greek text of the first sentence of this quotation is
defective. The sentence has been judged by recent editors to be either in whole or
in part an intrusion into the text of the *Letter to Herodotus*.
     [48]See above, p. 379, note 6.

or broken in transit, especially if they come from a long distance. The ultimate criterion is the confronted object or close-hand observation. The immediacy of the individual sensation or feeling carries with it its own validity. Sensation furnishes the contents or materials for knowledge. But the mind is active even in perception as it is set in motion by the impulse of idols. All our ideas or notions come from sense perceptions, either by actual contact, or by analogy, resemblance, or composition of these with the aid of reasoning. In addition to these operations, the mind by its attention selects from the images presented to it and may add or subtract from these presentations. It forms general notions or concepts (προλήψεις) which are based on the percepts which it stores up. Universal ideas are formed from the recollection of a number of presentations of an object. These general notions give us the notion of kinds of things by which we recognize instances of the kind and thus 'anticipate' perceptions of particulars. Presumably the mind may err in attributing the particulars to these general ideas, although the general ideas themselves Epicurus regards as reliable criteria. These general ideas are sharply distinguished from abstract ideas and assumptions not based directly on experience. Names attached to the general concepts serve to recall the general type and enable us to recognize and to refer to the particular instances when we meet them:

By preconception they mean a sort of apprehension or a right opinion or notion, or universal idea stored in the mind; that is, a recollection of an external object often presented, e.g. Such and such a thing is a man: for no sooner is the word "man" uttered than we think of his shape by an act of preconception, in which the senses take the lead. Thus the object primarily denoted by every term is then plain and clear. And we should never have started an investigation, unless we had known what it was that we were in search of. For example: The object standing yonder is a horse or a cow. Before making this judgement, we must at some time or other have known by preconception the shape of horse and cow. We should not have given anything a name, if we had not first learnt its form by way of preconception. It follows, then, that preconceptions are clear.[49]

The mind must make inferences from what it experiences to objects not immediately experienced because of distance or remoteness in time or from some other circumstance. It must also make inferences about what cannot be perceived nor confirmed by later confrontation.

[49]Diog. Laert., X, 33 (Hicks's translation slightly altered).

Here, too, there is chance of error. Hypotheses or assumptions which anticipate experience or ignore it for a purely rational test are contrasted with opinions. The mind makes judgments and interpretations from what is presented which may be verified by experience:

Again, we must suppose that nature too has been taught and forced to learn many various lessons by the facts themselves, that reason subsequently develops what it has thus received and makes fresh discoveries, among some tribes more quickly, among others more slowly, the progress thus made being at certain times and seasons greater, at others less.[50]

Lucretius gives to the mind and the senses an active role in perception. As there are countless idols available, some only of which are actually perceived, he attributes to the senses and the mind a kind of act of attention or even of intention in the selection and apprehension of idols.[51]

Language, at the beginning natural in origin, is developed conventionally by means of analogy and reason. It has been noted already the importance of understanding what it is that words denote.[52] A name refers to the general notion or idea of a class by which we identify or recognize the particular instance. The importance of language and its role in scientific theory must also be understood as a contribution of the mind in its use of the materials of sense and the extension of knowledge on the theoretical level. The concrete language of ordinary experience is preferred by the Epicureans. The metaphorical and abstract language of philosophers is attacked by them as remote from the thing-language of sense experience and as emotional. Philosophical language must be clear and informative.[53]

---

[50]Diog. Laert., X, 75.

[51]Lucretius, IV, 802–10: "Again, because they are fine, the mind cannot discern them sharply, save those which it strains to see; therefore all that there are besides these pass away, save those for which it has made itself ready. Moreover, the mind makes itself ready, and hopes it will come to pass that it will see what follows upon each several thing; therefore it comes to be. Do you not see the eyes too, when they begin to perceive things which are fine, strain themselves and make themselves ready, and that without that it cannot come to pass that we see things sharply?"

[52]See above, p. 377, note 2.

[53]See the comments on language in the fragments of Epicurus, *On Nature*, Bk. XXVIII, published with an Italian translation by G. Arrighetti in Epicuro, *Opere*, pp. 289–317; and Colotes' criticisms of Platonic language in Crönert, *Kolotes und Menedemos* (Leipzig, 1906), pp. 4–12.

8. *Idea of God*

Epicurus rejects atheism, maintaining that there are gods and that the knowledge of them is manifest:

First believe that god is a living being immortal and blessed, according to the notion of a god indicated by the common sense of mankind; and so believing, thou shalt not affirm of him aught that is foreign to his immortality or that agrees not with blessedness, but shalt believe about him whatever may uphold both his blessedness and his immortality. For verily there are gods, and the knowledge of them is manifest; but they are not such as the multitude believe, seeing that men do not steadfastly maintain the notions they form respecting them. Not the man who denies the gods worshipped by the multitude, but he who affirms of the gods what the multitude believes about them is truly impious. For the utterances of the multitude about the gods are not true preconceptions but false assumptions.[54]

The gods are not objects of experience in the sense of being perceived by the senses. However, idols too fine to be perceived by the senses affect the mind and we form notions of the gods from the succession of images streaming from them to our mind. These images are attended to usually in dreams when other distractions do not interfere. Cicero in the *De Natura Deorum* gives the Epicurean view in most detail with extensions of his own to fit the popular anthropomorphic conception.[55] The divine nature, as everything else, is made of atoms, but does not exist as a solid object in our world but in the interspaces between worlds where such conjunctions of atoms are able to maintain themselves eternally free from collisions from without which would make them mortal. The constant stream of similar idols or images which strike our mind is empirical proof of the continued unchanging existence of the gods and of their nature. They cannot, however, affect us, as they themselves cannot be affected by us. That they

[54]Diog. Laert., X, 123–24.

[55]Cicero, *De Natura Deorum*, I, 19 (Poteat translation): "Epicurus, then, who perceives clearly with the inner eye things that are shrouded in mystery and darkness, and still deals with them as though they were objective realities, declares that the gods are so formed and constituted that, in the first place, they are apprehended not by the senses but solely by the intellect—seeing that there is in them no corporeality and that they are not to be distinguished as individuals, like the solids which, because of their solidity, Epicurus calls *steremnia;* nay, identical images cross over to our minds and are received by them—identical images in an unending stream which has its source in the countless atoms and flows down to us. Thus, with ecstasy we earnestly apply reason and intelligence to these images, and so we learn the nature of beings who enjoy eternal bliss."

are of human form our ideas of them tell us; but to Epicurus they exist primarily as models for us of perfect bliss and tranquillity. As such they must be inactive and free from all ties of occupation. Thus as to the existence of the gods we are assured by empirical evidence, by our notions of them produced by idols emanating from them. Our ideas of the nature of the gods are derived then from what persistent and unchanging notions all men have of them—that they are human in form, of perfect beauty and happiness, and that they are eternal. As eternal, they are of different atomic composition from humans; i.e., they cannot be made of flesh and blood, for living creatures of flesh and blood are subject to death. The gods with perfect bliss somehow maintain themselves unaffected by external blows which would destroy their perfect tranquillity and cause their destruction. Their continued existence and permanent nature are proved by the constant succession of similar images of them received by us and by the common consent of mankind.[56]

The prime importance of the concept of the divine nature for Epicurus is to serve as the ethical ideal of perfect tranquillity and happiness. Men have the idea of perfect happiness, which must be everlasting, and corresponding to this idea must exist a real nature of the divine which produces this notion. Epicurus stresses the perfect bliss and eternality of the gods as two divine attributes which cannot be dispensed with; the other attributes of the divine nature presumably vary from people to people:

A blessed and eternal being has no trouble himself and brings no trouble on any other being: hence he is exempt from movements of anger and partiality, for every such movement implies weakness. (Elsewhere he says that the gods are discernible by reason alone, some being numerically distinct, while others result uniformly from the continuous influx of similar images directed to the same spot and in human form).[57]

The gods cannot touch us as they are not touched themselves. Being outside our world in the *intermundia*, the empty spaces between worlds, they have an existence immune from destruction and immune

---

[56]Cf. Philodemus, *De Signis*, xxvii: "Indeed, it is apparent that the gods and the first elements of things are indestructible and unborn, since this is a condition of their being such as they are, and since inductive inference from appearances has proved it."

[57]Epicurus, *Sovran Maxims*, 1, with the ancient scholium (Diog. Laert., X, 139).

from care and distress. Only thus could they remain as ethical patterns and ideals for men.

Epicurus endeavors to ground his theology empirically. Idols coming from an external source are guarantees of existent natures corresponding to them. Just as the continued existence and personal identity of external objects are based upon the continual succession of similar perceptions, so the continued existence of the gods (of some of whom we receive particular enough images to attribute individual identity) is attested by the constant flow of similar images received from them now and in the past by mankind. But the gods have no special metaphysical role. They are part of the natural scheme of things.

Epicurus prefers the expression 'the divine nature' to indicate the continuity and infinity of the chain of existence of nature. There is no reason why there may not be atomic arrangements unlike those in our world in some respects, yet like them in others. What is possible in the Epicurean view may be actual. Epicurus preaches reverence and worship of the gods as models of the ethical ideal. His anthropomorphic conception of the gods follows from his epistemological position of the real external origin of all our ideas and his metaphysical theory of the uniform nature of all existence. However, he attacks the popular anthropomorphism because of its relative and changing concepts and because it brings the divine nature into our world and makes it subject to the limitations within it. The eternality and happiness of the gods would thus be lost, and with them, any religious and ethical use. He denies to the gods any agency in the creation or maintenance of our world; for this cannot be empirically established, conflicts with the facts, and would again lose for them their status as ethical ideals. There is no supernatural. But there are innumerable worlds and interspaces between worlds which may contain other possible combinations and beings whose manner of existence and qualities are both like and unlike ours.

ESTELLE A. DE LACY

ROOSEVELT UNIVERSITY

ON SUBSTANCE AND PROCESS IN LEIBNIZ

I T IS AN IRONY of modern philosophy that Leibniz, who did more than any other thinker of his century to undermine the traditional doctrine of substance in the interest of a modern conception of change and dynamism[1] should, in the last twenty years of his life, have applied most of the time and energy left him for philosophical thought to what may well be the longest and most persistent debate on the nature of substance which records have preserved.

Moreover, since this debate was carried out with correspondents schooled in either the Scholastic or the Cartesian tradition (or in that strange combination of the two which prevailed so widely in the late 17th century) it is a part of this irony that Leibniz's expositions of his doctrine, which was approaching a functional simplicity, had to be written in the terminological tradition which they used, with the result that they seem only rarely to grasp his meaning adequately. It is rather in those simpler interpretations of his thought written in the last years of his life for the instruction of such interested laymen as Eugene of Savoy, Nicolas Remond, and Louis Bourguet that the clear, concrete, and empirically oriented accounts are to be found which still serve best as introductions (admittedly inadequate) to his thought.[2]

It is the position of this paper that Leibniz's mature doctrine of substance stands at midpoint between the traditional theory of his predecessors—that which was criticized by Berkeley and Hume—and the process philosophy of our own century, from which the category

---

[1]Cf. the new concept of *force* which resulted from his studies in dynamics, and was first given a metaphysical meaning in a published paper of 1694: *On the Correction of Metaphysics and the Concept of Substance, Philosophische Schriften,* ed. C. I. Gerhardt, 4 (Berlin, 1879), 468-70. (This work will hereafter be designated as G.)

[2]Particularly the *Principles of Nature and of Grace,* probably written for Eugene of Savoy but sent to Nicolas Remond de Montmort as well, and the so-called *Monadology,* which A. Robinet has recently suggested was sent to Remond to provide the basis for a new *De Natura Rerum* by the poet Fraguier. G. W. Leibniz, *Principes de la nature et de la grace fondés en raison, Principes de la philosophie ou monadologie,* ed. A. Robinet (Paris: Presses universitaires, 1954). The letters to Louis Bourguet also contain clear expositions, G, 3, 572-583.

is banished, at least in name, but in which its functions must still somehow be served. Our discussion of the debate will be restricted to the intellectual exchanges with three men: Pierre Bayle, Burcher de Volder, and Bartholomew des Bosses—the former two Cartesians of somewhat diverse interests; the last named a Jesuit Scholastic. Involved in this discussion will be, primarily, five perennial antinomies brought to the fore by Leibniz's new theory: the logical antinomy of universal and particular (and the ambiguity of their relation); the metaphysical antitheses of self-determinism vs. external interaction and of order vs. freedom; the psychological antithesis of disposition or habit vs. particular act, and the ethical antithesis of power and justice (now tempered with love). These are all aspects of the same general issue; they are all Platonic in origin and inspiration; and the one great generalization of Leibniz's theory of substance proposes to resolve them all.

I

In a detailed reply to some of De Volder's criticisms, Leibniz offers a compact definition of substance. In essence, it is a permanent law determining a temporal sequence or series of events.

That there is a certain persisting law which involves the future states of that which we conceive as the same—this itself is what I say constitutes the same substance. If anyone concedes to me that there is an infinity of percipients, in each of whom there is a fixed law of the progression of phenomena; that the phenomena of these different percipients correspond with each other; and that there is a common reason for both their existence and their correspondence in the being we call God—this is all I claim in the matter and all I think can be claimed.[3]

Thus a substance consists of two mutually dependent phases corresponding to the logical dimensions of intensionality and extensionality respectively—the "complete notion" or "the law of the individual," and the particular temporal series of "states" or perceptions which express this law. In traditional terms, the complete individual notion, concept, or law is the substance, which has two kinds of properties: the essences or enduring natures which are ingredient to it, and the particular events which change and which are particular actualizations of these essences. Logically speaking, it is a singular sub-

3Letter of Jan. 21, 1704, G, 2, 264.

ject in which all of its abiding and changing predicates inhere, and which is identical to them; the subject is equal to the whole of its predicates. In mathematical terms, it is a functional law which determines all of the particular values which inhere in its complexly interrelated variables. But it can equally well be regarded (as the second part of the quotation from the letter to De Volder shows) as a succession of events, understood as perceptive acts, continuously related to each other by an internal principle of order which determines them. Substance is thus a uniformly ordered succession of such events.

For Leibniz every individual thus consists of a combination of universal and particular in the new relationship or form (indeed, he revives the Scholastic designation of substantial form) and process. These two inseparable aspects do justice, the one to his panlogism, the other to his panpsychism. When the new concept of substance was first clearly explicated, in the *Discourse on Metaphysics* in 1686, Leibniz was engaged in logical studies involving the development, through the art of combinations, of *complete* or *integral* notions. This was to serve as the logical analog to the creation of individuals from the simple perfections of God.[4] Thus the *Discourse,* written for Antoine Arnauld and given the title, in its first draft, of "A Treatise on the Perfections of God," emphasized the panlogistic aspect of substance—the logical constitution of the individual concept.[5]

At the time of the correspondence with Arnauld which followed, Leibniz had not yet worked out clearly such detailed problems as the nature of composite substances and the relationship between individuals, particularly the relations between mind and body, nor had he simplified his theory of the action and passion of the individual into a theory of perception and appetite. The concept of force was still lacking. During the Italian journey which followed, his interest was centered, aside from his historical task, upon problems of mathematics and dynamics, with the result that his new theory of individual substance was further developed to include the conception of primitive force; this must be understood as the metaphysical exigency or striving of the ideas comprising the individual notions to actualize themselves, or in other words, as the operative power of the very per-

---

[4]For example, see the *Generales Inquisitiones de Analysi Notionum et Veritatum* (1686). Couturat, *Opuscules et fragments inédits* (Paris, 1903), 356-99.

[5]See particularly *Discourse,* sections 8-13, G, 4, 432-39.

fections of God as they are compounded and made complete in individual substances.[6] In *The New System on the Nature and Communication of Substance* (1695) Leibniz undertook the first published interpretation of his new doctrine, with particular emphasis upon the activism of the individual and the doctrine of harmony as an explanation of their relationships, but with a mere mention of "a kind of perception" as the act expressing this harmony. It was the *New System* which gave rise to the great controversy about substance. And it is worth noting that Leibniz's correspondents did not know the unpublished *Discourse* of 1686 in which the logical basis of his theory had been given. Thus his panpsychism, and its significance for dynamics, is clear in their minds, but his panlogism is obscured. Leibniz's last papers on logic were written in 1691-92, and mark no advance in his thinking about the metaphysical implications of logic.

But although Leibniz's analogies in these letters are drawn primarily from the functional concept of mathematics, the concept of force in dynamics, and the phenomena of life and consciousness, and although his thinking is increasingly occupied with time, process, and history, his concept of substance holds the panlogistic and panpsychistic aspects of his metaphysics together in inseparable union.[7]

II

From its earliest beginnings Leibniz's thought had converged upon this unity of logic and process. One may say that his early philosophical speculations, before the years in Paris (1672-76), were eclectic, and that his logical, juristic, and theological ideas were incompletely assimilated to each other. Yet there is underlying them all a metaphysical synthesis which assimilates Aristotle's doctrine of substance to Platonic souls and thus to the data of conscious life, without neglecting the mathematical Platonism of the new sciences of Kepler and Galileo. Certain phases of this combination may briefly be enumerated.

1. In the student work in which his mathematical logic of combinations and commutations was first proposed, the *Dissertation on*

---

[6] *On the Radical Origination of Things* (1697), (G, 7, 303) and the letter to Des Bosses (Feb. 5, 1712), G, 2, 435.

[7] See Jalabert, *La théorie Leibnizienne de la substance* (Paris, 1947), especially the concluding chapter. Jalabert agrees that though the panpsychistic aspects dominate the discussion after 1696, Leibniz never abandoned his panlogism.

the Art of Combinations (1666), there is a short metaphysical introduction which involves a metaphysics of ideas and their possible arrangements, in the course of which spatial, temporal, and dynamic
orders are derived. This theme was not developed, however, until the
first logical papers of the early Hanover years, ten years later, when
Leibniz had acquired the mathematical tools needed for a clearer
conception of logical addition—the ideas of variables and values in a
functional relationship, of a mathematical determinant which is resolvable into successive lower and more abstract orders of determinants until the lowest order of simple elements is reached, and the
physical device of a resolving of motion into momentary impetuses
or conations.[8]

2. Leibniz's early papers on theological and juristic problems,
written during his stay in Mainz, reflect a metaphysical theory of
creation which anticipates some of his later principles. It views creation as a process of multiplication of the divine ideas, required by
the infinite nature of God. Several quotations will show the Platonism involved.

The substance of things is an idea. Idea is the union of God and creatures, as
action is the union of agent and patient . . . N.B. Ideas are not in God except
insofar as there are things outside of him. Thus a point is not a center without
lines . . . The ideas of God and the substances of things are the same in fact,
different in relation, as are action and passion. And since the substances of
things are the action of God upon species, we must inquire how it is possible
that his action upon one species is numerically the same as his action upon
another.

Again,

In idea is contained ideally both passive and active power, both active and
passive intellect. Insofar as passive intellect concurs, there is form.[9]

This metaphysics of ideas provided the ground for his early doctrine
of harmony in theology, and of justice in jurisprudence.

---

[8]Cf. the marginal note to the Dialogue of 1677: "When God calculates and carries
out his calculations, the world is made." See also the paper on *Universal Synthesis
and Analysis, or the Art of Discovery and Judgement*, G, 7, 278-83, 351-59.

[9]*Prussian Academy* edition (hereafter referred to as PA) 6, i, 513. From a treatise
on transubstantiation from 1668. See also the letter to Magnus Wedderkopf (May,
1671), PA, 2, i, 117; Leibniz's first letter to Arnauld (1671) G, 1, 72-73, and *On the
Elements of Jurisprudence*, PA, 6, i, 437.

3. If the first two examples show Leibniz's early tendency to a panlogism, the next reflects his early panpsychism. In the a priori part of the *New Physical Hypothesis, The Theory of Abstract Motion,* published in 1761 and dedicated to the French Academy, Leibniz makes an early attempt to find a common component of body and mind in motion. In this he makes use of Hobbes's concept of *conatus* as a simple momentary motion. More than twenty years will pass before it becomes a momentary force.

No conatus without motion lasts longer than a moment except in minds. For what conatus is in a moment is the motion of a body in time. This opens the door to the true distinction between body and mind, which no one has heretofore explained. Every body is a momentary mind, or one lacking recollection *(recordatio),* because it does not retain its own conatus and the contrary one together for more than a moment. For two things are necessary to sense pleasure and pain—action and reaction, opposition and then harmony—and there is no sensation without these. Hence body lacks memory; it lacks the perception of its own actions and passions; it lacks thought.[10]

Remarkable here is the theory that sensory feelings are momentary oppositions or resistances between opposed impulses, and that memory or the retention of a series' own past actions and passions makes possible thought. There is no evidence that Leibniz at this time has related this conception of a dynamic series as a succession of momentary motions to the role of the individual idea in creation, but when he succeeds in refining both notions, in the post-Paris period, the essentials of his theory of substance will have been outlined.

4. The psychological aspect of the notion of a serial order of events is brought out in a paper of 1679 published by Grau. Entitled *De affectionibus, libide, potentia, actioni, determinatione,* it begins as a running commentary on Descartes' *On the Passions of the Soul,* but soon shifts to a description of the serial chains of thought (later, perceptions) which constitute the mind. Beginning with the basic proposition, *nos esse substantias,* Leibniz here resolves the mind into an interweaving of series of cogitations each of which is determined by an affect and aims at a perfection. Nowhere did he penetrate more deeply into a phenomenological study of consciousness, or anticipate Whitehead more closely, and it is regrettable that he never resumed

10G, 4, 230. The theory of *conatus* or *impetus* is generally accepted in Scholastic works on physics at the beginning of the century.

his thinking in this direction. A few quotations will show the nature of his analysis.

An affect is a determination of the mind toward thinking of a certain thing in preference to other things.

Attention is the determination toward thinking one thing above other things because these others are not remembered.

A series is a multitude with a rule of order.

The determination to a series of thinking is stronger to the degree that the rule of the series involves the more reality (or perfection).

A series is thus ingredient in (ingredimur) thinking, so that we may discover in (the confused parts of thought) something which we seek. It can happen that diverse series become progressively ingredient so that we may choose what we find in each.[11]

Thus the mind, conscious and unconscious, is constituted not merely by one "series with a rule of order" but by many which may determine each other, and sometimes envelop, one the other, or merge into each other. These subordinate series within the mind, or more generally, within the individual substance, provide a basis for the "subalternate maxims" (as Leibniz designates them in the *Discourse*) [12] or the laws of nature which are common to entire classes of individuals. It is to be regretted that Leibniz never developed this idea nor built it into his mature system. But the paper on the affections does mark one point in the development of Leibniz's thought at which his panlogism and panpsychism are firmly bound together through the principle that generative individual concepts or laws and serial acts are united inseparably in each substance.

In its essentials Leibniz's doctrine of substance was now complete, although it required his correction of Descartes' theory of motion and the conservation of momentum, and the development of the calculus, to provide him with his strongest analogical arguments from science and his clearest explanations of the relationship between a universal law and the particular instances or values of its variables.

[11]*De affectibus, libido, potentia, actioni, determinatione.* Printed by G. Grau, *G. W. Leibniz. Textes inédits,* 2 (Paris, 1948), 512-537. The quotations are from pages 525, 526, and 524.

[12]Sections 7, 17, etc., G, 4, 432, etc.

III

It will be useful to enumerate some of the gains which Leibniz had achieved by this doctrine.

1. *It eliminates the unempirical specter of a substance with spatial or temporal attributes but itself beyond definition.* This is the "substance" to which the Cartesians clung and which was found, by the time of Locke, to be without empirical support or rational necessity. Both souls and bodies are now reduced to continuous processes of active and passive states, the effects of forces originating in the ideas or laws which determined them. They are as habits which determine acts, as the fixed relations between variables which determine their values, as facts and the principles which describe their order. This is a concept of substance which lies well within the limits of scientific theory and verification (though complete verification would involve an infinite process of analysis).

2. *It claims to show the possibility that a perfect logical order may be coextensive with a spatio-temporal order of serial events.* There is necessary, of course, a narrowing of the logic of possibilities into a logic of the order of existence; this involves the principle of the best possible. But by identifying Aristotle's dictum that in an adequately analyzed proposition the subject must include its predicates, with the logical principle that the intensional meaning of a term must be equivalent to its extensional scope, Leibniz achieves a harmony of rational order with empirical totality.

Couturat considered it a mistake of Leibniz to have developed a logic of intensionality rather than of extensionality. But in fact his logical papers show the possibility of both types and the nature of their relation to each other. His metaphysics requires both. The modern trend toward nominalism, however, when it rejects intensionality, finds it impossible to explain order (save as a pragmatically justifiable verbal generalization by the observer). Metaphysically, the choice is one of explaining particulars in terms of an established order, as in Leibniz, or of explaining order as a function of the differing and chance particulars, as in Whitehead.

3. *It restores the old theological theory of the univocity of divine and creaturely attributes,* and develops it into an actual identity of the essences of created individuals with the perfections (finitely limited) of God himself. This brings to the center of discussion again the traditional metaphysical and ethical categories as attributes both

of God and of his creation, and pushes aside such relational categories as extension and thought (which Leibniz could not regard as simple). But in place of the Aristotelian hierarchical structure of genera and species terminating in infima species, Leibniz adopts Spinoza's conception of substance as self-determining and applies it to each individual substance as a complete essence causing its existence. Thus, as Leibniz's discussion of Locke's distinction between real and nominal essences shows, his theory of the essence or idea of the individual approximates the real essences which Locke considers unknowable, but which Leibniz regards as knowable imperfectly and in part.[13]

4. *Moreover, the shift which this theory of substance involves from a reference to things of ordinary perception to the micro-things resulting from analysis, and from spatial to temporal and dynamic relations* (a shift which was not fully apparent to his critics) *provided a more fruitful hypothesis for the explanation of physical as well as mental phenomena* than the alternative hypothesis of atoms. The new atomism stopped with space and motion, and failed to explain the qualities of composite bodies. Leibniz's theory supported the deepening of the physical sciences by the principle of force[14] and its conservation in closed systems of particles, and in the complex structures of life and mind as well.

5. In particular, *Leibniz's doctrine of substance provides his psychology with a firm basis for both acts and dispositions,* making the latter the ground for the former. It is true that the dispositional components of the mind (or of monads of a lower order) are conceived intellectually, as subalternate patterns of ideas ingredient in the complete notion of the individual. But they are not conscious ideas, though they may become known by inner perception or reflection. Indeed, this distinguishes self-knowledge from self-consciousness. To know oneself is by analysis and synthesis to penetrate as deeply as possible into the dispositional characters of which our complete law is the whole.[15] Acts proceed out of character, as particulars from uni-

[13]See the *New Essays on the Understanding,* trans. Langley (La Salle, Illinois: Open Court Publishing Co., 1949), 3, iii, 15-19, 315-18, 384-87.

[14]G, 4, 468-70. Leibniz here makes explicit the distinction between his conception of force and the Scholastic notion of potentiality. The force operative in the monad (primary force) is a specific impetus or conatus implicit in the law of the individual, but actualizing itself, if not impeded, as successive appetites and perceptions.

[15]See the *New Essays,* 2, 27, sec. 6-23, in reply to Locke's theory of personal identity on this point, G, 5, 215-27.

versals, and their variety and order is determined by the order and arrangement (literally, the disposition) of the constants and variables in our nature. For the method of psychology, Leibniz's conception of analysis is significant—and perhaps comforting—at this point. He frequently shows, using algebraic and geometric problems, that though the selected terms and operations of an analysis may differ, and analysis therefore differ in apparent results, the terminal result, if it can be achieved, must always be the same. We may set out to achieve a psychic profile, or laws of motivation, or a typology of personalities, but regulative for all of these methods is an ultimate individual nature defined in simplest terms and relations, even though we can never achieve this definition because truths of fact involve an infinite process of analysis.

6. In his new doctrine, moreover, Leibniz has now defined *the nature of the interrelationship between individual substances*. One of his less fortunate metaphors, it is true, deprives the monads of windows—a figure singularly inconsistent with that other one describing them as living mirrors. Windowlessness, however, excludes only the possibility of an external causality or "influence" upon the individual, but not perceptions from within. It emphasizes the completely self-determining nature of substances. Each, in every present state or act, "represents," "expresses," or "perceives" the entire world according to its point of view, or the restriction of its individual law. Every perception is the actualization of an idea, is internal to the perceiver but external to what is perceived (this is the realistic dimension of Leibniz's thought), and combines activity and passivity—the inert, material content of the perception which restricts it to "phenomena well founded." "Every mind is omniscient but confused."[16]

Such a harmony of interpenetrating perceptions, however, cannot assure the ontological harmony of the world, for, however complex the order of perceptions, they are all focused in the nature of the *percipient* and unattached, so to speak, to the *perceptum*. A world of such percipients would fall apart into a plurality of substances, as Bayle and others charged. The harmony of the existing world is assured, not by these perceptions but by the common ideas or perfections of God ingredient in the complete concepts of the monads. The unity of the world is made possible only by the presence of God whose

16From a fragment of the Paris period; Couturat, *Opuscules et fragments inédits*, 10.

very attributes inhere, with finite differences, in our natures. Hence "God belongs to me more closely than my body," as Leibniz says in one of his most mystical formulations of his thought.[17]

7. The conception of a harmonious order of distinct but (in spite of their differences) largely overlapping individual concepts thus supplies Leibniz with *a new notion of levels of generality and abstractness in the scientific laws imbedded in both natural and spiritual or mental events.* The process of combinatorial synthesis involved in the creation of this world may be grasped by the analogy to a matrix or determinant containing an infinite number of terms (the irreducible perfections of God) each of which will appear in this world in a particular range of finite values. The complete solution or resolution of this determinant will be an infinite number of complete notions, all containing each of the simple terms, but in a different order or disposition, and with varying values. This complete resolution is reached, however, in an infinity of stages in which each term serves as a parameter related to a subordinate order of determinants, each stage involving reduction of the order of these determinants until they disappear. Thus there appear, in the final complete concepts, various overlapping orders of identical configurations, each of which defines a class of events or abstract attributes and forms which constitute Leibniz's "subalternate regulations" or natural laws. No natural law, however, serves to define completely an individual monad. Each individual retains a uniqueness of nature.

8. Leibniz's monadology thus involves *a theory of causality approaching that of modern science* and more adequate than current positivistic theories. The individual monads and their concepts do not render mechanical laws unnecessary; mechanical laws are abstract aspects of God's creation of the monads. But they are descriptive and functional. All efficient causality resides in the individuals as *vis primitiva,* the actualization of the series; this is what Leibniz means in his frequently repeated remark that he had to return to the substantial forms of the Scholastics.[18] Scientific causality rests on the observation of *phenomena bene fundata* and consists of a description of the relationship between two regularly recurring types of observed events, one of which is relatively active, the other relatively passive, with respect to each other. These descriptive laws, however, are sub-

---

[17]*On the True Theologia Mystica.* Guhrauer, *Deutsche Schriften,* **2,** 411.
[18]*Discourse,* section 11. Cf. G, **4, 345, 471,** etc.

ject to such analysis as can be given to truths of fact; that is, when analyzed further, they may be seen to approach mathematical functions, and, ideally, the functional relations implicit in the monadic notions.[19] Thus science ideally involves a bridging of the gulf separating macrocosmic from microscopic events and the reduction of casual connections to functional dependencies, though these are actually achieved only in dynamics, where the quantifiable elements are fairly exact analogues to the monadic acts and contents themselves. In less exact sciences the scientist must content himself with descriptive and externally related causes and effects. Leibniz thus anticipates Hume's analysis of causality, but completes it with a metaphysical theory derived from mathematics.

9. Finally, *Leibniz's doctrine of substance also provides him with his doctrine of freedom.* For the "spontaneity" of the monad, whether natural or spiritual, consists of its self-determination, that is, the determination of its actions and passions by the law of its nature which inheres in them. And this individual nature, being complete and concrete, lies beyond the determination of any of the subordinate regulations which are abstractions from it. Reflexion and memory impart responsibility to spirit monads, but in no way supply their freedom; this resides in the exigencies of the law of each individual substance, and none of Leibniz's distinctions—between metaphysical and moral necessity, or between necessitating and inclining causes—can modify his determinism. The very important distinction between truths of reason and truths of fact, first introduced in the essay *On Freedom* written in the early years in Hanover,[20] supports the contingency of this world as a whole and provides an explanation for man's empirical sense of freedom in his inability to reduce empirical knowledge to logical necessities, but it offers no help toward modifying his determinism. Thus divine creativity enters intimately into man and nature, but only in a way to deprive them of any internal indeterminism or genuine creativity.

IV

It is remarkable that this theory of freedom seems to have satisfied

[19]See Leibniz to Conring (March 1678), PA, 2, 1, 400: "All things occur mechanically in nature; that is, by certain mathematical laws prescribed by God."

[20]*Philosophical Papers and Letters,* trans. Loemker, 1 (Chicago, 1956), 404-410.

all of Leibniz's correspondents; not even Bayle, the alleged free thinker, nor De Volder, the Cartesian, questioned it. Yet they all raised the same question which is closely related to it—how can one explain the lack of "uniformity" in serial events which are determined by internal principles of order? How can sudden changes and abrupt variations occur in any substantial series of events?[21]

It is no doubt true, as Peirce said of Leibniz, that "this great and singular genius was as remarkable for what he failed to see as for what he saw." But clearly his correspondents shared with him this myopia which kept them from considering discontinuity, indeterminism, and other implications of science and moral experience. They were all distrustful of "libertinism," with a greater concern for order and law than for man's willfulness, and a commitment to glorify God, the great monarch and father, rather than the independence of his subjects and children.

The obvious shift in Leibniz's own thinking after 1696 from an emphasis upon logic and panlogism to process, force, and panpsychism does not, however, bring him to regard his theory of substance with greater flexibility. He never relinquishes his theory of the completely determinant concept or law of the individual, though his physical studies of the total force of closed systems of bodies bring considerations of the nature of time, space, and composite bodies to the foreground of his thought, and his historical studies lead him to conjectures about the nature of progress.[22] One must regret the host of distractions, of uncertainties, and of diverse projects which prevented this great creative mind, in the last two decades of his life, from further adapting his metaphysical views to these new concerns. It is in the letters written in answer to his critics that we must find the last refinements of his thought about substance and any tendencies to modify it.

The criticisms of his friends—in particular, of Bayle, De Volder, and Des Bosses—may be treated under a few points:

1. The obscurity of the relationship between the law of the in-

[21]Antoine Arnauld was uneasy about this deterministic doctrine, not because it denied a genuine freedom of choosing alternative actions, but because it implied traducianism—the law of Adam's nature must include not only his own acts but also those of all of his descendents. Letters of March 13 and May 13, 1686, G, 2, 15, 29, etc.

[22]See the concluding paragraph of On the Radical Origination of Things, G, 7, 307-8; and the letter to Bourguet (Aug. 5, 1715), G, 7, 582-83.

dividual and the series of events involved in it. This leads De Volder to suggest several radically different theories of substance—Spinoza's monism on the one hand, and a reification or substantialization of momentary events on the other.

2. A difficulty in accepting the doctrine of preestablished harmony as a solution of the problem of the interrelationship between self-determining substances.

3. The problems of novelty and the need of God creating new monads to explain it.

4. The nature of the spatial, inertial, and dynamic unity of composite bodies. This involves the issue of whether composite bodies can be treated adequately as phenomena, or whether a metaphysical principle, more specific than that of harmony, is needed to explain corporeal unity.

Among the first critics to examine the conclusions put forth by Leibniz in the *New System* was Pierre Bayle, who raised the first two of the above points. He could not understand how a simple substance determined by a law, could undergo so rapid and abrupt a variety of states, even of contradictory states. Nor could he understand how the self-determination of the monad could be compatible with its entering into relations with other monads. Indeed, since a monad's states are expressions solely of a nature created directly by God, how could a monad know (assuming it to be a spirit monad) that other monads exist? Why should it not rather follow that either God and my monad alone exist or that in creating many monads God has created, not one universe but an infinity of them, each one private to an individual substance.[23]

Bayle himself preferred a direct interactionism on the ground that only direct causal intervention can explain the radical transitions which occur in successive states of consciousness.

I understand why a dog passes from pleasure to pain if we strike him with a stick just when he is very hungry and is eating some bread. But that his soul is constructed in such a way that he should feel pain at the moment he is struck even if no one were to strike him, and even if he were to continue to eat bread without difficulty or interruption—this I cannot understand.

---

[23]Des Bosses raises an objection similar to this but the obverse of it. If Leibniz's theory were correct, he says, it would force God, in creating one monad, to produce all the rest, since the monad consists of a series of perceptions of all of them. But this would be a serious limitation to the freedom of God, who is not forced to do anything, G, 2, 493.

To this figure Bayle adds, in the second edition of his *Dictionnaire historique et critique* (1702), a comparison of Leibniz's theory to a ship so constructed that it can arrive at a desired port by itself and without guidance.

In his replies Leibniz once more outlines the theory of harmony implicit in the agreements, i.e., the actual identities, contained in the laws of the different series of actions involved in a system. But the criticisms lead him to a reaffirmation and amplification of his mechanism. The apparent lack of continuity in the actions of an individual results from our overlooking the complex multitude of unconscious perceptions which flow, at every moment, from the law of our nature. Just as a simple (i.e., an irreducible) mathematical function in which one variable contains, in each of its successive values, all of the corresponding values of other variables, yet, in spite of its simplicity, contains maxima, minima, and other variations in curvature, so the present state of every monad is continuous with those which precede and follow, and radical discontinuity seems to appear only because we consider only those perceptions to which we are attentive, or of which we are conscious.[24]

To make a ship which could arrive at a desired port without guidance (which Leibniz admits would be contrary to the nature of a ship), God would have to impose upon it a "particular faculty" extrinsic to its nature. He could do this, but it would have to be, not a Scholastic faculty, but a principle derivable from the laws of mechanics and applicable to the internal forces in the ship. Man himself, Leibniz adds, could make a robot capable of walking about the streets of a city, turning the proper corners, and arriving at a planned destination at the proper time.[25] Similarly, the inbuilt law of the individual series involves a purpose or final cause to which each internal event leads.

Thus there is implicit in Leibniz's reply to Bayle an amplification of his mechanism to include internal controls of the timing of events and "feedbacks" to assure the properly timed adjustments to the monadic environment. In our own century, we are fully conscious of the possibility and the utility of this expanded conception of mechanism, and it is remarkable that Leibniz should have conceived it within

---

[24]G, 4, 518-19. See also De Volder (Jan. 21, 1704), G, 2, 264.
[25]G. 4, 555.

the limits of the mechanical techniques of his day.[26] Yet it is unfortunate that he never showed how such delayed and mutually adjusted actions could arise out of the compound law of the monad; it
would involve a delayed order of successive temporarily operating
principles, all of which must be defined in the complex total individual order. But since, as Leibniz frequently reasserts in the correspondence, time is nothing but the succession of events, as space is
their simultaneity, it is difficult to see how either could function as
principles of determination within the eternal laws themselves.

De Volder's criticisms of the doctrine of substance, though similar
at points to Bayle's, involve certain misunderstandings of Leibniz's
thought which grow out of his Cartesian convictions, and it is not
surprising that the tone of Leibniz's replies to his unyielding repeti-
tiousness sometimes changes from amicable deference to unconcealed
irritation. Yet, as we have seen, he evoked from Leibniz his clearest
and simplest definitions of both simple substances and composite, and
of their relationship.

It is on logical rather than metaphysical grounds that he finds the
doctrine unsupportable. Three points in his criticism are noteworthy.

1. If a substance is simple, as Leibniz claims, in the sense that it
has no parts, then each substance must have a simple attribute and
no two substances can have a common nature. Extension is such a
simple attribute. It follows, then, that contrary to Leibniz's analysis,
force must be a derivative mode of extension and therefore apply only
to composite bodies.

2. If substance is that which is self-contained and conceived in itself, then, as Bayle had maintained, it cannot give rise to such a
variety of divergent successive modes. Perhaps, then, it would be better to regard each momentary state as possessing its own essence and
nature, and therefore as being a momentary substance. Or, alternatively, it might be feasible to accept Spinoza's view that there is only
one eternal substance.[27]

3. How can a persisting law be related to a succession of changing

---

[26]His invention of devices for producing a uniform movement of the pumps of the
windmills used at the Harz silver mines, regardless of the speed of the wind, is an
example of such a mechanism. Leibniz includes the greatest feats of outstanding
arithmeticians in his mechanistic interpretation.

[27]Letter of April 13, 1702, G, 2, 235-38, etc.

states or acts? Or how can an extended body be related to (or appear as the result of) disparate unities?[28]

Leibniz's clearest replies to De Volder's objections (the last two of which both Bayle and Des Bosses also raise) are found in his letters of July 6, 1701, April, 1702, June 20, 1703, and (to the last) Jan. 19, 1706.[29] De Volder's proposals lead him not merely to reexamine the logical conception of substance and its implications for dynamic theory, but also to discuss such related problems as the spatial and temporal nature of intersubstantial relations.

Many years earlier he had criticized Spinoza's definition of substance as that which is in itself and is understood through itself; his comment was that though substance may be regarded as in itself (this being true of his monads) it cannot be understood through itself.[30] He had also had misgivings about Spinoza's definition of attributes. Now, to De Volder, he expresses his unhappiness with the innovation which attaches attributes to substance rather than to God, and gives a conclusive proof that substances with differing but simple attributes cannot ever undergo a series of modifications or enter into relationship with each other. The variations within things and the interrelatedness among them require that substances have complex essences with some simple natures in common. It is this latter requirement which makes possible the "sympathy" which exists between monads.[31]

Extension, Leibniz asserts, is not a simple attribute since it is compounded of number, continuity, and simultaneity; nor can it be a source of derivative force or power since the passive cannot give rise to the active. Extension is in fact an abstraction from the concrete temporal-spatial order of events given in our experience. In correcting Descartes' physics by accepting the primacy of force, De Volder must also make force prior to extension. Since "space is the order of possible coexistents and time is the order of possible inconsistents," both space and time "enter into all things," corporeal and incorporeal for "every change, spiritual as well as material, has its own place

[28]Letter of January 5, 1706, G, 2, 279.

[29]G, 2, 224-28, 239-41, 248-53, 280.

[30]In the *Notes on the Ethics of Spinoza* (1678), G, 1, 139.

[31]G, 2, 240. Years later Leibniz accuses Newton of having restored the old doctrine of the sympathists through his conception of gravity as a force acting at a distance. But this is in the realm of *phenomena bene fundata* where abstract descriptive laws prevail; Newton's famous scholium in the second edition of the *Principia* shows the two men to be in agreement.

(sedes), so to speak, in the order of time as well as its own situation *(situs)* in the order of space."[32] Time is a dimension of the serial order of monadic events, space a dimension of simultaneous events. Hence our experience of space rests upon the perceptual relations of the monads, and all perception has a spatial as well as a temporal dimension.

Leibniz's general answer to the question raised by all of his critics —what uniformity there can be in a series of acts and passions of such great apparent variation and continuity—is that given to De Volder: their only uniformity is that they follow from a uniform law.

To De Volder's suggestion that the problem of sudden and abrupt variations in serial events might better be solved by the Cartesian theory of the momentary creation by God of successive individual substances without duration, Leibniz makes no specific reply. Though he agrees that God's creativity is operative continuously in each monad, he cannot agree that the individual law or concept in which God's nature is effective can be eliminated from his creation, and the series reduced to momentary substantial complexes of perception, sensory feeling, and appetition. For this would remove any permanent dispositional ground for the unity of the monadic series, and no source of its primary force or dynamism.

It has remained for thinkers of our own times, notably for Whitehead, to develop the theory suggested by De Volder which resolves each temporal continuity of being into momentary occasions, though this is done in the interest, not of the divine power, but of an intrinsic novelty and creativity. But the modern view, in turn, has the problem of explaining the presence of enduring experiences and permanent dispositions in a continuous temporary succession of new events. The choice between Leibniz and Whitehead on this matter seems to be between deriving novelty and spontaneity from abiding order (which is impossible) or deriving order from spontaneity and novelty (which has its difficulties too).

The "perpetual progress" which Leibniz comes to see both in the life of the monad and in the world[33] would seem to involve novelty and creativity, but he prefers to consider it as growth determined by a

---

[32]G, 2, 253; see also 263. In another context, however, Leibniz writes to Des Bosses (May 26, 1712), G, 2, 444: "In themselves monads have no situation with respect to each other, that is, no real order which reaches beyond the order of phenomena."

[33]See note 22, above.

predetermined law, after the analogy of the biological preformation theories of his day. Each present is always considered as "a natural consequence of its preceding state, in such a way that the present is great with the future."[34]

Only one concession does Leibniz make toward the recognition of true novelty, and this is made reluctantly in the midst of the long correspondence on substance with Bartholomew Des Bosses. This discussion with a learned Jesuit mathematician and theologian turned about theological issues. It is known chiefly for the discussion of the *vinculum substantiale*, a metaphysical solution which had been proposed by certain post-Tridentine theologians to explain the unitary properties of extension, mass, and motion, of composite bodies and to give them the metaphysical status needed, among other considerations, in the doctrine of transubstantiation.

The concession forced by Des Bosses is related to this problem, but also to that of the origin of the soul. Leibniz has argued that a spermatic animal can develop into a rational animal, and therefore an unthinking, unreflective substance into a spirit monad. Des Bosses, who has earlier argued for a free interaction between monads as a source of the changes between them, maintains that this change from sperm to spirit would involve the creation, at a particular point of time, of a new monad, since the individual law of a dormant monad with only unconscious perceptions could hardly be the same as the law of a conscious, reflective monad. Leibniz, on the other hand, prefers to consider such a transformation a "transcreation" within the specifications of one single individual serial law. But he is willing at length to admit that

. . . it is possible for God to create new monads. Yet I do not assert that new monads have been created by God.[35]

"Transcreation" within a determinate serial order can hardly be considered as more than equivocation. The possibility of God's creating new monads as filiations of old ones moves in the direction of De Volder's suggestion of the creation of a succession of temporally lim-

34*Monadology*, section 22, G, 6, 61. Leibniz generally recognizes that monads grow in proportion to their activity, and that the law of their nature is thus not only teleologically defined but a law of growth. Cf. *Discourse*, section 15: "Whenever anything exercises its virtue and power, that is to say when it acts, it improves and enlarges itself in proportion to its action."

35To Des Bosses (April 30, 1709), G, 2, 371.

ited substances. But Leibniz could take no further step toward limited indeterminacy and creativity within creation. The demands of
his own panlogism on the one hand, and the theological temper of
the time on the other, which distrusted libertinism, prevented him
from drawing the consequences of his own belief in progress, spontaneity, and moral responsibility. The choice of actions remained
God's, the responsibility for them, man's.

The central issue underlying the discussion remains. It is this: admitted that individual substance involves a series of actions or events
determined by an immanent but perduring law, how is the unity of
the two to be conceived and expressed? To this question Leibniz has
no answer save the traditional one that law is to its included events
as subject which includes its predicates—(whether permanent or
changing) or as function to its variable values. This remains the
mystery of the Platonic idea, active in bringing about imitation and
participation, and Leibniz finally replies to De Volder as he had already done to Father Tournemine when that Jesuit leader had
pressed him on the nature of the union of soul and body: This union
"is not a phenomenon and there is no concept and therefore no
knowledge of it."[36] The only empirical clue, which does not reach
the mystery, is the dynamic force of conscious perceptions arising out
of habits or faculties.

V

The lasting force of Leibniz's doctrine of substance can be seen
in our own time, in spite of our nominalistic aversion to persisting
laws and determinants. His achievement was the reduction of substance to ordered process, and the criticisms of the traditional empiricists, aimed at a substratum theory, did not really touch it, since
the law of the individual, though not an object of experience, can be
approached, both in science and in reflective self-awareness, through
rational analysis.

It remains to ask, however, how his doctrine must be modified to
do justice to freedom, genuine spontaneity and creativity, a real responsiveness to environmental changes, and moral decision and responsibility. All of these seem to demand a linear continuity of actions

with momentary freedom from any total determinant—logical or mechanical.

In his letter of July 20, 1715, Des Bosses argues that a system of interacting substances is "in greater conformity with the divine wisdom" than one in which individuals do not so influence each other.

Which architect will deserve credit for greater wisdom in his art (he asks), one whose entire craftsmanship consists in his choosing stones that are not only already exactly square but also so fitted to each other by their nature that a most magnificent palace is put together out of them because of the mere fact that they have been brought together in one place . . . just as the Theban walls sprang up to the lyre of Amphion . . . Or is that architect rather to be preferred who constructs an equally beautiful palace from stones unfinished by nature and not corresponding to each other in such harmony, but which must be fitted by craftsmanship and adjusted in time and place?

Lebniz replies with a third alternative.

In reply to your analogy, I admit that the architect who rightly fits stones together acts with greater art than one who has found the stones already so prepared by someone else that they fall into order when merely brought together. But on the other hand I believe you will admit that the craftsmanship of the architect who can so prepare stones in advance will be infinitely greater still.[37]

Stones, it will be admitted, are poor analogies to monads. But their use does reveal an obliviousness on the part of both Leibniz and his critic, to the significance of his panpsychism. To fit contemporary thought one would have to force the analogy further in one of two possible directions. Either the living "stones," the individual components of the cosmic structure, can freely develop their own forms, without preformation by a determining architect or law, so effectively that through their efforts a beautiful palace comes into shape of itself, without architect—this is the way of creative intelligence, and many find it difficult to hold in our century. Or a builder—perhaps no longer an architect—is needed to assume a role, "consequent" to the individual's creative development of his own form, of redeeming the flaws and unfitnesses and building the best edifice possible under the circumstances. (Or there may be no building, and no possibility of one) .

Whitehead is right, it seems, in showing that the choice is not between a panlogism and a panpsychism, or between spontaneity and order, but rather about the proper relationship between the two. Life cannot be subjugated to logic, and the issue is how logic is properly subordinated to life. Recent metaphysics seems to be showing clearly that it is not necessary to reduce logic entirely to an instrument of creative purpose, but that a logically definable order may develop within a field of serial choices or self-determinations *and* interactions.

Such an order is needed as a regulative principle both for science and for human morals and values. Leibniz's theory provides the former, since his overlapping individual concepts or laws assure the validity of infinite empirical analysis, synthesis, and generalization. But he is deficient in the latter, for ethics requires that creativity burst through the determinism of law, but also that creativity operate with responsibility through the increasing regularity and persistence of disposition and purpose.

The traces of the development of a new notion of substance are to be found in recent discussions (though the new concept may be to the old very much as the lingering smile is to the vanished Cheshire cat). Russell has set up as a fundamental postulate of science the relationships of "compresence" and "causal linearity" among a pluralism of space-time events to explain the continuity of structure in space and time respectively.[38] Frederic Fitch follows him in asserting the individual sufficiency of "causal chains of primary occasions" which he calls substances.[39] And Nathaniel Lawrence has defined the person as a causal chain of primary occasions of longer duration, of greater discontinuity, but characterized by "value, volition, attitude, disposition, etc."[40] Thus substance as causal-formal "persistence" (Weiss) or "continuant" (Gotshalk) is reappearing in a reconsideration of the conservative aspect of fixation in creative serial orders. Yet the task of defining the proper relationship between the self-determination of an individual series and its interaction with other partly self-determined series is still incomplete. Leibniz was partly right;

[38]B. Russell, *Human Knowledge, its Scope and Limits* (New York, 1948), 196, 459, et passim.

[39]F.B. Fitch, "Sketch of a Philosophy," in I. Leclerc, *The Relevance of Whitehead* (London, 1961), 95-97.

[40]*Ibid.*, 163.

there is an individual nature which determines us, though not completely. But he was wrong in denying that our free choices can help determine our complete individual nature, and that the influence of other environing persons and things somehow also plays a role in this.

LEROY E. LOEMKER

EMORY UNIVERSITY

STUDIES IN THE PHILOSOPHY OF RELIGION

THE ELUCIDATION OF RELIGIOUS STATEMENTS

I T IS generally recognized that talk about God stands in need of clarification. In this paper I shall address myself not directly to that task of clarification, but to the prior task of determining how such clarification is to be carried out.

I

Consider the following statements:

(1) God made the heavens and the earth.
(2) God watches over the affairs of men.
(3) God has commanded us to love our neighbors.
(4) God forgives the sins of those who truly turn unto Him.
(5) God spoke to the prophets in days of old.
(6) God has comforted me in my distress.
(7) God will guide me in whatever I undertake.

It is no accident that this list is made up exclusively of action-sentences; they are the crux of the problem. It is essential for any religion, with the possible exception of extreme mystical sects and highly intellectualized fringe groups like Humanism, that God make effective contact with His worshippers and vice versa. This involves thinking of God as acting toward us and reacting to our actions. Moreover the other sorts of statements we make about God, e.g., attribute-statements, depend on action statements for their meaning. To call God merciful is to imply that He will sometimes perform acts of forgiveness. To call Him wise or just implies that His decisions, commands, judgments will exhibit wisdom or justice. God's freedom consists in the independence of His actions from any external compulsion.

These sentences are puzzling in a way that sentences about tables and chairs are not. We know perfectly well how to handle furniture-sentences in the contexts in which they are commonly used. It is only their "analysis" in some abstruse philosophical sense which is puzzling. But sentences about God are likely to seem strange even in their native habitat. In the course of using them in religion we are apt to become baffled over what implications they have, what they exclude or do not exclude, and how they are appropriately supported or attacked. It is the primary, garden variety sort of understanding that needs attention. Therefore what I want to ask is: how can one give an adequate account of what is meant by such a sentence?

II

It might seem that the task of elucidation falls into two parts, corresponding to subject and predicate. We need to make clear Who these statements are about (to Whom 'God' refers), and what is being said about Him (what 'made' or 'forgives' means in this context). With respect to any particular sentence these jobs are no doubt distinguishable. In (1) e.g., 'Who is God?' can't raise just the same problem as 'What does 'made' mean here?' They could receive the same answer only if the initial answer to the first question could be 'The maker of heaven and earth'. And to answer it in this way would be to interpret (1) as saying 'The maker of heaven and earth made heaven and earth'. Nevertheless over the long haul the questions merge. Although with respect to (1) we cannot answer 'Who is God?' by 'The maker of heaven and earth', we can only answer by using some other such phrase, 'the most perfect being', 'the father of our Lord Jesus Christ', 'He Who spoke to the prophets'; and these phrases raise exactly the same problems as the predicate terms 'is the most perfect being', 'is the father of our Lord Jesus Christ', and 'spoke to the prophets'. That is, the problem of explaining the subject-term is identical with the problem of explaining the meaning certain key predicate terms have when used in conjunction with this subject-term. It could be otherwse only if one could teach someone Who God is by means other than the citation of descriptive phrases, e.g., by pointing or in some way getting the pupil to notice the object. As there is no reliable way of determining whether an individual is noticing God at a given time, this method is not available.

III

In explaining "God forgives our sins" it is natural to begin with talk about men forgiving each other. Indeed this is what we always do when we teach a child to talk about God. We presuppose that he already knows what it is to speak of men forgiving, making, speaking, or comforting; if he doesn't, we see to it that he learns. Is there any alternative? Could we teach a child to talk about God before he has learned to talk about men? Only if we could do something like pointing to instances where God is forgiving, speaking, or making. And this seems impossible, for the reason mentioned in the last paragraph. In fact, the problem is even more acute here. To ostensively define the predicates we would need not only a reliable way of determining that a person was noticing God at a particular time, but also a reliable way of determining that he was noticing a particular activity of God. Otherwise there would be no reason to suppose that he was attaching the right meaning to the word.

Is this impossibility a matter of fact or of logic? Let us see whether we can envisage a state of affairs in which it would be possible. Let us suppose that I could tell whether someone is having an experience of the sort I would call an experience of the presence of God, without having to rely on the person's report that he is having such an experience. How I would tell is not important. It might be by a certain unique bodily attitude and demeanor. Or it might be that I had discovered that certain mental states or combinations of mental states for which there are objective criteria—e.g., humility, receptivity, or despair—are regularly correlated with that sort of experience. And now suppose that I teach a child to say 'God is forgiving me' every time I notice that he is having such an experience; and let us further assume that the child does not yet know how to talk of men forgiving each other, or indeed how to talk of men acting on each other in any way at all. If these conditions were satisfied, could I then teach a child to talk about God without having to depend on his mastery of talk about men? I fear not. From this instruction the child would simply have learned to use the words, 'God is forgiving me' to report, or express, a certain state of mind. It would be like learning to say 'God damn' to express irritation. Even if he is taught a whole range of God-sentences, he will have no basis for regarding the constant recurrence of 'God' as anything more than a reflection of a generic similarity in the experiences. He would miss the point. This brings out the way in which the objective reference of God-sentences is borrowed from the prior application of their predicate terms to human beings. We can use 'Jones has forgiven me' to talk about something objective, because we have public tests of its truth or falsity. It is our prior mastery of this sort of sentence that leads us to give 'God has forgiven me' an objective reference too, even in the absence of such tests. Take away the human model, and we are left, even in the conditions we are imagining, with an expression of a state of mind.

IV

Thus we get, and must get, the terms we apply to God from our talk about men. This is the first principle of religious semantics. And the second is equally important: in talk about God these terms no longer have their primary or literal meaning; their sense as well as their application has shifted. This is a familiar point, but lest familiarity breed contempt for the complexities involved, I want to consider it with some care.

Just how the senses differ depends on the ground rules for the particular religion, sect, or theology. A great many Christian theologians have felt called upon to deny that God exists in time. Mystical philosophies like the Vedanta deny that any distinctions at all can be made in God; this doctrine is found in a weakened form in Aquinas and other orthodox Christian theologians. Using these denials it is easy to show that action terms change their sense when applied to God. Surely it is logically necessary for a human command, supervision, or pardon to take time for its performance, and for a man's commanding to be distinguishable from his forgiving. But this is too easy. The rules look tailor-made for the occasion. In fact these denials, I believe, have been foisted onto the Judeo-Christian tradition by a coalition of mystics and speculative philosophers for purposes of their own, purposes which have little basis in religious thoughts, actions, attitudes, and feelings of most devout souls of this or any other tradition. In order to assure relevance to conceptions actually entertained in religious activity, I shall base my discussion on the very widespread denial that God has a body.

When I say 'My mother forgave me', I imply, or presuppose, that she performed some appropriate overt action, i.e., some action which could be publicly observed, i.e., would have been observed by any normal observer who was on the scene. There is no specific action, or sort of action, which I imply that she performed. It is not necessary that she said "I forgive you", or indeed that she said anything at all. Her forgiveness may have taken the form of a reassuring smile or a pat on the cheek. But if nothing of the sort took place, then she did not forgive me. I might still say "She has forgiven me in her heart". This does not imply that any appropriate overt action has taken place, or even that it will. She might conceivably go to her grave without betraying the fact that she has forgiven me, and continuing to act as if she still holds it against me. But it does imply that she might perform an overt act of the appropriate sort, and that she will do so in the absence of special reasons to the contrary. Thus it implies that it makes sense to talk of her performing such acts and that I would recognize them if they were performed.

Essential connections with bodily activity are found in other predicates from our initial list. 'Speaks' is a very clear case. If I say 'Smith spoke to me this morning' I certainly imply that Smith produced sounds which could be heard by any person with normal hearing who was close enough; and the standards for 'close enough' cannot be made impossibly strict. If other non-deaf people in the vicinity didn't hear anything, then Smith didn't really speak to me. I was 'hearing things'.

Clearly when we apply such predicates to an immaterial God, no such implications hold. I can say 'God has forgiven my sins' without being prepared to specify any utterance, embrace, or smile equally perceivable by all bystanders; I may say 'God has spoken to me' and stubbornly hold onto it in the face of a failure by others in the vicinity to hear anything. Nor would I be thought unreasonable, or deficient in understanding, in doing so. (It will be noted that I have shifted from general to particular God-sentences; e.g., from 'God forgives the sins of those who truly turn unto Him' to 'God has forgiven my sins'. But this is quite proper. I certainly cannot understand what it is for God to forgive sins in general, or in certain sorts of conditions, unless I understand what it would be for God to forgive my sins or your sins.)

All this comes out implicitly in ordinary religious instruction. The child who asks where God is, what He looks like, when He is coming, etc., is told that God can't be seen nor heard, nor is He located anywhere, because He is a pure spirit. What is not usually clearly recognized is the problem this raises. We begin by using 'makes', 'forgives', etc., as if we were using them in their familiar senses in which they apply to parents and neighbors, in order to give information about another person who is, unfortunately, out of sight. Then we stack the cards (or rather the cards are stacked by the nature of religion) so as to make these senses inapplicable. This raises, or should raise, the question: Then in what sense are these terms being used? Now obviously this sense, though different from the literal sense, is derived from it and has some continuity with it. Divine forgiving is more like human forgiving than it is like human commanding. That is the point of the necessity of the literal sense as a starting point. Hence the problem can be put: In just what way does the theological use of the term deviate from its 'anthropological' use? I now want to consider how one might go about answering this question.

V

At this point we might do well to turn to other cases where terms are given a derivative, non-literal use, and where we know how to handle the situation. The whole spectrum of metaphorical and figurative uses, so prominent in our discourse, plain and fancy, presents cases which fit this bill.
Consider:

> He blew his top.
> There is a power vacuum in the Middle East.
> Religion has been corroded by the acids of modernity.

Clearly 'blew . . . top' is being used here in a way derivative from its literal employment with respect to steam engines and oil wells. How could we go about explaining to a puzzled listener what is meant? There are at least three ways:
(1)   Provide a literal way of saying the same thing, i.e., a way which does not involve using any terms in a derivative sense. "He suddenly became violently angry".
(2)   Make explicit the features common to the top blowing off a boiler and a man becoming violently angry, i.e., the features which are common to the two senses of the term and make the derived sense appropriate. In this case they would include vigorous random motion, explosive sounds, a sudden discharge of energy.
(3)   Simply point out or describe a situation where the term would be used in the derivative sense, and instruct the pupil to find the common features. This is how the sensitive reader grasps fresh metaphors in poetry.
For talk about God (1) and (3) are not available, and for basically the same reason. (3) is out because, as we have seen, there are no reliable ways of showing someone a case of God forgiving, command-

ing, or making. We can *describe* such a case, but that involves using
words in the way we are trying to explicate. (1) is out because there
can be no literal way of talking about God. And this is because the
impossibility of ostensively defining any theological term leaves us no
alternative to deriving its theological use from a non-theological use.
Of course we can define some theological terms by means of others.
Thus we can define "omnipotent" by "able to perform any act". But
again the definiens contain words used in just the way about which
we are trying to get clear. We can even introduce new terms, e.g.,
"divine", "holy", which have their primary application to God; the
theological use of these terms is not derivative from their
non-theological use. But like 'God', their use has to be explained in
some way, and it seems that this can be done only by bringing in
words whose primary use is elsewhere. This recourse can be delayed,
but only delayed, by using other special theological terms which raise
the same problem. 'Divine' means holy. And 'holy' means, in part,
numinous. But now 'numinous' (or some further member of the
series) will have to be explained, as Rudolf Otto does, by bringing in
a lot of words which have a primary meaning elsewhere—'mysterious', 'powerful', etc. . . The situation can be exhibited more clearly
by talking in terms of uses rather than words. Any theological use of
a word is derivative from a non-theological use of *some* word; derivative just in the sense that the former cannot be taught without employing the latter. This is enough to invalidate method (1), an essential condition of which is that there be some way of saying the
same thing which does not raise the same sort of problems.

VI

This leaves (2). Is there any way in which we can specify the
components of the literal sense of 'forgives' which carry over to the
theological sense? When we remove all the bodily activity involved in
forgiving, commanding, etc., what is left? Perhaps a correlated mental
state. We must tread carefully here. It has often been assumed that
every deliberate action is the outward expression of a private mental
action, which is the real core of the performance and to which the
overt behavior is an inessential accompaniment. Thus when I say 'I
forgive you', my utterance is simply the outward manifestation of the
real forgiving which is taking place behind the scenes. Or at the least,

every deliberate or intentional action is prefaced by a volition to perform that action. Since this view has been decisively criticized by Gilbert Ryle and others, I shall not appeal to any such ghostly doubles of overt actions. But in the flush of victory over these hoary prejudices we should not lose sight of the fact that there commonly are private mental states accompanying overt actions, and that there is some pattern to these accompaniments. Volitions are psychological myths, but *sometimes* an action is preceded by a non-publicly observable decision, intention or resolution to perform the act. Acts of forgiveness and comforting are *often* accompanied by feelings of sympathy, compassion, and tenderness, and by private resolutions not to hold a grudge. Commands are *often* privately rehearsed before their official promulgation and are often issued in a stern frame of mind. Faced with the task of interpreting these words as applied to an immaterial being it is tempting to retreat to these private accompaniments and suppose that they are what is being asserted to go on. Thus 'God has forgiven X's sins' would mean something like 'God has said to Himself 'I forgive X's sins', God feels compassion toward X, and God does not feel grudges or resentments against X'. 'God watches over the affairs of men' would mean 'God has experiences which correspond exactly to what is going on in the world'. 'God commands us to love our neighbors' would mean 'God privately rehearses the command: Love thy neighbor as thyself'. I shall henceforth refer to this mode of explanation as the 'whittle-down method'.[1]

This sort of interpretation is less grotesque in some places than in others. It is not obviously absurd to think of God's judgments on my acts, or his knowledge of what I am doing (Divine knowledge involves some *very* thorny problems which I cannot go into here.) as consisting solely in private conscious states. But this obviously won't do for making, forgiving, commanding, and watching over. Forgiving me can't just consist in feeling well disposed and not feeling resentment, nor does watching over human affairs simply consist in registering sensations of what is going on. If these acts are to retain their religious point, they must involve some contact with the worshipper. God's private feelings and soliloquies are not enough. They must get

[1]This term was suggested to me by some remarks of I. M. Crombie. See *New Essays in Philosophical Theology*, ed. A. Flew and A. Macintyre (London: SCM Press, 1955), p. 122.

through somehow to the human being. The former might be enough for a deist, who simply makes a formal assent to the existence of God and passes on, but it is woefully inadequate to an actually functioning religion. Pure thought thinking itself is of no use to religion, whatever attractions it may have for speculation.

No doubt this can be patched up. Where some impact on the worshipper is involved in what we mean by 'God . . .', we can introduce a reference to such impacts into our explanation. Thus 'God has forgiven me' means not only that God has private mental states like those which accompany human acts of forgiving, but also that I have feelings of release from guilt, of being accepted, of a profound peace, etc., i.e., feelings like those I have when a man has forgiven me. And part of which is meant by 'God has spoken to me' will be that I have experiences something like those I typically have when a man for whom I have a very high regard speaks to me, e.g., hearing a voice speak with authority, being seized with a sudden conviction, having a sudden sense of illumination, etc. Of course no one of these experiences has to be present. And even an open-ended class of experiences has a very loose connection with the divine action. I may say 'God has forgiven me' when nothing like this happens. ("I know that God has forgiven me, for the Bible promises that He will forgive those who truly turn unto Him, but I still feel dreadfully oppressed and guilty. What is wrong?") But we can admit exceptional cases while continuing to insist that the presence for the most part, of experiences of this sort is part of what is meant by 'God has forgiven me'. If people did not often have such experiences when they said 'God has forgiven me', the concept of divine forgiveness would be quite different. Compare this with the meaning of 'sad'. It is logically possible for a person to be sad without looking droopy, acting in a lethargic manner, speaking quietly, brooding, etc. But it is not logically possible for people, as a rule, to be sad without exhibiting behavior of this sort. If a man consistently said 'I feel sad' when he was acting exuberant, we would conclude that he did not know the meaning of 'sad'.

VII

But patching up the account is futile. The whole approach is defective in very fundamental ways. To bring these out I shall ask whether one who had been given this instruction would be able to use 'God forgives the sins of those who truly turn unto Him'. Suppose the following questions are raised

(1) How can I know whether this is true?
(2) How can I tell whether I really believe this?
(3) How do I go about truly turning unto Him?
(4) Why should I truly turn unto Him? Why should I care whether God has forgiven my sins?

Has the instruction provided a basis for answering these questions?
   (1) Answers that might be given to (1) are

A. On the authority of the Bible.
B. You can't know, at least not now. Now you can only believe. You will know this to be the case only by the long range consequences of your actions. If, e.g., you humbly confess your sins now, and then lead a blissful existence after death, that will show that this statement is true, or at least be very strong evidence in its favor.
C. The only way one can know is by directly experiencing God's forgiveness. If you have not experienced it, proofs are of no avail; if you have, they are not needed.
D. This question cannot arise. There is no such thing as knowing this. When we utter this sentence we are simply expressing a sense of being forgiven, a sense of cosmic acceptance. We are expressing this feeling by telling a story about a supreme person. There is no point in asking how we know this is really so. The only questions are whether one has this feeling and whether this story is a good expression of it.

Does the whittle-down explanation help the pupil to choose between these answers? I can't see that it does. Its impotence is underlined by the fact that any of the respondents could have accepted the whittle-down explication. Each could have agreed that, as he talks about God, God's forgiveness is like a man's forgiveness only with respect to certain private mental states and certain typical feelings in the forgiven. Their divergences develop beyond this point. They all take the same basis from the literal use of the word, but then they do very different things with it, e.g., make predictions about the future course of experience, express a state of feeling, or report what one perceives (or thinks he perceives). It is *these* differences that are responsible for their diverse responses to the demand for justification. And the salient fact is that these differences cannot be expressed by drawing further similarities or dissimilarities between human and divine forgiveness. It is not that the person who maintains answer "C" thinks divine forgiveness is like, or unlike, human forgiveness in a way that doesn't agree with the person who offers answer "D". Their description of God's forgiveness might be couched in exactly the same terms. It is what they do with the whole description that differs. Just as two men might describe King Arthur in exactly the same terms, agree completely as to what he is like, while one meant to be giving an historically accurate account, the other to be creating or narrating a piece of fiction.

(2)   What is it to believe that God forgives my sins if I truly turn unto Him? The whittle-down explanation would suggest that it simply consists in entertaining the emasculated concept which has been derived, perhaps along with a feeling of conviction. But surely having a religious belief involves more than this; and this approach gives no hint as to what that something more might be. It tells us what it isn't, viz., having the sort of sensory expectations which would be involved in believing that a man would forgive me under certain conditions. But it does nothing to replace these deletions. (It might seem that on this approach the belief would involve expecting feelings of release from guilt, etc. after one had humbly confessed. But, as we have seen, one can believe that God has forgiven one, even when no such feelings occur.)

(3)   Our pupil will be at a loss when it comes actually to making the turn. The whittle-down approach gives no help here. How does one address an immaterial being? Why do it in one place, posture, or attitude rather than another? Should one make the address silently or aloud? Alone or in concert? However we do it, what constitutes it an address *to God*, rather than talking to ourselves or an imaginary conversation? The use of the word 'God' is not sufficient. I might use that word in an imaginary conversation. "But this isn't pretence. I firmly believe that God is aware of what I am saying." If God is omniscient, He is aware of everything that happens. This can't mark out certain utterances as being addressed to Him. "But I *intend* Him to hear these. They are directed to Him." This is where we started. What is it to direct a confession to Him? In functioning religions we find standard methods for doing this. Sometimes confessions are to be made through an authorized representative, sometimes with the accompaniment of certain gestures, sometimes in certain postures. But from the analogies exploited by the whittle-down method one could anticipate neither the existence nor the nature of these methods. The

method fails to connect sentences about God to the religious activities which they both guide and reflect.

(4) A salient feature of the logic of 'God' is the impossibility of indifference. God is a matter of "passionate interest" (Kierkegaard), an object of "ultimate concern" (Tillich). A man who says "Oh yes, I know God made and sustains me, judges me, and died for my sins to save me.", then yawns and turns to the sports page, is not merely idiosyncratic. He is exhibiting a semantic failure, a misunderstanding of 'God'. His yawn pragmatically contradicts what he said, in the way one would contradict himself if he said, "We must all work together for the common good", while making a killing in wheat futures on the basis of inside information. To define 'God' in such a way as to leave concern an open question is to commit an analogue of what G. E. Moore calls the naturalistic fallacy in ethics. And the whittle-down method does just that. A set of disembodied conscious states, with or without a pure ego or soul substance, may or may not inspire passionate interest. It will probably leave all but the speculative quite unmoved. To be sure, one could hardly be indifferent to the feelings of release from guilt, etc., but this does not help. It is surely a perversion of religious belief to be interested in one's religious experiences, but not in what God does or is. The problem is to exhibit their relationship in such a way that we see how the interest aroused by the former is also directed on to the latter. The most the whittle-down method can do to bridge the gap between these twin privacies is to take the divine conscious state as the cause (in some mysterious way) of the human feelings. But this won't really do; for, as we have seen, religious people are often prepared to say that God has forgiven them when no such feelings are forthcoming, and the divine forgiveness does not lose its interest on these occasions.

VIII

These deficiencies all have a common root and all point in the same direction. The basic trouble is that in removing overt behavior from forgiving, commanding, etc. (and even more if we remove temporal sequence too) we have taken these terms out of the language game in which they primarily function without replacing it by another. In etherealizing these action concepts we snip off the rules which normally govern their use—rules which stipulate what is relevant evidence for an application of the term, what constitutes believing that the term applies in a certain case, in what contexts it is appropriate to use the term, to what attitudes, if any, an application of the term commits one, etc. So long as we merely explain God's forgiveness, as being like human forgiveness except that there is no bodily activity, we have taken away an essential condition of the literal use of 'forgives' without indicating what is to be put in its place. At this point we have but a fragment of a meaning. We don't yet know how to use 'God has forgiven my sins'—we don't know what would count for or against its truth, what sorts of implications it has, or what to do about it.

There are other ranges of discourse in which similar problems arise, e.g., scientific explanations couched in terms of unobservable entities conceived by analogy with observable ones. Psychoanalytic theory is a good example. We find Freud saying things like:

At the very beginning all the libido is accumulated in the id, while the ego is still in process of formation or far from robust. Part of this libido is sent out by the id into erotic object—cathexes, whereupon the ego, now growing stronger, attempts to obtain possession of the object-libido and to force itself upon the id as a love-object.[2]

It is clear that this cannot be construed literally. The ego and the id are not different persons. We can hardly suppose that conflicts between the ego and *id* might take the form of a fist-fight, nor can we picture the ego making eyes at the *id,* or the *id* making a pass at the ego. Then what is being said? We could try to explain it by the whittle-down method. The *id* is like a lustful brute, but without a body, and not even a glimmer of reason, etc. The ego is like a prudent business man, except for analogous restrictions. We can picture each as a cartoonist's model in which all personality functions but one have atrophied. This gives us a picture, but we still don't know what to do with it. We don't know how to test the statement, when to say that this attraction has taken place, what role it might have in the formation of neuroses, etc. For that we must go beyond similarities and differences, and depict the use to which the picture is put, the rules which govern that use. We must make explicit the sort of behavior which is to be expected in particular cases when this attraction does or does not take place; we must specify some way of (at least roughly)

2S. Freud, *The Ego and the Id,* tr. J. Riviere (London: Hogarth Press, 1927), p. 65.

measuring the amount of energy possessed by the ego or *id* at a particular time. Until such jobs are done, we are merely amusing ourselves with fables.

It seems that the whittle-down method is effective when both literal and non-literal use belong to the same "language-stratum" (Waismann). This is the case with 'He blew his top' and 'There is a power vacuum in the Middle East'. The same *sort* of checks and tests, implication patterns, etc., hold for both 'That boiler blew its top' and 'Jones blew his top'; for example, both can be tested by observing the individual in question. Since they carry over from the primary to the derivative use they don't have to be explicitly mentioned in making the transition. We can confine ourselves to spelling out detailed differences between boilers blowing their tops and men blowing their tops. But when we go from an observable human being to a non-observable sub-system of the psyche, or from an embodied action to an action of a purely immaterial being, the usual sort of rules is no longer applicable, and we are forced to put something in their place explicitly. An immaterial person isn't simply another kind of person in the way a disagreeable or a talented person is, or even in the way a power vacuum is a different kind of vacuum from an air vacuum.

IX

The way forward is clear. By drawing analogies we get a picture, with taboos against using it in familiar ways. What is needed is a positive description of the ways in which it is to be used. More specifically the theistic picture could be, and has been, put to the following uses:

(1) Explanation of facts in the natural world.
(2) Matrix for predictions of the future course of events.
(3) Expression of feelings and attitudes.
(4) Imaginative presentation of moral ideals.
(5) Report of what is perceived in religious experience.
(6) Guide to worship.

This list is not complete. Furthermore it is obvious that these items are not necessarily mutually exclusive. But it serves as an indication of the diversity with which we are confronted. What we must do is to trace out in detail the various ways in which religious statements function in one or another of these dimensions. Clarification of talk about God awaits progress on this task.

WILLIAM P. ALSTON

UNIVERSITY OF MICHIGAN

DEVOTION AND FANATICISM

THE SEARCH for meaning is a basic aspect of human existence, and I believe that academic philosophy, as an attempt to help men fulfil this vital need in a careful and disciplined way, should be in close touch with life. At the present time, however, in the Anglo-Saxon countries there is a deep chasm between professional philosophy and existence as it is lived in the concrete, which I believe is not healthy for either one. One indication of this is the widespread tendency to identify existential engagement with a fanaticism and dogmatism which have no place in the unbiased, objective investigations of a free university. Since it is hard to exist as a human being without becoming concerned and "biased" in some way, this kind of argument has not helped to keep professional philosophy in touch with the objects of our concrete experience and with the concerns of living men.

I do not believe that this argument is sound, and in this paper I shall present an argument on the other side. I also believe that it is appropriate to present this to Charles Hartshorne, whom I have known for many years, and whom I regard as a disciplined and original thinker who is at the same time actively concerned with lived experience. All who know him are aware of his amazing capacity to bring out the meaning of a haphazard incident that arises during a taxi ride to an official meeting, or on a casual walk through a city park. He can bring basic aspects of his philosophy to bear on the call of a bird or the flavor of Indian tea. His reflections are not isolated in a separate compartment of his mind. They are merged and fused with his life. I believe that what he says and what he writes wells up from a deep personal concern for life, and for the current problems, aesthetic, moral, and religious, of living man. I think of him as a philosopher who is engaged, concerned. And yet, though I have been involved in controversies with him, I cannot think of him as fanatical or dogmatic. I have always found him ready to listen, and flexible in mind. Hence I present to him this attempt to distinguish between two kinds of commitment, the devoted and the fanatical. I do not, of course, suppose that he will agree with very much that I shall say. But I think he will understand the question, and that he has thought about it. Perhaps these few suggestions may stimulate him to find a better resolution.

The Life-World and the Universe of Objects

If there is an authentic way of existing and thinking that is concerned, and another way that is unauthentic and fanatical, we must first try to understand what it means to be concerned, or involved, in our thinking. Let us approach this question by examining the distinction that is found in ordinary language between opinion and real belief. As Aristotle pointed out, I have opinions about many things which do not affect my actions. Thus I may believe, on the basis of what I regard as good authority, that the moon has no atmosphere, and that the Hebrews escaped from Egypt about 1200 B.C. Such theoretical beliefs, as Aristotle pointed out, may be expressed by my words and my thoughts. They are not expressed by my actions. I say that I *have* such opinions. There are other beliefs, however, which express something about my way of life. I do not merely have them or possess them. They belong to my being. So I refer to them in another way as strong beliefs or convictions that enter into my way of life. I do not merely possess them; I am them. Thus I do not say: *I believe that I am an American*, but rather *I am American*. And a genuine Marxist will not say: *I believe that Marxism is true*, but rather *I am a Marxist...*

Aristotle glimpsed what we have in mind in his distinction between opinion (δόξα), from which we are relatively detached and which easily comes and goes, and practical insight (φρόνησις) as he called it, in which we are involved, and which, once acquired, is harder to lose. This much he saw. But several other things about this distinction he did not see. He believed that the opinion-forming faculty in man had access to a reliable knowledge of things as they really are, and of a great cosmic order in which we ourselves and our practical actions and deliberations are actually contained. He did not see that "practical planning" involved a whole human world quite different from any order of abstract objects to which theoretical reason, or science, has any access. This world has a peculiar order, or orders, of its own, which require a special mode of understanding that does not exactly coincide either with what he called *theoretical*, or with what he called *practical* understanding.

By the more recent methods of linguistic analysis, and by those of phenomenology, we are beginning to learn more about this world of our actual existence, which is expressed and revealed, to some degree of clarity, by our ordinary language, with its rich ambiguities and shades of meaning. Certain differences between it and the objective perspectives of science and reason, in the traditional sense, have now become quite clear. This is a world of engagement to which we have access only through our active concern. It is radically reduced and distorted when regarded as a set of objects from a detached point of view. It includes certain "subjective" and intentional factors which are absent from any objective perspective. Each of these perspectives abstracts its own special field of objects, and deals with them in isolation from the rest. Even within its own field, it proceeds analytically, first dealing with one class of objects until clarity is achieved, and then turning to the next. The idea is to pass from clarity concerning the parts to a synthetic clarity concerning the whole.

In the life-world, on the other hand, we must first become oriented with respect to the whole field of meaning before we can understand the particular "figures" in the field. Thus we would never become oriented with respect to a strange room by first abstractly analyzing the window, the ceiling, the wall, and the desk. It is only by first understanding something of the room that we can grasp what the window is, and the desk. Here we must pass not from the figure to the ground, but from the ground to the figure. Aristotle and his objectively minded followers held that "values" could be described from the outside, and arranged in hierarchical orders which were valid for all men everywhere. It has now turned out, however, that to observe the motions of a person pursuing a "value" from the outside is quite different from what the person himself goes through from the inside, and that the same term (value) cannot be used of both without equivocation.

It is not merely that they are qualitatively distinct. They actually occur in different world horizons, and it is proper to say that they are worlds apart. It is clear that the term "value," as it occurs in actual usage, refers not abstractly to observed behavior but rather to a lived experience in the life-world. Hence if we are to avoid confusion, it is better for us to speak of the objective perspectives of science, which are ordered by classes and laws, as being neutral to value. The life-world, on the other hand, is pervaded and ordered throughout by meaning and value. This world, however, appears in many versions that are radically distinct, and no one of them as yet seems likely to become valid for all men.

Traditional thought has held that these different versions of the world can be objectively observed from the outside, and then compared and contrasted in an unbiased and objective way without any reduction and distortion. But this also has turned out to be false. There are many differences, of which we shall have time to mention only one. When objectively observed, each version of the world becomes closed within itself, a finished system with nothing beyond, and isolated from all the others. Furthermore, it appears as only one possibility among many. This theoretical attitude, when rigidly adhered to, leads to the now influential position known as *relativism*. But the two characteristics of world objects we have noted do not apply to existence in the *Lebenswelt*, as the German philosopher Husserl called it. Lived versions of the world may become closed by fanaticism, as we shall see. But many versions are aware of mysteries which they know they do not know. Hence they remain open to the world which lies beyond, and are able to communicate, at least to some degree, with other versions. Furthermore, since the version in which I actually exist remains unfinished and open to further exploration, it is never experienced by me as only one objective possibility among many others. I live in it as the one and only world there is for me, and I have staked my life upon it.

The events that happen in this world and other versions of them, all its various realms and regions, are given meaning through the project in which I am actively engaged. It is in this world that I am faced not only with laws and uniform sequences but with active agencies and powers. Some of these are friendly, and with them I can cooperate. Others are hostile, and with them I must struggle sometimes to the death. It is in and through these struggles that the real world looms into view. It is not broken up into those separate world islands which the relativist observes from his objective point of view. These are only versions of a single world horizon which, at the same time, encompasses and yet transcends them all. The things in the world-field are constantly changing. But the field itself is also passing, and the new world-facts, with their differing phases, do not appear in neatly separated packages one by one. They appear all together, new discoveries in science, new policies, sickness, wealth, and genocide, —all at once. These diverse occurrences cannot be meaningfully gathered together without that type of global interpretation to which science is indifferent, but without which human existence in the *Lebenswelt* is impossible. Every way of life, whether it be of an individual or of a society, involves a world version of this kind.

Scientific facts are not oriented around any particular personal or social project, except that of science,—the disciplined observation of what can be seen by anyone, anywhere. The aim is, by such observation, to confirm as many theories from as many different points of view as possible, in order to achieve the widest synthesis, or what we shall call *breadth of mind*. My version of the life-world, on the other hand, centers around me, or the projects of my group. I need to take account of versions other than my own. But I cannot escape from myself and my situation in history. I cannot become another person, and then slip back into myself again. Hence there is no use for a living person to seek to live in the widest synthetic manner. By trying to exist as a primitive African, an Italian, a Buddhist, and an Eskimo, I would simply dilute my existence, and finally cease to be anything at all. The development of insight here involves not so much width as depth.

I have tried briefly to suggest what is now meant by the human life-world, which I cannot observe from the outside as an object, or set of objects, but which I inhabit and care for from the inside with my own existence. This *Lebenswelt* has peculiar structures of its own, quite different from those of any objective universe of discourse. No set of opinions about external objects, no matter how strange, can give me any access to this world. And yet every one of us understands it, though perhaps dimly and unthematically, in and through his acts of existing. But this understanding is of a different order and requires a logic of a very different kind, some aspects of which we have tried to suggest.

Devotion and Fanaticism as Ways of Existing

Now if this is the world of our concrete concern in which we exist and think, let us now turn to the distinction between fanaticism and devotion. They have their analogies in the realm of objective theory and opinion,—dogmatism and breadth of mind. But these are neither opinions nor ways of holding opinions. They are ways of thinking and existing in the life-world. Is passionate care, or devotion, merely a polite way of speaking of bigotry? Or is there a real distinction between the two? Both R. Niebuhr and G. Marcel have dealt with this distinction in recent works.[1] But their discussions rely, for the most part, on psychological categories, and fail to do justice to the sense in which two different ways of constituting the world are involved. The most thorough treatment with which I am familiar is that of W. Zuurdeeg.[2] In spite of his use of the psychological term *conviction*, he is aware of the depth of the issue involved, and realizes that it lies at a level more basic than what this term would suggest. However, though he makes many pertinent remarks, to which we shall refer, his failure to distinguish between *the* world and *versions of* the world, leads him, in the end, to question the very distinction that his penetrating observations would seem to justify (pp. 83-4).

Let us now turn to these two ways of being in the world, the devoted and the fanatical, Kierkegaard and Hitler, for example. Can they both be subsumed under a single concept, like that of fanaticism? Or is this a confusion of types? Is there a real difference between the two?

One difference is suggested by a bare reference to these two names, though they must not be thought of as paradigm cases. Other equally pertinent examples can be found. The world of devotion is ordered towards a mystery absolutely transcending our finite powers of understanding and appropriation. In Kierkegaardian language, it is a world of *infinite passion*. It is important to note that he does not say a passion for the infinite, since the infinite is no object which we can observe from the outside. It is a presence coming from beyond us, and yet working in us so that this passion itself, when it is felt, belongs to the mystery. The world, whose presence is felt through such a pas-

1R. Niebuhr, *The Self and the Dramas of History;* G. Marcel, *Man Against Mass Society.*

2*Analytical Philosophy of Religion* (New York: Abingdon Press, 1958).

sion, must transcend any human version of it, including that of the one who is feeling it and thinking it. Hence it is characteristic of such thinking to recognize itself as only a version, but as a version open to the transcending world. There are also other versions. But there is no need of trying to absorb them in a great synthetic whole, for this one is capable of infinite deepening. This way is not the only way. But it is felt to be open and authentic.

The world of the fanaticized consciousness, as Marcel calls it, on the other hand, is not open. Here the distinction between my version and the world of which it is a version is blurred in a way that is not always revealed by any examination of the words and concepts used. The language may be filled with extreme and hyperbolic terms. The confusion lies rather in the direction and movement of the thinking itself which seems to be enclosed within inflexible limits, and to be elucidating what is already there, instead of breaking through boundaries and opening itself to what is beyond. This kind of a world-version becomes rigid and fixed, and, finally, in place of any further exploration and creation, it gives itself over to aggression and defence against other views. Instead of an authentic way, it thinks of itself as the only way. Between the fanatical world and the world of impassioned devotion there is this basic difference. The one understands itself to be a version; the other to be the world itself. The one is open. The other is closed.

Both the fanatic and the man of devotion are engaged in tasks. But here we may see another difference closely connected with the one we have noted. Without betraying the ethos of his way, the zealot may give himself to a cause which might be fully realized and completed in human history. In fact, many examples of such fanaticism can be given. Hitler, for example, was fanatically concerned with the conquest of the world. This might have been actually achieved. What then? But the man of impassioned devotion, described by Kierkegaard, could not give himself to any such realizable goal without betraying the ethos of his devotion. This is because the infinite passion is concerned with and enveloped by a mystery which can be penetrated but never comprehended. Some advance, some satisfaction may be hoped for. But one cannot imagine the philosophic passion of Socrates ever being realized or satisfied in this life. It is an infinite passion which is capable of an endless deepening. But no matter how far it goes, it needs to be endlessly reinterpreted and reenacted by each succeeding generation. This is what Socrates means in his *Apology* where he speaks of human knowledge as worthy of little or nothing (23A) and of the young men coming after him (39D). And as Kierkegaard remarked in his study of Socrates, this infinite passion called forth by mystery, though never fully expressible by concepts and theories, can nevertheless be expressed by irony.[3] Here is another basic difference. The fanatic can attack his enemies by ridicule and satire. He is incapable of a self-reflecting irony.

From an objective and intellectualistic point of view, devotion and fanaticism are merged together under such general terms as emotional commitment, feeling, and especially passion, which has undergone an important change in meaning during our western history. For the Greeks, this term *passio* referred to the internal, subjective effect of some external agency. Such feelings, or passions, disturb the rule of reason, and must be suppressed or controlled so far as possible. Feelings are a kind of suffering in which we lose our rational autonomy, and simply give in to random influences from the outside. The word still carries this ancient rationalist meaning, for we speak of someone as being upset or disturbed by emotion. But we have now become aware of the cognitive value of feeling, and of certain things that we can come to know in no other way. The most exhaustive intellectual and physical analysis, for example, could never tell us the meaning of a threat. Hence we now speak of *feeling our way, feeling a person out*, and *having a feeling for art or music*. We are prepared to grant that feeling is even more closely connected with action than conceptual thought, and in our common speech, we often recognize that rational discourse, without feeling, is abstract and "cold." By personal "warmth," and "warmness of heart," we refer to attitudes which overcome this separation, and which involve a noteworthy interpenetration of thinking and feeling. Thus by a warmhearted person we do not ordinarily think of someone who is stupid, but rather of someone whose thinking and feeling work together in a harmonious way.

As a result of these "irrational" notions, which have long been active in our tradition, we now use the word *passion* in a novel way

---

[3] S. Kierkegaard, *Der Begriff der Ironie* (München: Kaiser Verlag, 1929), pp. 225-6.

quite foreign to the linguistic habits of traditional Greek philosophy. When we speak of Augustine, Kierkegaard, or Nietzsche as impassioned thinkers, we do not mean that they were constantly upset by random emotions. We mean rather that their lives have been dominated by overarching attitudes in which rational insight, together with intense feeling, have reached a remarkable agreement. This kind of agreement and integration is very rare and difficult to attain. For most of us, our rational insights lead us in certain directions, and our feelings in others. We are distracted by different interests, and torn apart by divergent loyalties to different purposes and causes. It is only very rarely, in exceptional cases, that an individual is able to achieve an almost undiluted personal integrity by such a union of far-reaching insight and intense mood and feeling. These are the men of infinite passion of whom Kierkegaard speaks, and among whom he was himself an outstanding example.

There are several ways in which this kind of integrity can be approximated. There are those who achieve an integrity of thought by wide-ranging systems of ideas. But they do not come very close, because their lives may remain distracted. Kierkegaard referred to them in his famous remark about the philosopher who built a marvelous and spacious palace on a beautiful hill, but lived in a shack on the swamp beneath. On the other hand, there are those, with no overarching insights and little perspicacity, who try to achieve integrity by sheer intensity of feeling alone. Instead of dwelling with this feeling and thinking it through to the depths, they attach it to some purpose, or cause, that they find already under way in their environment. Instead of taking this over responsibly and lifting it up into a new field of meaning of their own, they give themselves over to it with an intensity of blind feeling that may substitute for understanding.

Against such violence of feeling, the charges of irrationalism and irresponsibility are certainly justified. But this is a simulated passion, as we may call it, which is quite distinct from the infinite passion of devotion. It is outwardly directed towards something objective which abstracts from lived existence. This objective purpose, as we have seen, is one that may be achieved or realized by a quantitative proliferation in breadth rather than in depth. Finally, it is only a false imitation that is achieved, not genuine unity and integrity. Underneath this false façade, there is a buzzing swarm of competing loyalties and unities, that must be ignored or suppressed, and which bring forth a sense of insecurity in the agent. This is answered by a further outburst of passion for the one great cause in a vicious circle which is characteristic of fanatical existence. From the outside, this vicious circle is evident, as Zuurdeeg remarks (*op. cit.* pp. 80-1) even though it may be, for the most part, concealed from the person himself. It is also attended by further manifestations, which are not found in the world of devotion, to which we shall now turn.

One of these is the element of possessiveness. The fanatical consciousness is not wholly and integrally on the way which it has chosen. Many parts of it are uncommitted, or tending in other directions. But it wishes to be on the way, to be totally identified with it. Unable to attain this by giving itself to the way, it tries, by a reverse operation, to do something to the way, to bring it as close as possible into a position where it can be governed and controlled. The closest relation I can have to an external thing with which I wish to become identified is that of possession or ownership. Such a thing I can make my own by owning it, and by using it for my purposes, if I know what they are. Instead of taking the way and becoming a Marxist, for example, and being it through and through, I hold it as a set of opinions which I have, and a set of regulations which I follow to the letter. I am more concerned with the curves and dips of the way which lie immediately before me and over which I can exert some control, than with the ultimate end. This seems very distant and remote. Nevertheless having gained some external control over the instruments of the way, such as boots, binoculars, and a cane, it is easy for me objectively to identify the way with its ultimate end. After all, they are connected as objects, and part of it is already mine. So I soon hear myself thinking of my way, my devotion, my faith, and my God, as though the whole path from beginning to end, were already in my possession, as one who is ambitious to play, and owning an instrument, but as yet knowing only a few scales and bars, may readily identify with exquisite finished productions, and may speak not only of his instrument, but also of his style, and his kind of music.

Zuurdeeg has noted this tendency of the religious fanatic to identify the ultimate end with the way thereto, so that he himself, and the group to which he belongs, are taken up into the divine, and become, with little effort on their part, also holy. He points out that the term *fanatic* is derived from *fanum,* meaning temple. For the bigoted believer, his group is a privileged and holy domain where he is relieved from all hidden worries and insecurity (p. 81). He himself, his *fanum,* and his God all belong together in a special, sacred area, apart from the trials and problems of everyday life, and not subject to ordinary standards and criticisms. This type of fanatical devotion is not restricted to religious groups. It is found wherever groups are bound together by basic, global purposes which are not easily understood, and where intense feeling has replaced careful and disciplined thought, as in the existing nation-state, the superior white race, the Communist Party, etc.

In spite of the ubiquity of such devotion, there is another kind. Though easily confused with the former when regarded externally from an objective point of view, it can be distinguished, in those rare cases where it actually occurs, by those who will take the trouble to use their imaginations in following this type of existence as it is lived from the inside. Such authentic devotion, as we may call it, differs from the fanatical type in all the respects we have just mentioned. In the first place, intense feeling is not only directed to a global view of life, but this view is carefully thought through, as in the case of Kierkegaard, and related to concrete daily tasks. Through this union of thought and feeling in a grand and overarching passion, the whole of life may be taken over, and lifted up into a coherent world which makes sense to the living person. He is then in a position to choose a way of life that is supported by this world, and through this choice, to achieve a genuine integrity, following this way with the whole of himself, all that he is and has been, up to the end.

Nothing will have to be ignored or suppressed. He will not have to hold himself back and gaze on the way with a longing detachment. He will be on the way. He will not try to have and to hold it as a possession which he can identify with himself. He will try rather to be this way, and to identify himself with it. He will no longer speak of my devotion, but of my devotion to. . . . He will think of the way as a whole, and especially of its final destination and source, rather than of the immediate twists and turnings. With respect to these, he will remain flexible, and will be indifferent to specific regulations and to the use of this instrument or that. He will rather constantly aim to be on the way. And while he is moving towards it, both with his thoughts and his limbs, he will never be able to confuse himself and his mobile position with that of his destination. This will be especially true if he is climbing upwards,—if his goal has any transcendence in it. He will be quite clear that this goal is not and never will be in his possession, even if he reaches the mountain top. It is not a thing or a place to be possessed. It is rather a mystery that may be compared to a sunset or a sweeping view from the heights that is not obtained, but suddenly given and granted.

By devoting his every effort to climbing higher and thus transcending himself, he becomes aware of heights to which he can never climb, and of that which completely transcends himself and all he ever can be. No one actually devoted to a project of this kind will ever confuse himself and his group and his instruments with the goal that is luring him on. It is by his own blood and sweat that he knows the difference. These are human, all too human. He has no access to any special area separated from the trials of everyday life. This is only a false escape. These trials and problems must be taken over and given meaning. It is precisely in and through them that he must find his way. Once we get a sense of such devotion as it is actually lived, we see that it is sharply distinct from the fanatical type. But there are other differences which are even more clear.

The unconditionally committed person is supposed to be subjectively certain of his own beliefs, unable to bear the thought of being disappointed, unwilling to bear serious questioning, and hostile towards other groups and persons following different ways. These criticisms certainly apply to fanatical modes of existence. In so far as I fall into one of these modes, and there are very few of us who do not, it is not only myself but my relevant doctrines and feelings that become identified with the divine end, and come to share in its infallibility. One can say that this is especially true of the doctrines, since I myself am never fully and integrally committed. But the doctrines I possess concerning the holy are identified with the holy. Hence they are absolutely certain. They cannot lead me astray. The very thought of missing the promises they contain is unthinkable and unbearable. Since the fanatical mind, like any other, can and does think such a thought, it is goaded to more and more frantic actions and protestations of faith.

This attitude is sharply contrasted with that of the father in the *New Testament* who said: *I believe, Oh Lord, help Thou mine unbelief.* (Mark, 9,24), and with that of a "believer," like Kierkegaard, who recognized that there could be no objective or divine certainty in matters of faith. There is a risk involved, as in the accepting or non-accepting of any global interpretation of the world. Kierkegaard goes even farther than this in his discussion of infinite resignation, where he says that the believer must be resigned to ultimate disappointment, and the frustration of all his hopes.[4] This kind of devotion is not to be confused with the objective proofs and certainties of fanatical belief. It is true that the fanatic mind resists all questioning and is unable to question itself. But if we are right in thinking of Socrates as an example of impassioned concern for an unfinishable project, it is hard to believe that every commitment belongs to this type. It is hard to deny that he questioned himself. And Kierkegaard is another example.

The fanaticized consciousness is aggressive and hostile to other ways than its own. They offer threats to its sense of security. Hence it is interested in universal agreement concerning matters of life-interpretation, and in the quantitative proliferation of its point of view by numbers of adherents. But this comes from a failure of integral engagement. There is another type of devotion which, though it recognizes a real risk, is sure enough of itself to be on the way. And once on the way, it is free from such threats. It knows itself to be taking one way, and knows that there are others also open to the truth. It has enough questions and difficulties of its own to face. So it has no time for hostility and aggrandizement against others. It defends itself against them only in so far as it must defend itself against itself. It does not feel strengthened by crowds on its side. It is able to stand alone.

I think that we have adduced enough evidence to show that there is a contrast between two types of devotion. The one that we call authentic is guided by an overarching union of thought and feeling known as passion, and understands itself to be a version. The other is guided by uncriticized feeling, and thinks of itself as the only way. Fanatical consciousness thinks of this way as an object which it possesses from beginning to end. Authentic devotion, on the other hand,

---

[4]Kierkegaard, *Abschliessende unwissenschaftliche Nachschrift*, Zweites Teil (Jena: Diederichs, 1925), IV.

is on its way to something transcendent. With respect to rules and regulations the one is flexible, the other literal and strict. The one thinks of its faith as a special region apart from the problems and questions of profane existence, while the other works out its way in and through the trials and difficulties of daily life. Fanatical commitment finds itself to be certain of its beliefs, is unwilling to face serious questioning, and is aggressive towards other ways. Authentic devotion, on the other hand, is aware of the risks of its global project, self-conscious, self-critical, and unaggressive. This is the nature of the contrast we have suggested.

But we must end with a warning first cogently presented by Zuurdeeg (*op. cit.* pp. 83-4).

We have referred to ideal cases in our attempt to bring out a distinction that is only implicit and latent in everyday life. From an objective point of view that simply observes behavior and language, the two types are indiscernible. The same observable acts may be performed; the same words and expressions may be used. To grasp the distinction clearly, it is necessary to follow the lived experience imaginatively from the inside, and to grasp its meaning for the agent. But even here, though the boundary is clear, it is readily crossed from the one to the other, and each type in our lived existence is usually mixed with the other, and is hardly ever pure. Authentic devotion, in particular, is constantly threatened by the danger of fanaticism. Nothing in fact, is more fanatical than the claim to be the only non-fanatic view. Authentic devotion in its purer forms, as we have suggested, is very rare and difficult to maintain. It is, nevertheless, a distinct, existential mode to which every person has access, and which can be achieved in varying degrees. Fanaticism, on the other hand, is something far more familiar. It is proper for us all to realize that if we have not already fallen into it, we are very near the edge.

A Further Question: Which Is the Broader Horizon?

But now we must raise a further question. The distinction between fanaticism and devotion, which we have attempted to clarify, is found in ordinary language. It seems to be commonly recognized, and neither arbitrary nor artificial. Why then, we must ask, is there the widespread tendency, at least in certain contexts, to slur over it and to confuse the two? We have already suggested an answer to this question by distinguishing between two perspectives, that of objective reason and science, and the horizon of the *Lebenswelt,* as we have called it, in which we exist both as individuals and as members of active groups. In the former, we observe and theorize about objects from a detached point of view. This is the perspective of science in which we try to abstract from bias and other "subjective" factors, in order to get an impartial and objective view. But this attitude extends far beyond the limits of science in the strict sense. In much of our ordinary conversation, we assume this attitude of objective impartiality, trying to take account of all the known facts, and to synthesize them into a sweeping view. From the time of the Greeks until recently, our Western philosophy has been dominated by this kind of objectivism. From this standpoint, it is better to suspend judgment than to run the risk of error by jumping to hasty conclusions. Authentic thinking of this kind demands suppression of personal feeling and bias, detachment, and a tentative withholding of judgment.

What we have called *devotion,* however, involves a violation of all these standards. It is dominated by personal feeling and passion, is completely committed, and is, finally, based on a global decision which goes beyond the available evidence, for as James pointed out, our finite existence confronts us with forced options. We have to make global decisions of this kind. So it is not surprising that, from this point of view, what we have called *devotion* is identified with fanaticism as a kind of dogmatism which is a constant threat to objective clarity and breadth of mind. This explains one part of the antinomy with which we are concerned.

But we also have to exist in the human life-world which we have, at least in part, ordered and constructed. And here, as James pointed out, we are confronted with forced options. We cannot wait indefinitely for further evidence to come in. We have to live in one way rather than in another. Hence we have to make global decisions of the most far-reaching kind on insufficient evidence. The scientific evidence will never be adequate, for it abstracts from "subjective" factors which have to be taken account of in life, and the life-world also involves obscurities and mysteries which will probably never be exhausted by any mode of approach. Hence it is not surprising that, in this horizon, the distinction between devotion and fanaticism, with which we have been concerned, makes sense, and that it is found in ordinary speech, the language of the *Lebenswelt.* This explains the other part of the antinomy.

Why then, should we not let the matter rest at this point?

As human beings, we participate in two noetic enterprises. One is that of objective reason and science which are concerned with all objects that can be observed from a detached point of view. This calls for suppression of bias and for other specific virtues. Authentic thought is impartial, tentative, and wide in scope. Unauthentic thinking is dogmatic, that is, partial, biased, and narrow. The other is an attempt to understand our own existence in the *Lebenswelt*. It is concerned not only with objects, but with our own subjective attitudes and meanings as we live them. We cannot detach ourselves from this world to gaze at it from the outside. We have to understand it, if at all, from the inside by a thinking that attends our action, and reveals it as it goes along. Since the evidence is insufficient, we must here be guided not only by conceptual insight but by feeling as well. This calls for global understanding and integrity, for passion and depth, in short, for the authentic devotion we have described. Its proper vice and corruption is fanaticism.

This resolution is sound, so far as it goes. But it is incomplete, and raises many further questions. For example, can these two worlds be separated in such a neat way? Have not the procedures of science changed the whole world in which we live? Have they not revolutionized our way of life? Have not reason and science emerged from the life-world in its history? Are these two worlds not closely intertwined and interdependent? Can they be sharply disconnected from each other as two self-enclosed islands? Are they not phases of one single world, not two?

These questions cannot be evaded. We must now face the issue as to how these two horizons are related. As we are using the term, a *horizon* indicates a certain limited range of revealing power, and two horizons may either coincide, or one may be more inclusive than the other. In the case before us, it is clear that the universe of science and the life-world do not coincide. They reveal different phases of being in different ways. We are, therefore, left with only two alternatives. Either the objective universe of science is wider in range and includes the life-world, or the latter includes the former. Which of these alternatives is true? The dominant traditions of Western thought have in the past favored the former alternative, and in more recent times they have often used the ambiguous term *subjective* in establishing their case. The objective universe, revealed by reason and science, extends more widely, both in space and in time. What we have been calling the *Lebenswelt* is a "subjective" human perspective much narrower in range, and even contained within the private experiences of the human subject or group. This position is still very much alive, and is accepted today by positivistic and naturalistic philosophers, as well as by relativistic thinkers in the social sciences.

The Life-World vs. The Objective Universe: A Testing of Hypotheses

Let us now test this thesis in terms of our analysis of these two horizons and their respective authentic and unauthentic modes. Let us call the authentic mode of objective reflection *impartiality,* its unauthentic mode *dogmatism,* and let us continue to call the authentic and unauthentic modes of existential disclosure *devoted* and *fanatical* reflection respectively. We are asking now which of these horizons is the broader, and in particular whether the relation of these modes to one another can shed any light on this question. We have found, for example, that the characteristic virtue, as we may call it, of objective reflection, impartiality, is quite dissimilar to devotion, the characteristic virtue of existential disclosure. On the other hand, the two characteristic vices, dogmatism and fanaticism, are quite similar. We have already noted the tendency of scientific thought to identify them. We shall now go further and point out that, on the basis of the analysis we have made, there is a basic similarity between the two which we shall explain by a brief analysis.

We have found that the fanatical consciousness is guided by uncriticized feeling rather than by painstaking analysis, that it thinks of its way as a set of objects which it possesses from beginning to end, that it takes rules and regulations literally, that it regards its own theories and their objects as occupying a special region not subject to the normal procedures of verification and refutation, that it is unduly certain of its beliefs, unwilling to face serious questioning, and aggressive towards other views (pp. 11-3). We do not need a protracted examination to see how closely this agrees at each point with the phenomenon of dogmatism. The dogmatic mind is uncritical, and allows itself to be governed by irrelevant emotions and feelings. It is a mode of objective reflection which believes itself, without adequate justification, to master its objects from beginning to end. It is apt to become obsessed with matters of detail, and is strict about minor regulations of procedure. Even after he has been clearly and definitely refuted, the dogmatist will think of his theories as in some sense exceptional and free from the rules of ordinary procedure. It is, in fact, or at least pretends to be certain of facts and meanings that are unstable and equivocal. It neither questions itself, nor is it able to face fair questioning. Finally, it is hostile and aggressive towards other views. The two phenomena correspond very closely, point for point. No wonder that they are closely connected both in rational thought and in ordinary speech. It is fair to say that dogmatism is a definite kind of fanaticism, working in a special and perhaps more restricted region.

Let us now turn to the two horizons we are examining. Their characteristic modes of authenticity are radically distinct. Their characteristic modes of unauthenticity are closely similar. Let us now ask if these facts, and others like them, have any bearing on the relative ranges of the two fields in question. The following phenomenological examination of field structure will have to be brief and schematic, but it may provide us with clear evidence pointing towards a defensible answer. We shall adopt the following procedure. First, we shall choose an example of two fields of thought and action, one of which is broader than the other, and where the relations between their respective modes of authenticity and unauthenticity are clear. After pointing out what these relations are in what we are taking to be a typical case, we shall use these results to help us decide which is the broader of the two fields with which we are concerned. When these two fields are not properly ordered with respect to breadth, the relations between their modes of authenticity and unauthenticity should fail to correspond. When they are properly ordered, these relations should correspond to those of the typical case. We can think of this as a phenomenological investigation of world structures.

As our typical case of a wider and a narrower field, let us take the two styles of thought and action which are involved, on the one hand with the concern for mankind, now exemplified in the United Nations, and on the other, with that narrower concern for the nation-state now exemplified in the many forms of national patriotism. Now each of these has an authentic and an unauthentic mode. Thus there is a genuine concern for the collective welfare of mankind, and an unauthentic version of this, which uses it only as a cloak for world conquest which we shall call *imperialism*. There is also an authentic patriotism which is concerned with the preservation of the national culture and the welfare of the state as a whole. But opposed to this, there is an unauthentic mode which uses it only as a cloak for the pursuit of its own special interests, and which we shall call simply *selfish interest*. Let us now compare these perspectives in five different ways: (a) the two authentic modes with respect to their similarity and difference; (b) the two unauthentic modes with respect to their similarity and difference; (c) the way in which the two less inclusive modes (patriotism and selfish interest) appear to the more inclusive, authentic mode (concern for mankind) ; (d) the way in which the two more inclusive modes (world-concern and imperialism) appear to the less inclusive, authentic mode (patriotism) ; and finally, (e) the way in which the two authentic modes (concern for mankind and patriotism) appear to the unauthentic modes.

(a) When we compare them, we find that the two authentic modes, patriotism and concern for mankind, are strictly different, both as ways of thought and as ways of action. We cannot say that concern for mankind is simply a broader form of patriotism, a whole made up simply of the different parts taken together. To take them together, in this way, leaving them as they are, leads to chaos and conflict, as we now know, not to world order. Mankind is more than all the nations added together, and concern for mankind involves a new and distinctive mode of thought quite different from that of patriotism. We do not have time here to spell out this distinction in detail. We shall mention only one basic difference. In authentic world thought there may be an affirmative mode of competition for the welfare of mankind, but no negative competition against autonomous, national rivals. The negative element of winning against, or over, another group is missing. There are also other differences. But this will be sufficient for our purposes. These two modes of thought, proceeding authentically at different levels, are quite distinct. But concern for mankind is certainly the broader and richer conception.

(b) The two unauthentic modes, selfish interest and imperialism, are very similar. Imperialism, since it is a privative version of concern for mankind, is a richer structure which involves more factors. But like selfish interest, it is an attempt of the part to dominate the whole, which may be fairly described simply as selfish interest on a larger scale. It would be fair to say that imperialism is an extreme form of selfishness. Every form of imperialism would have to be selfish, but every form of selfishness on a small scale would not have to be imperialistic.

(c) From the standpoint of concern for mankind, the distinction between authentic patriotism, as a sort of enlightened selfishness, and crude self-interest can be made. Patriotism, indeed, has a certain place. But if unqualified and unrestrained, it will be understood ultimately as a masked form of self-interest which is radically opposed to the broader concern for mankind, and will be closely linked with imperialism, as an imperialism temporarily suppressed under ideal disguises, but ever ready to emerge as an urge for further conquest.

(d) On the other hand, patriotism, from its more restricted point of view, will tend to identify concern for mankind with a masked form of imperialistic self-seeking. Each of these is simply a mode of selfishness magnified to a vast size, and each of these, including world-concern, is radically opposed to its own narrower, but legitimate interest in the national and cultural welfare.

(e) Finally, the selfish zealot will understand the imperialist simply as a more successful version of himself. From his point of view, both patriotism and concern for mankind will be linked together as airy pretenses having no real foundation in the facts. They are hidden forms of self-seeking, but world concern is the more false and more extreme version of the two. World concern is a magnified version of patriotism.

Now I believe that (a), (b), and (c) are, on the whole true, and that (d) and (e) are false versions of the situation. But I believe that whenever one world horizon includes another that is narrower, a conflict of modes of understanding emerges which falls into a pattern of this kind. Now let us turn to the two horizons with which we are concerned, that of the life-world, involving devotion and fanaticism as its unauthentic mode, and that of objective reason, involving what we have called breadth of mind and dogmatism. Let us now test two alternative hypotheses, first, that the latter includes the former, and second, that the former includes the latter. It will, of course, be easy to place each of them formally in the pattern we have just worked out in the case of patriotism and world concern.

But as we do this, let us ask the question as to which of them falls into this normal pattern more readily with the least strain over against the known facts. If, when placed in this standard pattern, one hypothesis forces us into strained relations which do not fit the facts, we shall rule it out. If the other corresponds with what we know of the relations, and fits the facts, we shall accept it. Let us now apply this test first of all to the view that reason and science give us the broader horizon which includes that of the *Lebenswelt*. In this case, in terms of our standard example, breadth of mind and dogmatism will correspond to world-concern and imperialism in our standard example, and devotion and fanaticism to patriotism and selfish interest. Let us now see if we can work out this hypothesis without undue paradox and strain.

(a) The two authentic modes, breadth of mind and devotion, are strictly different, as we have seen in our preceding analysis. So this fits the facts without strain. But when we try to think of breadth of mind as the broader and richer perspective analogous to world-concern as against patriotism, we find ourselves under a strain. The attitude of detached observation is, in fact, narrower and more abstract, since it sees only objects, and misses our lived existence. It is also less rich, since it fails to include itself and its own intention as they are lived. These suppositions are against the facts.

(b) Turning now to the two unauthentic modes, fanaticism and dogmatism, corresponding to self-interest and imperialism in our analogy, we find, as we have seen, that they are very similar. But when we try to think of dogmatism as a more fully realized and more extreme form of fanaticism, or, in terms of our analogy, selfishness as a more fully realized and more extreme form of imperialism, we find ourselves under a strain. Imperialism is rather a highly developed form of selfishness, on a grand scale, so to speak. Similarly it does not seem true to say that dogmatism is fanaticism on a grand scale. One can be selfish without being able to turn it into imperialism. A small child can be selfish in a kindergarten. But it is hard to think of a fanatic who is not also dogmatic. Once again we are in trouble with the facts.

(c) From the standpoint of breadth of mind (the widest objective view of things), we can see how devotion might seem to be a disguised form of fanaticism, and both might seem to be linked with dogmatism. In the case of our analogy, the corresponding judgment would be: concern for the welfare of mankind is either an empty phrase or a masked form of imperialism, rooted in selfishness, which works against the real interests of a particular nation-state. This is the perspective of a narrow, nationalistic patriotism. But it gives us a false and twisted version of the situation. It is rather this narrow patriotism which is a masked form of selfishness in international affairs, and both contain the germs of imperialism. But in this case, the point of view of what is presumably the wider horizon is false to the facts, and, as we may say, necessarily distorted.

Devotion is not a disguised form of fanaticism, and is quite distinct from dogmatism. Here what is presumably, by hypothesis, the broader and more adequate point of view gives us a reduced and false view of the facts. This certainly raises a serious doubt as to whether it is, in fact, the wider and richer point of view. Once again we are in difficulty.

(d) Devotion, on the other hand, is, according to the hypothesis, the less adequate and more restricted point of view. It will see dogmatism, when it is generalized and applied to existence, as a form of fanaticism, which it is. It will recognize that breadth of mind, which sees everything as an object, turns every open version of the world into a closed system, and thus leads us towards relativism. This objectivist view is closely related to fanaticism, for it misinterprets devotion as a closed world, and thus makes existential truth impossible. But when every attempt to think through a world interpretation is equally false, the only recourse is to blind feeling.

This point of view is not the sort of reduced and distorted version we should expect from our hypothesis, and from the analogy. It is basically in agreement with our analyses of devotion, breadth of mind, and their unauthentic modes. Hence from a point of view which, on the basis of our hypothesis, should be narrow and inadequate, we are getting the broader and less inadequate analysis. This also does not increase our confidence in the hypothesis.

(e) Turning now to the standpoint of fanaticism, it will see breadth of mind as a magnified version of devotion or, in terms of our analogy, patriotism as a magnified version of concern for mankind. But this is clearly out of line with the facts, for devotion and concern for mankind are the wider and richer horizons. It will also link them both together as hidden forms of fanaticism, as though concern for mankind and patriotism were mere expressions of personal selfishness. This is hard to reconcile not only with the facts of our standard example, but with our analysis of devotion, and even with common speech.

The results we have attained from this hypothesis are not encouraging. They would lead us to suppose that breadth of mind and dogmatism are more highly developed and richer than devotion and fanaticism, and are out of line with several other facts which are implicitly recognized by the uses of ordinary language, and more explicitly by our analyses. But the most serious difficulty is to be found in the presumed revealing power of the different perspectives. That one (c) which, according to our standard analogy, gives us the wider and sounder point of view on the whole situation, and which, according to our hypothesis, should do so, as a matter of fact gives us one that is narrow and distorted. On the other hand, that one (d) which in the analogy is narrow and distorted, and which, according to the hypothesis, should be so, as a matter of fact is wider and more true to the facts. We must conclude that this hypothesis is dubious. It fails to meet the test.

So let us now turn to the other hypothesis that the *Lebenswelt* is the wider and richer horizon, let us test it in the same way in relation to our standard example. Since we have covered many relevant points in our previous discussion, we may now be more brief. We need remember here only that, according to our present hypothesis, devotion and fanaticism, the attitudes of the life-world, represent the broader, while breadth of mind and dogmatism represent the narrower point of view.

(a) The two authentic modes, devotion and breadth of mind, are, of course, strictly different. But according to our present hypothesis, devotion is the broader and richer horizon, and this seems to be true. It is broader because it must take account of "subjective" as well as of objective factors. It is richer, since it is aware of itself and its own intentions in the very act.

(b) The two unauthentic modes, fanaticism and dogmatism, are closely similar, and one seems to be a more far-ranging and fully developed version of the other. According to our hypothesis, this is now fanaticism. Dogmatism is a less developed mode which contains it in germ, and this seems to be true. The dogmatist is rigid and narrow in the opinions he holds about objects. But the fanatic is rigid and narrow in his vital attitudes which involve "subjective" as well as objective factors. We can say that he is "dogmatic" not only with respect to the objects with which he is concerned, but with respect to his very concerns themselves. One can be dogmatic as a youth in certain fields or regions of opinion without being a full-blown fanatic. But one cannot be a fanatic without also being dogmatic. It is the more extreme and more fully realized version of the other. These observations fit the facts.

(c) From the standpoint of the hypothesis we are now assuming, it is devotion which has access to the more authentic and far-ranging perspective. Hence by centering the other attitudes around itself, it should be able to give us the sounder interpretation of the situation. Concern for mankind played this role in our analogy. From the point of view of devotion, dogmatism is a germinal version of fanaticism, which, as we have just seen, fits the facts. Furthermore, just as patriotism, when it becomes closed and generalized, readily turns into imperialism, in the same way, when objective analysis (breadth of mind) closes every individual and cultural life-pattern into a separate world, and generalizes itself into some form of relativism, it readily turns into a fanatical mode of life. Just as selfishness and fixed forms of patriotism are germinal forms of imperialism, so dogmatism and objective breadth of mind are germinal forms of fanaticism. This interpretation agrees with our standard analogy. It seems on the whole sound, and fits the facts.

(d) According to the present hypothesis, breadth of mind is not the more adequate perspective for grasping the whole situation involved in an overlapping of perspectives. Its point of view is partial and abstract. Hence when it places itself in the center, and interprets the other factors, we should expect certain reductions and distortions to arise, as in the case of our analogy, when patriotism generalizes itself and reduces world-concern to imperialism, and sees both of them as only blown-up versions of selfishness. In the same way, when objective analysis makes itself the center, and interprets everything in relation to itself, devotion is reduced to fanaticism, and both of them are seen as only expanded versions of dogmatism. This may, indeed, be true of fanaticism. But it is not true of devotion. As we should expect from our assumptions, this limited perspective distorts the whole situation, and forces the facts.

(e) Turning now to the standpoint of dogmatism, on the basis of our hypothesis the least adequate and authentic of the four, when it is generalized, it will make itself the center, and will regard the other perspectives as expanded or distorted versions of itself. This is a mistake that might be expected from the limited position granted it by our hypothesis. However, in judging the relative ranges of the different perspectives, it will not be mistaken. Just as selfishness recognizes in imperialism a further development of itself, and in world-concern a more extreme version of patriotism, so will dogmatism recognize in fanaticism a further development of itself, and in devotion a more extreme version of breadth of mind. These judgments are correct.

We may conclude from this test of the second hypothesis, that the horizon of the life-world is broader and richer than that of objective reflection. In the first place, this hypothesis agrees with the pattern of our standard example. In both cases, the first three sets of relations (a), (b), and (c) are truly recognized as they are, and the last two sets (d) and (e) are recognized with only those distortions of perspective we should expect, but with the basic facts untwisted. They also agree with the independent evidence of ordinary usage, and with our phenomenological investigation of devotion, fanaticism, breadth of mind, and dogmatism which made this evidence more explicit. We conclude, therefore, that this hypothesis is, on the whole, correct, and that the life-world is broader and richer than the objective perspectives of the sciences. We conclude, further, that this horizon of the *Lebenswelt* is not a mere chaotic confusion, as many traditional thinkers have believed, but that it is structuralized in certain distinctive patterns that are open to disciplined, phenomenological investigation.

In line with these conclusions, we suggest that the exploration of the human life-world in which we exist, though long neglected and postponed, is now a matter of major importance for the living thought of our time, and that it may offer us a radically new approach to the genuine problems of what have been traditionally called, logic, epistemology, ethics and metaphysics.

JOHN WILD

YALE UNIVERSITY

THE TWO STRANDS IN NATURAL THEOLOGY

§ 1. Throughout the history of Western philosophy there have been two competing conceptions of divinity, which will be called the self-sufficient and the outgoing. The object of this paper is to see if it is possible to maintain both conceptions at the same time, and, if so, on what conditions. The issue appears to be of the first importance to natural theology, because it would be permanently impoverished if either conception were dropped, and yet there is a *prima facie* contradiction between them.

On the one hand, in the Western tradition, God is said to be complete in Himself, and does not require to be supplemented by His creation. He moves the world, as Aristotle said, "by being loved," and not by any active manifestations on His own part; for that would indicate that He was previously inadequate. He is eternal and unchangeable, unaffected by anything that can happen, within or without Himself. It would make no difference to Him if the creatures did not exist at all. He does not suffer with their sufferings: even in the Christian orbit, to suppose that He does is to admit to the heresy—my favourite heresy—of Patripassionism. He is ineffable, motionless and utterly alone.

On the other hand, in the Western tradition, God is a creator: He brings into being what was not; "we love Him because He first loved us"; He intervenes in the world and faces towards the world; He is accessible to prayer; it is a matter of concern to Him that the world should be as good as it can be; and on one famous occasion He worked six full days in the week. And (lest it be thought that we are drifting too far from nature to revelation) Thomas Aquinas, speaking as a philosopher, exulted in the variety of things: "the diversity of creatures was primarily intended by the prime agent": and he was followed in this by the heretical Giordano Bruno; "the gods take pleasure in the multiform representation of multiple things"; though Bruno was indiscreet or indifferent enough to write "gods" in the plural. And, finally, there was Leibniz, who attached the creatures to the creator by the iron chain of sufficient reason.

Now these two aspects of the Western tradition are *prima facie* opposed to each other. How can the immobile move anything? How can the unchangeable have purposes? How can the eternal deploy itself in time? How can creatures be at once of no account and of high concern? If, as would appear, we are confronted with contradictions, is it then possible to adjust them so that they are contradictions no longer? Or, alternatively, is it possible that one or the other is a mistake, and that the tradition henceforward should run on one engine rather than on two? One thing is certain: that until these problems are faced, natural theology is living in (let us say) a natural's paradise.

It is customary with theologians to say that these two persisting tendencies are Greek and Hebrew respectively. Whether the second or outgoing side of the tradition exhausts the Hebrew contribution experts must judge; but the fashionable theologians' view about the Greeks is certainly a mistake. The doubleness (some might say duplicity) of the Western theological tradition existed already in Greek philosophy, and especially in Plato. Over against the mysticism of the *Symposium* and the sixth book of the *Republic* we must set the creationism of the *Timaeus* and the tenth Book of the *Laws*. We must also add that in the formation of the Western tradition in the Middle Ages the *Timaeus* counted for more than all the other dialogues put together. Now the *Timaeus* is at once a statement of the conception of God as outgoing (there is no envy in Him, and He wished the world to be as good as it can be (30b)), and an attempt to reconnect it with the conception of God as self-sufficient. Plato succeeded, like so many after him, by deducing the world from God's *goodness:* not having any ground for envy, He can afford to be generous: and like so many after him, he did not pause to consider how a God who is generous, who "desired" the world to be like Himself, can be wholly and timelessly self-sufficient. To be generous, or even to desire, is to look outside oneself. And, with the additional credit of creation, God is more perfect afterwards than he was before.

This, it is true, is to anticipate. For the moment our object is to show that the discrepancy which splits natural theology down the middle also split Plato down the middle, and does not arise solely from the strain between Greek and Hebrew influences in the early Christian church. There are however good reasons for the error. In the first place, Aristotle's God is more like the Form of the Good than He is like Plato's God: a sort of magnet operating from an arm-chair.

In the second place the Christian church encountered Platonism in its "neo-Platonic" revival, and the neo-Platonists did everything they could to suppress the activist tendencies of the *Timaeus*. They lived too soon to be consoled by A. E. Taylor with the suggestion that Plato never meant it, and they fell back on allegorical interpretations. Aided by Plato's fatal modesty in describing his cosmogony as a "likely story," they spirited it away into their own realm of abstractions, and treated it as a mythological disguise for logical emanation. Now it was Aristotle who was "the philosopher" for the Middle Ages, and it was the neo-Platonists who challenged and were outfaced by, but infiltrated, the Christians of Alexandria. In both cases the Greek philosophical tradition which encountered the new religion was that God (or the Whole, or Reality) was immobile and self-sufficient. Consequently, anti-philosophical creationists have denounced Greek philosophy together with the undoubtedly unbiblical attribute of self-sufficiency. If they had remembered the *Timaeus* (and with it the *Philebus,* where the mixed life is preferred to the pure), they would have realized that the problem was presented to Western culture before it ever heard of the Hebrews.[1]

§ 2. Having, it is hoped, shown that the discrepancy goes deeper than a conflict of cultures, we can now examine the two strands in Western natural theology in greater detail. (i) The first, which we shall call the "immobilist," we shall illustrate by referring to the second book of Plato's *Republic*, which contains a frontal and revolutionary attack on the popular religion of Ancient Greece. The myths, whether poetic or obscene, purported to show forth the divine by metamorphosis; thus God is known as such by His magical power of becoming something else. Plato's response to popular religion was that while it might be good enough for gods it was not good enough for his commonwealth; and he set about reforming the gods by turning them into highlights of the rationalist state—a process finally completed only in *Laws* X. His first step was to insist that what is divine (singular or plural), being perfect, cannot change; for if what is perfect changes, it will not be as perfect as before (381b). This applies particularly if the change comes from outside, for that would

---

[1]Plato, *Timaeus, passim.* It should be added that from Philo onwards the method of allegory was applied also to the Old Testament. The operative Jewish tradition in Roman times was not the Old Testament unqualified.

mean that God is being pushed about by extraneous forces; but applies also to voluntary change (one thinks of Zeus becoming a bull to abduct Europa) , and even to the simulation of change by the actually changeless, for simulation is a form of lying appropriate (I use Plato's language) not to gods but to poets. Changelessness, then, is the central character of deity; and one can see in this conviction both the indignation of a religious reformer and an expression of the philosophy of Forms.

But if the gods are changeless, there must be a world of change which is intercepted and left outside the divine perfection. Otherwise there would be no point in the contrast: in a homogeneously changeless world no one would call *anything* changeless. Further, that world is not *because* of divine perfection, but in spite of it: it may aspire after it; when self-conscious it may discipline itself to attain to it; and in a few cases it may actually succeed. But in those cases the mortal is "translated," and the rest of mortality remains behind him. It is thus entailed in the notion of a changeless God that that which changes is outside his province. He is out there, beyond, an eternal lure to both mind and heart, but totally unresponsive—how could He respond, seeing that to respond is to change? So it is thus further entailed that the cosmos is a dualism with the gods and the Forms on one side and all changing things on the other. This conclusion is in conflict with much else in the Western theological tradition, but it is certainly what happens if the changeless is taken neat. What has made it palatable is being diluted with its opposite.

Further, that which is changeless is self-sufficient. Indeed, for the Greeks, it might be more accurate to say that that which is self-sufficient is changeless; αυταρκεια, self-sufficiency, was the more familiar conception; it was the watchword of city-state economics. But, either way, the entailment holds. What is changeless has need of nothing, and what has need of nothing has no need to change. What the idea of self-sufficiency in theology amounts to (again, when taken neat) may be gauged from a revealing passage of the *Eudemian Ethics,* which, if not Aristotle, is so near to the source that it hardly matters: "The self-sufficient man neither needs useful people nor people to cheer him, nor society; his own society is enough for him. This is most plain in the case of a god; for it is clear that, needing nothing, he will not need a friend, nor have one."[2]

§ 3. (ii) To the activist strand we now turn: and the best introduction to it is through the philosophical difficulties of the alternative.

As long as the mind is on the upward path, receding from the temporal scene to the unimaginable heights of reason, it does not have to face the question, How and why does the temporal scene exist at all? The temporal scene is the starting point of the dialectic in which it is to be transcended. But, from the point of view of the changeless, the temporal scene is strictly superfluous. And yet it is not nothing. In the *Republic* Plato declared it both being and not-being, and used the metaphors of participation and imitation to explain its relation to being. But this is no more than an honest statement of the problem. The temporal scene has being, in a sort of a way, but there is nothing in the nature of being to suggest why. The same problem will always arise when the standpoint of the ascent is taken as final. Even when it is trying to surpass itself, the finite can never be final. There is just *no* reason why the temporal scene should have the being it does have: if it is there, it bears testimony to something in the world other than reason, with which reason is only just on speaking terms. This is where there creeps into the picture the dualism which the centralizing force of the good should have dissipated. But as long as no reason is given for the temporal scene being what it is and is admitted to be, the dualism must persist.

The problem is in no way peculiar to Plato; it attaches to the *via remotionis* in theology whenever it recurs. But it is instructive to follow it up in Plato, because Plato, in later middle age, had the resilience to go into reverse on some major issues in order to solve it. Beginning with the mystical hint in *Republic VI* (509b) that the very being of the objects of knowledge comes from the Good, as well as their being known, he then asserts (*Phaedrus* 254E) that soul is the only source of motion, proceeds (Sophist 248Eff) to put soul on the same level of being as Forms, then argues that the "mixed" and (we

---

[2]*Eudemian Ethics,* trans. Solomon, Oxford translations, 9, 6, 1244 b6. I have replaced the translator's "independent" by "self-sufficient," the usual translation of ἀυταρκής.
At this point tradition would insist on a discussion of the further attribute of necessity. It is true that the changeless and self-sufficient God is also claimed to be necessary; but God might still be claimed to be necessary without being timeless or self-sufficient.

should add, this-worldly) life in which wisdom is blended with pleasure is better than the life of wisdom alone (*Philebus*, especially 22A) ,[3] adding that the mixture requires an agent to arrange it; and finally (*Timaeus, passim*) depicts God as the creator of the worldsoul and as the source of nature's remarkable mathematical adjustments. The notion of agency creeps in and enlarges itself because it provides a reason why physical objects should *be:* they *are* because they are creatures, and they have such order as their frailty allows because their creator likes mathematics.

Thus, swinging round from immobilism to activism, Plato was able to explain what in his earlier dialogues remained a mystery. But he never had to carry the full burden of the problem, because his outgoing deity is also a limited deity. He looks to the Forms as His model and the material He has to handle is refractory. God is a demiurge but not a providence. In many ways this picture is helpful: in particular it does not raise the problem of evil, which can be attributed to the backward pull of "chance and necessity." But, precisely because it does not push divine activity to the limit, bringing it in rather as a subsidiary though necessary device, it does not compel us to state our own problem squarely. That problem emerges in its acute form only when the notion of *cosmic* sufficiency is paired with the notion of *cosmic* activity. Either, taken as the handmaid, or the complement, of the other can be compatible with the other. The two notions are in contradiction only when both claim to be characters of the same absolute. But this is just what does happen in the classical natural theology, because it affirms that the God who creates is also the absolute which is self-sufficient.

But we have anticipated. It is time now to turn to the second or outgoing strand of our theological tradition.

The central conception here is that of creation. Now a creator differs from a demiurge in having no pre-existing models or materials. Everything that is, He has made. There is therefore no difficulty about dualism; if there is a difficulty, it is that there appears to be no room for the minimum of dualism which most people hanker after. There is also a sure foundation, as there is not under immobilism, for the uniformity of nature.[4] Again, there is a natural alignment, at least

---

[3] In this dialogue occurs the famous phrase γένεσις ὲις ὀυσίαν, which I insist on taking technically and seriously: 26D.

[4] This point was admirably made by Collingwood in his *Essay on Metaphysics*, p. 253.

in the West, between this kind of theology and personal religion. An immobile God is inaccessible: to pray to Him is merely to commune devoutly with one's own thoughts. The God who moves can also be moved. And here difficulties arise, for a god who can be moved is no longer self-sufficient; He has "passions," which even the accommodating Thirty-Nine Articles declare He has not; and He moves on from one point to the next, which is inconciliable with the Greek dogma of timelessness. Indeed, the moment we talk of creation, the whole problem of time arises to plague us. For either creation is in time or it is not; if it is not, it differs hardly, if at all from emanation, which is hardly, if at all, activity; if it is, the usual barrage of questions about what happens before creation is strictly in order, and if anything happens before creation, time is not a creation but part of God's nature.

These are not historical accidents; they are implicit in the original concept. Activity is necessarily in time, even in the form of creation. Only a stationary God can be eternal. The practical difference to the believer may be slight; for him "from everlasting to everlasting" is as good as "eternal"; in fact he does not distinguish between them. But for the creationist philosopher "from everlasting to everlasting" is opposed to "eternal," and is the only logically acceptable formula. (It is the believer's best formula anyhow, for it is far more biblical). For to create, in even the most attenuated sense, is to be the reason why something is which formerly was not; and the operative word is "formerly." The state of affairs before the thing happened *differs* from the state of affairs afterwards. It is just not possible to say that creating makes no difference to the creator, for the something which is there, and formerly was not there, is in relation to Him: He is related where formerly He was unrelated.

Thus the second strand in natural theology, left to itself, arrives at conclusions which are in contradiction with the first strand, left to itself. But our theological tradition does not wish to leave either of them to itself. We must therefore find some way of getting rid of the contradiction.

§ 4. Here, then, are the possibilities.

(1) Immobilism may be wholly mistaken and outgoingness entirely satisfactory.

(2) Outgoingness may be wholly mistaken and immobilism entirely satisfactory.

(3) Immobilism may be the formula for the whole, but outgoingness may be provided for within it. This is the orthodox view of actual theologians.

(4) Outgoingness may be the formula for the whole, but it may need the support of immobilist elements. This is the view we shall try to maintain.

On these possibilities, it may be observed that, for reasons already adumbrated, (1) and (2) are most unlikely to be true; we shall deal with them summarily. The real choice lies between (3) and (4), and these will receive most of our attention.

(1) The defects of this thesis have already emerged in the course of exposition. A God who was nothing but a creator would have nothing, so to speak, to stand on. What gives order and stability to the created world is that order and stability have gone to their making. A mere kaleidoscopic whirl could not create, any more than (to take the nearest human analogy) a chaos of mental events could compose music. Yet that is what creation apart from permanence would amount to: what the immobilist doctrine contributes to theology, and it is an indispensable contribution, is, at the very least, that God does not come and go; He is there even when He seems most absent. Whether this minimum should be rendered "timeless" or "everlasting" is a point to be considered by philosophers; but at least as reduced to "everlasting" the contribution of the immobilist has to be maintained.

Moreover, the everlasting, even if it is not timeless, but only coexistent with all possible time, forestalls the dialecticians like the Franciscan radical, Joachim of Flora, who regarded the three persons of the Trinity as successive phases of an evolution, the one giving way as the next appears on the scene. It is one thing for God to move, or even to be moved; it is another for Him to change His nature. The sea-god Proteus is no less elusive for tricking himself up in triads. To catch him one still has to tie him down. Otherwise, divinity might be anything or anywhere. It is the everlasting in whom there is no shadow of turning which saves creationism from passing over into pantheism—as was demonstrated, at considerable cost, in the story of German romanticism from Herder to Hitler.

(2) The defects of pure immobilism have also been indicated, and all that is here required of us is a *resumé*. An immobilist God must be finite; He can operate on the changing world only as a lure and not as a power: He is essentially alien to it; He cannot create; and He cannot respond to worship or prayer. To perform any of the

functions assigned to Him by the Western (and the near Eastern) religious tradition He has to borrow attributes from his opposite, and the result is intellectual confusion. The only way of establishing Him is to say that the whole tradition is intellectually mistaken. But if so, the whole associated system of prayer and practice is futile and invalid. The culmination of religion would be just to stare into an infinitely receding distance. And in that case, "God" has no resemblance to the Christian God, who is involved, concerned and responsive, and has established a religion which culminates in action—Why call ye me Lord, Lord, and do not the things which I say?

It might be replied that congruity with the life and concepts of religion is one thing and truth is another, and that immobilism, while certainly incompatible with what religion demands, is none the less true. We should not, it might be added, be dismayed that the word "God" should thus be detached from its normal frame of reference: we are discussing, not words, but things; if the immobile and eternal is the truth of things, we are entitled to call it "God," which is our general term for the best we know. But if we prefer to use "God" to mean "object of worship," then we can turn round and say that God is not the last word in the scheme of things, even if he is (as Bradley thought) the last but one. The immobilist doctrine must be tested not by verbal protestations but by argument.

The argument, however, is not far to seek. If the immobile God is the whole truth, nothing else can be true at all, not even God as active. For if He is the *whole* truth, everything temporal is an illusion. If the argument is naive, so is the position it controverts. If, in the manner of Hegel or Bradley, the immobile God (now called, more appropriately, the Absolute) is held to have degrees of reality within Himself, then His immobility is not the whole truth even about Him: if there are appearances of the Absolute the Absolute would not be what it is without its appearances. And this takes us from the present hypothesis to the next on the list. As far as the present hypothesis is concerned, argument coincides with the postulates of personal religion: and it eliminates one of the possible solutions of our main problem. It was suggested that the two strands of natural theology, as they stand, might not be as contradictory as they look. We now know that they are.

§ 5. We now move to the second type of solution, which is to scale down one of the factors till it takes its place in the scheme of the other. And we begin with the attempt to scale down activity and creation: the normal procedure of Western natural theology. Of theology, be it said, for it is very far from the practice of Western religions.

Supposing, then, that we start from the God of Aristotle, the first philosopher's God in Western history. It must be shown how the contingent derives from the necessary, the dependent from the self-sufficient, the fruitful from the eternal, and, consequently, change from the changeless. Note the form of the question: we could have asked instead whether there is such a thing as necessary or timeless or self-sufficient being, and that, in fact, is the *usual* question. Our question starts one stage further on: assuming that there is necessary and timeless and self-sufficient being, how could it be related to other kinds of being?[5]

It is the merit of Aristotle that he attempts to answer this question. God, he says, "moves without being moved" (Metaph. 1072 a25), in the way that objects of desire and objects of thought do: as a "final cause, which produces motion by being loved" (107264), He is "impassive and unalterable" (1073 a12), and is still a "first mover," for He is the lure which draws us on. The answer saves what Aristotle wanted to save: the divine attributes of changelessness and self-sufficiency. But he still assumes that there is a world of change, and he does not tell us how it came to be. It is what the Absolute Idealists used to call "brute fact." Aristotle just accepts it, looks beyond it, finds in its final cause the source of such order as it possesses, and admits that at the far end it fades off into the indeterminacy of "prime matter." There is a reason why it is what it is, but no reason why it is.

As an account of how movement issues from immobility, Aristotle's theory is highly ingenious: but it depends on there being already a propensity to movement, if not movement in actuality, in the thoughts and desires of man. Certainly, mathematicians think about triangles; for all I know, they may even love triangles; and triangles are not in time. But mathematicians are; and the lure of eternal triangles operates on them in their temporal medium. Given *their* temporality,

[5]This way of putting the question does not preclude, but neither does it entail, the elimination of "necessary being," etc.

triangles (or God) can operate without having any. It is only the thought or desire for triangles (or God) which is time-bound.

And so Aristotle discerns a relation between God and the world which is temporal from the side of the world, but not temporal on the side of God. His discernment marks the zenith and the fulfilment of the classical tradition. By absorbing Plato's God into Plato's Form of the Good, thus at the same time de-activating Him and making Him absolute, and deriving activity from the attraction of the final cause, in the best classical tradition, Aristotle answered our question so convincingly that his authority continued to weigh on the minds of Christian philosophers whose boast should have been that they had escaped from the classical tradition. But he started with the assumption that divinity was inactive and activity was not divine.[6] To carry his conclusions over into the Semitic orbit of primitive Christianity was an act of intellectual desperation.

For, with the acceptance on the religious plane of the God by whom all things were made, the whole cultural situation was altered. Instead of a God upheld by the love of men, there were men saved by the love of God. Instead of a "realm of imprecision" fading at the far end into the indeterminacy of "prime matter," there was a realm of precision governed in every detail by divine law.[7] In that context the focus of activity is no longer in man but in God. What has to be effected is no longer the conjunction of an impassive God and the longings of men (a synthesis which Aristotle handled with consummate skill) but the conjunction of passivity and activity in God Himself. To such a situation the Aristotelean answer no longer applies.

Nevertheless, classical civilization was the intellectual incunabulum of the Christian faith: and though it was only among intellectuals that the faith encountered any spiritual (as opposed to administrative) opposition, when it came to formulate itself, the only available categories were those of Greek philosophy. And so, from an early stage, the conception of eternity, construed as timelessness, took the place of the Biblical everlastingness, and the conception of self-

---

[6]Aristotle's God is not inactive, so to speak, internally, for he is busy with an eternal self-contemplation; he is even described as ζῷον ἀίδιον, "an eternal living object." But in this concentrated centre of the world's desire there is absolutely no response: externally, God *is* inactive, and, insofar as the human being becomes god-like, so is *he*.

[7]As Collingwood pointed out, *Essay in Metaphysics*, p. 254, the Christian revolution had to be accomplished before there could be natural science.

sufficiency, incongruously paired with justice or mercy, corroded or transformed the Biblical omnipotence. The church did not evolve its own philosophy but grew to maturity in borrowed clothing. The intellectual stresses of this imperfect merger continued till the Reformation.

But, leaving for a moment the history of the matter, let us consider on what terms, if at all, the synthesis of the two conceptions of Godhead could have been effected.

(1) It would have been easy to keep the Greek categories for the intellectuals and to dispense the primitive Christian categories as mythology for the multitude: easy, because both would thus have followed their natural bent. In fact, and fortunately, this did not happen: what that way leads to can be seen in the intellectual sterilization of Islam after Averroes, who, *mutatis mutandis,* made precisely this distinction. Both categories persisted (though with differing emphasis) both in natural theology *and* in the creeds to which all subscribed. The category of activity was not consigned to revelation and discarded from philosophy. The philosophical problem, on the contrary, was fairly faced on both levels.

(2) In revealed theology, it was all too convenient to assign the diverse attributes to different persons of the Trinity. In general, the God of the Old Testament was provided with Aristotelean attributes, and activity of Godhead was assigned to the Son.[8] This nest of confusions is strictly beyond the scope of this paper; we may simply quote "I and the Father are one," "He that hath seen me hath seen the Father," and above all, "My Father *worketh hitherto,* and I work." It is mentioned because it provides an allegedly Christian escape from our dilemma: the divergent attributes can be assigned to the different Persons. Unfortunately,[9] it is the first Person of the Trinity which appears in Aristotelean garb, and it is the first Person of the Trinity that is discussed in natural, as opposed to revealed, theology. Hence the revealed dissociation of Persons helps to maintain, for the philosophers, the immobilist conception of God.

(3) Thus there is no way round: we have to accept both the Aristotelean and the Hebrew inheritance, and let them sort them-

[8] As Collingwood points out, *Essay in Metaphysics,* p. 226.

[9] As well as unnaturally: The God of the Old Testament is particularly non-Aristotelean.

selves out as best as they can. How, then, starting with immobilism, eternity, and self-sufficiency, can we derive the attributes of creativity, justice and mercy?

(a) One device is to say that we just can't, and can't be expected to: so great a mystery can't be explained at all, it has to be accepted, humbly and empirically, as a fact. Such an attribute is fair enough at the moment of worship, when analysis is suspended; but it is improper in natural theology, which is committed to gettng the analysis straight.

(b) Another device is to develop the notion of self-sufficiency so as to *include* the notion of outgoingness. Its merit is that it maintains the note of one-sided dependence which is undoubtedly part of religion and which the notion of self-sufficiency conveys, but not quite so well. A self-sufficient God may easily encourage self-sufficiency in men; in fact, the "divine" man, i.e., the sage, is a sort of prefiguration of Him. An outgoing God, by His generosity, elicits both generosity in others and gratitude to Himself. The passage from self-sufficiency to outgoingness has thus been made acceptable to Western religion; and it has the advantage of requiring the co-operation of no other force outside God Himself. "Outgoing" is a metaphor designed to express what happens when the abundance of God can no longer be contained in God and has to spill over into creation. Unhappily, the notion of self-sufficiency does not cohere with that of abundance, but excludes it. For (1) what is self-sufficient cannot add to its inward resources any more than it can be lacking in them. (2) Only through an addition to the inward resources of God could there be an overflow. (3) And principally, both operations postulate a passage of time for the self-sufficient timeless God to deploy Himself in. Time is thus installed in the centre of the divine being, and the "eternal" is overthrown. To develop self-sufficiency by means of "overflowing" is therefore suicidal and if "overflowing" is acceptable, for religious or philosophical reasons, self-sufficiency will have to go.

(c) Yet another attempt to combine the incompatible is to be found in the conception of God's goodness. Aristotle himself presents God as good; and the general notion that what is one and what is good are somehow the same is a leading motif of Greek psychology and politics. Now the oneness and the goodness of God was precisely what had to be stressed by early Christian theologians in their struggle with pagan polytheism and the Manichees. Here, if anywhere, it might be said, there should be continuity.

On the oneness of God we may agree: on this issue Aristotle was with his Christian adapters against the Greek tradition. But the senses in which "goodness" was understood in the two environments were so different that the bridge proves to be no more than verbal. In Aristotle the "good" is that to which everything tends; God is good as the finally satisfying object of the world's desire. To be good in this sense does not entail *doing* anything. But the goodness of God in the Old and New Testaments is displayed in His justice and His mercy and these are unquestionably thought of as activities. They are, moreover, activities which no self-sufficient deity, enthroned above time, could possibly engage in; for Him, they would be a descent: "omnis determinatio est negatio," as Spinoza was to say later on. Nor is it any use saying that on the Christian view there *was* a descent; *if* there was, it was because God was in some way pledged to this world, i.e., He is not self-sufficient.

(d) Nothing has been said about the attribute of "necessity" so commonly taken to distinguish the being of God from other kinds of being: partly because everything cannot be said at once, but mainly because "necessary being" might be shown not to be inseparable from self-sufficiency and timelessness, and these are the attributes under scrutiny. It might, in fact, be possible to transpose the arguments for necessary being into the temporal mode. This will be argued in the next paragraph. All that is here said is that self-sufficiency and timelessness must stand on their own feet; and this we have now seen they have some difficulty in doing.

To conclude: any attempt to expand the Aristotelean account of deity to take in the traditional attributes of Semitic-type religions— even Christianity, despite its early Hellenistic conditioning—ends in contradiction. What it is intended to include persists in breaking the container. The attempt to scale down divine activity to accord with divine impassivity must be pronounced a failure. Let us now see if we succeed any better with the alternative policy: that of scaling down divine impassivity to accord with divine activity.

§ 6. The first proposition in this policy in unorthodox. Seeing that all activity is in time, divine activity is in time, and God, like all being, is temporal being. That is the pre-suppostion with which the traditional attributes will somehow have to be brought into line. From it follow other propositions equally disconcerting. One is that God grows, e.g., after creation, God is more God than He was previously, to match the world which is also more than it was previously. Another is that God is affected by what happens outside Himself; however adequate to all situations, He has to cope with situations. A third, and still more unpalatable consequence, this time of special concern to philosophers, is that, being temporal, and therefore not eternal, though perhaps everlasting, God is part of the empirical world, and therefore subject to the tests of experience. Such is the picture of God which, if natural theology is not to be broken into two, must absorb and find place for the attributes assigned to Him by Greek philosophy, and by the theologians in their more professional moods.

The second general point is this. It is not proposed to *substitute* a temporal account of God for the eternal. It is proposed to inquire whether the eternal can be *incorporated* in the temporal. This could happen in two ways. Either the eternal might be re-presented empirically as "everlasting," i.e., co-eval with all possible time but never out of time; or there could be eternal elements persisting or recurring in the history of temporal being, carried along with it, but remaining unchanged. The element of eternity will either be scaled down throughout to its "empirical counterpart," or it will retain its character unaltered in an enveloping temporal context. It will be argued that both these operations are necessary, and that when they have been carried out the two strands in natural theology will be as well adjusted as the final mystery allows.

There is one respect in which the approach from this side is encouraging. There is no analogy anywhere for the self-mobilization of immobility, but there is an analogy both for continuity of character and for immobilities in time. The favoured analogy for hints about God is that of human personality; take the continuity of character in a well-rounded human life and extend it indefinitely, and it is possible, without importing extraneous factors, to depict a God who should be everlasting. On the other hand, character is built round recurring patterns, as indeed the physical world is built round recurring structures; and once again all one has to do is to contemplate these things, with due regard for the difference between finite and infinite. The scheme of continuity and recurrence is already there;

they belong to experience, and to the world, intrinsically, and they do not have to be introduced from without.

There are, however, the following difficulties.

(1) Continuity in human character is based on limitation: it is this and not that. Can God be so conceived?

(2) There is always time extending both ways from any human experience, but how can there be time extending either way from the everlasting?

(3) How can God change without becoming more God or less God? If He is perfect, neither of these things is possible. For if He becomes more God, then He was previously not perfect, and if He becomes less God, He will be less perfect in the future.

(4) The God who is apprehended in time will be apprehended empirically: vouched for, no doubt, by a cloud of witnesses, but not existing necessarily.

These are the questions which have sent the theologians scuttling back to the defences of changelessness and impassivity. But, if they do, they are condemned to oscillate between incompatibles, for they cannot let go the concept of divine activity. On the answers depends the possibility of a rational theology.[10]

The first difficulty is easily answered. *Of course* God is this and not that: He is God and not His creatures. To deny it is to say that God is everything, that is to say, nothing. God is not all being: He is supreme being. There is an ambiguity in our question about "limitation." It would be derogatory to speak of God as having limited excellence or limited power: it is not derogatory to speak of God as determinate: as maker rather than as made. On the contrary, to speak of Him as *in*determinate, i.e., as nothing in particular, *would* be derogatory; and it would lay statements about Him wide open to the current charge of "vacuity."

The second question has a more threatening aspect, but it is based on a *petitio principii*. To ask what happens before time is like asking, from the immobilist point of view, what *is* when there is no being? On the assumption now being elaborated, time is just given, and that which is everlasting is coincident with it. What it is necessary to assert

---

[10]And that matters: a merely kerygmatic religion, indifferent to intelligence, must produce in these days a schizophrenic culture.

is not that God is out of time, but that there is no moment of time which is without Him.

The third question is especially instructive, because it introduces us to the "schematization" in time of characters traditionally held to be timeless.[11] Perfection, schematized, is actively complementary to a given state of affairs. The God who was perfect in relation to an earlier state of affairs would *have* to change in order to be perfect in relation to a later state of affairs. He was perfect then, He is perfect now, He will be perfect hereafter, but only by being now more than He was then, and by being more hereafter than He is now. And if it be objected that in that case God is relative to His creatures, the answer is that if He were not, He would soon be inadequate to His creatures. The perfection of God, so far from rejecting change, depends upon it.

This brings us to the fourth and final problem. If God is in time, then, like anything else in time, he just happens to be there; there is no reason why he *has* to be there. No doubt He goes on happening to be there; but this is not sufficiently reassuring. As the weaver in Cebes' parable (*Phaedo* 87B) outwears cloak after cloak but dies in the end, so a God who merely happens to be there might outlast generations and then disintegrate. Where God is concerned, we cannot dispense with necessity.

Several answers come to mind. The first is that of the ordinary believer, convinced of the presence of God, and untroubled by metaphysics. I am blest in what I find; I am confirmed by finding that other people find what I find; and, for the rest, I live by faith, and leap the fire-break between the now and the everlasting. That God should happen to be there is so marvellous that there is no time to look past it: I just have to keep telling the story as it found me. In the mood of worship, the distinction between empirical and necessary does not arise at all.

A second thought, however, which may occur to the worshipper in his more reflective moods, and provides a possible way of escape for the philosopher, is to stress the sense of necessity of God in the act of worship and to say that it is the work of faith. Necessity does not belong to the *being* of God, but is *imputed* to Him on the basis

[11]The phrase is Kant's, but he used it of the categories in their relation to experience. It never occurred to him to schematize the traditional attributes of deity, and that is why he had to be agnostic about them.

of the records of Scripture, continuous testimony, and the constraining recapitulation of both scripture and testimony in one's own experience. Our knowledge of Him is empirical, and our faith takes care of the gaps and the future. On this showing, the argument does not require us to transcribe necessity into the temporal mode, because, temporal or non-temporal, it falls outside the sphere of argument. Our *philosophy* of religion is empirical, and the demand for necessity represents the total religious response, with its persistent practical orientation.[12]

This dichotomy, however, although it meets all practical needs and maintains the complete objectivity of God as an object of worship, will not satisfy those who require of a temporalist translation that it should re-present the being of God as *logically* necessary. For these, there is nothing for it but the traditional proofs, trimmed to suit the ubiquity of time.

Now if there is a being compassing every *possible* moment of time, that being exists both temporally and necessarily. In such a conception there is no contradiction whatever. The only question therefore is, Is there a being compassing every possible moment of time? Now the difficulty of there existing such a being is no greater than the difficulty of there existing a being wholly beyond time. All that is required is that the arguments for necessary being beyond time should be "schematized." Of these, only the cosmological proof and the argument from value have any significance. The argument from design can never establish anything more than a demiurge, and the ontological proof runs on purely logical lines and cannot be converted to a temporalist gauge.

In some of its aspects (e.g., the argument from motion) the cosmological proof argues to a first cause from the absurdity of temporal regress. By hypothesis, this consideration now loses its sting, for a temporal regress is no longer absurd. But "contingent" in the argument, means far more than "temporally caused." It means "dependent," and it means "imperfect." These notions are the mainspring of the proof; if they cannot carry it, nothing can. Power and excellence which proceed from strength to strength are no less non-dependent and no less perfect than power and excellence anchored

---

[12]It was defended by the present writer to the *Journal of Religion*, 36, No. 1, Jan. 1956, and he is still prepared to stand by it.

in eternity: and they are much closer to the needs of personal religion. And that is all the argument requires of us. We are concerned with the adjustment of the strands and not with the separate justification of each of them. Those who are dissatisfied with the cosmological proof as a *whole* will probably remain unconvinced, but it might pay them to examine the suggested temporalist version of it, to see if it removes any causes of complaint.

As for the argument from value, this in no way depends on the absurdity of a temporal regress. If the world in which value is embodied had only existed for half an hour, in its own right and not merely as a projection of our preferences, it would still be pertinent to argue (as those who favour this type of argument have argued) that the impersonal objectiveness of values requires a sufficient personal source. That values cannot be impersonal; that we who are subject to them, cannot be the persons giving rise to them, and that they must derive from a being in whom they are fully personalized, are statements and conclusions which are perfectly at home in a temporal universe, and indeed much more so than in eternity: for there can be no personalized value in pure inaction. The very terms in which this argument is usually conducted point to a temporalist interpretation.

So far we have argued that timefulness in God is no derogation of divinity, provided that it is not a limited timefulness. None the less, we have been holding on to the traditional attributes in temporalized form. And that is only part of what we proposed, and are required to show. For there are some features of the world which are in fact immutable. It is these factors which in Greek times formed the model for the immutable God. There are, in the first place, mathematicals; triangles take no account of time. And, secondly, there are the μέγιστα γένη of Plato's *Sophist* and the mediaeval "transcendentals"—the constitutive structures of the world subjectively rendered by Kant as "categories." These do not merely endure and grow, they remain unaltered: they not merely are, but they cannot be otherwise. Whether their being otherwise would be a contradiction in things or in thought does not matter: for in the context of creation, in which we are here considering them, any contradiction in things could only be the reflexion of a contradiction in God's thought. As is well known, the Platonic Forms (or Ideas), became, in the hands of

Augustine, part of the furniture of the mind of God.[13] In setting them aside God would be setting Himself aside, and, as Thomas Aquinas observed, "God cannot do that which is in itself impossible."

There are thus in God's nature eternal elements as well as temporal, and it is these which save us from the spectre of arbitrary deity. But they belong to a nature which is progressive, responsive and creative, and provide a balance for its unbounded energies. God is everlasting and not eternal, but his everlastingness takes shape and form from the eternal elements within it.

§ 7. At the beginning of the previous section, we set out to see what would happen if we started with divine activity and tried to accommodate divine immobility. We have now redeemed our promise. We have shown how many of the attributes of those associated with eternity can be represented in time by "empirical counterparts"; we have shown how a hard core of eternal attributes can function as a framework for divine enterprise; and we have shown how by schematization on the one hand and by the re-affirmation of eternity as a constituent attribute on the other, the two kinds of natural theology can be consolidated without violence. Such was our original objective; we have now settled on the terms which make it possible.

There are three necessary epilogomena. The first is to explain further how it is that the temporal form of deity can contain the eternal, while the eternal cannot contain the temporal. The second is to relate our conclusions to practical religion. The third is personal, and it will appear in its proper time.

The first, which is the main point of the paper, may be extricated from the argument and re-stated thus; that if once we start from eternity and immobility, we cannot get activity out of them; that when we talk of the eternal and immutable as "outgoing" or "overflowing" we are smuggling activity into them; that the only consistent statement of the eternalist position was Aristotle's, which is inherently dualistic and places motion only in the creature, God being merely its occasion; that the proper corollary is that which Aristotle in fact adopts, that the most perfect movement is not progress but movement in a circle; that both the position itself and its corollary are irreconcilable with the notions of divine agency proclaimed in the Jewish-

13And only with the secularization of philosophy in the 17th century was the word "idea" used to describe the furniture of the human mind.

Christian tradition, and with the modern world's expectation of progress, which rests in part on an analysis of technology, but far more profoundly on the Old and the New Testaments: and that in general the attempts to derive agency from eternity contradict themselves by taking for granted what they have to deny. On the contrary, activity is distinguished from mere flux firstly by its continuity (in the case of God an unending continuity) and secondly by its primary structures (in the case of God appearing both subjectively as intellect and objectively in His creation). Activity is the mediating term between flux and eternity, and already contains in itself the synthesis which cannot be extracted from eternity alone.

(2) The advantages of this conclusion for a working religion stand out at once. It is a commonplace of religion that God is a power in the world making for good; and that power can be exercised only in time. To take God out of time is to transfer power from God to our thinking about Him. It may be said that He draws or invites our thoughts: but even that is *doing* something. If God is not in time, He might, in some odd sense, exist, but He could not "make for good"; *we* might make for good by contemplating Him, but there would be nothing except ourselves to ensure good in this world, and the more we became like God the less we should be able to do it. These paradoxes cut religion at the root. They make nonsense of prayer, they demean action; and worst of all, they are neutral on the central issue of religion: is this world an accident, to be seized upon by opportunists for their own aggrandisement, or is it a creation in which we are assured that God's will shall one day be done? In this conflict between cynicism and reverence the motionless God takes no sides, and in such a matter neutrality is a victory for the cynics.

It is eminently satisfactory that our philosophical disputation should conclude by returning contemplation to its proper context in the field of practice. There is a persistent tendency, not least among theologians, and especially among theologians influenced by contemporary British philosophy, to deprecate the empirical element in religion, and to exalt God beyond the reach of human contact. What we claim to have shown is that if He is so represented it will be impossible to get Him back again: whereas if we start from the assumptions of ordinary religion, we shall be able to include in a subordinate role the insights of the philosophers.

(3) Throughout this discussion, I have purposely refrained from

consulting or citing Professor Hartshorne's treatment of these issues in *Man's Vision of God*. Now, however, seeing that this collection is in his honour, I wish to repair the omission, and to confess that my guiding inspiration comes straight from Professor Hartshorne himself. It is he who has insisted for two dreary decades during which even philosophical theology has taken on a protective colouring of triviality that its reform is the greatest single problem of philosophy; and it is he who made the crucial distinction between absolute and relative perfection (*op. cit.*, p.7.), thus revealing the cleft within the orthodox philosophical theology of today. Whether this contribution, which owes so much to him, is in keeping with his present convictions, I do not know: I suspect that I am more disconcerted by eternity than he is, and he might prefer to preserve a balance between the outgoing and the eternal components of deity, instead of giving pride of place to the outgoing. But I am very conscious that I have been working in his own special field, and proud to have the opportunity.

A. BOYCE GIBSON

UNIVERSITY OF MELBOURNE

BULTMANN'S DEMYTHOLOGIZING AND
HARTSHORNE'S DIPOLAR THEISM

I

DURING a period in which some of the most prominent voices have affirmed the contrary, Rudolf Bultmann has been notable for his insistence that the work of the Christian theologian is properly dependent on the work of the secular philosopher. Bultmann himself has remarked that this insistence, as expressed in his "efforts to make philosophy fruitful for theology," is what has accounted for his increasing opposition to Karl Barth.[1] And this remark is readily understandable; for wherever Barth's extraordinary influence has prevailed, theologians have generally been anxious to declare their independence of philosophy in the interests of a purely "biblical" or "church" theology. To be sure, there have always been exceptions to this rule, and at the present time especially, there are important signs that at least some of the younger generation of Barthian theologians have moved toward a much less defensive position. But it is significant that the chief source of such signs—namely, the Basel theologian Heinrich Ott—is one of the most knowledgeable students of Bultmann's achievement and is scarcely less indebted to it than he is to that of Barth himself.[2] The point, in any case, is that Bultmann has consistently rejected the Barthian demand for a nonphilosophical theology and has urged instead that the theologian has every reason to be gratefully, though not uncritically, dependent on his colleagues in philosophy.

In this, of course, Bultmann has not stood alone. We in America have long had reason to give thanks that a theologian as eminent as Paul Tillich has forcibly defended an essentially similar position. And there have been others as well who have been just as emphatic in

---

[1]Schubert M. Ogden (ed.), *Existence and Faith: Shorter Writings of Rudolf Bultmann* (New York: Meridian Books, Inc., 1960), p. 288.

[2]Cf. especially Ott's two major works, *Geschichte und Heilsgeschichte in der Theologie Rudolf Bultmanns* (Tübingen: J. C. B. Mohr, 1955) and *Denken und Sein: Der Weg Martin Heideggers und der Weg der Theologie* (Zollikon: Evangelischer Verlag, 1959).

rejecting the anti-philosophical demand of Barth's narrow biblicism. Even so, Bultmann's view has a certain interest all its own, and not least because his lifelong preoccupation with the problem of theological method has enabled him to argue for it with perhaps as much self-consciousness as can be found anywhere in contemporary theology.

The logic of his argument is simple and convincing.[3] If, as he maintains, the task of theology is the adequate conceptual statement of Christian faith, its object, basis, and consequences, then obviously the primary concern of the theologian must be to secure concepts in which this task may be effectively accomplished. He must attempt to discover a "conceptuality" *(Begrifflichkeit)* in which he can appropriately state what faith itself affirms and, at the same time, so express its affirmations that they can be clearly understood by the contemporary hearers who are addressed by them through the church's proclamation. But this implies, Bultmann argues, that the theologian inevitably becomes dependent on the work of the philosopher; for it is not the task of theology as such, but rather of philosophy, to provide the concepts by which the theologian must carry out his responsibility.

Bultmann does not mean by this, naturally, that no one individual is able to pursue both of these tasks, so that no theologian can be, as it were, his own philosopher. He means, rather, that the responsibility of adequately conceptualizing the generic features of our experience is one that properly falls to philosophy rather than theology, and that a theologian who attempts to exercise such responsibility is himself insofar a philosopher.

It follows, however, Bultmann believes, that the theologian has every warrant to learn as much as he can from secular philosophy. For just as in general, having something to say does not guarantee that one also commands resources for saying it, so the theologian cannot assume that he disposes of concepts in which he can explicate Christian faith in the most appropriate and understandable way. The task of adequately conceptualizing the basic realities given in our experience is a task all by itself, and it requires all the skill and attention that the professional philosopher alone is able to bring to it. Therefore, if the theologian is to carry out his responsibility, he

---

[3]The most important sources for this discussion, as for that in the next section, are *Existence and Faith*, pp. 92–102, 302 f.; H. W. Bartsch (ed.), *Kerygma und Mythos*, 2 (Hamburg: Herbert Reich-Evangelischer Verlag, 1952), 187 ff., 191–197, 201; and *Jesus Christ and Mythology* (New York: Charles Scribner's Sons, 1958), pp. 45–70, 74.

does well to become scholar to the philosopher and to learn from him how to speak more adequately of the realities of which he is commissioned to speak.

This he may do without anxiety, Bultmann claims, because, if philosophy is properly pursued, it is simply the attempt to analyze the essential features of experienced phenomena and to express these features in appropriate and understandable concepts. Its method is phenomenological analysis, and its goal, as distinguished from the goal of the special sciences, is properly ontological. It abstracts from all particular being (*das Seiende*) in order to focus on the being in general (*das Sein*) of which particular beings are all instances. This it may do initially, and for the purpose of securing a starting point, by developing an ontology of some special kind of being such as the being of man, which is immediately accessible to analysis. But its final goal is to develop a completely general ontology, a conceptuality or categoreal scheme in which it is possible to interpret every reality given in our experience.

If this is so, however, the theologian need have no scruples about becoming dependent on the work of the philosopher. So far from compromising the proper autonomy of his theological work, such dependence can only serve to assist him at the point of his greatest need—to secure concepts in which he may adequately express the affirmations of faith, all of which refer to the realities encountered in man's experience of himself and his world.

This assumes, of course, that the philosophy from which the theologian attempts to learn has properly pursued the philosophical task. And so Bultmann's argument concludes with the statement that the most important question the theologian has to answer is the question of the "right" philosophy. Which of the philosophies currently available so analyzes and expresses the basic realities of our experience that it provides the "right" conceptuality for understanding them, and thus supplies the theologian with concepts in which he, too, may adequately speak?

Bultmann's own characteristic answer to this question is the existential analysis of the early Martin Heidegger. Although he is fully aware that conclusive results are no more to be had in philosophy than in any other inquiry, he obviously believes that Heidegger's *Sein und Zeit* is an impressive philosophical achievement. Indeed, there are, to my knowledge, but one or two places in all his writings where he acknowledges any dependence on philosophical resources other than those provided by Heidegger's early work. Just as for Thomas Aquinas, the words "the philosopher" had a unique and unmistakable reference, so also for Bultmann, philosophy and the early Heidegger are practically indistinguishable. I do not mean by this that Bultmann's dependence on Heidegger is uncritical, any more than I should wish to make such a charge about Thomas' relation to Aristotle. It seems clear to me, rather, that he has what he, at any rate, regards as good reasons for his high opinion of Heidegger's work. The point, however, is that his dependence on Heidegger, at least to judge from his explicit statements, is quite complete and thoroughgoing. With the few exceptions noted above, all he says by way of presenting his own answer to the question of the "right" philosophy points to Heidegger's existential analysis and to it alone. As a matter of fact, he has repeatedly attempted to defend this answer even in the respects in which many of his critics have regarded it as most open to objection.

This suggests, however, that it is precisely Bultmann's espousal of Heidegger's existential analysis as the "right" philosophy that has provoked the major criticism of his theological program. He has presented his famous demand for a "demythologizing" of the Christian proclamation as having the positive significance of a demand for, in John Macquarrie's words, "an existentialist theology," i.e., a theology that expresses faith's affirmations in the concepts of Heidegger's analysis of human existence. But just this has been his chief cause of offense to the majority of his critics. Nor is this true solely of those who repudiate in principle anything other than a "biblical" or "church" theology. Even those who are sympathetic with his insistence that the theologian is properly dependent on the philosopher have difficulty agreeing that the early Heidegger is the philosopher on whom they should be dependent. On the face of it, they claim, Heidegger's existential analysis alone is unable to provide adequate concepts for Christian theology.

The reason for this is that the reality to which the affirmations of faith refer is not only or even primarily man, but rather God and man together, and in that order of priority. Faith's first concern, these critics argue, is not with man's possibilities of self-understanding, but with God's gracious action as Creator and Redeemer, through which alone man and his possibilities have their basis and significance. But precisely this concern is impossible to express within the limits of

Heidegger's philosophy. God not only is not the primary object of his existential analysis, but does not figure in his analysis at all; and while this may not mean that Heidegger's philosophy is "atheistic," one can scarcely claim that it by itself provides the "right" concepts for an appropriate Christian theology. Or, at any rate, such a claim can be made only by renouncing all direct speaking of God and his action and reducing the affirmations of faith solely to statements about human existence. In that case, however, faith can hardly be distinguished from a purely subjective self-understanding, which is lacking in any divine basis or object.[4]

Bultmann has repeatedly tried to meet this criticism and to silence the question whether Heidegger's existential analysis is really the "right" philosophy for the Christian theologian. But of more importance is that he himself, particularly in his more recent writings, has indirectly voiced the same question. In his earnest attempts to defend his program of demythologizing, and especially to make clear that it does not involve a renunciation of all direct speaking of God and his action, he has stepped well beyond the limits of Heidegger's existential analysis and thus has in effect conceded the point for which so many of his critics have contended.

I recognize it may seem strange that a theologian who is obviously as self-conscious as Bultmann should make use of philosophical resources of which he fails to give any accounting. And in the strict sense, I should be unwilling to defend the proposition that this is so; for, as I noted, there are at least some places where he acknowledges his dependence on resources other than the early Heidegger. Nevertheless, the fact that such acknowledgments are made in the context of some of his most determined defenses of Heidegger's philosophy— defenses that go so far, indeed, as even to justify Heidegger's "atheism"—suggests that his position on this matter is far from being clearly worked out. Even so, he unquestionably depends in part on philosophical resources that are not directly supplied by Heidegger's analysis of human existence. In fact, the merit of his theology is that the conceptuality it employs is ampler than seems to be allowed for by his characteristic answer to the question of the "right" philosophy.

[4]Probably the best statement of this criticism by one who is sympathetic with Bultmann's general view of the relation of theology and philosophy is John Macquarrie's, especially in *An Existentialist Theology: A Comparison of Heidegger and Bultmann* (London: SCM Press Ltd., 1955).

In saying this, however, I have no concern to maintain that Bultmann's theology is free of deficiencies in its philosophical foundations. He himself has frequently pointed out that no theology can be adequate unless it is in critical and self-conscious command of the philosophical concepts in which it makes its assertions. And, in part at least, his own work provides a model of such mastery in turning Heidegger's existential analysis to the purposes of an adequate theological anthropology. But in the other part of his theology, which has to do directly with God and only indirectly with man, one looks in vain for anything like the same kind of command. Although he clearly intends to speak directly of God as well as of man, he repeatedly defends a philosophy that hardly allows for such speaking, and, in his actual practice, speaks of God relatively infrequently and, even then, with almost none of the conceptual mastery that so uniquely distinguishes his speaking of human existence.

In short, the philosophical foundations of his theology are anthropologically strong, but theologically weak. He is handicapped in realizing his own concerns because he insufficiently develops the specifically *theological* component in an adequate philosophical conceptuality.

But this means that anyone, who, like myself, is concerned to follow Bultmann in his intentions, has no alternative but to work through the problem of the "right" philosophy in a rather different way than he has done. And this is where the philosophical theology of Charles Hartshorne becomes immensely significant. I do not mean, of course, that this is the only reason for holding Hartshorne's work to be important. I should gladly allow that there are any number of other reasons for regarding his achievement as the most impressive of its kind to have been produced in the twentieth century. My point, however, is that one of the ways in which his immense significance is proven is that his "dipolar" theism supplies precisely the philosophical resource that Bultmann obviously needs but can hardly secure by depending solely on Heidegger's existential analysis. If it can be shown, as I believe it can, that Hartshorne provides an analysis of *divine* existence that closely parallels and complements Heidegger's analysis of *human* existence, then we shall have found a means for overcoming the inadequacy in Bultmann's conceptuality that fully honors and expresses his own intentions. The way will be open to a better answer to the question of the "right" philosophy than he himself has given, and the cause for the chief criticism of his theological program should be removed.

The tasks to be accomplished in the remainder of the essay are now before us. First, I should like to develop the point that Bultmann in fact depends on, and in part acknowledges, philosophical resources beyond any supplied by Heidegger's analysis of human existence. Second, I want to show that these additional resources, which Bultmann himself presents only fragmentarily, are most adequately provided in Hartshorne's dipolar analysis of the nature of God. Finally, and in the light of the preceding, I want to offer an alternative answer to the question of the "right" philosophy and, in so doing, point to a larger task that seems to be required if this answer is to be really convincing.

II

I noted that the major criticism of Bultmann's theological method is that it makes impossible a direct speaking of God and therefore is insecure against the dangers of subjectivism. I also noted that Bultmann has been sensitive to this criticism and, in at least one or two places in his later writings, attempts to overcome it in a way that goes well beyond the mere defense of his characteristic position. In his reply to his critics in the second volume of *Kerygma und Mythos*, and in the parallel passages in *Jesus Christ and Mythology*, he states emphatically that it is no part of his intention to preclude a direct speaking of God and his action. "If speaking about God's act is to be meaningful, *it must indeed be not simply a figurative or 'symbolic' kind of speaking* [i.e., simply a way of designating man's own subjective self-understanding], but must rather intend a divine act in the fully real and 'objective' sense."[5]

To justify this position, Bultmann introduces a distinction between "myth" and "analogy," which, so far as I am aware, is explicitly made in none of his earlier writings. "Myth," he says, speaks of God and his action only by using concepts that properly apply solely to the "world," to the realm of the wholly "objective," which is the correlate of the kind of thinking represented by scientific research. Accordingly, an adequate theology has no alternative but to reject such mythological speaking; for not only has myth been rendered incredible by

[5]*Kerygma und Mythos*, 2, 196; cf. *Jesus Christ and Mythology*, pp. 60–70.

the world-picture of modern science, but, even more important, myth seriously misrepresents the transcendence of God and his action as Christian faith understands it.

This does not require, however, that *all* direct speaking of God be precluded. On the contrary, Bultmann argues, there is another realm of man's experience, and so also the possibility of other concepts, than the realm of the "world" as disclosed by the concepts of the special sciences—namely, the realm of man's distinctively personal existence as clarified and conceptualized in *Sein und Zeit*. By constructing "analogies" on the basis of Heidegger's existential analysis, and thus representing God as eminent existence, it is possible to speak of him in "the fully real and 'objective' sense" without involving oneself in the double inadequacy of myth. For, although even the concepts of existential analysis involve "objectification," they objectify man precisely as subject and therefore as transcending conceptualization in his concrete existence. Thus, when they are applied to God by way of analogy, they do not reduce him simply to an object of conceptual thinking and consequently entail neither a conflict with science nor a misrepresentation of the divine transcendence.

With even less clarification of what he means by analogy than this summary suggests, Bultmann simply refers to the discussion of the concept in Erich Frank's *Philosophical Understanding and Religious Truth*. In doing so, however, he evidently records a philosophical indebtedness beyond any he could possibly owe to the early Heidegger.

It is interesting that Bultmann's discussion of analogy has gone almost completely unnoticed by his readers. In fact, until quite recently, there was only one English-speaking critic who even seemed to be aware of it, and he was of the opinion that the distinction between myth and analogy is invalid, given Bultmann's original definition of myth.[6] This opinion can hardly be maintained, since it rests on a failure to observe an important limitation to which Bultmann's concept of myth is subject. But because Bultmann himself devotes so little attention to clarifying his distinction, one cannot feel too hard toward the critic for failing to see its validity. Nor can one be completely unsympathetic even with those who neglect Bultmann's discussion of analogy altogether; for the place occupied by this discus-

---

[6]Cf. Ronald W. Hepburn's essay in Antony Flew and Alasdair Macintyre (eds.), *New Essays in Philosophical Theology* (London: SCM Press Ltd., 1955), pp. 229 f. and 237.

sion in the total structure of his theology is so inconspicuous that it is hardly surprising it has been so universally overlooked.

Even so, it would be a serious mistake to suppose that what Bult-mann says in this discussion is unimportant or that it is nothing more than an *ad hoc* solution to a difficulty posed by his critics. I have no doubt that his attempt to explicate the notion of analogy has in fact been occasioned by his more recent critics' objections. But I am equally confident that the notion itself, so far from being novel or arbitrary, is more or less clearly implied in the vast bulk of his writings. If his actual practice is any indication, then he does not mislead when he says he has no intention of denying that God as well as man is the direct object of theological discourse. For all of his concern with existential interpretation and with presenting the affir-mations of faith as expressing a certain possibility for man's self-under-standing, he continually speaks of God himself in "the fully real and 'objective' sense," and does so, moreover, in the very way he indicates—namely, not mythologically, but in terms of analogies drawn in the concepts of existential analysis.

Nevertheless, his conceptuality is so anthropologically one-sided, so insufficiently developed in its specifically theological component, that it is far from meeting the requirements of an adequate theology. And this inadequacy also is everywhere reflected in his practice. If he con-tinually speaks directly of God, as well as of man, this is not his usual mode of procedure. Rather, his predominant approach is to present the affirmations of faith in terms of the self-understanding they express, and thus to develop theology primarily in the form of anthropology.

In short, Bultmann presents an anomaly. On the one hand, he clearly does not wish to deny that theology must speak as directly of God as it speaks of man; and he himself not only continually engages in such speaking, but even attempts to justify it by his fragmentary theory of analogy. On the other hand, he so stresses the procedure of existential interpretation as apparently to preclude the very direct speaking of God he has no intention of denying; and this impression is confirmed by his resolute defense of the early Heidegger, even to the point of claiming that Heidegger's "atheism" is a positive philo-sophical virtue. The question now is whether this anomaly can be explained.

I believe it can. In the first place, Bultmann is well aware, as many of his critics are not, that faith so understands God and man and their relationship that to speak appropriately of either is in fact to speak of both. The objection that existential interpretation is inherently incomplete because faith speaks not only of man but also of God runs the risk of implying that the relation between God and man is wholly external for one or both of the two relata. That some of Bultmann's critics are not secure against this risk seems evident from the way they present their alternatives to his kind of existentialist theology. He, on the other hand, almost never forgets that the relation between God and man is internal on both sides of the relationship: that to speak of man is indirectly to speak of God, and to speak of God—of God as fully actual here and now—is indirectly to speak of man.

In the second place, he recognizes that direct speaking of God, while proper and necessary, is nevertheless open to dangers as serious as those of subjectivism and perhaps even more rarely surmounted in the history of theology. To speak of God—even indeed, in existential analogies—is impossible without "objectifying" him. Therefore, there is always the double danger that he himself will be regarded as nothing more than a reified abstraction and that faith in him will be misunderstood as a form of conceptual thinking. Anyone acquainted with Bultmann's writings will recognize that this twofold danger is precisely what his whole theology is an attempt to avoid. His marked opposition to myth, as well as his critical attitude toward all forms of philosophical idealism, has its basis in the concern that faith and the God to whom it refers be freed from such distorting objectifications. But one way to implement this concern, obviously, is to focus attention less on the reality to which faith is directed than on faith itself. By making clear that faith is not a species of conceptual thinking, but a certain kind of existential self-understanding, one not only secures faith against the misunderstanding that it is a "world-view" *(Weltanschauung)*, one also undercuts the notion that God himself is nothing more than a hypostatized object of thought. For, as the inclusive term of my self-understanding, God cannot be an abstract object of conceptual thinking, but only a concrete subject of existential encounter.

I believe that some such rationale as this explains the overriding stress in Bultmann's practice on existential interpretation and on presenting Christian faith primarily as a possibility of self-understanding. It also explains why the specifically theological component in his conceptuality is so insufficiently developed as compared with its anthropological component. He declines to work out a complete philosophical theology, not because he holds that a direct speaking of God is illegitimate or impossible, but because he is so acutely aware of the perils of such speaking as represented in traditional theistic doctrine. Furthermore, the same rationale serves to account for his high opinion of the early Heidegger. He values Heidegger's work so greatly because it provides him with the conceptual tools for appropriately clarifying the nature of faith as self-understanding, and thus for also making clear indirectly that the reality to which faith is directed does not have the being of an abstraction but of a concrete actuality.

But this is not all. These same reasons also help to explain, at least to an extent, why Bultmann goes so far as to defend Heidegger's philosophical "atheism." If his argument on this point is carefully examined, it will be seen to turn on his conviction that God, as faith understands him, is not an object of thought, but a subject of encounter.[7] In the back of his mind is the kind of view—especially, it would appear, idealism with its *deus in nobis*—that presents God as simply the inclusive object of conceptual thinking, and therefore as immanent in man's own nature as rational spirit (*nous*; *Geist*). As against *this* kind of theism, Bultmann argues, Heidegger's "atheism" is distinctly preferable; for if Heidegger fails to speak of God at all, he also does not misspeak of him; and by supplying concepts in which faith in God can be appropriately clarified, he at least provides for an indirect speaking of God such as faith requires.

This much of Bultmann's defense of Heidegger's "atheism" seems to me to be understandable given the reasons discussed above; and I myself have much sympathy with the motive that underlies his argument. But it is a fair question whether he does not go on from this point and so overstate his case as seriously to obscure yet another of his basic intentions. When he claims that "an analysis of human existence without regard for God is not only possible, but alone makes sense"[8] he seems to call in question the whole point at stake in his theory of analogy. The purpose of this theory is to establish that demythologizing does not entail the renunciation of direct speaking of God and his action. But if such speaking is possible, then God as well as man must in some sense be the object of philosophical anal-

7Cf. *Kerygma und Mythos,* 2, 193 ff., and especially *Jesus Christ and Mythology,* pp. 57 ff.

8*Kerygma und Mythos,* 2, 194.

ysis; for, on Bultmann's own view, it is not theology, but rather
philosophy, that provides the concepts in which the theologian must
speak. Yet this very implication is what Bultmann appears to deny
when he applauds Heidegger's philosophy for not involving God in
its existential analysis.

In other words, Bultmann seems to be confronted with a dilemma.
If he claims that God is in no sense the proper object of philosophical
analysis, then his theory of analogy completely falls to the ground. On
the other hand, if he insists that an analogical speaking of God is not
to be precluded, then he is forced to say that God is as susceptible to
philosophical analysis as man, and this can only mean that Heidegger's
"atheistic" philosophy, while perhaps preferable to an inadequate
kind of theism, is far from satisfying the demands of an adequate
conceptuality.

I have already offered reasons for thinking that Bultmann avoids
this dilemma by conceding the point of the second line of argument.
Both his actual practice and his fragmentary theory of analogy
constitute a *de facto* acknowledgment that Heidegger's existential
analysis provides something less than the "right" philosophy. Nevertheless, the cloud of uncertainty cannot be completely dispelled, and
this in large part because Bultmann, for some reason, fails to exploit
an insight already at his disposal that would perfectly reconcile his
apparently conflicting concerns.

It is characteristic of him, as also indeed of Heidegger, that he has
never fully shared in the common existentialist disparagement of
"objective" thinking. Unlike Karl Jaspers, for example, he has never
claimed that there can be no such thing as a scientific analysis of
man's distinctively personal life. On the contrary, he has followed
Heidegger in asserting that, while human existence indeed eludes the
concepts of the natural and social sciences (what Heidegger speaks of
as "categories"), one can nevertheless develop other concepts (namely
"existentials") through which the structure of existence can be appropriately analyzed. To be sure, he has wavered on the question of
whether such an analysis should be regarded as "objective." But his
motives in this are transparent, and the position he wants to maintain
is reasonably clear: existential analysis does "objectify" man's being,
but it objectifies him precisely as subject and thus makes clear that
his actual concrete existence transcends objectification. In short, Bultmann maintains that, although man in his actual concrete existence

(*Existenz*) is always subject and never object, the essential structure of his existence (*Existentialität*) *can* be the object of conceptual analysis.

The strange thing, however, is that he never really seems to see that an exactly parallel thing may be said about God, and that by saying it he would be able to do justice to both of the motives he wishes to express. There are, to be sure, a few scattered places where something like this appears to be implied, as when he tells us that, although "it is wrong to speak of God as acting in general statements, in terms of the formal analysis of man's existence," one nevertheless can "explicate the conception of God and of God's action."[9] But, as this statement itself suggests, the insight here is nowhere fully worked out in the way one has the right to expect from his own principles. He never says clearly and unambiguously that the essential structure of the divine existence may very well be made the object of phenomenological analysis without in any way precluding that God in his concrete action can never be conceptualized, but only encountered.

This is precisely what must be said, however, if his theology is to be freed from the shadow of suspicion that now hangs over it. The claim of his critics that he avoids the dangers of objectivism only by opening himself to an equally dangerous subjectivism will hardly be silenced solely by his theory of analogy. Nor can this theory by itself complete a conceptuality that is otherwise insufficiently developed in its theological component. What is required, rather, is, first, the unambiguous acknowledgment that God, no less than man, is in one sense as properly the object of philosophical analysis as he is in another sense solely the subject of existential encounter; and, second, the full and uninhibited development of the philosophical theology for which this acknowledgment provides the basis. Only in this way can Bultmann's own intentions, as well as the legitimate motive in the objection of his critics, be given proper expression.

III

This is the point at which Hartshorne's dipolar theism presents itself as a most significant resource.[10] For the chief distinction of

[9]*Jesus Christ and Mythology*, p. 66.

[10]Practically all of Hartshorne's major writings are relevant to this discussion, but it presupposes especially the more extended statements of his position in *Man's Vision of God* (New York: Harper & Brothers, 1941) and *The Divine Relativity* (New Haven: Yale University Press, 1948).

Hartshorne's achievement is that he has succeeded in working out with an unprecedented scope and depth precisely the kind of philosophical theology to which Bultmann's concerns clearly point, but which he himself has barely more than postulated in his theory of analogy. In saying this, I do not wish to imply that Hartshorne is in any way directly dependent on Bultmann or that he has consciously tried to parallel Heidegger's analysis of human existence in developing his dipolar doctrine of God. My point is simply that the actual logic of his doctrine, quite apart from the question of its origins or of its possible dependence on other systems of thought, closely parallels the logic of existential analysis. It presents an understanding of the being of God that directly—or, better perhaps, analogically—corresponds to Heidegger's understanding of the being of man.

Hartshorne himself has often indirectly pointed this out. In the Preface to *The Divine Relativity*, for example, where he notes the connections between his view and several others, he has the following to say about its relation to what he speaks of as "crisis theology."

With Crisis Theology, which in a fashion is existential, our theory can agree that God is personal and self-related to the creatures, and that his acts of self-relationship are not rationally deducible, but require to be 'encountered.' However, as Barth and Brunner seem not to see, this is compatible with there being an essence of God which is philosophically explicable and knowable. . . . Philosophy seeks that general principle or essence of the divine being of which such concrete actions of God are mere contingent illustrations. But from a religious point of view, it is the illustrations that count. Thus the religious and the philosophical attitudes are complementary, not conflicting.[11]

If this statement is compared with what Bultmann has to say about Heidegger's existential analysis, the parallels are striking. Just as Bultmann argues that there can be "a science that speaks of [*sic* human] existence without objectifying it to worldly being,"[12] so Hartshorne argues to exactly the same effect about divine existence. And the reasoning is precisely identical: God can be the object of philosophical explication without in any way being objectified to worldly being because what philosophy seeks to explicate is not God

---

[11]*The Divine Relativity*, pp. xi f. Hartshorne makes this same point in his discussion with Martin Buber. Cf., e.g., Charles Hartshorne and William L. Reese (eds.), *Philosophers Speak of God* (Chicago: The University of Chicago Press, 1953), p. 306.

[12]*Kerygma und Mythos*, 2, 187; italics deleted.

as concretely actual, but rather God's abstract essence—just as, by analogy, the object of existential analysis is not man as concrete existence *(Existenz)*, but rather the abstract form or principle of such existence *(Existentialität).*

According to Bultmann (and in this he simply follows Heidegger), it is imperative to distinguish between two senses of the word "understanding." On the one hand, there is what may be called *"existentiell* understanding," which is man's immediate and highly personal understanding of himself as concrete existent in relation to other concrete existents. This kind of understanding is entirely a matter of free personal decision in the moment of encounter, and therefore transcends philosophical analysis. On the other hand, there is the kind of understanding—Bultmann speaks of it as *"existential* understanding"—that philosophy itself exemplifies. It has to do not with concrete existence as such, but with "existentiality," with the abstract essence or structure that all concrete existence necessarily embodies. Bultmann's point in making this distinction is to establish that, although these two kinds of understanding must be distinguished, each of them has its proper and necessary function. So far from being incompatible, they mutually complement one another.

But notice that Hartshorne makes a precisely parallel point when he says that "the religious and the philosophical attitudes are complementary, not conflicting." The religious attitude, or, as he says elsewhere, "faith," is directed to God as concretely actual, as *my* God here and now, and therefore as fully personal and self-related both to myself and to the environing world of fellow creatures. In this pole of his being, God is the eminent subject who transcends conceptual analysis; and, correspondingly, faith in him is not a form of "reason" or conceptual thinking, but what Hartshorne speaks of as "life-trust."[13] For philosophy, on the other hand, God is not the inclusive term of trust or devotion, but the eminent object of rational understanding. Its focus is the abstract pole in his being, the essential structure or form that individuates him as God and thus is concretely embodied in all his actual states. Indeed, Hartshorne could perfectly express his point by simply applying analogically the Heideggerian

---

[13]Cf. especially *Reality as Social Process* (Glencoe, Illinois: The Free Press, 1953), pp. 163–176, where Hartshorne clarifies the meaning of "faith" and "reason" in a way that is even verbally similar to Bultmann's. Cf. also his review of Nels F. S. Ferré's *Faith and Reason* in *The Review of Religion*, 11 (1947), 409-413.

distinction between "existence" and "existentiality." The theme of philosophical theology is not the divine "existence," but the divine "existentiality."

It is because this is so, of course, that he can parallel Bultmann's argument that the two kinds of understanding—*existentiell* and *existential*—are not conflicting, but complementary. In affirming that God himself is solely the subject of existential encounter, one need not deny that the divine essence is properly the object of philosophical analysis. But, quite as important, one can affirm that God's essence is philosophically explicable without in the least calling in question that God as fully actual can be known by faith alone.

In one sense, of course, God as concrete is also knowable to reason. Just as existential analysis abstracts not from human existence altogether, but simply from its specific instances, so the theme of philosophical theology is the divine existence, although considered in abstraction from any of its particular actualizations.[14] Even for philosophy, Hartshorne argues, God is something different from a reified abstraction; for while philosophy can deal with God only by objectifying him, it objectifies him precisely as eminent subject or actuality. To be sure, the philosopher as such is unable to deal with God's specific acts or with God himself as fully actual. But what he is able to do is to explicate the structure of the divine action and therewith to make clear that God in his very being is a God who acts, who primordially realizes his essence through concrete acts of love and judgment in which the succeeding worlds of creatures have their beginning and end. Thus, in spite of Pascal, Hartshorne maintains that the God of the philosophers (provided, of course, they properly fulfill their task) is not a different God from the God of religious faith—just as, according to Bultmann, the existence explicated by existential analysis is not some other reality than the existence actually lived. What the philosophers speak about is the same God in whom faith places its trust, albeit under a different aspect from that in which faith alone is able to know him.

Up to this point, I have been trying to show that the logic of Hartshorne's dipolar theism corresponds analogically with Heidegger's

14The apparent contradiction with what has just been said is removed by observing that Hartshorne's use of "existence" corresponds to the Heideggerian-Bultmannian "*Existentialität*," rather than "*Existenz*." For the latter, Hartshorne's equivalent is "actuality." Cf. *Reality as Social Process*, pp. 204–207.

existential analysis. But in doing so, I have implied something else—namely, that Hartshorne's view not only parallels Heidegger's, but also complements it at its weakest point. Whereas Heidegger holds that it is possible to analyze man's existence without any reference to God, Hartshorne denies this and insists that man and God together are the only proper object of philosophical analysis. Just as what is given in my immediate experience or "faith" is not simply myself, but myself in relation to God, so the theme of rational reflection is not merely human existence, but human existence as the analogical counterpart of the eminent existence of God.

Hartshorne is aware, of course, of the apparent possibility of atheism, and, indeed, in its practical as well as its theoretical form. But just as Bultmann argues that there is no reason in principle why there cannot be a valid existential analysis, and that even the in-authentic man can discern the structure of authentic existence, so Hartshorne offers a parallel argument concerning our knowledge of God. Neither man's openness to error nor his lack of perfect trust precludes the possibility of an adequate philosophical theology; for to be human at all is to have some confidence in the meaningfulness of life, and thus some awareness of God that can be conceptually explicated, provided it is made the object of sufficient care.

Indeed, Hartshorne claims that we can be clear about what we mean by man only when we first become clear about what we mean by God. He rejects "the conventional view that we know directly and literally what we mean by human 'experience,' while we have only a vague, symbolic, or perhaps negative grasp of divine experience." The truth, rather, is that the analogy between God and man

may be used to shed light in both directions. On neither side of the compar-ison do we have simply direct, literal understanding, or wholly indirect, non-literal understanding. Rather, on both sides, we have something literal, but inadequate, needing to be helped out by the analogy with the other.[15]

Thus, in his own way, Hartshorne endorses the motive of Karl Barth in urging the *analogia fidei* against the *analogia entis* of traditional philosophical theology. He insists that "self-knowledge and knowledge of God are apparently inseparable" and that "neither is clear unless both are somehow clear."[16]

[15]"Process as Inclusive Category: A Reply," *The Journal of Philosophy,* 52 (1955), 99.

[16]"The Idea of God—Literal or Analogical?" *The Christian Scholar,* 39 (1956), 136.

But Hartshorne complements Heidegger's work in yet a deeper sense. He not only asserts that human existence can be properly analyzed solely in conjunction with a corresponding analysis of the being of God, but he has actually produced just such a divine phenomenology. In several books and a vast number of essays and articles, he has subjected our knowledge of God to as thorough and painstaking an analysis as can be found anywhere in twentieth century philosophy. In fact, one may say without exaggeration that his dipolar doctrine of God, in its fidelity to experience and logical power, equals and perhaps even surpasses the achievement represented by Heidegger's analysis of the being of man. But one may also say that the significance of his work for Christian theology is correspondingly great. It presents a fully developed conceptuality in which the theologian can speak directly of God with the same kind of critical command that Bultmann displays in speaking of man.

But the important thing is that it does this without in any way sacrificing the motive that accounts for Bultmann's own failure to work out such a conceptuality. If Bultmann's position is inadequate because it insufficiently develops specifically theological concepts, the *reason* for this inadequacy—namely, that God and faith must not be falsely objectified—is nevertheless a valid reason that cannot be disregarded in an adequate theology. This must be emphasized because it is so rarely taken seriously by Bultmann's critics. In rightly urging against him that God as well as man must be a direct object of theological discourse, they nevertheless fail to make clear how this can be so without God's being reduced to a hypostatized abstraction and faith in him to a form of conceptual thinking. Indeed, most of them do not even seem to be aware of the problem, as is evident from their uncritical appeal to the very kind of traditional theism in which this point is obscured. But with Hartshorne, the situation is quite different. He makes clear how God can be the proper object of knowledge and speech without in the least ceasing to be the subject whom faith alone can know in the fullness of his actual being. In fact, so far from compromising Bultmann's concern at this point, Hartshorne's dipolar theism provides the most direct means for expressing it.

It can be objected, of course, that Hartshorne provides this means only by paying the price of renouncing the kind of theism that Christian theology has classically presented. But this is hardly a conclusive objection. Bultmann has frequently pointed out how the anthropological concepts of classical theology, oriented as they are to the tradition of Greek antiquity, have again and again distorted the New Testament understanding of man. And in a similar way, Hartshorne himself has convincingly demonstrated that the Christian understanding of God has suffered equally serious distortions as a result of the "monopolar" prejudice of the classical theistic tradition. In any case, Hartshorne provides a conceptuality in which God may be directly spoken of, even while honoring Bultmann's concern that God not be robbed of his subjectivity. And if one is convinced, as I am, that this concern is a concern of Christian faith itself, then he has more than sufficient reason for gratefully appropriating Hartshorne's work.

IV

I can now summarize the preceding argument by offering an alternative answer to the question of the "right" philosophy to the one Bultmann has characteristically given. The "right" philosophy for Christian theology is not Heidegger's analysis of man alone, but his analysis in conjunction with Hartshorne's dipolar doctrine of God. If the reality to which the affirmations of faith refer is not simply man, but man in relation to God, then Heidegger's analysis by itself cannot meet the demands of an adequate conceptuality. Nor can these demands be met solely by Bultmann's theory of analogy and the somewhat ampler conceptuality for which it is the rationalization. Rather, what is required is a fully developed philosophical theology in which God as well as man is made the object of phenomenological analysis and which therefore provides a means for speaking of God and his action with the requisite conceptual command. But, quite as important, such means must honor the concern of faith that God be understood as the eminent subject who can be fully known solely in his gracious action in the present and solely through the personal decision of faith. The merit of Hartshorne's dipolar theism is that it meets this double requirement for the theological component in the "right" philosophy.

In presenting this argument, however, I have not intended to imply that Hartshorne alone stands to make an independent contribution to an adequate conceptuality. I have stressed, to be sure, that it is Heidegger's work that is incomplete and in need of being complemented by Hartshorne's. But I should readily agree that a somewhat similar judgment can be made the other way around. The situation is not exactly the same because Hartshorne is hardly as lacking in a philosophical anthropology as Heidegger is lacking in a philosophical theology. Nevertheless, Hartshorne has not devoted the same care and attention to the doctrine of man that he has devoted to the doctrine of God, and this undoubtedly handicaps his philosophy for theological employment. One of the great strengths of his work, of course, is that its sensitivity for the non-human realms of nature is a much needed corrective to the tendency of existentialism to preoccupy itself with the narrowly human to the exclusion or depreciation of the wider world of created being. But the fact remains that the theologian's central theme is the divine-human relationship, and this means he has a special need for a carefully developed analysis of the being of man. That Heidegger's early work offers such an analysis has been brilliantly proven by Bultmann's use of it. And anyone who, like myself, is concerned to make Hartshorne's work fruitful for theology has every reason to acknowledge the valuable complement Heidegger provides.

The obvious reply to this argument is that it is arbitrary, simply a forced attempt to bring together two quite different lines of influence that happen to have been significant for my own development. I am aware of the force of this reply and should not in the least wish to deny that Bultmann and Hartshorne have in fact been the decisive influences on my approach to the theological task. I also recognize that the only way really to answer it is to do what has been impossible here—namely, to show by an extensive comparative analysis that Bultmann and Hartshorne, for all their differences, express or imply essentially the same general ontology. Unless I am mistaken, however, the interpretation of the two positions I have presented is sufficiently faithful to their authors' respective intentions to escape the charge of serious misunderstanding. And if this is so, I think I may claim to have shown that the connection I have alleged between them is something more than a rationalization of my intellectual autobiography. I might add that I am encouraged in affirming such a connection because Hartshorne himself, in his review of *Sein und Zeit,* long ago remarked the parallels between Heidegger's burgeoning ontology and his own.[17]

17Cf. *The Philosophical Review,* 38 (1929), 284–291. Cf. also *Beyond Humanism* (New York: Harper & Brothers, 1937), pp. 298-305.

Even so, there remains the larger task of thinking through together in an integral way Heidegger's and Hartshorne's respective contributions to a general ontology such as an adequate theology requires.18 If the present essay can succeed in suggesting that such a project promises to be fruitful for philosophy and theology alike, it will have amply served its purpose.

SCHUBERT M. OGDEN

PERKINS SCHOOL OF THEOLOGY
SOUTHERN METHODIST UNIVERSITY

18The relevance of the later Heidegger to this task is more problematic. If Ott's interpretation is correct (cf. *Denken und Sein, passim)*, the parallels with Hartshorne in Heidegger's more recent work are suggestive and occasionally striking. On the other hand, subsequent study leads me to think that the basic direction of Heidegger's later thought is different from Hartshorne's, and Hartshorne himself has recently commented on its "frankly antirationalistic" and "eccentric" character (*The Logic of Perfection and Other Essays in Neoclassical Metaphysics* [LaSalle, Illinois: Open Court Publishing Co., 1962], pp. x and xiii). The least to be said, perhaps, is that Heidegger's questions, if not his answers, contribute toward developing an ontology that overcomes the chief inadequacies of classical Western metaphysics.

SOME REFLECTIONS ON NECESSARY EXISTENCE

THE present note assembles some brief reflections inspired by an all too rapid, but deeply interested, reading of Professor Hartshorne's forthcoming book, *The Logic of Perfection*.[1] I have read it in proof, a mode of confrontation which always makes me aware how difficult it must have been to read Aristotle in the scroll: the rewards for this effort were in this case fortunately commensurate. I am contributing my note to the *Festschrift* for Professor Hartshorne, partly because I want to keep my foot in the door of the argument, and partly because I wish to pay a tribute to Professor Hartshorne for his originality and courage in bringing the whole topic of necessary existence back into circulation and philosophical respectability, and for having done this in so systematic and persuasive a manner. Part of the thoroughgoing rehabilitation of the great philosopher who sleeps in Canterbury Cathedral had of course been begun by Professor Malcolm in a recent article, but this may have seemed to many—though not to myself—as a strange intellectual excursion of Professor Malcolm's, an intrusion of a personal Kierkegaardianism into a field where such quirks are merely curious. The 'infinite guilt' felt by Professor Malcolm for delinquencies unapparent to the secular eye, seem a poor reason for making major innovations in the sphere of modality. Professor Hartshorne, however, by being Anselmian in so well-worked out and contemporary a fashion has at least shown that the theses and arguments called 'ontological' are no trivial sophisms, but have the same sort of place in philosophy as the arguments of Zeno, of which refutations are numberless, but which, by their uniform survival, have revealed more of the essence of space and time than any merely positive analyses. Anselm's notion of the one unique case where existence cannot be accidental seems to point to some pole or horizon of discourse, a perfectly well-defined limiting ideal position or region, which can be too easily judged void of actual

---

[1]The Logic of Perfection and other Essays in Neoclassical Metaphysics (La Salle, Illinois: The Open Court Publishing Co., 1962).

occupancy, if we expect its geography and geometry to conform to those of nearer regions.

It is not possible for me, within the limits of my time and this paper, to consider all Professor Hartshorne's detailed theses and arguments, nor do I indeed know how I stand towards many of them. My thought on the topics with which Professor Hartshorne deals is itself in motion, and in directions not unlike his own: I have moved far from my simple *Mind* 'disproof' of God's existence, and I cannot say how far from each other we shall ultimately find ourselves. I have been powerfully moved by Professor Hartshorne's suggestion, so strange to theological tradition, that it may be feasible to recognize both a necessary and a contingent 'side' in God, that they in fact require each other and fill in each other's defects, and so enable us 'to eat our cake and have it' in the way religion needs, and that my *Mind* 'disproof' judged impossible. My aversion from theism, even when qualified as 'panentheism' is, however, constitutional: like Professor Hartshorne I have been much influenced by Gotama Buddha, the best man in my acquaintance, and I always recur to his battle under the Bo-tree against the spells and threats of positive religion. I certainly dislike the thought of 'one up there', whether developing or undeveloping, who seems to retain something of distinct existential status, and to act otherwise than through rational personal insights and decisions. There is an externality, a suggestion of being one among others, even in Professor Hartshorne's fine portrait: it makes deity 'finite' in the Hegelian sense, and so a defective object of religious deference. The best way to rationalize these protests is, however, to develop them fully, and I shall therefore try to reconsider in my own idiom, the feasibility and propriety of affirming categorically necessary existence, as well as the sort of object to which one might apply it.

I shall say, at the outset, that I do not think the sort of question under consideration can be dealt with in a formal way, whether this formalism achieves the final formalization of symbols, or the mere fixity of clear, closed, rigorously functioning ideas. No formal treatment can tell us whether or not we should include among possible axioms the assumption that there is, or necessarily is, any sort of object, nor whether we should so choose our axioms, definitions or patterns of inference that this follows from them. As little could it tell us whether we should or should not postulate a necessary God or a necessary giraffe. It cannot tell us these things, since they are not the sort of things a formal system can tell us: they involve asking what we should say in a situation where there are as yet no rules and principles to go by, a type of question precisely excluded by the notion of formality. If a formal system can without absurdity be made to refer to a part of itself, and to comment on its own structure and workings, and if it can be so extended as to include evaluations of its own assertions, asserting some to be valid, some contravalid, and some neither, and perhaps also to include prescriptions to the effect that this or that should be asserted, or this or that inferred from that, its assertions about itself will still never be more than idle endorsements of its actual procedures, and condemnations of those it does not follow. It can never rise to a consideration of what should be asserted or inferred in a situation where there are no rules to go by, or rules to which we are not committed, or a plurality of conflicting rules among which we must choose. It is plain that the issue under debate is one that requires the free, unformalized thought that lives in the interstices of formal systems, and that may be called 'dialectical' in a valuable and appropriate sense, a form of reasoning that tries out reasonings and assertions and sees how it likes their outcome, and which is not even clear as to the borderlines of its concepts till it has found out whether the picture they yield has the satisfactory contrasts and unity which make for 'intelligibility'.

All this would be trivial, were it not so readily forgotten. And it is forgotten whenever the exigencies of logic, in an august and truly important sense, are confused with those of some formal system. I am not clear whether Professor Hartshorne makes such a confusion or not. He wishes to make the existence of God a logical necessity, not anything relative or natural or psychological, but he defers greatly to existent formalisms, and he wishes to bring in his theology as an 'interpretation' of these logics (see p. 99) rather than as a new version of logic altogether. This deference to existent formalisms is, in my view, misguided. Formalization has no other philosophical merit but to show up the resources and limitations of certain basic conceptions and assumptions, so that we may freely decide whether to adopt them, add to them, alter them or reject them totally. By itself it can be construed to recognize anything or suppress anything, to bring out any distinction anyone finds important, or to relegate it, by a suitable *lettre de cachet*, out of all sight and mention. A formal system can be constructed so as to imply the determinism of the future or to leave it open and undetermined, to imply an ontology of at least one, or of a definite or indefinite finite number of individuals, or of an infinite number of individuals, or of no individuals at all, or of individuals variable in number through time, and capable of dividing or coalescing. It can likewise be so constructed as to admit of any number of irreducible categories for which anyone might find a use. But, however constructed, it is, like all formalisms, potentially sinister: we can be tempted to read a philosophy out of it, instead of putting one into it. This is not a senseless warning. One has but to think how Russell became the prisoner of his own formalisms, still pliant and malleable when the *Principles of Mathematics* were being written, but set beyond remoulding once *Principia Mathematica* had been published. One has but to think how he imprisoned whole generations after him, so that even today a great logician dares to connect ontologies with odd issues of quantification and the use of variables. I do not accuse Professor Hartshorne of these errors. But he has not demoted symbolism and formalism to the quite ancillary part it should play in discussions of the sort he is conducting, the place of a secretariat invaluable in preparing or executing philosophical decisions, but quite unfitted to take part in them.

Decisions regarding the notion of necessary existence as applied to deity will, however, require general decisions regarding *existence* and *necessity*: one must determine their content and mode of functioning. Here I can do no more than indicate, without making out a full case, how I stand on these points. I reject all Russellian approaches to existence: that something exists does not mean that something or other has certain properties, or that a certain description has application. Existence is not primarily connected with descriptions or with general notions: it is primarily applicable to individuals, or to abstracta thought of as quasi-individuals. It is I, you, the butcher, Professor Hartshorne, Julius Caesar, the number 10, the quality of mercy, etc., that exists or has existed, not primarily men in general, or number or qualities in general. And it does not matter whether the entities said to exist are named or merely described: St. Teresa existed not otherwise than the saint of Avila. If men in the plural or numbers in the plural, can be said to exist, it is because individual men or specific numbers exist—John, Paul, Harry, 124, 209, etc.—and the existence of men or numbers does not mean that the properties of being a man, or of being a number, apply to something. The reasons for my somewhat startling denial are many, and can only be given summarily. One reason lies in the almost universal rejection of Russell's equation by those not specially drilled to accept it: all those who have taught the 'theory of descriptions' to pupils know how relentlessly they say 'There is something that is King of France, etc.', before acquiring the aseptic 'Something is King of France, etc.', thereby showing their unextinguished sense of the difference between the *existence* of the something that is King of France, and the mere fact that he *is* King of France. Another reason lies in the way in which it prejudges the whole issue of the possibility of there being nothing at all, and so furnishes a gratuitous ontological proof of the existence of something or other, a prejudgment which even Russell saw to be a defect. Another reason lies in our plain need for what may be called judgments of acknowledgement, or judgments of 'hailing', judgments expressed in such words as 'There's that!', 'There's something!' or simply 'John!', 'Something!', 'That!' Whitehead admirably suggested the symbolic forms 'Lo *a*!' and 'Lo *x*!' as the the general expressions of such judgments. The judgmental character of our attitude appears in the possibility of a negation: we can always say 'No John!' or 'Nothing!' or 'That's gone!' Another reason lies in the fact, manfully acknowledged by Moore, that while it may be *strange* and redundant to say of an entity before us 'This exists', it still is significant since it excludes the plain possibility that *this particular entity*, not another, *should not have existed*, should not have been part of the universe at all. To think of the possible non-existence of an entity is implicitly to recognize its existence. And a last reason lies in the grammar of desire and of other intentional experiences. For plainly to desire that there *should* be something having certain properties, e.g., a beautiful bride or child for oneself or for someone else, is *not* to desire that one or other among actually existent things should have been, or should become, such a bride or such a child. It is to desire nothing concerned with the mere character of anything, but with the prior existence of what shall sustain such a character: to make it impossible for us to utter this intelligible thing is to create a dangerous form of aphasia. We are driven unavoidably towards drawing a distinction between what Meinong called facts of *Sein* (being *simpliciter*) and facts of *Sosein* (being such and such), even if we refuse to take his further audacious step of making *Sosein* independent of *Sein*. To assert character, we may hold, implies, though it does not actually assert, existence, just as to assert existence demands, though it neither implies nor makes, some further assertion of character. All this must not be forgotten because it is often obscure whether we mean to assert existence, or character, or both.

As regards necessity, we need not be so contentious. We must say, however, that the necessity to be considered must not be the merely arbitrary necessity of some formal system, nor yet a necessity dependent on the existence or actual states and relations of things which exist in the world, whether this necessity circumscribes the 'nature' of open classes of existent things (the so-called 'laws of nature'), or of particular things in particular predicaments. It must be a necessity which emerges as we deepen our hold on our notions, and avoid all facile applications, identifications and subsumptions, and it will show itself, not so much in a passive, descriptive *Wesenschau*, but in what may be called the profound protest of our ideas, their screaming fight for significant survival, when subjected to various dialectical manhandlings. It is the sort of thing we encounter when we see that something which, at a facile, formal level, is free from contradiction, and would have taken in a Hume, does not, at a deeper level, admit of being thought out clearly, or when we see that some innocent simplification or substitution really mauls, maims, deforms or rends asunder the whole tissue of organized discourse. And in the battle for significant survival no holds are barred: ideas change their form and their characteristic strategy, positions are abandoned and lines reformed, examples and counterexamples serve to reinforce or to wear down. The battle for ideal survival is normally conducted in words: it is in fact necessary that it should be so. It has been as honourably and as well fought by many who have professed merely to investigate the use of words as by some who have professed to deal in naked essences. It has, however, always involved going beyond mere words or their actual use, to the live protest of our notions, to what we feel we must or cannot on reflection say. And the necessity it brings to light is always the upper limit of a long series of notional probabilifications, of cases where notional protest is muted rather than wholly absent. There are things that we can conceive, but only with strain: they are rebarbative, grotesque, intellectually repellent. There are things whose contradictories can only be entertained with strain, which make doubtful sense: it is these whose upper limit is true notional necessity. There are also things that we can conceive as well as, or nearly as well as, their alternatives: here is the field for all that 'saying what one likes' of which recent philosophy has been so profligate. The final outcome of the steady rise in the acceptability of a notion is its formal canonization: its content and working is set forth in a system which it would seem self-destroying to question. It is not my task to enquire how far we have reached, or may hope to reach, this peak of philosophical uninterest.

I shall now proceed to apply these broad reflections to the question of necessary existence in general, and of God's necessary existence in particular. Here what I have said of the distinction between assertions of existence and assertions of character is extremely relevant. Anselm thought, or can be interpreted as thinking, that one can reason from a mere determination of the divine character, of the sort of thing a God would be, if He were at all, to the fact of God's actual existence, and he rightly included in that character the higher-order property of existing necessarily. A being who might or might not be, would, however excellent, not lie at the point of intersection of all those exacting demands which make up religion, and could not therefore be a perfect being or a God. And there is nothing obviously wrong in a notion of necessary existence in which it functions as a higher-order part of a thing's character. Things, if any, of which it was true that there had to be such things, would certainly deserve to be distinguished from things of which this was not true, and the attribution to *them*, as a character, of such a feature of the fact that they are, would be no more oblique and far-fetched than any other higher-order attribution, e.g., having all the properties of a great general. What remains clear, however, and what the whole traditional criticism has emphasized, is that the existence of anything cannot be inferred from anything in its character or concept, even if this includes a reference to existence, since its character or concept only tells us what sort of thing it would be *if* it existed, from which no conclusion involving existence can be inferred. I do not think Professor Hartshorne has shaken this traditional line of criticism nor am I sure that he wished to do so. The only hint that he may have wished to do so stems from the fact that in his formal proof (pp. 51-2) he argues to God's existence from the logical possibility of perfection. The suggestion is that this possibility is a small thing to concede, and that, once conceded, its immense conclusion follows. But the possibility of a necessary existent is no ordinary possibility, precisely because it is not a possibility if it is not also more than one, i.e. an actual fact, so that, in consideration of this immense consequence, one might well find the option of impossibility more attractive. There is, therefore, no route to existence from anything notional or characterizing, even if the latter in some way relates to existence.

If there is to be a valid ontological argument it must proceed, not from concept or character to existence, but in the reverse direction, from existence to concept or character. One must be clear, in the first place, that there must be something, and it must then follow that only what is of a certain character can necessarily be. Or perhaps the two could be established in unison, as it were: one could be clear that there must be something of a certain sort. The principle thus arrived at is not really derived from higher premises: it can at best be buttressed indirectly by showing that all other affirmations or denials of existence of anything else alike presuppose it, which is rather a means of exhibiting its axiomatic character, than of deriving it from anything. The Cosmological Proof, enlarged to argue equally *a contingentia mundi* and *a contingentia absentiae mundi* would be a better expression of this line of argument than the Ontological Argument: Kant was wrong in giving the latter the prerogative. But it would not be a strict proof, but rather the sort of 'elevation of thought' that Hegel held the theistic proofs essentially to be: the sudden decision, informed by insight, to shape one's thought and one's language so that, whatever may be or not be, divinity certainly is. We must now ask whether we are prepared to 'take off' in such an 'elevation of thought'. Do we feel, in reflecting deeply on all we can conceive or assert or deny, that we are always residually committed to affirming the existence of something, and of something presumably exalted and unique?

There are much stronger grounds for holding that we are, and should be thus committed than are commonly allowed. Even Russell showed such commitment when he shaped his logic so that, on his own admission, it 'contains the admission that there is something'. And Wittgenstein made it in the *Tractatus* in failing to provide explicitly for the possibility that there might be no linkages among 'objects', and so no 'world'. Many people feel, and Professor Hartshorne among them, that something at least must exist to make affirmations and denials significant, though there need be nothing necessary in the number or kinds of what thus exists. I myself am not hospitable to this conviction, since it seems to me to belong to a confused family in which what is incapable of illustration and fulfilment *for us*—placed as we are placed, and for reasons that we quite well understand and that are involved in what we mean—is confused with what is intrinsically and absolutely incapable of illustration and fulfilment. There is a predicamental difficulty in picturing one's own funeral which is quite different from the logical difficulty of imagining the end of infinity, and the difficulty of conceiving that there should be nothing whatever seems to me to belong to the former class. If the possibility of there being nothing whatever is to be ruled out, it must be on stronger ground than that we should not then be there to talk or think, or that someone is unable to imagine what such a situation 'would be like'.

It appears to me that the one hope for a successful ontological argument lies in the region of value: we must be able to show the existence of something to be necessary because it would be good. That it lies here is perhaps felt by Anselm and Professor Hartshorne when they connect necessity with perfection: the trend of their argument is, however, logical and ontological, and the 'must' of greatness rather than the 'should' of value predominates. That it should be possible to argue from what is to what should be, is of course a suggestion now universally suspect and evocative of horror, but suspicion and horror pale before an argument from what should be to what is, especially when the 'should be' hangs in the void, and depends on nothing beyond itself. None the less such an argument seems to me to have force, and force of that ultimate, notional kind that deserves the name of 'logical'. Despite all that I have read about the emotive or prescriptive or non-natural character of ethical utterances or their content, I cannot call anything 'good' or 'fitting' in full seriousness, without thinking it likely, and intrinsically likely, that it will recommend itself to others, and I cannot do so without thinking it to some degree likely, and intrinsically likely, that even *things* will show some tendency to conform to what I feel to be good and fitting rather than the opposite. I call the likelihood in question 'intrinsic' because it is neither based on experience nor capable of being removed by experience, though experience may possibly increase it. And that it is intrinsically likely is shown by the fact that I do not think reasons need be given, in certain profound and ultimate cases, when things are as they should be, but only when they *deviate* from this state. It is not, e.g., at all remarkable, nor requiring explanation, and yet not a matter of definition, that things should reveal themselves more and more completely when studied by science, and that our observations should more and more chime in with scientific expectations, whereas it would be remarkable if they did not do so. Many will of course see in my remarks no more than a relic of teleological superstition. Everyone knows, it will be said, that the 'survival of the fittest' explains the adaptiveness of things, that the order of nature is what our minds and our language put there, that all science is fortunate guesswork, etc. I am unrepentant. I find in my deepest thought a persistent linkage between the 'should' of likelihood and the 'should' of value, so that I cannot conceive, except facilely and superficially, what either would mean without the other. And I detect a similar linkage in the thought even of those who would reject it most explicitly. There may be divergence in detail, but there cannot be systematic contrariety or mutual irrelevance between the two 'shoulds'. It is not, however, necessary to argue this point strongly, nor to resuscitate any grand-scale traditional teleology. It is only needful to ask whether, if such a linkage obtains at all, it will entail the existence of anything, and in particular of anything of a superlative and unique kind.

It might appear plain that, *if* there is an argument from value to existence, then it would surely prove the existence of what is perfect, the synthesis of all values in their highest form. This argument would previously not have held water, since the notion of perfection seemed plainly self-contradictory. Not only did it involve a purely conceptual necessity of existence, which seemed absurd, but it involved also a synthesis of countless incompatible ways of being good or an impossible choice among them, as also the notion of an apex where no apex is conceivable. Professor Hartshorne has suggested a way out of *one* of these difficulties: a synthesis of the necessary and the contingent in the being and nature of God. That there should be a God is necessary, and that, being a God, He should have certain deific properties, e.g., capacity for realizing all excellence, uniqueness etc., is likewise necessary, but that God should reveal Himself in this way rather than that—in *some* way He must—is not necessary but contingent, and necessarily contingent. This contingency in God would affect, presumably, not only His relation to His creatures, but also His intrinsic being: capable of all things, He might elect to be one sort of God, e.g., a somewhat austere mixture of justice and mercy, rather than another. Professor Hartshorne has given this divine marriage of necessity with contingency a temporal form. God, rather like the immortal soul in Kant, seems bent on removing the element of contingency in His being by realizing an ever wider round of possibilities: if He cannot achieve all goodness at once, He will at least achieve it by endless approximation—an aspiration in my belief vain, since the *order* in which goodness was realized would remain contingent. Possibly I am reading more into Professor Hartshorne's picture than he really would allow: I am interested but not deeply moved by his notion of a developing deity. His conceptual marriage of the necessary and necessarily contingent seems, however, to be an important idea, and one in which I can see no obvious flaw,: that it should be necessary for something to be, and that what thus necessarily is, should necessarily have these or those properties, not only does not *exclude* its having farther contingent properties, but even *entails* that it *should* have some, since no complete being can avoid 'coming down' among various incompatible possibilities. Nor is such 'coming down' necessarily an imperfection, since it merely reflects an incapacity for the impossible, and since it does not affect the divine power to achieve each incompatible possibility separately. God, in short, cannot be *actus purus,* since the idea is, in this connection, self-contradictory, and He has never, outside of the pronouncements of official theology, been thought to be so. His necessary nature necessarily completes itself in a freely chosen contingent nature—He is by preference the God of Jacob and not of the Edomites, by preference forgiving rather than absolutely exacting, etc.—and possibly the thought of the creative Logos, or Second Person of the Trinity, was framed to express this fact. The possibility opened by Professor Hartshorne smites me with awe, but I cannot say that I wholly like it. Perhaps I feel obscurely that I might not personally care for the sort of God God has contingently chosen to be.

In another direction, however, I do not think Professor Hartshorne has worked at all hard enough to remove contradictions in the notion of perfection. His God presumably enjoys a personal consciousness distinct from that of contingent beings, though He sums up and sympathetically relives all that they do and suffer. I am not able to see how this squares with Hartshorne's 'panentheism', or even with the perfection of God. For a God that has even the exclusiveness involved in being one conscious person among others, even though reliving all that the others live through and more besides, has not in my view the absoluteness necessary for a perfect, truly religious object.

I feel, therefore, that the antinomies in the idea of deity have not been eliminated, and, moreover, that one does not perhaps wish them to be so. I am not sure that religion really desires a possible, and therefore an actual God. If the divine lineaments emerge from conceptual mists there is always something dreadful about them (religiously dreadful), and they make those whose thought about them is not nebulous into somewhat dreadful people. Or if one approaches the matter from the standpoint of an argument from value to fact, I am not sure, paradoxically, that it would be good for there to be something perfect, or not in any straightforward, first-order sense of perfection. The argument from value to fact is in any case never felt to be a rigorous one, as, e.g., Plato felt when he held that divinity only made things as good as possible. We do not feel, further, that it could conceivably be made rigorous: the being of the good cannot rise above probability. If it is absurd to conceive of a complete divergence between what is and what should be, a complete coincidence seems as inconceivable, and as destructive of either notion. These are old antinomies, part of the deep 'duplicity' of our value-consciousness, that nothing has overcome. It seems to be the case that the perfect or best, in an ultimate sense, is also always a higher-order perfect or best, and that it demands, as part of its meaning, the *non-existence* of what is straightforwardly perfect or best. The really best, in short, is a state where rational purposive activity always has some work to do, and this, it would seem, is a state from which the redundant, ready-made perfection of a God is necessarily absent (though it has, of course, unlimited room for saints and gods, of which I hope there are many). All this is what I believe Hegel understood by 'the Idea' and its 'reconciliation with error and finitude', which practically amounts to making our own world, and our own rational struggle in it, when looked at in a special transfiguring light, as both being what necessarily is, and what is as it should be. So that if I were to believe in any sort of necessary existence—a plunge I have not yet taken—I should make my necessary existent something much more like the Hegelian Idea than Professor Hartshorne's developing and suffering deity. I am not concerned to argue for such a conception. What I am concerned to argue is that Professor Hartshorne's defence of Anselm has left the whole question open: one is still in doubt whether to say anything necessarily exists, or to say that it is of this or that sort. This, however, is precisely Professor Hartshorne's merit: he has reopened a question that for so long had seemed closed.

J. N. FINDLAY

KING'S COLLEGE
UNIVERSITY OF LONDON

THE PERFECTION OF PERFECTION

HARTSHORNE has argued that if it is possible that something is perfect, then it is necessary that something is perfect.[1] His argument uses standard principles of modal logic together with the reasonable assumption that if something is perfect then it is necessary that something is perfect.

In this brief paper I wish to give a similar but somewhat different argument. I will show that if it is possible that something is perfect, then the attribute perfection itself is perfect.

I assume that there are degrees of perfection, and that we may regard some things as more nearly perfect than others. If anything is perfect, then nothing else is more nearly perfect.

The point of view that I take will exclude the assumption that there is a realm of "possible entities" or "conceived entities", some of which have "existence" (or "reality" or "actuality") and others of which do not. My reason for rejecting this assumption is that every self-consistent attribute would have to be exemplified in such a realm by an entity (either "existent" or "non-existent") having that attribute. For example, the attribute of being a green giant is a self-consistent attribute, hence there should be a green giant among the "possible" entities, who exemplifies green-gianthood by being both green and a giant. But the attribute of being an "actual" green giant would also be a self-consistent attribute, so there should be an "actual" green giant who is just as "actual" as he is green and a giant, and who, since he is "actual", is one of those fortunate "possibles" which is not *merely* "possible", but "actual" as well. But we know there is no "actual" green giant.

In excluding the assumption that there is such a realm of "possible" entities, I also exclude the assumption that existence (or actuality) is an attribute in the same sense that greenness and gianthood are attributes. Rather, any statement of existence is regarded as a

[1]Charles Hartshorne, "The Logic of the Ontological Argument," *The Journal of Philosophy*, 63, No. 17, 471-473.

statement to the effect that a certain attribute is non-empty.[2] Thus the assertion that there is a perfect being is regarded as an assertion that the attribute perfection is non-empty.

The traditional ontological argument, on the contrary, seems to take the view that since perfection is a self-consistent attribute, there is a perfect entity in the realm of "possibles", and that this entity cannot be truly perfect without also having the attribute of "actuality".

The problem, from my point of view, is simply to show that the attribute of perfection is non-empty. It is *not* to show that some subsisting "possible" entity has an attribute of "actuality" or "existence". I refuse to believe that there is any such attribute of "actuality" or "existence" except in the sense of "non-emptiness" (as applying to attributes and relationships), or in the sense of "truth" (as applying to propositions). Similarly, I would regard the attribute "possibility" as applying properly only to relationships, attributes, and propositions, and as meaning "possibly non-empty" in the case of relationships and attributes, and "possibly true" in the case of propositions.

I wish to begin by assuming that perfection is a possible attribute, in other words, that it is possible for something to be perfect. This can be taken to mean that it is possible for something to be such that nothing else is more nearly perfect.

My purpose is to show that the attribute perfection is itself perfect. Suppose, on the contrary, that the attribute perfection in some respect fails to be absolutely perfect itself. (Of course, whatever the attribute perfection *applies to*, if anything, is perfect, but this is not the same as saying that the attribute itself is perfect.) If perfection is not itself perfect, consider the consequences that ensue for anything x that might happen to be perfect. Since x possesses only an imperfect kind of perfection, it is clear that x lacks the fullest sort of perfection, and so is not perfect after all. There is a greater degree of perfection than that possessed by x, that is, the degree of perfection that would be possessed by something having a *perfect* attribute of perfection instead of an imperfect attribute of perfection. Thus perfection in the fullest sense of that term is perfection of the sort that something has

2For more detailed accounts of my conception of existence see my papers, "Actuality, Possibility and Being," *Review of Metaphysics*, 3 (1950), 367-384, and "Some Logical Aspects of Reference and Existence," *Journal of Philosophy*, 57 (1960), 640-647.

if it has *perfect* perfection rather than imperfect perfection. If it is *this* sort of perfection that we assume to be possible for something to have (and how could we mean less than this by "perfection"?) then it is clearly required that perfection itself be perfect.

It might be objected that all we have shown is that if it is *possible* that something is perfect in the fullest sense, then it is *possible* that something has a perfect kind of perfection, and hence *possible* that perfection is perfect. In reply to this objection, it must be conceded that the argument we are using tacitly assumes that the perfection of perfection is a non-contingent matter. It assumes, in other words, that if perfection is perfect, it is necessarily perfect, and if perfection is imperfect, it is necessarily imperfect. From the fact that perfection is possibly perfect, and therefore not necessarily imperfect, we may then conclude that perfection is not imperfect, since otherwise perfection would be imperfect but not necessarily imperfect, contrary to the tacit hypothesis of the non-contingency of the perfection of perfection. Since perfection is not imperfect, it is perfect.

From the assumption that it is possible that something is perfect, we have therefore reached the conclusion that something *is* perfect, namely the attribute perfection itself. We have reached the conclusion that the attribute perfection is non-empty, since perfection itself has the attribute perfection. But if perfection is really perfect, it cannot have any deficiencies. It cannot be *merely* an attribute. Besides being an attribute, it must be whatever else is required of it in order to be perfect. Thus the perfect being, among its other attributes, has the attribute of being itself an attribute. If there is any contradiction in this, then there must have been a contradiction in our original assumption that it is possible for something to be perfect (in the fullest sense of "perfect").

The classical form of the ontological argument, when divested of its talk about "possible" entities or "conceived" entities, could be restated as follows: "If the attribute perfection is an empty attribute, then, indeed, perfection is imperfect because of the deficiency involved in its emptiness. But perfection cannot be deficient in any respect and cannot involve any sort of imperfection. Hence perfection cannot be empty, and hence there must be a perfect being." This restatement of the argument already presupposes that perfection is itself perfect. The perfection of perfection is used as the justification of the non-emptiness of perfection. But if perfection is perfect, then we know not merely *that* there is a perfect entity, but also *what* it is.

The attribute of perfection can be defined in such a way that there can be at most one perfect entity. This is done by defining something as perfect if it has a higher degree of perfection than any-thing else. If we assume that it is possible for something to be perfect in this sense, then we not only can show (as before) that perfection is itself perfect, but also that nothing else is perfect. In this case perfection would be a "unit" attribute (an attribute applying to only one thing) and the only thing it would apply to would be itself. There are systems of logic in which there appear to be attributes of just this sort, attributes each of which applies to itself and only to itself.[3] Apparently perfection is such an attribute. But, as already noted, per-fection is also more than an attribute, since it is also whatever else it needs to be to be perfect. On the basis of the foregoing argument, we can also conclude that imperfection is imperfect, since only perfection is perfect.

A similar type of argument can be used to show that the attribute of maximal imperfection is the only thing that is maximally imperfect, assuming, of course, that it is possible for something to be maximally imperfect. It is also clear that maximal imperfection, besides being an attribute, has whatever deficient properties it needs to have in order to be the most defective and imperfect entity in the world.

FREDERIC B. FITCH

YALE UNIVERSITY

[3] F. B. Fitch, "Self-Referential Relations," *Proceedings of the XIth International Congress of Philosophy,* 14, 121-127.

RELIGIOUS NATURALISM AND THE PHILOSOPHY
OF CHARLES HARTSHORNE[1]

MY INTENTION here is to examine some relations between the
philosophy of Charles Hartshorne and the general philosophy
of naturalism, especially in the area of religious philosophy. I shall
do this first, by explaining the meaning that I understand "naturalism" to have, in terms of its principles for interpreting the world,
knowledge, and value; second, by showing the extent to which Hartshorne exemplifies these principles; and finally, by discussing those
points where his philosophy seems to develop, or to deviate from
naturalism.

Central to this discussion is the issue of whether a naturalistic
philosophy can be also a genuinely religious philosophy. Specifically,
can one be a naturalist in his interpretation of the world and at the
same time, within that naturalistic framework, also believe in a deity
that is natural? The earliest Western philosophers, the Milesians and
Ionians, were naturalists, and they criticized the traditional supernatural religions. And naturalists in modern times, from Comte, Marx,
Nietzsche, Santayana, and Russell, to the logical empiricists, have
questioned whether religion could be at the best anything more than
a beautiful fairy-tale, and at the worst anything more than an opiate,
a mischievous fiction, or sheer nonsense. In general naturalists have
opposed religion because they have opposed supernaturalism, nearly
always linked with religion. At the same time religion has not always
been linked with supernaturalism, and some religious people have
claimed to be naturalists and have even claimed to worship a natural
God or seek to maximize some ultimate though natural value. The
Milesians, Taoists, Stoics, Buddha, Zen masters, Bruno, Spinoza, and
Dewey, so far as they may be called naturalists, developed religious
philosophies that seemed to be organic to their naturalism. Therefore,

[1]Numbers in parentheses indicate page numbers in Charles Hartshorne, *Reality
as Social Process* (Glencoe, Illinois: The Free Press; Boston: Beacon Press, 1953).

just how compatible religion and naturalism can be will be an implicit theme of this discussion.

I

Like many of the grand old terms and labels in philosophy, "naturalism" has a hard core of fixed and common meanings and a nebulous fringe of varying and idiosyncratic meanings. Further, it would probably be impossible to get perfect agreement among philosophers as to just what that hard core of meaning is. Still, there is large agreement in the literature as to what "naturalism" means.[2] I define it as follows:

(1) Reality, or Nature, is constituted by events which occur, and things which exist, in space and time, along with the qualities of, and the relations between, those things and events. Whatever is real is natural, and vice versa; whatever is claimed as being real and also beyond Nature cannot be real—its definition is a contradiction in terms. There are no disembodied possibilities, ideals, relations, souls, heavens or gods. If these entities are real—then they participate in some spatio-temporal order of occurrences or existents. Aristotle's doctrine of substance, and Whitehead's ontological principle, are illustrations of this proposition of naturalism.

(2) The things and events, the qualities and relations, which constitute Nature are objective. Nature, in its parts and as a whole, is real in its own right and by its own operations, and is not dependent on any other order of reality. Its parts and its whole are independent of our thinking and of any thinker. Thus subjective idealisms, supernaturalisms, and transcendentalisms are ruled out. Every item of the experienced and hence every item of knowledge is an item in Nature. Likewise every experiencer is participant in Nature, depending on the reality of the external world for his knowledge. All objects and all subjects are therefore natural entities.

(3) Nature is pluralized. Individual things and events are as real as anything. Contexts, relations, and wholes in which they participate do not impair or destroy their reality. They are not reducible to anything else—universals, or God. They are just what they are. Nature

[2]Y. H. Krikorian, ed., *Naturalism and the Human Spirit* (New York: Columbia University Press, 1944). Dale Riepe, "What is a Scientific Naturalist at Mid-Century?", Journal of Philosophy, 55, No. 17 (August 14, 1958), 726–734.

may be one at the same time that it is many, but, contrary to Plato, the many, far from being an appearance or an image of the real, are real themselves. Whitehead's Category of Objective Diversity, and Aristotle's doctrine of substance, illustrate this pluralism.

(4) Nature is continuous. Events are contiguous in space and time and interact. Nature in its various aspects—things, events, qualities, relations—displays certain common categories. These are objectivity, subjectivity, energy (matter), space, time, identity, difference, value, evil, etc. While Nature exhibits discontinuities in the form of individualities and temporal successions, its parts are also bound together by common structures of being. Nature, in short, though individualized, is not bifurcated. It does not admit of any dualism, be it spirit-matter, mind-body, value-fact, possibility-actuality, one-many, religion-science, God-man, or whatnot. Every entity is connected, directly or indirectly, in itself or through others, with every other entity. Thus there is no dualism within man, or between man and the rest of nature. This principle is illustrated by Peirce's doctrine of synechism.

(5) Every entity that is real, can, in principle, be known. Contrapositively, what cannot be known in principle cannot be real. As stated above in (2) every entity in Nature is objectively independent of every other entity. It is thus available for the experience of some subject—"universal objectivity." (70) In short, what is an object can be known; and what is not an object cannot be known. Contrapositively, what cannot be known by any subject is not an object; and what can be known by some subject is an object. This notion of naturalism eliminates all claims to knowledge that go beyond the rational-empirical methods, and all assertions of a supernatural world. To say that only natural entities can be known by man, who is a participant in Nature, is to say that only when man is connected with his object of knowledge, only when some bond of contiguity or similarity obtains between subject and object, can there be knowledge. In Whitehead's words, "If anything out of relationship, then complete ignorance as to it." Naturalism generalizes this principle to say, "If an object is out of relation to all subjects, then it cannot be real."

(6) Experience, analyzed and synthesized, is the only reliable way to knowledge. Experience is the objectification of a portion of Nature (a neighbor) in a subject, and in turn the objectification of the subject in another subject. Experience is an interaction or, in Dewey's term, a transaction. When the elements and relations in experience are

discriminated and related so as to correspond to what is the case, then true knowledge occurs. The means for producing this correspondence are rational coherence and operations upon the object of knowledge. Thus naturalism rejects claims to nonexperiential knowledge as infallible. Because direct apprehension (or prehension) of an object is the first step and one of the final steps in reliable knowledge, insight or intuition is not to be discounted. But as an unanalyzed and unrationalized whole it cannot be accepted as reliable knowledge. For the latter to occur the patient who has been subject to the influence of his neighbor must in turn become an agent, moving to objectify himself in the neighbor. He must act back on that neighbor, proceeding with some hypothesis or set of expectations deduced from his prior observations and acting so as to observe whether future observations fulfill those expectations. Knowledge is incomplete until it is thus transactional. It involves reception of data, analysis and organization of these data by rational reflection, the inferring of new data in consequence, and then action to test out the organization and the inferences. Reasoning is abstract and instrumental; it enables us to organize and to predict our concrete experiences.

(7) The most reliable knowledge is public and probable. No subject can experience the totality of its objects. To do so would be to become those objects. Thus all experience is relative and partial to the objects experienced. It is perspectival. This is Peirce's principle of *probabilism* or *fallibilism*. At the same time, for knowledge to be reliable it must be public—i.e., it must be communicated. To communicate our experience is to give proof that the objects of our experience are genuinely objects, i.e., that they are "out there" available to other subjects. For the definition of an object is that it is something available to *any* subject that is in a position to experience it. The effort to be reasonable in our claims is an effort to publicize and even universalize our private standpoint. Thus reason is the transition step between our own immediate experiences on the one hand and the immediate experiences of our fellow subjects on the other.

(8) Value is inherent in Nature. Wherever else in Nature value may reside, it is found in the experiences of subjects and is a function of some subject's response. Value is not supernatural or in any way transcendent of Nature. It is continuous with "fact." It is not imposed on Nature and man but is organic to them.

II

To what extent does Hartshorne's philosophy exemplify these principles of naturalism?

(1) Hartshorne identifies his religious philosophy with a developing trend of "natural theology." (23) After Whitehead, his philosophy may be called "actualism." (207) By actuality is meant reality in its full concreteness—"the most concrete and complete form of reality." (204) Actuality is the actualization of possibility, the determination of the indeterminate. Actuality occurs as the may-be moves through becoming into being. It is process, temporal process, the process of concrescence. It is to be contrasted with possibility. And it is to be distinguished from existence, which is the common form binding together a set of actual experiences through time, and from essence, which is comprised by the abstract properties defining this common generic form. (204-205) There are no "timeless or immutable" existents. (134) Possibilities are known and are effective only as they relate themselves to some particular process of actualization. "The whole in its actuality includes all that is actual, and in its potency all possibility." (120) Such possibilities are always more or less real, i.e., always more or less close to actualization, though never identical with what is realized. (98) Thus a man knows more possibilities than a molecule. So far as the whole domain of possibilities are together, they must be grasped in the experience of an all-inclusive existent, namely, God. For God, to be real, must partake of the traits of an actual entity. God must be concrete and hence contingent, or He is nothing. "There can be no exception to a metaphysical principle," (130) and one of the prime principles of Hartshorne's metaphysics is that reality consists in concrete particulars to which the categories of possibility, existence, and essence must relate themselves if they are to be real at all. " 'Humanity' is absolutely independent of Socrates, though not of there being *some* suitable concrete instances or other." (72)

(2) Hartshorne upholds the principle of "objective independence." "An 'object,' or that of which a particular subject is aware, in no degree depends upon that subject." (70) Thus the actual events and things of nature which are observed or experienced are not swallowed up in the experiencer, be he human or divine. They have an autonomy of being which no other entity can efface. If such events and things are to be known, they must be known in their concrete character. (78-84)

Likewise, every subject or experient is participant in Nature. It "always depends upon the entities of which it is aware, its objects." (70)

(3) For Hartshorne, as for Whitehead, the individual events and existents of Nature are real for to deny them is to deny the actual facts of our experience. To hold that they are mere parts in some absolute system, or mere appearances of an underlying reality, or complete derivations of universals or of past events (87) is to violate the fact of relativity and to produce a contradiction. For a relation that swallows up the relata becomes no relation at all, just as a secular or divine determinism that determines every event in detail has nothing left to determine. (97) Relativity is the inherent structure of a universe of particulars. In Hartshorne's terms, "reality is social process" (17) by which the many particular entities relate themselves one to another and weave the structure of the actual world. But without particulars nothing can be relative to anything else and the world collapses. Apart from such particulars there would be no actual world, for actualization is a process of particularization, of definition. The particular is non-deducible from general concepts and from antecedent particulars. (87) This is so because actuality is not the unfolding of an equation but an artistic process of creation.

(4) In this philosophy the various events of Nature are continuous concretely. They are experient subjects sympathetically responding to one another. Whatever else actual entities may be, they must be social in this sense; sociality is their generic character. "To live alone," said Aristotle, "one must be a god or a beast." For Hartshorne the tie that binds the world together is love—reciprocal sympathy of the individual being supplementing the far greater, cosmic sympathy of God. (180) Personal identity is seen as what exists over a period of time and over a region of momentary experiences when there is sympathy of present experients for past experients, i.e., memory. (102) We may say then that because of this generic category of love—of which God is the primordial and supreme case—all other forms of continuity are possible, and all opposites and dualities are reconciled as aspects of this concrete and universal fact.

(5) Hartshorne asserts with naturalism that every entity that is real can, in principle, be known. He even goes farther to maintain that the knower need not be a human subject, and therefore to eliminate the "in principle." For whatever is actual is known or will eventually be

known. This is a corollary of his principle of "Universal Objectivity" which requires that every entity is or will be an object for *some* subject or other. (70) It is the very nature of things to transmit their experiences (in part) to other things. What binds things together is this subject-to-subject sharing of experiences. To be objective or real, whether in the realm of actuality or possibility, is not only to have a being independent of other beings and not reducible to them; it is to become available for objectification in other entities, namely, subjects.

(6) Hence Hartshorne's insistence on experience (44)—taking human experience as the paradigm—as the source of knowledge, provided that experience becomes reflective and is coherently analyzed. Experience is the process by which the feelings of an "object" are communicated to some subject. It is the means by which we become directly aware of happenings beyond us. Indeed, Hartshorne argues that the meaning of an "object" becomes unintelligible save as it is conceived as an independent subject which is then objectified in another subject. (Ch. IV) "We know nothing of a form of concreteness other than that of subjects." (84) This is the principle of "Universal Subjectivity." (70) The function of reason is not to legislate the basic character of the world as we find it in experience. To say that it is, is to twist the facts to fit our ideas. Reason should enable us to make theoretical and practical decisions by taking account of the basic factors in the world—and these are both necessary and contingent. (92-93) Philosophical (or metaphysical) reason should define and refine basic meanings applicable to all experience until they describe unrestrictedly, unexceptionally, and coherently that experience. (85, 130) Experience is the starting point and the testing ground of all knowledge, and reason is instrumental to our prediction, control, understanding, and final enjoyment of it.

(7) The probability of knowledge in Hartshorne's philosophy follows from the relativity, particularity, and definiteness of all experience. Definiteness is exclusion. Hence only a portion of any given object of knowledge can be known. While an experience in itself is a concrete synthesis of materials from beyond, it is an abstraction from those subjects offering themselves to the experient subject. Every experience is infected with the limitations of particularity.

Similarly, the effect of philosophy to express generic and coherent principles applicable to all of experience is necessarily partial and incomplete. ("It would be presumptuous," remarks Hartshorne, "to offer the social view as proved.") (43) But the effort to communicate our experiences and to put them into some public and hence testable form—to rationalize experience—is both required and possible. It is required because we are social, communicating creatures who have discovered that reason thus put to use can be productive of more value for us and others. And the effort to make our private experiences public and to share them and have them tested on a universal scale is possible and promissory of success precisely because we are sympathetic creatures who yearn for the widest possible identification with our fellow creatures both human and non-human. Hartshorne's method of uniting opposites into contrasts illustrates the ideal of inclusive sympathy, which is the implicit aim both of our common life and of philosophy.

Further, the probable and the public aspects of knowledge require each other. "Common experience" is the final appeal in metaphysical knowledge (130) not because private experience does not reveal truth but because the only way to approximate removal of the limitations (probabilities) of uncommon experience is to discover what is necessary and inescapable in *all* such uncommon experiences. But even metaphysical formulations are liable to error. "Both secular reason and revelation are fallible," (130) else, we may say they would not be human knowledge but would be divine in the sense of absolutely necessary and unalterable.

However, Hartshorne departs from naturalism in holding that "necessary" propositions are something more than mere tautologies dictated by rules of language. They express the very (existential) structure of actuality. They pertain to the inescapable categories of all experience, and are reached through a logical analysis of meanings and an elimination of those meanings that are unclear, inconsistent, inconceivable, and derivative. Yet such structures are not disembodied —naturalism's principle (1). They are exemplified—everywhere. But they are logically prior to experience, and can be known only through logical analysis. As necessities of thought, they are necessities of experience.

In the next section I shall explore this important difference between Hartshorne and naturalism.

(8) "Experience is an act; and every act at least strives to realize a value . . . value is unity in contrast, beauty in the broadest sense. The supreme example of such unity is the social harmony which is

called love." (44, 100) Thus Hartshorne agrees with the naturalistic principle that value is inherent in nature—in particular, in some experience. He goes beyond the "scientific" or "materialistic" principle in holding that value is more concrete than matter of fact and that no fact can be understood apart from some value-experience.

III

Let us turn now to an evaluation of Professor Hartshorne's philosophy.

Perhaps the most important—certainly the most radical—feature of this philosophy is its theory of reality as social process. This theory is by no means new. Yet it hardly goes back beyond the modern period ("Leibniz was its Newton") (31) and its chief development has come within the last hundred years or less. It is a protest against the Newtonian doctrines of substance and of "vacuous actuality." Simultaneously, the isolated individual and the deadness of matter have been done away with. Individuals are not knocked about on the billiard ball of Nature by forces at a distance or by a Cosmic Cuestick. "Simple location" gives way to temporal succession, experience, and interaction, and what was called vacuous or dead becomes sentient. The Fallacy of Windowless Monads and the Apathetic Fallacy disappear together. What societism does is to reveal that the windows of Nature are open and the residents have feelings. It is not accidental that this radical reconstruction in metaphysics has led to a radical reconstruction in religious philosophy—namely (like many such reconstructions in religion), a rediscovery of the insights of the Gospels. There, the doors and windows of the creatures are open one to another (if not, one should knock) and the souls of men are their feelings, for themselves, for one another, for the rest of Nature, and for God.

Societism has important implications for human action. The principle of atomic and rugged individualism, which dominates so much of our life in the United States (and which, as someone remarked, produces so many ragged individuals), makes the welfare of individuals independent of each other and indeed mutually exclusive and antagonistic save as the "invisible hand" of the market and the sacred "law of supply and demand" adjust the conflicting interests of those individuals. Hartshorne properly (though guardedly) criticizes this view as assuming selfishness, separating chance or individuality from tragedy, and "denying the primacy of love." (108) Societism entails a thorough transformation in man's order of living and of making a living. Not only must man's relations to man be reorganized so as to make fellow-feeling and mutual aid the primary principle; man's relations to all living things, and indeed to the rest of Nature, must undergo a similar change. As the one occurs the other will also tend to occur.

What this means is that animals, plants, and even stones have their rights. This is not so merely because stones, for example, can become the foundation on which first lichens, then moss, then ferns, then flowering plants, and eventually animal life and man arise. The rights of these "lower" things are not contingent on man's rights or his welfare, though man's own enlightened self-interest would alone dictate a concern for them. Their rights reside in the things themselves because they are forms of being—centers of experience, if you will, which are affected by, and which act upon, the world. They were here in the universe before man came on the scene and probably will be here after he is gone or has been superseded by higher forms.

What is a right? It is a claim to be and to become. Everything that is actual (or its atomic parts) exercises such a claim. It possesses an "objective independence" (70) that spells its autonomy, not reducible to other things with their claims and purposes. At the same time every such entity is or will be available to some other entity's experience; i.e., every such entity exercises its power toward and for some subject ("universal objectivity"). (70) It is sensitive and responsive in some degree (however low) (134) and thus commands the respect of similar subjects. It is independent, and this independence is known as it presses itself against some recipient and is felt in that recipient's experience. To have a "healthy respect" for the reality of a thing is to acknowledge its intrinsic sensitivity and the press and the claim of that thing. Man cannot justifiably claim the right to curtail or destroy the rights of other entities (minority races or nations, whales, buffalos, whooping cranes, termites, mosquitos, or stones) save as such curtailment produces in the long run a greater wealth of value-experience. (The man who shows concern for a falling sparrow gives signs of a cosmic sympathy).

These entities are "lower" in the sense that they preceded later forms and formed an order of being by means of which the later arose and evolved. And if it is a fact that any one of them usually, though not invariably, is capable of less value-experience than that of a man

—and hence is "lower" in this capacity—this does not give man the right to do as he pleases toward these beings. Not without reason do we fear a man who is unkind to animals, or who in the pursuit of his own immediate interests neglects the care of the vegetation and soil on the land he "owns." A man who is that shortsightedly selfish with these things is apt to be so with other human beings. For lack of foresight or reason in planning one's own life in relation to the environment indicates lack of sympathy toward that environment, whether that environment include animals or birds or plants or soil or men. Sympathy toward the lower beings does not mean that we will "turn and live with the animals" and forget the "higher" values which civilization has reared. Rather it means the highest kind of intelligence in the guidance of human affairs, because it means the greatest sensitivity and responsiveness toward that total cosmic environment in which human affairs and *all* value-experience must take place.

Someone might ask whether cancer cells have a right to live. If panpsychic societism is correct then cancer cells must be considered on their own merits, intrinsically and extrinsically; they cannot be arbitrarily destroyed. The general problem is that of the justification of human control over toxic and injurious processes and things in Nature. Man's blind eradication of certain vegetation and insects has destroyed birds and birdsong and the balance of Nature; elimination of "dirt" has washed tons of harmful detergents into the rivers and destroyed wildlife in and around those rivers; and nuclear testing may have altered the equilibrium which viruses and other micro-organisms have achieved over a billion or more years in a complex and delicate Nature. It may well be that cancer should be destroyed or controlled so far as possible. But in doing so it is important for us to know the consequences of our action and the reasons for it. Hartshorne points out that the necessary order of nature involves chance or freedom and hence conflict and tragedy, (99, 107) and therefore any effort to tidy up the world after our own ideals will only be met by some unseen defiance and disorder. The universe is inexpugnably wild, and the law of compensation takes its revenge on those who wish to domesticate it down to the last detail. While it is better to be a healthy man than an ill one, it is also better to be an ill man than a healthy pig, provided that in his illness a man is bound to a community of life that can redeem the suffering of illness through the stronger power and joy of health.

The merit of Hartshorne's analysis at this point is not only that he shows that self-love and other-love are compatible; he reveals that they are different forms of the same fundamental act of sympathy. (101 ff.) When I love myself, my present experience sympathizes with my past or future experiences, drawing them into a bond of unity. When I love others, my present experience similarly sympathizes with the experiences which are beyond this present and either past or future to it, and whose original loci are the beings ("existents") of others. The answer to the ancient egoism-altruism problem, over which ethicists have spilt much ink, nations much blood, and ordinary people many tears, is as simple as that. When the Jews enjoined one another to love others as they loved themselves they had found a profound principle. But men have agonized over the problem of the self and others because they did not love themselves with sufficient intensity, range, and consistency. Respect for others grows with the growth of respect for self. Fromm has pointed this out, and has suggested the method of generalization as the clue: genuine respect for oneself reaches down to the generic humanity which one shares with others. Mead traced this generalizing to "taking the role of the other." But in no case would this role-taking be possible or be anything more than "enlightened" self-interest or abstract selfish calculation unless it were undergirded by the concrete act of sympathy of one feeling for another feeling.

When we ask for the ultimate meaning of illness and suffering we are asking a religious question. But, someone will ask, what can "God" mean? A lasting contribution in the social theory of reality is that deity must be just as fully receptive, passive, affectable, and changeable, as it is productive, active, influential, and unchanging. (136 ff.) God, in other words, must be social, or He is nothing—provided that reality is generically social process.

The problem of understanding God is first a problem of choosing an image that is appropriate; then of refining that until it is rationally coherent and capable of universal application; and then of looking to its consequential meanings in direct experience. The selection of an image is all-important. For example, God has been imagined as a monarch, a military leader, a shepherd, a father, a lover, a deliverer, and the like. Thus as men from Xenophanes to the ink-blot soothsayers have been fond of reminding us, our images of God tell more about us than about God. But this need not be so. The ego-centric predicament can be resolved if the ego can raise its blinds and even open its windows. True, our apprehension of the light coming from beyond will always be framed and colored by our own particular windows.

Our ideas of God mirror the depths of our selves. But so far as our selves are in the world and the world is in them, our ideas mirror the world. Hence our ideas of God are functions of our sympathetic responsiveness to what in the world and in ourselves can legitimately be called God. Hartshorne observes that our deficiency in understanding deity for what deity truly is—namely, sympathy—arises from our incapacity to endure the suffering that invariably accompanies our sympathetic experience of others (147-148). As we are magnanimous our understanding of God can accordingly rise to his magnanimity. This means not that we inevitably make God in our own image but rather that we have found eyes with which to see and that our windows have been opened to the Sun and its Light.

Shall deity be initially imaged as what is like us, or as what is different from us? Hartshorne takes the former alternative. "If we refuse to conceive God by analogy with our virtues, that is to say, our other-regarding desires, and habits of acting upon them, we shall end by conceiving him by analogy with our vices, for example, our most truly and deeply 'selfish' wish for self-sufficiency." (142) I think the warning of this last clause is apropos. Surely much of the history of theology is the autobiography of men who rejected the world—misanthropes who painted their autistic fantasies and wish-fulfillments in cosmic terms. But I do not think this conclusion necessarily follows from the premise. If we conceive God by analogy with our defects, then God may well be a compensatory substitute for our weakness. But God might also be an objective factor in the world which is able to create and redeem our values in a way that we cannot do and in a way that is *different* from our way. Such a concept of God would not deny the principle that God is kindred to us because He participates in Nature. But it would be the outcome of a different analogy from Hartshorne's. His analogy grows out of societism's concept of experience. Hartshorne's argument that subjects can know only subjects seems to me equivocal. What I know here and now of this desk is in my subjective experience, but the desk as such is not. But what can the desk be? A subject, or a set of subjects, he says, since there is no other way of conceiving it. But it can be conceived as an I-know-not what, a pure independent object. Even if it is conceived as a subject through and through, *my* knowledge of it is not identical with it; hence there is a hidden side to it which I can never come at. To assume that every whit of this hidden side is *like* my own subjective states is to swallow up difference in similarity. It may be admitted that there is a continuum of subjective states enabling us to infer vaguely what those unexperienced states might be. But evolutionary studies suggest that there are deep differences and qualitative leaps in Nature which no discernment of similarities can wipe out. Hartshorne says that God redeems the imcompatibilities of the world in a way that we cannot do, but deity for him is always a supreme case of what the creatures do. While this emphasis corrects the dualistic thinking of most of traditional theology, it also introduces the danger of forgetting that man's limitations are not just quantitative but are qualitative, and of overlooking that fact that our feelings, our meanings, and our relations with others and the world are created in such a way that we do not foresee or control the outcome—and in a way that is sometimes contrary to what we desire although good (in Hartshorne's sense of deepening sympathy and intensity of felt contrasts) in the long run.

While analogy from human experience is important and inescapable in understanding God, disanalogy is no less needful and significant, for as the former indicates what we can know the latter sets the limits of our knowledge. For a thoroughgoing naturalism, Nature is filled with divergent forms, and, as George Gaylord Simpson and others have shown, evolution is radial. Organisms adjust in ways quite different from cerebral-manual-linguistic intelligence; for most do not have cerebrums, let alone nervous systems. Feelings among organisms, moreover, while similar, probably differ vastly, so that while human feelings may give an intimation of what other things are like they do not afford a skeleton key to all of Nature's mysteries. Naturalism holds that the principle of pluralism—radical pluralism, if you will—is just as true as the principle of continuity. Further, naturalism's emphasis on the objective world as the prime source of knowledge and its consequent appeal to experience *of* that world seems to entail a certain skepticism toward human reason in giving an exhaustive or definitive account of the world. Thus naturalists do not ascribe as much importance to beliefs as do spiritualists and others.[3] For naturalists Nature on one side is a surd that cannot be penetrated; the mystical and analytic ways (sometimes in the same person) join in saying that man must remain mute before this mystery. Reason does not tell at all, and her claim to be or provide a paradigm of Nature's ways gets its validation from reason itself, or from experience. Surely reason can and will speak for herself. But how for the rest of Nature? That is a legislative power reason assumes autonomously. And experience does not detect that Nature in her infinite variety repeats the subjective and affective pattern of man's esthetic experience—from the quantum up to God. Nature does not seem so neat.

In our conceptions of Nature, so much depends on our initial point of view. If we survey the world, taking our own subjectivity as the "root metaphor," then our conception of it grows and flowers into a community of free subjects, harmoniously interacting and (usually) coordinated in the experience of the supreme subject, God. ("I am the vine, ye are the branches.") But if we begin with ourselves as objects, divided and disparate, then we conceive the world similarly —it is a congeries of unknowns and induplicables, neglected or imposed upon by powers standing over against them, dismembered by processes they are not aware of, sacrificed to purposes they are blind to, dependent for their good on what lies below and around them. Then the divine is thought of as a power that creatively transforms man as man cannot. It may even crush man; and its best working may require man's weakness. ("My strength is sufficient for thee; for my strength is made perfect in weakness.")

If we think of ourselves as unitary, complete, and fulfilled, as whole or potentially whole, then the world and God are thought of as similar. They are echoes and elaborations of the same themes expressed in us, confirming our being. Interaction with them yields an ever-growing harmony of subjective differences. But if we think of ourselves as plural, incomplete and unfulfilled, as broken or ever breakable, then the world and God are seen as standing over against us, diverging from and threatening us. They sting and cross us, opposing our being. Interaction with them as opposites demands a continuous struggle to maintain and deepen our unity. In the first alternative, God supple-

---

[3]Elsa A. Whalley, *Individual Life-Philosophies in Relation to Personality and to Systematic Philosophy: An Experimental Study* (Ph.D. Dissertation, University of Chicago, 1955), pp. 88–89.

ments man's nature by receiving his achievements (even a failure is a minimal achievement) into his absolutely receptive nature. In the second, God complements man's nature by acting upon it, breaking it, opening it to new unities, and positively supplying the good it lacks. The temptation of the first view is absolute idealism; of the second, agnosticism. An adequate metaphysics and theology, beginning inescapably with certain clues in man's direct experience, must take account of both the analogical and disanalogical features in the world and in deity. Both methods are given in the Western tradition (Judaic, Christian, Moslem) and in the Hindu tradition.

Hartshorne makes the important point that prediction and control exclude one another. (90) So far as we cannot or do not exercise control, novelty tends to increase, provided of course that a sufficient amount and kind of order obtain to prevent novelty from becoming self-nullifying. The assertions of science, far from being categorical as the popular mind supposes, are conditional for just this reason. They refer not merely to what is (i.e., has been) but to what might be; they are "existential" and also "actual"—actual in the sense that they are probabilistic. What power does man have to create his future actuality? Complete control over present conditions rules out the need for prediction, as complete foresight into the future already produces the future in the present, thus collapsing time into one punctiliously omniscient moment. Yet, between these extremes, prediction and control are, within a certain range, inversely proportional to each other, each requiring the other. What enables us to predict? Insight into the qualities and relations of things and events here and now. Do we create our own insights? If by "we" is meant our genetic identities (102) enduring through time, then it might be said that we, as informed and free, choose which identity is to dominate our experiences. Even so, the range of choices available to us is not entirely in our control. Alternatives of identity emerge before us as real possibilities only as things and events and relations beyond our control are favorable. If by "we" is meant our particular experiences, the same limitations in our control as well as our predictive power seem to prevail. It is true that the energies associated with my body and the effort I put forth and the decisions I have made and am now making all determine the particular experiences I have. But to deny that other factors beyond these help to create my particular experiences is to deny the social theory of reality. Thus, though God's way of creating

Himself may well be analogous to human creation—and may well be, in some respect, hidden to us—His way of creating us seems to be *different* from the way in which we create ourselves. We create within the limits of the energies and forms and contexts over which we exercise control. He creates and recreates those energies and forms and contexts.

Whether deity is to be conceived as fundamentally similar to man or fundamentally different from man is a matter of personal decision. In a matter of this kind, decision seems to be a function of temperament, and temperament of constitution. Some temperaments emphasize the similarities of experience, some the differences.[4] It may be objected that the function of philosophy is to overcome temperamental differences and to formulate that which is common to all temperaments. Just so. But what *is* common to all temperaments? The "leveller" will say that what men have in common with one another, with the world, and with God is their similarities. The "sharpener" will contend that what men have in common is the fact of their differences. Philosophy is conducted by men, and men do genuinely see the world differently. It may be answered that they see it similarly too, else we could not call them men. The resolution of this problem would seem to lie in the recognition of differences as well as similarities in men and in the world, without reducing the one to the other.

Since we can't get away from temperament, the realistic attitude is to face it as an inescapable fact—without at the same time forgetting to seek the objective factors in our experience which are differentially filtered, interpreted, and judged by different temperaments. The naturalistic principle of experience demands acknowledgement of temperament (compare James), but its stress on the public character of reliable knowledge pushes us to look for what is common to temperaments.

The conception of deity as the superlative case of experience, taking human experience as indicative of the general pattern, leads to further questions about the character of deity.

Hartshorne describes God as the being in whom there is "complete preservation" of all experiences whatsoever. (211) He is "the all-cherishing or cosmically social being . . . the storehouse of beauties

---

[4]George S. Klein, "The Menninger Foundation Research on Perception and Personality, 1947-52: A Review," *Bulletin of the Menninger Clinic*, Vol. 17, No. 3 (May, 1953), pp. 93–99. See also Elsa Whalley, *op. cit.*

which is the divine memory . . . from whose consciousness nothing can die away and be lost." (42) God is the all-encompassing, all-retaining, infallible rememberer of the creatures' experiences. Why is memory the primary metaphor for conceiving God? Once an experient event has occurred, it becomes past. The meaning of such an occurrence or actualization is that it is known, or can become known, to another experient event. ("Known to" means objectified in or referred to.) In other words, what has once occurred must always be; otherwise the objective character of the past and of time disappears. What is true once is forever true. But for truth to be, some experient event must refer to the occurrence which the truth describes. Now no finite experient can perfectly grasp and hold in memory even a small number of past events. Hence, for the past and the truth about the past to be maintained as coherent conception of the past seems to require, an infinite experient or rememberer is required. God is thus conceived as the supreme memory of the universe. The reason is that God is no exception to metaphysical first principles and must have the same generic character as any being, namely, sociality; and further, "only a socially constituted, all-retaining memory can give all of life a long-run meaning." (42) There is a human "need" for "escape . . . from loss of precious experiences." (42) Now the value of experience is satisfaction; it is the enhancement of feeling achieved through unified contrast. But no creature can achieve in its own experience *all* such values. It is finite in what it can grasp; and its memory is weak and infallible. Nor can posterity be adequate to the individual need to be remembered. (41, 212) So "what is needed for a logic of good is some conception of how values can contribute to an all-inclusive value or satisfaction." (193)

What is the relation between human need and a metaphysical understanding of God? So far as man is man, he needs to understand —discover meaning in—his experiences. Implicated in this need to find what "stands under" the relatively changing elements of experience— is the need to find and experience a certain kind of significance or value. What is the essential character of such significance? And what is it that can provide such significance—which exists in some way, and which gives to man a sense of fulfillment when he comes into proper relation to it? Hartshorne's account suggests that for man's life to be significant there must be (1) complete preservation of all values (and hence happenings) and (2) an all-inclusive and continuous integration of such values. But are these the *sine qua non* of all men's religious concern? True, many men have believed these because of custom. Yet some men have been able to give themselves to the value-process of the world, in the trust, persistence, and risk of faith, *without* requiring belief in these propositions to provide their faith with significance. But to be engaged in religious faith at all, men do implicitly require that *some* value, *somewhere*, be preserved and continued; that they have an opportunity to contribute to that value-process; and that there be some enrichment—entailing integration—of values in the value-process. But this demand does not necessitate complete preservation and all-inclusive integration of values.

Naturalists are convinced that the future status of present value, and the status of values in the future when they do emerge, is unknown not only to God but also to man. For Dewey and Russell, for example, the tie between past values and future ones is one of conditional necessity: the future depends on man. This is true for Hartshorne, except that for him there would be a future if we were no more. Here Hartshorne and naturalists divide on their views of the past. For the latter the past derives not only meaning but significance from its perceived and appreciated effects in and on the future. "The meaning of a statement is its method of verification," and this principle entails present action with future effects. Hartshorne accepts this verifiability (and valuability) principle—though for him the effects of the past need not be confined to human subjects. But he goes on to assert that the past also has meaning only as it is preserved intact in some everlasting subject. For Hartshorne, the meaning of an object is its method of objectification. If every subject is real as it *is,* and if this isness is not to be removed and hence contradicted by not being preserved in some memory, but once is always *is;* and if every achieved reality is a form of value—then *something,* an everlasting subject, is required to preserve all value. Deductive system as well as the principle of naturalism that God is not to be treated as an exception to metaphysical first principles, may demand this conclusion. But the fact is that some men find justification for value and their pursuit of value in something less than such philosophical justification.

As for Hartshorne's argument, naturalists are disposed to be suspicious of speculation where not even a peephole of direct inspection is permitted. They agree that all events that have occurred may in principle be known, but whether they *will* be known is another question. In fact, many events will never be known by man; and to say that such events, unknown to man, will transmit their effects to other events, only means that in so far forth they continue to be candidates for discovery and hence truth. They form the ground for potential truth. But that is different from realized truth.

If it is answered that knowledge or truth is subjective appropriation of the past, naturalism, if it does not differ with the definition of truth, sharply distinguishes human truth from existents that human subjectivity cannot apprehend. While naturalism may not deny the objectivity and indefinite continuance of the past in some form, it cannot fully convert all objects into subjects, potential truth into actual truth, and actual truth into everlasting truth. Naturalism reasons from events to truth, and its principle of empiricism does not allow it to reverse this procedure. Some naturalists have the grace to grant that such everlasting truth *may* exist, but it could be known only to an everlasting subject. And then the argument returns to the question of how such a subject can be known.

Does man need an all-remembering God to be justified in a life of value? What is the justification of value? In one sense, the question is a pleonasm. An experience of value—of joy, or even a kind of suffering—carries its own reward. As such, it needs nothing beyond to fulfill it. Hartshorne recognizes this. "If I presently feel concern for another and act on this concern, I do now what I now want to do, and it is absurd to ask a reward for doing what one wants to do. That I, the present self, am privileged to act out my wishes is reward enough." (104-105) "To really love others is to find reward now in promoting their good." (209) "The locus of decision . . . must be in the act of the given moment." (96) And value is the particularization of feeling here and now by means of such decision. (96)

Thus the *practical* justification of value is just the value-experience itself. This is the meaning of "intrinsic": "self-justifying," or "self-evident." And if a value is not intrinsic then to partake of any value at all it must be instrumental to some intrinsic value. Thorndike's Law of Effect, reformulated in recent psychology, indicates that a primary, ever-present motive of man is the search for value—though of course man may be mistaken.

When men become reflective this organismic demand extends itself to the search for some connection between values. Men demand that values be connected in time and space; that they have "meaning" in the sense that present values conserve, transform, or in some way enrich and consummate past values, and that they in turn anticipate, prepare the way for, and facilitate future values; and that some measure of integration be achieved between contemporary values. *Reflective* justification of value thus consists (1) in some form of "validation" which appeals to a system of metaphysics and axiology and adduces data in support of such a system via deductive reasoning; and (2) in some form of "vindication"[5] which appeals to the conditions and consequences of choosing certain values.

Similarly *reflectively religious* justification of value consists in an appeal to a system of theology, on top of metaphysics and axiology, deduction, and the analysis of empirical data.

But the points to be noticed are these. At the unreflective, practical level, men have a sense of justification in the life of value if they experience *some* value or have some prospect of doing so, or if they anticipate that *others* will experience some value in consequence of what they are doing. They may be justified by faith, more or less blind, with very little rational assurance concerning the ground, end, or guarantee of values. At the reflective level, some men require for justification *some* continuity and integration of values but not a complete system involving no loss or irremediable discord. Finally, at the reflectively religious level, where men are "ultimately concerned," their faith in values and the value-enterprise may be as semi-agnostic, pluralistic, humanistic, existential, and fragmentarily rationalized as Buddha's, Camus', or Zen's. While the excellently religious man does not live by faith alone (totally devoid of reason), he normally is or can be justified with much less rational system and assurance than traditional theologies have provided.

Let us consider, finally, the case for the philosophical justification of the immortality of the past—the perfect preservation of all values. Hartshorne's argument rests not only on the "need that our lives, our experiences just as they are, should have permanent value," (143) but on a necessity of thought. If the past must be preserved, and if God is the supreme subject, then it is preserved in Him. Thus God is con-

[5]Herbert Feigl, "Validation and Vindication: An Analysis of the Nature and the Limits of Ethical Arguments," in *Readings in Ethical Theory*, edited by Wilfrid Sellars and John Hospers (New York: Appleton-Century-Crofts, Inc., 1952), pp. 667–680.

ceived as a super-case of, rather than an exception to, metaphysical first principles. For man's memory is limited; but God's is not.

Naturalism's ontological principle (1) that whatever is real must be an actual event in space and time or ingredient in some event, its principle (4) that Nature is continuous (there are no exceptions to metaphysical first principles), and (7) its principle of relativity or probability, require that God be actual (or nothing), that God share in all the generic categories applicable to events, and that there be limitation or definiteness in God. Hartshorne denies that there is any elimination or loss of value in God's experience of the created world. To this extent he goes beyond naturalism. For naturalism, the category of experience, which includes memory, involves limitation—selection, incompatibility, elimination, and loss.[6] New experiences are additions to those of the past that are funded in the present. But addition here involves subtraction, for the same reason that P involves non-P. Why is it not so with God?

Suppose we grant that God as primordial is absolutely necessary and hence having no alternative excludes nothing as abstract. Then God on His contingent and finite side *responds* to the world. He is receptive and sympathetic to it. In short, He *loves* it. "The parts determine, *in interaction with* the radically superior determining power of the whole-being, the accidental *de facto* state of that being (the contingent content of its experience)." (122-123, my italics). But love, or creative synthesis, even in the supreme case, would seem to involve a principle of limitation, even if the general category of creative love seems to be a necessary, categorial feature of the world. Love involves some minimum of decision and hence exclusion. By "exclusion" I mean not destruction (the extreme and self-contradictory case) but some degree of attenuated emphasis. If, as Hartshorne says, God is moved to sympathize with all happenings, if in loving and suffering He takes unto Himself the vast, particularized variety of the actual universe moment by moment, how can He avoid decision in His receptive, creative act? For the events are not harmoniously arranged before they pass into God. Indeed, they are contemporaneously independent and in the heat of conflict seem incompatible. Hence God must arrange them. But God's arrangement involves decision. For if the consequent order of concrete events in God were foreordained

[6]F. C. Bartlett, *Remembering* (New York: The Macmillan Co., 1932), p. 213.

there would be no need of their passage into God; or, they would already be in God, and would, in their temporal aspects, be no more than a movie image of an Eternal Reel. To remove such decision from God destroys the distinction between freedom and necessity and makes "love" meaningless as applied to God.

Apart from the problem of arrangement, it would appear that in one aspect God remembers the past in a limited way. For He everlastingly experiences completed subjects just as they really are. But their realities involve selective remembrance and love. If God absorbs such realities, then He feels the past, through his feeling of them, in just that limited way. But, says Hartshorne, the data of the world are "transparently immortalized with the maximal contrast-value and harmony into which they are capable of entering."[7]

It may be that "even though contemporary events are independent, they are becoming determined in patterns as well . . . and by the time they become past, they are fully patterned."[8] But that account does not explain how the living immediacy of contemporary events enters into God nor does it answer the question of how events that appear to be incompatible in the rest of nature become compatible in God. Further, if it is true that "Hartshorne's position is that God changes the world by changing himself; [not] change of the past [but] somehow a change in the possibilities which lie before the world in the antecedent nature"[9]—it is not clear how a change in God's nature as a growing whole can fail to affect those definite contents of his nature which He derives from the world—if only by a shift in emphasis. If God is a super-case of love and His love is devoid of any selective principle, then either the love we experience is not necessarily selective or God's reception of the world (as described by Hartshorne) cannot be properly and analogously called "love."

Is God then at this point in Hartshorne's philosophy an exception to naturalistic first principles, or merely a super-case? So far as Hartshorne otherwise adheres to naturalism, I think God is here an exception. Naturalism (as I have stated it) allows for a continuum of better and worse memories or loves, and therefore to assert a memory or love that imposes no principle of limitation and hence produces

[7]"The Philosophy of Creative Synthesis," *Journal of Philosophy*, 55, No. 22 (October 23, 1958), 953.

[8]Professor William Reese, in correspondence with the writer.

[9]*Ibid.*

no effect on the data remembered or loved, is to assert an exception. (Of course, to avoid making God an exception, one may always redefine the ordinary meanings of "memory" and "love.") If "super-case" means literally a "non-limited" form of the species, then naturalism considers it an exception. For, for naturalism, "definition is the soul of actuality."

One who loves is not only receptive; he acts back upon the world. Wherein does God's activity on the world consist? How do we know God as a being in process? Can naturalism's principle (5) that every real entity can, in principle, be known, apply to God? And its principles (6) and (7) that experience, analyzed and synthesized, is the only reliable way to knowledge, and that all reliable knowledge is public? The merit of Hartshorne's approach is that he defines God (in part) societally, i.e., triadically, as an actuality interacting with other actualities, and thus avoids the difficulties of an unqualified monadic approach (mysticism) or a strictly dyadic approach (dualism)—which so often crop up in traditional formulations. But exactly how men know God empirically is not made plain—because God is known "vaguely." Such an account will perhaps satisfy the man with a strongly esthetic response to the world; but men of action demand that they come to grips with a tangible deity that makes a difference to perception and conduct.

Although the social category requires that God give to and receive from the creatures (136), interacting with them, we are not told how God *distinctively* acts upon us or other concrete beings. It is true that God disposes the primary order of events so that he sets "the best or optimal limits to freedom," (41) mixing his own necessary nature with the contingency of events. But that action, if it may be called action, is abstract. How is God apprehended concretely?

The whole idea of religion . . . is precisely that we can know God as he is in himself (though vaguely), for we know him through love, and love is "taking the standpoint of the other" (Mead) . . . God as cause is *in* his effects, and God as cause is God himself . . . we know ourselves and everything else in relation to our dim but direct sense of God's love, with which we are one by our subconscious but inalienable returning love for him.[10]

It may be that under a societal account of deity, this is the closest we can come to describing our experience of God. If so, then it be-

10Charles Hartshorne, *Man's Vision of God and the Logic of Theism* (Chicago and New York: Willett, Clark and Co., 1941), p. 127.

comes difficult experientially to distinguish God's love from man's love. But naturalism requires that whatever exists must be in principle distinguishable from other things and relatable to them. It requires that God as love, for example, must be perceived or experienced *as different* from man's love—granting of course that "experience" may include a small or a large degree of the conceptual element. Nor does naturalism, in employing the method of difference, deny "necessary" features of experience and reality. But it does demand that where we arrive at "necessities of thought" these can have no status as truth or as adequate guides of conduct until *some* perceptual elements, directly corresponding to them or deducible from them, have been discovered in experience.

Moreover, to take the social conception of reality seriously means that we always perceive and hence conceive deity under the limitations of a perspective, and that the very "meaning" we give at any moment to deity is always—i.e., necessarily—determined in a contingent way. In short, *our* necessities of thought are not in every respect identical with the necessities of existence; they are tinged with our perspectival contingencies. Hartshorne's argument is that for thought that is sufficiently reflective "there *must* be *something* contingent, since otherwise contrast, and therewith meaning, would collapse; and for the same reason there must be *something* necessary."[11] Thus *"all* arguments for the necessary being [i.e., "unconditionally necessary" being] are essentially of one type, and all must in some sense be a priori."[12] But I do not see how this abstract conclusion of our limited minds decides the question of whether God's creative synthesis (love, memory) is limited in the way suggested. Logic or "meaning" requires *that* God is; but it does not tell *what* God is except in a most general way.

But of course naturalism faces this same problem. The dilemma of metaphysics at this point is that its necessary statements turn out to be empty formalities whereas its statements that apply to experience are contingent, probable, and improvable. Naturalism, so far as it searches for or accepts necessities, occupies an uneasy position between these two alternatives, seeking to formulate necessities of thought and then to confirm them in some way in experience. How is mind con-

---

[11]"The Philosophy of Creative Synthesis," p. 952.
[12]*Ibid.*

nected with matter, subject with object, concept with percept, the permanent with the changing, God with the world? In religious thought, "God in Christ," and the concept of Buddhahood, are formulas for solving the dilemma; but they do not on their face tell what Christ or the Buddha nature may be, except in vague language like "divine love."

One way through the dilemma for naturalism is to regard the necessities of thought as linguistic forms which are created, revised, passed down, and shared in a given culture, and which interact with the concrete, perceived data of the culture. Thus the emergent meanings acquire slowly increasing clarity and self-consistency as they are communicated and used in relation to their objects and contexts. In turn, they give form and direction to such experience. And the demands of human subjects and their objects, joined in the connections conferred by human activity—practical, contemplative, esthetic, religious—press certain adjustments upon established meanings. Thus the occurrence of patterns of such meanings are experiential necessities apart from which distinctively "human" existence (i.e., linguistic experience) could not be. But the patterns themselves are by no means universally or easily agreed upon.

It is curious that in commonsensical and scientific experience we do not argue about empirical, existential, contingent, and hypothetical statements; for we have established methods of testing them. But we do argue about what lies at the level of the rational, essential, necessary, and categorical. We argue about which set of linguistic patterns is—or is to be—applied to matters of perceived fact. The reason for this is not that empirical statements are "objective" and pertain to things available for inter-subjective testing and that rational statements are "subjective." For meanings may be tested in inter-subjective ways. Nor do we always so argue because some men differ in virtue of differing personal decisions as to which set of basic linguistic patterns they adopt for interpreting and dealing with the world. Some pattern is necessary. But which? Can we discover a pattern or meaning of human experience which is necessitated for all men as men?

To live, and to achieve for himself and others any value whatsoever—above the level of the non-human—a man must choose a set of basic meanings; and to increase value, to fulfill himself, he must grow in his meanings. Here are two necessities for man as man—the necessity of choice and the necessity of growth in meanings. The fact that men do change their minds, that meanings grow, indicates the cause of their differences and arguments. But it also indicates a dialectic between meaning and brute fact that makes possible increasing clarity, consistency, and pragmatic utility of meanings, as well as a growing consensus among men as to the genuine necessities of a given culture and the whole human community.

In naturalism, the existence of "necessary" meanings or "categories" does not mean that the method of difference (transformed into the method of concomitant variations) may not be used in discovering such categories. Thus religious naturalism (in one form) holds that the creativity of God varies in the lives of persons as the conditions of those lives vary. But such a demonstration still does not prove that God's creativity is continuous. The difficulty is that this "proof" would have to consist in a continuous (and hence unconscious) intuition, common to all men if not all creatures, or in an abstract chain of deductions. But both of these methods, for naturalism, leave something to be desired. If intuitions are unspeakably golden, then speech is sounding brass. But if such intuitions are communicable, then they acquire a definiteness and abstractness that adulterates their power and necessary nature. We are back then to inference.

In this essay I have tried to think through some of the relations of Hartshorne's philosophy of religion to the philosophy of naturalism. Hartshorne's approach and purpose, as significant as his conclusions, raise the question of how the new naturalism must be modified or transcended to accommodate the experiences, intuitions, insights, and deductions that arise in religion and religious thought. The world of science has challenged traditional notions of reality, value, knowledge, and deity. Hartshorne's societism is a major attempt to reconstruct those notions boldly and systematically, in a way akin to the way of naturalism but different from it. Can a religion, as conceived and practiced within the bounds of naturalism, be wholly adequate for man? And how must traditional religious meanings be accommodated to naturalism? In response to the impact of science, the religious thought of both West and East has for some time been ready for a re-orientation. Hartshorne has fashioned one of the few philosophies of religion that speaks comprehensively to such a readiness. Having taken account of modern science, logic, and religious experience, Hartshorne presents such a re-orientation. His work offers fresh insights into nature and a novel vision of God.

HOWARD L. PARSONS

COE COLLEGE

RELIGION AND HUMAN NATURE IN THE
PHILOSOPHY OF DAVID HUME

O F THE MANY ambiguities that characterize Hume's philosophy none is so deep or so puzzling as his treatment of religion. We find statements in Hume's writings that would do credit to the most reverent orthodoxy and other statements that criticize religious beliefs with such excessive violence that they go beyond the boundaries of good taste. Perhaps his own attitude is best expressed at the end of his *Natural History of Religion* where he says that, "the whole is a riddle, an aenigma, an inexplicable mystery."[1] But a careful study of Hume's works give us some clues for resolving at least that part of the riddle which has to do with his own views about religion. In this essay I shall try to show that the commentators have largely failed to grasp the main point of Hume's anti-religious polemic. In placing the emphasis on his refutations of the proofs for the existence of God, or on his skeptical doubts concerning miracles, students of Hume have overlooked his most powerful anti-religious weapon. As a result they have been unclear about Hume's own theory of religion.

Hume had both generous and bitter things to say about traditional religion. There are passages in which he speaks with seeming reverence about "our most holy religion"[2] and in which he advises us to "fly to revealed truth with the greatest avidity."[3] These are opposed by passages in which he asserts that most religious principles must be viewed as nothing but "sick men's dreams . . . or the playsome whimsies of monkies in human shape."[4] The interpretation of these passages has posed a problem for students of Hume and has led most of them to conclude that whenever he says anything appreciative about

[1]David Hume, *The Natural History of Religion* (Stanford: Stanford University Press, 1957), p. 76.

[2]David Hume, *Enquiry Concerning Human Understanding* (Selby-Bigge edition; Oxford, 1902), p. 130. Cf. *Treatise of Human Nature*, p. 250.

[3]David Hume, *Dialogues Concerning Natural Religion,* ed. Norman Kemp Smith (2d ed.; London, 1947) p. 227.

[4]*Natural History of Religion*, p. 75.

religion it is either sarcastic or else in deference to the social utility of religion. But in leaving the matter there they overlook what is most important.

Religion posed problems that occupied Hume deeply. In the introduction to his *Treatise* he expresses the hope that human knowledge in its various branches will be much advanced by his investigations, but he is especially confident that "The improvements are the more to be hoped for in natural religion."[5] This initial concern was sustained throughtout his life. Not only did he take elaborate care to insure the posthumous publication of his *Dialogues Concerning Natural Religion,* but he even made revisions in the manuscript during the last year of his life.[6] For more than twenty-five years he had kept the manuscript of this work and returned to work on it on more than one occasion. How shall we explain Hume's life-long preoccupation with religion? What were the improvements for which he hoped? Why, if he was convinced that religion was little more than "sick men's dreams," did he continue to devote intense thought to the subject?

The answer, I believe, lies in another area that concerned Hume deeply, namely human nature. We concentrate so much on Hume's epistemology and his criticism of metaphysics that we tend to forget that the title of his first and largest book is *A Treatise of Human Nature.* E. C. Mossner, in his *Life of David Hume,* brings the crucial issue to our attention with a most effective rhetorical device. Mossner opens his book with a dedication, "To a young David in the hope that he, too, will never lose faith in the dignity of human nature." He concludes the biography with a chapter entitled, "The Dignity of Human Nature." What is eminently clear is that we are being told that the preservation of human dignity was the profoundest interest of Hume's life. I believe that Mossner is correct and that Hume's struggles with religion stem largely from his desire to maintain the dignity of human nature.

In the Western world claims about human dignity have traditionally grown out of a religious foundation.[7] The biblical description

---

[5]David Hume, *A Treatise of Human Nature* (Selby-Bigge ed.; Oxford, 1951), p. XIX.

[6]*Dialogues,* p. 5 of Kemp Smith's Introduction.

[7]Hendel maintains this point when he says of Hume, "We have seen him showing reverence for persons. Where reverence dwells in human nature, there religion has

of man as created in the divine image was the ground for belief in the intrinsic worth of each man, as such, and in the superiority of men over all other creatures. Even when religious writers denigrated man it was primarily because they saw him as fallen away from his ideal possibilities. Both Judaism and Christianity depend on a view of man as unique and superior to all other earthly creatures. These religions view man as God's special concern. Divine revelation is addressed only to man; the hope of final redemption is held out only to man; and in Christian teaching God saves man by assuming a human form. Explicitly or implicitly Western morality is closely tied to this way of thinking about man. All earthly existence is in the service of man. The best animal may be sacrificed, if necessary, to preserve the life of the most unsavory man.

So long as man is understood to be but "little less than God"[8] because he is God's special creature it is easy to maintain the usual claims about the dignity of man. Hume, however, faced an aggravated problem. He rejected Christian orthodoxy, but wanted to maintain the moral attitudes and the reverence for man which had for centuries been based on that orthodoxy. It is a credit to his rigorous intellectual honesty that he did not make the task easier for himself by closing his eyes to the proper conclusions of his own naturalism. As we shall show, he pursued his line of argument relentlessly, even when it forced him to conclusions that were not to his taste.

In his thinking about human nature Hume was far more deeply influenced by certain of his non-religious predecessors than by the religious tradition. There is a long line of thinkers, stretching from antiquity to Hume's own time, who deny all superiority to man. Hume had close acquaintance with many of these thinkers and was deeply influenced by them. The most famous ancient source is in Plutarch's *Moralia* in the section "Beasts are Rational." Odysseus has been given an opportunity to speak with Gryllus, formerly a man now transformed into a swine. If Odysseus can persuade Gryllus that the human state is superior, Circe will change him back into a man. But Odysseus fails. Gryllus argues most impressively in defense of the superiority of beasts, showing that "The soul of beasts has a greater natural capac-

its roots." Charles W. Hendel, *Studies in the Philosophy of David Hume* (Princeton: Princeton University Press, 1925), p. 14.

[8]Psalms, 8:6. This is a literal translation.

ity and perfection for the generation of virtue"[9] than the souls of men and also that "animals have a natural endowment of reason and intellect."[10] This work of Plutarch's and the opening of Book VII of Pliny's *Natural History* are the most familiar standard sources in classical antiquity which argue for the superiority of animals.[11]

As a student of classical literature Hume certainly knew these passages, but there were closer and more immediate influences. While early Renaissance humanism had stressed the superiority of man, by the late sixteenth century Montaigne and other writers had again reduced man to the beasts or even less.[12] And in the eighteenth century Pierre Bayle marshalled arguments and evidence against the superiority of man. In the article "Rorarius" in his *Dictionary,* Bayle gives us the sources and grounds for the view of Rorarius who "undertook to shew . . . not only that beasts are rational creatures, but that they make better use of their reason than man."[13] Hume had read Montaigne and Bayle carefully. From them, as from Plutarch and Pliny, he learned to think of man as nothing more than an animal.[14]

It is this view of man which constitutes Hume's most powerful anti-religious weapon. Christianity and Judaism are not seriously threatened by refutations of proofs for the existence of God. In their lack of demonstrative evidence for the existence of God men of religious faith are not in worse condition than are philosophers who believe in the existence of bodies or in the uniformity of nature without sufficient evidence. "Thus the sceptic still continues to reason and believe, even tho' he asserts, that he cannot defend his reason by rea-

[9]Plutarch, *Moralia* (Loeb edition), p. 501 = 987B.

[10]*Ibid.*, p. 531 = 992C.

[11]For additional sources see A. O. Lovejoy and George Boas, *Primitivism and Related Ideas in Antiquity* (Baltimore: Johns Hopkins University), Ch. XIII.

[12]Montaigne, *Essays,* trans. E. J. Trechmann (Oxford: Oxford University Press, 1927), "Apology for Raymond Sebond," *passim.*

[13]Pierre Bayle, *Dictionary, Historical and Critical,* 8 (London, 1739), 757; cf. the entire article, "Rorarius."

[14]In his *Philosophy of David Hume* Norman Kemp Smith writes: "We know that Hume read extensively in Bayle's *Dictionary* . . . Bayle, too, is often simply the mouthpiece of Montaigne—one of the few modern writers to whom Hume makes explicit reference." (p. 325).

We also know that Hume had studied Cicero and other ancients who make man superior to animals. But on this point they did not persuade him.

son; and by the same rule he must assent to the principle concerning the existence of body, tho' he cannot pretend by any arguments of philosophy to maintain its veracity."[15] If Hume's attack on religion depended only on invalidating the proofs for the existence of God it would have been trivial. And it would have come with poor grace from a man who was driven to admit that though almost all of our supposed knowledge goes beyond what is justified by the evidence, we nevertheless continue to believe.

The real danger to religion is to be found in those relatively unnoticed sections of Hume's works in which he considers the nature of man in comparison with animals. In his essay "Of the Dignity or Meanness of Human Nature" Hume has given us a valuable key to understanding his position properly. He begins by commenting on the widely varied views that have been advanced concerning the dignity of man, and then suggests that authors should decide whether to argue in behalf of man's dignity or his meanness only on the basis of which view best fits their rhetorical talents. In this essay his own qualified argument in behalf of human dignity must also be seen as a rhetorical exercise, for he tells us explicitly that society is better served when man is exalted. "The sentiments of those who are inclined to think favourably of mankind, are more advantageous to virtue, than the contrary principles which give us a mean opinion of our nature. When a man is prepossessed with a high notion of his rank and character in the creation, he will naturally endeavour to act up to it, and will scorn to do a base or vicious action, which might sink him below that figure which he makes in his own imagination."[16] The same motivation which causes him at times to speak kindly of

---

[15]*Treatise*, p. 187.

[16]"Of the Dignity or Meanness of Human Nature," in *Essays Moral, Political, and Literary by David Hume,* eds. T. H. Green and T. H. Grose I (New York, 1898), 151. Hume speaks of various "sects" in the opening paragraph of his essay and makes the following observation: "The most remarkable . . . are the sects, founded on the different sentiments with regard to the *dignity of human nature;* which is a point that seems to have divided philosophers and poets, as well as divines, from the beginning of the world to this day. Some exalt our species to the skies, and represent man as a kind of human demigod, who derives his origin from heaven, and retains evident marks of his lineage and descent. Others insist upon the blind sides of human nature, and can discover nothing, except vanity, in which man surpasses the other animals, whom he affects so much to despise. If an author possess the talent of rhetoric and declamation, he commonly takes part with the former: If his turn lie towards irony and ridicule, he naturally throws himself into the other extreme."

religion is operating here. "In one respect only does he recognize Christianity as standing by itself, namely, that for him and his contemporaries in Britain the Reformed Church teaching stood officially for religion, and that the good citizen was therefore in duty bound to pay it outward deference . . . while yet none the less reserving his right to critize it freely in his own thoughts, and subject to certain recognized conventions also in his own writings."[17] When speaking about human dignity in a popular essay Hume must exalt man for the sake of preserving public morality. But when he considers man in his serious philosophic works he attacks without restraint. In the *Treatise* man is reduced to being nothing more than any animal. This reduction, as we shall show, is neither accidental nor casual. It is carefully planned and worked out in meticulous detail and is given such a strategic place in the ordering of the parts of the *Treatise* that it cannot escape the attention of any careful reader of that book. By way of this reduction of man to animal Hume deals the severest of all blows to religion.

The religious position depends on the belief that man is essentially different from animals, that the difference is not one of degree but of kind. It is this very claim that Hume denies. In his view, we cannot know the essence of human nature, "and any hypothesis that pretends to discover the ultimate original qualities of human nature, ought at first to be rejected as presumptuous and chimerical."[18] Since we cannot have any direct knowledge of human nature we can only study it by way of analogy. In religious thought man is analogized to God, and the human ideal is expressed as *imitatio dei*. The same is true of those classical philosophers who see man as unique and superior to all other creatures. Plato, for example, speaks of man's soul

---

[17]*Dialogues*, p. 10 of Kemp Smith's Introduction. Cf. *Enquiry Concerning Human Understanding*, p. 147: "Men...draw many consequences from the belief of a divine existence, and suppose that the deity will inflict punishment on vice, and bestow rewards on virtue . . . Whether this reasoning of theirs be just or not, is no matter. Its influence on their life and conduct must still be the same. And, those, who attempt to disabuse them of such prejudices, may, for aught I know, be good reasoners, but I cannot allow them to be good citizens and politicians; since they free men from one restraint on their passions, and make the infringement of the laws of society, in one respect, more easy and secure."

[18]*Treatise*, p. xxi.

as being like the unseen, the unchanging, and, above all, the divine.[19] Hume finds the analogy with God useless, since we know nothing about God. This is perhaps the strongest point that is made in the *Dialogues Concerning Natural Religion*—that we find neither justification nor meaning in attempts to analogize man and God. In the *Treatise* Hume does not even attempt such an analogy, but tries instead to understand man on the model of animals.

Of all the claims to man's uniqueness none has persisted more than the belief that man is the only rational animal. Yet Hume begins his discussion of reason in animals by saying that "no truth appears to me more evident than that beasts are endowed with thought and reason as well as men."[20] In fact, human reason can only be understood, according to Hume, on the model of animal reason. "Reason is nothing but a wonderful and unintelligible instinct in our souls,"[21] an instinct exactly like the instincts of animals. At the end of the *Treatise* Hume concedes a limited natural superiority to man, but this is only a superiority of degree. "Men are superior to beasts principally by the superiority of their reason; and they are the degrees of the same faculty, which set such an infinite difference betwixt one man and another."[22] It is worth noting that this admission of limited superiority occurs in Hume's discussion of morals, a fact the significance of which we shall explain later. But when he is comparing human and animal reason under the rubric "Of Knowledge and Probability," men seem to come out second best. Reason is an instinct, and no man can act instinctively in complex matters with the unerringly elaborate and delicate skill with which, for example, a bird builds its nest. In his fumbling efforts to adapt means to ends man is

---

[19]*Phaedo*, 78b-81a. Norman Kemp Smith in his *Commentary on Kant's Critique of Pure Reason* makes the observation that Kant approached these problems "from the point of view of the difference rather than the kinship between man and the animals." This approach "leaves him free from that desire which exercises so constant, and frequently so deleterious an influence, upon many workers in the field of psychology, namely to maintain at all costs, in anticipation of conclusions not yet by any means established, the fundamental identity of human and animal intelligence." (p. xlviii)

[20]*Treatise*, p. 176.

[21]*Treatise*, p. 179.

[22]*Treatise*, p. 610; cf. *Enquiry Concerning Human Understanding*, p. 107, note 1. In the *Dialogues* he speaks with contempt of "This little agitation of the brain which we call thought." (p. 148) See also Norman Kemp Smith, "The Naturalism of Hume," *Mind*, N. S., 14, 1905, 155.

far inferior to many animals, rarely rising to the level of "those more extraordinary instances of sagacity" which occur among animals. Hume destroys the belief in human rational superiority, and with it one of the firmest foundations of the religious view of man's nature. To make his argument especially effective he sets it at the end of Part III, "Of Knowledge and Probability." He seems to want to make certain that his readers will carry away as their final thought a conception of human reason which cannot be used to exalt man in any way above the animals.

Near the end of Book I of the *Treatise* Hume strikes another blow against the religious conception of man. The substantial identity of the individual person is an important element in orthodox religious doctrine, without which the belief in the immortality of the soul and the hope for reward and the fear of punishment make no sense. That Hume had great trouble with the problem of personal identity is well known. What we need to take note of in the present discussion is the fact that he explains human identity by analogy with animal identity and denies any significant distinction between them. "The identity," he says, "which we ascribe to the mind of man, is only a fictitious one, and of a like kind with that which we ascribe to vegetables and animal bodies. It cannot, therefore, have a different origin, but must proceed from a like operation of the imagination upon like objects."[23] Again we see Hume eliminating a traditional distinction and thus denying man's uniqueness and superiority.

Lest it be thought that these views may not have been consciously anti-religious on Hume's part it might be well to provide unmistakable evidence that he knew exactly what he was doing. In his discussion of vice and virtue he concludes that virtue is closely connected with pride and vice with humility. This seems so blatantly opposed to Christian morality that Hume cannot let the matter pass in silence. He reveals his hand unambiguously when he says that, "There may, perhaps, be some, who being accustomed to the style of the schools and the pulpit, and having never considered human nature in any other light, than that in which *they* place it, may here be surprised. . ."[24] Hume explicitly announces that he views human nature in a light significantly different from that "of the schools and the

[23]*Treatise,* p. 259; cf. pp. 253ff.
[24]*Treatise,* p. 297.

pulpit." This instance is characteristic of his treatment of human nature, a treatment which is consistently and consciously opposed to the views "of the schools and the pulpit."

In Book I of the *Treatise* Hume reduced human knowledge to a set of idiosyncratic psychological processes shared by men and animals. It might be thought, however, that as a feeling passional creature man may be different from animals and that this is the ground of his claims to uniqueness. But in Book II Hume turns vigorously against this view as well. His elaborate analysis of the human passions is punctuated by the regular identification of human and animal emotions. Part I, "Of Pride and Humility," concludes with a section on pride and humility in animals. Part II, "Of Love and Hatred," ends with a section on the love and hatred of animals. Part III ends in a similar though somewhat less obvious way. In all these sections Hume stresses two points. First, that man is to be understood only by analogy with animals. Second, that there are no essential differences between animal and human psychology.

At the end of the discussion of pride and humility Hume argues that "all the internal principles, that are necessary in us to produce either pride or humility, are common to all creatures; and since the causes, which excite these passions, are likewise the same, we may justly conclude, that these causes operate after the same manner through the whole animal creation."[25] Love and hatred, the subject of Part II, offers a more revealing instance of Hume's reduction of man to an animal. He begins by asserting that "The object of love and hatred is evidently some *thinking person*." In the next sentence, speaking of the cause of these passions he broadens his category and speaks of them as "always related to a *thinking being*." That "thinking person" and "thinking being" are not synonymous becomes clear in the next sentence when he says that "The cause of love and hatred must be related to a person *or* thinking being."[26] Lest we have any doubt as to what these "thinking beings" may be, Hume clarifies the matter a little later in the discussion when he asks us "to observe the force of sympathy through the whole animal creation, and the easy communications of sentiments from one thinking being to another."[27]

[25]*Treatise*, p. 328.
[26]*Treatise*, p. 331, my italics.
[27]*Treatise*, p. 363.

Here we see clearly that animals are thinking beings for Hume, and the logic of his position causes him to eliminate the supposed differences between "thinking persons" and animals. At the end of the exposition of love and hatred his view is stated explicitly. "But to pass from the passions of love and hatred . . . as they appear in man, to the same affections as they display themselves in brutes; we may observe . . . that love and hatred are common to the whole sensitive creation. . . . Every thing is conducted by springs and principles, which are not peculiar to man, or any one species of animals."[28]

Part III of Book II of the *Treatise* is entitled "Of the Will and Direct Passions." Hume allows no distinction between men and animals in his treatment of this topic. Instead he is so convinced of their similarities that he does not even find it necessary to discuss them. He concludes his exposition by saying, "I waive the examination of the will and direct passions, as they appear in animals; since nothing is more evident, than that they are of the same nature, and excited by the same causes as in human creatures."[29] Men and animals are essentially alike in their passional life as in their rational life. In this way Hume concludes the book on the passions, leaving us with a final note that underscores his systematic elimination of the differences between men and animals. In each case he has set the crucial passage at the end of a section, thus seeking to make sure that it would be noted and that it would leave a lasting final impression.

There is, however, an oddity that needs to be explained and integrated into our analysis. A final section is added to the end of Book II which deals with "Curiosity or the Love of Truth." Though this discussion does not fit into the ordered pattern of the *Treatise* Hume, nevertheless, feels that it would be strange if in a philosophic analysis of the passions he ignored the love of truth completely. However, he acknowledges that, " 'Tis an affection of so peculiar a kind, that 'twould have been impossible to have treated of it under any of those heads, which we have examined, without danger of obscurity and confusion."[30] How does this section fit into the scheme of our analysis?

At first glance Hume seems here to want to save a bit of face for man. After having told us repeatedly that human psychology is only

[28]*Treatise*, p. 398.
[29]*Treatise*, p. 448.
[30]*Ibid.*

one instance of animal psychology, he seems to be saying to his worried readers, "Fear not! At least man has his love of truth, and this is not shared by animals." Love of truth is equated with philosophy, and it might heal our wounded pride a bit to remind us that philosophy is a peculiarly human activity. This is the impression that one might get from a quick and cursory reading of the section. However, a closer and more careful reading will show that, in a subtle way, Hume is only strengthening his case against the uniqueness of man.

To begin, we should note that philosophy or love of truth is reduced by Hume to a passion—a most undignified state for what is normally supposed to be the highest activity of human reason. Hume adds an even more severe blow when he proclaims that "There cannot be two passions more nearly resembling each other, than those of hunting and philosophy, whatever disproportion may at first sight appear betwixt them."[31] The only other analogy he offers is between philosophy and gambling (which has the same motive drive as hunting). In effect, while seeming on the surface to exalt man because he alone philosophizes, Hume has actually brought man down from all his claims to eminence. It is true that in this section he makes no explicit comparison between men and animals. But the comparison is not made because it is not necessary. Hunting is very much an animal activity. If man's love of truth is understood as nothing more than a variety of hunting, then philosophy has lost all claim to special status. Man, the philosopher, is only carrying on another animal activity. Good taste may have prevented Hume from saying directly that philosophers are animals. It did not prevent him from suggesting that an animal stalking his prey and a philosopher pursuing truth are engaged in essentially similar activities.

The strongest traditional fortress of human uniqueness and superiority is man's moral nature. Even those theologians who refuse to place their trust in the uniqueness of man's reason affirm that man is unique in his moral capacity. It is as a moral agent that we see in man reflections of the divine. As the serpent puts it to Eve, when tempting her to eat the forbidden fruit, "You will become like God, knowing good and evil." If it can be maintained that morality distinguishes man essentially from all creatures we can still preserve our

[31]*Treatise*, p. 451.

belief in man as a special being. However, Hume does not allow us even this ego-saving comfort.

As might be expected, when he deals with morals Hume is more circumspect than when dealing with reason or the passions. There are distinct social advantages in maintaining the dignity of man as a moral agent, advantages which Hume wants to preserve. He is not ready, however, to preserve them at the cost of intellectual dishonesty. "When any opinion leads us into absurdities, 'tis certainly false; but 'tis not certain an opinion is false, because 'tis of dangerous consequence."[32] Hume is anxious to reduce the dangerous consequences, so far as he can, but he will not restrict the development of his inquiry because he fears that his conclusions may be dangerous. Thus, in Book III of the *Treatise* he makes no *explicit* statement that reduces human morality to an animal activity. Such a statement would be needlessly hazardous. Yet, a careful reading of his treatment of morals leads inevitably to just such a reduction.

Early in his discussion he seems even to deny that there is animal morality. In arguing that morality does not consist in relations he makes his point by showing that though animals and men exhibit the same relations these relations do not evoke identical moral judgments. For example, "incest in the human species is criminal . . . and the same relations in animals have not the smallest moral turpitude and deformity."[33] To many readers Hume seems to be saying here that morality is a peculiarly *human* phenomenon. All he actually says is that those who conceive of morality as consisting in relations will be forced to admit "That every animal must be susceptible of all the *same* virtues and vices, for which we ascribe praise and blame to human creatures."[34] This extreme proposition Hume will not grant. However, his denial is not based on the principle that animals have no morality, but only on the conviction that it is a mistake to conceive of virtue and vice as relations. An analysis of Hume's theory of morals will show that it offers us no ground for the claim that there are any essential distinctions between human and animal nature.

In Hume's view moral distinctions are derived from a moral sense. "To have the sense of virtue, is nothing but to *feel* a satisfaction of

32*Treatise*, p. 409.
33*Treatise*, p. 467.
34*Treatise*, p. 468, my italics.

a particular kind from the contemplation of a character. The very *feeling* constitutes our praise or admiration. We go no further; nor do we enquire into the cause of the satisfaction."[35] If this is all there is to man's moral awareness it is hardly a ground for asserting that man is either unique or superior. The moral sense may be peculiar to man, but various other animals have peculiar senses of their own. Possession of any given sense cannot be taken as evidence that a creature is more than a mere animal. No one would argue that a dog is a being of special status and value merely because dogs are able to hear sounds that men cannot hear or to smell odors that men cannot smell. Moreover, the moral sense involves certain feelings of approval and disapproval, and Hume admits without hesitation that animals also have such feelings. In some cases, the causes or the objects of the feelings may be unique to man. But this does not confer on him any special status.

When we follow the development of Hume's analysis of morals we are left with no doubt that he meant to eliminate the presumed distinctions between men and animals even in the moral sphere. There are two kinds of virtues, natural and artificial. The prototype of the artificial virtues is justice, and it is under the rubric "Of Justice and Injustice" that the artificial virtues are dealt with. That animals do not exhibit the artificial virtues is not a defect on their part. Quite the contrary, justice and the other artificial virtues result from man's inferiority. "Here then is a proposition, which, I think, may be regarded as certain, *that 'tis only from the selfishness and confined generosity of men, along with the scanty provision that nature has made for his wants, that justice derives its origin.*"[36] Justice and the other artificial virtues that are concerned with property are no indication of man's superior God-like nature. They seem, rather, to make man lower than the animals. For the animals are both better favored by nature and better able to provide for their wants without the elaborately contrived artificiality of human morality. The artificial virtues are a mark of man's degradation, not of his exaltation.

Defenders of man may quickly rise to the challenge by pointing out, quite correctly, that, according to Hume, justice and the other artificial virtues arise not merely from man's self-concern, but also

35*Treatise*, p. 471.
36*Treatise*, p. 495.

from his sympathy with other men. "Thus self-interest is the original motive to the *establishment* of justice: but a *sympathy* with public interest is the source of the *moral approbation* which attends that virtue."[37] "Thus it appears, that sympathy is a very powerful principle in human nature, that it has a great influence on our taste of beauty, and that it produces our sentiment of morals in all the artificial virtues."[38] If sympathy constitutes the real ground of human morality, is it not here that we see the significant superiority of man over the animals? This hope is quickly shattered when we recall that Hume explicitly finds sympathy among animals, and, moreover, that he understands human sympathy on the model of animal sympathy. All we need do is to "take a general survey of the universe, and observe the force of sympathy through the whole animal creation."[39] Sympathy in man is not a high-minded piece of altruism, divine in nature, but an animal response common to all the members of the animal kingdom.

If man is not guaranteed his superiority by possession of the artificial virtues, then he will certainly not be helped by the natural virtues. For these virtues depend on pleasure and pain and are expanded through sympathy. But animals respond to pleasure and pain, and, as we have shown, they, too, exhibit sympathy.[40] Human nature is animal nature, and natural virtue in man is nothing but an elaboration of responses that are part of man's animal nature. In a fitting conclusion to this attack on the superiority of man Hume rejects the common distinction between natural abilities and moral virtues.[41] In so doing he removes the last possibility of separating man from the animals. If moral virtues and natural abilities are essentially the same, if the attempts to distinguish them turn out to be "merely a dispute of words,"[42] then nothing of moral significance that is possessed by man can be denied to animals. Hume has set his views down in an unmistakable way here at the end of his *Treatise*. He leaves no room for doubt that he believes that man is nothing more than an animal. As knower, as passionate being, and as moral

[37]*Treatise*, pp. 499-500.
[38]*Treatise*, pp. 577-8.
[39]*Treatise*, p. 363.
[40]Cf. *Treatise*, pp. 574-6.
[41]Cf. *Treatise*, pp. 606ff.
[42]*Treatise*, p. 606.

agent, man is basically like other animals. When theologians and philosophers ascribe special status to man, when they compare him to God, they render a false and misleading account of human nature.

Much as he wanted to support a belief in the dignity of man Hume was unable to find any evidence for man's natural and intrinsic superiority.[43] If, nevertheless, he continued to affirm human dignity it was not on any sound theoretical grounds. All he could do, as he admitted in the essay on "The Dignity or Meanness of Human Nature," was to employ his rhetorical skills in praise of man, knowing that in human society the strategies of rhetoric are generally more effective than the intricacies of philosophical argument. At the start of his philosophical career, in his Introduction to the *Treatise*, he reminds us that in most cases " 'tis not reason, which carries the prize, but eloquence; and no man needs ever despair of gaining proselytes to the most extravagant hypothesis, who has art enough to represent it in any favourable colors. The victory is not gained by the men at arms, who manage the pike and the sword; but by the trumpeters, drummers, and musicians of the army."[44] As a man of humane social concern Hume was ready to employ his eloquence to preserve decency in human society. As a philosopher he followed out his inquiries to their most unpleasant and most dangerous conclusions.

In developing this view of human nature Hume has rejected the most fundamental claims of the religious tradition. If he can salvage anything at all, it can only be a thin and attenuated natural religion. Among the most fundamental beliefs of Judaism and Christianity is the doctrine that man is a special creature, specially endowed by God, and of special concern to God. It is this creature that receives God's revelation, and it is to this creature that the hope of salvation is extended. The God of Western religion is not only the Lord of nature, but also the Lord of history, concerned with the affairs of men. This relationship presupposes a conception of human nature such as was developed in the religious tradition. Clearly these doctrines are impossible for Hume. In fact, he not only reduces man to an animal, but suggests in his *Dialogues* that we might do the same to God. If

---

[43]Cf. Hendel, *op. cit.*, p. 328: "Hume seems to have been increasingly alive to the reality, and even the mystery of human personality. Despite his inability to show any warrant for our idea of a person he had continued to employ it, and had even emphasized it, in his later studies of sentiment and morality."

[44]*Treatise*, p. xviii.

man is only an organism, and if all we claim to know of God is that he is analogous to man, then why not conceive of God as an animal as well?[45]

Revealed religion depends on the existence of a direct relationship between man and God. The strongest anti-theistic arguments in the *Dialogues* are those that deny any such relationship. The main reason for introducing the discussion of the problem of evil in the *Dialogues* is to show how little ground there is for asserting that God has a special concern for man and his world. But this is only an extension of the conception of man that Hume had arrived at in the *Treatise*. Even orthodox theologians puzzle over the problem of evil. What gives power to Hume's posing of the problem is that he does so on a base which has already made it impossible to take seriously any notion of God's providential concern for man. All that can remain for Hume is the highly attenuated natural religion which is devoid of all religious substance. If, as Hume asserts, "The dispute concerning theism . . . is merely verbal,"[46] it is because he has purged rational theism of its traditional doctrinal content. In its place he has left us with a single conclusion which is "the whole of natural theology. That the cause or causes of order in the universe probably bear some remote analogy to human intelligence."[47] He goes on to say that if this proposition is not thought of as having any significance for human life or human action, then everyone should be able to assent to it. That is to say, even natural religion can command assent only when it is reduced to a single trivial proposition.

One wonders if this was the great improvement in natural religion that Hume hoped for in his early years. One wonders whether he was willing to rest here. There is no decisive evidence, but merely the conjectures of the commentators—conjectures which more often reveal their own attitudes than those of Hume. This much is certain—that he could find no philosophical grounds for believing in the preeminence of either the God or the man of traditional religion. It is equally clear that he wanted very much to strengthen the fabric of civilized society and to preserve our belief in human dignity. What we cannot know with certainty is how he viewed the strategic situa-

[45]*Dialogues*, p. 161.
[46]*Dialogues*, p. 218.
[47]*Dialogues*, p. 227.

tion. The appeal to faith at the end of the *Dialogues*, and elsewhere in his works, may have been written with an ironic tongue in Hume's cheek.[48] It may also be that Hume saw how deeply his naturalistic conclusions threatened the humane values which he cherished, and that he was serious when he wrote that, "A person, seasoned with a just sense of the imperfections of natural reason, will fly to revealed truth with the greatest avidity."[49] Whatever his intention he made the issues and the choices clear and the need for decision inescapable.

MARVIN FOX

OHIO STATE UNIVERSITY

[48]Kemp Smith contends that Hume learned from Bayle "That there is no surer method of rendering religion doubtful than to subject it to the tests of reason and evidence, and at the same time to speak of it as resting solely on revelation." (Introduction to the *Dialogues*, p. 41.)

[49]*Dialogues*, p. 227.

PUBLISHED WRITINGS OF
CHARLES HARTSHORNE

PART I–PHILOSOPHY

BOOKS

The Philosophy and Psychology of Sensation. Chicago: The University of Chicago Press, 1934. Pp. 288.

Beyond Humanism: Essays in the New Philosophy of Nature. Chicago: Willett, Clark & Company, 1937. Pp. 324.

Man's Vision of God and the Logic of Theism. Chicago: Willett, Clark & Company, 1941. Pp. 360. [After 1948 published by Harper & Brothers Publishers, New York.]

The Divine Relativity: A Social Conception of God. The Terry Lectures, 1947. New Haven: Yale University Press, 1948. Pp. 164.

Whitehead and the Modern World: Science, Metaphysics, and Civilization, Three Essays on the Thought of Alfred North Whitehead. By Victor Lowe, Charles Hartshorne, and A. H. Johnson. "WHITEHEAD'S METAPHYSICS" by Charles Hartshorne, pp. 25-41. Boston: The Beacon Press, 1950.

Reality as Social Process: Studies in Metaphysics and Religion. Glencoe: The Free Press and Boston: The Beacon Press, 1953. Pp. 223.

Philosophers Speak of God. (With William L. Reese) Chicago: The University of Chicago Press, 1953. Pp. 535.

The Logic of Perfection. LaSalle, Ill.: The Open Court Publishing Company, 1962. Pp. 335.

COLLECTED PAPERS OF CHARLES SANDERS PEIRCE. Edited by Charles Hartshorne and Paul Weiss. Cambridge: Harvard University Press.

Vol. I. *Principles of Philosophy,* 1931. Pp. 393.

Vol. II. *Elements of Logic,* 1932. Pp. 535.

Vol. III. *Exact Logic,* 1933. Pp. 433.

Vol. IV. *The Simplest Mathematics,* 1933. Pp. 601.

Vol. V. *Pragmatism and Pragmaticism,* 1934. Pp. 455.

Vol. VI. *Scientific Metaphysics,* 1935. Pp. 462.

ARTICLES FROM JOURNALS,* SYMPOSIA, AND BOOKS

1. Review of *Sein und Zeit* by Martin Heidegger and of *Mathematische Existenz* by Oskar Becker, from *Jahrbuch für Philosophie und phänomenologische Forschung*, Achter Band. *The Philosophical Review*, May, 1929. xxxviii, no. 3, pp. 284-293.
2. "CONTINUITY, THE FORM OF FORMS, IN CHARLES PEIRCE." *The Monist*, October, 1929. xxxix, no. 4, pp. 521-534.
3. "ETHICS AND THE ASSUMPTION OF PURELY PRIVATE PLEASURES." *The International Journal of Ethics*, July, 1930. xl, no. 4, pp. 496-515.
4. "CONTINGENCY AND THE NEW ERA IN METAPHYSICS (I)." *The Journal of Philosophy*, August 4, 1932. xxix, no. 16, pp. 421-431.
   "CONTINGENCY AND THE NEW ERA IN METAPHYSICS (II)." *The Journal of Philosophy*, August 18, 1932. xxix, no. 17, pp. 457-469.
5. "FOUR PRINCIPLES OF METHOD—WITH APPLICATIONS." *The Monist*, January, 1933. xliii, no. 1, pp. 40-72.
6. "THE INTELLIGIBILITY OF SENSATIONS." *The Monist*, July, 1934. xliv, no. 2, pp. 161-185.
7. "REDEFINING GOD." *The New Humanist*, July-August, 1934. vii, no. 4, pp. 8-15.
8. "THE NEW METAPHYSICS AND CURRENT PROBLEMS (I): MEDIEVALISM, HUMANISM, AND BEYOND." *The New Frontier*, September, 1934. i, no. 1, pp. 24-31.
   (II): *The New Frontier*, Nov.-Dec., 1934. i, no. 5, pp. 8-14.
9. "ETHICS AND THE NEW THEOLOGY." *The International Journal of Ethics*, October, 1934. xlv, no. 1. pp. 90-101.
10. "THE PARALLEL DEVELOPMENT OF METHOD IN PHYSICS AND PSYCHOLOGY." *Philosophy of Science*, October, 1934. i, no. 4, pp. 446-459.
11. "PATTERN AND MOVEMENT IN ART AND SCIENCE." *Comment; The University of Chicago Literary and Critical Quarterly*. Winter Quarter, 1935, iii, no. 2, pp. 1-2, 11.
12. "METAPHYSICS FOR POSITIVISTS." *Philosophy of Science*, July, 1935. ii, no. 3, pp. 287-303.

*Most of the published Book Reviews by Charles Hartshorne (c. 100) are not included here, this selection being limited to his Review Articles and a few others especially chosen by C.H.

13. "On Some Criticisms of Whitehead's Philosophy." *The Philosophical Review,* July, 1935. xliv, no. 4 [whole no. 262], pp. 323-344.
14. "The Compound Individual." In *Philosophical Essays for Alfred North Whitehead.* New York: Longmans, Green and Co., 1936. Pp. 193-220.
15. "The New Pantheism—I." *The Christian Register,* February 20, 1936. cxv, no. 8, pp. 119-120.
    (II): *The Christian Register,* Feb. 27, 1936. cxv, no. 9, pp. 141-143.
16. "The Philosophical Limitations of Humanism." In "A Symposium on Humanism." *The University Review,* Summer, 1937. iii, no. 4, pp. 240-242.
17. "The Reality of the Past, the Unreality of the Future." *Hibbert Journal,* January 1939. xxxvii, no. 2, pp. 246-257.
18. "The Method of Imaginative Variations." In "Notes Concerning Husserl." *The Journal of Philosophy,* April 27, 1939. xxxvi, no. 9, pp. 233-234.
19. Discussion: "The Interpretation of Whitehead (Reply to John W. Blyth)." *The Philosophical Review,* July, 1939. xlviii, no. 4, pp. 415-423.
20. "A Critique of Peirce's Idea of God." In "Abstracts of Papers to be read at the Joint Meeting of the Eastern and Western Divisions of the American Philosophical Association, Columbia University, December 27, 28, and 29, 1939." *The Journal of Philosophy,* December 7, 1939. xxxvi, no. 25, pp. 683-684.
21. "Husserl and the Social Structure of Immediacy." In *Philosophical Essays in Memory of Edmund Husserl.* Cambridge: Harvard University Press, 1940. Pp. 219-230.
22. "Santayana's Doctrine of Essence." In *The Philosophy of George Santayana*: The Library of Living Philosophers, Vol. II. Evanston and Chicago: Northwestern University, 1940. Pp. 135-182.
23. "The Three Ideas of God." *The Journal of Liberal Religion,* Winter, 1940. i, no. 3, pp. 9-16.
24. "Whitehead's Idea of God." In *The Philosophy of Alfred North Whitehead*: The Library of Living Philosophers, Vol. III. Evanston and Chicago: Northwestern University, 1941. Pp. 513-559.
25. "Charles Sanders Peirce's Metaphysics of Evolution." *The New England Quarterly,* March, 1941. xiv, no. 1, pp. 49-63.

26. "ANTHROPOMORPHIC TENDENCIES IN POSITIVISM." *Philosophy of Science,* April, 1941. viii, no. 2, pp. 184-203.
27. "A CRITIQUE OF PEIRCE'S IDEA OF GOD." *The Philosophical Review,* September, 1941. 1, no. 5, pp. 516-523.
28. "A PHILOSOPHY OF DEMOCRATIC DEFENSE." In *Science, Philosophy, and Religion: Second Symposium.* New York: Conference on Science, Philosophy and Religion in Their Relation to the Democratic Way of Life, Inc., 1942. Pp. 130-172.
29. "ELEMENTS OF TRUTH IN THE GROUP-MIND CONCEPT." *Social Research,* May, 1942. ix, no. 2, pp. 248-265.
30. "ORGANIC AND INORGANIC WHOLES." *Philosophy and Phenomenological Research,* December, 1942. iii, no. 2, pp. 127-136.
31. Review: "WHITEHEAD'S THEORY OF KNOWLEDGE," by John Blyth. *Philosophy and Phenomenological Research,* March, 1943, iii, no. 3, pp. 372-375.
32. Discussion: "IS WHITEHEAD'S GOD THE GOD OF RELIGION?" *Ethics,* April, 1943. liii, no. 3, pp. 219-227.
33. Communication: Rejoinder: "ELY ON WHITEHEAD," *The Journal of Liberal Religion,* September, 1943. v, no. 2, pp. 97-100.
34. Discussion: "REFLECTIONS ON THE STRENGTH AND WEAKNESS OF THOMISM." *Ethics,* October, 1943. liv, no. 1, pp. 53-57.
35. "A MATHEMATICAL ANALYSIS OF THEISM." *The Review of Religion,* November, 1943. viii, no. 1, pp. 20-38.
36. Radio Discussion: "HOW CHRISTIANS SHOULD THINK ABOUT THE PEACE." By Edwin Aubrey, Charles Hartshorne, and Bernard Loomer. The University of Chicago Round Table, April 9, 1944, no. 316, pp. 1-20.
37. "THE FORMAL VALIDITY AND REAL SIGNIFICANCE OF THE ONTOLOGICAL ARGUMENT." *The Philosophical Review,* May, 1944. liii, no. 3, pp. 225-245.
37a. Discussion: "ON HARTSHORNE'S FORMULATION OF THE ONTOLOGICAL ARGUMENT: A REJOINDER." *The Philosophical Review,* January, 1945. liv, no. 1, pp. 63-65.
37b. Discussion: "PROFESSOR HARTSHORNE'S SYLLOGISM: REJOINDER." *The Philosophical Review,* September, 1945. liv, no. 5, pp. 506-508.
38. "PHILOSOPHY AND ORTHODOXY." *Ethics,* July, 1944. liv, no. 4, pp. 295-298.
39. "GOD AND MAN NOT RIVALS." *The Journal of Liberal Religion,* Autumn, 1944. vi, no. 2, pp. 9-13.

40. Entries: *An Encyclopedia of Religion,* ed. by Vergilius Ferm. The Philosophical Library, N. Y., 1945.

> Acosmism; analogy; anthropomorphism; anthropopathism; Aristotle and Aristotelianism; axiom; Berkeley, George; Carneades; cause; Copernican astronomy; eternal; eternity; ether; etiology, aetiology; foreknowledge, Divine; Gerson, Levi ben; God, as personal; Hume; infinite; Kant, Immanuel; omnipotence; omnipresence; omniscience; panentheism; panlogism; pantheism; Peirce, Charles Sanders; perfect, perfection; Ptolemaic astronomy; Renouvier, Charles; Spencer, Herbert; Spinoza, Benedict; time; transcendence; Whitehead, Alfred North.

41. A Review Article: "Efficient Causality in Aristotle and St. Thomas." *The Journal of Religion,* January, 1945. xxv, no. 1, pp. 25-32.

42. "A New Philosophic Conception of the Universe." *The Hibbert Journal,* October, 1945. xliv, no. 1, pp. 14-21.

43. Review Article: "The Philosophy of Bertrand Russell," ed. by Paul Arthur Schilpp. *The Journal of Religion,* October, 1945. xxv, no. 4, pp. 280-284.

44. Communication: "Reply to Father Meehan." *The Journal of Religion,* January, 1946. xxvi, no. 1, pp. 54-57.

45. "Relative, Absolute, and Superrelative: A Formal Analysis." *The Philosophical Review,* May, 1946. lv, no. 3, pp. 213-228.

46. "Tragic and Sublime Aspects of Christian Love." *The Journal of Liberal Religion,* Summer, 1946. viii, no. 1, pp. 36-44.

47. "Theological Values in Current Metaphysics." *The Journal of Religion,* July, 1946. xxvi, no. 3, pp. 157-167.

48. "Leibniz's Greatest Discovery." *Journal of the History of Ideas,* October, 1946. vii, no. 4, pp. 411-421.

49. "Ideal Knowledge Defines Reality: What Was True in Idealism." *The Journal of Philosophy,* October 10, 1946. xliii, no. 21, pp. 573-582.

50. Review: "Faith and Reason," by Nels F. S. Ferré. *The Review of Religion,* May, 1947. xi, no. 4, pp. 409-413.

51. "God as Absolute, Yet Related to All." *The Review of Metaphysics,* September, 1947. i, no. 1, pp. 24-51.

52. "Two Levels of Faith and Reason." *The Journal of Bible and Religion,* January, 1948. xvi, no. 1, pp. 30-38.

53. "The Rationalistic Criterion in Metaphysics." *Philosophy and Phenomenological Research,* March, 1948. viii, no. 3, pp. 436-447.

54. "EXISTENTIAL PROPOSITIONS AND THE LAW OF CATEGORIES." *Proceedings of the Tenth International Congress of Philosophy*, Amsterdam, August 11-18, 1948. Ed. by E. W. Beth, H. J. Pos, and J. H. A. Hollak, Fascicule 1. North-Holland Publishing Co., Amsterdam. Pp. 342-344.

55. Review: "THE PHILOSOPHER'S WAY," by Jean Wahl. *The Philosophical Review*, September, 1948. lvii, no. 5, pp. 509-511.

56. "EIN THEOLOGISCHES PARADOXON NACH ARNAULD." *Philosophisches Jahrbuch*, 69/2, 1949, pp. 250-251.

57. "NOCH EINMAL DIE ZUFÄLLIGKEIT DER WELT UND NOTWENDIGKEIT GOTTES." Erwiderung an Dr. Ferdinand Bergenthal. *Philosophisches Jahrbuch*, 69/2, 1949, pp. 469-471.

58. "DAS METAPHYSISCHE SYSTEM WHITEHEADS." *Zeitschrift für philosophische Forschung*, III/4, 1949, pp. 566-575.

59. "THE SYNTHESIS OF IDEALISM AND REALISM." *Theoria*, March 12, 1949. xv, pp. 90-107.

60. "CHANCE, LOVE, AND INCOMPATIBILITY." (Presidential Address read before the meeting of the Western Division of the American Philosophical Association at Columbus, Ohio, April 29, 1949.) Published in *The Philosophical Review*, September, 1949. lviii, no. 5, pp. 429-450.

61. "WHITEHEAD'S METAPHYSICS" in *Whitehead and the Modern World: Science, Metaphysics, and Civilization, Three Essays on the Thought of Alfred North Whitehead*. By Victor Lowe, Charles Hartshorne, and A. H. Johnson. Pp. 25-41. Boston: The Beacon Press.

62. "PANPSYCHISM." Chapter thirty-five, *A History of Philosophical Systems*, ed. by Vergilius Ferm. New York: The Philosophical Library, 1950. Pp. 442-453.

63. "LE PRINCIPE DE RELATIVITÉ PHILOSOPHIQUE CHEZ WHITEHEAD." *Revue de Métaphysique et de Morale*, Janvier-Mars, 1950. 55° Année, No. 1, pp. 16-29.

64. "THE DIVINE RELATIVITY AND ABSOLUTENESS: A REPLY." *The Review of Metaphysics*, September, 1950. iv, no. 1, pp. 31-60.

65. "GOD IN GENERAL PHILOSOPHICAL THOUGHT." In *The Encyclopedia Hebraica*, Vol. III, 1951 (in the Jewish Calendar 5711). Jerusalem: Encyclopedia Publishing Company. Pp. 467-478.

66. "STRICT AND GENETIC IDENTITY: AN ILLUSTRATION OF THE RELATIONS OF LOGIC TO METAPHYSICS." In *Structure, Method, and*

Meaning: Essays in Honor of Henry M. Sheffer. New York: The Liberal Arts Press, 1951. Pp. 242-254.

67. "Philosophy of Religion in the United States." *Philosophy and Phenomenological Research,* March, 1951. xi, no. 3, pp. 406-410.

68. Discussion: "Arthur Berndtson on Mystical Experience." *The Personalist,* Spring, 1951. xxxii, no. 2, pp. 191-193.

69. "The Relativity of Nonreality: Some Reflections on First-ness." In *Studies in the Philosophy of Charles Sanders Peirce,* ed. by Philip P. Wiener and Frederic H. Young. Cambridge: Harvard University Press, 1952. Pp. 215-224.

70. "Radhakrishnan on Mind, Matter, and God." In *The Philosophy of Sarvepalli Radhakrishnan:* The Library of Living Philosophers, Vol. VIII. New York: Tudor Publishing Company, 1952. Pp. 313-322.

71. "Tillich's Doctrine of God." No. 7 in *The Theology of Paul Tillich:* The Library of Living Theology, Vol. I, ed. by Charles W. Kegley and Robert W. Bretall. New York: The Macmillan Company, 1952. Pp. 164-195.

72. "La Philosophie de la religion aux Etats-Unis." *Les Etudes philosophiques,* Janvier-Juin, 1952. Septième Année. No. 1-2, pp. 50-56.

73. "Time, Death, and Eternal Life." *The Journal of Religion* April, 1952. xxxii, no. 2, pp. 97-107.

74. "Politics and the Metaphysics of Freedom." In *Enquête sur la liberté,* Fédération internationale des sociétés de philosophie. Publié avec le concours de l'u.n.e.s.c.o., Hermann & Cie., Editeurs, Paris, 1953. Pp. 79-85.

75. "Noch einmal, das Wissen Gottes." *Philosophisches Jahrbuch.* 62. Jahrgang/2. Halbband, Verlag Karl Alber, Freiburg-München 1953, pp. 409-411.

76. "Spirit as Life Freely Participating in Life." *The Biosophical Review,* 1953. x, no. 2, pp. 31-32.

77. "The Monistic Theory of Expression." *The Journal of Philosophy,* July 2, 1953. 1, no. 14, pp. 425-434.

78. "The Immortality of the Past: Critique of a Prevalent Misinterpretation." *The Review of Metaphysics,* September, 1953. vii, no. 1, pp. 98-112.

79. Symposium: "ARE RELIGIOUS DOGMAS COGNITIVE AND MEANING-FUL?" *The Journal of Philosophy*, March 4, 1954. li, no. 5, pp. 148-150.

80. "THE KINDS OF THEISM: A REPLY." *The Journal of Religion*, April, 1954. xxxiv, no. 2, pp. 127-131.

81. "MIND, MATTER, AND FREEDOM." *The Scientific Monthly*, May, 1954. lxxviii, no. 5, pp. 314-320.

82. Review Article: "WHITEHEAD'S PHILOSOPHY OF REALITY AS SO-CIALLY-STRUCTURED PROCESS." *Chicago Review*, Spring-Summer, 1954. viii, no. 2, pp. 60-77.

83. "BIOLOGY AND THE SPIRITUAL VIEW OF THE WORLD: A COMMENT ON DR. BIRCH'S PAPER." *The Christian Scholar*, September, 1954. xxxvii, no. 3, pp. 408-409.

84. "RUSSIAN METAPHYSICS: SOME REACTIONS TO ZENKOVSKY'S HIS-TORY." *The Review of Metaphysics*, September, 1954. viii, no. 1, pp. 61-78.

85. "CAUSAL NECESSITIES: AN ALTERNATIVE TO HUME." *The Philosophical Review*, October, 1954. lxiii, no. 4, pp. 479-499.

86. Review: "LA PREUVE RÉELLE DE DIEU: ÉTUDE CRITIQUE," by J. Defever, S. J. *Philosophy and Phenomenological Research*, December, 1954. xv, no. 2, pp. 285-286.

87. Review: "THE NATURE OF THOUGHT," by Brand Blanshard. *Philosophische Rundschau*. 3. Jahrgang, Heft 1/2, 1955. Pp. 119-120.

88. "PROCESS AS INCLUSIVE CATEGORY: A REPLY." *The Journal of Philosophy*, February 17, 1955. lii, no. 4, pp. 94-102.

89. Review: "GOD AND POLARITY: A SYNTHESIS OF PHILOSOPHIES," by Wilmon H. Sheldon. *The Philosophical Review*, April, 1955. lxiv, no. 2, pp. 312-316.

90. Panel Discussion: 1955 Edward Gallahue Seminar in Religion and Psychology at The Menninger Foundation, *passim*.

91. "SOME EMPTY THOUGH IMPORTANT TRUTHS." *The Review of Metaphysics*, June, 1955. viii, no. 4, pp. 553-568.

92. "THE UNITY OF MAN AND THE UNITY OF NATURE." *The Emory University Quarterly*, October, 1955. xi, no. 3, pp. 129-141.

93. "SOME EMPTY THOUGH IMPORTANT TRUTHS: A PREFACE TO META-PHYSICS." In *American Philosophers at Work: The Philosophic Scene in the United States*. Ed. by Sidney Hook. New York: Criterion Books, 1956. Pp. 225-235.

94. "ROYCE'S MISTAKE—AND ACHIEVEMENT." The *Journal of Philosophy*, February 2, 1956. liii, no. 3, pp. 123-130.
95. Panel Discussion: 1956 Edward Gallahue Seminar in Religion and Psychology at the Menninger Foundation, *passim*.
96. Colloquium No. 8: "THE IDEA OF CREATION." *The Review of Metaphysics*, March, 1956. ix, no. 3, pp. 464-465.
97. "THE IDEA OF GOD—LITERAL OR ANALOGICAL?" *The Christian Scholar*, June, 1956. xxix, no. 2, pp. 131-136.
98. Discussion: "NEW PROPOSITIONS AND NEW TRUTHS." *The Review of Metaphysics*, June, 1956. ix, no. 4, pp. 656-661.
99. "TWO STRATA OF MEANING IN RELIGIOUS DISCOURSE." In Symposium on Philosophy of Religion. *The Southern Philosopher*, October, 1956. v. no. 3, pp. 4-7.
100. "SOME REFLECTIONS SUGGESTED BY H. WOLFSON'S PHILOSOPHY OF THE CHURCH FATHERS, VOL. I, FAITH, TRINITY, INCARNATION." In *Collection of Reviews*, Southern Society for Philosophy of Religion, March 9, 1957. J. R. Cresswell, bibliographer. Pp. 1-10.
101. "WHITEHEAD AND BERDYAEV: IS THERE TRAGEDY IN GOD?" *The Journal of Religion*, April, 1957. xxxvii, no. 2, pp. 71-84.
102. "CHARLES PEIRCE, PHILOSOPHER-SCIENTIST," No. 1 in Charles Sanders Peirce—A Symposium. *Journal of Public Law*, Spring, 1958. vii, no. 1, pp. 2-12.
103. Discussion: "WHITEHEAD ON PROCESS: A REPLY TO PROFESSOR ESLICK." *Philosophy and Phenomenological Research*, June, 1958. xviii, no. 4, pp. 514-520.
104. "SCIENCE, INSECURITY, AND THE ABIDING TREASURE." *The Journal of Religion*, July, 1958. xxxviii, no. 3, pp. 168-174.
105. "OUTLINES OF A PHILOSOPHY OF NATURE." Part I. *The Personalist*, Summer, July, 1958. xxxix, no. 3, pp. 239-248.
   "OUTLINES OF A PHILOSOPHY OF NATURE," Part II. *The Personalist*, Autumn, October, 1958. xxxix, no. 4, pp. 380-391.
106. "FREEDOM REQUIRES INDETERMINISM AND UNIVERSAL CAUSALITY." *The Journal of Philosophy*, September 11, 1958. lv, no. 19, pp. 793-811.
107. "METAPHYSICAL STATEMENTS AS NONRESTRICTIVE AND EXISTENTIAL." *The Review of Metaphysics*, September, 1958. xii, no. 1, pp. 35-47.
108. "'THE LOGICAL STRUCTURE OF GIVENNESS." *The Philosophical Quarterly*, October, 1958. viii, no. 33, pp. 307-316.

109. "The Philosophy of Creative Synthesis," I in Symposium: Creativity as a Philosophical Category. *The Journal of Philosophy*, October 23, 1958. lv, no. 22, pp. 944-953.

110. Discussion: "The Structure of Metaphysics: A Criticism of Lazerowitz's Theory." *Philosophy and Phenomenological Research*, December, 1958. xix, no. 2, pp. 226-240.

111. "Four Unrefuted Forms of the Ontological Argument," *The Journal of Philosophical Studies*, January, 1959. xl, no. 1. [Japanese text, pp. 1-15; English Summary, pp. 1-2 of the Outlines] Published Monthly by the Kyoto Philosophical Society (The Kyoto Tetsugaku-Kai), Kyoto University, Kyoto, Japan.

112. "A Philosopher's Assessment of Christianity." In *Religion and Culture: Essays in Honor of Paul Tillich*, ed. by Walter Leibrecht. New York: Harper, 1959. Pp. 167-180.

113. "John Wisdom on 'Gods': Two Views of the Logic of Theism." *Downside Review* (Bath, England), Winter, 1958-59, pp. 5-17.

114. "The Principle of Shared Creativity." Unitarian Symposia No. 6, *What Can Religion Offer Modern Man?*" April, 1959, pp. 1-8.

115. "The Philosophy of Creative Synthesis" (reprinted from *The Journal of Philosophy*, supra.), *Americana: A Monthly Journal of Humanities, Social Sciences, and Natural Sciences*, August, 1959. v. no. 8, pp. 80-90. [In Japanese]

116. "Freedom, Individuality, and Beauty in Nature." *Snowy Egret*, Autumn, 1960. xxiv, no. 2, pp. 5-14.

117. "Equalitarianism and the Great Inequalities." *The Emory Alumnus*, November, 1960. 36, no. 7, pp. 24-25, 49.

118. "The Buddhist-Whiteheadian View of the Self and the Religious Traditions." *Proceedings of the IXth International Congress for the History of Religions*. Tokyo and Kyoto, 1958. Tokyo, 1960, Maruzen. Pp. 298-302.

119. "Whitehead and Contemporary Philosophy." In *The Relevance of Whitehead: Philosophical Essays in Commemoration of the Centenary of the Birth of Alfred North Whitehead*. Ed. by Ivor Leclerc. London: Allen and Unwin, 1961. Pp. 21-43.

120. "Metaphysics and the Modality of Existential Judgments." *Ibid.*, pp. 107-121.

121. "Hume's Metaphysics and Its Present-Day Influence." *The New Scholasticism*, April, 1961. xxxv, no. 2, pp. 152-171.

122. "THE SOCIAL STRUCTURE OF EXPERIENCE." *Philosophy,* April and July, 1961. xxxvi, no. 137, pp. 97-111.

123. "THE STRUCTURE OF GIVENNESS." *The Philosophical Forum,* 1960-61. xviii, pp. 22-39.

124. "GOD'S EXISTENCE: A CONCEPTUAL PROBLEM." No. 26 in *Religious Experience and Truth: A Symposium,* ed. by Sidney Hook. New York: New York University Press, 1961. Pp. 211-219.

125. Discussion: "PROFESSOR HALL ON PERCEPTION." *Philosophy and Phenomenological Research,* June, 1961. xxi, no. 4, pp. 563-571.

126. "TILLICH AND THE OTHER GREAT TRADITION." *Anglican Theological Review,* July, 1961. xliii, no. 3, pp. 245-259.

127. "THE LOGIC OF THE ONTOLOGICAL ARGUMENT." *The Journal of Philosophy,* August 17, 1961. lviii, no. 17, pp. 471-473.

128. Discussion: "ABSOLUTE OBJECTS AND RELATIVE SUBJECTS: A REPLY." *The Review of Metaphysics,* September, 1961. xv, no. 1, pp. 174-188.

129. "MAN IN NATURE." No. 6 in *Experience, Existence, and the Good: Essays in Honor of Paul Weiss,* ed. by Irwin C. Lieb. Carbondale: Southern Illinois University Press, 1961. Pp. 89-99.

130. "WHITEHEAD, THE ANGLO-AMERICAN PHILOSOPHER-SCIENTIST." *Proceedings of the American Catholic Philosophical Association,* The Catholic University of America, 1961. Pp. 163-171.

131. *Saint Anselm, Basic Writings: Proslogium, Monologium, Gaunilon's On Behalf of the Fool, Cur Deus Homo,* translated by S. W. Deane, with an introduction by Charles Hartshorne. Second Edition. Open Court Publishing Company, La Salle, Illinois, 1962. Pp. 1-19.

132. "THE MODERN WORLD AND A MODERN VIEW OF GOD." *The Crane Review,* Winter, 1962. iv, no. 2, pp. 73-85.

133. "RELIGION AND CREATIVE EXPERIENCE." *Darshana, an International Quarterly of Philosophy, Psychology, Psychical Research, Religion, Mysticism and Sociology,* Jan., 1962, ii, no. 1, pp. 47-52.

134. "WHAT DID ANSELM DISCOVER?" *Union Seminary Quarterly Review,* March, 1962. xvii, no. 3, pp. 213-222.

135. "LA CREATIVIDAD PARTICIPADA," (translated by Sira Jaen). *Revista de Filosofía de la Universidad de Costa Rica,* Jan.-June, 1962. iii, no. 11, pp. 237-244.

136. "RELIGION AND CREATIVE EXPERIENCE." *The Unitarian Register and the Universalist Leader,* June, 1962. 141, no. 6, pp. 9-11.

137. "MIND AS MEMORY AND CREATIVE LOVE." In *Theories of the Mind,* ed. by Jordan M. Scher, New York: The Free Press of Glencoe, 1962. Pp. 440-463.

138. Discussion: "HOW SOME SPEAK AND YET DO NOT SPEAK OF GOD." *Philosophy and Phenomenological Research,* Dec. 1962. xxiii, no. 2, pp. 274-276.

139. "PRESENT PROSPECTS FOR METAPHYSICS." *The Monist,* Winter, 1963, 47, no. 2, pp. 188-210.

140. "INDIVIDUAL DIFFERENCES AND THE IDEAL OF EQUALITY." *New South,* Feb., 1963, 18, no. 2, pp. 3-8.

141. "MARTIN BUBER'S METAPHYSIK," in *Martin Buber,* herausgegeben von Schilpp und Friedman. Stuttgart: Kohlhammer Verlag, 1963, pp. 42-61.

142. "FURTHER FASCINATION OF THE ONTOLOGICAL ARGUMENT: REPLIES TO RICHARDSON." I, *Union Seminary Quarterly Review,* March, 1963. xviii, no. 3, Part I, pp. 244-245.

143. "WHITEHEAD'S NOVEL INTUITION," In *Alfred North Whitehead: Essays on His Philosophy,* edited by George L. Kline. Englewood Cliffs, N.J., Prentice-Hall, 1963, pp. 18-26.

144. "SENSATION IN PSYCHOLOGY AND PHILOSOPHY," *The Southern Journal of Philosophy,* Summer, 1963, 1, no. 2, pp. 3-14.

145. "RATIONALE OF THE ONTOLOGICAL PROOF." *Theology Today,* July, 1963, 20, no. 2, pp. 278-283.

146. "WHITEHEAD'S CONCEPTION OF GOD" and "WHITEHEAD'S THEORY OF PREHENSION." *Actas-Segunda Congreso Extraordinario Interamericano de Filosofia,* 22-26 Julio, 1961. August 1963 [dated 1962] Imprenta Nacional, San José, Costa Rica, pp. 163-170.

147. Communication: "FINITE OR FINITE-INFINITE?" *Philosophy and Phenomenological Research,* September, 1963, xxiv, no. 1, p. 149.

148. "REAL POSSIBILITY." *Journal of Philosophy,* October 10, 1963, lx, No. 21, pp. 593-605.

149. "MAN'S FRAGMENTARINESS." *Wesleyan Studies in Religion,* 1963-1964, 56, no. 6, pp. 17-28.

150. "ABSTRACT AND CONCRETE IN GOD: A REPLY." The Review of Metaphysics, December, 1963, xvii, no. 2, pp. 289-295.

151. "SANTAYANA'S DEFIANT ECLECTICISM." *The Journal of Philosophy,* January 2, 1964, lxi, no. 1, pp. 35-44.

PART II—ORNITHOLOGY

1. "First Encounter with Hawaiian Songbirds." *Elepaio* (Hawaii), June, 1952. xii, no. 12, pp. 76-78.
2. "A Foreigner's Impression of the Lyrebird's Singing." *The Victorian Naturalist* (Australia), September, 1952. lxix, no. 5, pp. 73-74.
3. "Musical Values in Australian Bird Songs." *The Emu* (Australia), June, 1953. liii, Part 2, pp. 109-128.
4. "The Monotony Threshold in Singing Birds." *The Auk* (U.S.A.), April, 1956. lxxiii, pp. 176-192.
5. "The Phenomenon of Bird Song," *The Emory University Quarterly* (U.S.A.), October, 1956. xii, no. 3, pp. 139-147.
6. "Some Biological Principles Applicable to Song-Behavior." *The Wilson Bulletin* (U.S.A.), March, 1958. lxx, no. 1, pp. 41-56.
7. "The Relation of Bird Song to Music." *Ibis* (Great Britain), 1958. c, no. 3, pp. 421-445.
8. "Freedom, Individuality, and Beauty in Nature." *Snowy Egret* (Shorter Apts., Rome, Ga.). xxiv, no. 2, Autumn, 1960. (See Item 116, Part One, this bibliography.)
9. Review of *A Treasury of New Zealand Bird Song: An Album of Three Records. The Wilson Bulletin*, December 14, 1960. 72, no. 4, pp. 421-422.
10. "Sketch of a Theory of Imitative Singing." *The Oriole*, June, 1961. xxvi, no. 2, pp. 23-27.

APPENDIX B

BIBLIOGRAPHY OF WRITINGS BY AND ABOUT ALFRED NORTH WHITEHEAD IN LANGUAGES OTHER THAN ENGLISH*

Compiled by George L. Kline

PART I: TRANSLATIONS OF WHITEHEAD'S WORKS[1]

1. THE AXIOMS OF PROJECTIVE GEOMETRY (1906)

French

"Introduction logique à la géométrie," *Revue de Métaphysique et de Morale* (Paris), 15 (1907), 34-39. (Translation of Ch. I, "Fundamental Considerations.")

2. PRINCIPIA MATHEMATICA (with Bertrand Russell) Vol. I (1910).

German

Einführung in die mathematische Logik (die Einleitung der 'Principia Mathematica'). Trans. Hans Mokre. Munich: Drei Masken, 1932. viii, 167 pp. (Introduction.)

3. AN INTRODUCTION TO MATHEMATICS (1911).

Arabic

Muqaddima li-al-riyadijat (trans. Muhyi al-Din Yusuf), Baghdad: Matb. al-Rabita, 1952. 242 pp.

German

a. *Einführung in die Mathematik.* (Trans. Berthold Schenker), Vi-

---

* Sincere thanks are due to the following persons who, through their published writings or personal correspondence, have brought certain of the items listed in this Bibliography to my attention: Ahn Byung-uk, Joseph Breton, S.J., William A. Christian, Constantino Láscaris C., Victor Lowe, Mou Jun-sun, David S. Nivison, Jacques Ruytinx, Donald W. Sherburne; the reference librarians at the Seoul National University Library and the University of Tokyo Library.

[1]Whitehead's works are listed chronologically. In cases where a given work has been translated into more than one language, the various translations are listed alphabetically by language. Chinese, Japanese, and Korean names are given in Far Eastern order, i.e., surnames first, and are alphabetized by surname.

enna: Humboldt, 1948. (Sammlung "Die Universität," Bd. 3.), 222 pp.

b. *Eine Einführung in die Mathematik* (trans. Berthold Schenker), Munich: Dalp, 1958 (Sammlung "Dalp"). 152 pp.

Icelandic
Staerfraedin (trans. Gudmundur Finbogason), Reykjavik: Isafold-arprentsmidja H.F., 1931. 171 pp.

Italian
Introduzione alla matematica (trans. Gian Mario Crespi), Florence: Sansoni, 1953. 187 pp.

Japanese
Sûgaku nyûmon (trans. Kôno Isaburô), Tokyo: Sôgensha, 1953. 222 pp.

Polish
Wstep do matematyki (trans. Władyslaw Wojtowicz), Warsaw: E. Wende i Ska., 191—(?) (Biblioteka Naukowa Wendego, Tom. 3). 226 pp.

Russian
Vvedeniye v matematiku, Petrograd, 1916.

4. "THE PRINCIPLES OF MATHEMATICS IN RELATION TO ELEMENTARY TEACHING," *Proceedings of the Fifth International Congress of Mathematicians* (1912), Cambridge: Cambridge University Press, 1913, Vol. II, pp. 449-454. (Reprinted as ch. v of *The Organization of Thought*, 1917.)

French
"Les Principes mathématiques et l'enseignement élémentaire," *L'Enseignement Mathématique.* 15 (1913), 111-112. (Abstract printed together with original English text.)

5. THE CONCEPT OF NATURE (1920)

Italian
Il Concetto della natura (trans. Massimo Meyer), Turin: Einaudi, 1948 (Biblioteca di cultura filosofica, 5). x, 178 pp.

6. SCIENCE AND THE MODERN WORLD (1925)

Dutch
De natuurwetenschap in de moderne wereld, (trans. Jan van Rheenen), Utrecht-Antwerp: Aula-Boeken, 1959. 210 pp.

French
La Science et le monde moderne (trans. A. d'Ivéry and P. Hollard), Paris: Payot, 1930 (Bibliotèque scientifique). 271 pp.

German
  a. *Wissenschaft und moderne Welt* (ed. by Walter R. Corti, preface by Leopold Deuel, trans. by Gertrud Tschiedel and François Bondy), Zürich: Morgarten, Conzett and Huber, 1949 (Erkenntnis und Leben, Bd. 3). 283 pp.
  b. "Gott," in Arthur Hübscher, *Denker Unserer Zeit,* Munich: Piper Verlag, 1956, Vol. II, 318-327. (A translation of ch. xi.)
  c. "Die Abstraktion" in Max Bense, *Zwischen beiden Kriegen: Die Philosophie,* Frankfurt: Suhrkamp Verlag, 1951, pp. 333-352. (A translation of ch. x.)
Italian
  a. *La Scienza e il mondo moderno* (trans. and intro. by Antonio Banfi), Milan: Bompiani, 1945 (Idee nuove, vol. 19). 237 pp.
  b. Part of ch. vi included (in Banfi's translation) in Enzo Paci, *Il pensiero scientifico contemporaneo,* Florence: Sansoni, 1950, pp. 88-94.
Japanese
  Kagaku to kindai sekai (trans. Ueda Yasuharu and Murakami Shikô), Tokyo: Sôgensha, 1954. 381 pp.
Korean
  Gwahag gwa hyeondae (trans. by Kim Chin-sup), Seoul: Eulyoo, 1956. 306 p.
Spanish
  La Ciencia y el mundo moderno (trans. Marina Ruiz Lago and J. Rovira Armengol), Buenos Aires: Losada, 1949 (Biblioteca Filosófica, ed. by Francisco Romero).
  7. RELIGION IN THE MAKING (1926)
French
  Le Devenir de la religion (trans. and intro. by Philippe Devaux), Paris: Montaigne, 1939 (Philosophie de l'Esprit, collection dirigée par L. Lavelle et R. Le Senne) . 192 pp.
  8. SYMBOLISM: ITS MEANING AND EFFECT (1927)
Japanese
  Shôchô sayô; Kako no kenkyû; Yoken ni tsuite (trans. Ichii Saburô), Tokyo: Kawade Shobô, 1955. 331 pp. (Includes "The Study of the Past" from *Essays in Science and Philosophy* and "Foresight" from *Adventures of ideas;* all bound with the above-listed Japanese translation of *Science and the Modern World* as Vol. 17 in the series,

"Leading Thinkers of the World: Section of Philosophy and Literature"—"Sekai Daishisô Zenshû. Tetsugaku, Bungeishisô-hen.")

9. PROCESS AND REALITY (1929)

Spanish

Proceso y realidad (trans. J. Rovira Armengol), Buenos Aires: Losada, 1956 (Biblioteca Filosófica, ed. by Francisco Romero). 474 pp.

10. THE FUNCTION OF REASON (1929)

Italian

a. Translation of pp. 1-7 by Enzo Paci included in his *Il Pensiero scientifico contemporaneo*, Florence: Sansoni, 1950, pp. 94-99.

b. *La Funzione della ragione* (trans. and intro. by F. Cafaro), Florence: La Nuova Italia, 1958. xx, 104 pp.

11. THE AIMS OF EDUCATION AND OTHER ESSAYS (1929)

Italian

I Fini dell'educazione e altri saggi (trans. and intro. by F. Cafaro), Florence: La Nuova Italia, 1960.

Japanese

Kyôiku no mokuteki (trans. Motono Yoshikatsu), Tokyo: Kyôiku Shorin, 1955. 278 pp.

Korean

Gyoyug eui mogjeog (trans. Yu Hyeong-chin), Seoul: Eulyoo, 1960. 256 pp.

12. ADVENTURES OF IDEAS (1933)

Japanese

See listing under No. 8, above.

Spanish

Aventuras de las ideas (trans. Carlos Botet), Barcelona: Miguza, 1947. 374 pp.

13. NATURE AND LIFE (1934)

Italian

Natura e vita (trans. and intro. by G. M. Crespi), Milan: Bocca, 1951 (Nuova biblioteca filosofica, Vol. 1). 112 pp.

Spanish

Naturaleza y vida (trans. and intro. by Risieri Frondizi), Buenos Aires: Universidad de Buenos Aires, 1941. 88 pp.

14. MODES OF THOUGHT (1938)

Spanish

Modos de pensamiento (trans. Joaquín Xirau), Buenos Aires: Losada, 1944 (Biblioteca Filosófica, ed. by Francisco Romero). 199 pp.

15. "MATHEMATICS AND THE GOOD" (1941)

French

"Les Mathématiques et le bien," in Cesselin, *La Philosophie organique de Whitehead,* pp. 220-225. (Abridged.)

16. "IMMORTALITY" (1941)

French

"Immortalité," in *ibid.,* pp. 226-235. (Abridged.)

17. ESSAYS IN SCIENCE AND PHILOSOPHY (1947)

Chinese

"Hua-te-hai Tzu-chuan," *Ta-hsüeh Sheng-huo* (University Life), 8,
7, pp. 23-30. (Trans. by Yü Yung-chia of "Autobiographical Notes,"
first published in 1941.)

German

Philosophie und Mathematik (trans. Felizitas Ortner), Vienna-
Stuttgart: Humboldt, 1949. (Selections.)

Spanish

"Harvard: El futuro," *Revista de Filosofía de la Universidad de
Costa Rica,* 2, 5 (1961), 45-46. (Trans. by Ligia Herrera of "Harvard: The Future," first published in 1936.)

PART II. WORKS OF WHITEHEAD ORIGINALLY
PUBLISHED IN LANGUAGES OTHER
THAN ENGLISH

1. "Note," *Revue de Métaphysique et de Morale,* 13 (1905),
916-917. (Response to P. Boutroux, "Correspondance mathématique et relation logique," *ibid.,* pp. 621-637, esp. p. 627n.)
2. "La Théorie relationniste de l'espace." *Revue de Métaphysique et de Morale,* 23 (1916), 423-454.

PART III. STUDIES OF WHITEHEAD'S THOUGHT
IN LANGUAGES OTHER THAN ENGLISH[2]

A. BOOKS AND UNPUBLISHED DISSERTATIONS

1. Ludovico Actis Perinetti, *Cosmologia e assiologia in White-*

---

[2]Listed alphabetically by author under each of the first three sections: A. Books
and Unpublished Dissertations, B. Chapters or Sections of Books, C. Articles. Listed
chronologically by work under D. and E. (Reviews). Listed alphabetically by author
under F.

head, Turin, 1954. (Studi e Ricerche di Storia della Filosofia, No. 12). viii, 61 pp. (Comprises the author's three articles, listed under C. 2-4, below, plus a two-page preface and three-page bibliography.)

2. Marc-André Béra, *A. N. Whitehead (un philosophe de l'experience)*, Paris: Hermann, 1948. 55 pp.

3. Eberhard Bubser, *Die spekulative Philosophie Alfred North Whiteheads* (unpublished dissertation: University of Göttingen, 1958). An abridgement of ch. III was published as an article in 1960; see C. 12, below.

4. Félix Cesselin, *La Philosophie organique de Whitehead,* Paris: Presses Universitaires de France, 1950. 248 pp.

5. Hsieh Yu-wei, *Huai-hei-te Hsüeh-shu* (An account of Whitehead's Philosophy), Taipei: Chung-yang Wen-wu Kung-ying She (Central Cultural Supply Co.)

6. Ichii Saburô, *Whitehead no tetsugaku* (The Philosophy of Whitehead), Tokyo: Kôbundô, 1956. 216 pp.

7. Concetta Orsi, *La Filosofia dell'organismo di Whitehead,* Naples: Libreria Scientifica [1956]. 159 pp.

B. CHAPTERS OR SECTIONS OF BOOKS

1. Nicolà Abbagnano, "Whitehead" in STORIA DELLA FILOSOFIA, Turin: Unione Tipografico-Editrice Torinese, 1950, Vol. II, pp. 611-616.

2. Ludovico Actis Perinetti, "Whitehead," in ENCICLOPEDIA FILOSOFICA, Venice-Rome, 1957, Vol. IV, cols. 1751-1756.

3. Felice Alderisio, "Il realismo e il razionalismo di Whitehead," in SAGGI DI FILOSOFIA CONTEMPORANEA, Salerno, 1952.

4. Max Bense, "Bertrand Russell und Alfred North Whitehead," in ZWISCHEN BEIDEN KRIEGEN: DIE PHILOSOPHIE, Frankfurt: Suhrkamp, 1951, pp. 86-104.

5. I. M. Bocheński, EUROPÄISCHE PHILOSOPHIE DER GEGENWART, Bern: A. Francke, 1951 (second ed.). Whitehead: pp. 231-242. (English translation: CONTEMPORARY EUROPEAN PHILOSOPHY, Berkeley and Los Angeles, 1961. Whitehead: pp. 226-237.)

6. A. S. Bogomolov, "A. N. Uaitkhed i yevo 'filosofiya protsessa'" ("A. N. Whitehead and his 'Process Philosophy'"), pp. 272-319: ch. vi of IDEYA RAZVITIYA V BURZHUAZNOI FILOSOFII XIX I XX VEKOV (The Idea of Development in Nineteenth and

Twentieth-Century Bourgois Philosophy), Moscow: Izdatel'-
stvo Moskovskovo Universiteta, 1962.

7. ──────, also a chapter with the above title in
FILOSOFIYA ANGLO-AMERIKANSKOVO REALIZMA (The Philosophy
of Anglo-American Realism), Moscow: Izdatel'stvo Moskovskovo Universiteta, 1962, pp. 57-78.

8. Philippe Devaux, "La Philosophie en Grande-Bretagne et aux
États-Unis aux xixᵉ et xxᵉ siècles. De Coleridge à Whitehead"
in PHILOSOPHY IN THE MID-CENTURY (ed. R. Klibansky), Vol.
IV, Florence, 1959, pp. 187-199. (Whitehead: pp. 194-195.)

9. ──────, LOTZE ET SON INFLUENCE SUR LA PHILOSOPHIE
ANGLO-SAXONNE: CONTRIBUTION À L'ÉTUDE HISTORIQUE ET CRITI-
QUE DE LA NOTION DE VALEUR, Brussels, 1932, 48 pp. (White-
head: pp. 15n, 31-44, 46.)

10. José Ferrater Mora, "Whitehead," in DICCIONARIO DE FILOSOFÍA,
Buenos Aires: Sudamericana, 1958 (fourth ed.), pp. 1425-1426.

11. Guillermo Francovich, TOYNBEE, HEIDEGGER Y WHITEHEAD,
Buenos Aires: Raigal, 1951. 81 pp. (Whitehead: pp. 61-79.)

12. Risieri Frondizi, "Conceptos fundamentales de la metafísica
de Whitehead," printed as an introduction to the author's
Spanish translation of NATURE AND LIFE, Buenos Aires, 1941,
pp. 13-30.

13. Juan D. García Bacca, NUEVE GRANDES FILÓSOFOS CONTEM-
PORÁNEOS Y SUS TEMAS, Vol. II: James, Ortega, Whitehead.
Caracas: Imprenta Nacional. 1947. 360 pp. (Whitehead: pp.
187-360.)

14. Paul Ginestier, LA PENSÉE ANGLO-SAXONNE DEPUIS 1900, PARIS:
Presses Universitaries de France, 1956. 134 pp. (Russell and
Whitehead: pp. 32-34; Whitehead: pp. 66-71.)

15. Arthur Hübscher, DENKER UNSERER ZEIT, Vol. I, Munich:
Piper Verlag, 1956. 363 pp. (Whitehead: pp. 327-330.)

16. Ichii Saburô, "Alfred North Whitehead," TETSUGAKU KÔZA
(Philosophy Series), Tokyo: Chikuma Shobô, 1949, Vol. I, pp.
239-242.

17. ──────, "Jisshô shugi e no hanpatsu" (The Rejection
of Positivism), AMERICA SHISÔSHI (History of American
Thought), Tokyo: Nippon Hyôron-sha, 1950, Vol. 4, pp.
271-298.

18. Iino Norimoto, "Whitehead no ingasetsu" (Whitehead's Vew of Causality"), BUNSEKI TETSUGAKU NO SHOMONDAI (Problems of Analytic Philosophy), ed. by Ueda Seiji, Tokyo: Waseda Daigaku Shuppan-bu, 1957, pp. 253-299.

19. Alfred Koort, KAASAEGSET FILOSOOFIST, I (Contemporary Philosophy [Estonian]): *Nietzsche, Bergson, Dilthey, Scheler, Jaspers, Heidegger, Brunschvicg, Meyerson, Alexander, Whitehead,* Tartu, 1938. 127 pp.

20. Kôsaka Masaaki, GENDAI TETSUGAKU (Contemporary Philosophy), Tokyo: Kôbundô, 1952. (Whitehead: pp. 63-80.)

21. Jean Laporte, L'IDEE DE NÉCESSITÉ, Paris: Presses Universitaires de France, 1941. xii, 156 pp. (Whitehead: pp. 53-55.)

22. Tina Manferdini, ONTOLOGISMO CRITICO E FILOSOFIE DELL' ESPERIENZA CONCRETA, Reggio Calabria: Edizioni "Historica," 1954. 26 pp. (Whitehead: pp. 18-20.)

23. Rudolf Metz, DIE PHILOSOPHISCHEN STRÖMUNGEN DER GEGENWART IN GROSSBRITTANIEN, Leipzig: F. Meiner, 1935. (Whitehead: Vol. II, pp. 136-169.) Translated as *A Hundred Years of British Philosophy,* London: Allen and Unwin, 1938. (Whitehead: pp. 589-622.)

24. Gianfranco Morra, "Religione e sociologia nel pensiero di A. N. Whitehead," FILIOSOFIA E SOCIOLOGIA, Bologna: I. L. Mulino, 1954, pp. 230-237.

25. Gustav E. Müller, AMERIKANISCHE PHILOSOPHIE, Stuttgart: F. Frommann, 1950 (second ed.). 336 pp. (Whitehead: pp. 183-185.)

26. Maurice Nédoncelle, LA PHILOSOPHIE RELIGIEUSE EN GRANDE-BRETAGNE DE 1850 À NOS JOURS, Paris: Bloud et Gay, 1934. 233 pp. (Whitehead: ch. iii: pp. 109-142.)

27. Noda Matao, "Yûkiteki shizen—Whitehead no tetsugaku" (An Organic View of Nature—the Philosophy of Whitehead), in KINDAI SEISHIN SOBYÔ (Portraits of the Modern Mind), Tokyo: Chikuma Shobô, 1947, pp. 252-283.

28. Enzo Paci, TEMPO E RELAZIONE, Turin: Taylor, 1954. 314 pp. (Whitehead: *passim.*)

29. —————, DALL' ESISTENZIALISMO AL RELAZIONISMO, Messina-Florence, [1957]. 398 pp. ("Whitehead e il relazionismo," pp. 85-139. Reprint of articles C. 45 and C. 47, listed below.

30. Guido de Ruggiero, "Whitehead e la dottrina delle scienze naturali" in *Filosofi del Novecento,* Bari: Laterza, 1934.
31. Shin Il-chul, "Alfred Whitehead," pp. 273-284 of *Hyeondae sasang-ga sam-sib-in* (Thirty Contemporary Thinkers), vol. 9 of *Hyeondae sasang gangjwa* (Series on Contemporary Thought) , Seoul: Dong-Yang Publishing Co., 1960.
32. Doroteia C. Macedo Steffens, "La correlacción entre la percepción sensorial y el pensamiento científico según Alfred North Whitehead," *International Congress of Philosophy* (São Paulo, Brazil), 1954. vol. 3, 14 p.
33. Takagi Sadakazu, "Whitehead: Shizen ninshiki no shogenri" (Whitehead: An Enquiry Concerning the Principles of Natural Knowledge, GENDAI SHIZENKAGAKU KÔZA (Contemporary Natural Science Series) , Tokyo: Kôbundô, 1952, Vol. 8 pp. 125-128.
34. Ueda Seiji, "Whitheead no shizen tetsugaku" (Whitehead's Philosophy of Nature), ANGLO-SAXON TETSUGAKU NO DENTÔ (The Tradition of Anglo-Saxon Philosophy) , Tokyo: Tôkyôdô 1947, pp. 161-213.
35. Jean Wahl, VERS LE CONCRET, Paris: Vrin, 1932. 269 pp. (Whitehead: Préface, *passim;* "La Philosophie spéculative de Whitehead," pp. 127-221. Revision of two-part article C. 60, listed below.)

C. ARTICLES

1. Nicolà Abbagnano, "Whitehead e il concetto della ragione," *Revue International de Philosophie* (Brussells) , No. 56-57 (1961) , 204-216.
2. Ludovico Actis Perinetti, "Filosofia e scienza nella filosofia della natura di Whitehead," *Filosofia* (Turin) , 3 (1952) , 251-266.
3. ————, "Studi su Whitehead," *Filosofia,* 5 (1954) , 191-214.
4. ————, "Cosmologia e assiologia in Whitehead," *Filosofia,* 5 (1954), 658-674. (2, 3, and 4 reprinted as A. 1, listed above.)
5. A. Z. Bar-On, "Waithed ve-ha-Mesoreth ha-Filosofiah ha-Modernith" (Whitehead and the Tradition of Modern

Philosophy), *Iyyun: A Hebrew Philosophical Quarterly* (Jerusalem), **13** (1962), 13-29.

6. Max Bense, "Kosmologie und Literatur. Über Alfred N. Whitehead und Gertrude Stein," *Texte und Zeichen: Eine Litterarische Zeitschrift* (Stuttgart), **3** (1957), 512-525.

7. H. Bergmann, "Whitehead der Physiker," *Kreatur* (Berlin), **2** (1928), 356-363.

8. Piero Bertolini, "Aspetti e problemi dell'educazione in Whitehead," *Aut-Aut* (Turin), No. 28 (1955), 320-340.

9. Ján Bodnár, " 'Process-Philosophy' — filozofia subjectivneho idealizmu" ('Process Philosophy'—a Philosophy of Subjective Idealism), *Filozoficky Časopis* (Bratislava), **9** (1954), 252-262.

10. ――――――, "Teória organicizmu, úrovni a finitizmu v súčasnej filozofii prírodných vied" (The Theory of Organicism, Levels, and Finitism in the Contemporary Philosophy of the Natural Sciences), *Otázky marxistickej filozofie* (Bratislava), **18**, 3 (1963), 215-228.

11. Lamberto Borghi, "Aseptti religiosi e morali del pensiero americano contemporaneo," *Il Saggiatore: Rivista di Cultura Filosofica e Pedagogica* (Turin), **3** (1953), 37-61. (Whitehead: pp. 56-61.)

12. Eberhard Bubser, "Sprache und Metaphysik in Whiteheads Philosophie," *Archiv für Philosophie* (Stuttgart), **10**, No. 1-2 (1960), 79-106. (Abridged third chapter of a University of Göttingen dissertation on Whitehead, 1958, listed as A. 3, above.)

13. Felix Cesselin, "La Bifurcation de la nature," *Revue de Métaphysique et de Morale,* **55** (1950), 30-49.

14. Chao I-wei, "Huai-te-hai ti Wen-hua Che-hsüeh" (Whitehead's Philosophy of Culture), *Ta-lu Tsa-chih* (Mainland Magazine: Shanghai), **4**, 3 (1935?), pp. 10-13.

15. ――――――, "Huai-te-hai Yu-chi Shih-tsai-lun chien-chieh" (A Brief Introduction to Whitehead's Organic Theory of Reality), *San-min Chu-i Pan-yueh-K'an* (The Three People's Principles Fortnightly: Chungking), No. 3 (1942?), pp. 8-13.

16. ――――――, "Huai-te-hai Che-hsüeh Kai-shu" (A Survey of Whitehead's Philosophy), *Hsüeh-shu Chi-K'an* (The Scholarly Quarterly), **3**, 1, pp. 52-61.

17. Angelo Crespi, "Alfred North Whitehead: L'Ultimo dei platonisti inglesi," *Il Ponte* (Florence), 4 (1948), 1139-1144.
18. Gian Mario Crespi, "La Filosofia di Whitehead," *Rivista di Filosofia Neoscolastica* (Milan), 40 (1948), 293-331.
19. Philippe Devaux, "L'Esprit du néo-réalisme anglais," *Revue Internationale de Philosophie*, No. 3 (1939), 499-541. (Whitehead: pp. 504, 510, 512, 518-525, 532-539.)
20. –––––––––––, "Le Bergsonisme de Whitehead," *Revue Internationale de Philosophie*, No. 56-57 (1961), 217-236.
21. D. Emrys Evans, "Platon ac A. N. Whitehead," *Efrydiau Athronyddol*, 5 (1942).
22. Charles Hartshorne, "Das metaphysische System Whiteheads," *Zeitschrift für philosophische Forschung* (Meisenheim), 3 (1948-1949), 566-575.
23. –––––––––––, "Le Principe de relativité philosophique chez Whitehead," *Revue de Métaphysique et de Morale*, 55 (1950), 16-29.
24. F. De Hovre, "Prof. Alfred North Whitehead: Wiskundige, Natuurkundige, Wijsgeer en Paedagoog," (Prof. Alfred North Whitehead: Mathematician, Physicist, Philosopher, and Educator), *Vlaams Opvoedkundig Tijdschrift* (Antwerp), 28, No. 4 (1948), 161-171.
25. Hsieh Yu-wei, "Huai-hei-te Lun Li-hsing ti Chih-neng" (Whitehead on the Function of Reason), Part I: *Min-chu P'ing-lun* (Democratic Critique: Hong Kong), 11, 22 (1959), p. 9; Part II: *Ibid.*, No. 23, p. 10; Part III: *Ibid.*, No. 24, pp. 12-16.
26. –––––––––––, "Huai-hei-te Lun 'Li-chich' " (Whitehead on "Understanding"), *Min-chu P'ing-lun*, 12, 20 (1960), pp. 10-15.
27. –––––––––––, "Huai-hei-te Lun Li-ch'eng ti Hsing-shih" (Whitehead on the Forms of Process), *Min-chu P'ing-lun*, 13, 4 (1961), pp. 6-10.
28. –––––––––––, "Huai-hei-te Lun 'Wen-ming ti Yü-chou'" (Whitehead on the "Universe of Civilization"), *Min-chu P'ing-lun*, 13, 5 (1961), pp. 7-12.
29. –––––––––––, "Huai-hei-te ti Tsung-chiao Kuan" (Whitehead's Philosophy of Religion), *Min-chu P'ing-lun*, 13, 8 (1961), pp. 2-8.
30. –––––––––––, "Huai-hei-te Lun Chung-yao" (Whitehead on

Importance), *Ta-hsüeh Sheng-huo* (University Life), **6**, 21, pp. 11-19.

31. ――――――, "Huai-hei-te Lun Piao-hsien" (Whitehead on Manifestation), *Ta-hsüeh Sheng-huo*, **6**, 23, pp. 4-7; *ibid.*, No. 24, pp. 17-22.

32. Huang Tzu-t'ung, "Huai-t'i-hei ti Shih K'ung Kuan" (Whitehead's Conception of Space and Time), *Che-hsüeh P'ing-lun* (Philosophical Review: Peiping), **6**, 1 (1936), 46-57.

33. Ichii Saburô, "Whitehead," *Risô* (Tokyo), January 1950, pp. 55-63.

34. ――――――, "Alexander yori Whitehead e" (From Alexander to White), *Risô*, May 1954, pp. 43-51.

35. ――――――, "Whitehead no sensô heiwa shisô" (Whitehead's Views on War and Peace), *Shisô* (Tokyo), No. 3 1960, pp. 13-22.

36. Kao Ming K'ai, "Huai-t'i-hei chih Hsin Hsing-erh-shang-hsüeh" (The New Metaphysics of Whitehead), *Che-hsüeh P'ing-lun* (Philosophical Review: Peping), **5**, 2 (1933), 12-34.

37. René Kremer, "L'Evolution du néo-réalisme en Angleterre," *Revue Néo-Scholastique de Philosophie* (Louvain), **30** (1928), 5-17. (Whitehead: pp. 12, 16, 17.)

38. André-Louis Leroy, "Science et philosophie chez Alfred North Whitehead," *Revue de Synthése* (Paris), 3ᵉ Série, No. 22-24 (1961), 43-66.

39. A. Lichtigfeld, "Yaspers u-Waithed" (Jaspers and Whitehead), *Iyyun: A Hebrew Philosophical Quarterly* (Jerusalem), **13** (1962), 30-35.

40. Gottfried Martin, "Neuzeit und Gegenwart in der Entwicklung des mathematischen Denkens," *Kant-Studien* (Cologne), No. 45 (1953-1954), 155-165. (On Husserl and Whitehead.)

41. ――――――, "Metaphysik als *scientia universalis* und als *ontologia generalis*," *Kant-Studien, Ergänzungsheft* 81, Cologne, 1961, pp. 221-232. (On Leibniz and Whitehead. First published in an English translation by Eva Schaper in Ivor Leclerc ed., THE RELEVANCE OF WHITEHEAD, London: Allen & Unwin, New York: Macmillan, 1961, pp. 219-231.)

42. Carlo Mazzantini, "La Filosofia di A. N. Whitehead," *Quaderni di Roma*, **2** (1948), 175-193.

43. Enzo Paci, "Presentazione di Whitehead," *Aut-Aut* (Turin), No. 12 (1952), 507-517.

44. —————, "Prospettive empiristiche e relazionistiche nel Whitehead prespeculativo," *Aut-Aut*, No. 16 (1953), 279-297.

45. —————, "Definizione e funzione della filosofia speculativa in Whitehead," *Giornale Critico della Filosofia Italiana* (Florence), 32 (1953), 304-334. (Reprinted, with additional footnote references, as pp. 85-125 of the author's B. 29, listed above.)

46. —————, "Sul primo periodo della filosofia di Whitehead," *Rivista di Filosofia* (Turin), 44 (1953), 397-415.

47. —————, "Whitehead e Russell," *Rivista di Filosofia*, 45 (1954), 14-25. (Reprinted as pp. 125-139 of the author's B. 29, listed above, unchanged except for one paragraph on p. 130.)

48. —————, "Über einige Verwandtschaften zwischen der Philosophie Whiteheads und der Phänomenologie Husserls," *Revue Internationale de Philosophie*, No. 56-57 (1961), 237-250.

49. Annibale Pastore, "Whitehead e Hedigger control Kant circa la natura emotiva del tempo," *Rivista di Filosofia*, 38 (1947), 181-190.

50. Karl Pichl, "Überwindung des Geschichtspositivismus. Der englische Beitrag: Whitehead, Russell und Toynbee," *Wort und Wahreit: Monatschrift für Religion und Kultur* (Vienna), 4 (1949), 748-763. (Whitehead: pp. 749-754.)

51. D. H. Prins, Jr.; Two-part article: "De natuurfilosofische denkbeelden van Whitehead" (Whitehead's Views on Natural Philosophy), *Physica* (The Hague), 7 (1927), 122-142; "De kritische Snelheid der relativiteitstheorie" (The Critical Velocity of Relativity Theory), *ibid.*, pp. 156-162.

52. Shin Il-chul, "Whitehead eui 'Sageon' gaenyeon" (Whitehead's Concept of Event); Saeroun hyeong-i sanghag e-eui gil, *Cheolhag Yeon-Gu* (Seoul), 1, 1 (1955), 65-77.

53. —————, "Whitehead eui jayeon-gwan" (Whitehead's Concept of Nature); Whitehead cheolhag yeon-gu, *Cheolhag Yeon-Gu*, 2, 2 (1958), 67-100.

54. ————————, Saeng-e wa sasang" (Life and Thought), Whitehead, *Sasangge Monthly* (Seoul). 7, 2 (1959), 223-231.
55. ————————, " 'Sin' eui hyeoungseong gwajeong" (Concept of God) : Whitehead wa gwanryeon hayeo, *Sasangge Monthly,* 8, 2 (1960), 184-190.
56. Georg Siegmund, "Alfred North Whitehead," *Philosophisches Jahrbuch* (Fulda), 58 (1948), 177-178. (Obituary notice; includes a long quotation from Bocheński's *Europäische Philosophie der Gegenwart,* 1947, pp. 216f.)
57. Takenaka Nobutsune, "Whitehead no shûkyôron" (Whitehead on Religion), *Chûgai Nippô* (Kyoto), March 8-15, 1947.
58. J. W. van der Horst, "De methode van de metafysica volgens Alfred N. Whitehead" (The Method of Metaphysics according to A. N. Whitehead), *Algemeen Nederlands Tijdschrift voor Wijsbegeerte en Psychologie* (Assen, Netherlands), 52 (1959), 103-111.
59. C. H. van Os, "Over de philosophie van A. N. Whitehead," *Synthèse* (Utrecht), 4 (1939), 221-238.
60. Jean Wahl, "La Philosophie spéculative de Whitehead," *Revue philosophique* (Paris), 111 (1931), 341-378; 112 (1931), 108-143. (Reprinted—with revisions—in the author's B. 35, listed above.)
61. Edgar Wind, "Mathematik und Sinnesempfindung. Materialien zu einer Whitehead-Kritik," *Logos* (Tübingen), 21 (1932), 239-280.
62. Ramón Xirau, "A. N. Whitehead: tres categorías fundamentales," *Filosofía y Letras* (Mexico City), 23 (1952), 311-325.
63. A. A. Yakushev, "Subektivno-idealisticheskii smysl teorii simvolizma A. Uaitkheda" (The Subjective-Idealist Significance of A. Whitehead's Theory of Symbolism), *Voprosy Filosofii* (Moscow), No. 12 (1962), 117-128.

D. REVIEWS OF WHITEHEAD'S WORKS[3]

1. A TREATISE ON UNIVERSAL ALGEBRA (1898)
   Louis Couturat: *Revue de Métaphysique et de Morale,* 8 (1900), 323-362.

---

[3]Whitehead's works are listed chronologically. In cases where there is more than one review of a single work, reviewers are listed alphabetically by name.

2. PRINCIPIA MATHEMATICA (WITH BERTRAND RUSSELL) 1910-1913
   a. Rudolf Carnap: *Erkenntnis* (Leipzig), 2 (1931-1932), 73-75. (Review of second edition, Vols. I-III, 1925-1927.)
   b. Henri Dufumier: *Revue de Métaphysique et de Morale,* 20 (1912), 538-566. (Review of Vol. I.)
   c. P. E. B. Jourdain: *Jahrbuch über die Fortschritte der Mathematik,* (Berlin), 44 (1913—published in 1918), 68-71. (Review of Vol. III.)
   d. Giuseppe Peano: *Bolletino di Bibliografia e Storia delle Scienze Matematiche* (Turin), 15 (1913), 47-53, 75-81. (Review of Vols. I and II.)
3. THE CONCEPT OF NATURE (1920)
   a. Gian Mario Crespi, *Rivista Critica di Storia della Filosofia* (Milan), 6 (1951), 237-240. (Review of Italian translation of 1948.)
   b. Hans Driesch: *Kant-Studien,* 26 (1921), 204-205.
   c. F. Selvaggi, S. J., *Gregorianum,* 31 (1950), 313-314.
4. SCIENCE AND THE MODERN WORLD (1925)
   a. Philippe Devaux: *Archives de la Société Belge de Philosophie,* I, No. 3 (1928-1929), 9-24.
   b. Ch. Hummel: *Neue Schweizer Rundschau* (Zürich), 20 (1952), 434-437. (Review of German translation of 1949.)
5. SYMBOLISM, ITS MEANING AND EFFECT (1927)
   Cleto Carbonara: *Logos* (Florence), 13 (1930), 373-376.
6. ADVENTURES OF IDEAS (1933)
   P. de Saint-Seine, *Archives de Philosophie,* 10, 4 (1934), 65-76.
7. ESSAYS IN SCIENCE AND PHILOSOPHY (1947)
   a. Félix Cesselin: *Revue de Métaphysique et de Morale,* 53 (1948), 81-84. (Reprinted—with revisions—in the author's *La Philosophie organique de Whitehead,* 1950, pp. 237-243.)
   b. José Pemartín: *Revista de Filosofia* (Madrid), 7 (1948), 593-604.
8. DIALOGUES OF ALFRED NORTH WHITEHEAD (edited by Lucien Price) (1956)
   Francisco Pérez Navarro: *Cuadernos Hispanoamericanos* (Madrid), 26 (1956), 386-387.

E. REVIEWS OF WORKS ABOUT WHITEHEAD

1. Leo A. Foley, *A Critique of the Philosophy of Being of Alfred North Whitehead in the Light of Thomistic Philosophy*, Washington, D. C., 1946. Carlo Mazzantini: *Rivista di Filosofia*, 39 (1948), 275-285.

2. E. P. Shahan, *Whitehead's Theory of Experience*, New York, 1950. Félix Cesselin: *Revue Philosophique*, 77 (1952), 88-95.

3. Félix Cesselin, *La Philosophie organique de Whitehead;* Paris, 1950. André Lentin: *La Pensée* (Paris), No. 45 (1952), 141.

4. Ivor Leclerc, *An Introduction to Whitehead's Metaphysics*, London, 1958, and William A. Christian, *An Interpretation of Whitehead's Metaphysics*, New Haven, 1959. Anon.: *Revue de Métaphysique et de Morale*, 65 (1960), 363.

5. William A. Christian, *An Interpretation of Whitehead's Metaphysics*, New Haven, 1959, and Tulane *Studies in Whitehead's Philosophy*, New Orleans, 1961. André-Louis Leroy: Revue Philosophique, 87 (1962), 552-555.

6. Ivor Leclerc, ed., *The Relevance of Whitehead*, London and New York, 1961. Jacques Ruytinx: *Revue Internationale de Philosophie*, No. 56-57 (1961), 289-293.

7. A survey of recent literature in: André-Louis Leroy, "Introduction à la philosophie contemporaine d'expression anglaise," *Revue Philosophique*, 87 (1962), 433-466. (Whitehead: pp. 457-461.)

F. TRANSLATIONS OF ARTICLES ON WHITEHEAD ORIGINALLY PUBLISHED IN ENGLISH

1. Samuel Alexander, "Alfred North Whitehead," *Neue Auslese aus dem Schrifttum der Gegenwart* (Munich), 3, 3 (1948), 85-88. Original: *Manchester Guardian*, Dec. 31, 1947 (but written in 1935).

2. A. H. Johnson, "La filosofia de la historia de Whitehead" (trans. Mauricio A. López), *Philosophia* (Mendoza, Argentina), 4 (1947), 128-139. Original: "Whitehead's Philosophy of History," *Journal of the History of Ideas*, 7 (1946), 234-249.

3. Paul Kecskemeti, "Whitehead und der Aufstand gegen die Metaphysik," *Amerikanische Rundschau*, 4, 19 (1948), 40-50. Original: "Whitehead and the Revolt against Metaphysics," *The Modern Review* (New York), 2, 5-6 (1948), 247-260.

4. Ivor Leclerc, "Whitehead: La transformación del concepto de substancia," *Convivium* (Barcelona), 1 (1956), 181-208. Original: "Whitehead's Transformation of the Concept of Substance," *Philosophical Quarterly*, 3 (1953), 225-243.
5. Bertrand Russell, "Tsai Lo-su Hui-i chung ti Huai-t'e-hai" (trans. by Wang Yü), *Min-chu P'ing-lun* (Democratic Critique: Hong Kong), 13, 14 (1961), p. 15. Original: "Whitehead" in *Portraits from Memory*, New York, 1956.

ADDENDA: (To Part III.C)

Hsieh Yu-wei, "Huai-he-te Lun 'Yüan-ching'" (Whitehead on "Foresight"), *Min-chu P'ing-lun* (Democratic Critique: Hong Kong), 13, 1 (1961), 10-15.
Walter Jung, "Über Whiteheads Atomistik der Ereignisse," *Philosophia Naturalis*, 7, 3-4 (1962), 406-441.

APPENDIX C

THE CONTRIBUTORS

WILLIAM ALSTON was educated at Centenary College (B.M.) and The University of Chicago (Ph.D.). Since 1949 he has taught philosophy at the University of Michigan where he is now Professor of Philosophy. He has also taught at the University of California at Los Angeles and Harvard University. In 1955-56 he held a fellowship from the Western Division of the American Philosophical Association for work on the meaning of religious statements. He has written for *The Journal of Philosophy, Review of Metaphysics, Philosophical Review, Philosophy of Science, Philosophical Studies, Philosophy and Phenomenological Research, Mind,* and *Philosophical Quarterly.*

A. Cornelius Benjamin was educated at the University of Michigan (A.B., A.M., Ph.D.). He has taught at the University of Illinois (1923-32) and the University of Chicago (1932-45). He has been John Hiram Lathrop Professor of Philosophy at the University of Missouri since 1945. He has written *The Logical Structure of Science,* Kegan Paul, London, 1936; *An Introduction to the Philosophy of Science,* Macmillan, New York, 1937; and *Operationism,* Charles C. Thomas, Springfield, Ill., 1955. He has written many articles.

Arthur Berndtson was educated at The University of Chicago (Ph.D.). He is currently chairman of the Department of Philosophy at the University of Missouri. He is a contributor to various journals, including *Philosophy and Phenomenological Research, Revue Internationale de Philosophie, Journal of Aesthetics,* etc., and *History of Philosophical Systems,* ed. Ferm.

Milič Čapec was educated at King Charles University of Prague (M.A., M.Sc., Ph.D.) and has also studied at Sorbonne, Paris and the University of Chicago. He has taught at the University of Nebraska (1944-46), University of Olmutz, Czechoslovakia (1946-47), Carleton College (1948-57), and Boston University (1962-until the present). He has written *Bergson and the Trends of Contemporary Physics,* University of Prague Press, 1938; and *The Philosophical Impact of Contemporary Physics,* Van Nostrand, Princeton, 1961. He has also written numerous articles.

Lucio Chiaraviglio was educated at the University of Chicago (B.Sc., M.A.) and Emory (Ph.D.). He has taught at Emory University (1962-63) and is now at the University of Delaware. He was research assistant, Department of Microbiology, Division of Basic Health Services at Emory University in

1960-1962. He has written, "Strains", *The Journal of Philosophy* Vol. 58, No. 19, Sept. 14, 1961; "Whitehead's Theory of Prehensions" in *Alfred North Whitehead, Essays on His Philosophy*, edited by George Kline, Prentice Hall, Inc., 1963, and "The Pragmatics of Truth Functions" with A. Sweet, *Notre Dame Journal of Formal Logic* (in press).

William A. Christian was educated at Davidson College (A.B.) and Yale University (Ph.D.). He has taught at Smith College (1935-1951), and has been visiting professor at Swarthmore College and the University of Chicago. He is presently teaching at Yale University. He has written *An Interpretation of Whitehead's Metaphysics*, 1959, and has also written many articles and essays in various symposia.

Bowman L. Clarke was educated at Millsaps College (B.A.), University of Mississippi (M.A.), and Emory University (B.D., M.A., Ph.D.). He has taught at the University of the South, Sewanee, Tennessee (1959-60), and is presently Assistant Professor of Philosophy at the University of Georgia. He has written "Whitehead's Cosmology and the Christian Drama," *The Journal of Religion*, 34 (July, 1959); and has written articles for the *Anglican Theological Review*, and *The Monist*.

Estelle Allen DeLacy was educated at the University of Washington (A.B., A.M.) and the University of Chicago (Ph.D.). She has taught at the University of Arkansas, Central YMCA College, and Roosevelt University. She is co-author of *Philodemus: On Methods of Inference, A Study in Ancient Empiricism*, American Philological Association, 1941; *Euclid and Geometry*, F. Watts, 1963; and has contributed various articles to the *Philosophical Review, Sophia*, and *Telugu Encyclopedia*.

William Earle was educated at the University of Chicago (Ph.D.), and de l'Universite Aix-Marseilles (Doctorat). He has taught at Yale University, Harvard University, Stanford University, and is presently Professor of Philosophy at Northwestern University. He has written *Objectivity* (Noonday, 1956), and has contributed numerous articles to various journals.

John N. Findlay was educated at Oxford (M.A.) and Graz (Ph.D.). He has taught at the University of Otago, New Zealand (1934-44); Rhodes University, South Africa (1945); Natal University, South Africa (1946-48); King's College, Newcastle-on-Tyne, (1948-51); King's College, University of London (1951 to the present) and was visiting professor at Carleton College, Minnesota (1961) and the University of Texas (1962). He has written, in addition to numerous journal articles, *Meinong's Theory of Objects and Values, Oxford*, 1st ed. 1933, 2nd ed. 1963; *Hegel: A Re-Examination*, Macmillan Co., 1958; *Values and Intentions*, Allen & Unwin, 1961; and *Mind, Language and Value*, Allen & Unwin, 1963.

Frederic Brenton Fitch was educated at Yale (B.A., Ph.D.). He has taught at Yale since 1937, where he is now Professor of Philosophy. He had a Guggenheim Fellowship in 1945 and was Director of Graduate Studies in Philosophy at Yale (1951-56). He was President of the Association for Symbolic Logic 1959-61. He has written *A Mathematico-Deductive Theory of Rote Learning* (Yale University Press, 1940) (jointly with C. L. Hull and others); *Symbolic Logic: An Introduction* (Ronald Press, 1952); and has written articles in the *Journal of Symbolic Logic, Philosophy of Science, Mind,* and other scholarly journals.

Marvin Fox was educated at Northwestern University (B.A., M.A.) and the University of Chicago (Ph.D.). He has taught at Ohio State University since 1948. He is the editor of Kant's *Fundamental Principles of the Metaphysics of Morals,* Liberal Arts, 1949; and is the author of numerous essays, including "Some Problems in Buber's Moral Philosophy," for the forthcoming volume of the *Library of Living Philosophers* on Martin Buber to be published by Open Court in 1964; "The Diversity of Methods in Dewey's Ethical Theory," *Philosophy and Phen. Research,* 1951; "Kierkegaard and Rabbinic Judaism," *Judaism,* 1953; "The Trials of Socrates: An Analysis of the First Tetrology," *Archiv für Philosophie,* 1956; and Tillich's "Ontology and God," *Anglican Theological Review,* July, 1961.

Eugene Freeman was educated at the University of California at Los Angeles (A.B.), and the University of Chicago (Ph.D.). He taught at Illinois Institute of Technology, and is now at San Jose State College. He is editor-in-chief of The Open Court Publishing Company of LaSalle, Illinois, Editor of *The Monist* and a member of the Advisory Board of *The Library of Living Philosophers.* He is the author of *The Categories of Charles Peirce,* Open Court, 1934; the editor (with D. Appel) of *The Great Ideas of Plato,* Lantern Press, 1952, reprinted as *The Wisdom and Ideas of Plato,* Premier Books, Fawcett World Library, 1956, 1959, and 1962; and the editor of the forthcoming Festschrift for Paul A. Schilpp, *Crisis in Philosophy—The Role of Philosophy in the Atomic Age.* He has written articles on the philosophy of visual perception, on professional ethics, and on integration.

Alexander Boyce Gibson was educated at Melbourne (B.A.), Oxford (M.A.) and Cambridge (D. Litt.). He has been Professor of Philosophy at the University of Melbourne since 1935. He has written *The Philosophy of Descartes; Should Philosophers be Kings?; Thinkers at Work,* with A.A. Phillips; and *Towards an Australian Philosophy of Education.* He has also written numerous articles.

Richard Hocking was educated at Harvard College (B.S.), Harvard University (A.M.), and Yale University (Ph.D.). He has taught at the University of Minnesota, Williams College, University of California, University of Chicago University of Frankfurt and is currently Professor of Philosophy, Emory University. He has written "The Problem of Truth," in *Truth, Myth, and Symbol,* ed. Altizer, Beardslee, and Young (Prentice-Hall, 1962); "Process and Analysis in the Philosophy of Royce," in *Josiah Royce's Seminar, 1913-1914: As Recorded in the Notebooks of Harry T. Costello,* ed. Smith (Rutgers University Press, 1963); and has contributed to *Emory University Quarterly, Bulletin of the General Theological Seminary, Philosophy East and West, Journal of Philosophy, and Review of Metaphysics.*

George L. Kline was educated at Boston University, Columbia College and Columbia University. He has taught at Columbia, The University of Chicago, and Swarthmore College, and is at present Associate Professor of Philosophy and Russian at Bryn Mawr College. He is one of the Editors of the *Journal of Philosophy* and was the Special Editor of the *Whitehead Centennial Issue* of the *Journal of Philosophy* in 1961. He is the author of *Spinoza and Soviet Philosophy* (1952); the translator of Zenkovsky, *History of Russian Philosophy* (1953); and the Editor of *Alfred North Whitehead: Essays On His Philosophy* (New York: Prentice-Hall, 1963).

Ivor LeClerc was educated at Cape Town (M.A.), and London (Ph.D.). He has taught at the University of Glasgow and is now Senior Lecturer in Logic and Metaphysics there. He was Visiting Professor in Philosophy at Bonn University in 1961. He has written *Whitehead's Metaphysics,* 1958; edited *The Relevance of Whitehead,* 1961; *Whitehead's Philosophical Writings,* (German-English ed.); and translated *An Introduction to General Metaphysics* with Eva Schaper, 1961.

Albert William Levi was educated at Dartmouth (A.B.), the University of Chicago (M.A., Ph.D.). He has taught at Dartmouth, University of Chicago, Black Mountain College (where he also served as Rector), University of Graz, University of Vienna, Washington University. He has written *Rational Belief* (Harcourt, Brace and Co., 1941); *General Education in the Social Studies* (American Council on Education, 1948); *Varieties of Experience* (Ronald Press, 1957); *Philosophy and the Modern World* (Indiana University Press, 1959); *Literature, Philosophy and the Imagination* (Indiana University Press, 1962); and has edited *The Logic of Language* (Dartmouth College, 1939); and *J. S. Mill: The Great Humanistic Essays* (Pocket Books, 1963).

Leroy Loemker was educated at the University of Dubuque (A.B.) and Boston University (S.T.B., Ph.D.). He has taught at the University of Dubuque (1921-24) and Emory University since 1929. Since 1946 he has been Dean of the Graduate School at Emory. He is the editor of *Gottfried Wilhelm von Leibniz: Philosophical Papers and Letters.* 2 vols., University of Chicago Press, 1956. He has also written articles and reviews in the *Journal of the History of Ideas, Journal of Philosophy,* etc.

Richard Martin was educated at Harvard (A.B.), Columbia (A.M.), and Yale (Ph.D.). He has taught at Princeton University and the University of Chicago (1942-46), at Bryn Mawr College and the University of Pennsylvania (1945-59) and has taught at the University of Texas and New York University since 1959. He has been Guest Professor at Universität Bonn in 1960 and 1961. He has written *Truth and Denotation* (Chicago: University of Chicago Press, 1958); *The Notion of Analytic Truth* (Philadelphia and Oxford: U. of Pennsylvania Press and Oxford U. Press, 1959); *Toward a Systematic Pragmatics* (Amsterdam: North-Holland Publishing Co., 1959); and *Intension and Decision* (New York, Prentice-Hall, 1963). He is a member of the Editorial Board of *The Monist*.

Schubert M. Ogden was educated at The University of Chicago (B.D., Ph.D.), Ohio Wesleyan University (A.B.). He is currently Associate Professor of Theology, Perkins School of Theology, Southern Methodist University. He has written *Christ Without Myth: A Study Based On the Theology of Rudolf Bultmann* (New York: Harper and Brothers, 1961); and is editor and translator of *Existence and Faith: Shorter Writings of Rudolf Bultmann* (New York: Meridian Books, Inc., 1960).

Robert M. Palter was educated at Columbia University (A.B.), and The University of Chicago (Ph.D.). He has taught at Northwestern University and is presently Chairman of the History and Philosophy of Science staff at the University of Chicago. He has written *Whitehead's Philosophy of Science* (Chicago: University of Chicago Press, 1960); and edited *Toward Modern Science: Studies In Ancient, Mediaeval, and Renaissance Science* (Noonday, 1961).

Howard L. Parsons was educated at the University of Chicago (B.A., Ph.D.). He has taught at the University of Southern California, University of Illinois, University of Tennessee, Teacher's College of Columbia University, Idaho State College, Victoria College (B.C.) and is currently at Coe College, Cedar Rapids, Iowa. He contributed to *Symbols and Society,* Harper and Row, 1955; *The Nature of Man,* Harper and Row, 1962; and *The Empirical Theology of Henry Nelson Wieman,* Macmillan, 1963. He has written articles for many philosophical journals.

William L. Reese was educated at Drury College (A.B.) and the University of Chicago (B.D. & Ph.D.). He has taught at Drake University (1947-1957) and Grinnell College (1957-1960). Since 1960 he has been professor and chairman of the Dept. of Philosophy at the University of Delaware. His writings include *Studies in C. S. Peirce* (symposiast), Harvard University Press, 1952; *Philosophers Speak of God* (with Charles Hartshorne), Univ. of Chicago Press, 1953; *The Ascent From Below,* Houghton Mifflin Co., 1959, and *Philosophy of Science, the Delaware Seminar,* Vols. I and II. (General editor), Interscience Publishers, a Division of John Wiley & Sons, 1963.

Huston Smith was educated at Central College (A.B.) and The University of Chicago (Ph.D.), and was awarded Doctor of Humanities, Central College and Doctor of Letters, Concord College. He has taught at the University of Denver (1945-47), University of Colorado (Spring, 1947), Washington University (1947-58), and is currently Professor of Philosophy at Massachusetts Institute of Technology. He has written *The Purposes of Higher Education* (Harpers, 1955); *The Religions of Man* (Harpers, 1958; Mentor, 1959); and

The Search for America, editor and co-author (Prentice-Hall, 1959). He has contributed articles to *The Journal of Religion, The Journal of Religious Thought, Philosophy East and West, The Saturday Review, The Saturday Evening Post, The Nation,* and in *The Empirical Theology of Henry Nelson Wieman.*

John E. Smith was educated at Columbia University (A.B., Ph.D.) and Union Theological Seminary (B.D.). He has taught at Vassar College (1945-46); Barnard College, Columbia University (1946-52), and Yale from 1952 to the present. He has lectured at the University of Michigan (1958), Union Theological Seminary (1959) and was Dudleian Lecturer at Harvard in 1960. He is a member of the Editorial Board of *The Monist.* He has written *Royce's Social Infinite,* New York, 1950; *Reason and God,* New Haven, 1961, and *The Spirit of American Philosophy,* New York, 1963. He is the translator of R. Kroner, *Kant's Weltanshauung,* Chicago, 1955 and the editor of *Treatise Concerning Religious Affections,* by Jonathan Edwards, New Haven, 1959.

Paul Weiss was educated at Harvard University (Ph.D.), and was awarded an LHD from Grinnell. He is currently Sterling Professor of Philosophy at Yale University. He is founder and editor of *The Review of Metaphysics* and founder and past president of the Metaphysical Society of America, and a trustee of Middle East Studies. He has written *Reality; Nature and Man; Man's Freedom; Modes of Being; Our Public Life; The World of Art; Nine Basic Arts; History: Written and Lived; Religion and Art,* etc. With C. Hartshorne he edited *Collected Papers of C. S. Peirce,* 6 vols.

John Wild was educated at Harvard University (M.A.), University of Chicago (Ph.D.), and was awarded an LHD from Ripon and an LLD from Monmouth College. He has taught at the University of Michigan (1926-27), Harvard University (1927-1960), Northwestern University (1960-63), and is currently Professor of Philosophy at Yale University. He has written *Spinoza, Selections* (Scribner); *Plato's Theory of Man* (Harvard University Press, 1946); *Challenge of Existentialism* (Indiana University Press, 1955); *Human Freedom and Social Order* (Duke University Press, 1959); *Existence and the World of Freedom* (Prentice-Hall, 1963).

Daniel Day Williams was educated at the University of Denver (A.B.), the University of Chicago (M.A.), the Chicago Theological Seminary (B.D.), and Columbia University (Ph.D.). He was Dean of Chapel and instructor in religion at Colorado College (1938-39); professor of constructive theology, The Federated Theological Faculty of the University of Chicago and the Chicago Theological Seminary (1939-54); associate director of the Survey of Theological Education (1954-55), and Roosevelt Professor of Systematic Theology, Union Theological Seminary, New York from 1955 until the present. He has written *God's Grace and Man's Hope,* Harper & Bros., 1949; *What Present Day Theologians are Thinking,* Harper & Bros., 1952, 1959;

Advancement of Theological Education (co-author), Harper & Bros., 1957, and *The Minister and the Care of Souls,* Harper & Bros., 1961.

Sewall Wright was educated at Lombard College (B.S.), University of Illinois (M.S.), Harvard University (Sc.D.), and was awarded Sc.D. degrees by Univ. of Rochester, Yale University, Harvard University, Knox College, Western Reserve, Univ. of Chicago, and the Univ. of Illinois, and an LLD from Michigan State University. He has taught at the University of Chicago (1926-1955), University of Wisconsin (1955-1960), Univ. of California (Berkeley; Spring, 1943), and Univ. Edinburgh (1949-50). He has written about 160 papers on genetics of characters of the guinea pig, effects of inbreeding and cross-breeding on the guinea pig, theory of path coefficients, theory of genetics of populations and evolution.

INDEX OF NAMES

INDEX OF TOPICS